The Nature of Boats

Insights and Esoterica for the Nautically Obsessed

Dave Gerr

International Marine
Camden, Maine

To Pamela, my favorite sister; to Dave and Donna,
who never take me too seriously; to Chris and
Barbara and Gordon, who seem to take me any way
at all; to Paul and Helle, who take my advice (occa-
sionally); and to Bob, who wins all our bets.

First paperback printing, 1995.
Published by International Marine
10   9   8   7   6   5   4   3   2   1
Copyright © 1992 International Marine,
a division of The McGraw-Hill Companies.

Library of Congress Cataloging-in-Publication Data
Gerr, Dave
    The nature of boats : insights and esoterica for the
nautically obsessed / Dave Gerr.
      p. cm.
    Includes bibliographical references (p. 407) and index.
    ISBN 0-07-024233-X
    1. Boats and boating—Miscellanea. 2. Yachts and yachting—
Miscellanea. I. Title.
GV775.G47 1992
797.1—dc20   92-10623
                                    CIP

Questions regarding the content of this book should be
addressed to: International Marine,
P.O. Box 220, Camden, Maine 04843

Questions regarding the ordering of this book should be
addressed to: The McGraw-Hill Companies, Customer Service
Department, P.O. Box 547, Blacklick, OH 43004,
Retail Customers: 1-800-822-8158, Bookstores: 1-800-722-4726

Design by Ann Aspell.
Typeset by Farrar Associates.
Edited by Jon Eaton, Tom McCarthy, and Dorothy Chocensky.

Contents

Part 1. Boats to Note—Designs and Types Worth a Noodle

1. The Earliest Yachts—a Gift from the Dutch 3
History of the first yachts / Discussion of different types of Dutch sailing yachts and their pros and cons

2. The Dory—The Seaman's Sea Boat 10
Some famous dory adventures / Types of dories / Why dories don't sail well (as a rule) / The Offshore Skiff / *Shellback*, a 65-foot dory motor cruiser

3. Sharpshooters—The Catboats that Never Were 18
Discussion of the "Bahama Sharpshooter" Catboat / Comparison of Cape Cod Cats and Sharpshooters / Design of a 22-foot pocket cruising Sharpshooter

4. Sea Skiffs: Sea Bright and Otherwise 24
History of the Sea Bright skiff, why they'd make fine yachts / What makes a sea skiff, their pros and cons

5. The Best of Both Worlds 31
Discussion of a motorsailer that will perform as well under power as under sail

6. A Cruise Aboard *Crackerjack* or An Imaginary Cruise in a Dream Boat 37
Dream boat designed specifically for cruising

7. Presto and Sharpie: The American Answer to the Dutch 44
American shoal-draft sailing cruisers, sharpies, and Commodore Munroe Presto boats

8. A Tug of the Heart Strings 53
Modified tugboat as a liveaboard cruiser

9. My Own Double-Enders 58
Seagoing advantages of the double-ender / Examples of the canoe stern I invented (I think) and favor

Part 4. How Fast Will She Go?

Part 5. Fads, Trends, and History

Part 6. The Iron Breeze

Part 7. Electricity and Water Sometimes Mix

Part 8. Analyzing the Eggbeater

Part 9. Catching the Wind: Sailing Simplified

Part 10. You Built Her of What? Construction for Everyone

Part 11. People Power or Your Boat Should Fit Like a Glove

Part 12. Getting Where You're Going

Acknowledgments

I was standing on a boatshow dock drenched in the August sun. "You make a tapered eye splice with a brass ring in it. Wrap it around here," I was explaining. Someone suggested, "Why don't you write a piece and tell our readers about it?" The speaker was Tom Baker, then editor of *Small Boat Journal*. It wasn't many months later that Herb Gliick—editor and publisher of *Offshore* magazine— called. He was wondering if I had any interest in writing a column . . . .

A surprising span of years, and some hundred or more articles later, I'm still at it. All this work owes its existence to the many editors who thought I had something worthwhile to say, and encouraged me to do so—Tom and Herb; Keith Lawrence of *Boatbuilder* magazine; Michael Crowley of *National Fisherman*; Dennis Caprio of *Soundings*; Alex Agnew and Tim Queeney of *Ocean Navigator*; and most definitely not least, Jonathan Eaton of International Marine. Without their encouragement and support—over many years and through many projects—this book would never have been written.

A Note on Metrics

Because the world is moving inexorably to the metric system, I've made a point of giving all measurements in both English and metric units, the idea being that—no matter what system you're familiar with—you'll have no trouble following along. Converting from metric to English (and vice versa) is not always convenient, however. A measurement of exactly 2 feet converts to 0.6096 meter (m) or 60.96 centimeters (cm), while 10 pounds works out to 4.5359 kilograms (kg). Accordingly, whenever possible I've used *soft conversions*. A soft conversion rounds the metric (or English) value to the nearest *convenient* figure: 2 feet would be 0.6 m, or 60 cm; 10 pounds, 4.5 kg.

Occasionally, I've used *extremely soft conversions*. These I employ when exact values aren't critical, and round, whole numbers can be used arbitrarily to make a point: 2 feet might then be 0.5 m or 50 cm; and 10 pounds, 5 kg. Of course, in those instances where precision is required, I've used hard or exact conversions accurate to two or three decimal places.

With a few exceptions, speeds are given in knots, since this is the universal standard of both sea and air. Where weights are in tons, they are long tons of 2,240 pounds. Long tons have not usually been converted to metric tons, as the difference between them is very small—about 1.6 percent.

Under Metric Pressure!

One problem unique to metric measure is pressure. The metric system seems to have more units for measuring pressure than you can shake a stick at. To start with, to the metric engineer, a kilogram is not simply a kilogram; no indeed, when measuring force it has to be a *kilogram of force* (kgf). This keeps you from confusing it with *kilogram of mass* (plain "kg"—no "f"), which—as long as you remain on planet Earth—is effectively the same as a kgf. Anyway, in converting from the rather consistent English-measure pounds per square inch (psi), one is supposed to use kgf.

Now, you'd think that 1 psi would equal some number of kgf per square centimeter, and it does—0.0703 kgf/cm^2, or (the other way around) 1 kgf/cm^2 equals 14.223 psi. But, sensible as this seems to me, few engineers use this unit. Nope, for years—when dealing with pressure—*newtons* (N) have been substituted for kgf. One kgf equals 9.8066 newtons (N). This means that 1 kgf/cm^2 also equals 98060 N/m^2. *Newton meters squared* (N/m^2) thus becomes the engineer's unit of pressure. To make things still more entertaining, there's yet another unit of force, the *dyne*. Accordingly, there's still another unit of pressure—dynes per centimeter squared. Dynes are largely used by physicists, so we can forget them completely. But isn't it nice to know they are there?

Follow so far? Good, because we're not finished. For some reason, several years back it was decided to rename the N/m² as the *pascal* (Pa)—exact same unit but a new name. (What's in a name?) Finally, pascals—which are really newton meters squared, which are the same as kilograms of force per square centimeter (forget about dynes)—happen to work out to be very large numbers. Accordingly, pascals are almost always given in kilopascals or megapascals—kPa or mPa. This keeps pressure figures manageably small.

If this weren't enough, the old kgf/cm² yields conveniently sized numbers—200 psi is about 14 kgf/cm², for example. Nevertheless, the kgf/cm² has essentially been declared obsolete. In spite of this, I've used kgf/cm² throughout this book. I've done so because I believe it is easier for nontechnical readers to understand. Even engineers will understand, though they'll probably shake their heads at "poor practice." I've also dropped the "f" from kgf, because I'm betting you plan to do all your boating on this planet. For your reference, however:

From English to Metric
> *1 kgf/cm² = 14.223 psi*
> *1 kg/cm² = 1 kgf/cm² (as long as you're on planet Earth)*
> *1 psi = 0.0703 kgf/cm²*
> *1 psi = 6,895 N/m² (you see, big numbers)*
> *1 psi = 6,895 Pa (exactly the same as N/m²)*
> *1 psi = 6.895 kPa*
> *1 psi = 0.00689 mPa*

Within the Metric System
> *1 kgf/m² = 0.0001 kgf/cm²*
> *1 kgf/cm² = 98060 Pa or N/m²*
> *1 kgf/cm² = 98.06 kPa*
> *1 kgf/cm² = 0.09806 mPa*

Let's hope there isn't another all-new, improved metric unit of pressure on its way.

Introduction

We made the experiment; and the fruit is before us. Look at it—think of it. Look at it, in its aggregate grandeur, of extent of country, and the number of population—of ships, and steamboat, and rail.

Abraham Lincoln, from a fragment of writing, 1854

There's something special about boats. They hint at escape and adventure, speed and ease, comfort and challenge. Agile, strong, stout, and beautiful, their handmade hulls seem to clothe a living spirit.

Their lure and fascination often grow from a small seed—a childhood cruise, a weekend fishing. The cool bite of salt breeze, the soothing chuckle of waves, the excitement of weathering the first storm or landing the first big fish—all cleave somehow deep into memory. Underlying all is the boat itself. The craft that takes you out and keeps you safe. This leads to a sort of benign mania—boat noodling.

What's boat noodling?

In its milder forms, boat noodling's no more than pondering why the vessel at the next slip has different props from yours, even though she's the same size and fitted with identical engines. It might be mulling over your standing rigging: Is it stout enough for that long-planned passage offshore? Or perhaps it's figuring if there might be a way to add additional tankage—fuel or water, or both (now there's the ticket)—without harming performance.

More-dedicated noodlers may study the pros and cons of repowering. Contemplating their next vessel, they may compare the seakeeping qualities of different designs. Or, they may embark on a campaign to eliminate the one annoying feature of their current *Sea Gull*—adding ventilation, increasing stability, perhaps beefing up flimsy engine beds or tracking down and liquidating an annoying source of vibration.

Then there's the terminal boat noodler. These fearless souls won't stop at simple modifications. Instead, they'll dream of finishing off a bare hull; of building their own *Vivacious Viking* from scratch; or even of designing their next vessel—every nut and bolt of her. Such dreams call for some mighty noodling indeed—weeks, months, even years spent in the planning stages alone. This is a full-blown benign madness; hours of hard work that somehow wind up unalloyed satisfaction.

It's not, of course, as if the boat noodler had much choice in the matter. Once you've started noodling you're almost inexorably hooked. You may be sitting at the office honestly trying to earn your paycheck, when suddenly you realize you've spent the last twenty minutes considering the options on your latest boat project. In fact, if you've picked up this book simply to see what it contains, you're just about certain to be beyond help. Even if you manage to put *The Nature of Boats* back on the shelf and tiptoe away—a stealthy retreat is usually best—it won't be long before you'll be back to sketching ideas on envelope flaps and arguing hull shapes or cockpit configurations with equally hapless fellow noodlers.

Boat noodling's nothing more (or less) than sketching, scheming, analyzing, and planning boats. I've yet to meet a boatowner who doesn't do most, if not all, of the above. Not only is it half the fun (perhaps more), but it also improves your understanding how and why boats do as they do—the nature of boats. This can't help but make you a better and safer sailor—knowing what to expect from your craft, and from others, reduces the chance that you'll be taken by surprise. It also increases the odds that you'll make the right decision in a hard chance, when the chips are down.

In fact, a real seaman (or seawoman) will strive to develop a working knowledge of all types of watercraft. A sailor who knows how and why powerboats behave as they do will be less likely to tangle with trolling gear or be surprised by the effect of a prop wash. By the same token, the powerboater who understands how sailboats go about getting from point A to point B will be less likely to run afoul of racing fleets. He or she will know why some courses—on some occasions—are just about impossible on a sailboat. There will be less likelihood of white-knuckled evasive maneuvers, swerving away from that sloop to port and its (to the uninitiated) seemingly suicidal maneuver.

By understanding all types of boats—power and sail, race and cruise—you'll also be in a position to judge when assistance might be needed, and to deliver it safely. Even better, you'll be sure to pick up useful ideas and solutions to many a problem by looking at how the other fellow did it. (Solution swiping is a time-honored tradition in boat noodling.) The design of a helm station for a lobsterboat, for instance, may well have many fine features for use on an auxiliary or motorsailer. Knowing how sailboat rigging is proportioned would certainly help you install a boat hoist or steadying sail on your trawler yacht.

The Nature of Boats was written as a browser's reference to understanding how boats tick: how you can judge and evaluate different hulls; make improvements; or even start doodling up a new design from scratch. It's written in plain English, not highfalutin technical jargon, and there's little math included here that's more difficult than adding up your grocery bill. Rules of thumb and simple charts make everything from estimating hull thickness to specifying a sailboat's rig to proportioning engineroom vents to selecting propellers and more, simple and straightforward. Of course, I couldn't possibly squeeze everything in here, but you should find a good clear start to answering many a boat noodler's question. Harry S Truman used to talk about "plain dealing." You should find *The Nature of Boats* "plain speaking."

It was difficult to know where to start *The Nature of Boats*. Should it begin by investigating construction or hull shape, or would delving into the principles of stability, displacement, and performance be better? Which should come first? It's difficult to examine construction without reference to hull shape, but clearly shape is influenced by construction and all are controlled by fundamental principles. (Did I hear a chicken clucking, or was that an egg hatching?) There was only one way out; I decided to start with the boats themselves—twelve chapters on boats of historical or practical interest. From there on, well, I went with the flow.

PART 1

Boats to Note— Designs and Types Worth a Noodle

I'm not bad—I'm just drawn that way.

Jessica Rabbit to Eddie Valiant,
in *Who Framed Roger Rabbit?*

One might well ask—in fact you may be asking yourself—why I selected the follow-
ing boats from among all those to choose from. The truth is there's no special rea-
son. The chapters that follow describe fine vessels, craft with special abilities,
proven worth, or unique appeal. Many aren't as well known as they deserve to be,
and all would make wonderful cruisers, yachts, or workboats, but certainly they're
not the only such craft.

The list of craft I could have added is long enough to stretch from gooseneck to
masthead: Tancook whalers, double-wedge launches, whaleboats, wherries,
Whitehall boats, Japanese yamato boats, Saint Lawrence skiffs, bugeyes, Great
Lakes racing scows, multihulls (power and sail), dhows in all their many flavors
(baghlas, booms, sambuks, balms), North Sea motor trawlers, Baltimore clippers,
Danish coastal seiners, Hawaiian power sampans, Chinese junks, Chesapeake Bay
skipjacks, Lafitte skiffs. . . . Well, you see the problem.

The boats included here for some reason came to the top of this wonderfully
long list. Some I was asked to design, others seemed to fill a special need at some
particular time, still others just struck my fancy. The remainder still beckon invit-
ingly. Let's see . . . the sampan would make a fine cruiser. What we'd want to do
is . . . .

CHAPTER 1

The Earliest Yachts—a Gift From the Dutch

She still had a bright black eye and jet black hair, was comely, dimpled, plump and tight as a gooseberry, and though she was not exactly what the world calls young, you may make an affidavit, on trust, before any mayor or magistrate in Christendom that there are a great many young ladies in the world (blessings on them, one and all!) whom you wouldn't like half as well or admire half as much as the beaming hostess of the Blue Dragon.

Martin Chuzzlewit, Charles Dickens

Although even the ancient Egyptians would poke about the Nile for pleasure, the first modern form of yacht appeared during the late 1500s or early 1600s, in Holland. At this time, the Dutch had one of the greatest naval trading empires the world had ever seen. Not surprisingly, they had their share of trouble with smugglers and the like. Accordingly, they evolved small, handy, shoal craft for pursuing illegal traders—sounds familiar, doesn't it?—and they called these vessels "jaghts." This comes from the Dutch word "jagen," meaning to hunt—after all, they were hunting smugglers. Of course, it's not much of a step from "jaght" to "yacht," and this is where our English word "yacht" comes from.

A King Has Fun at Sea

It wasn't long before wealthy Dutch ship owners and government officials discovered that just messing about on the company jaght was, well—fun. Indeed, it became such a sign of wealth and status that in 1660 a "jachtschippen"—the *Mary*—was given as a royal gift to Charles II of England on his return to power. Old King Charles (he was young at the time) took to his new toy so well he actually started designing yachts himself. Naturally, this snazzy craze quickly spread through the aristocracy of the British Isles, France, Germany, and—well, the rest is history.

Massive is the Word

Incredibly, if you visit the Netherlands today, you'll have no difficulty finding numerous private yachts that are astoundingly similar to the *Mary* of 1660. She, like all her kin, was fantastically massive and bluff-bowed by modern standards. Fifty-two feet (15.8 m) overall, with 19 feet (5.8 m) of beam, she is said to have displaced just over 100 tons; however, this seems impossibly high. (A solid block of these dimensions would just displace 100 tons.) Sixty-five to 75 tons is almost certainly nearer the mark. Even so, these figures are nothing short of amazing.

Assuming just over 70 tons, the *Mary*'s displacement-to-length ratio (see Chapter 13) was 600 (a typical modern yacht is well under 350, usually under 280) and her length-to-beam ratio was 2.7 to 1. By current theory, such a boat couldn't sail out of its own way. Nevertheless, these boats did and do sail quite well. Modern Dutch yachts are less extreme than the *Mary,* but still very, very bluff and heavy by our current standards.

Of course, there isn't just one form of Dutch yacht; a number of types evolved independently over the years, usually from fishing and trading craft as well as the smuggler chasers. The best known of these is the "boier," closely followed by the "botter" and the lesser-known "hoogaar." All have many similarities. They're all heavy-displacement and extremely shoal; 60-footers (18.5 m) drawing just 2 feet 8 inches (80 cm) are not at all uncommon. They also share that well-recognized peculiarity—leeboards. The leeboard is the ancestor of our centerboard. It's seldom used in the United States except on dinghies, and—if you ever own a boat equipped with them, as I have—you may find your friends making com-

A botter in a one-reef breeze. (Courtesy Netherlands Board of Tourism)

ments about boats with wings, frequently accompanied by demonstrative gesticulations.

Working the Wings

Through unfamiliarity, most American sailors are downright suspicious of leeboards, but they shouldn't be. Not only is a pair of leeboards simpler and less expensive to install than a single centerboard in a trunk, but the leeboards are actually a bit more effective for their size. Why is this? Well, when your centerboard is down it operates only from the bottom of the hull (centerboard slot) down. The leeboard, on the other hand, is fully effective from the waterline down. This means that for the same overall draft, the leeboard has several square feet of additional effective area.

The drill when tacking with leeboards is to call "helm's alee," drop the upwind board and put the helm over. As soon as the tack is completed, the newly dropped weather-board becomes the leeboard, and the former leeboard becomes the weather-board and is hoisted. It's not actually

A fleet of racing boiers in light air. Note the leeboard down. (Courtesy Netherlands Board of Tourism)

necessary to raise the new weather-board immediately, as it is free to pivot harmlessly out away from the hull and so trails like a broken wing until you have time to get it in. It simply adds a small bit of resistance and a rather pleasant swooshing sound. During short tacking, as in picking up a mooring, you can leave both leeboards down and ignore them completely until you're hooked on safely.

Leeboards: Strong and Simple

Another nice feature of leeboards is that they make for a much stronger boat. Centerboard slots actually cut the hull structure in half transversely right at the center of the vessel. In Northern Europe, tidal ranges are huge by U.S. standards, and there are many shallow tidal estuaries and inlets—as Erskine Childers's marvelous spy tale, *Riddle of the Sands*, makes clear. This is the reason

Bow view of a botter in a race of botters. The fantastically bluff bow, curved gaff, and raised weather leeboard are clearly visible. (Courtesy Netherlands Board of Tourism)

the Dutch yachts have such shoal draft. These craft are designed specifically to dry out with the tide day in and day out, often in less than ideal conditions. Thus, they require unusually strong bottoms. By opting for leeboards instead of centerboards, these vessels are eliminating a potential source of structural weakness and also any chance for a centerboard to be jammed with gravel and sand forced in during a grounding.

The Usual Rig

Almost all the Dutch yachts are sloop rigged with a gaff mainsail—the *grootzeil*—having a short, curved gaff. Customarily, a single large jib—the *fokzeil*—is set to the stemhead and a second flying jib—*kluiverzeil*—is set on a removable or housing bowsprit. (The Dutch claim that a housing bowsprit isn't a bowsprit at all, and who knows, they may be right. They call their housing non-bowsprits *kluivers*.) In modern times, many of the larger of these craft have been given ketch rigs and even, on rare occasions, schooner rigs. After all, the sails on a 100-ton sloop would be quite a handful.

Boiers, Botters, and Hoogaars

The principal difference among the boier, botter, and hoogaar is in their hull shapes. The boier is a fully round-bilged hull. Massive, bluff, and shoal as they are, such craft have no flat spots or chines anywhere. The boier's near cousin—the botter—has nicely rounded topsides, but her bottom is quite flat and meets the topsides at a hard chine. From the chine up the botter and the boier are so close in appearance that few experts can tell them apart in the water. This has caused endless confusion over the years as—to the uninitiated—it seems that the terms "boier" and "botter" are used interchangeably. Very little difference in the performance of the boier and the botter is evident, and the botter's only apparent advantage is that it will sit perfectly level when dry on a sandbank, whereas a boier might occasionally heel over as much as, oh, four degrees.

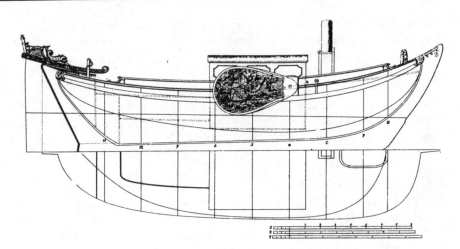

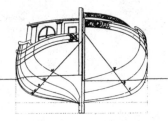

A 25-foot 4-inch (7.7 m) boier reproduced from the 1768 naval architecture text Architectura Navalis Mercatoria, *by F.H. Chapman. Her beam is 8 feet 4 inches (2.5 m) and her draft 2 feet 5 inches (74 cm). She is described, even as late as 1768, as a "Dutch scout or boyert," the term "scout" indicating the original purpose of these boats: hunting smugglers and charting tidal estuaries. Modern boiers are remarkably similar in form.*

Hoogaars are a bit different. Where both the boier and the botter have rounded topsides and very bluff vertical bows, the hoogaar has a flat bottom and simple, flat sections to her topsides. Additionally, the hoogaar's bow, although bluff, rakes out and forward at a pronounced angle. This makes the topsides easier to plank and also gives these craft a distinctive appearance. Originally, the slightly simpler form of the hoogaars made them the workingman's alternative to the somewhat more elegant botter and boier. Today, this distinction is nearly lost. Hoogaars are usually under 50 feet (15 m) or so and built lapstrake. Vessels over 50 feet (15 m) with the hoogaar's shape are usually smooth or carvel planked and are called "schokkers." (Perhaps Dutch seamen found such boats shocking.)

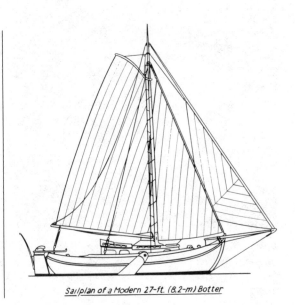

Sailplan of a Modern 27-ft. (8.2-m) Botter

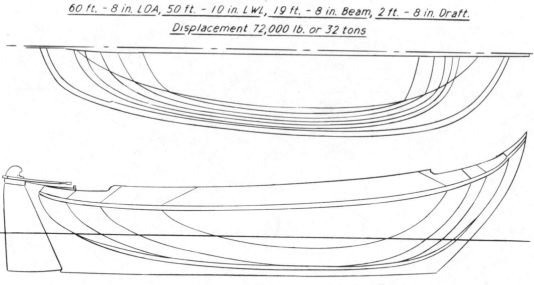

60 ft. - 8 in. LOA, 50 ft. - 10 in. LWL, 19 ft. - 8 in. Beam, 2 ft. - 8 in. Draft.
Displacement 72,000 lb. or 32 tons

Lines of a Typical Botter

The Question of Performance

Of course, the great question is how do these boiers, botters, and hoogaars sail? Although I built and owned a leeboard yacht some years ago, I've never sailed a true botter or one of her kindred. I do know, from personal experience, that handling leeboards is no problem at all. The sailing performance of true botters, boiers, and hoogaars, however, has long been a matter of debate.

Naval architect L. Francis Herreshoff made great claims for these craft. He said:

> . . . These fine little vessels seem to tromp the waves under them instead of cutting through them, and they really do go to windward remarkably well in a sea. They also have an easy motion and the larger ones have high bulwarks, so that altogether this type of craft is well thought of by yachtsmen of Great Britain as well as Holland.

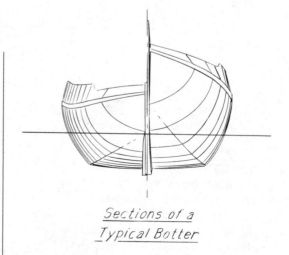

Sections of a Typical Botter

On the other side of the coin is the experience of famous turn-of-the-century British yachtsman Claud Worth. He cruised the coast of England and Europe extensively from 1900 through the next several decades. A friend of his named Bennet fell in love with a boier—which Worth mistakenly

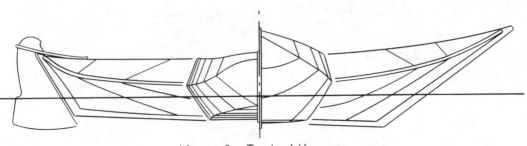

Lines of a Typical Hoogaar

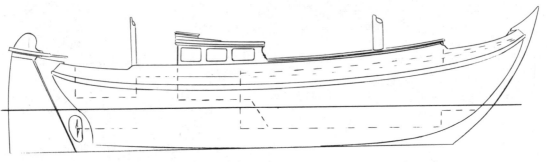

Profile of a 60-ft. (18.3-m) Botter with Small Pilothouse

calls a botter—and asked Worth to help him sail her. Worth recounts their experience:

We tried her during two week-ends in the Thames Estuary, but she was altogether too slow and heavy for the purpose. The sails were light to handle, and her powerful winch made the ground tackle easy enough to work, but she made a very poor show to windward, except with a good breeze and a favorable tide. In light airs she was quite helpless.

Bennet thought he would like to try her in more open waters. We sailed with a fair wind down to Dungeness, and brought up for the night in the east roads. Next morning there was a fresh breeze W.S.W. We cleared the Ness at about 7 a.m. and at first made

fair progress to windward. But when the sea began to get up, she soon showed us that she was not designed for this kind of work. She had to be sailed hard to keep going at all. When she pitched into the trough of the sea, instead of rising gently over the next sea, she would ram it hard with her square bows, completely stopping her way. There was as much wind as she wanted with a single-reefed mainsail. The sea was rather high, but easy and regular.

So, who's right? I suspect both accounts are on target. The Dutch yachts will sail wonderfully from a close reach on down. They can also be made to go to weather quite respectably in moderate to strong wind and relatively smooth seas. The one thing they will not do well, and the one thing that Claud Worth was looking for, is go to windward in light or moderate airs and steep seas. This is not what these vessels were designed for.

Retiring Afloat

For sheer room and comfort, however, these boats are nearly unequaled. If you're ever seriously considering living aboard, a 45- to 60-foot (13.7 to 18.3 m) botter or boier would be hard to beat. Easy motion, fantastic roominess, and their massive, solid feeling will keep you comfortable blow high or low. Even better, the modern marine engine eliminates the problem of working to windward in tough conditions. A fair-sized diesel driving a large, controllable pitch, fully feathering propeller would take care of this one weakness handily. Additionally, most boiers, botters, and hoogaars have their masts stepped in tabernacles and neatly counterbalanced for quick and easy raising and lowering, which makes it possible to take them into all those tight, interesting places that seem to be guarded by bridges.

Hmm . . . I'd spend the summer in New England, a couple of months working leisurely down the Intracoastal Waterway in the fall, poke about the Caribbean through winter, and back north in spring—all without stirring from my large three-bedroom home. I think I could just manage to endure such a life.

CHAPTER 2

The Dory— The Seaman's Sea Boat

There was slack time at noon, and the dories began to search for amusement. It was Dan who sighted the Hope of Prague *just coming up, and as her boats joined the company they were greeted with the question: "Who's the meanest man in the Fleet?"*

Three hundred voices answered cheerily: "Nick Bra-ady."

It sounded like an organ chant.

Captains Courageous, *Rudyard Kipling*

Dory! The name alone evokes the tang of salt air, fresh fish, and the sound of ships' bells clanging mournfully through a fog. For well over a century, these craft have seen every sort of hard service imaginable. They are found in nearly every port of the world. They have been riverboats, ocean fishermen, yachts, and utility craft. Steeped in legend, they figure in many barroom tales.

The Indomitable Captain Blackburn

One of these yarns comes from the days of the Grand Banks fishing fleets. Just before the turn of the century, Howard Blackburn was crew on a Gloucester fishing schooner. As was the custom, he and a mate were dropped off in their dory for an afternoon of longlining until the mother ship returned to pick them up. In just a few short hours, however, a raging snowstorm blew in, the schooner couldn't find them, and the two seamen were lost. "Astray," as they termed it then—the greatest fear of any doryman. Three hundred miles from the coast of Newfoundland, the only hope—and it wasn't much of one—was to row to shore. With no other chance for survival they did just that, rowing across 300 miles of freezing Atlantic in their trusty dory.

Blackburn's companion didn't survive the frigid voyage, but Blackburn did—losing his fingers, which he allowed to freeze around the oars when they could no longer grip. So tough a character was Captain Blackburn that he later sailed transatlantic alone several times, always in boats under 25 feet (7.6 m) long. He even won one of the first solo transatlantic races, beating a sailor named Andrews in 1901. Years later, Blackburn retired to the old sailor's most pleasant job—and natural shoreside haunt—running a saloon. He was happy there until it was closed during Prohibition, whereupon Blackburn died—some claimed of a broken heart. "The sea couldn't get him," they said, "but the law did."

Slocum Builds a Dory

At about the time of Blackburn's many adventures, none other than the most famous solo sailor

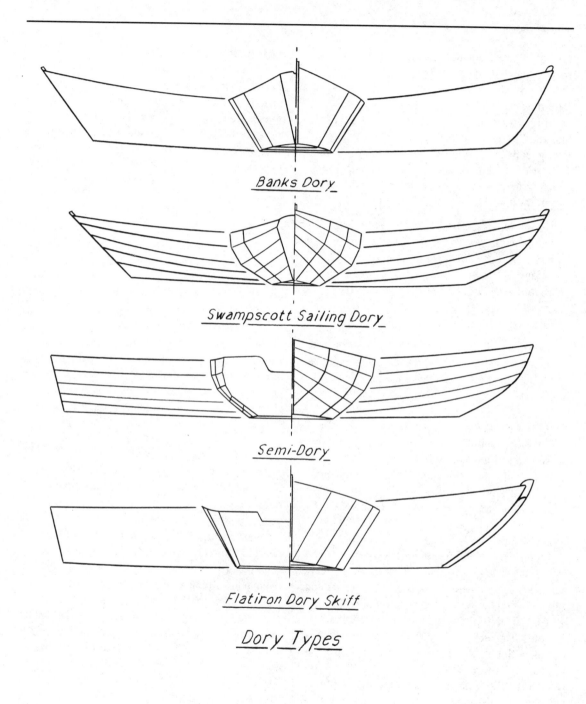

Banks Dory

Swampscott Sailing Dory

Semi-Dory

Flatiron Dory Skiff

Dory Types

himself, Captain Joshua Slocum, called on a dory to get him out of desperate straights. Slocum's command, the 326-ton bark *Aquidneck,* sank, stranding Slocum and his entire family in Brazil. Destitute, with no resources other than his skills and the salvage from the wreck, Slocum and his family built a modified Cape Ann dory, 35 feet (10.6 m) long, and rigged her as a Chinese junk. (Cape Ann dories were modified banks dories rigged for longshore sailing.) Slocum himself said:

> *Seaworthiness was to be the first and most prominent feature in our microscopid ship; next to this good quality she should sail well; at least before free winds, for we counted on favorable winds; and so they were experienced the greater part of the voyage that followed.*

With his family as both crew and passengers, Slocum's dory, the *Liberdade,* lived up to expectations, scudding the entire Slocum clan home safe and sound.

The Dory's Two Great Advantages

It is the combination of these two attributes, seaworthiness and ease of construction, that have made the dory so popular. A dory offers more boat for the dollar—and more safe and reliable boat, at that—than nearly any other sort of craft.

Types of Dories

There are, of course, quite a few types of dories. The best known is the banks dory, these being the above-mentioned boats used by the fishing schooners off the Grand Banks. Although often lap-straked, their topsides are dead flat, as are their bottoms. The largest working version of the banks dories is the St. Pierre dory. These craft are frequently as large as 35 or 40 feet (11 to 12 m)—although 25 to 30 feet (7.6 to 9.2 m) is more common. Open or half-decked, with a cuddy cabin and a small, slow-turning engine, they have established a remarkable reputation for thrift and reliability.

Narrow Bottoms—Tender Ships

One of the dory's few faults—if you can call it that—is that it is very narrow on the bottom. This inclines dories to be fairly tippy initially, even though their great flare gives them plenty of reserve stability. For this reason, many pleasure dories are built with widened bottoms. Not only does this stiffen them and give them a bit more room, it also adds extra planing surface, for higher-speed types.

Dory Skiffs

Taken to the extreme for high-speed outboards, widening the bottom yields the semi-dory and the flatiron dory skiff. The semi-dory and dory skiff both have wide, flat bottoms aft and resemble typical planing outboard boats in their proportions, but with the handsome dory sheer and plenty of flare to their topsides. The chief difference between the semi-dory and the dory skiff is that the semi-dory has the two or three upper planks of its topsides laid on at varying angles, giving a round-bilge appearance, whereas the dory skiff has flat topsides like a banks dory.

The Problem With Sailing Dories

Dories are principally powerboats. (Rowboats are the earliest form of powerboat.) With their low initial stability, they don't sail well upwind. As you could see from Captain Slocum's comments earlier, he was well aware of this. He charted the course of *Liberdade* carefully to avoid sailing hard on the wind. Although there have been many attempts at making sailing yachts from a dory, they haven't met with much success. In fact, the only truly fine sailing dory is the sailing Swampscott. These craft are usually between 18 and 25 feet (5.5 to 7.6 m) long, with narrow beam and low topsides. Their lapstraked hulls are so finely modeled that, for all practical purposes, they are really round-bottom boats with a broad, flat keel. As lively daysailers, the Swampscott dories are a delight. Their hulls are so fine, however,

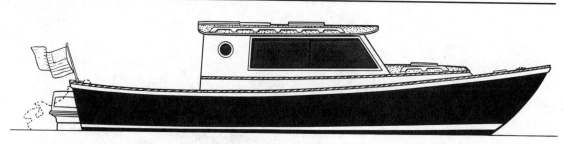

Profile of the 28-foot (8.5 m) sheet plywood Offshore Skiff.

that you'd have to build a 40-footer (12 m) just to get minimum weekender accommodations.

More Boat for the Buck

Of course, banks dories and St. Pierre dories have been modified to sail with some success, but you have to fight their lack of stability all the way. Better to start with a hull that's more suited to sailing. For a power cruiser, though, an enlarged dory—either a dory skiff or a banks or St. Pierre dory—offers more boat for the buck than nearly any other craft.

The Offshore Skiff—An Economical Cruiser/Commuter

At 28 feet 3 inches (8.6 m) overall, 24 feet (7.3 m) on the waterline, 8 feet beam (2.4 m), 5,400 pounds (2,450 kg) displacement, and drawing a scant 15 inches (38 cm) to the bottom of her hull (26 inches or 66 cm to the bottom of her outboard), The Offshore Skiff is a good example of what can be wrought from the dory concept. Large enough to do an honest day's work and small enough not to ruin your savings account, her hull is a cross between the semi-dory and the flatiron dory skiff. These well-proven traditional hulls have a great reputation for speed and seaworthiness.

A single 75-hp (56 kw) outboard would give her an easy cruising speed of 16 knots with a top speed of 19 knots. In any ordinary weather, The Offshore Skiff will cover roughly 200 miles in 12

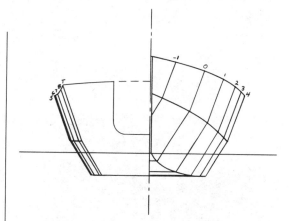

Sections of The Offshore Skiff. Her shape is derived from the flatiron dory skiff and the semi-dory.

hours without strain. With 120 gallons (454 l) fuel tankage, her cruising range is some 370 miles. You could run from Narragansett Bay out to Block Island, past Montauk Point and on into Shelter Island in a single afternoon. Boston Harbor to Martha's Vinyard would take just over 7 hours, and you'd finish with 70 percent of your fuel still left in the tanks. New York Harbor to Cape May, Eastchester Bay to New London, or Coney Island to Point Judith all leave you half a tank of fuel or more in reserve.

Speed demons could fit The Offshore Skiff with up to 150 hp (112 kw), which would give her a cruising speed of 23 knots and a top speed around 26. With the same 120 gallons (454 l), this would reduce range to 260 miles, but you'd get there in

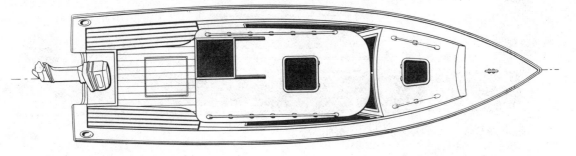

Deck plan of The Offshore Skiff.

Bow view of The Offshore Skiff.

just over 11 hours. The drawback is that your fuel bill will be higher. Also, at 23 knots or more, a light, flat-bottom hull like this will start to jump out of the water and pound when the seas pick up. You'll have to slow back down to 16 or 17 knots in rougher conditions, at which time the 150-hp (112 kw) engine will be running far less economically than the 75-hp (56 kw) machine would be.

Like most dories, The Offshore Skiff's hull is easy to build. In fact, she's of tape-seam (or epoxy-chine) sheet-plywood construction, which is about the simplest method of boatbuilding. There are no chine logs to bend into place and bevel, the cabin sides all have exactly the same slope, and all the deck crowns are constant. Framing is nearly

all off-the-shelf standard lumberyard stock, and the hull and cabin are all of ⅝-inch (16 mm) marine plywood, sheathed in glass laid in epoxy. Couldn't make a hull much simpler!

The arrangement plan shown here crams a lot of living room into a 28-footer (8.5 m). The cockpit is 7 feet (2.1 m) long. The wheelhouse/cabin has 6-foot 4-inch (193 cm) headroom throughout. She's fitted with an enclosed stand-up head with telephone handset-type shower, a full galley with over 6 feet (1.8 m) of counter space, and a 6-foot 4-inch (193 cm) settee berth and dropleaf table to starboard. The table folds down and the berth extends to create a small double berth. Forward is a small stateroom with sitting headroom and a vee berth, with 8 feet (243 cm) of sleeping length to port and 6 feet 6 inches (198 cm) to starboard.

The forward wheelhouse windows fold completely open. The forward half of the side windows slide back, and the skylight, companionway slide, and forecabin hatch can be left open for ventilation. With all this fresh air, it'll feel like being under a bimini top outside rather than being enclosed in a cabin. A couple can take a very comfortable vacation in a layout like this, while there's plenty of room for a day party of four to six.

If you're after less accommodations and more working space, The Offshore Skiff can be built as an open, center-console vessel, with no cabin at all or just a small cuddy forward. The center-console version of The Offshore Skiff would serve admirably as everything from a sportfishing platform to a dive

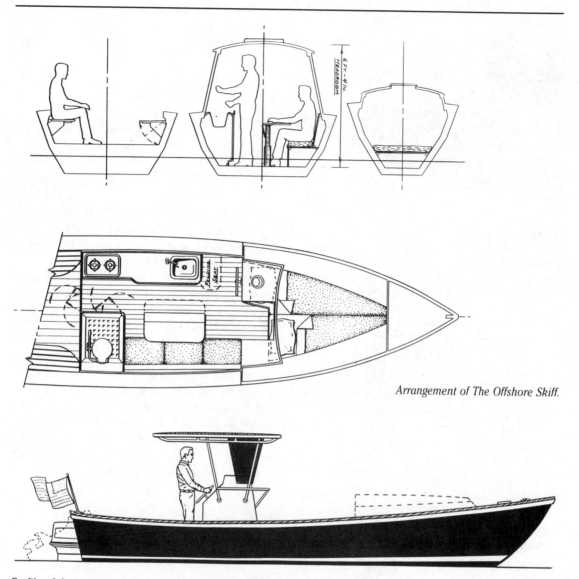

Arrangement of The Offshore Skiff.

Profile of the center-console version of The Offshore Skiff.

boat, longshore lobsterman, or even a small long-liner. Take your pick.

Shellback—A Liveaboard Dory Motor Cruiser

The illustrations show the 65-foot (19.8 m) dory cruiser Shellback—the dory form taken to the max. If you've ever dreamed of retiring afloat and cruising the coast and the Caribbean under power, a boat like this would seem to fill all the requirements. She is large enough to offer all the comforts of home—three private double cabins; two heads, one with a full-size bathtub; a washer/

This open, center-console Offshore Skiff was built by Captain Steve Ellis in just over two months. He reports that—fitted with a single 70-hp outboard—she does 21 knots light-loaded and climbs fully onto plane at just 11 to 12 knots. A commercial fisherman, Steve runs his skiff in all sorts of weather. "She goes nicely without pounding at just under plane [10 knots or so] in short, steep, 5- to 6-foot seas," he says. He beaches the boat routinely. (S. Ellis photo)

dryer; a large refrigerator/freezer; plenty of big hanging lockers; an enclosed wheelhouse for steering out of the weather; and a huge, unencumbered flush deck, with deep bulwarks for lounging about in the sunshine. Add in a full 6-foot 6-inch (198 cm) headroom throughout, and room on

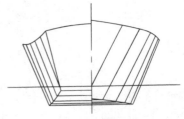

Sections of Shellback. Her hull is that of a modified banks dory.

deck for a really large 14-foot (4.3 m) ship's launch complete with proper hoisting gear, and you've got the perfect retirement home. What's more, she'll cruise at a comfortable 14 knots with twin 150-hp (112 kw) engines—smaller than those installed in many 35-foot (11 m) sportfishermen—giving her a range of 1,000 miles on a single 650-gallon (2,460 l) fill-up.

Shellback was designed for sheet-steel construction—one of the least expensive ways to build a boat one-off at any commercial yard. Sheet aluminum or epoxy-saturated sheet plywood—like a scaled-up version of The Offshore Skiff—would do equally well. Kept simple—leave the fancy electronics and hand-carved teak interior out (at least until you've got her launched)—the 65-foot (19.8 m) Shellback could be built for less

Profile of the 65-foot (19.8 m) sheet-steel or sheet plywood dory motorcruiser Shellback.

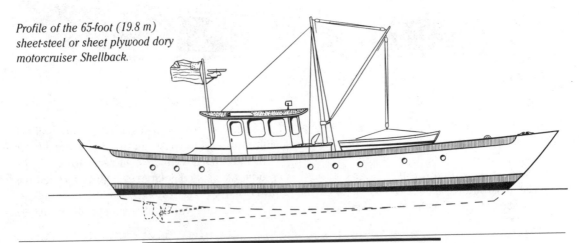

than the cost of many a production 45-footer (13.7 m)—and operate for less too. Naturally, if your plans are not this ambitious, you could build a 45-foot (13.7 m) or so dory motor cruiser for about the price of a 30- or 35-foot (9 to 11 m) production power cruiser. Keep the overall design simple and the dory's strengths and weaknesses in mind, and your imagination is the only limit.

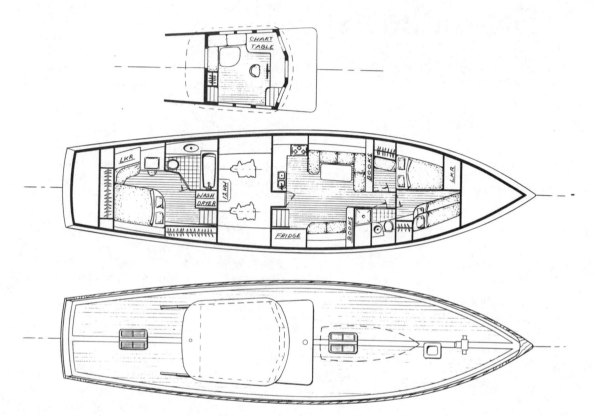

Arrangement and deck plan of Shellback.

CHAPTER 3

Sharpshooters— The Catboats That Never Were

"... and what I can see, I can hit at a hundred yards, though it were only a mosquito's eye. Be ready to clench!"

The Pathfinder, James Fenimore Cooper

Catboats! Rare indeed is the sailor who doesn't harbor some deep fondness for these homely craft. Their wide, plain hulls tromp purposefully across the seas like graceful hippopotami. Elegant in their simplicity and sporting a single great butterfly wing—a gaff sail bowed to the breeze—they remind us of an era when, on the water, work and pleasure alike were carried out under oars or sail. Horace, Charles, and Herbert Crosby, C.C. Hanley, and Fenwick C. Williams—they're still names to conjure with. Their creations, imbued with the immortality of spare utility and common sense, sail on.

The One Ingredient for a Catboat

Of course, the one feature that truly makes a catboat a catboat is that she has only one sail and one mast—it really doesn't matter what kind of sail or rig. I suppose you could have a square-rigged catboat, though she'd be a queer duck indeed. In fact, the British for a time were calling catboats "una boats"—"una" for one sail. I'm thankful this term never caught on here; somehow, it seems a soulless sort of moniker for vessels with so much character.

Catboats from the Cape

Of all catboats, the most common—the type you're probably visualizing now—is the Cape Cod cat. They evolved from Newport Point boats (keel boats), through practical centerboard fishing craft, into thoroughly impractical sandbaggers (racing craft with booms and bowsprits each longer than the hull). The standard Cape Cod cat, however, has a reasonably proportioned rig, is nearly half as wide as she is long, and has a shoal underbody so flat that her draft is usually less than 10 percent of her length—a true skimming dish. A 25-footer (7.6 m) might have 12 feet (3.6 m) of beam and draw just 2 feet 3 inches (68 cm)—including skeg—with her centerboard raised.

Given just the right reaching breeze, the Cape Cod catboat will pick up her skirts—petticoats and all—and take off. Otherwise, these vessels

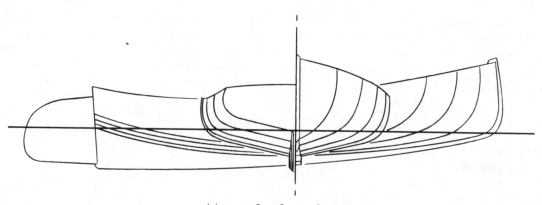

Lines of a Cape Cod Catboat

aren't notably fast, particularly upwind where their bluff, shoal hulls butt rather than slice through the chop. Further, for all their splendid simplicity—beamy, stable, and shoal—the Cape Cod cats are really longshore boats. Their wide, shallow hulls can give a false sense of security; though hard to start over, once heeled too far—they capsize. This lack of weatherliness and reserve stability is the bane of all skimming-dish craft.

Requirements for Something Different

Accordingly, when the publisher of *Offshore* magazine asked me to draw up a catboat for him I paid special attention to his requirements. Herb Gliick was going to keep his boat on Buzzards Bay, where it breezes up regularly with a short, steep chop, yet he wanted a boat that would be a pleasure to sail and safe and secure in anything he was likely to encounter. He and his wife didn't want to feel skittish about their craft if they had to work their way home some afternoon in a 25-knot headwind. They also wanted a rig that would be easy to handle and simple to maintain.

A Boat from the Bahamas

Immediately, another form of catboat sprang to mind—the Bahama sharpshooter. Described glowingly in the pages of Howard Chapelle's *Amer-*

ican Sailing Craft, the Bahama sharpshooter is a keel boat—surprisingly similar to the Newport Point boat. Her beam is a seagoing 33 percent or so of her length, and her draft (with keel) is a good 15 to 18 percent of her length. A 25-footer (7.6 m) would have 8 to 9 feet (2.4 to 2.7 m) beam and 3 feet 9 inches to 4 feet 9 inches (1.1 to 1.4 m) of draft. These are much more seakindly proportions than those of the longshore Cape Cod cat.

Leg-o-Mutton Anyone?

Even better, the sharpshooter has a leg-o-mutton or jibheaded sail rather than the traditional Cape Cod gaff rig. This makes for less weight and windage aloft, fewer halyards, and easier handling. What's more, the sharpshooter's mast is raked far aft. This not only gives her a jaunty look but serves to keep the center of effort of the reefed sails close to the fore-and-aft location of that of the unreefed sail. Where the Cape Cod cat is notorious for its strong, difficult-to-manage weather helm in heavy air, the sharpshooter balances nicely in these conditions.

The Catch

There was only one problem. Like Fenimore Cooper's sharpshooter Hawkeye, from this chapter's opening quote, the Bahama sharpshooter is largely the figment of one man's imagination. The man? The very same Howard I. Chapelle, perhaps the most respected and prolific of all marine historians. His books—much thumbed and covered with handwritten notes—line the shelves of my office, and I'm sure those of many other designers. It would be impossible to overestimate his contribution to understanding and preserving information about the history of ship and boat design.

Yet Chapelle had his weaknesses. It was not unknown for him to "improve" the lines of a traditional boat when he measured and recorded them; he was known to be less than eager to do detailed weight calculations on his own boat designs; and he occasionally based the entire premise for the origin of historical vessels on rather skimpy research.

It was just such abbreviated research that sired the Bahama sharpshooter. Chapelle claimed, strangely enough, that the Bahama sharpshooter, although developed in and for the Bahamas, was created by a New Yorker from Staten Island—a fellow named Benjamin Morton. A boatbuilder by trade, according to Chapelle, Morton was advised sometime in the late 1850s to take a voyage to the West Indies for his health. He wound up on Eleuthera Island, to the east of Nassau, and found it so much to his liking he stayed. (Ah, those were the days.) At any rate, Morton soon found himself in need of a reliable boat. Fishing, daysailing, and carrying light cargo were all required. He also needed an able boat that could safely weather the stiff tradewinds and ragged storms that blew through the area regularly. He named his boat *Sharpshooter.* Again, according to Chapelle, she lived up to all expectations, and the name stuck.

The Truth

In fact, Chapelle had only had time to visit Eleuthera Island rather briefly. He scouted Tarpum Bay, but never got to the major boatbuilding areas on Ragged Island, on the Abacos, or at Andros. Actually, no Bahamian ever called a boat a "sharpshooter," and this general type of vessel had existed years before the Yankee Morton arrived.

Unfortunately, the locals—mostly of African descent—were less than dirt poor. Although they built, worked, and fished boats with considerable industry, these craft were finished in the crudest fashion, with incredibly ragged and baggy sails, rotten and chafed line, worn paintwork, and cobbled-together fittings. It appears that Chapelle fell victim to the prejudices of his day, and it never occurred to him that these dark sailors and their rough craft were the true origins of a fine type. He must have assumed that Benjamin Morton's yacht-quality copy was the inspiration, and the

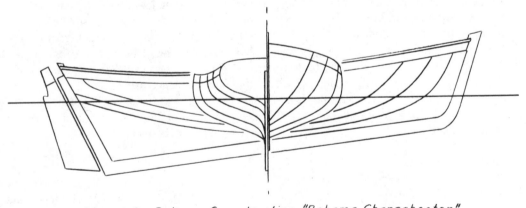

Lines of a Bahama Smack, alias "Bahama Sharpshooter"

Bahama sloops (alias "sharpshooters") still sail today, specialized for racing. Here is one of the most famous of these boats, Tidal Wave. *With lower freeboard and much larger sail plans than their working ancestors, in a breeze these craft are held up by the "pry," a hiking plank or board on which as many as a dozen crew will perch. (Art Paine photo)*

Bahamian's own craft mere imitation. In reality, the reverse was the case. Rather than "sharp-shooters," the Bahamian sailors simply called these boats "smacks," "sloops" (when they were sloop rigged), or "bare-headed smacks" (in the larger catboat sizes).

Turning Her into a Pocket Cruiser

Whatever the name or origin, however, a boat of this type would make a wonderful cruising boat. Secure, weatherly, and easily handled, she can be relied on to sail you out of a hard chance. Herb Gliick had one additional requirement, and that was very shoal draft. Accordingly, his *Elisily II* was designed with a centerboard all the way aft. This unusual centerboard location was necessary to get the right helm balance with the well-raked rig; it worked out very nicely. The centerboard trunk doubles as a gigantic cockpit drain and is entirely out of the cabin, creating plenty of unimpeded, sprawling space.

The Unsinkable *Elisily II*

All sharpshooters or Bahamian smacks have a much greater range of stability than Cape Cod cats, and *Elisily* is no exception, but to get the ultimate in safety we fitted her with full foam flotation. Not only is she stable over a wide range of heel, but she's totally unsinkable as well. On a small boat like the 21-foot 6-inch (6.5 m) *Elisily II*,

Sail plan of Elisily II.

flotation is fairly easy to work in. You just install foam under large portions of the sole, the berths and seat flats, under the cockpit seats, and in the lazarette. Being a daysailer and overnighter, *Elisily II* doesn't have to carry much in the way of stores or gear. On larger cruising boats, though, finding space for all this foam is quite difficult. Everywhere you want to put foam, you also want to stow gear and install tanks and equipment. This is one of the principal reasons you seldom find larger vessels fitted with foam flotation—though it can and has been done.

Oceangoing Bahamian Smacks

Most of the Bahamian smacks were 25 feet (7.6 m) or less overall. Chapelle records Morton's *Sharpshooter* as being 36 feet (10.9 m) long. In fact,

Sections of Elisily II.

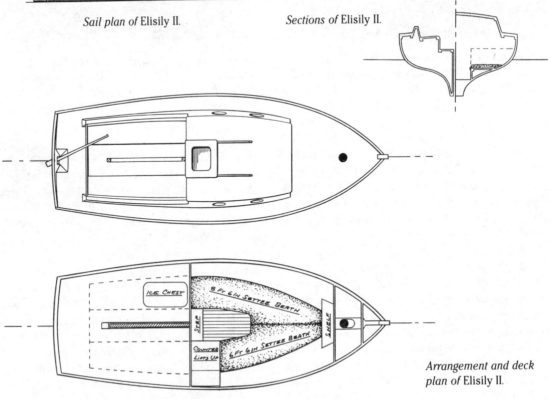

Arrangement and deck plan of Elisily II.

Bahamian smacks or sharpshooters as large as 55 feet (16.7 m) or so have been built. In this size, they make wonderful, safe, voyaging liveaboards. The Bahamian smack is heavier-displacement than most modern cruisers and so has more room for a given length and an easier and steadier motion. Some years ago, I met naval architect Morgan Mac-Donald and his wife aboard their smack at the Newport Wooden Boat Show. They'd purchased a 30-plus-footer (11 m) and converted her into a home.

Mac is quite a sailor, and he and his wife had just voyaged from the Bahamas through a hurricane. When I asked him if they'd had a hard time of it, he replied, "Nope, it was a pretty nice hurricane. This was my fifth or sixth one, no problems at all." This says volumes for Mac and his wife's seamanship—not to mention their stamina—but it says something about the Bahamian smacks as well. And she was so cozy and handsome that Mac's boat was one of the few larger wooden craft to sell on the spot, right at the show.

A Liveaboard Smack

Mac's Bahamian smack had been rerigged as a sloop. This is because, in larger vessels, the single large sail can be a bear to manage shorthanded—although in stiff breezes, Mac would drop his jib and sail under reefed main alone. Breaking the sail plan up into jib and main cut the individual sail sizes roughly in half. A still better arrangement might be a cat ketch—a ketch rig without headstays or headsails. Such a rig on a 45-foot (14 m) Bahamian smack would make for exceptionally safe, simple voyaging. Without headsails to worry about, the rig would remain particularly agreeable to handle. Additionally, you'd have the ability to

lie hove-to at will. Just drop the main and sheet the mizzen flat, and presto, the cat-ketch-rigged smack will weathercock into the wind and lie safe and steady under consummate control—try that on a conventional sloop! Finally, when the spirit moves, you could set a great mizzen staysail that would pull you along fiercely on a reach.

At 45 feet (13.7 m) overall, beam would be about 14 feet (4.2 m) and draft 6 feet (1.8 m)—or perhaps 4 feet 6 inches (1.4 m) with a centerboard—with full standing headroom throughout. All manner of accommodation plans would fit in handily. In fact, if I were planning to cruise the Caribbean, investigate the coast of Nova Scotia, or explore the South Pacific, I might very well choose a cat-ketch-rigged craft.

An interesting benefit of the deepish—by modern standards—Bahamian smack's hull is that at 45 feet (14 m) or so it would have full standing headroom under a flush deck. Not only does this simplify construction and increase strength (flush decks have no exposed cabin sides to get stove in by heavy seas), but it creates tremendous additional visible space below decks. A standard 45-foot (14 m) trunk-cabin boat with 14-foot (4.2 m) beam would have a visible interior cabin width of just 11 feet (3.3 m) or so. Obviously, a flush-decker with the same 14-foot (4.2 m) beam would have nearly her full 14 feet (4.2 m) of clear transverse inside space—a 27 percent increase in real and psychological elbow room. Additionally, on deck, the flush-decked vessel offers you one huge, unobstructed surface—a veritable floating backyard. By comparison, usable, livable deck area on most trunk-cabin boats is restricted to the cockpit, narrow side decks, and a small patch of foredeck.

CHAPTER 4

Sea Skiffs: Sea Bright and Otherwise

"Everybody keep his place! This is a federal raid!"

The words were no sooner out than four revolvers hit the floor and four pairs of arms shot into the air. They stood rigid, heads swiveling to the rear as the door from the back room crashed open and Lahart and the prohibition man who had accompanied him burst into the barroom.

The Untouchables, Eliot Ness

If you were to stalk the shoreline of New England and ask sailors to name the most seamanlike and handsome workboat around, you'd find that nine times out of ten the word "lobsterboat" would burst out emphatically. This is hardly a surprise. Lobsterboats are both handsome and seamanlike, and then some. If you venture a bit farther south—southern Connecticut, New York, New Jersey—you'll start hearing a few folks name "the Sea Bright skiff" or "the Jersey skiff." In fact, it's a shame that the lobsterboat—wonderful as it is—has so overshadowed these fine Jersey Shore boats. In some respects, the Sea Bright skiff makes a better all-around boat than the lobsterboat, particularly since it tends to be lighter and thus somewhat more easily driven and more buoyant.

The Sea Bright Skiff

The true Sea Bright skiff developed in the last half of the 19th century and the first half of the 20th. Before dredged and marked channels, there were few usable bays and inlets on the Jersey Shore south of Sandy Hook. If you wanted to fish, you had no choice but to launch off the beach, through whatever surf happened to be running. If you fished for a living and your boat couldn't handle the launching conditions, well, you didn't make any money that day. Clearly, this called for boats that were light and able but very strong, and boats that had good directional stability. It also required a hull that would sit upright and level on the sand.

Box that Garboard

The true Sea Bright skiff evolved gradually to meet these specific requirements. (Not surprisingly, most of the principal early builders were located in or near Sea Bright, New Jersey.) Their hulls are light and strong and their bottoms dead flat athwartships for as much as a third of their beam. The bottom is also fairly flat fore-and-aft, although there may be a slight rocker or curve to the bottom as viewed from the side. The most peculiar

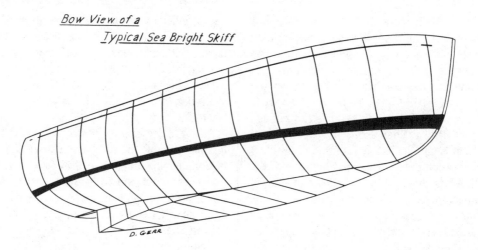

Bow View of a
Typical Sea Bright Skiff

D. GERR

thing about a true Sea Bright skiff, and the feature that really sets it apart from all other boats, is its hollow box garboard or skeg.

You can see on the drawings that a Sea Bright skiff's bottom continues aft flat and level while her hull body sweeps up in the normal manner. To close the gap between the flat bottom aft and the hull above it, the bottommost plank, or garboard, was "rolled" down or twisted.

This box garboard or skeg has many real advantages. A hull of this shape can poke into shoal water and dry out on the tide without a care. In single-engine craft, the prop shaft projects aft out of the center of the after post of the box skeg. The old-time fishermen used to fit their Sea Brights with two-bladed wheels. When beaching, they'd simply lock these props with the blades aligned athwartships, well protected by the box skeg and safe from damage. Even with standard three- and four-bladed wheels, deepening the box skeg slightly or fitting a U-shaped skeg bar below provides complete propeller protection.

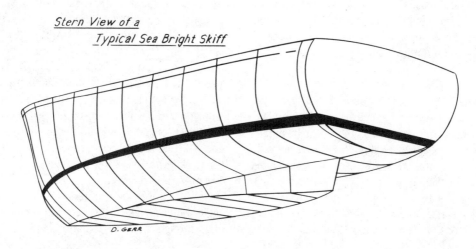

Stern View of a
Typical Sea Bright Skiff

D. GERR

Room Down Under

Another plus of these box skegs is that they create plenty of additional volume low down on the centerline of the hull aft. Since the bottom of the engine can nestle down into the top of the skeg box, Sea Bright skiffs are one of the few relatively light boats that can fit engines low enough to have virtually no shaft angle (that is, their propeller shaft is parallel to the waterline). Low shaft angles mean improved thrust and higher efficiency. At the same time, getting the engine this low in the hull improves stability and reduces rolling, and what's more, frees up room above the engine for storage, work space, or accommodations. Keeping weights low is one of the most important contributors to making a good sea boat, and I wouldn't be surprised if this feature alone accounts for much of the Sea Bright skiff's ableness.

Of course, the box garboard or skeg also acts—who would have guessed it?—like a skeg. In other words, it provides good directional stability. Clearly, this was critical when beaching a boat through surf, but it's also a wonderful feature when maneuvering in choppy seas or any sort of crosswind.

As you follow a Sea Bright skiff's hull forward, you find that the flat bottom tapers to a point well aft of the stem. Accordingly, the Sea Bright skiff's entry is quite sharp. Gently rounded topsides mate with her bottom and stem in a shapely forefoot. Her topsides have a noticeable flare forward, changing gradually to pronounced tumblehome aft.

Carrying a Load

Perhaps the finest thing about Sea Bright skiffs is that they are good at nearly everything. This claim is made for many hulls, but—unfortunately—is seldom so. Sea Bright skiffs, however, are easily driven at low, moderate, and even at semiplaning and low-end planing speeds. They carry large loads very well. A 30-foot (9 m) pound net boat—one of the larger fishing Sea Brights—could carry a load of nearly 15 tons, while a 40-footer (12 m) could safely

haul as much as 25 tons, even through surf! The Sea Bright skiffs' shoal draft and beachability make them ideal gunkholers, yet their stability, buoyancy, and easy motion make them excellent rough-weather boats. In fact, a 32-foot (9.7 m) Sea Bright skiff cabin cruiser made the passage from New Jersey to Bermuda as early as 1928.

Now, a Sea Bright skiff won't ever be quite as fast and as able at true planing speeds as a vee-bottom planing hull (some vee-bottom Sea Brights have been built and were quite successful), but the Sea Bright will still operate at these high speeds fairly well. More important, the Sea Bright skiff will be superior to a planing vee-bottom hull in comfort, efficiency, and handling at low speed. Not only does this mean that you're not, well, *obligated* to run at planing speeds, but it is a great safety factor if caught out in rough weather and steep seas, when you have to slow down. By the same token, a pure displacement hull will slip along with slightly less resistance than a Sea Bright skiff at low (displacement) speed, yet the Sea Bright skiff comes close to this low-speed efficiency while at the same time being able to kick up her heels and go!

Speeding Up—or a Rum Deal

The early Sea Bright skiffs were rowing craft—occasionally sail assisted—and not intended for high speeds. As engines replaced muscles, though, the search for swiftness was on. At first, Sea Brights had too little bearing aft—their sterns were not wide and flat enough. Thus, they squatted at high speed. Builders soon realized—obvious to us now, not so obvious back when—that widening and flattening the stern would control this problem. On the East Coast, in fact, many of the best—or most infamous—Prohibition-era rumrunners were true Sea Bright skiffs in every regard, complete with box skeg or garboard.

At first, these rumrunners were powered with single engines like their fishing counterparts. Soon, though, the Coast Guard was ordering Sea

King 28-Foot "Speed Sea Skiff"

A true Sea Bright skiff Produced by King Boatworks in the 1920s & 30s
these craft cruised at 22 knots with a single 150-HP inboard

Bright skiffs for themselves. It was the only way to stay in the hunt. Often, a Coast Guard chase boat and a rumrunner would be under construction, side by side, in the same yard. It must have made for some interesting, ah, conversations over the sawdust piles!

Twin engines with more power were the natural result of all this excitement. Rumrunner power frequently came from a pair of surplus World War I aircraft engines. Liberties, Vickers, Wright Cyclones, and Sterling Vikings—these are still engine names to conjure with. The Sterling Viking, for instance, delivered 565 hp (420 kw), from eight cylinders, each with an 8-inch (203 mm) bore and a 9-inch (228 mm) stroke—I'd call this a no-nonsense power plant. A pair of these machines producing in excess of 1,100 hp (820 kw) would sort of tend to move you along. Rumrunners regularly sped along at around 30 knots while loaded with 500 cases of bootleg liquor! Yet, for all this power (these engines were not small or light) and all their cargo—remember the 40-footer's (12 m) 25-ton carrying capacity—many of the rumrunners managed to remain decent sea boats, operating well at low and high speed and riding fairly level on plane.

The Practical Sea Bright

Clearly though, the demands placed on rumrunners, namely staying out of reach of the friend-ly neighborhood Coast Guard cutter, pushed the Sea Bright skiff to extremes. In their last days, these boats were overpowered, overloaded, and a bit squirrelly. A moderate Sea Bright skiff, however, can make nearly the speeds of the rumrunners, with lighter modern engines, and retain all the Sea Bright's other fine attributes. The hull form shown in the drawings could be powered to a speed-length ratio of 4 to 5. If she were a 36-footer (10.9 m) of, say, 33 feet (10 m) on the waterline, she'd comfortably make 23 knots. She'd also do this with modest power, say, just under 300 hp (224 kw)—not bad!

Sea Bright skiffs have all the attributes for the perfect family cruiser: comfort, speed, seakindliness, shoal draft, and economy. They make ideal cabin cruisers, sportfishermen, day boats, and, yes, workboats. With modern flared bows and modern cabin styling, they need not look like traditional boats—though I have to confess to liking the salty appearance of some of the old plumb-stem cabin cruisers. They have been mass-produced by Ulrichtsen, among others, into the late 1960s, but are harder to find these days. Hopefully, this will change.

The DR Northwest Cruiser

Although her styling is reminiscent of Northwest Coast fishing boats, the DR Northwest Cruiser is a true Sea Bright skiff complete with box skeg. She's a moderate family cruiser, with a range of 2,000 nautical miles at 7.6 knots. You can see how her box skeg allowed engine installation entirely beneath the wheelhouse sole, with a horizontal prop shaft.

The bottom of the DR Cruiser's keel is fitted with a ½-inch (12 mm) copper-nickel plate, which serves as ballast and as grounding armor. With her prop well protected and a draft of just 2 feet 9 inches (84 cm), this is one powerboat that can take the ground safely at will. Her wide keel-flat and low weight placement ensure she'll sit level and stable till the tide comes back in.

Although the DR Northwest Cruiser is shown with a 46-hp (34 kw) engine for long-range, dis-placement-speed cruising, she'll function efficiently with a 200-hp (150 kw) machine that'd give her a speed of 16 knots or so.

Interestingly, the DR Cruiser is designed to be trailerable; her beam's just 8 feet 6 inches (2.6 m). At 16,000 pounds (7,260 kg) and 34 feet (10.4 m) overall, she's about as large a boat as can realistically be trailered. You'd need a small truck—at least—with a *big* engine, carefully beefed up suspension, load-leveler hitch, and a *strong* custom trailer. Even so, transporting a craft this size overland is no picnic. Still, it's nice to know that once or twice a season you can pick her up and move her hundreds or even thousands of miles overland to new cruising grounds, or just to store her in your backyard. If we hadn't set out to make her

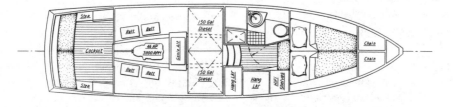

Profile of the 34-foot (10.4 m) DR Northwest Cruiser, a true Jersey Sea Bright skiff with Northwest-coast styling.

The arrangement plan shows an ideal long-range cruiser for two. Note the no-nonsense chain lockers, sheltered cockpit, and chart table by the helm.

trailerable from the outset, I'd have given the DR Cruiser another 18 inches of beam, which would have opened her accommodations up a bit more.

Jersey Sea Skiff—A Different Kettle of Fish

Naturally, given the fine characteristics and well-deserved reputation of the Sea Bright skiff, there are boats being marketed as Sea Brights that just aren't. Some of this is natural confusion. Since the box skeg that makes a Sea Bright skiff a Sea Bright skiff is hidden below the water, it's easy to be misled. Additionally, there's another fine Jersey Shore boat that is known simply as the sea skiff or Jersey sea skiff. It's not uncommon for the sea skiff to be mistaken for the Sea Bright skiff, but although related, they're not the same.

The sea skiffs were a natural development of the true Sea Bright skiff. For really high planing speeds, the Sea Bright skiff's box skeg and rounded stern sections don't work well—too little lift and too much drag. To get a Sea Bright skiff to operate efficiently at speed-length ratios greater than 5—high planing speed—the bottom has to be flattened out and the box garboard eliminated.

The Triangular Bottom

As you can see in the drawing, this is exactly what makes a sea skiff, or Jersey sea skiff—now, no longer a Sea Bright skiff at all. Their bottoms are dead flat and very wide at the transom for maximum planing lift. At the same time, the flat bottom tapers to a sharp point at the stem. In fact, the sea skiff's bottom appears a bit odd at first. It's so wide aft and so narrow forward it looks nearly triangular. Nevertheless, sea skiffs are fine boats in their own right.

Get Up and Go

Usually built in sizes under 30 feet (9 m) overall, with the right horsepower, sea skiffs get up and go like a scared cat. A 20-footer (6 m) would do close to 44 knots with a 150-hp (110 kw) outboard hung on her tail—a speed-length ratio of 10 plus! Even in a deep-vee hull, though, speeds like

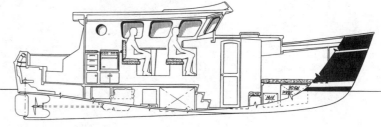

Inboard profile of the DR Northwest Cruiser. Note how the engine, tanks, and machinery all fit below the wheelhouse sole, making for open accommodations and low weight placement.

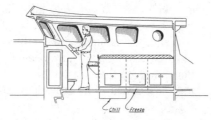

Starboard inboard profile of the DR Northwest Cruiser. Headroom is 6 feet 4 inches (193 cm).

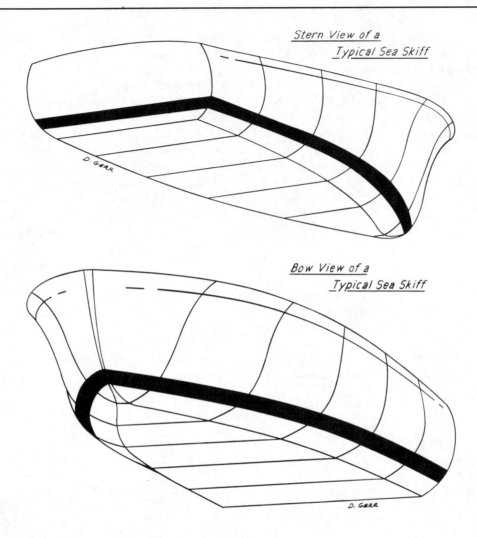

Stern View of a
Typical Sea Skiff

D. GERR

Bow View of a
Typical Sea Skiff

D. GERR

this aren't exactly comfortable. The wonderful thing about sea skiffs—like their cousins, the Sea Bright skiffs—is that they work well at low speed, high speed, and in between. The same sea skiff we were blasting around in with a 150-hp (110 kw) engine would comfortably and economically do 21 knots with a 35-hp (26 kw) outboard, and 12 knots with a 15-hp (11 kw) motor. You could go racing in the morning, come home for lunch, switch to the 35-hp (26 kw) engine, and go fishing in the afternoon. Especially inshore and on lakes and rivers, sea skiffs are about the ideal all-arounders. They're pretty fine sea boats as well, and make great craft for skimming around the bay or getting out to the fish on a fine day. Being small, flat, and open, however, they are not up to crossing to Bermuda as is a well-found Sea Bright skiff.

CHAPTER 5

The Best of Both Worlds

And the best of all ways
To lengthen our days
Is to steal a few hours from the night, my dear.

The Young May Moon, Thomas Moore

One of the easiest ways to get up an argument among sailors is to mention the word "motorsailer." Some folks think quite well of them, but others ... well, the expletives have been deleted. They'll claim—with considerable justification—that there's a built-in problem with motorsailers: they're neither fish nor fowl. Because of their rigs and keels, they don't motor as well as pure powerboats, and because of their large propellers and relatively heavy engines, they won't sail as well as dedicated sailboats or auxiliaries. It was this that led to the old, informal rating system for motorsailers. You'd have 50%–50%, 60%–40%, or 30%–70% motorsailers, and so on. A 50%–50% motorsailer would perform 50 percent as well under power as a motorboat, and 50 percent as well under sail as a sailboat. A 30%-70% was only 30 percent sail and 70 percent power, and so on.

Motorsailing Comfort

In spite of the old limitations on motorsailer performance, advocates also have strong arguments on their side. Anyone who's done a lot of cruising knows that beating against a stiff headwind offshore for days at a time gets stale quickly. Even worse is being becalmed after a five-day passage just hours from your port of call. The motorsailer crew never faces these difficulties. They can fire up the iron genny and carry on easily. In fact, this is what motorsailers are all about—long-range cruising in comfort. With their enclosed helm stations and substantial power plants, bone-freezing watches and athletic feats of close-quarters sail handling become things of the past.

I well remember a chill four-day blow in Newport one year. The wind didn't drop under 25 knots the whole time—gusts frequently peaked at 45. As we lay bobbing in our sloop, a traditional motorsailer powered easily through the steep swell and confused chop to drop anchor. Peering over into that warm, snug wheelhouse, we saw her crew lounging back sipping hot coffee. It put a new edge on the word "envy!"

Limiting Roll

From the powerboater's perspective, motor-sailers offer still another comfort advantage. Their substantial sail plans are superb roll dampers. Many's the sailer who seldom gets sick on a sailboat, but who—in a few hours of roll, roll, roll—will end up feeling pretty peaked on a powerboat off soundings. Setting a decent bit of sail makes the deep, rhythmic powerboat roll vanish as surely as if it had never been there at all.

Combining the Pluses

If you could combine this sort of comfort with solid performance under *both* sail and power, you'd really have something, and not too long ago a client asked me to do just that. He wanted comfortable accommodations for three couples and a large enclosed wheelhouse and saloon for steering and

Sail plan of the 57-foot (17.4 m) high performance motorsailer Quicksilver.

lounging out of the weather, but even more important, he wanted speed. Cruising speed, under power, was to be 12 to 13 knots, with a top speed of 14 knots. Further, he wanted race-boat performance under sail. He set a goal of achieving 14 knots in ideal conditions, reaching in 35 knots true wind; of having enough sail to drive the boat well in light air; and of being close-winded—under sail alone—in light and heavy air. In short, he was asking for a motorsailer that would be a true 100%-100% in the old rating system—a proper motorsailer.

Thirty or more years ago, this couldn't have been done, but modern materials and engines have combined to make it possible at last. By using light composite construction, hull weight and overall displacement could be kept down. We could make the ultimate motorsailer. The resulting design was named *Quicksilver,* and in fact, her displacement-length ratio of 158 is as low as that of many racing machines. At the same time, she's fitted with a huge, tall rig—1,583 square feet (147 m²). Her sail area–displacement ratio is 20.6 (see Chapter 13), which, again, is as high as many racers.

Keel Removal?

Now, however, we faced the inevitable compromise. With all the weight and windage of the sail plan and the drag of the keel, speed under power would be limited. There's really nothing you can do about the rig. (You can't reasonably expect to drop the rig on a 57-footer (17.4 m) at will. At least, I don't.) But we could do something about the keel. It lifts into the hull at the touch of a button using a solid bronze screw-jack powered by an electric motor, all of which is high up in the wheelhouse out of the wet and the weather. (There's a manual backup, of course.) In this way, *Quicksilver* drastically reduces appendage resistance under power. At the same time, she's equipped with a 19,000-pound (8,620 kg) lead bulb on the bottom of her lifting fin keel. Fully lowered, this bulb significantly drops the center of gravity, greatly increasing sail-carrying power on the wind.

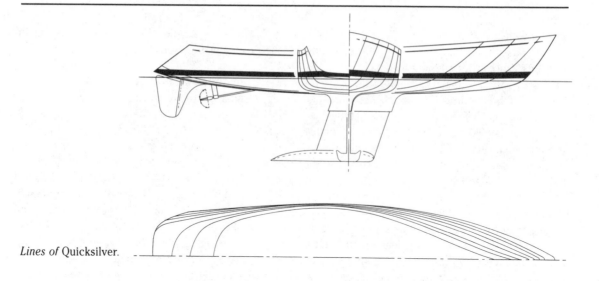

Lines of Quicksilver.

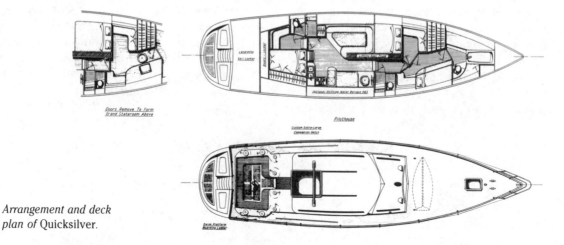

Arrangement and deck plan of Quicksilver.

All Heavy Gear—Down and Center!

Another critical aspect of performance—for any boat—is to keep weights low and near midships to decrease pitching and increase stability. With older engines—engines that were larger and heavier for the power they delivered—this was nearly impossible. On *Quicksilver,* though, we were able to fit both engine and generator under the wheelhouse sole, about smack in the middle of the boat and with their centers of gravity well below the waterline. Thirty or so years ago this would not have been possible. It took modern, low-profile, turbocharged diesels to permit this feat.

Power to the Water

In fact, in order to drive a 43,000-pound (19,500 kg) boat with a 49-foot 6-inch (15 m) waterline at 14 knots—a speed-to-length ratio of 2—we needed 270 horsepower (200 kw). Lehman's Super 275, delivering 275 hp (205 kw), weighing just 1,300 pounds (590 kg), and sitting only 33 inches (84 cm) high, filled the bill. Considering the engine, however, brings us right back to the other side of the motorsailer equation—transferring this power to the water efficiently. An ordinary motor cruiser would use a solid three- or four-bladed propeller. If such a gizmo were hung on *Quicksilver*'s tail, she'd lose at least a knot and a half—if not two or three—off her top speed under sail. The solution was to use a very large-diameter, slow-turning two-bladed folding propeller. As a true folder, this prop has extremely low drag under sail. By the same token, going large on diameter allowed sufficient blade area to absorb engine power effectively (see Chapters 32 and 33). *Quicksilver*'s geared folding prop is a full 38 inches (97 cm) in diameter and turns at just 750 rpm. It delivers honest thrust at both high and low speed. This is an approach that can be used to advantage on any motorsailer or auxiliary, assuming there's sufficient clearance under the hull at the prop, or in the prop aperture (see Chapter 34).

Traditional versus Modern

Comparing the modern *Quicksilver* with a traditional motorsailer is interesting. The drawing shows the lines of a traditional motorsailer of 55 feet (16.7 m) length overall, 48 feet (14.6 m) on the water, and 13 feet 9 inches (4.2 m) beam. (*Quicksilver* is 57 feet (17.4 m) LOA; 49 feet 6 inches (15 m) WL; and 14 feet 9 inches (4.5 m) beam.) Although 2 feet (60 cm) shorter than *Quicksilver,* she displaces over 40 percent more, at 61,200 pounds (22,760 kg). Yet, though she's substantially heavier than *Quicksilver,* her sail area is much less—just 1,070 square feet (100 m²). In other words, the traditional motorsailer's sail area–displacement ratio is just 11—barely enough to move her in a whole gale. (Generally, a sail area–displacement ratio of 16 is considered the minimum for good cruising performance. A sail area–displacement ratio of 17 to 19 is typical of faster performance cruisers, while competitive racers may have ratios of 20 to 22 or so. *Quicksilver*'s sail area–displacement ratio is 20.6. See Chapter 21.)

A further look at the lines shows that the tra-

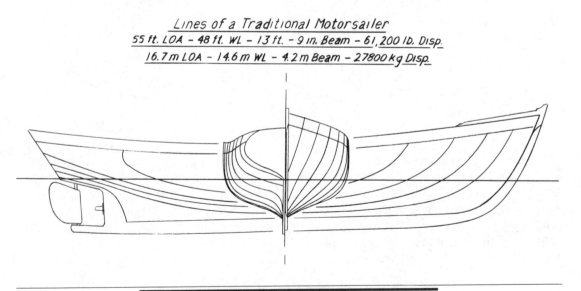

Lines of a Traditional Motorsailer
55 ft. LOA – 48 ft. WL – 13 ft. – 9 in. Beam – 61,200 lb. Disp.
16.7 m LOA – 14.6 m WL – 4.2 m Beam – 27,800 kg Disp.

ditional motorsailer's underbody has little effective keel, reducing her upwind sailing ability. She also has pronounced deadrise (the vee shape of her underbody), which—combined with her greater weight and sharply upswept buttocks aft—indicates she can never be driven faster than a speed-to-length ratio of 1.4 or so (see Chapter 18). This gives the traditional motorsailer a top speed under power of 9.7 knots and a cruising speed under power of around 9.2 knots.

By virtue of her light weight, flat floors aft (a good semiplaning surface) and shallow buttock angles aft, *Quicksilver*—by comparison—will cruise comfortably at 12.5 knots, with a top speed of 14. Even more interesting is that the heavier traditional motorsailer needs nearly as large an engine as *Quicksilver* to make less speed—220 hp (165 kw) versus *Quicksilver*'s 275 (205 kw). This means that the crew of the traditional motorsailer is paying almost the same fuel bill per hour, and a heck of a lot more per mile.

There's No Such Thing as the Perfect Boat

Of course, you can't have everything. There is, sadly, no such thing as the *perfect* boat. (I'm not so sure *I* should be sad about this. If someone does come up with the perfect boat, I'll be out of a job!) Anyway, *Quicksilver*'s rig, being so much larger than the traditional motorsailer's, requires more gear and more care. Thirty years ago, short-handing a rig this large would have been considered risky, if not foolhardy. Again, however, modern sail-handling gear reduces this difficulty tremendously. *Quicksilver*'s headsails are all powered luff roller furlers, winding in or out at the touch of a button (naturally, with full manual backup). Her main's equipped with a powered halyard winch, the Dutchman lazyjack system, and single-line slab reefing, which also make it possible to set, douse, or reef sail at the touch of a button. You can't set up an easier way to manage nearly 1,600 square feet (147 m²) of sail; still it *is* there to be considered and dealt with. Obviously, we wouldn't get *Quicksil-*

ver's impressive performance under sail without her large sail plan.

The Comfort Compromise

Modern sail-handling systems do make *Quicksilver*'s large rig manageable even for a singlehander or husband-and-wife crew; however another trade-off has been made for speed. The heavier displacement and pronounced deadrise of the traditional motorsailer give her hull a slow, stately, comfortable motion. (They also give her a slow, stately speed.) *Quicksilver*'s lighter, flat-floored hull will make her motion quicker and jerkier. The inertia of her lead bulb and high rig will help this, but—in severe conditions—the traditional hull will be more comfortable. There's a flip side even to this, though; *Quicksilver*, being faster, will spend less time out in those conditions than the slower, traditional motorsailer.

Quicksilver and the traditional motorsailer shown are at the two extremes of the motorsailer spectrum. A wide variety of production motorsailers is available, ranging from virtual reproductions of 1920s craft, to performance-oriented cruisers and high-powered auxiliaries—really pure sailboats with larger-than-usual engines and a small, enclosed helm niche or solid dodger. At present, I don't know of any vessels that have exploited the full range of modern technical advances employed in *Quicksilver*.

All motorsailers could benefit from these approaches. Speed and performance potential mean safety. Few craft, for instance, could claw their way off a lee shore as reliably as a motorsailer like *Quicksilver*. With only her staysail set for roll reduction and extra drive, her powerful engine can push her to weather and safety when other sailing craft would be dropping anchor and hoping fervently that their ground tackle's *really* strong.

It's not actually necessary to go quite as far as *Quicksilver* to reap many of the advantages of a 100%-100% motorsailer. (In any craft, going for it all is costly, and *Quicksilver*'s certainly not an inexpensive boat.) *Quicksilver* has not only a lifting bulb keel, but also optional, shifting water ballast. The water ballast is really just for showing off. When it's breezing up hard, you can pump the windward tank full (at the touch of a button, of course), instead of tying in a reef, and proceed to blow by almost any boat around. (They'd all probably think you'd switched the engine on.) Similarly, the lifting bulb keel is for ultimate upwind performance. By settling for a modest loss of top-end upwind speed, a 95%-95% or 90%-90% motorsailer could be built along the principles of *Quicksilver* as a keel centerboarder or even with a shoal keel. Obviously, shifting water ballast tanks are always optional. You could replace them with long-range fuel tanks and head for Bora Bora.

CHAPTER 6

A Cruise Aboard *Crackerjack* or An Imaginary Cruise in a Dream Boat

. . . he lighted the running lights before he went back to the wheel. The clouds had scattered around, so there were spaces with stars, and Guido began to sing and kept it up. With all the jolts I had had in the past two days, I wouldn't have been surprised if Wolf had joined in . . . .

The Black Mountain, Rex Stout

Pulling his cap down lower to shield his face from the spray, Gordon peered about. *Not the greatest way to start a cruise,* he thought. "Why don't you keep her at a dock?" he called plaintively above the launch's engine.

"Oh, I used to," Quinn replied, "but I just decided I liked the privacy of being out on a mooring. Besides, it's cheaper." A wavetop crested over the side of the launch, slapping him in the face.

"You sure this is a good weekend for a cruise?" Gordon queried his friend.

"Yeah, it'll be fine. The weather's already breaking. The wind's down and this slop'll fade away in an hour or two. In fact, I think those guys on *Sandlewood*"—Quinn pointed to a crew readying a sailboat—"are in for a disappointment today. They'll have a bit of breeze out, then nothing. A slow trip home for them.

"You can see *Crackerjack* pretty well now." Quinn gestured forward.

Looking away from *Sandlewood*, Gordon took in the lines of his friend's boat. *Crackerjack* was lying head to the wind, veering slightly from side to side and plunging sedately to the swells. Unlike many modern glass powerboats, she had a bold sheer and curved stem. You could see in her the time-tested tradition of the lobsterboats that so many fishermen relied on for their daily bread—boats that had to get them there and back in all sorts of weather, safely and reliably.

Gordon, a confirmed sailor, wondered momentarily how he could find himself going for a weekend cruise on a powerboat, but consoled himself that at least she was a real little sea boat and not some metal-flake job with a fake rollbar. *Besides,* he thought, *that enclosed wheelhouse looks inviting.* He turned up his collar against the fine, steady drizzle—all that remained of last night's squalls.

The launch operator swung next to *Crackerjack* and, reversing the engine, drew them neatly alongside. Grabbing his duffel, Quinn bounded

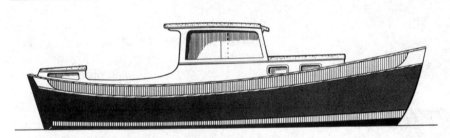

Profile of Crackerjack. *She's 28 feet (8.5 m) LOA, 24 feet 9 inches (7.5 m) beam, draws 2 feet 3 inches (68 cm), and displaces 9,300 pounds (4,230 kg). Cruising speed is 15 to 18 knots; top speed is 20 knots.*

aboard. As the operator held the vessels close, Gordon passed up their groceries and his bag. Then he hopped aboard himself. He gazed about as the launch motored away.

The first thing he noticed was how much steadier and drier than the launch *Crackerjack* felt. Of course, she was bigger and higher, but he also realized that the deep bulwarks all around *Crackerjack*'s deck gave him a feeling of security. His kit lay at his feet, right against the rail, without the slightest danger of going over the side.

"You can admire her just as well from in here," Quinn jibed from the wheelhouse.

Gordon clambered over the cockpit rail, onto the after cockpit seats, and into the cockpit. A few steps brought him under the wheelhouse roof. *Dry and out of the wind and spray! Too bad there's no*

way to put up a wheelhouse on my sloop, he thought.

The cockpit stretched a good 10 feet (3 m) aft and was fully 6 feet (1.8 m) wide. Way at the stern was a small aft cabin, and just forward of it were the built-in cockpit seats. Farther forward, in the middle of the cockpit, was the engine box, which also served as a seat or work table.

"It's a grand arrangement," Quinn said. "The cockpit sole's just high enough to be fully self-bailing, but it's so deep and well protected that you feel comfortable and safe even in really rough going. There's a wet locker tucked under the starboard deck in the wheelhouse." Quinn pointed. "It's not large—just big enough for a couple of pairs of oilskins. But it sure is nice not to have to drip water all over the cabin. Over there," Quinn

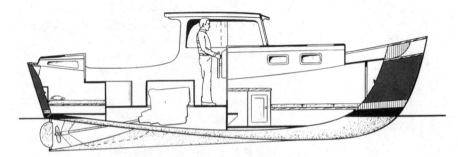

Inboard profile of Crackerjack.

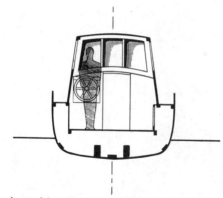

Crackerjack's midships section.

said, pulling at a drawer to port, "are drawers and cabinets for engine spares and tools."

To port was the helm—all the engine controls, radio, loran, fishfinder/sounder. Gordon noticed a lever by the throttle he'd never seen before. "What's that," he asked, "trim tabs?"

"Nope," Quinn responded looking a bit sheepish. "I told you that I wanted *Crackerjack* to be simple—less cost and less to go wrong. Well, that's my one extravagance. A bow thruster. Actually, the smallest jet thruster made. You see, there's one drawback to a single-screw vessel with a high bow. Crosswinds can make things a bit unpredictable.

"It isn't a problem 98 percent of the time, but when you're docking in a crowded spot, well . . . it can lead to some embarrassment. With a twin-en-gine boat, you can control the attitude of the bow by alternately backing and forthing opposite motors. In a single-screw craft—if a sudden breeze hits you broadside at the wrong moment—there's sometimes not much you can do. Anyway, with the bow jet I can work *Crackerjack* into the most difficult berths without fuss or worry. Besides, the entire jet installation costs one heck of a lot less than a second engine."

Quinn popped the motor box open and inspected the machinery. He poked and prodded while peering about. "I always give her a once-over—fluid levels, hoses, belts—before I start her up," he explained. "Cheap insurance." Grabbing his keys, he cranked *Crackerjack*'s motor, surveying the engine instruments carefully as she came up to idle. "We'll let her warm up at a low idle for a few minutes," he said. "High revs on a cold machine'll wear it out quick. Got to give the old oil a chance to warm up, thin out, and spread around." He made what Gordon charitably assumed was intended to be a "spreading" gesture. Then, opening the cabin door, Quinn led the way below.

Gordon was surprised at how quiet the engine was. He could feel it through the cockpit sole more than hear it. "Shoot! Your engine must be a hundred times quieter than my outboard."

Quinn grunted agreement. "Outboards are about the noisiest kind of engine you can own. There's no reason, though, for an inboard to be any louder than your family car's engine. In fact, it

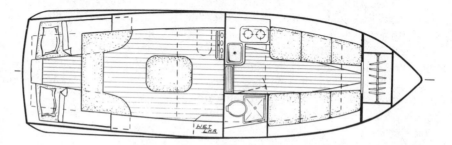

Arrangement of Crackerjack.

ought to be quieter, since it can be sealed in an insulated compartment. *Crackerjack* has three inches of lead/foam sound insulation all around the engine and immediately above the prop as well. She runs very quiet. When I see—or rather hear—some fellow powering by and kicking up a racket, I can't believe my ears. Not only does all that noise wear you out, but you can't hear the water or the birds or anything else you're supposedly out on the water to enjoy."

Below, *Crackerjack* was light and airy. Her cabin was painted a soft eggshell beige, the sole was dark teak, and the overhead was a high-gloss white. Dark mahogany trim edged the cabinetwork. *She could practically be a sailboat,* Gordon thought.

Port and starboard, forward, were a pair of long settee berths. Quinn opened a door all the way forward, which to Gordon's surprise proved to be a really large hanging locker. Aft, to port, was a compact galley, and to starboard was an enclosed head with shower.

"She has a good five feet (152 cm) of headroom in the cabin," Quinn explained. "Any more would have hurt her looks and her performance. This is plenty of room to be comfortable, and with the six-foot four-inch (193 cm) headroom under the wheelhouse, you can stand up and stretch 'indoors,' even when the weather's bad. I did worry about the shower, but it's just fine taking a sit-down bath using a telephone-handset shower head. I asked the designer to raise the height of the cabin roof inside the wheelhouse over the shower, but he talked me out of it. Said it wouldn't be worth the cost or the sacrifice in appearance, and I think he was right."

"What kind of windows are those?" Gordon asked. He indicated the five opening windows in the forward cabin. They had an odd frame around them with a pair of wedges stuck in behind each pane.

Quinn leaned forward, pulled the wedges out of the nearest one, and allowed the pane to fall

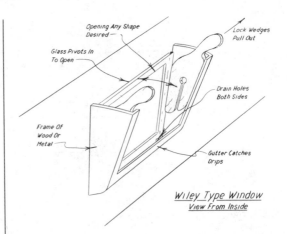

Wiley Type Window
View From Inside

inboard. Then he jammed the wedges back in, locking the window open. "They're Wiley windows," Quinn answered. "They're not expensive, and you can keep them open longer in worse weather than most other sorts of opening ports without taking in water. You see, the rain and spray hit the angled pane and drain outboard through the weep holes. I usually leave the four side windows open underway and open the forward windows at anchor. When it's really hot you can take the panes out altogether for even more air. You can never have enough ventilation below decks." He proceeded to open the remaining windows.

Gordon hung up his few clothes and then Quinn led him outside to the aft cabin. Already the drizzle had nearly ended and the sun was showing serious signs of a long-term appearance.

Quinn slid back the companion slide and removed the drop boards of the aft cabin hatch. The boards stowed out of the way, in a pair of clips along the inboard faces of the cockpit seats. "The biggest drawback to aft cabins like this," he said, "is that the hatch faces forward and you tend to get a lot of spray inside. *Crackerjack*'s high wheelhouse, though, shields her aft cabin from most of this."

Stepping down, Quinn and Gordon tucked

themselves into the cabin. "Your suite sir," Quinn quipped. There was plenty of sprawling space, and the berths here were actually larger than those in the forward cabin. They were just as long and a few inches wider. Narrow Wiley windows on either side and a skylight in the hatch admitted a lot of light. Gordon chucked his duffel on the port berth and stretched his legs.

"The two separate cabins are wonderful," Quinn said. "Just think, we won't have to listen to each other snore! Seriously, though, Janet and I can take the kids cruising and after bedtime they're out of sight and out of mind. Of course, when we cruise with another couple, the advantages are obvious."

The two men climbed on deck, and Quinn sent Gordon forward to cast off. Again, Gordon was impressed by the security of *Crackerjack*'s high bulwark rail. The rain had stopped altogether now, and Gordon sat on the forward edge of the cabin roof. Contemplating the harbor scene, he waited for Quinn's instructions.

Quinn had slid the port wheelhouse window open, and leaning out, he broke Gordon's reverie with the call, "Cast off!"

Stepping forward, Gordon knelt and freed the mooring pendant from its cleat. "We're loose!" he called back as he flung it overboard. He looked aft and watched as Quinn let the wind blow *Crackerjack* away from the floating pendant. Then he felt more than heard the surge of power as *Cracker-*

jack's engine was put in gear and brought up to speed. She plunged into the first swell and then, gaining speed, lifted higher for the next one. By the third she climbed over smoothly.

To a sailor like Gordon, the speed seemed terrific. He clambered aft and joined Quinn in the wheelhouse. "How fast are we going?" Gordon asked.

"Oh, about 12 knots," Quinn responded, pointing to the speedo. "I'd keep her a lot slower if we were further in among the moorings, but, as you can see, *Crackerjack*'s on the outside. Still, I don't like to take off too fast. We'll open her up a bit more in a minute, when the engine's fully warmed and our wake won't bother anyone."

A few moments later, Gordon felt *Crackerjack* rise higher onto a plane. Her motion was easy as she worked her way solidly into the oncoming swell. The wind was dead on the nose, and although it was no longer strong, the waves were still a few feet high. *Crackerjack* took each oncoming crest in stride. She'd plunge into it only slightly, her flared spoon bow lifting her over with certainty. There was little pounding—just a rhythmic feeling of power against power as *Crackerjack*'s engine drove her through the elements, each wave a small but easy triumph.

"She's surprisingly comfortable bashing into this," Gordon commented appreciatively.

"Well, this isn't much. She can work her way into considerably worse slop," Quinn replied. "Still, her motion's very comfortable. Of course,

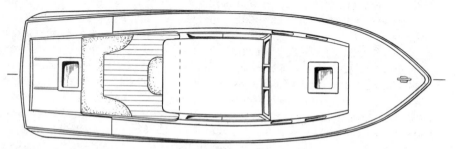

Deck plan of Crackerjack.

that's partly due to the fact that I don't drive her hard. I cruise *Crackerjack* at 15 knots or nearly 18 miles per hour—a very comfortable speed. It's only when you start trying to go 30 to 35 knots or more that pounding gets fierce in ordinary conditions. Besides, 15 knots is fast enough to get you pretty much anywhere in reasonable time. We cover 45 nautical miles in three hours. That's well over a day's sail for you sailboat guys, particularly as *Crackerjack* doesn't have to tack into it, which, as you know, increases the distance covered by about 40 percent."

"What'll she do if you open 'er up?" Gordon inquired.

"I seldom twist her tail," responded Quinn. "But, at 3,500 rpm she'll get up to 19 knots or just about 22 miles per hour. I've seldom done it, but you can force her to 3,700 rpm and go 20, 21 knots or so, but for what? You'd be straining the engine and banging up the boat. If I wanted a speedboat I'd have gotten a deep-vee muscle boat. Not my cup of tea, though I suppose it could be lots of excitement to go 60 knots or so from time to time.

"One of the nice things about keeping speed moderate is that you can get by with a much smaller engine. *Crackerjack* has a Volvo TMD40C diesel that delivers 136 horsepower (101 kw) at 3,600 rpm. Of course, I cruise at 2,500 rpm, at which speed the engine will last a good long time. If I'd wanted to go 25 knots *Crackerjack* would've required 300 or more horsepower (224 kw)—more money, bigger engine, more fuel. There's not much to be gained by driving her that hard."

"Diesels are better than gas, I suppose," Gordon commented.

"Well," Quinn answered, "the designer originally drew *Crackerjack* with a gas engine. But I argued him out of it. You know, I worried about explosions. But, now—after the fact—I think he was right. There're literally thousands of gas I/Os and outboards running everywhere without many problems. The advantages of gas engines in this size are tremendous. *Crackerjack*'s diesel weighs

just about half a ton with the reduction gear. If we'd used a gas engine it'd only have weighed 550 pounds (250 kg) or so. What's more, it would've cost a lot less and, of course, it wouldn't have the unpleasant diesel smell.

"The only thing I'd change about *Crackerjack*, if I could, would be to put in a gas engine. Still, the diesel is plenty solid and reliable. She's a good little ship as is."

They'd worked their way out of the bay now, and Quinn put the helm over. *Crackerjack*'s motion changed dramatically. In place of the solid surging and butting of the upwind course, they were now running at an angle across the swell. *Crackerjack*'s progress was smooth and unruffled, but she rolled and heaved in the seas. "I hope you took your Bonnine," Quinn grinned. "She handles this stuff beautifully, but like any powerboat, without sails to steady her, she rolls a bit in a beam sea."

Gordon knew what it was to be seasick, but he'd remembered to take the pills, and felt fine. "Mind if I take her for a while?" he asked.

"Sure," Quinn replied. He stepped aside and handed the wheel over to his friend. He went over the engine gauges carefully—oil pressure and temperature, water temperature, fuel, rpm. "The oil pressure and temperature are the main thing," he expounded. "If they move much from where they are now, give a shout. Keep her about 62 to 63 degrees magnetic. You can pull out the folding seat if you want. I'll bring up some breakfast."

Gordon reached down and lifted the chair. Seated, he tried to get the feel of *Crackerjack*'s helm. The trick seemed to be to adjust for the effect of the waves on this course. Eventually, he got it—giving her a quarter spoke to weather as she crossed a swell and a quarter spoke the other way as she surged down the other side.

Quinn emerged from the galley with coffee and some hot, buttered scones. Grabbing an offered mug with his free hand, Gordon sniffed the potent brew. Its aroma mingled with the smell of the salt spray blowing by the open wheelhouse windows. The clouds were fading into the distance and, with the wind dying, the swell was growing less and less by the minute. The regular hum of the engine and the faint rhythmic vibration of the prop mingled with the sound of the water rushing by. *Maybe next time I can manage a four-day cruise,* Gordon thought. He bit into a scone and watched *Crackerjack*'s bow drive purposefully through the water. *Powerboating ain't so bad after all,* he considered.

Off the starboard bow a gull swooped low and dove for a fish.

CHAPTER 7

Presto and Sharpie: The American Answer to the Dutch

As I said, with 30 inches [76 cm] under you, you roam along, carefree.

The Good Little Ship, Vincent Gilpin

Shallow waters make shallow ships. The Dutch developed their bluff leeboard jaghts for their tidal estuaries. But shoal waters can be found everywhere, and so can shallow craft. In the United States the oystermen around New Haven, Connecticut, were employing vessels about as radically different from the bluff boier and botter as can be imagined. They're called sharpies, and in spite of their popularity no one really knows how they came to be, or even where the name "sharpie" comes from. They were long and lean—usually with length-to-beam ratios of between 4.5 and 5 to 1—and they had absolutely dead flat bottoms that were remarkably shallow. Their drafts were usually between $\frac{1}{35}$ and $\frac{1}{40}$ of their length overall. A 28-footer (8.5 m) would draw just 9 inches (22 cm) with her centerboard raised.

Boats for the Working Man

These sharpies are ideal workingman's boats. They're cheap to build, carry a fair load, can be hauled up on the beach on a whim, and will float the oysterman over the mudflats that provide his income. Even better, with so little boat, as it were, under the water, sharpies are remarkably fast off the wind. I can attest to this from personal experience, having built and owned a 20-foot (6 m) sharpie years back. Downwind, I used to take great pride in screaming by keel sailboats that had cost 10 times as much and were twice my boat's size. Of course, the flip side to this is that upwind everyone would leave me behind with ease. Though they *can* go to weather reliably, even with substantial centerboards, true flat-bottom sharpies can never approach the upwind performance of a modern keel sailboat. The New Haven oysterman, however, wasn't especially concerned with upwind performance, and the simple flat-bottom sharpie suited him just fine.

Shallow Rewards

The sharpie's extreme shoal draft goes a long way toward compensating its poor windward qualities. There's very little as satisfying as nosing your way over a bar into an unexplored little nook and laying over with the tide, your boat resting upright, safe and stable on the sand. It also eases your navigating chores. Especially in good weather, anywhere there seems to be water is probably good enough. If it's not, well, no harm done. You can almost always back off and refloat with ease.

Sharp Yachts?

Because of the pleasure of shallow draft combined with the sharpie's low cost, there have been many sharpie sailing yachts designed in the past. Having owned such a boat, I'm not sure this is a good compromise. The true flat-bottom sharpie gives away too much interior room—it's hard to get even sitting headroom in less than a 30-footer (9 m). They have low reserve stability (though they *have* proved remarkably able in rough seas). Also, their lack of upwind ability is too pronounced. Finally, sharpies tend to pound, not underway when their chine's heeled over to cut the

water, but at anchor, when they're sitting upright and you're trying to relax.

Without Parallel?

These drawbacks became apparent early on, and modified sharpies are the result. The earliest sharpie modifier was probably Thomas Clapham, who built sharpie yachts (and a few workboats) in Roslyn, Long Island, in the late 1800s. Clapham's innovation was to keep the flat bottom amidships but introduce vee to the bottom fore and aft (or sometimes either fore or aft alone). The results were excellent, and these boats were known as "nonpareil sharpies" or "Roslyn sharpies."

A Star is Born

The working flat-bottom sharpie and the modified sharpie spread around the country, and variations could be found everywhere from the Pacific Northwest to the Chesapeake to Florida. In fact, the modified vee bottom was also built as an arc bottom, which worked better still. It increased

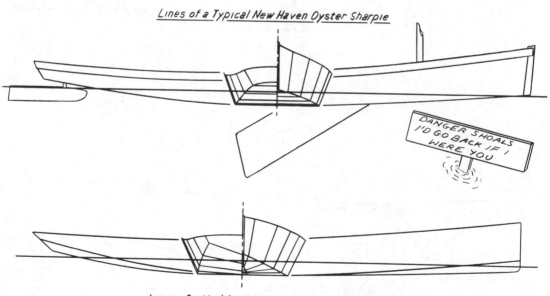

Lines of a Typical New Haven Oyster Sharpie

DANGER SHOALS I'D GO BACK IF I WERE YOU

Lines of a Modified, Nonpareil or Roslyn Sharpie

hull draft slightly, but also allowed ballast to be carried lower, increasing reserve stability, initial sail-carrying power, and—not incidentally—headroom. The most famous sharpie, in fact, is found all around the world—though most people don't realize she's a sharpie at all. It's an 85-year-old one-design—the Star.

The Star was drawn up in 1907 in the New York City office of William Gardner, as a modification of an earlier and somewhat smaller vessel known inauspiciously as the Bug. (No wonder the original class didn't catch on.) The new, larger Star drawings were prepared by Francis Sweisguth and remain the basis of not only the first true one-design class, but one of the most popular and successful one-designs ever. The hull is pure arc-bottom modified sharpie. Adding the steel-plate

fin keel and ballast bulb gave these boats improved initial stability, reserve stability, and plenty of lateral plane. The Star's a sharpie that's come full circle; she's truly able upwind but no longer has shallow draft!

Presto!

In Florida, however, another designer was modifying the sharpie into what's probably the finest cruising boat possible. His name was Commodore R.M. Munroe, and according to L. Francis Herreshoff he was the only designer ever to influence The Wizard of Bristol, Captain Nat Herreshoff. Based in Coconut Grove, Florida, Munroe owned a true flat-bottom sharpie, *Egret*. She'd proven fast and able—though not weatherly—in very rough water, and he decided to try an arc-

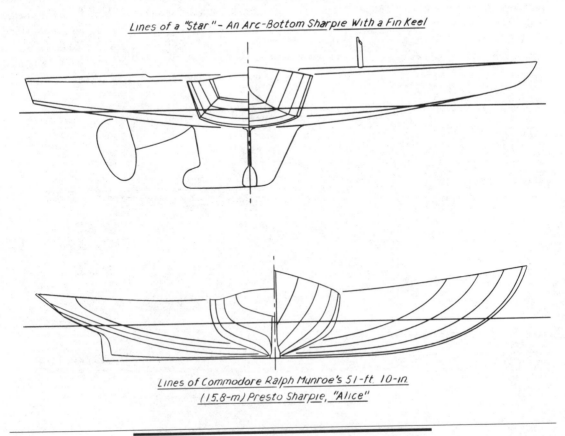

Lines of a "Star" – An Arc-Bottom Sharpie With a Fin Keel

Lines of Commodore Ralph Munroe's 51-ft. 10-in. (15.8-m) Presto Sharpie, "Alice"

bottom sharpie, slightly deeper and with round bilges instead of a chine. He called this first 40-footer (12 m) *Presto,* and she lived up to all expectations. In fact, to this day most similar craft are called "presto boats." Retaining the sharpie's shoal draft, the presto boat's round (sometimes slightly veed) hull is stronger and doesn't pound. By placing the ballast outside, the center of gravity can be brought low enough to get self-righting through 120 degrees or more—ocean capable—and the somewhat deeper hulls have room for adequate accommodations and headroom.

A Presto Cruiser

Mollyhawk is a presto boat I designed for Donald Farrar, who is—among other things—a professional aeronaut (balloonist) and an experienced builder of some very handsome canoes and kayaks. He and his wife had cruised extensively in these, not only in the United States, but in the Car-

ibbean as well. Don didn't want to sacrifice the extremely shoal draft he'd become used to with his L. Francis Herreshoff–designed leeboard ketch *Meadow Lark.* He wanted another extremely shoal craft that would be large enough to live aboard for several months of the year, with full standing headroom throughout. "I'd like to keep draft to 30 inches [76 cm], though," he said. At the same time, he wanted enough reserve stability to venture offshore safely and a rig that was easy to handle. *Mollyhawk* fills the bill nicely, except that her draft is all of 31 and not 30 inches (79 rather than 76 cm). Don's an understanding and easygoing sort, and he graciously overlooked the extra inch (2.5 cm).

Mollyhawk

Mollyhawk is 41 feet 11 inches (12.7 m) overall, 11 feet 6 inches (3.5 m) in beam. Her displacement-to-length ratio is 277, which is moderate—just right

Sail plan of the 41-foot 11-inch (12.8 m) presto boat Mollyhawk.

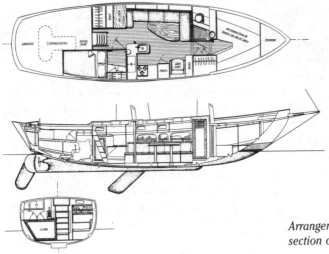

Arrangement, inboard profile, and midships section of Mollyhawk.

for this sort of cruising. Sail area—displacement ratio is 17, which is also moderate—again, just right for the cruising intended.

Flush Deck

A critical aspect of *Mollyhawk*'s design is her flush-deck construction. The flush deck gives a host of advantages. First, it is the easiest form of deck to build. Instead of having to fabricate a complicated trunk cabin, the builder simply bends sheet ply over deck beams and that's it. Second, the flush deck is the strongest construction known. Trunk cabins—even on well-made boats—can be stove in during a knockdown offshore. Flush-deckers don't have this weakness. Third, the flush deck dramatically increases freeboard. *Mollyhawk,* at 20 degrees of heel, has a full 2 feet 6 inches (76 cm) of reserve freeboard on the lee side! This not only makes for a secure feeling, but—most important—greatly increases her range of stability. Accordingly, even with her extreme shoal draft, *Mollyhawk*'s positive range of stability is 125 degrees. Finally, the flush deck dramatically increases interior room. From inside, *Mollyhawk*'s cabin is a full 11 feet (3.3 m) wide. If she'd been a trunk-cabin craft, the maximum width of the trunk cabin would have been only 9 feet (2.75 m) or so.

The Broadhead Schooner

The rig's a leg-o-mutton schooner rig with Broadhead (single, full-length, top-batten) sails—pioneered by Sailspar Sailmakers of Stamford, Connecticut. *Mollyhawk* spreads plenty of area in small increments for easy handling—the largest sail's only 401 square feet (37 m²). The relatively low rig, with its low center of effort, is critical to getting good upwind performance in a very shoal hull. The full-length top-batten Broadhead rig provides essentially the same area as a gaff rig without the weight, windage, or complication of the gaffs. It's very similar in concept to L. Francis Herreshoff's short gaffs, which he favored for such hulls and used on his leeboard sharpie *Meadow Lark* and leeboard presto boat *Golden Ball.*

Simply dropping the foresail reduces *Mollyhawk*'s total sail area to 625 square feet (58 m²). She's then happy as a duck under this canvas to 25 knots or so—perfectly balanced and in good control. The jib's on a club and is equipped to be roller reefing and roller furling. Thus, you can set, douse, and reef the jib without stirring from the

Large Sailing Vessels and Shoal Draft

One of the most intractable problems with the design of large sailboats is draft. As we've seen, 2- to 3-foot (60 to 90 cm) draft is wonderful for poking about in tight corners and unspoiled anchorages. It's achievable in craft under 40 or 50 feet (12 to 15 m), but what about 70-, 80-, or 90-footers (20, 25, or 30 meters)? Well, there's simply no way to build a 70-foot (20 m) plus vessel with 3-foot (90 cm) or less draft. Nevertheless, the shallower the better. In fact, the most common requirement is that—no matter what else— a boat is to draw less than 6 feet (1.8 m). The presto hull type is absolutely the finest solution here.

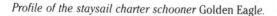

Profile of the staysail charter schooner Golden Eagle.

LOA	71 ft. 7 in.	(21.8 m)	Sail Area	2,152 sq. ft. (200 sq. m)	
LOD	64 ft. 0 in.	(19.5 m)	Power	Perkins 6.3544 (M),	
LWL	54 ft. 5 in.	(16.6 m)		250 hp (186 kw) at 2,800 rpm;	
Beam	17 ft. 8 in.	(5.4 m)		3.79:1 reduction gear	
Draft(CB up)	4 ft. 0 in.	(1.2 m)	Generator	Northern Lights 8 KW	
Draft (CB down)	12 ft. 8 in.	(3.8 m)	Fuel	200 gal. (757l) diesel	
Disp.	38 tons		Water	500 gal. (1892l)	

continued

The drawings show *Golden Eagle*, a 71-foot (21 m) staysail charter schooner designed for American Eagle Yachts. Her hull—not surprisingly—is strikingly similar to Commodore Munroe's *Alice*. In spite of her size, she draws a mere 4 feet (1.2 m) with her centerboard raised. A 100-footer (30 m) of this form would draw just 5 feet 6 inches (1.7 m)! Although *Golden Eagle*'s styling is that of a traditional schooner, the presto hull form below that water can mate with modern styling above equally well.

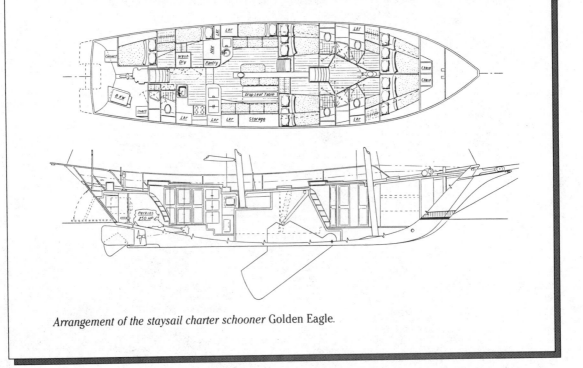

Arrangement of the staysail charter schooner Golden Eagle.

cockpit (or venturing onto the bowsprit). The club makes the headsail self-tending, as are all of *Mollyhawk*'s sails. And—set on the stemhead, aft of the tack—the club automatically acts as a whisker pole when running downwind. This both holds the sail out and increases the depth of camber for best efficiency.

Pulling in a reef or two in the main and a few feet (a meter or so) of furling line on the jib keeps *Mollyhawk* happy to 35 or 40 knots. Of course, on

any schooner, the foresail's the survival sail. With all other sails dropped, *Mollyhawk* is perfectly balanced and able under foresail alone. It'd be difficult to imagine anything short of a hurricane that could overwhelm her in this configuration.

Leeboard Pluses

As we saw in Chapter 1, and as the Dutch know full well, leeboards are *the* ideal solution to getting sufficient lateral plane on very shoal hulls that take ground frequently. Not only do they produce a stronger structure, but there's no centerboard trunk to ruin the accommodations and no centerboard slot to jam with silt and gravel, to keep clean, or to weaken the bottom structure.

Mollyhawk could never have had both her extreme shoal draft and her wide-open accommodations with a centerboard. Her flush deck and large, open salon eliminate the railway car feel found on many boats. Unobstructed visual space is 15 feet long by 11 feet wide (4.6 m by 3.4 m), with an irregular bite taken out of the aft starboard corner for the sleeping cabin. The off-center companionway, off-center forward bulkhead door, and corner easy chair help create a slight feeling of asymmetry that completely dispels any tunnel effect.

Bumper Ballast

Total ballast is 9,000 pounds (4,090 kg) of lead. It's 5 inches (12.5 cm) thick and 2 feet (60 cm) wide amidships, tapering fore and aft. This long, wide,

flat lead keel provides *Mollyhawk* with an ideal "bumper" for grounding. Thanks to this and her long skeg, you can let her dry out on the tide just about anywhere, anytime, with complete peace of mind. The keel is also wide and flat enough to ensure that *Mollyhawk* remains upright and level without the need for grounding legs or similar paraphernalia—just brew a pot of coffee, sit back, and watch the water gurgle away out to sea.

Sharp Power

Though many folks aren't aware of it, sharpies also make excellent power craft. The drawing shows a 36-foot (11 m) modified power sharpie—a Florida mullet skiff. The flat bottom aft gives these boats excellent planing performance for their power, and there's enough vee or deadrise forward to minimize pounding. Additionally, the flat floors and hard chines make mullet skiffs stable working platforms.

Like the Sea Bright skiff, the mullet skiff's

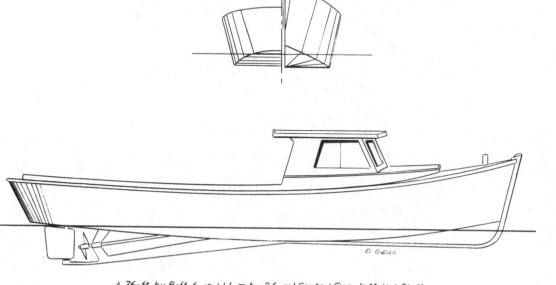

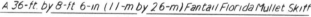

A 36-ft. by 8-ft 6-in (11-m by 2.6-m) Fantail Florida Mullet Skiff

speed, ableness, and shoal draft made it an ideal rumrunner during Prohibition. A further advantage was that the modified sharpie hulls were inexpensive and quick to build—no mean consideration when the Coast Guard might well confiscate three or four of your boats every few months.

Mullet skiffs have been built in sizes ranging from 20 to 80 feet (6 to 24 m), fitted with widely differing deckhouses, and used as everything from swordfishermen to commuters, sportfishermen, gillnetters, and dive-and-salvage boats. It's important to keep two things in mind, however. One is that—like any narrow, shallow craft—mullet skiffs must have low superstructures to maintain sufficient stability. The other is that they require substantial skegs and rudders aft; otherwise, at low speed in rough water their relatively deep-veed forefoot will dig in and cause difficult steering or even broaching. A deep skeg and rudder aft control this nicely (see Chapter 53).

CHAPTER 8

A Tug at the Heart Strings

The little fleet, still lashed tightly together, was worried over that last mile by the anxious tugs.

The Ordeal of the Ohio
(Run to Malta, 1942), Terrance Robertson

Bound with gammon irons and festooned with jib-boom guys, martingales, bobstays, and netting, a tangled forest of bowsprits projects into the street. Behind that towers an imposing wall of rigging—yardarms, crosstrees, ratlines, and stays. Surging in the swell, brigs, barques, ships, and schooners are packed and squeezed together. They dip and roll as stevedores and seamen hustle about their decks. Lighters squat between the ships while pulling gigs and sloops glide about the river beyond. The clamor of horse-drawn carts and the shrill of boatswain's whistles mingle with the flap of an awning, the slap of the waves, and the smell of salt water, oakum, and ripe fish. Barely beyond living memory, this was the scene at New York City's South Street, at Boston Harbor, and at many other seaports the world 'round.

Flags Across the Water

The Blue Peter, a square blue flag with a white square center, blooms from the foretruck of the barque *Heimdall*. Her lines singled up, her rigging overhauled, the Blue Peter announces she's ready to make sail. An ensign breaks from low in her main rigging.

Before radio, it was flag signals that spanned the harbors: The owner's flag, when dipped a few feet below the top of the main truck, solicited the water boat; an ensign from the topgallant backstay summoned the pilot boat; while an ensign hoisted low in the main rigging was the call for a tug. Waiting at their stations or patrolling the harbor, these hard-working vessels scanned the horizon for trade.

Easing Out

In a short time, *Heimdall*'s crew sees a cloud of smoke and hears several short toots on a steam whistle. Their tow has arrived. Once, windjammers waited days for the right wind—the "right slant" it was called—to sail out of a tight anchorage. Vessels of several hundred tons had to be worked by brawn and guile. Kedging, warping, towing with the ship's boats, and backing and filling against wind and tide were arduous chores requiring fine judgment. The "sailing master" had better be just that!

By *Heimdall's* day, though—the last great days of sail—the tug was the windjammer's friend and confidant. Nestled close, tugs maneuvered their charges in tight corners and nudged them free of obstructions. They towed them to drydock and led them clear of harbor traffic on the way out to sea. All this was no small task for the tug's master, but far surer, easier, and safer than in the age before steam.

Making Steam

To this day, there's something comforting about a tug. Slow and solid, they've evolved to be tough and hardy. They can take rough water and hard knocks. Bluff and low, they give a feeling of confidence. In *Heimdall's* era, tugs were driven by steam. Almost inevitably they were fitted with Scotch boilers—a horizontal fire-tube configuration—tanks of water with horizontal pipes opening to the firebox below, thence running through the boiler to maximize heating surface. Basically no more than giant—though complex—tea kettles, these Scotch boilers had an indecent propensity to explode!

Later, safer water-tube boilers were introduced. Steam boiler types—not to mention steam engine types—came in bewildering variety. In addition to the risky and ubiquitous Scotch boiler there were: gunboat, firebox, Stanley, water-leg, submerged-tube, Merryweather, Mumford, and Field boilers, to name just some of the fire-tube options. Water-tube boilers came in an even wider array. One of the latest of these—the Babcock & Wilcox single-pass, sectional-header boiler (now that's a mouthful)—is still in service on many older ships today.

Modern Tugs—Specialized Machines

Present-day tugs, however, are virtually all diesel or diesel-electric. A 60-footer (18 m) may fit an engine rated at nearly 1,000 hp (750 kw), while a 90-footer (27 m), might hold a 2,000-plus-hp (1500 kw) machine. The modern harbor tug, in fact, is a very specialized mechanism. These vessels have their underbodies designed to maximize stability. (Tying up to and tugging on a liner that's four times higher and 100 times heavier than you are is asking to capsize should something go wrong.) Further, these big engines require great hull volume. Fuel tanks are correspondingly large, and the tug's entire afterbody is shaped to fit a monstrous propeller. After all, this prop has really been sized to push a 12,000-ton liner *and* the tug—it needs to be *big!*

These factors don't make a true harbor tug a very practical platform for modification to a liveaboard cruiser, though for some reason folks are always trying to do just that. To be manageable, you'd need to replace the immense engine with something economical. Imagine the cost of pulling a 14,000-pound (6,350 kg) engine. (Nope, that's not a misprint.) Even if you pass this hurdle, you still have a very full-bodied hull to push along, and—for cruising purposes—a queerly shaped run.

A Tug Cruiser?

Nevertheless, a tug-inspired cruising yacht has a great deal to recommend it. The low, deep hulls have plenty of room and great stability. High bulwarks make walking about on deck secure and comfortable. Heavy construction fits these craft well, giving you a solid, shippy feel seldom found on small vessels.

What's called for is a craft that retains the tug's advantages without overdoing it. We want lots of stability, plenty of interior volume, and a stout structure. We don't want a hull shaped to swing a gigantic prop or equipped with five times the power we need for ordinary cruising—just think of the fuel bills!

Iron Kyle

Iron Kyle ("Kyle" is the Scottish word for "harbor") is such a craft. At 45 feet (13.7 m) overall

LOA	45 ft. 1 in.	(13.7 m)
LWL	40 ft. 5 in.	(12.3 m)
Beam	13 ft. 8 in.	(4.2 m)
BWL	12 ft. 7 in.	(3.8 m)
Draft	5 ft. 3 in.	(1.6 m)
Disp.	22.5 tons	
Power	Cat 3304-B, 136 shp (101 kw) at 2,000 rpm;	
	3.79:1 reduction gear	
Generator	Northern Lights 12 kw	
Fuel	1,480 gal. (5,600 l) diesel	
Water	275 gal. (1,040 l)	
Speed	9 knots max	
	8 knots cruise	

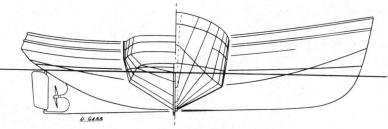

"Iron Kyle" a 45-foot cruising tug

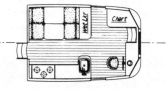

Lines of "Iron Kyle"

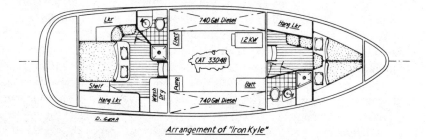

Arrangement of "Iron Kyle"

and 13 feet 8 inches (4.2 m) beam, drawing 5 feet 3 inches (1.6 m), she's small enough to be managed easily and to poke her nose into some tight corners. Yet she retains plenty of interior room.

Iron Kyle's hull is of hard-chine welded steel, an ideal material for a small tug. Heavy, welded-steel construction—for small craft—is about as close to truly indestructible as it's possible to get. If you run into something, it will be it (or them) you'll be worried about, not *Iron Kyle*. What's more, welded-steel construction like this is ideally suited to economical one-off building at any of the many small commercial yards dotting the coastline. Of course, *Kyle* could be built in heavy, solid fiberglass and would do just fine, but somehow this would make her seem a bit less, well, tug-like.

The View from the Wheelhouse

An interesting feature of *Iron Kyle* is her forward-raked wheelhouse windows. The fact is that many tugs built today have their wheelhouses mounted high up with the windows on all four sides raked outward—even at the rear. The reason for this is the same as it is for the outward slope of windows at airport control towers. Visibility on a working boat (not to mention at the control tower) is of paramount importance. The outward slope of the panes reduces glare and reflections from the instruments at night, and sheds rain and spray more quickly and cleanly than other configurations.

Some modern tugs place such great emphasis on 360-degree visibility (if you see it first you can probably get out of the way before it hits you—or vice versa) that they mount their bridges on hydraulic or mechanical lifts. These lifts telescope up or down like gigantic periscopes, or alternately like immense scissor cranes. With the bridge on top, lifting 10 or 12 feet (3.0 to 3.7 m), these gizmos permit a skipper to see over his tow. (It must be comforting to know what's going on over there on the other side!)

A telescoping bridge would be a bit of overkill

on *Iron Kyle*, but her forward-raked windows will make visibility clearer in all weather. Of course, *Iron Kyle* has high bulwarks all around, so you get that enclosed, secure feeling on deck. Amidships, at the wheelhouse, the bulwarks are actually 26 inches (66 cm) high. Forward and aft they're 14 inches (35 cm). *Kyle* also has room aft to carry a 9-foot (2.7 m) dinghy along with proper, permanent hoisting gear.

Comforts of Home

The wheelhouse itself fits a 6-foot 6-inch (198 cm) dinette that converts to a double berth as needed. In ordinary use, the inboard leaf of the table folds over on top of the outboard leaf to create more lounging space. Large windows on all sides, a chart table, and large galley round out the wheelhouse.

Aft, *Iron Kyle*'s master cabin is equipped with a queen-size berth, a 7-foot (2.1 m) hanging locker, a settee, and a head with separate shower. She even has room back there for a stackable washer and separate dryer. Forward, the guest stateroom has a king-size vee berth, settee, head, and 6-foot (180 cm) hanging locker. It's the tug's voluminous form that permits such spacious accommodations in 45 feet (13.7 m) without building her up high. Tall superstructures may add room, but they also decrease stability and increase windage—not ideal for serious voyaging.

A Heart of Iron

In the center of her engineroom beats *Iron Kyle*'s heart—a Caterpillar 3304-B diesel. Delivering 136 shaft horsepower (101 kw) at just 2,000 rpm, a relatively low-speed diesel like this means long engine life and a quiet ride. With her 3.79:1 reduction gear, *Kyle*'s prop lazes over at a bare 460 rpm at cruising speed. Not only is this efficient and easy on *Iron Kyle*'s gear, but any slight vibration will be at the low, comfortable, thump-thump speed of an old steam launch.

Again, the tug form permits plenty of room to work all around the engine—pleasant maintenance and no grumbling from the mechanic. It also allows space for generator, electric panels, pumps, and batteries. Perhaps best of all, the twin 740-gallon (2800 l) fuel tanks give *Iron Kyle* a cruising range of 2,100 nautical miles—the entire East Coast, the Caribbean, the Great Lakes are just routine hops with this sort of capacity. (Three-thousand-mile transoceanic capacity could be squeezed in, at some sacrifice in engineroom access and storage space.)

Easy Does It

If you're a speed demon, tugs probably are not for you. There's no way to get a shape like this to go faster than hull speed, no matter how much power you cram in. On the other hand, if getting about on the water safely and comfortably is your number-one concern, and if you prefer to take your time and savor the passing scene, then *Iron Kyle* and her cruising-tug sister ships will fill the bill perfectly.

CHAPTER 9

My Own Double-Enders

"By Jove, John," said Luxton, at the same time tapping me on the shoulder, "I thought sure it was all off with us when we hove to and I saw that big sea in front of us, but to see this little canoe going over the top of those big monsters without rolling or tumbling about is most wonderful. . . ."

The Venturesome Voyages of Captain Voss,
Captain John Claus Voss

It was once a common scene. The end of a hard day's sail, the hook just set firm, and the crew easing chilled bones, windburned cheeks, and salt-split fingers around a crackling stove. Outside the wind moans, and inside legs brace and fundaments shift as each sailor adjusts to the swell. The tang of hot coffee, rum, or whisky intertwines with pungent wood smoke and the salt steam rising from damp woolens.

"Now, that's what I call a sail!" someone comments, draining a cup for emphasis. "Pretty exciting, all right," comes the reply. "It was over 35 solid the last few hours." A momentary gust shivers the boat demonstratively. Everyone tenses just a trifle. The thought flits by: *Is the anchor holding?* "The old gal took it fine, though," the skipper says, patting her mahogany ceiling affectionately. Reaching into the coal bin, he pops the stove lid, judiciously adding a half shovelful. "Yeah, she's a good little ship," someone agrees. "But, you know, for the ultimate storm, I'd say 'give me a double-ender'." Sage nods all around and discussion about whose turn it is to cook dinner.

Once the Safest Boats

Until the last 20 years or so it was generally agreed that, in extreme conditions, the safest and most forgiving hull form was the double-ender. These days, when seakeeping and comfort are often neglected, the double-ender's advantages are seldom considered. Certainly a well-proportioned transom-stern boat can be comfortable and safe in the worst conditions offshore; however—all other things being equal—double-enders do offer some real advantages. Their sterns are inherently stronger and less prone to damage from wave action than transom sterns. They won't pound uncomfortably in a quartering or following sea. They also have somewhat less tendency to yaw in these conditions, and if their steering gear, house, and hatches are up to it, they can even lie stern-to safely.

Double Drawbacks

Naturally, nothing's perfect; double-enders have their drawbacks as well. One of these is that, for the same length overall, a double-ender has less usable room. Another is that it's very hard to get a wide, flat run—the form needed for high speeds (see Chapter 18). Wide, flat runs, on the other hand, make for temperamental handling in a quartering sea. As usual, you can't have everything in one boat.

The Oldest Shape

It's difficult to know for sure, but I'd bet that double-enders were the earliest type of boat (rafts excluded). Traditional canoes are double-ended (a natural shape to get out of a hollow log), and most ancient seagoing craft were as well. Greek and Phoenician galleys, often named for the arrangement of men at their oars—pentekonters, hecatoners, trieres, and penteres, for instance— were the backbones of ancient navies and essentially double-enders. Farther north and a millennia or so later, double-ended Norse longboats enabled their Viking crews not only to roam and master most of coastal northern Europe, but to cross the Atlantic and trade with the Mediterranean. The squared-off or transom stern, it seems, is a "modern" innovation.

The Small-Craft Preference

Though the double-ender was generally abandoned for large vessels by the 1600s or so, small craft—coasters, fishing vessels and launches— have commonly remained double-ended to this day. Whaleboats and surfboats, in particular, were likely to be double-enders. A typical example—a "Greenland Pinnace, for Whale fishery"— appears in one of the earliest texts on naval architecture, *Architectura Navalis Mercatoria 1768*, by F.H. Chapman. The need for predictable handling in confused seas and surf made the sharp stern a virtual necessity.

Redningskoites?

There are, not surprisingly, many types of double-enders—Block Island boats, pinkies (see *Papoo*, Chapter 48), and Tancook whalers, to name just a few. All of these, in their day, were particularly respected as rough-water boats. If any single craft, however, perpetuated the double-

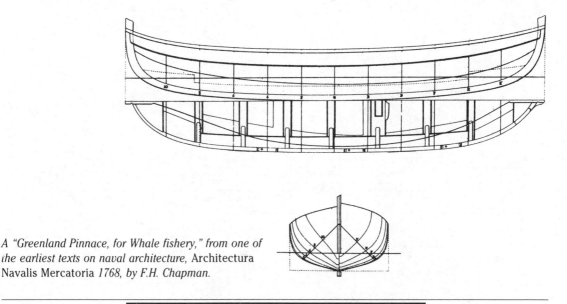

A "Greenland Pinnace, for Whale fishery," from one of the earliest texts on naval architecture, Architectura Navalis Mercatoria *1768, by F.H. Chapman.*

ender's reputation for seaworthiness, it was the Norwegian sailing lifeboat or Redningskoite designed by Colin Archer around the turn of the century. Rescue service in the cold, steep, short seas and high winds of the Baltic and North Seas required nothing less than the hardiest craft. It wasn't long before "Colin Archer double-ender" became synonymous with safety at sea. For many, many years, ocean voyagers selected such craft above all others. A pure Colin Archer double-ender was being manufactured even as recently as the 1970s—the fiberglass production boat Westsail 32, which sold extremely well for some time.

North Sea Lifeboats Aren't Yachts

Perhaps it is this fascination with the Colin Archer-type boat that has led to the mild backlash against double-enders I sometimes encounter. Archer's North Sea craft were designed for their environment. They had very heavy displacement and were underrigged for ordinary cruising purposes. What's more, their hulls had slack bilges and considerable displacement low down. This adds volume and eases motion, but detracts from sail-carrying power. The short-rigged Norwegian sailing lifeboats can't simply be given taller rigs;

they wouldn't stand up to it. This isn't a fault of the Redningskoites; they were specifically designed to operate in high winds and rough seas, and other considerations were secondary. They are not, though, a good starting point for yachts, at least not if you plan to get anywhere fast.

Gerr's End

It was thus that—almost by accident—I gradually developed my own double-ender, a hull form that, though it looks traditional, copies no preexisting type. What I wanted was a double-ended or canoe-stern boat that would minimize the drawbacks of double-enders while retaining their virtues. Additionally, I needed a hull with firm bilges and flat floors to generate the initial stability required to stand up to a tall rig, and to keep displacement moderate.

Sisters—Big and Little

Madrigal and *Serenade*—little and big sisterships—were the result. You can see that, compared to the Colin Archer type, they have very flat underbodies and firm bilges indeed.(*Madrigal's* lines are shown in chapter 17.) *Madrigal* is a keel-centerboarder fitted with a half-ton of ballast on

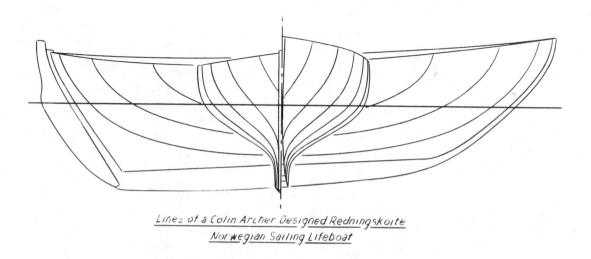

Lines of a Colin Archer Designed Redningskoite
Norwegian Sailing Lifeboat

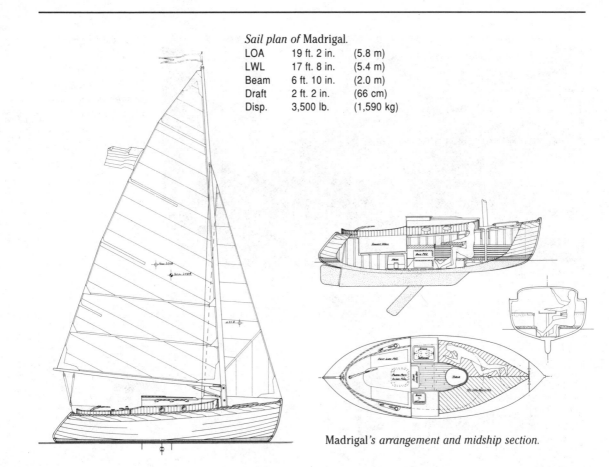

Sail plan of Madrigal.

LOA	19 ft. 2 in.	(5.8 m)
LWL	17 ft. 8 in.	(5.4 m)
Beam	6 ft. 10 in.	(2.0 m)
Draft	2 ft. 2 in.	(66 cm)
Disp.	3,500 lb.	(1,590 kg)

Madrigal's arrangement and midship section.

the bottom of her keel. Her centerboard's long and narrow (high-aspect) and housed entirely in the keel proper, without projecting into the cabin at all. In fact, many a guest has clambered into her cabin, stretched his legs across the smooth sole and then, looking startled, inquired, "Where's the board?"

Although—like any double-ender—she's a trifle cramped for space astern, Madrigal's quite spacious inside. Clearly, she's got only sitting headroom, but it's honest and comfortable sitting headroom—room enough, in fact, for my 6-foot 6-inch, 250-pound (200 cm, 114 kg) friend (not surprisingly known as "Big Dave") to sit up with a

couple of inches (5 cm) clear over his noggin. Being just 19 feet 2 inches (5.8 m) overall, Madrigal's a small boat, and this leads to another surprise. Step on her rail and she feels solid and stable—the direct result of her hard bilge and flattish underbody. It's this that enables her to stand up to her sail plan. Of course, a canoe stern ought to look handsome as well. You can judge Madrigal's for yourself from the photo.

A Voyaging Double-Ender

Serenade is Madrigal's big sister. At 13,600 pounds (6,180 kg) to Madrigal's 3,500 (1,590 kg) she's nearly four times larger, even though she's

Madrigal *leaving her builder, North River Boatworks. Frank Houde—North River partner number two—seems to have something important to announce.*

Stern view of Madrigal. *The author and his wife are in the cockpit. Howard Mittleman, one of the partners at North River Boatworks, tends the bow line.*

Madrigal *working upwind on an evening breeze.*

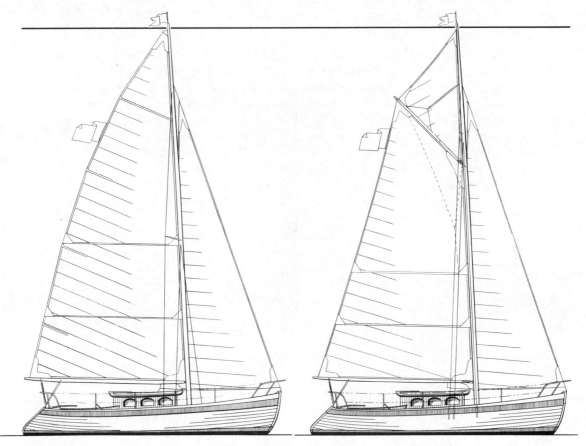

Serenade's *jib-headed sail plan:*

LOA	30 ft. 3 in.	(9.2 m)
LWL	27 ft.10 in.	(8.5 m)
Beam	8 ft. 8 in.	(2.6 m)
Draft	4 ft. 8 in.	(1.4 m)
Disp.	13,600 lb.	(6,180 kg)

Serenade's *gaff-rig sail plan.*

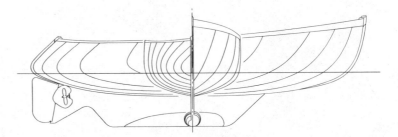

Arrangement and lines of Serenade.

only one and a half times longer—a classic example of the laws of relativity and similitude at work (see Chapter 13). Where *Madrigal* is a coastal cruiser, *Serenade* is up to real voyaging. Her full keel supports a 5,000-pound (2,270 kg) lead-ballast torpedo along its bottom to give her great reserve stability as well as sail-carrying power. Still, *Serenade* draws just 4 feet 8 inches (1.4 m). She can work her way into some pretty tight spots. Her rudder and prop are well protected from impact and grounding, so with her long keel she can take bottom safely.

Gaff vs Jib-Head

Nick Robison, who commissioned *Serenade,* is a traditionalist at heart. He just had to have a gaff rig—I couldn't talk him out of it. I must say that the gaff rig looks handsome with this hull, but the jib-headed rig makes an instructive comparison. Both the gaff and jib-headed rigs set about the same sail area on about the same height. The jib-headed rig, however, has fewer and lighter spars and fewer halyards and control lines. One of the most unpleasant experiences a sailor can have is to be becalmed in a sloppy sea with a gaff rig. The gaff and all its attendant gear bang about fearfully for hours or days at a time. In addition, decreasing weight and windage aloft dramatically improves performance and comfort. This isn't to say that the gaff rig won't work just fine. Gaff riggers were masters of the coast and fishery trades for several centuries, and Nick will cover many pleasant ocean miles in his gaff *Serenade*. It's simply that the jib-headed rig will be better still.

CHAPTER 10

The Ultimate Sportfisherman

I have laid aside my business, and gone afishing

> *The Compleat Angler,* Izaak Walton

New boats always start as a gleam in someone's eye. In this case, the gleam began—as it so often does—after hundreds of hours on a boat that once had seemed good enough, but no longer quite lived up to expectations.

When a sailor gets really serious about sportfishing, he or she wants the best tools available—rods, reels, fish finders, loran, and so on. For offshore fishing, though, one of the most crucial tools is the machine that takes you out to the fish, serves as your working platform, and gets you and your haul back safely.

An ex-submariner and a no-nonsense, no-holds-barred fisherman, Jim Melley decided his old boat wasn't up to his current requirements, and that he needed just such a serious fishing machine. He haunted boat shows, visited builders, and kept an eagle eye on other sportfishermen, watching their performance and questioning their skippers: "How does she ride? Does she pound or plow? Does she snap roll? Can you back her down under good control?"

There are plenty of good fishing boats out there, and Jim found several he liked. None of them, however, had all the features he had in mind: "If the cockpit were just a bit larger. If she only had more room for electronics. If the cabin weren't so cramped." Soon, Jim found himself frequently wandering over to a nearby boatbuilder. Off Soundings Yachts of Manorville, Long Island, was producing nice 21- and 27-footers (6.4 and 8.2 m), and they were already considering setting up for a boat in the 33-foot (10 m) range.

It wasn't long after this that my phone rang. It was Steve Krivacsy, the owner of Off Soundings Yachts. He had offered to design Jim's new boat, and he certainly could have done an acceptable job, but Jim wanted something more than acceptable. In fact, it became clear to me, after we'd talked for a brief time, that what Jim wanted was nothing less than the *ultimate* sportfisherman.

Defining the Ultimate Sportfisherman

Now, there can be considerable discussion regarding what constitutes the ultimate sportfisherman. To some, "ultimate" conjures up visions of 90-foot (28 m) gold platers with alligator-skin lounge seats and onyx-and-ebony inlay on all the joinerwork. Others might not go this far, but would want to see a flybridge boat with plenty of cabin space. Jim, however, wanted a boat that was for sportfishing first and last. He wasn't planning to cross oceans or to carry 20 friends or charter customers from place to place. In fact, Jim definitely didn't want a boat that was so big he'd have to charter her out just to be able to afford to keep her. Nor was he planning to spend long periods of time cruising and living aboard with his friends and family. He needed a cabin, sure, but just room enough to be really comfortable for a night or two out at the Canyon from time to time.

If there was one feature he did want, though, it was cockpit space—lots of it. The cockpit is the work area on a sportfisherman, and the bigger it is the more work it can handle. A real fisherman needs room for a fighting chair, large, easily accessible fish boxes, a bait prep station, tackle storage, transom door, and so on. In fact, if the cockpit were large enough, several fishermen could be working these different functions at once without getting in each other's way. Finally, Jim had less interest in gold-plated bathroom fixtures than he does in pink Cadillacs. (At least, I presume he's not interested in pink Cadillacs; I've never asked him.) A real fishing machine is a tool. You'd no more want ebony inlay and alligator-skin lounge seats in a serious sportfishing machine than you would want solid gold casing built onto a fine lathe.

Settling on the Right Length

After considerable discussion and sketches of designs of various lengths, we settled on 34 feet (10.4 m) or so as the ideal length. At this size, we had a boat that was big enough to take plenty of rough weather, had room for a comfortable cabin and a roomy helm station, and still provided a really large cockpit. Jim also had his heart set on Caterpillar's new 3116TA engines. Just becoming available, these new Cats produce almost the same horsepower as the old, reliable Cat 3208TA, but they are nearly 6 inches (16 cm) lower in profile and over 6 inches (16 cm) narrower. Additionally, these engines are almost 400 pounds (180 kg) lighter than the 3208s. Of course, other powerplants could be fitted if desired, but knowing the boat length, power plant, and type of service, we were ready to firm up the design. The Off Soundings 34 was the result.

Moderate Beam Equals Seaworthiness and Speed

Our next important decision was to keep beam moderate. A serious sportfisherman has to be a good all-weather sea boat. Many folks equate beam with room, but this just isn't so. Room is volume, and volume—in a boat—is displacement. If you have two boats of the same displacement, and one is wide and short and the other long and lean, they will have the same usable room and cost about the same, but the leaner boat will go faster with the same power and, even better, be much more comfortable and more easily handled in rough weather.

Of course, a sportfisherman shouldn't be truly narrow, but too much beam leads to pounding and an uncomfortable jerky roll. Further, a wide transom—in comparison with a boat's length—increases the tendency to broach in following or quartering seas. This is because, as waves strike the transom from behind or underneath, the wide-sterned boat has proportionately more of its buoyancy at the transom. It thus lifts and slews more at each passing wave. Keeping beam moderate greatly reduces this tendency.

Hull Design for Seakindliness and Comfort

In addition to moderate beam, the Off Soundings 34's lines incorporate several other features

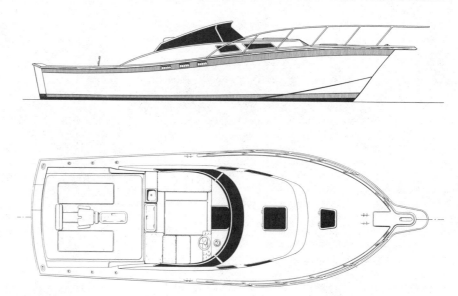

Profile and deck plan of the 34-foot 6-inch (10.5 m) by 12-foot 1-inch (3.7 m) Off Soundings 34, a twin-diesel sportfisherman.

that are critical to making a good sea boat. The deadrise (entry) forward is very fine to eliminate pounding. Further, the chine forward is quite high, which also reduces pounding. Slight convexity has been worked into the sections forward to give sufficient buoyancy for operation at low speed (as well as at high speed) in a seaway.

The chine/spray knocker is shaped to curl water back down where it belongs. This creates a dry boat and gives additional planing lift and dynamic stability. This chine increases in width aft (generating even more lift), where it will not cause pounding. An additional benefit is that the wide immersed chine aft gives a very stable fishing platform—it damps out any tendency to snap roll.

The sections aft have only slightly less deadrise than at amidships, but they are narrower and have less volume. This gives the same benefits as decreasing deadrise while keeping plenty of vee to minimize the chance of pounding at the stern when trolling or drifting.

Obviously, there's a lot more that goes into a set of lines. The buttock angles in the run for both the hull and the chine have been adjusted to give proper planing trim (approximately 4 to 5 degrees); the engine and propeller locations affect hull shape; and the longitudinal center of buoyancy and prismatic coefficient are just some of the features that required careful juggling—see Chapter 18.

To Flybridge or Not to Flybridge

Not loading up the boat with the height, weight, and windage of a flybridge/cabin made it possible to give the Off Soundings 34 a sleek, low look. This pays off in more than just appearance, as windage is reduced for greater speed and the center of gravity is kept lower for better roll characteristics. Of course, for those who want to do less fishing and more cruising, we did design the Off Soundings 34 hull to take a flybridge/cabin; you may even see one motor by someday. The fly-

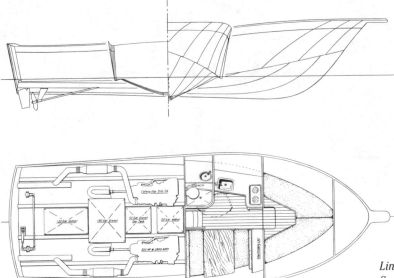

Lines and arrangement of the Off Soundings 34.

bridge version, though, gets away from Jim's "ultimate sportfisherman" concept.

Deck and Cockpit Layout

The Off Soundings 34's cockpit is a bit under 10 feet (3 m) beam inside the coaming and just over 10 feet (3 m) beam to the sheer. As we mentioned earlier, some fishermen look at beam as the principal indicator of room. You shouldn't be deceived by beam alone, however. The Off Soundings 34's cockpit is huge for a boat of this size—over 93 square feet (8.6 m²).

In the cockpit, forward to port, is a tackle counter with bins and drawers (facing aft into the cockpit) for all the fishing gear that accumulates so quickly. Above the counter is a sink, and stowed below is a deck washdown hose on a reel. Forward, to starboard, is a live-bait well. A hinged bait-prep counter lifts up (dotted line) for plenty of work space. Temporary rod stowage is fitted under the cockpit gunwales, port and starboard. (Long-term rod stowage is in the cabin. Rod racks

are fitted under the headliner over the dinette and vee-berth, where the rods can be locked up securely out of the salt and wet.)

The bridge deck steering station is fitted with a wide helm seat to starboard, and a 5-foot (150 cm) cooler with cushions on top forms a seat to port. The sole of the bridge deck is well raised to make room for the engines and, more importantly, to give really good visibility. Access to the bridge deck from the cockpit is by a three-foot-wide step that forms still another tackle box. An important safety feature of this configuration is that even with the transom door wide open, a large wave will be confined to the cockpit and cannot get forward and below.

Although the Off Soundings 34 has the stability to support a full-size tuna tower, she's usually fitted with a smaller marlin tower. This is the kind of personal decision that drives fishermen to distraction. The taller tuna tower gives greater range of visibility for both eyes and radar, and it allows you to see deeper into the water. Unfortunately,

The Off Soundings 34 runs home after catching her limit.

The Off Soundings 27—the 34's little sister built by Steve Krivacy's Long Island yard—heads out to look for fish on a fine day. (Off Soundings Yachts photo.)

the taller tuna tower also increases roll and creates additional windage that slows you down and makes handling more difficult in a stiff crosswind. The smaller, lighter marlin tower doesn't give quite the visibility of a tuna tower, but it generates less windage and roll, making for a better sea boat.

Cabin Arrangement and Engine Access

The Off Soundings 34's cabin is equipped with a dinette that forms a full-size, 6-foot 4-inch–long (194 cm) double berth, and forward vee-berths that are 6 feet 6 inches (198 cm) long and a full 2 feet (60 cm) wide. A removable filler wedge transforms the vee-berth into a king-size bed. An enclosed head with stand-up shower, a full galley with fridge, and a hanging locker complete the interior. Headroom is 6 feet 4 inches (194 cm) throughout.

The twin Cat 3116s fit nicely under the bridge deck. Engine access is through three lifting panels on the bridge deck sole. The center panel is always ready for quick opening. By lifting out the helm seat and cooler, the remaining two panels can be opened, giving totally unobstructed engine access the full width of the boat.

Speed Counts

Jim, sensibly, plans to cruise at around 20 to 25 knots; however, he wanted top speed in ex-

cess of 30 knots. Fully loaded, the Off Soundings 34 delivers as follows:

RPM	KNOTS	MPH	RANGE (NAUTICAL MILES)
2800	33.2	38.2	321
2400	26.4	30.3	412
2000	20.0	23.1	510

Being able to run at over 30 knots gives a fisherman the ability to dash out quickly to where the fish are biting, to keep ahead of a threatening squall, and, of course, to show off a little.

Tankage, Range and Trim

Seventy-five gallons (340 l) of fresh water and 300 gallons (1,360 l) of diesel form the standard tankage. The tanks are located around the boat's center of buoyancy and center of flotation so there will be a minimum change of trim running empty or full. Additionally, trim can be adjusted by pumping from the after to the forward fuel tank, or vice versa. A nice feature is that you can draw from the aft fuel tank on the way out. Then the weight of the fish hauled aboard and stored in the fish boxes will be balanced out by the emptying of the aft tank. You can run back in on the forward tank, which holds a few more gallons than the aft tank—a nice reserve.

Variable Displacement

Many sailors tend to think of a boat's displacement as being fixed. In reality, displacement changes all the time depending on loading. The Off Soundings 34's design or reference displacement is 14,630 pounds (6,640 kg). Topped up with ice, fuel, water and a large crew, though, she'd run out at around 15,500 to 16,000 pounds (7,030 to 7,260 kg) or so. Without ice and with a small crew and low fuel she'd be down around 13,500 pounds (6,120 kg).

Maneuverability Is Critical

Serious sportfishermen need good maneuverability even at low speed and while backing down for fighting and boating fish. Accordingly, the Off Soundings 34 has slightly larger than normal rudders for improved steering. The rudders are entirely tucked under the transom—no part projects aft to snag lines and fish.

A Mean Machine

If I were a fish and saw a boat like the Off Soundings tear by, I'd just roll over and jump in the cockpit. This might, however, take some of the fun out of sportfishing. Jim was considering having Off Soundings install "fish reflectors" to control this problem, but we'll hold off on 'em 'til absolutely necessary.

CHAPTER 11

The Sutherland Paddle Boat

Oh well for the fisherman's boy,
That he shouts with his sister at play!
Oh well for the sailor lad,
That he sings in his boat on the bay!

Break, Break, Break, Alfred Lord Tennyson

On the upper reaches of the Hudson—tucked into an out-of-the-way corner of Albany—is a small boatbuilder. North River Boatworks (the North River has long been the Hudson's second name) is the kind of builder that makes a designer look good. In fact, every designer knows that, no matter how beautiful a set of drawings he or she produces, it's the builder who quite literally makes it come to life. A good builder can transform even a mediocre design into something special, while a poor builder can make hash of the most exquisitely conceived detail drawings.

Several years ago, North River had just finished their second project for me—my canoe-sterned sloop *Madrigal*—and we were proudly displaying her at the Newport Wooden Boat Show. Her all-varnished, lapstrake, mahogany-and-cedar topsides glowed in the sun; her polished bronze fittings gleamed; and her canoe stern bobbed gracefully as if she were eager to get going. Naturally, I was sure she'd be the hit of the show. Naturally, I was wrong.

Taking a Scow for a Spin

The fellows at North River hauled a diminutive, nondescript scow out of the back of their pickup. It was about 5 feet (1.5 m) long and 2 feet (60 cm) wide, and it had little hand-cranked paddles—sidewheels—sticking out on either side. Howie and Frank (two of the three partners at North River) shoved her unceremoniously into the water and Dan (partner number three) clambered in. He knelt down, grabbed the two crank handles and motored(?) from dock to dock.

I can tell you from direct observation that, if you ever want to make friends at a boat show, all you have to do is paddle by in a Sutherland paddle boat. Soon, there was a line of kids and grown-ups—and some in between—forming for rides. It wasn't long before North River had to charge admission just to keep things in hand. They quickly had the longest line of any exhibit at the show.

The Sutherland paddle boat was invented by

A paddleboat skipper powers his vessel along. The characteristic paddle swirl indicates that an attempt at real acceleration is underway.

The original smaller paddleboat was a bit skimpy on freeboard. This didn't seem to detract from the fun much—especially on hot days!

Dan's grandfather, Earnest Sutherland (a builder of fine skiffs in the 1920s), and the fact is, his brainstorm is plain good fun. She isn't big or fancy or expensive, but all you have to do is set a kid down at her cranks and his face will light up. It's hard to pry them out of the boat when their turn is up. Just take a look at the photos.

Rolling Your Own

The Sutherland paddle boat is so small and simple that you can easily make one of your own in a few weekends. The accompanying drawings give her overall dimensions and layout, as well as showing the paddle mechanism. There are a few minor improvements over the original model. Most important, the original 5-foot-long (1.5 m) hull had a bit too little buoyancy for both a captain and crew, as you can see in the photo. Getting in and out of the original model, with her low freeboard, or powering through a bit of chop was sometimes a wetter experience than one desired. The version shown has the same beam, but it's 2 feet (60 cm) longer. This gives her plenty of extra buoyancy and freeboard—drier and safer.

The paddlewheels themselves throw a distinctive swirl of water—half the fun I think—and can get you pretty well doused as well. To help in

this department, I've shown a pair of optional splash guards. They're simply screwed to the outside of the hull at the paddlewheels. Quarter-inch (6 mm) Plexiglas would be the ideal material, but any scrap plywood would do fine. You could paint your paddle boat's name around the perimeter of each splash guard. I'd suggest something like *Indomitable* or *Courageous*. The splash guards can be added at any time, so you might want to try your paddle boat without them first, to see how she goes.

Obviously, the final dimensions aren't critical to a Sutherland paddle boat. Just get the general shape and approximate lengths shown. If you end up an inch or two off, you can declare yours to be an extra-special, souped-up experimental model. (A bit of port and starboard symmetry is worth striving for.)

The Scantlings

The hull may be made from a single sheet of ¼-inch (6 mm) plywood. Or you can save yourself

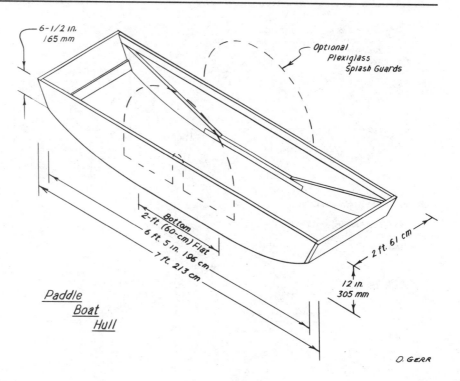

6-1/2 in.
165 mm

Optional
Plexiglass
Splash Guards

Bottom
2-ft. (60-cm) Flat
6 ft. 5 in. 196 cm
7 ft. 213 cm

2 ft. 61 cm

12 in.
305 mm

Paddle
Boat
Hull

O. GERR

the work of fastening chines and sheer clamps to the ¼-inch (6 mm) ply by using ¾-inch (18 mm) plywood for the sides and the bow and stern transoms. (You should still use ¼-inch (6 mm) ply for the bottom, because ¾-inch (18 mm) won't make the bend.)

For the all-¼-inch-ply (6 mm) version the scantlings (the construction thickness and descriptions) should be about as follows:

- Sides and bottom: ¼-inch (6 mm) plywood
- Middle chines (at flat bottom): ¾-inch by 1½-inch (18 by 35 mm) pine, fir, or mahogany
- Forward and after chines: ¾-inch by 4-inch (18 by 100 mm) pine, fir, or mahogany; saw to the curved bottom shape
- Sheer clamp (gunwale): ¾-inch by 1½-inch (18 by 35 mm) pine, fir, or mahogany
- Bow and stern transoms: ¾-inch-thick (18 mm)

pine, fir, or mahogany plank, or ¾-inch (18 mm) ply
- Splash guards: ¼-inch (6 mm) Plexiglas or plywood

Crank and Paddle

The paddlewheels themselves also are easy to assemble. Their hub is simply a solid wood block 4 inches by 4 inches by 4 inches (10 cm by 10 cm by 10 cm). The paddle blades are ½-inch-thick (12 mm) fir, pine, mahogany, or plywood. (They can be thicker if you have some scrap ¾-inch (18 mm) stock left over to use up.) The only tricky part is the cranks. These are made from ¼-inch-diameter or ⅜-inch-diameter (6 or 9 mm) steel rod, bent to shape as shown. The important thing to remember is that the two paddlewheel cranks are separate. They *are not connected* at the center.

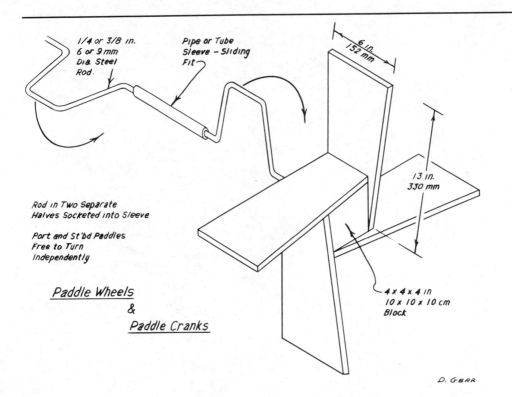

1/4 or 3/8 in.
6 or 9 mm
Dia Steel
Rod.

Pipe or Tube
Sleeve – Sliding
Fit

6 in.
152 mm

13 in.
330 mm

Rod in Two Separate
Halves Socketed into Sleeve

Port and St'bd Paddles
Free to Turn
Independently

4 x 4 x 4 in
10 x 10 x 10 cm
Block

Paddle Wheels
&
Paddle Cranks

D. GERR

By keeping each paddlewheel free to turn independently, you can crank one forward and the other backward for maneuvering. Without this feature, the Sutherland paddle boat would have only two courses—straight ahead and straight astern. At the centerline, the two cranks meet in a sleeve of pipe or heavy tube with a sliding fit. This sleeve should be about 7 inches (18 cm) long and should fit just snug enough to allow the cranks to rotate freely and independently. (You might want to drill a small hole at the center of the sleeve and squeeze a drop of oil into it once or twice a season.)

The fittings to attach the rod to the paddlewheel hub block and to the hull need to be welded. (It is about as simple and inexpensive a welding job as can be imagined; any local welder will be able to do it in a few minutes.) To attach the rod to the paddle, a 3½-inch (9 cm) square plate is welded to each end, drilled for four 3/16-inch (5 mm) bolts, and bolted on.

Fastening to the Gunwale

The bearings at the gunwale, port and starboard—the fittings that hold the cranks to the hull—are made from two steel channels welded back to back to form an "H." The lower channel is fitted over the gunwale and through-bolted on. The upper channel is drilled for the crank rod, and a bearing is made by cutting some of the sleeve pipe or tubing to fit in the channel and welding it in place. Just bend to shape, assemble all your crank and paddle pieces, and bring them to your local welder. Remember, though, to put the crank rod through the bearing on the channel *before* the plate is welded to the rod end. Sliding it in after the plate is welded on would be a neat trick, but it's one that I, at least, haven't mastered.

Take your two welded-up cranks home and, fitting the center crank sleeve over the center ends, drop the entire assembly onto your boat. Bolt the channel bearings to the hull and the paddlewheels to the plates on the crank and you're ready to go for a spin—not a pun, I think.

Races Anyone?

With birthdays, Christmas, and similar occasions always just around the corner, you can probably have a Sutherland paddle boat ready in time for one or the other—if you start soon. Be warned though: If you have more than one kid, you may end up having to make a second paddle boat. Not only will this keep the peace, but you can stage races.

CHAPTER 12

Nester Dinghy and The Terribly Trying Dinghy Dilemma

I received in succession our stores, and stowed the cargo as best I could, while the dinghy sank lower and lower in the water, and its precarious superstructure grew higher.

The Riddle of the Sands, Erskine Childers

"Where am I goin' a put the gosh durn thing?!" I've sworn up and down at hapless dinghies more frequently than I care to remember. What's more, I'm not alone. Not only do fellow designers join in, but most of my clients and three-quarters of the boating world do the same. The sad fact is, on boats under 45 feet (14 m) or so it just isn't easy to find a place to store a really good dinghy.

Cruising without a good dinghy is no fun. You need a safe, reliable way to get from your boat to shore when anchored in strange—and thus interesting—places. A proper dinghy should be able to take you exploring into all those inviting nooks and crannies the mother ship couldn't even approach. At the very least, the dink should be stable; row and power well; and have room for four adults (six in a pinch) and a respectable amount of gear—all at the same time!

Dinghy Requirements

Now, it's a simple matter to determine the shape and dimensions of the minimum boat that will live up to these requirements. To honestly seat four to six grownups and leave room for their duffel, she'd have to be somewhere between 10 and 12 feet (3 and 3.6 m) long, with a beam, say, around 4½ feet (1.4 m). For stability, she'd require a flat bottom. To get the most room and the most stability, she ought to have a pram bow.

The drawing of *Pippin* shows a design of mine that meets all these requirements perfectly. *Pippin* is so stable that I can stand on her rail without swamping her. She has the bonus of sail, which is fun, but not necessary for a good dinghy, and she rows and powers very handily indeed.

So, Where Do I Put Her?

Naturally, the old sea dogs reading this are chuckling to themselves: "She's no dinghy. You couldn't fit her on board anywhere!" But of course, that's the point. A boat like *Pippin* does everything a dink ought to do, but you couldn't squeeze her onto anything less than a 50-footer

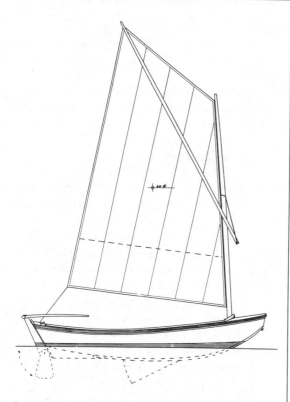

Sail plan of the 11-foot (3.3 m) sailing garvey Pippin.

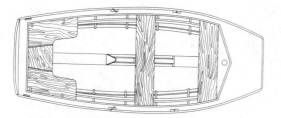

Arrangement of Pippin.

(15 m)—and a 60-footer (18 m) would be more likely.

The most common solution is to compromise on a small dinghy. You can often manage to just squeeze an 8- or 9-footer (2.4 to 2.7 m) on most small cruisers—though it isn't easy. At a bare 8 or 9 feet (2.4 or 2.7 m) long, though, these little craft

Pippin *ghosting along the upper Hudson.*

aren't up to a serious day's work. They're certainly better than nothing, but far from ideal.

Another approach to this problem is to forget all the dinghy has to do and design it simply to be stowed as easily as possible. Obviously, for sheer stowing convenience, you can't beat the inflatable. They're fairly stable, and they can be blown up to any size—any size they were designed for, that is—so room for crew and gear isn't a problem.

The difficulty with inflatables is that they aren't all that good as boats. Sure, with an outboard strapped to its posterior, an inflatable will get you where you want to go, but they're wet and, well, rubbery the whole while. The time spent inflating and setting them up (or taking them apart) is tiresome, and stowing them below wet leads to imaginative accumulations of mildew and salt crusts.

Towing Can Be a Drag

Another approach to the dinghy problem is to use the hard dinghy of your choice and forget about stowing it aboard—just tow it everywhere. Now, this has some real advantages. Not only is the stowage problem eliminated, but the trusty tender is always ready for instant use. You don't even have to hoist her overboard.

The drawbacks, unfortunately, are obvious. Several summers ago, we towed a dink—affectionately named *The Black Brick*—wherever we went. The convenience was so great that we didn't blow up our inflatable (always aboard) even once. Nevertheless, *The Black Brick* ultimately proved to be a real drag. On one occasion, working upwind in a 20-knot breeze, we had to tack to avoid colliding with a tug and barge train. (We generally try to avoid hitting barges so as not to cause them undue damage). Three times in a row *Madrigal*—usually swift and sure in stays—failed to tack. I think we got to count the weld seams on each of those barges! Of course, the culprit was *The Black Brick*. She was generating so much drag that we'd lose way as our head came into the wind, with the stiff breeze and short chop. Then we'd fall off onto our original tack.

Offshore, towing a dinghy presents additional problems. She can easily become swamped in a storm, in which condition she'll make a nifty sea anchor—though this isn't exactly the best way to go about rigging one. In fact, any time it gets rough you stand a real chance of losing your dinghy altogether. Tow ropes seem to have a special fondness for parting late at night in a howling nor'easter.

Even in fair weather you often have to adjust the length of the tow rope to match the waves. If the rope isn't the right length, your dinghy will snub up hard every few waves with a pronounced jerk and audible thwang. Or—just to make matters as exciting as possible—your dink can surf down the front of a wave, accelerating so fast that she overtakes her mother ship. The obvious solution is to break out cutlasses and rig to repel boarders. Just when you're sure you've prevented the attacking dink from climbing into the cockpit, she'll take a dive and smash into the transom at the waterline.

Cut Her Right in Two!

So what is the solution? Well, there isn't really a perfect solution. That's why the dinghy dilemma is so terribly trying. No matter what approach you choose, you're in for a compromise.

Probably, the best compromise is a good nesting dinghy. This is no more than a proper dinghy that breaks in two, with the shorter half stowing (nesting) inside the longer portion. You can have a good-size hard dinghy, well shaped and properly proportioned for rowing and for power. You can tow her behind you inshore during short hops, and—when you need to get her squared away on deck—she'll only take up about half the room a regular (non-nesting) dinghy would.

Nester Dinghy

The drawings show the lines of Nester Dinghy, which fits all these requirements. Open, she's a full 11 feet (3.3 m) long and 4 feet 6 inches (1.4 m) wide—the same size and carrying capacity as the non-nesting *Pippin,* yet when broken and stowed, Nester Dinghy lies upside down on deck in a space just 5 feet 10 inches (1.8 m) long by 4 feet 6 inches (1.4 m) wide. This is considerably less space than the usual "minimum" 8-foot (2.4 m) dink requires. Combine this with a nested height of just 1 foot 9 inches (53 cm), and you can find room for Nester Dinghy on nearly any cruiser.

Nester Dinghy is designed for tape-seam sheet-plywood construction, which is both easy and light. Loaded and ready to go, she weighs in at around 130 pounds (60 kg). This is light enough to hoist aboard easily with a tackle rigged to the boom or with any small davit. Nester Dinghy's two

The Smallest Nesting Boat?

Perhaps the most compact nesting boat anywhere is the one I drew up for Doug Goldhirsch of Piece Boat Water Craft, of Noank, Connecticut—the Piece Boat Solo. She's just 48 inches (1.2 m) long nested and weighs a mere 35 pounds (16 kg). Open, she's 10 feet 6 inches (3.2 m) overall, and can carry a 200-pound (90 kg) man easily.

The three-piece Piece Boat Solo stowed and nested—48 inches (1.2 m) long, 28 inches (70 cm) beam.

The three pieces coming out for assembly.

All the pieces out for inspection.

Doug Goldhirsch takes the Piece Boat Solo for a spin. His 6 feet and 180 pounds (182 cm, 82 kg) is no problem for the small Piece Boat. Assembly time—from start to launch—is a bare 1 minute 15 seconds.

halves float independently, however, so you can take her apart in the water and hoist each section up individually.

Keep Her in Your Closet

Naturally, being light and compact, Nester Dinghy is ideal for car-topping and/or stowing at home in tight spaces. If you're an apartment dweller, you could even stick her in the back of a large closet and carry her down the elevator for a fishing trip every weekend. Of course, you could take her fishing from your 40-footer (12 m) too—a picnic basket, an ice bucket, the grapnel anchor over the side, a shade umbrella jammed into an oarlock. . . .

Okay, Go Ahead and Build One

A dink like this is an ideal home project. The first thing you need to do is draw the frame and transom shapes on a sheet of plywood, taking dimensions from the table of offsets and the lines drawing. Deduct the plank thickness ($\frac{1}{4}$ inch—6 mm) and measure the bevel for each frame and transom. (The plank thickness deducted at the bow and stern transoms has to be adjusted for their rake.) Nester Dinghy has been designed specifically so that the bevels are constant on a given frame's panel section. So on, say, frame 1, the bevel is the same from the top to the bottom portion of the upper side panel. The same is true for the bilge panel, the bottom panel, and every frame.

You can now cut out the frames using this information and erect them vertical and square at the proper station locations on a strongback of 2×4s. Screw and bolt temporary wood supports and cross-braces to the frames to hold them to the strongback. Make sure that your strongback is rigid and square, and also—very important—make sure that you can turn the whole boat and strongback over together (right side up) to work on the interior.

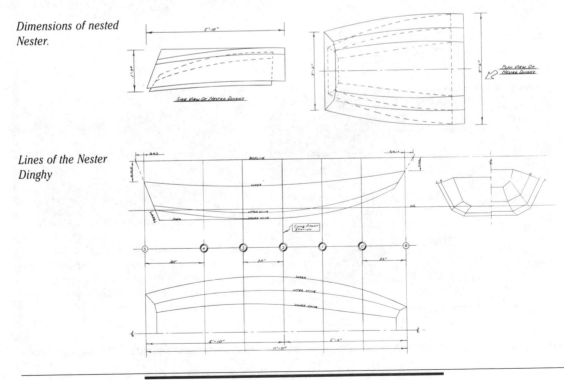

Dimensions of nested Nester.

Lines of the Nester Dinghy

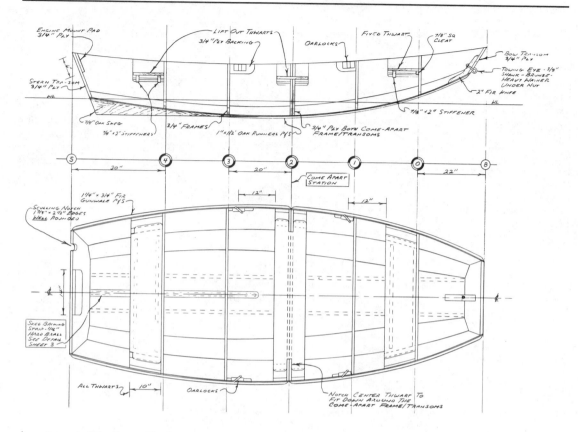

Arrangement of the Nester Dinghy

Planking Panels

Erect the bow and stern transoms at the proper angles and you're ready to begin planking. Tack the ply panels for the side and bottom in place temporarily and mark them for cutting to shape. After trimming them to size, you can glue and screw permanently to the frames. Now, do the same with the bilge panel. Once you have a good fit for the bilge panel, screw and glue it to the frames and stitch it to the top and bottom panels with temporary wire ties. (A number of builders have found they needed hardly any ties—just two or three in the whole boat.) Simply drill small holes at 6-inch to 8-inch (15 to 20 cm) intervals and poke wire twist-ties through (twisting them tight from the outside with pliers).

Chines of Plastic

Roll your Nester Dinghy over and, using the fillet tool shown, apply the epoxy fillets or epoxy chines on the inside. Finish these with two layers of glass cloth, as depicted on the chine detail, and roll Nester Dinghy upside down again. Untwist and pull out the temporary wire ties (you can also grind the ties off, leaving bits embedded in the wood) and grind the outer chine corners round.

****** TABLE OF OFFSETS — DESIGN NO. 45 — GERR MARINE, INC. — 1/4/89 ******								
—————————————————HEIGHTS FROM BASE LINE———————————————								
STATION	S	4	3	2	1	0	B	STATION
SHEER	0,10,0	1,0,2+	1,0,6+	1,0,3+	0,11,3	0,9,4	0,6,2	SHEER
UPPER CHINE		2,0,4+	2,1,6+	2,1,4+	1,11,2	1,6,6		UPPER CHINE
LOWER CHINE		2,3,4	2,4,6	2,4,6	2,2,6+	1,9,7+		LOWER CHINE
STATION	S	4	3	2	1	0	B	STATION
——————————————————————HALF BREADTHS——————————————————————								
STATION	S	4	3	2	1	0	B	STATION
SHEER	1,7,1	2,1,1	2,2,7+	2,2,6	2,0,4	1,7,7+	0,11,3	SHEER
UPPER CHINE		1,6,5+	1,8,0	1,7,7+	1,6,3+	1,3,0+		UPPER CHINE
LOWER CHINE		1,0,7+	1,1,6	1,1,0+	0,10,7+	0,8,2		LOWER CHINE
STATION	S	4	3	2	1	0	B	STATION
DIMENSIONS IN FEET, INCHES & EIGHTHS OF AN INCH								
A "+" SIGN AFTER A NUMBER INDICATES AN ADDITIONAL 1/16 INCH								
ALL REGULAR STATIONS SPACED 20 in.								
22 in. BETWEEN STA. "0" AND STA. "B" — 30 in. BETWEEN STA. "4" AND STA. "S"								

Table of offsets for Nester Dinghy.

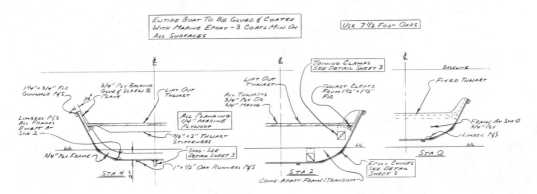

Nester's construction sections.

Then saturate the outside with three or more coats of epoxy and lay a single layer of glass cloth tape over the chines.

This can be faired off nicely by using epoxy grout. Apply the lightest-weight, easiest sanding epoxy grout lightly with a flexible plastic trowel and sand smooth after cure. The basic hull of your Nester Dinghy is now complete. You need only add the gunwale, thwarts, runners, oarlocks, and miscellaneous details shown on the plans.

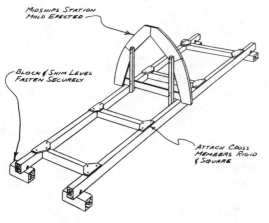

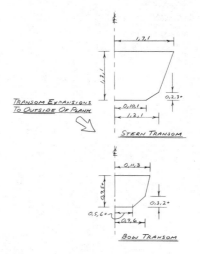

Typical strongback. (The frame shown is not for the Nester dinghy.)

Bow and stern transoms for the Nester Dinghy.

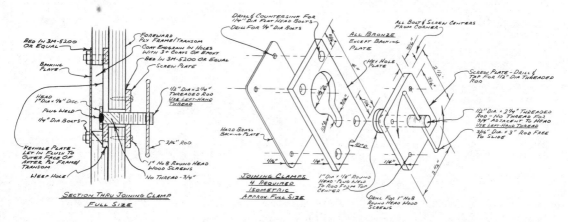

Nester's joining clamp.

Joining Clamps

The most important of these details, however, cannot be left to last. Instead, it must be done at the very beginning. This is the installation of the joining clamps. The four bronze (or stainless) joining clamps shown in the detail are not cheap. (They're the only thing about Nester Dinghy that isn't inexpensive.) But they'll be worth every pen-

ny you pay for them. Unless you're a pretty good machinist, however, you won't be able to make the joining clamps yourself, so you'll have to bring the drawings to a local machine shop and pay to have them fabricated there.

The greatest problem with folding or come-apart boats is that their fastening is usually weak and flimsy. This makes them short lived and

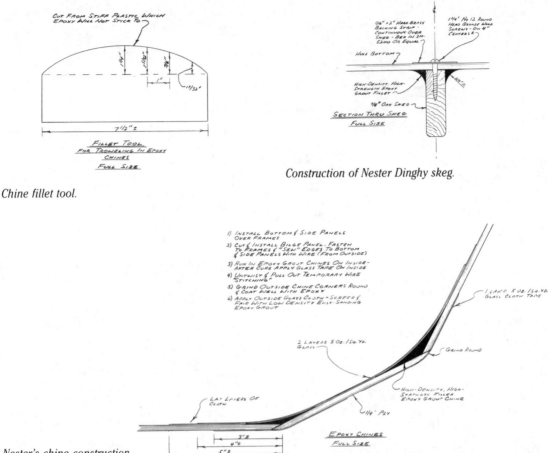

Chine fillet tool.

Construction of Nester Dinghy skeg.

Nester's chine construction.

doesn't instill confidence when you're working them into a steep chop. The joining clamps I drew up for Nester Dinghy are *strong*, with a very positive locking action. They don't require that you carry any special tools; there's nothing to go astray or fall overboard; and you can assemble or disassemble Nester Dinghy with these clamps in a bare minute or two—anywhere, anytime, in or out of the water.

Put Her Together—Take Her Apart

The joining procedure is as follows: Make sure the threaded rod screws are extended about ½ inch. Insert the projecting threaded screws from the forward half of Nester Dinghy, into the large holes on the key plates of the after half's transom. Push down to seat the rods in the narrow portion of the key plates and tighten down. Tighten good and tight by hand, but no harder (exactly like tightening a woodworker's C-clamp). Drop the middle thwart over the joint (notched around the two joining frame/transoms) and drop the after thwart into place. Nester Dinghy's ready to go! Until you loosen the joining clamps for disassembly, she'll be so rigid and tight you'll never know she's of separate halves.

Main components of one of Nester Dinghy's joining clamps.

Begin at the Beginning

To make everything line up properly, when building, however, you have to *start* construction with the joining clamps and the two joining frame/transoms. Cut these frames to shape and coat them well with epoxy. Clamp them together with ordinary C-clamps—after the epoxy has cured, of course, so they don't stick together. Carefully locate and mark the holes for the four joining clamps. Be very careful to cut the holes and align the joining clamps so that the two joining frame/transoms will remain even and true all along their edges when the clamps are fully installed and tightened down.

Now, unclamp the two joining frame/transoms and install the joining clamps permanently. Bed the joining clamps well with 3M-5200 or equivalent bedding compound. (Be sure to saturate the endgrain in the holes for the joining clamps *thoroughly* with epoxy.) After the clamps are installed and all the epoxy has cured, place some heavy plastic sheeting between the joining frame/transoms—to keep them from sticking together—and assemble the two joining frame/transoms again, this time hold-

A stern view of Nester all spruced up and ready to go.

Mike Powell alone makes a very light load in his Nester Cinnamon.

Nester is one dink you can stand up in.

Cinnamon *sits easily on a standard car roof rack. Another Nester owner carries her inside his VW microbus.*

ing them together with the newly-installed joining clamps. Erect the joined frame/transoms at station 2 as shown, and use them—held together by the joining clamps—while assembling the hull. (The plastic sheeting should project a couple of inches (5 or 6 cm) out from all the edges to keep the forward and after plywood plank panels from being glued together on the outside.)

After the hull structure is all glued up, as described earlier, you can loosen the joining clamps and separate the two halves of Nester Dingy. Peel off the plastic sheet and finish off the outsides of the joining transoms. (Of course, you have to take care not to get epoxy or paint on the joining clamps.)

A dinghy or tender like Nester Dinghy is really a workboat. She'll take all sorts of knocks and bangs during her years of service. If you want to give her the ultimate in armor coating, you can finish her outside with a single layer of Xynole polyester cloth laid in epoxy before you paint her (and before installing the gunwale and the runners). This sheathing isn't required, but it will make her stand up to a fantastic amount of abuse.

All the drawings and the table of offsets required to build Nester Dinghy are included here. You're welcome to build one for yourself directly from this. (If you plan to set up for mass production, you'll need permission from Gerr Marine first.) The full set of scale drawings is available directly from Gerr Marine, Inc., for $45 postpaid in the United States. They'll save your eyes and make it easy to take miscellaneous measurements directly from the drawings.

PART 2

Theory for Everyone
or
Why Boats Do What They Do

There be three things which are too
* wonderful for me,*
Yea, four which I know not:
The way of an eagle in the air;
The way of a serpent upon a rock;
The way of a ship in the midst of the
* sea;*
And the way of a man with a maid.

Old Testament, *Proverbs* 30 : 18,19

CHAPTER 13

How Big is She Really?

"Use your imagination, man. Consider the top of the first cube in relation to the top of the second; that's cube number three. The two bottom squares, then the front faces of each cube, the back faces, the right hand, the left hand—eight cubes," he pointed them out.

"—And He Built a Crooked House—,"
Robert A. Heinlein

You hear a lot of talk about how large a boat is: "Jim just bought a 50-footer (15 m)"; or "I don't know how they could've lived on a 25-footer (7.5 m) for three months!" The only problem with these descriptions of size is that they don't give any concrete indication of how big the boats truly are. Length overall simply doesn't do the job. In fact, it's just possible that Jim's 50-footer (15 m) is smaller than the 25-footer (7.5 m). An ultralight catamaran of 50 feet (15 m) could easily have far less living room aboard than a heavy, traditional, 25-foot (7.5 m) houseboat.

The only reliable indicator of a boat's size is her true displacement or actual weight loaded and ready for sea. Armed with this figure and a boat's dimensions—length, beam, draft—you can make some intelligent comparisons.

Relativity and Similitude

One of the most common jobs a naval architect is asked to do is to take a given hull and make it either larger or smaller. This can be quite a challenge, because you run smack up against the laws of *relativity* and *similitude*. Understanding these little beasties gives you a whole new perspective on design.

Basically, these laws say that if you double (2^1, or times 2) the size of a vessel—or anything else for that matter—evenly all around, you'll increase its surface area by 4 times (2^2) and its volume by 8 times (2^3). Even more spectacular, you'll increase stability by an incredible 16 times (2^4). The same thing happens in reverse; so if you make a boat half the original size it will weigh 8 times less and have 16 times *less* stability.

Doubling a Cube

This all sounds nearly impossible, but if you take an ordinary cube and double its size things become a bit less mysterious. Say your cube is 1 foot (or 1 meter) on a side. This works out to—surprise—1 square foot (or 1 square meter) of area per side (1 ft. × 1 ft. = 1 sq. ft. , or 1 m × 1 m = 1

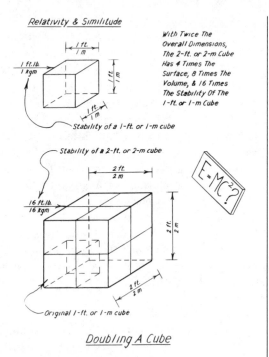

Relativity & Similitude

With Twice The Overall Dimensions, The 2-ft. or 2-m Cube Has 4 Times The Surface, 8 Times The Volume, & 16 Times The Stability Of The 1-ft. or 1-m Cube

1 ft.lb.
1 kgm

1 ft.
1 m

1 ft.
1 m

1 ft.
1 m

Stability of a 1-ft. or 1-m cube

Stability of a 2-ft. or 2-m cube

E=MC²?

16 ft.lb.
16 kgm

2 ft.
2 m

2 ft.
2 m

2 ft.
2 m

Original 1-ft. or 1-m cube

Doubling A Cube

m^2). Since most of the cubes I have seen have six sides, the total surface area is 6 square feet (or meters). Just as surprising is that the volume of your cube is 1 cubic foot, or 1 cubic meter (1 ft. × 1 ft. × 1 ft. = 1 ft.^{3}, or 1 m × 1 m × 1 m = 1 m^3). (We'll look at stability a bit later.) So what happens if you decide you must have a cube twice the size?

Well, each side is now 2 feet (2 m) long and 2 feet (2 m) high. Son of a gun, each side is now 4 square feet or 4 square meters (2 ft. × 2 ft. = 4 sq. ft., or 2 m × 2 m = 4 m^2) and the total surface area is 24 square feet or meters (4 sq. ft. × 6 sides, 4 m^2 × 6 sides). Your giant cube is playing the same tricks when you figure its volume. This time you have 2 ft. × 2 ft. × 2 ft. = 8 ft.^{3}, or 2 m × 2 m × 2 m = 8 m^3.

You may have started out to get a cube twice the size, but you've ended up with one that is 8 times the volume and 4 times the surface area. In fact, there's no way you can have a cube that's both twice the size in surface area and in volume

as the original, as these factors change at a different rate. Since volume (weight) is so critical in boats, this is the factor most designers use to judge size. If you wanted your cube to be twice the volume you'd increase its linear dimensions by 1.26—roughly the cube root of 2—1.26 ft. × 1.26 ft. × 1.26 ft. = 2 ft.^{3}, or 1.26 m × 1.26 m × 1.26 m = 2 m^3 and a tiny smidgen over.

Stability works out in much the same way. If you want to tip over your cube by pressing sideways on an upper edge (like the wind on sails) you'd have to overcome its weight of 1 pound or kilogram (our cube just happens to have a density of 1 pound per cubic foot, or 1 kilogram per cubic meter) times the width of the base or footing. Well, 1 pound (or kilogram) times a 1-foot-wide (1 m) base equals 1 foot-pound or 1 kilogram-meter (amazing what you can do with higher math). But . . . if we try the same thing with the 2-foot (2 m) cube we have to overcome its weight of 8 pounds (8 kilograms) times its base of 2 feet (2 m)—2 ft. × 8 lb. = 16 foot-pounds, or 2 m × 8 kg = 16 kilogram-meters. Sure enough, the 2-foot (2 m) cube has 16 times the stability of the 1-foot (1 m) cube. Boats aren't one whit different. They may have more complicated shapes and constructions, and they may give your designer fits—finding their centers of gravity and such—but the same laws of relativity and similitude are always at work.

Now the real difficulty in shrinking, expanding, or comparing vessels is not that surface area, volume, and stability change, but that they change so much relative to each other. A design that was in just the right proportion at a certain size can easily end up with too much or too little stability or volume if you shrink or expand it. So you can see that comparing boat size can be tricky indeed.

Relativity Costs

A surprisingly small increase in overall size can often yield a really significant increase in usable interior volume. This is why a 40-footer (12.2

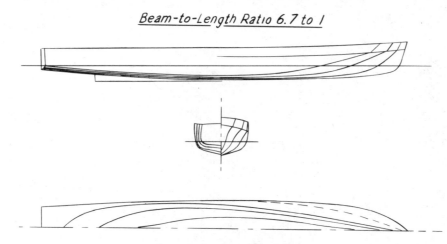

Beam-to-Length Ratio 6.7 to 1

Lines of a German S-Boat

m) can be so much bigger than, say, a 36-footer (11 m). It's also because of the laws of relativity and similitude that boat prices increase dramatically as you progress from a 20-foot (6 m) daysailer, through a 35-foot (10.7 m) cruiser, to a 55-foot (16.8 m) liveaboard. The 55-footer (16.8 m) is actually 21 times larger than the 20-footer (6 m)—assuming generally similar overall proportions—and she'll cost accordingly. Being more complicated—what with accommodations, diesel, electric wiring, and such—the 55-footer (16.8 m) will cost even more than that. All this explains why you can buy a nice 20-footer (6 m) for $8,000 to $12,000 (in 1991 dollars), but a 55-footer (16.8 m)—just 2¾ times longer—could run you well over $350,000.

The size and weight of the 55-footer's (16.8 m) gear is similarly proportioned. Where the 20-footer's (6 m) mainsail could weigh less than 20 pounds (9 kg), the 55-footer's (16.8 m) might easily come in at more than 160 pounds (73 kg)—quite an armful for one man on a slippery deck.

Forces, stresses, and strains throughout the whole 55-footer (16.8 m) are equally large by comparison. For instance, ⅜-inch (10 mm) headsail

sheets, with working loads of around 700 or 800 pounds (300 to 400 kg), would be ample on the 20-footer (6 m). If you got your fingers caught under the sheet at the winch you might get them back again. On the 55-footer (16.8 m), though, you'd have ½- to ¾-inch (12 to 20 mm) sheets, with working loads around 4,000 pounds (1,800 kg). You wouldn't get a second chance if you fouled up at the winch.

Relativity and the Rule

Another effect is that large sailboats very seldom have trouble carrying large rigs, but smaller vessels are often tender. This is one of the fundamental reasons for the complexity of current rating rules like the IOR and IMS. These rules are trying to compensate mathematically for the laws of relativity and similitude. They are attempting to *handicap* larger boats for their inherent ability to carry proportionally more sail per pound of boat than their smaller counterparts.

When a designer plays games with the rating rules, he or she is trying—among other things—to outsmart the fellows who were struggling to make

Beam-to-Length Ratio 6.5 to 1

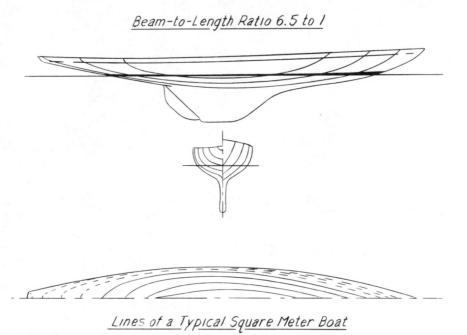

Lines of a Typical Square Meter Boat

things fair in the first place. Take away all the beam-max's and second, supernumerary, third-quarter, half-after-girth measurements and the wily designer is simply juggling volume, surface area, and stability to get a hull that's faster than the rule says it should be for its size.

Power is Relative Too

It's not surprising that power requirements go up very fast as boats get bigger. This is because power-to-weight ratio and resistance due to friction (surface area) are critical. An 8,000-pound 32-footer (3,600 kg, 9.7 m) would have a wetted surface area of about 320 square feet (30 m²) and require around 350 hp (260 kw) to cruise at, say, 18 knots. If you take the same hull and enlarge it evenly all around to only 40 feet (12.2 m)—just 25 percent longer—it will weigh in at about 16,000 pounds (7,200 kg) with a wetted surface of about

500 square feet (46 m²). Suddenly, you need around 700 hp (520 kw) to maintain the same 18 knots. Just think of the fuel bills!

Stretching Your Boat

Now, more games can be played with the laws of relativity and similitude. What happens if you take a boat, say, 25 feet (7.6 m) long and make it twice as long but keep her beam and draft the same—in other words, stretch her like a piece of taffy. This time, you do actually end up with a boat that's twice as big all around. You have twice the volume or weight, about twice the surface area, and twice the stability.

It would be like taking the original 1-foot (1 m) cube and sticking another, identical 1-foot (1 m) cube in front of it, producing a long, narrow rectangular prism. Obviously, all you need do is double most of the numbers, although the surface is a bit less as you will have lost two exposed sides—the sides of the two cubes where they meet. If you stretched your boat (or cube) sideways—instead of fore-and-aft—you'd get similar results, but you'd dramatically increase stability. In this case, doubling the width would up the stability four times. Since the resulting wide rectangle would have greater frontal area, however, you'd also be increasing its resistance to being driven through the water.

The long and narrow approach has a lot to recommend it. All other things being equal, a longer, narrower boat is more easily driven at a higher speed and in rougher conditions than a shorter, fatter one. Give a designer half a chance and he'll probably urge you to try a long, narrow craft. The squall on the horizon here (there's usually a squall lurking about somewhere) is that dockage and storage fees are based on length. Things being what they are, this could up the cost of owning your long, narrow vessel pretty fast. If you are able to get around this storage problem, take a look at some long, lean designs. You won't be sorry.

E-Boats and Square Meters

Two of the most spectacular examples of long and lean are the German E-Boats of the Second World War and the extraordinary square-meter boats popular in Scandinavia before the war. Inexplicably, although these boats are known as "E-Boats" in both the United States and Great Britain, no German ever used the term. In fact, no one even knows how or why this confusion got started—though it's persisted for 50 years. The proper designation, in their home ports, was *S-Boote* for *Schnell Boote,* meaning—not surprisingly—fast boat.

These vessels were mostly built at the Lurssen Werft yard, which is still in operation today. They developed from fast yachts in the 70- to 90-foot (21 to 28 m) range, but quickly grew to carry war sundries like torpedoes and anti-aircraft guns. Standard S-Boats were 114 feet (35 m) long and just under 17 feet (5.2 m) in beam, for a beam-to-

length ratio of nearly seven to one (around three or four to one is considered normal these days).

Almost all were fitted with triple supercharged 12- or 16-cylinder Daimler-Benz or M.A.N. diesels that could deliver 7,500 horsepower (5,600 kw) total. Top speeds were over 44 to 45 knots—not bad for craft that displaced 114 tons. Further, S-Boats could maintain well over 25 knots in weather that had most everyone else chugging around at 16 or less. In spite of their high speed, these craft had round bilges and thus were known for their remarkable comfort at speed in a seaway. (Comfort at speed in a seaway is always a relative thing. In the Navy, they call small fast boats—114 feet (35 m) is real small for the Navy—"young men's boats.")

The square-meter boats were the result of a rating rule that penalized sail area heavily. Thus all the boats in, say, the 30-square-meter class were to have very nearly the same sail area. Naval architects thus concentrated on squeezing every ounce of true speed out of their hulls. Length/beam ratios of six-to-one or more were not uncommon.

I once had the pleasure of owning a boat that was stored next to one of the few square-meter boats designed and built in the United States. This was the L. Francis Herreshoff-designed *Oriole.* Sighting down the length of her underbody was an experience to take your breath away. A vessel of this general type, with a fin keel and a bulb at the bottom, could carry substantially more sail than the old square-meter rule would allow. Such a boat would fly!

Oriole is an ideal example of how deceptive it is to judge size by length overall. She's just a bit under 40 feet (12.2 m) from stem to stern; however, she displaces only 5,500 pounds (2,490 kg)—talk about a low displacement-to-length ratio! (See the next chapter.) Her cabin's no bigger than that of many 20-footers (6 m), with strictly sitting headroom—not exactly what you'd expect from a 40-footer (12 m). Of course, in return for this, *Oriole* has been *reliably* clocked at 12 knots—now

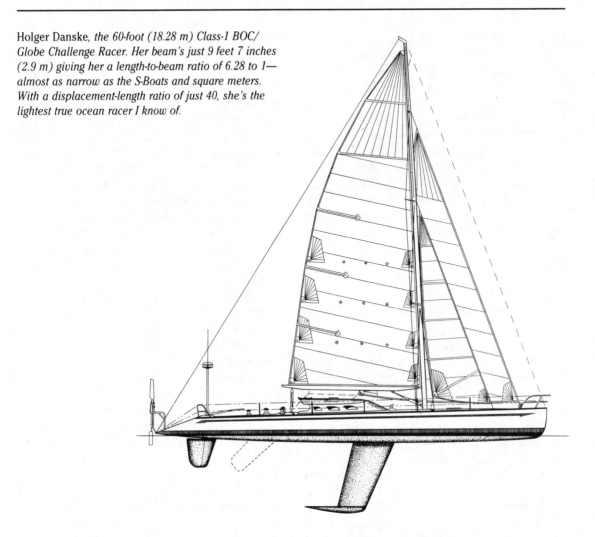

Holger Danske, *the 60-foot (18.28 m) Class-1 BOC/ Globe Challenge Racer. Her beam's just 9 feet 7 inches (2.9 m) giving her a length-to-beam ratio of 6.28 to 1— almost as narrow as the S-Boats and square meters. With a displacement-length ratio of just 40, she's the lightest true ocean racer I know of.*

that's sailing! Obviously, she wasn't doing 12 knots the whole time. Sometimes she was going slower, but other times she must have been going a whole lot faster. No 20-footers (6 m) and few monohulls this size can match this kind of speed under sail.

The Ultimate Sailboats

Some square-meter boats around 64 feet (19.5 m) overall yet under 11 feet (3.3 m) in beam were built. These craft, called 75 Square Meters, had all the room required for family cruising and displaced around 23,000 pounds (10,500 kg). Full standing headroom, separate cabins, and a complete galley are no problem at this volume. A modern version of one of these 75 Square Meters would not only be roomy and beautiful but would be one of the fastest boats in her area.

Such a vessel, of fiberglass, aluminum, or cold-molded wood, would have shorter overhangs

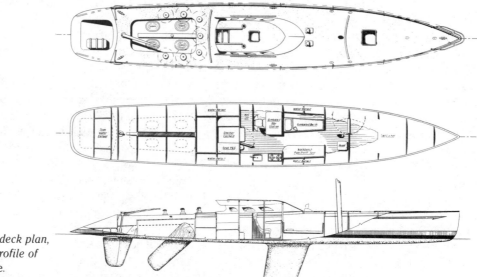

Arrangement, deck plan, and inboard profile of Holger Danske.

The 60-foot (18.28 m) Holger Danske awaiting launch. Her skipper/builder, Paul Harder Cohen, stands on her aft deck. The white object resting under the starboard bow is the boom. Holger Danske's high-tensile steel fin keel was replaced with a high-tech vacuum-bagged, post-cured, composite keel, fabricated entirely of unidirectional S-glass laid in epoxy. You can see it, unpainted and resting on blocks, just forward of the bow. Even though the new keel is 2.5 feet (76 cm) deeper than its steel predecessor, it weighs half a ton less. Holger Danske's draft is now 14 feet (4.26 m)

Construction: wood/epoxy strip plank unidirectional S-glass composite; originally with a high-tensile steel fin keel. Keel is now a unidirectional S-glass fin.

LOA	60 ft. 0 in.	(18.28 m)
LWL	57 ft. 0 in.	(17.36 m)
Beam	9 ft. 7 in.	(2.91 m)
Draft	11 ft. 6 in.	(2.91 m)
Disp.	16,800 lb.	(7,620 kg)
	7.5 tons	(7.62 Mtons)
Ballast	7,200 lb.	(3,266 kg)
Total Sail Area	987 sq. ft.	(91.7 sq. m)
Area Main	672 sq. ft.	(62. 4 sq. m)
Area 100% Δ	315 sq. ft.	(29.3 sq. m)
Mast Height	59 ft. 0 in.	(19.9 m)
Water ballast	439 gal.	(1662 l)
SA/Disp $^{2/3}$	24	
LOA/Beam	6.3	
Ballast/Disp.	43%	
Disp/WL	40	

(a longer waterline) than her predecessors and slightly more beam, with a deep bulb fin keel. Thus, she'd stand up to substantially more sail. Accommodations would be spread out well along her length for great privacy. But remember, she'd only have 11 or so feet (3.3 m) of beam on 64 feet (19.5 m) of length overall, so don't expect to make a houseboat of her. Still, I imagine most people would be able to make themselves comfortable on a craft like this. To my mind, these long, lean boats with their tall rigs are very nearly the ultimate sailboats.

Many years ago, there was even a 150 Square Meter built. At about 77 feet (23.5 m) overall and 11 feet (3.3 m) in beam she'd be likely to attract your notice as she sailed by. Somehow, I doubt you'd catch her.

Holger Danske

Of course, for racing boats this approach has obvious appeal. The illustrations show *Holger Danske,* a Class-1, BOC/Globe Challenge racer of my design. With a beam of 9 feet 7 inches (2.9 m) on a length of 60 feet (18.3 m), she's just about as narrow as either the old square meters or the S-Boats. Thanks to modern construction materials and a stripped-out racing interior, she's even lighter than either and can do 20 knots-plus. (At this writing, I believe her to be the lightest true ocean-racing monohull in the world.) Clearly, it has to be blowing pretty hard for a sailboat to reach this sort of speed. In fact, at the start of the 1989–1990 Globe Challenge, off the coast of Normandy, it was gusting 30 to 35 knots. The ultralight offshore racers were screaming along at 15 knots or more, but the vee-bottom runabouts— intended as photographer's chase boats—could hardly keep up in the rough conditions. In smooth water they'd have buzzed circles around the sailboats, but in choppy seas the runabouts would have done better if they'd been longer and narrower!

CHAPTER 14

Displacement and Shape— The Practical and the Forgotten

The feature that made these boats such weatherly craft was their heavy displacement, being very burdensome for their length, though not so very wide. . . .

Ships of the Past, Charles G. Davis

Although most of the sailors (power and sail) I know enjoy discussing their boat's speed or how roomy she is (or isn't), less thought seems to be given to their vessel's handling characteristics and reliability at sea: her motion, strength, and the margin of safety in her design. This is a radical departure from the sailors of earlier generations. Back then, such considerations were paramount. Of course, the sea hasn't changed, and these neglected aspects of boating ought to be given more thought.

Light as a Feather

The prevailing attitude these days seems to be that a boat has to be light—as light as possible—otherwise she just won't get out of her own way. Such is the current mania for lightness that manufacturers and dealers are often reluctant to give out accurate displacement figures. If they want to sell boats they have to make it *appear* as if they don't weigh much. One well-known magazine, for instance, recently featured an article on a small sailboat of about 21 feet (6.4 m). The article claimed an amazingly low displacement for the boat (a common practice); but on closer examination, it became clear that what the writer was calling "displacement" was the weight of the hull, deck, joinerwork, and rig only—light trailering weight. The weight of the crew, stores, sails, outboard, and so on were totally neglected. In fact, on a boat of this size, adding these weights produces a *real* displacement figure almost 50 percent larger than stated.

Powerboats are not immune to this sort of thing. At a recent boat show, my eye was drawn to a practical 30-foot (9 m), open sportfisherman. I wandered over to ask the dealer what she weighed and was astonished to hear him say, "About 2,000 pounds" (900 kg). When I asked him if this included the weight of the twin outboards, fuel, water, and her crew, he shrugged sheepishly, replying, "No." He must have thought I'd lose interest if she seemed "heavy." Quite the contrary—

if she'd really weighed so little, I'd have thought her flimsily constructed.

The shame of all this is that both these boats were fine vessels—yep, even at their real displacements. It shouldn't have been necessary for their builders and dealers to hedge on displacement figures to move their boats. Things being what they are, though, they couldn't take the chance on losing sales because their vessels didn't *appear* to be light enough. It's time folks realized that there's nothing necessarily wrong with "heavy" boats.

Make the Comparison Yourself

This whole problem seems to have gotten a bit out of hand, and many's the poor boating-magazine editor who has fallen into the lightweight-numbers trap. The results can be quite misleading. For instance, another magazine published my *Madrigal* design—17 feet 8 inches (5.4 m) on the waterline. The editor seemed to have genuinely admired her; however, he or she couldn't help putting in the comment, "Despite her displacement of 3,500 pounds (4,590 kg) she features plenty of sail area and a long waterline." The key word here is *despite*. The editor had unthinkingly accepted the idea that she was a "heavy" boat, and that "heavy" is a drawback. Ironically, on the same page was another design of similar size—17 feet (5.2 m) on the waterline. She was supposed to displace a mere 1,450 pounds (658 kg)! Wow! Now that is light weight—a displacement-to-length (Disp/L) ratio of 131! (Displacement-length calculations are explained later in this chapter.) But is it? Could such a vessel really be so light?

This is an important question, and one you ought to ask yourself when comparing boats. The displacement figure for *Madrigal* was her full-loaded weight with crew and stores aboard—in short, the weight that actually will have to be pushed through the water. Let's take a look at the other design. She has berths for four and must carry food and water for this many for at least a weekend. She'd also carry a small outboard and, say, 6

gallons (23 l) of gas, plus an anchor, fenders, and the like.

Okay, let's subtract all this weight from her 1,450-pound (658 kg) "displacement":

Four crew	600 lb	272 kg
Food, water, and gear for		
two days, approx.	90 lb	40 kg
Anchor, chain, and line	20 lb	9 kg
Two-thirds tank gas		
(4 gallons) and tank	25 lb	12 kg
Outboard	25 lb	12 kg
GRAND TOTAL	760 lb	345 kg

Actually, there are plenty more items whose weights we could add in, but let's see where we stand: 1,450 pounds displacement minus 760 pounds equals 690 pounds; 658 kilograms displacement minus 345 kilograms equals 313 kilograms.

That's it! The entire hull, cabin, deck, joinerwork, mast, and rigging must weigh only 690 pounds (313 kg). But wait a moment, she's a ballast keel boat. If we assume an average ballast ratio (weight of ballast divided by displacment) of 35 percent, then her ballast weighs 507 pounds (230 kg). When we subtract 507 pounds (230 kg) of ballast from 690 pounds (313 kg), we get 183 pounds (83 kg) for the entire hull, deck, cabin, and interior?! This is obviously silly—hardly enough weight for a moped.

Clearly, what was given as "displacement" is—again—actually trailering weight. To get this boat's real displacement we should add all these weights to her trailering weight. In this case we get a true displacement of 2,210 pounds (1,002 kg). Now we're talking sense. We can finally compare these two designs fairly. *Madrigal* has a Disp/L ratio of 283 and the other vessel has a Disp/L ratio of 206. Yes, the other boat is lighter (and, incidentally, a fine design), but it is not nearly as light as you might have been led to believe. In fact, *Madrigal* will usually sail lighter than 3,500 pounds

(1,590 kg), while the other craft will most likely sail somewhat heavier than 2,210 pounds (1,002 kg), as that's still cutting things a bit close.

Trade-Offs for Light Weight?

There's little question that—all other things being equal—a lighter boat is faster and livelier than a heavier vessel. Unfortunately, all other things are seldom equal. To see displacement from this angle alone is quite misleading. Some of the finest yachts ever built were of what we would now call very heavy displacement. (Remember the Dutch vessels from Chapter 1.) Don't let weight alone affect your choice of a new boat; take in the whole design. Finally, remember that the figures produced by this lightness mania make it difficult to compare boats. Ask questions; poke around; be nosy—get the straight dope!

She Can Carry Only So Much

Except for small, light daysailers and flat-out, round-the-buoys racers, all boats need to carry loads of passengers, gear, food, fuel, water, and stores. Now, it's an unavoidable fact that for most monohull sailboats, the weight of crew and stores equals about 7 to 9 percent of her total weight (true loaded displacement)—8 percent's a good average. Since your boat will be fully loaded at the start of the cruise and nearly empty at the finish, you'd use only 60 percent of your total load to calculate the required displacement. This assumes the vessel will sink an inch or two when fully loaded and rise an inch or so above her designed waterline when empty (see Chapter 16). Of course, some extreme craft are one or two percentage points above this; nevertheless, the majority of vessels follow this rule.

Small, light daysailers don't behave this way, because their crews weigh so much in proportion to total boat weight that they act as shifting ballast. This drastically reduces the percentage of total weight such craft carry as keel ballast (many have no keel ballast). Their load-carrying relationship is very different. Of course, you're not likely to cruise the Caribbean in, say, a Lightning.

Powerboats come in such a wide range of types—planing and displacement, single- and twin-engine, inshore skiff and ocean cruiser—that it's impossible to apply anything like the 8-percent rule to determine the displacement required. You simply have to use common sense. Ask yourself: Is there enough room for your gear and stores? Does she have the fuel capacity for the range you require? Does she have enough power to drive her at the speed you want when she is fully loaded? Long-range cruisers in the 35- to 55-foot (10 to 17 m) range will often require Disp/L ratios of 250 to 300 or even higher.

How Much Boat Do You Need?

For the average cruising sailboat or cruiser/racer, the sailor armed with the above information can make a good estimate of how big a boat he or she needs in terms of displacement. Simply take the total weight of crew and stores you'll carry and multiply it by 7.5. This is—for those of you who want to know—the reciprocal of 8 percent times 60 percent loading—$[(1 \div .08) \times 0.6] = 7.5$. The answer is the displacement you'll need, plus or minus 10 percent.

What Does All That Gear Weigh?

How do you figure the weight of crew and stores you'll need? Well, the crew part is easy. Simply multiply the number of crewmembers by 160 pounds (72 kg). As for the stores: Allow 6 pounds (2.8 kg) per person per day for food and 8.5 pounds (3.8 kg) for water—14.5 pounds (6.6 kg) total. (When calculating for food and water you should always multiply your result by 1.5 to allow for a safety reserve. See Chapter 47.) For personal gear and stores, figure the average sailor will carry on board around 5 pounds (2.3 kg) per day for ordinary cruising (up to a maximum of around 120 pounds (55 kg) per person, which is about all a normal bloke's likely to lug around).

Liveaboards, however, should use a fixed figure of about 400 pounds (180 kg) per permanent crewmember. (For a truly permanent home afloat, even 400 pounds (180 kg) is too low. For real comfort, 1,000 pounds (450 kg) per person isn't unheard of. After all, imagine the weight of personal belongings you've tucked away about your home; just visualize the last time you packed to move.)

Calculating a Cruiser

Let's figure the displacement required for a crew of four on an ordinary 10-day vacation cruise:

4 × 160 lb. = 640 lb. crew

4 crew × 10 days × 14.5 lb./day × 1.5 reserve = 870 lb. food and water

4 crew × 10 days × 5 lb./day = 200 lb. personal gear

TOTAL: crew, food and water, personal gear = 1,710 lb. (³⁄₄ ton !)

1,710 lb. × 7.5 = 12,825 lb. displacement

Plus or minus 10% = 11,540 lb. to 14,100 lb. required displacement

   or

4 × 72 kg = 288 kg crew

4 crew × 10 days × 6.6 kg/day × 1.5 reserve = 396 kg food and water

4 crew × 10 days × 2.3 kg/day = 92 kg personal gear

TOTAL: crew, food and water, personal gear = 776 kg

776 kg × 7.5 = 5,820 kg displacement

Plus or minus 10% = 5,240 kg to 6,040 kg required displacement

That's it. This is the size (weight or displacement) vessel you'd need to carry this crew comfortably and safely for this length of time.

Too Little Displacement Takes a Toll

What would happen if you tried to do this sort of cruising with a lighter, smaller vessel? Three things: First, you'd be forced, through lack of stowage space, to carry less food, gear, and stores than was comfortable or safe. Second, your boat would be excessively loaded. This would make her wetter as she'd lose freeboard and not rise to the seas as well. Additionally, you'd have raised her center of gravity with all the additional weight and thus decreased stability. Third, your vessel's hull and rig would be strained; the extra weight creates forces above and beyond those your craft was designed to withstand.

Of course, for coastal cruising you can easily extend range, or get by with a smaller vessel, by making frequent stops for supplies. This enables you to reduce the amount of food and water according to the number of days between stops. For an honest ten days out with four people, a displacement in the range given is about it.

Waterplane Area Does Not Equal Cargo Capacity

We come now to another common misconception regarding load carrying in both sail and powerboats. A number of articles have been published claiming that a boat's waterplane area is the most important factor governing load-carrying capacity. Nothing, unfortunately, could be further from the truth! Because of this bit of misinformation, sailors are purchasing light-displacement boats with large waterplanes, confident that they can carry great loads. In reality, the factors that contribute to load carrying are displacement, stability, freeboard, and robust construction. After all, load carrying is nothing but cargo carrying. When was the last time you saw a light-displacement freighter or barge? Such vessels are designed with large (and variable) displacements in mind. They couldn't do an honest day's work without it.

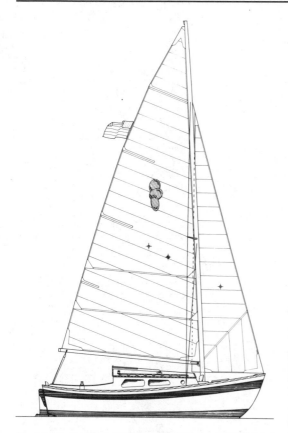

Doubloon, *the 25-foot (7.6 m), 8,160-pound (3,710 kg) voyaging sloop.*

Pounds Per Inch/Kilograms Per Centimeter

The waterplane is simply the area you'd have if you sliced the hull right across—from side to side—at the water's surface. You can estimate it fairly accurately by multiplying your vessel's waterline length times her waterline beam and multiplying by 0.76. (More on the waterplane can be found in Chapter 16.)

Basically, the waterplane area of a boat indicates how much load it takes to sink that boat one inch or one centimeter—a figure that naval architects have given the catchy name of "pounds per inch immersion" or "kilograms per centimeter im-

mersion." This is a handy number. To figure it, take the waterplane area of your boat in square feet and multiply it by 5.34 to get pounds per inch. (Multiply waterplane area in square meters by 10.25 to get kilograms per centimeter.)

If your *Shangri-la* has a waterline of 20 feet 4 inches (6.2 m) and a waterline beam of 6 feet 7 inches (2 m), her waterplane area would be 102 square feet (9.4 m²)—20.34 ft. × 6.58 ft. × .76 = 101.7 sq. ft., or 6.2 m × 2 m × 0.76 = 9.42 m². Thus, *Shangri-la's* lb./in. would be 545, or her kg/cm would be 97. Now, this tells you that when your crew of four 160-pounders (72 kg) clambers aboard, *Shangri-la* will sink just over 1 inch (about 3 cm). It doesn't give you the slightest information as to whether *Shangri-la* can carry, say, a 2,000-pound (900 kg) load safely.

Cargo Capacity—Light and Heavy

Let's compare a couple of different designs with similar waterplane areas—*Doubloon* and *Dart. Doubloon's* waterplane is 120 square feet for 640 lb./in. imersion (11.1 m² and 140 kg/cm), and *Dart's* waterplane is 115 square feet for 613 lb./in. immersion (10.7 m² and 110 kg/cm). According to the waterplane theory, both boats should have roughly similar load-carrying abilities. Well, let's see what happens if we try this. *Doubloon* displaces 8,160 pounds (3,710 kg) and has been designed to carry an average load of 1,000 pounds (450 kg). Actually, *Doubloon* can carry in the neighborhood of 1,900 pounds (860 kg) safely for a really long cruise. (This is an unusually high load capacity. *Doubloon* can carry this large load because of her high freeboard, great stability, and unusually robust hull and rig—the real factors governing cargo capacity.)

If we assume that *Doubloon's* been allowed to sink 2 inches (5 cm) to carry this load (she's 1 inch (2.5 cm) high when light and 1 inch (2.5 cm) down when loaded), we're left with a generous figure of 6,900 pounds (312 kg) for her hull and deck structure, joinerwork, accommodations, rig, and

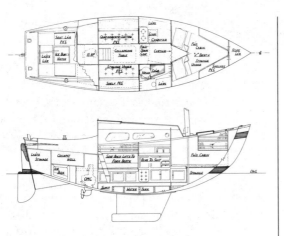

Arrangement of Doubloon.

ballast. Since *Doubloon*'s ballast ratio is 40 percent, she has 3,260 pounds (1,480 kg) of lead, leaving 3,640 pounds (1,650 kg) for hull and deck structure, rig, and so on—all pretty reasonable.

Let's try this with the 3,900-pound (1,770 kg) *Dart*. If we allow *Dart* to sink 2 inches (5 cm), we're left with only 2,674 pounds (1,215 kg) for the entire hull and deck structure, joinerwork, accommodations, rig, ballast, and so on. Since *Dart*'s ballast ratio is also 40 percent, she carries 1,560 pounds (707 kg) of lead. This leaves a mere 1,114 pounds (506 kg) for *Dart*'s entire hull structure, joinerwork, rig, and outboard, which is quite low. At 22 feet (7.8 m) overall and 8 feet (2.4 m) beam, *Dart*'s hull is a heck of a lot bigger than a full-size station wagon. (*Dart*'s actual hull structure weighs in at around 2,000 pounds—900 kg.)

Another way to approach *Dart*'s loading problem is simply to add the 1,900 pounds (860 kg) to *Dart* as she floats at her original designed waterline. In this case, *Dart* would sink about three inches (7.5 cm), and instead of displacing 3,900 pounds (1,770 kg), she'd displace 5,800 pounds (2,630 kg)—an increase of nearly 50 percent. In this state, *Dart*'s actual ballast-to-displacement ratio would be a puny 26 percent; her sail area–dis-

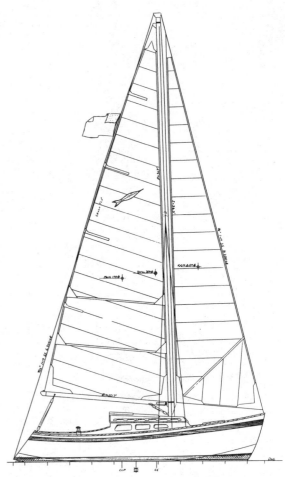

Dart, a 22-foot (6.7 m), 3,900-pound (1,770 kg) weekender.

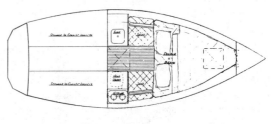

Arrangement of Dart.

placement ratio (see Chapter 21) would be equally poor. In addition, *Dart* would strain her hull and gear. Her stability would suffer, and she'd show an increase in her tendency to pound and pitch. Either way, an attempt to make the light-displacement *Dart* carry the kind of load that the heavy-displacement *Doubloon* can would be simply foolish.

How the Volume Is Distributed: Displacement-to-Length Ratio

All this is well and good. It's nice to know how much displacement you require to carry a given load, and that a certain amount of displacement is necessary, but doesn't displacement make a boat slow? Well, no—not necessarily. The factors that determine speed are power-to-weight ratio (for sailboats this is the sail area–displacement ratio) and the length on the waterline.

In the case of our 10-day cruise for four, we've decided on the displacement we need to carry our load, but we haven't decided on how this displacement should be distributed. We could choose a 12,000-pound (5,440 kg) boat with 25 feet (7.62 m) on the waterline, or we could choose a 12,000-pound (5,440 kg) boat with a 32-foot (9.75 m) waterline. To differentiate between long, spread-out hulls and short hulls, designers use the displacement-to-length ratio we've been referring to in the preceding chapters. This is nothing more than a boat's displacement in tons divided by 1/100 her waterline in feet cubed (multiplied by itself three times), or:

Displacement-to-length ratio (Disp/WL)
$= Tons \div (WL\ ft. \div 100)^3$

Displacement-to-length ratio (Disp/WL)
$= Tons \div (WL\ m \div 30.5)^3$

The ranges of Disp/WL ratio considered heavy or light have shifted some over the years. At present:

50 and under is super ultralight
50 to 120 is ultralight
120 to 250 is light
250 to 320 is medium
320 to 380 is heavy
380 and over is very heavy

The 25-foot-waterline (7.62 m) version has a Disp/WL ratio of 343 (a "heavy" boat), while the 32-foot-waterline (9.75 m) craft has a Disp/LWL ratio of 163 (a "light" boat.) Notice that both boats actually weigh the same, although one is "light" and the other is "heavy."

What we're really talking about is distributing the weight or volume of a boat over a longer waterline—remember stretching a cube. This generates less resistance and a higher hull speed for that weight. There's no question that the longer boat will be faster and livelier. The question is how much faster and what, if anything, you are sacrificing to obtain this speed.

The Price of Light Displacement

For both power and sail, there are two notable drawbacks to light displacement. The first of these is structural. In order to get the long, light hull required for a low Disp/LWL ratio you must greatly reduce the scantlings (dimensions, thickness, sectional areas, etc.) of the hull, joinerwork, and rig. It is a fascinating and challenging engineering task to accomplish this and still maintain adequate strength. Even with the best of modern materials, though, there are limits to what can be done.

The Ignorance Factor

When designing a structure to take certain strains, an engineer always uses a safety factor (2 to 4 is fairly typical). This means that if an engineer's calculations show there will be a 100-pound (50 kg) load on a particular component, he or she will actually design it to withstand 200 to 400 pounds (100 to 200 kg). Why? One of the best designers I've ever worked with used to say, "Factor of safety–factor of ignorance." What he meant is that no matter how carefully a structure is designed, you can't know *everything* about it. You can't know if it was built correctly; if it might be damaged or worn out at some future time; or if some unusual circumstances might subject it to larger loads than anticipated. Accordingly, the engineer makes his or her best guesstimate—it's usually a very detailed and carefully calculated guesstimate—of the loads, and adds the standard safety factor for that type of structure. This is a system that's been proven to work quite reliably for over a century.

As structures get lighter, however, the designer is forced to use lower safety factors and/or new or experimental construction materials to save weight. Aircraft, for instance—where weight is the paramount consideration—may have components with safety factors as low as 1.1 or less. Two things should be kept in mind here. First, the lower the safety factor and the newer the material and method, the more expensive it is to design and build a structure. (For example, the design alone of a single component of a single model of an airplane can cost hundreds of thousands of dollars.) Second, and even more important, the lower the safety factors and the newer the materials and methods, the more inspection and maintenance is required. It's common practice for an airplane to receive half an hour—or more—of inspection and maintenance for every hour of flight time. This is a necessary result of aircrafts' light weight and close design tolerances. Huge amounts of time and money must be spent reducing the "ignorance factor" to permit using lower safety factors—all to save weight. At the other end of the scale are structures like tunnels and bridges, which may receive little if any inspection and maintenance for months or years, yet are in continuous use. Structures such as this are designed with safety factors of 5 to 10 or even more. Boats fall somewhere between these two extremes.

When a boat is in the water, it's in nearly constant use. Even at anchor it's "flying," so to speak. Yet the average yacht receives only a few dozen hours of inspection and maintenance per season. Even if you only counted actual motoring or sailing time, this is too infrequent a schedule to allow for low safety factors, though many "space-age" materials have reached a stage where they are a safe, reliable way to reduce weight somewhat.

Of course, in boats specifically designed to be experimental, such as OSTAR multihulls, ultimate-30s, and C-class cats, cutting weight to the bone *is* the name of the game. Tearing along on the edge is a terrific thrill—the wind rips at your clothes, the whole vessel fairly quivers beneath you, and she seems to leap from wave to wave. Clearly, though, most such craft aren't for cruising. Further, you have to be able to afford the high cost-per-pound of such boats, as well as the cost of their maintenance and repair. Breakdowns, crashes, and sundry related surprises are the rule, not the exception.

Light Boats Under Stress

A grim reminder of what can happen to lightly constructed cruiser/racers offshore was the Fastnet Race of 1979, where many sailors lost their lives. Interestingly, in spite of the many injuries and fatalities, most of the boats remained afloat even though some were abandoned. A common problem—especially in the smaller and lighter craft—was that the internal joinerwork came loose because the motion of the boat was so extreme and the hull was flexing so much. As a result, no one could stay below. They were likely to be impaled or crushed by some careening piece of joinery.

A less tragic example was experienced by a friend of mine in the 1984 Bermuda Race. He was aboard a modern, light 40-footer (12 m)—a boat built by a top yard and designed by a well-known architect. During an ordinary gale in the Gulf Stream, this boat leaked through every deck opening because her hull flexed too much to allow for any real seal. Even worse, the main bulkhead, just forward of the mast, popped out of position by a good two inches. This sort of thing detracts from a crew's sense of security, to say the least. Light boats can and do stand up to these conditions, but it takes very careful engineering and construction. It's also difficult for such vessels to achieve quite the reserve of structural safety that a heavier, more robustly constructed craft would have.

Light, planing powercraft are seldom out in such extreme conditions (most aren't meant for that kind of service), and when they are, they can slow way down to reduce strain. Ocean cruising or "trawler"-type power vessels are usually fairly heavily built; they're intended to take quite a beating. This, however, shows in their displacement-to-length ratios, which are frequently around 300 or more.

Standing Up to a Punch

A second structural problem of light craft is their lack of impact resistance. In order to make a vessel light, her hull shell or skin must be made quite thin. (The planking or skin is one of the heaviest components of most boats.) In doing so, the designer uses various combinations of stiffeners, frames, and cores to obtain the rigidity and strength required. With the hull skin so thin between stiffeners (or over cores), though, there can be little to resist localized impacts, such as running into a floating log. Personally, when I go to sleep in a boat underway offshore, I like to think my vessel has a reasonable chance of withstanding such blows.

This can be a real design challenge on moderate- to high-speed power craft. At 20 to 30 knots and more, they pack quite a wallop should they smack into something. In larger vessels especially, it is very difficult to make a light hull that can resist such strikes. In fact it was just such an impact that sank Richard Branson's gas-turbine-powered catamaran a bare 200 miles off the British coast, on his first attempt at the transatlantic record under power. Light weight combined with high speed is a tough combination to make safe off soundings, although with lots of money and careful engineering it can be pulled off.

Heave Ho!

Perhaps the most neglected aspect of boat design and performance is boat motion and comfort at sea. Here again, modern light-displacement boats have some drawbacks. There are actually two ways to make a boat light for her length. One is to stretch her without increasing beam. The other is to decrease the amount of underbody in the water, keeping the same beam and waterline length. If you go far enough in this direction, you get a nearly flat underbody (with a small fin keel or centerboard on sailboats).

Because of current racing rules and because the cost of storage is based on length overall, it is this second wide-flat option that is most common today. Hulls like this generate very high initial stability. Thus they carry large, tall sail plans to drive light hulls—a good formula for speed. Unfortunately, light boats with high initial stability simply must have a vicious snappy roll (see the next chapter). Most modern sailors seem to give this matter little if any thought. That one boat may be more comfortable than another in a seaway by virtue of her hull shape is hardly ever discussed. Not so long ago, such concerns were at the top of many sailors' minds.

A Plank on Edge

The antithesis of the current trend was the old English plank-on-edge cutter. Where the modern trend is toward low Disp/WL ratios with wide, shallow underbodies and fin keels, the English cutter has an extremely deep hull body—narrow and heavy, with slack bilges. This is why they were called "plank-on-edge"; they were so deep and narrow that this is what they resembled. Vessels like this often had Disp/LWL ratios over 400. Most of their stability was generated by a truly immense weight of lead or iron in the keel. Like anything carried to extremes, many of these boats were so heavy and narrow that they sailed on their "ear" and rose to the seas so slowly that, in a real blow, they were constantly awash with green water—proverbial half-tide rocks. Moderate versions of these cutters, though, are very seaworthy indeed.

Ahh . . . Comfort

I've been lucky enough to sail on one of these moderate English cutters. It was designed by the superb English naval architect Albert Strange, just after the turn of the century. Let me tell you that I have never experienced or imagined motion as comfortable as on this vessel. On Long Island Sound, I hardly knew there was any wave action at all. The reason for this is two-fold. First, her great weight has an inertia that resists sudden changes in direction, thus naturally dampening out much motion. Second, with her relatively slack bilges and narrow beam, her initial stability's proportionately less for her displacement than that of her light, modern counterparts. This means that she rolls slowly, steadily, and gently, picking up stability gradually but certainly as she goes over. Nothing short of a tidal wave would be likely to get her over more than 70 degrees. The effect is most gratifying.

At the same time that I went sailing on this cutter I owned a beamy, shallow-bodied, bulb-fin-keel sloop with hard bilges. Although she was an old boat (though not nearly as old as the cutter), she is more or less representative of the current approach. Her motion in a seaway could most charitably be described as "exciting." In fact, there were more than a few times, at anchor in a stiff nor'wester, when we could hardly wait to get off her onto the relative comfort of the launch.

Many people go shopping for boats or searching for designs without ever stopping to consider how comfortable their motion will be. Boats of the current light, shallow-bodied type cannot be con-

sidered very comfortable at all in comparison with Albert Strange's fine old cutter. This does *not* mean that modern boats are "bad." It simply means that vessels of this sort don't excel at this particular aspect of sailing. I'm certainly not recommending that you go out and get yourself a turn-of-the-century cutter. However, if comfortable motion is at all important to you, you ought to consider some of the "heavier" and more traditional designs on the market.

Heave and Waterplane Loading

One excellent indicator of how comfortable a boat will be in a seaway is her rate of heave—how fast she bobs straight up and down. A rapid heave means many quick vertical accelerations that will keep you hanging onto things for support when you'd much prefer to be relaxing. A boat with a slow heave has a solid, shippy feel. Luckily, it's not actually necessary to calculate heave accelerations to compare boats. The rate at which a vessel lifts vertically to the waves is controlled by the amount of buoyancy she has at the waterline as compared to her total weight or displacement—the relationship of her displacement to her waterplane area.

As we saw earlier, if your boat were 30 feet (9.1 m) on the waterline and 7.5 feet (2.3 m) beam, her waterplane would be about 171 square feet (15.9 m²). (See also Chapter 16.) If she displaced 4.9 tons, she'd have a waterplane loading of 0.028 ton per square foot, or 64 pounds per square foot (310 kg/m²). This is an ideal loading for comfort, for craft of this size.

If the waterplane had been larger—say, if her waterline beam had been 8.5 feet (2.6 m)—or her displacement less, then her heave motion would be quicker and more uncomfortable. If the waterplane had been smaller or her displacement greater, heave would be slower and more comfortable. (You can go too far here; boats with very slow heaves need ample freeboard and flare to keep their decks dry.)

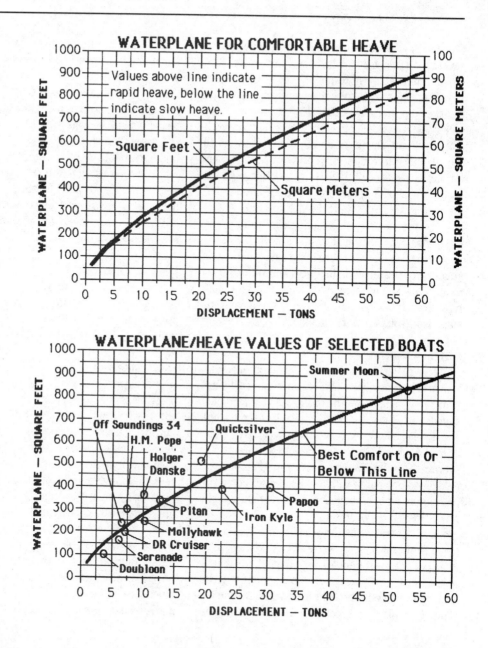

WATERPLANE FOR COMFORTABLE HEAVE

Values above line indicate rapid heave, below the line indicate slow heave.

Square Feet

Square Meters

WATERPLANE — SQUARE FEET

WATERPLANE — SQUARE METERS

DISPLACEMENT — TONS

WATERPLANE/HEAVE VALUES OF SELECTED BOATS

Summer Moon

Off Soundings 34
H.M. Pope
Holger Danske
Quicksilver

Best Comfort On Or Below This Line

Papoo
Pitan
Iron Kyle
Mollyhawk
DR Cruiser
Serenade
Doubloon

WATERPLANE — SQUARE FEET

DISPLACEMENT — TONS

The "Waterplane for Comfortable Heave" chart will enable you to check on heave comfort for any boat whose dimensions you know. Just estimate the waterplane area and run across from that value to the intersection of her displacement.

If the location's above the comfort line, heave will be more rapid than ideal; if on or below the line, heave will be comfortable.

The second chart, "Waterplane/Heave Values of Selected Boats," shows the same comfort line (here in English measure only) with the values for several vessels from this book plotted in. The most comfortable—in terms of heave—for serious voyaging are the pinky schooner *Papoo* and the cruising tug *Iron Kyle*—they'll have an extremely steady, shippy feel. Most of the remaining craft fall just about on the optimum line. Note that all the planing powerboats fall above the best-comfort line. It's very difficult to avoid this on such craft; they need ample planing surface and moderate to low weight. The three lightest and fastest vessels are *Quicksilver, Holger Danske,* and *H.M. Pope.* You can see that they all fall well above the best comfort line. In order to get their high speeds, low waterplane loadings and quick heave motions were unavoidable. As always, you can't have everything in a single boat. There have to be some trade-offs for performance.

Is Heavy Slow?

This brings us back to the question of whether heavy- or high-Disp/LWL–ratio boats really are slow. It depends on the boat. At displacement speeds, a heavy vessel with a well designed hull and a generous rig or powerplant will move along at a very good clip. If you take two more-or-less average boats of the same waterline length—one heavy and one light—and make all other comparable factors equal, their top and average speeds will be very nearly the same.

Both vessels must have similar sail area–displacement ratios or power-to-weight ratios. This is a perfectly attainable design goal for heavy boats. These two vessels will have speeds that are very close indeed. The light craft will have the advantage of quicker acceleration, quicker maneu-

vering, and bursts of speed over the theoretical maximum hull speed. The heavy vessel will be better in light to moderate air in a chop that would tend to slap and pound the light boat to a stop, and she will have a more comfortable motion. (Extremely light vessels with Disp/WL ratios under 100 can go significantly faster than theoretical hull speed, but these are not average craft.)

For vessels that are designed to operate at semiplaning and planing speeds, low weight is necessary. As we've seen, this usually generates hulls with more uncomfortable motions than ideal—the price of high speed.

Keep an Open Mind

By now, of course, you might think that I dislike light boats and don't recommend then. Not so. I think light boats are super! *Holger Danske,* with a Disp/WL ratio of just 40 (!) is—to the best of my knowledge—the lightest true ocean racer ever, and *Quicksilver* and *H.M Pope* are quite light as well. It's just that light boats do have some real drawbacks that are seldom discussed these days.

Heavy craft, too, have their place. For some purposes, such as serious voyaging or living aboard, these heavier vessels just can't be beat. It's a shame that the current fashion for lightness is keeping many sailors from considering boats of a type that could give them much satisfaction and pleasure. Further, this trend is encouraging people to buy boats that are more lightly constructed and with less comfortable motion than is best. Lightness might be just the thing for you in your next boat. On the other hand, a heavier vessel might be much better for your needs. Keep an open mind and evaluate each type on its real merits.

CHAPTER 15

The Great Stability Mystery

There isn't no call to go talking of pushing and pulling. Boats are quite tricky enough for those that sit still without looking further for the cause of trouble.

The Fellowship of the Ring, J.R.R. Tolkien

Few aspects of boat design are more inscrutable than stability. You can't see it. It's difficult to measure, and when you do measure it, it's not easy to say just what your nice numbers mean. Of course, you can feel stability (or at least its effects), but even this can be misleading. For instance, it's not unusual for a "stiff" boat to be more prone to capsize than a "tender" one! Also, stability affects comfort. A boat that's too stiff will snap back and forth so quickly that she'll jar your socks off. On the other hand, an excessively tender boat will roll so deeply and regularly that you're more than likely to leave your stomach at the bottom of the bay.

Like so many seeming mysteries, however, stability's really just a combination of a few fairly simple effects. You don't need higher math or complex graphs to understand it.

Stability Comes in Two Flavors

The first thing we have to do is realize that two completely different types of stability are at work, at the same time, in any vessel. Both of these types occur in everyday life ashore. The first is called *initial* or *form stability*. The second type is called *reserve* or *ultimate stability*. Generally, it's form stability that's more apparent and more easily measured. Form stability causes a boat to be stiff or tender—stable or easily rolled.

Initial Stability

The principle behind form stability is simplicity itself: The wider and flatter something is, the harder it is to tip it over. If you have a long, narrow card table (say 2 feet by 4 feet, or .5 meter by 1 meter) you can put it in your backyard and explore this yourself. Tie a rope around the tabletop and pull sideways on it until the table starts to tip over. (If you want to be scientific, you can put a spring scale on the rope.) You will easily be able to feel that it takes much less force to tip the table when you're pulling it in the transverse (2 ft., .5 m) direction than in the long (4 ft., 1 m) direction.

The reason for this is that the table has a cer-

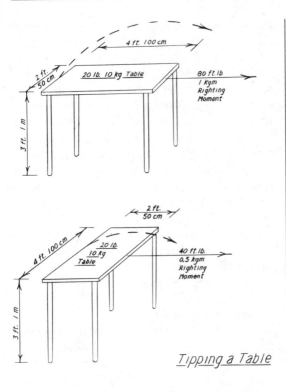

Tipping a Table

times a distance. In this case, 2 feet times 20 pounds equals 40 foot-pounds (50 cm × 10 kg = 500 kgcm, or 5 kgm). Since we know that we need 40 foot-pounds (5 kgm), and our rope is attached to the table at its top (3 ft. or 1 m high), we can figure just how hard we have to pull to get our capsize. The table's 40 foot-pounds (5 kgm) of moment is its stability or *righting moment.* Take this 40 foot-pounds (5 kgm) and divide by the 3-foot or 1-meter height (*heeling arm*) and you get 13 pounds or 5 kg of pull (40 ft.-lb. ÷ 3 ft. = 13.3 lb., or 5 kgm ÷ 1 m = 5 kg).

Here's where things get a bit confusing. If you'd attached the rope halfway up on the legs, at 1½ feet, you'd divide 40 foot-pounds by 1.5 feet and get a required pull of 26 pounds (40 ft.-lb. ÷ 1.5 ft. = 26.67 lb., or 5 kgm ÷ 0.5 m = 10 kg). Thus you'd need twice the force with only one half the lever arm. If you'd attached the rope to the very bottom of the table legs and pulled sideways, the table wouldn't tip over no matter how hard you hauled—you'd have a zero lever arm. (It would probably slide sideways at a good clip.) This is one of the reasons low and wide vessels feel stiffer than vessels that are high, even at the same width. If you repeat the experiment, pulling the table sideways the long way, you'd also need twice the force to tip it. This is because the table's stability (righting moment) in this direction would be its length of 4 feet (100 cm) times its weight of 20 pounds (10 kg), or 80 foot-pounds (10 kgm): 4 ft. × 20 lb. = 80 ft.-lb., or 100 cm × 10 kg = 1,000 kgcm, or 10 kgm.

Wide, Flat, and Heavy Makes Her Stiff

Now you can see that the two factors that affect form or initial stability are breadth (beam) and weight (displacement). The wider, lower, and heavier a boat is, the more initial stability it will have. A vessel like a barge loaded with bricks is both very wide and flat and very heavy. Such craft are almost impossible to capsize, at first. Remember the "at first"—it's crucial!

tain weight, say 20 pounds or 10 kg. In order to get the table to tip over, you have to lift the weight of the table and swing it up and toward you against the lever arm of the table's width. If you pull the table over far enough its center of gravity will no longer be over its legs, but beyond the legs, toward you. At this point the center of gravity is not being held up by anything—there's just empty space below it. With nothing under the table's center of gravity to hold it up, it falls to the ground on its side—capsize!

Righting Moment and Heeling Arm

Since the table is 2 feet (50 cm) wide, 4 feet (100 cm) long, and weighs 20 pounds (10 kg), it will require 40 foot-pounds (500 kgcm, or 5 kgm) of moment to tip over sideways. Now, don't let the word "moment" scare you off. It's just a force

Obviously, if you'd had a friend sit on the table, it would've taken a lot more strength to tip it over by pulling sideways on your rope. If your friend weighs 150 pounds (70 kg), you'd have to generate 340 foot-pounds (40 kgm) of heeling moment to tip him or her and the 20-pound (10 kg) table over (150 lb. + 20 lb. = 170 lb., and 170 lb. × 2 ft. width = 340 ft.-lb.; 70 kg + 10 kg = 80 kg, and 80 kg × .5 m width = 40 kgm). Since you're still pulling on a rope 3 feet (1 m) up, you'd have to generate 113 pounds (40 kg) of pull—340 ft.-lb. ÷ 3 ft. height = 113.3 lb. pull, or 40 kgm ÷ 1 m height = 40 kg—I hope you've been lifting weights.

Reserve Stability

Here we begin to touch on reserve or ultimate stability. With your friend sitting on top of the table you'd have to overcome his or her weight to tip the table; however, once you had the table angled far enough over it would come crashing down—friend and all. If you took the same table (and presumably the same friend) and repeated the whole exercise with the table upside down, things would be very different. (By this time your neighbors will, no doubt, consider you certifiable.) In this new configuration the table has the same width and weight as before, but its weight or center of gravity is positioned much lower, like adding lead ballast or low tanks and stores. What happens?

Interestingly, if you attach your rope to the top of the table legs (they're now sticking rather foolishly up into the air) you'll still have a 3-foot (1 m) lever arm, so you'll still need the same 113 pounds (40 kg) to lift and tip the table. But—and this is the big but—before, the table would have crashed onto its side when you had levered it over to about 25 to 35 degrees. Now, you'll find that even when you have the table hauled over to 60 or 70 degrees, it will not capsize, but will fall back to its initial position the minute you release the rope. This assumes that your friend is acrobatic enough to hold tight in one place while all these shenanigans are going on.

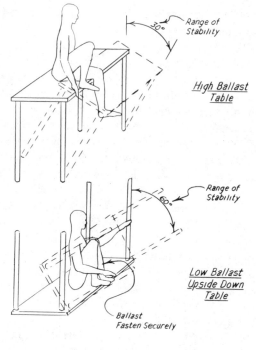

Ballasted Table Tipping

By turning your friend into ballast you've increased the table's range of stability (the number of degrees at which it is stable). This is what reserve stability is all about. In fact, reserve stability usually is measured in degrees of heel (tipping). A sailboat that reaches the point of capsize at 90 degrees has a *range of stability* of 90 degrees and is, incidentally, not considered stable enough to venture offshore. A sailboat that has a range of stability of 180 degrees will turn herself rightside up even when knocked completely upside down. Most well-found cruising sailboats have a stability range of around 120 to 145 degrees—more never hurts.

An Energetic Consideration

At first, all this may seem a bit strange. How can it take the same amount of force to tip the table with more reserve stability as the table with very little reserve stability? The answer is that you pull with the same amount of force but you have to keep exerting that force for a greater distance. This adds up to more work and more energy (work and/or energy are nothing more than a force times a distance). In order to overcome the upright table's stability and bring it to the point of capsize, you had to swing it through, say, 1.5 feet (.5 m) exerting a pull of 113 pounds (40 kg). This means that the table absorbed 169 foot-pounds (20 kgm) of energy before falling (1.5 ft. × 113 pounds = 169.5 ft.-lb.; .5 m × 40 kg = 20 kgm).

At the same time the upside-down (low-ballast) table had to be swung through 2.75 feet (.9 m) with the same 113 pounds (40 kg) of force. In this configuration, the table absorbed 311 foot-pounds (36 kg) of energy (2.75 ft. × 113 lb. = 310.5 ft.-lb.; .9 m × 40 kg = 36 kgm)—about 80 percent more energy! This is the fundamental reason that reserve stability is so important. It takes much larger waves and much stronger winds to pack the energy required to capsize a vessel with a great range of stability .

Hold That Ballast

If your friend were to let go and tumble down toward you, he or she would actually increase the table's tendency to capsize by shifting the center of gravity toward the down side. This is just what happens when heavy ballast or machinery comes loose at sea—an extremely dangerous situation. It's also some of what can go on in a vessel's tanks if they have insufficient baffles. In extreme cases this *free surface effect* can cause a vessel to capsize. Of course, the solution is to make darn sure that nothing heavy can come loose, that your ballast is very secure, and that your tanks are well divided with strong baffles to limit sloshing. You could also try lashing your friend to the table, but that might be carrying the pursuit of realism too far.

Reserve Versus Initial Stability

By getting the weight or center of gravity of the table (and friend) down low, we've created re-

serve, or ultimate stability. Here we run into one of the conflicts that confuses the stability question. A narrow, deep boat will have tremendous reserve stability but little initial stability. This makes the narrow boat seem tippy or tender at first; however, such a boat could be knocked down flat on her ear, or even further, and still right herself. A broad, flat boat with no low ballast or weights will seem very safe and reassuring to begin with. In fact, she can give one a false sense of security. Such craft could carry sail in a gale of wind before heeling more than 20 degrees, but once something gets it over more than 50 or 60 degrees—capsize!

Somersaults at Sea

This sort of unpleasantness has been occurring for years. In 1876, for example, the schooner *Mohawk* was anchored and just ready to hoist her hook for a sail. She was a notably stiff boat, broad and shoal draft, typical of the American boats of her day. Unexpectedly, she was struck broadside by a strong gust and heeled over beyond the point of no return. In just a moment she capsized. Her owner, his wife, and a crewman were drowned.

Only a few years ago, the trimaran *Gulf*

The yacht Mohawk, *drawn by Charles R. Parsons, from* Traditions and Memories of American Yachting, WoodenBoat Publications, 1989.

Streamer was hit by a rogue wave and rolled past her point of no return. There she floated in the Atlantic until her skipper, the indomitable Phil Weld, was rescued. In fact, multihulls like *Gulf Streamer* are the most stable vessels for their size and weight in the world. Yet they're classic examples of tremendous initial stability and virtually no reserve stability.

A big cat or tri gives one a very secure feeling, but there's always the question of that point of no return. Just as it was for the table with your friend on top, this is the point at which you no longer have to exert any force to tip her further. From this point on, gravity will do all the work. At sea, there's nothing you can do once this point is past. (Reserve stability isn't the only criterion for a safe boat. There are many extremely safe and reliable cruising multihulls. Keep in mind that most multihulls *can't* sink, whereas most monohulls—even completely self-righting ones—can. Capsizing a well-designed and properly sailed cruising multihull is no more or less likely than holing and sinking a well-designed cruising monohull.)

Neither size alone nor miles at sea guarantee protection from capsize. Even quite recently (1986), the *Pride of Baltimore* was struck by a terrific gust and capsized in the Gulf Stream. She was a large (by yacht standards) topsail schooner and a beautiful vessel by any reckoning, with many ocean miles to her credit, but neither the expertise of her crew nor her size could compensate, in this instance, for her lack of ultimate stability.

Self-Righting

On the other side of the coin are deep, heavy, monohull cruising sailboats. These craft—usually with 35 percent or more of their weight down very low as ballast—can literally be rolled over 180 degrees, till their masts point straight down, and then right themselves. Such boats have no "point of no return." No matter how far over they go, they'll always come upright again on their own. An example of ultimate stability at work in extreme conditions is the performance of Naomi James's *Express Crusader.* She was capsized and rolled 360 degrees by a tremendous wave in winds over force 10. Not only did *Express Crusader* right herself, but her already damaged rig remained standing. *Crusader* and Dame Naomi went on with their circumnavigation, eventually besting Sir Francis Chichester's globe girdling time.

The Buoyancy Shifts

Of course, a boat doesn't have legs (at least none of mine ever did) so it's not as easy to find the righting moment of a boat as it was to find the table's. Take the motor yacht *Golden Mermaid,* for instance. As in all vessels, her stability's generated by the buoyancy of her hull. When she's at rest, her center of buoyancy, *CB*, is amidships and directly in line with her center of gravity, *CG*. As soon as she rolls, though, her center of buoyancy shifts sideways to the down or immersed side. This is the heeled center of buoyancy, *CB1*. The reason this happens is that *Mermaid's* hull is no longer symmetrical in the water. At vertical, her hull is the same shape port and starboard; however, when heeled her immersed side presents a substantial bulge to the sea. This is why few boats have circular sections. Such hulls would remain essentially symmetrical when heeled and thus have little form stability.

While all this is going on, *Golden Mermaid's* center of gravity stays in the same spot—unless, that is, you've been chopping her up and sliding pieces of her around. The result of all this is that there's now a transverse distance between *Mermaid's* center of gravity and her heeled center of buoyancy—a distance designers call *GZ*. This is exactly like our card table experiments. Since a boat's buoyant force is equal to her displacement, it's simple to find *Golden Mermaid's* stability—known as *righting moment* or *RM*. The designer calculates where her heeled center of buoyancy falls at a given angle and where her *vertical center of gravity, VCG,* is, then measures the transverse distance, the GZ, between them. If *Golden Mermaid* displaces 24,000 pounds (10,890 kg) and the transverse distance between her center of gravity and her heeled center of buoyancy is 1.2 feet (37 cm) at 30 degrees, then her righting moment is 28,800 foot-pounds or 4,030 kgm, at 30 degrees (1.2 ft. × 24,000 lb. = 28,800 ft.-lb.—0.37 m × 10,890 kg = 4,030 kgm).

Naval Architects Earn Their Keep

Unfortunately, three things make stability calculations a real chore. The first is that *Golden Mermaid*'s (or any boat's) center of buoyancy is at a different location at every different angle of heel. Second, since hulls have irregular shapes, it's a long, laborious task to compute the position of the heeled center of buoyancy for each angle. Finally, determining a boat's vertical center of gravity requires adding up pages and pages of weights and

multiplying them by appropriate distances. All this amounts to a lot of number crunching for the designer. Luckily, computers make the whole process less onerous. Even better for you, if you want to estimate the stability of your boat, you don't have to go through any of this. You can perform a simple roll-timing experiment.

Powerboaters will want to determine if they have sufficient stability to venture off soundings, or to add additional weight high up—tuna towers, heavy dinks and davits, radar arches, and such. Sailors considering rerigging, modifications to improve upwind performance, or the effects of adding heavy gear aloft need to know their boat's righting moment.

Time to Roll

Naval architects use a number of complex formulas to check on powerboat stability; however,

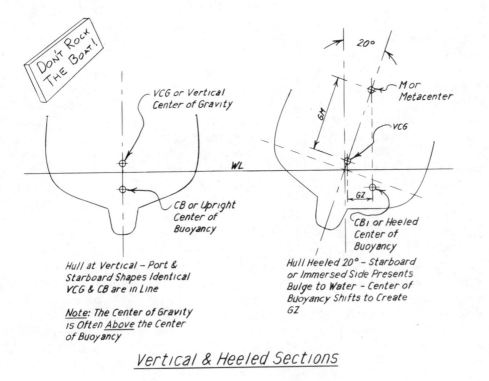

Vertical & Heeled Sections

GM

In reading about stability you'll occasionally encounter the term *GM*. Designers use this value to perform precise stability and roll-timing calculations. What is GM? Well, it's an imaginary distance between the vertical center of gravity of your boat and the point where a vertical line through the heeled center of buoyancy crosses the boat's vertical centerline—a point called the *metacenter (M)*. Yipes!! Don't worry. You can see how GM (also called the *metacentric height*) is defined in the illustration, but you don't really have to deal with GM to estimate it for your boat. In fact, using roll timing, determining GM is quite simple.

To find the GM take 44 percent of the beam in feet (79.7 percent of beam in meters) and divide that by the roll time in seconds. Then square the answer (multiply it by itself). Or, in math: $GM = ((0.44 \times Beam\ in\ ft.) \div Time\ in\ sec.)^2$—$GM = ((0.797 \times Beam\ in\ m) \div Time\ in\ sec.)^2$. For *Golden Mermaid*, we get a GM of 2.2 feet, or 0.67 m—$((0.44 \times 12.5\ ft.) \div 3.7\ sec.)^2 = 2.2\ ft.$, $((0.797 \times 3.81\ m) \div 3.7\ sec.)^2 = 0.67\ m$.

an amazingly reliable rule of thumb is that for maximum comfort and safety you'll want a roll time in seconds to equal between 1 and 1.1 times the boat's beam in feet divided by 3.28, or simply the vessel's beam *overall* in meters. (For simplicity's sake this is referred to as "roll time equal to beam.") Note that vessels with an unusual amount of flare—whose beam at the waterline is less than 90 percent of the beam overall—should use 111 percent of the waterline beam, not beam overall.

Craft that have longer roll times have less stability and are uncomfortable offshore to boot. Such boats roll very slo . . oo . . owly! You get a sickening drunken feeling as you grab hold of the nearest support while she gradually rotates farther and farther. *Will she come back?* you'll wonder fearfully. Then—most of the time—she will right herself, only to repeat the process in the other direction—back and forth, over and over. Not only is this terribly uncomfortable, but there's always the real danger that—with stability so marginal—one time she won't come back upright.

Vessels with roll times much less than their beam in meters (or beam in feet $\div$ 3.28) have plenty of initial stability. They, in fact, have too much for comfort. They'll snap back and forth in rapid jerks that'll rattle your teeth. On some types of craft, there's little you can do to reduce this problem. Planing powerboats, in particular, have quick roll times—sometimes as rapid as $\frac{1}{2}$ the beam. This is an unavoidable result of the wide, relatively shallow, hard-chine hull shapes and large, heavy engines such vessels require. They can be fine sea boats in other respects, but their roll motion will be uncomfortably jerky.

Timing the Roll

Let's see how *Golden Mermaid* works out. Tie her up at the dock on a nice, calm day and slack off the dock lines. Now, stand with one foot on the dock and the other on her rail (you may need several friends to join in). Push down rhythmically on *Mermaid's* rail (the singing of sea chanties is allowed). Adjust the rhythm of your pushes so that you get her rolling as well and deeply as possible. At this stage, wait till she's reached a full downswing toward your side (the dock side) and yell "Stop!" Lift all feet clear and, using a stopwatch, time her *complete* roll from side to side. A complete roll is from all the way starboard to all the way over port and then back again all the way starboard. Repeat this entire process three or so times and average the results.

Now, *Golden Mermaid* has a beam of 12 feet 6 inches (3.8 m), and we've averaged her roll times at 3.7 seconds. Dividing her beam in feet by 3.28 gives 3.81 (her beam in meters), and 3.7 seconds divided by 3.81 equals 0.97. This is close enough to 1 to be about perfect. Indeed, a roll time of exactly one indicates plenty of stability for rough-water work but not too much for comfort. Being just under 1 indicates *Mermaid* has enough reserve stability to take some additional weight on deck or aloft, should extra gear be desired.

Of course, there are other factors to consider before going off soundings—hull strength, power plant, freeboard, and so on. However, if you own an average powerboat with a roll time greater than 1.1 times beam it would probably not be prudent to operate her in conditions that will roll her deeply; she could pass the point of no return. On the other hand, if your roll time works out to well under 1 times the beam, you may want to ask yourself if your vessel is as comfortable as you'd like. She probably has a corky snap roll—more stability than you want. One way to fix this is to add weights up high—just don't add enough to slow her roll time to more than 1.1 times beam. (Stability's a complex subject. Check with a naval architect before adding very large, heavy weights high up.)

How To Spell Comfort

In this chapter and the last, we've spelled out two of the most critical factors in ensuring comfort—comfortable motion that is. A craft that has waterplane area on or below the recommended comfort line (see the previous chapter) and also has a roll time between 1 and 1.1 times beam in meters will have comfortable motion in rough conditions. She'll be more pleasant lying at anchor as well, particularly in rough, unprotected anchorages.

Remember, though, that for some craft—fast boats in particular—it's a necessary compromise to settle for quicker heave and roll motions than ideal. This doesn't make fast vessels "bad"; it simply means that you can't have everything in one boat. When evaluating different designs, heave and roll motion—comfort—should be among *many* factors you consider. They don't have to be the most important factors, unless of course you're contemplating a voyaging liveaboard.

Exceptions That "Prove" the Rule

Wide, shallow boats, such as houseboats, have very great initial stability. This results in very short roll times. Such craft could easily take additional tophamper; however, they are not suited to ocean voyaging. Their reserve stability is too small (often virtually nonexistent) and their pounding too great.

The Right Moment

For sailboats, simply knowing the roll period isn't enough. In order to determine sail-carrying power—or to give sparmakers the information they need to make up a new rig—you need actual righting moment, exactly as we found with our table. Happily, you can make fairly accurate estimates of righting moments—up to about 30 degrees of heel—from the roll time. First you have to determine the righting arm (called *GZ*), which is exactly the same as the width of the table in our table-tipping experiment. Then—just as with the table—you multiply the righting arm by the weight, which—for a boat—is simply her displacement.

The two critical heel angles for finding righting moment are 20 degrees and 30 degrees. The moment at 20 degrees is used to determine sail-carrying power, and the moment at 30 degrees is used by sparmakers for calculating rigging loads.

To find the righting moments for your *Swan Song* you'd do a roll-timing, exactly as we did on *Golden Mermaid*. Then determine righting arm (GZ) as follows:

$$GZft\ 20° = \frac{(BWL\ ft \div Sec)^2}{14.84}$$

$$GZft\ 30° = \frac{(BWL\ ft \div Sec)^2}{11.0}$$

$$GZm\ 20° = \frac{(BWL\ m \div Sec)^2}{4.53}$$

$$GZm\ 30° = \frac{(BWL\ m \div Sec)^2}{3.35}$$

(BWL is the waterline beam.)

If *Swan Song* weighs 8,000 pounds (3,630 kg), has a 9.7-foot (2.95 m) beam on the waterline, and her roll time was 2.6 seconds, we'd find her righting arm or GZ at 20 degrees to be 0.93 feet or 28 cm (9.7 ft. ÷ 2.6 sec. = 3.73, and 3.73 × 3.73 = 13.9, then 13.9 ÷ 14.84 = 0.93 ft.—or 2.95 m ÷ 2.6 sec. = 1.13, and 1.13 × 1.13 = 1.27, then 1.27 ÷ 4.53 = 0.28 m). Multiplying by her displacement of 8,000 pounds (3,630 kg) gives her a righting arm, at 20 degrees, of 7,440 foot-pounds (1,016 kgm). You can find the righting moment at 30 degrees the same way.

Both roll timing and inclining measure primarily a boat's initial stability; though if you haul a boat all the way over on her beam ends with a strong tackle with scale attached to her mast, you can check her stability to 90 or even 100 degrees. The only other way to find a vessel's reserve stability is to locate her center of gravity (this can be done by roll timing, but is too complicated to go into here), and then calculate her stability at many angles of heel from her lines drawing. The higher the ballast ratio and the lower the keel, however, the more ultimate stability your vessel

will have. Similarly, for powerboats, low superstructure and low engine and tank weights increase reserve stability. Powerboats with low superstructures are more suited to offshore cruising.

An unfortunate side affect of the IOR rule has been that, since stability increases the ability to carry sail and thus increases speed, it was actually penalized (!) for some time. This has now been corrected somewhat; however, boats built under the influence of this rule have a smaller range of stability than you'd expect from keel sailboats.

Nailing Down Wind Pressure

Knowing the righting arm of your boat, you can estimate her sail-carrying power. One of the methods designers use to determine how much sail a boat can stand up to has the catchy name of "The Wind Pressure Coefficient Method." Although you practically have to have a Ph.D. just to say it, it's really no big deal. It's simply a way of calculating (actually estimating) the wind speed that will generate enough force to heel the boat 20 degrees. The trick here is choosing the right wind pressure coefficient, *WPC*.

WIND PRESSURE COEFFICIENTS

	English	Metric
Daysailers	0.9 to 1.1	4.3 to 5.2
Racers, Performance Cruisers	1.1 to 1.4	5.2 to 6.7
Heavy Cruising Boats	1.2 to 1.5	5.7 to 7.1
Ocean Voyagers	1.3 to 1.7	6.2 to 8.1

In the case of *Swan Song*, we know she has a righting moment of 7,440 foot-pounds (1,016 kgm). She carries 400 square feet (37.2 m²) of sail. Is she able to stand up to this much sail? This will depend on how high her rig is. A taller rig is more efficient than a shorter rig of the same sail area, but it also has a longer heeling arm. The wind pressure coefficient formula says that the WPC equals the righting moment at 20 degrees divided by the sail area times the heeling arm times 0.88 (at 20 degrees), or:

$$WPC = \frac{RM\ 20°\ (ft\text{-}lb\ or\ kgm)}{SA\ (ft^2\ or\ m^2)\ \times\ HA\ (ft\ or\ m)\ \times\ 0.88}$$

We can measure *Swan Song*'s sail plan (see Chapters 21 and 37) to find that *Swan Song*'s sails have a center of effort 15.1 feet (4.6 m) above the waterline. To this we add 40 percent of her draft, or 2.2 feet (0.67 cm). This gives a total heeling arm of 17.3 feet (5.27 m). Now, just plug the numbers into the formula and multiply on any handy calculator, and you will find that her wind pressure coefficient (WPC) is 1.22 (5.9)—7,440 ft.-lb. ÷ (400 sq. ft. × 17.3 ft. × 0.88) = 1.22, or 1,016 kgm ÷ (37.2 m² × 5.27 m × 0.88) = 5.9. Referring back to the table of wind pressure coefficients, we can see that a WPC of 1.22 (or 5.9) falls nicely into the range of performance cruiser and cruising boats. We'd probably want a higher WPC (1.3 or 6.2 or more) for globe girdling, and could add more sail (getting by with a lower WPC) for coastal cruising and round-the-buoys racing.

Tote That Ballast

The other way to increase stability in a sailboat, besides making her wider or giving her deeper ballast, is to use shifting ballast. It's the use of such ballast that makes planing sailboats possible. Except for multihulls, no other scheme could produce enough stability to stand up to a rig generating the power needed for planing speeds.

Everybody to Weather!

Usually, the shifting ballast is you—the crew. On a small planing daysailer such as a Laser or Lightning, crew weight can be more than the weight of the whole vessel. If you move that much weight to windward (the up side) you get a heck of a lot of righting moment in proportion to the boat's weight and sail area. In fact, if you have three 150-pound (70 kg) crewmen hiking out on the weather rail and the boat's beam is 6 feet (2 m), then you're adding around 2,000 foot-pounds (288 kgm) of righting moment. (About 4.5 feet from center of buoyancy to center of crew weight, times 450 pounds—3 × 150 lb.—equals 2,025 ft.-lbs, or 137 cm × 210 kg—3 × 70 kg—equals 288 kgm.)

Sandbaggers

In the "good old days" sandbags were used on some boats, in addition to crew weight. Such vessels became known—not surprisingly—as sandbaggers. Crews on these craft were notorious, to say the least. Picked for heft and brawn, these stalwart fellows shifted not only themselves from side to side on every tack but dozens of 50- and 100-pound bags as well. When the fleet anchored for the night such crews had reputations that caused most folk to stay safely indoors. Crew loyalty could be fierce, and protests and other disputes between vessels could result in melees that spilled out onto the streets. All of this was liberally spiced with heavy outside betting and sensational newspaper stories—kinda' makes the IOR and the America's Cup seem tame.

The Incredible *Annie*

As exciting as they were, sandbaggers quickly developed into an unsafe class. They encouraged wide, flat hulls with little or no permanent ballast. Their rigs were so huge that some had booms one and a half times as long as the boat! *Annie*, a sandbagger from 1880, was 29 feet (8.8 m) long, 12 feet 6 inches (3.8 m) beam, and only 2 feet (60 cm) draft. She had a mast 36 feet 6 inches (11.1 m) tall; a gaff 18 feet (5.5 m) long; and her incredible boom was 42 feet (12.8 m) long. Imagine a mainsail of nearly 1,000 square feet (93 m²) on a 29-footer (8.8 m), with a bowsprit about half the length of the boat! Even more remarkable, *Annie* was not all that unique for her time. As usual, cruising boats tended to emulate the racers, and the result was a large number of boats with great initial stability

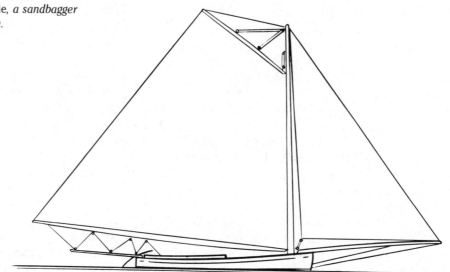

The incredible Annie, *a sandbagger with a 42-foot boom.*

and huge rigs but no reserve stability. Sandbagger capsizes were not at all uncommon.

The Shifting Ballast Ban

Very much as a result of these craft, today's racing rules usually prohibit shifting ballast. Thus, small daysailers that tend to stay inshore rely on shifting crew weight, but larger vessels can't carry enough crew to make a really big difference. It would take an awful lot of hefty fellows to heel a 27-ton vessel significantly. Such boats have to rely on the usual combination of form stability and low ballast for sail-carrying power and safety. There are some exceptions to this, however. Recently, a few production sailboats have been built with wings at the sheer to enable the crew to clamber way out to windward. Also, various OSTAR, BOC, and Globe-Challenge racers have used shifting ballast. (See *Holger Danske,* and *Quicksilver,* elsewhere in this book.)

Water Ballast

These vessels have water tanks port and starboard. By pumping the windward tank full, the crew can dramatically increase the righting moment or sail-carrying power. Under the right conditions, vessels of 40 to 60 feet (12 to 18 m) have approached planing speeds. The danger here is similar to that faced by the old sandbaggers. In the quest for speed, designers are tempted to use less and less fixed, low ballast and more and more shifting ballast, which is more effective pound for pound in generating stability. If the windward ballast tanks are not full, though, and the boat is struck by a sudden strong gust, such boats can easily be knocked down. Even worse, if the starboard tank were full and the vessel were to be hit by a strong gust from port, the water ballast would actually help to capsize her. Generally, such gear is best left to serious racers. When used carefully, however, water ballast can be safe enough.

The current BOC rule requires that shifting ballast water tanks not be too large. The rules won't accept an entrant that can be heeled more than 10 degrees by shifting ballast alone. This seemed a safe compromise originally; however, wily designers have found a way to beat the system. They've been making their BOC and Globe-

Challenge creations wider and flatter. By doing so, they've dramatically increased initial stability. Accordingly, they're able to carry less and less ballast in the keel and more and more in the water tanks without exceeding the 10 degrees heel limit. The end result, though, is boats with great initial stability and little reserve stability. In fact, in a recent Globe Challenge, one of the widest of these craft went over on her side and stayed that way! She had to be towed upright and was disqualified.

The Swinging Keel

An even odder approach to shifting ballast was proposed by L. Francis Herreshoff. He suggested that instead of using high, shifting ballast, the whole ballast keel be pivoted athwartships and swung from side to side. When you wanted to increase stability, you'd crank the entire keel to weather. The cat ketch *Red Herring* was built to this idea some time ago. She proved fairly fast and stable. Most important, since the ballast stayed low—even when shifted—reserve stability was not harmed.

Unfortunately, there are two serious draw-backs to this scheme. Shifting the fin-and-ballast keel to windward places it at such an oblique angle to the water that it's useless in counteracting leeway or generating lift. Thus, additional fore-and-aft centerboards are required. This leads to the other drawback of the scheme: It is a devilishly complicated engineering job. I once did considerable design work on a 64-foot (19.5 m) vessel that was to have water ballast and a swinging keel. This keel not only was to swing from side to side, but also to pivot up like a normal centerboard to reduce draft. She proved too complicated; all the mechanisms add excessive weight, and the design was not a success.

Even stranger devices have been used to increase stability. One experimenter is working on using mercury ballast pumped from port to starboard bilge keels—I doubt the EPA would approve! L. Francis Herreshoff—never at a loss for ideas—proposed a sliding arm proa; and Dick Newick, the multihull designer, has been trying out new-moon-shaped outer hulls on some of his trimarans to generate dynamic lift to increase righting moment at speed.

CHAPTER 16

Flotation and Trim

. . . where he decided to stow the other ten tons would make all the difference to Atropos, *could add a knot to her speed or reduce it by a knot, could make her stiff in a breeze or crank, handy, or awkward under sail.*

Hornblower and the Atropos, C.S. Forester

In the past few chapters we've discussed the waterplane from quite a few angles—how it affects behavior at sea, and how it can be used (or not used) to gauge carrying capacity. The waterplane, we've seen, affects how a boat responds to loading—where a boat will float and how she'll react to changes in weights and their locations. Designers use this information extensively and—if we take a more exact look at the waterplane and its effects—you can do the same for your own *Quickening Quahog.* If your *Quahog* floated, say, three inches below her boottop, you could determine how much weight to remove to get her to float higher again. Similarly, you could find the effect of adding additional tanks. Or, if *Quahog* were down a few inches by the bow, you might want to know how much trim ballast to add aft to get her level again.

Flotation and Trim Are Not the Same

Although most folks tend to use the words "flotation" and "trim" interchangeably, to the naval architect they're different and specific terms. *Flotation* is the amount a boat rises or sinks vertically with the addition of a relatively fixed load—it's also known as *sinkage.* (*Heave* is similar, but it is caused by the external force of wave action and it can be quite rapid.) *Trim* is the amount your vessel is angled up or down by the bow—again, as the result of more or less fixed internal loads. (*Pitch* is the equivalent motion caused by wave action—again, quite rapid.)

Waterplanes of Different Vessels

We've seen that the waterplane determines how much your *Quahog* will sink with a given load. Earlier we estimated the pounds per inch immersion simply by multiplying waterline beam by length on the waterline and taking 76 percent of that—which gives the approximate area of her waterline plane.

Actually, 76 percent is a fairly rough average. You can get more accurate results by using the following:

Light, Fine-Ended Sailboats	68%
Heavy, Full-Ended Sailboats	71%
Fine-Ended Displacement Power Craft	74%
Full-Ended Power Craft and Planing Vessels	80%

Say *Quickening Quahog* is a planing power craft 32 feet (9.75 m) on the waterline and 10.5 feet (3.2 m) waterline beam. Her waterplane would be:

32 ft. × 10.5 ft. × 0.80 = 269 sq. ft.

9.75 m × 3.2 m × 0.80 = 24.9 m²

That Sinking Feeling

The depth that some particular load will sink *Quahog* is the same as the buoyancy at the waterline (the weight or buoyancy of seawater 1 inch deep across the waterplane). So for square feet, we'd multiply by 5.34 pounds—the weight of 1 square foot of water 1 inch thick. For square meters we'd multiply by 10.25 kilograms—the weight of one square meter of water 1 centimeter thick. Then:

269 sq. ft. × 5.34 lb. = 1,436 lb./in.

24.9 m² × 10.25 kg = 255.2 kg/cm

In other words, if we add a 1,500-pound load, *Quickening Quahog* will sink 1 inch; or if we add 250 kilograms she'll sink 1 centimeter. Of course, if we remove 1,500 pounds or 250 kilograms, she'll rise the same amount.

Sinkage with New Tanks

Say, for instance, you've decided to increase *Quahog's* fuel capacity from 200 to 400 gallons (760 to 1,520 l) of diesel by adding a second 200-gallon (760 l) tank—a big increase. You'd have added over half a ton to her tank capacity, and the

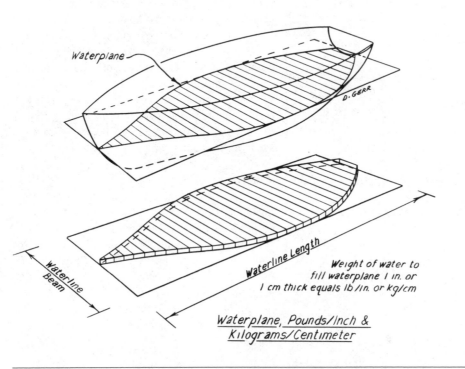

Waterplane

Waterplane Length

Waterline Beam

Weight of water to fill waterplane 1 in. or 1 cm thick equals lb./in. or kg/cm

D. GERR

Waterplane, Pounds/Inch & Kilograms/Centimeter

total weight difference, from empty to full tanks, would be 2,840 pounds or 1,290 kg (a gallon of diesel weighs 7.1 lb.—0.85 kg per liter). Accordingly, *Quickening Quahog* would rise or sink 2 inches (5 cm) from full tanks to empty (2,840 lb. ÷ 1,436 lb./in. = 1.97 in.—1290 kg ÷ 255.2 kg/cm = 5.0 cm).

With her original 200-gallon (760 l) capacity *Quahog* would've changed flotation by half this, or just under 1 inch (2.5 cm). Obviously all this doesn't account for the additional weights of crew, stores, and fresh water, which will sink her deeper still. (You can estimate these weights and calculate fairly accurately how much sinkage they'll cause in your boat.) On a craft the size of *Quickening Quahog*, an additional 200 gallons (760 l) of fuel or so might easily call for painting her boottop higher.

How Does She Trim?

Of course, we've been assuming that the new tanks lie conveniently over *Quahog*'s center of buoyancy, in which case she'd rise or sink straight up or down. (We have, in fact, been making this simplifying assumption throughout the previous chapters.) Clearly, matters are almost never this simple. There's seldom room amidships for large tanks or other heavy gear, generators, compressors, batteries, and all the gizmos that—stuffed into boats—make life more enjoyable. Accordingly, such weights often end up either well aft or well forward.

This brings us to trim. The farther from the center of buoyancy the new gear is, the more it puts a vessel out of trim—angled up or down by the bow or stern. A hundred pounds (45 kg) right over the center of buoyancy wouldn't cause a boat to trim by the bow or stern at all. She'll simply sink evenly into the water. Move that 100 pounds (45 kg) 5 feet (1.5 m) aft of the center of buoyancy and it'll create 500 foot-pounds (67.5 kgm) of moment to sink the boat down by the stern. This is where the term *moment to trim* comes from.

Trimming Moment

Moment to trim is the moment, in foot-pounds or kilogram-meters, required to change the trim of a boat by 1 inch or 1 centimeter; it's also known as MT1. An excellent method for determining MT1 is to take the square of the waterplane area, multiply that by 0.35 for square feet or 0.68 for square meters, and divide the result by the waterline beam. For *Quickening Quahog* this works out as follows (her waterplane, we estimated earlier, is 269 square feet or 24.9 m^2):

269 sq. ft. squared = (269 × 269) = 72,361

then 72,361 × 0.35 = 25,326

and 25,326 ÷ 10.5 ft. waterline beam = 2,412 ft.-lb./in.,

so Quahog's *MT1 = 2,412 ft.-lb./in.*

  or

24.9 m^2 × 24.9 m^2 = 620

then 620 × 0.68 = 422

and 422 ÷ 3.2 m = 132 kgm/cm,

so Quahog's *MT1 = 132 kgm/cm.*

If the combined centers of gravity of her two tanks—new and old—fell at 4 feet (122 cm) aft of her center of buoyancy then the moment of the tanks would be:

4 ft. × 2,840 lb. = 11,360 ft.-lb.

11,360 ft.-lb. ÷ 2,412 ft.-lb./in. = 4.7 in.

  or

1.22 m × 1,290 kg = 1,574 kgm

1,574 kgm ÷ 132 kgm/cm = 11.9 cm

This means that with her new 400-gallon (1,520 l) tanks full, *Quickening Quahog* will be about 4¾ inches (11.9 cm) out of trim—down by the stern. Of course, when the tanks are empty she'll be about 4¾ inches (11.9 cm) up by the stern or down by the bow.

Estimating the Center of Buoyancy

If you don't know the location of the center of buoyancy of your boat, it's usually about 55 percent of the waterline aft of the bow on sailboats and displacement-speed powerboats, and as much as 65 percent of the waterline aft of the bow on planing powerboats—aft of the bow at the waterline, that is. For most powerboats, 60 percent of the waterline aft of the bow is a good average. *Quickening Quahog*'s center of buoyancy then falls about 19.2 feet (5.8 m) aft of the waterline at the bow (32 ft waterline × 60% = 19.2 ft.—9.7 m × 60% = 5.8 m). Since her new tank is 4 feet (122 cm) aft of this, it must be 23.2 feet (7 m) aft of the bow or somewhere under her cockpit sole—not an unusual place for tanks—if it hasn't been used for something else already.

Adding the Effects of Flotation and Trim

What does all this mean, precisely? Well, a boat trims around her center of buoyancy like a seesaw pivoting about its support. Accordingly, roughly half the amount out of trim is at the bow and roughly half is at the stern. A better estimate is:

Sailboats	55% at the bow and 45% at the stern
Displacement Powerboats	55% at the bow and 45% at the stern
Planing Powerboats	60% at the bow and 40% at the stern

For *Quahog*, a planing powerboat:

4.7 inches × 0.6 = 2.8 inches—up by the bow, tanks full
4.7 inches × 0.4 = 1.9 inches—down by the stern, tanks full

or

11.9 cm × 0.6 = 7.1 cm—up by the bow, tanks full
11.9 cm × 0.4 = 4.76 cm—down by the stern, tanks full

(The opposite, naturally, with tanks empty.)

Accordingly, *Quickening Quahog*'s bow would be up just about 2⅞ inches (7 cm) and her stern down just under 2 inches (4.7 cm). Remember, though, that *Quahog* will also sink 2 inches (5 cm) deeper overall as a result of the weight of her full tanks.

This is how *Quahog* will float with her tanks full, taking into account the effects of both flotation (sinkage) and trim:

2.8 in. up at bow – 2 in. sinkage = 0.8 inch up at bow
1.9 in. down by stern + 2 in. sinkage = 3.9 inches down by stern

or

7 cm up at bow – 5 cm sinkage = 2 cm up at bow
4.8 cm down by stern + 5 cm sinkage = 9.8, say 10 cm down by stern.

How Much Change is Safe?

As a rough guide, average yachts can be allowed to rise or sink—above or below their design waterlines—a combined total (trim and flotation) of one percent of their waterline length. (As we saw in Chapter 14, heavy-displacement craft with high freeboards and robust construction can take more, and light craft with low freeboard less.) *Quahog*'s 32-foot (9.7 m) waterline divided by 100 gives 3.8 inches or 9.7 cm. Being down 4 inches (10 cm) at the stern is pushing this a trifle—in and of itself—but bearable. Keep in mind, however, that *Quickening Quahog* also has water tanks as well as passengers and gear. If many of these weights were aft, they'd sink *Quahog* even further by the stern, putting her well above the 1/100-waterline recommendation—a potential indication of a seriously out-of-trim and/or overloaded vessel. On the other hand, if these additional weights were added forward, they wouldn't hurt much, bringing the bow—formerly up 2.8 inches (7 cm)—down some, and lowering the stern very little.

Armed with the above information, you can determine how your boat will behave with any new weights—additional water tanks, new ballast keel, stores, new engine, tuna tower, flybridge, or whatever. An hour or two's noodling some evening, armed with no more than a scratch pad and a pocket calculator, will give you all sorts of useful information. In fact, you should find the moment-to-trim and flotation figures for your boat and scribe them on the front flap of your ship's log or some other readily accessible location. Commercial operators consider trim and flotation information so important that they have detailed trim and flotation charts and tables, often bound into books, giving complete information for almost every imaginable combination of fuel, cargo, and passenger loading.

PART 3

Shaping Her Up or What's Hull Form All About, Anyway?

. . . for the only way that a description of this art could have been written would have been in poetry, for this method of geometric procedure is nothing more nor less than an orderly arrangement of curves and dimensions to result in a shape of complete harmony. . . .

The Common Sense of Yacht Design,
L. Francis Herreshoff

CHAPTER 17

Defining Her Shape

The survey of the schooner had shown that her red coppered surfaces blended well with the white, that the slight apple to the bows gave way at the water-line to a fine-cut entrance beneath, that the bilges were hard, while the run, noticeably fine and forming the only concave lines extended an unusual distance forward.

The Saga of Cimba, Richard Maury

One of the most delightful, challenging, and fascinating things about boats is their shape; they're curved everywhere. Sweeping sheers meld with bold tumblehome and arced buttocks. Hollow entries and powerful runs harmonize with graceful diagonals. Even hard-chined power craft have few straight lines, though—on a lines drawing—some of the sections may appear straight. What's more, most lines curve not just in one direction, but in two or even three. It is this that produces the sensuous appeal of a well-proportioned hull. It's also this that can make boats daunting to build or repair. If you wanted to install some shelves in your living room at home, you'd just slice a few straight boards to suitable lengths and you'd be set. However, adding even something as simple as a single shelf over, say, the settee of your *Faultless Flyer* would require painstaking measurement of subtle curvature.

To really understand boats you need to be able to compare hulls, to deal with their complex shapes, to judge whether a vessel's heavy or light, stable or tender, suited to high speed or low. A large portion of this information is spelled out in the lines drawing. To a naval architect, this drawing is the heart of a design. Everything else—structure, accommodations, machinery, rig—must either fit in or work with the shape the lines describe. Knowing how to read a set of lines will help you understand your present boat better and make intelligent choices when you're studying boat plans, searching for your next *Dauntless Dancer.*

Hull Flavors—Smooth and Bumpy

There are three basic hulls—round bottom, vee bottom, and flat bottom. Round-bottom boats are usually the most attractive and strongest, with vee-bottoms coming in a close second. Flat-bottom boats are, broadly speaking, the least attractive and least strong; however, you must remember that these are only generalizations. Each and every one of these types can be beautiful and serviceable, and each is best suited for particular uses. Flat-bottom boats, for instance, are generally easier to build and have more initial stability for their weight than a comparable vee- or round-bottom boat. In fact, for small, simple, longshore craft such as rowing and power skiffs, and for dinghies, the simple flat-bottom vessel is frequently the best choice. On the other hand, if you're after an ocean cruising sailboat, then a round-bottom hull would most likely be superior—although a vee-bottom can be made to do very well indeed. Of course, planing powerboats almost invariably perform best as vee-bottom craft.

Multiple Bumps

There are also, of course, boats with hull shapes that fall somewhere between the vee-bottom and the round-bottom types. These are vessels with *multi-chined* hulls. Essentially, such hulls have hard corners, like vee-bottom and flat-bottom craft, but they have more of them. This allows the multi-chine hull to more nearly approach a true round-bottom shape while maintaining the flat surfaces—in one direction anyway—that can make construction a bit easier. This is an advantage principally for the one-off builder, though it may show up in slightly reduced costs for short-run semi-production craft. Swampscott sailing dories are really finely modeled multi-chine hulls, while semi-dories and flat-iron dory skiffs—like The Offshore Skiff—are good examples of more straightforward multi-chine hulls.

Lines Drawing Building Blocks

I often think of the lines drawing as sculpture in two dimensions. Not only does it define a complex three-dimensional shape precisely, but it can enable a practiced eye to visualize exactly what the finished hull will look like. Even without a practiced eye you can get plenty of valuable information from a lines drawing. You simply have to understand its fundamental building blocks.

A set of lines (the lines drawing) is made up of a series of "slices" taken through the hull at regu-

lar intervals, as well as the perimeter lines defining the edges or corners of the vessel. One of these perimeter lines is the *sheer* line, which is the line on the boat where the sides meet the deck. There is also a line or group of lines that determines the bottom of the boat at the centerline. At the *bow* (front of the boat) this line is called the *stem*, and at the bottom it is called the *keel* line. At the *stern* (back of the boat) this line is called the *sternpost*. Or it may be several lines that spell out the rear wall or aft side of the boat, called the *transom*. The transom usually is defined by a series of lines that show its outline where it intersects the sides of the hull and deck. Actually, these perimeter lines may be further divided. On vee-bottom, planing powerboats, the keel might come to a single point or line along the hull bottom; however, most vessels have keels with some width to them. Sailboats, naturally, have keels that project down from the hull bottom. The perimeters of such keels are defined by a series of edge lines instead of a single line down the centerline.

All lines drawings show three views of the boat: a side view or *profile,* a top view or *plan,* and a combined end-on view (from ahead and astern), called the *sections* or *body plan.* The perimeter lines alone—even on all three of these views—aren't sufficient to define a hull. They permit you to see the outline of the hull shape, but don't show the nature of curvature and shape within these boundaries. To establish this, the hull is cut into imaginary slices at right angles to each other and at regular intervals. The contours made by these slices clearly establish the curvature of the hull. This is exactly like the contour maps or topographical maps found in many atlases.

Sections or Stations Give Body

The principal reference lines are the *section* or *station* lines of the body plan. They are the shapes or curves created by cutting the hull from side to side and top to bottom just as you normally slice a loaf of bread. Usually they're at regular intervals to make it easier for the builder to measure them and lay them out full size. However, where the hull curves markedly, as at the bow and stern, additional, intermediate stations are often added in between the regular, standard stations. These additional stations help to clarify the shape in areas where there can be sudden, surprise changes.

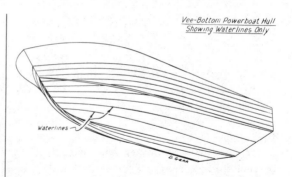

*Vee-Bottom Powerboat Hull
Showing Waterlines Only*

Waterlines

Waterlines

Waterlines are also curves created by "slicing" the hull, but here the hull is cut from side to side and from front to back. This is like slicing your loaf of bread along the top from front to back—you'd probably have some difficulty fitting such slices in your toaster. Standard practice is to single out the "design or datum waterline" (DWL) or "load waterline" (LWL). This is roughly—but only roughly—the line at which the boat is expected to float when normally loaded. (In reality, as we saw in the last chapter, boats seldom float exactly at their DWL. Sometimes they're more heavily laden and float deeper, and at other times they're nearly empty and so sit higher. Or, changes in loading may trim a vessel up or down by the bow or stern.)

Usually, the DWL is used as *the* fundamental reference line. Heights for defining most other lines—as well as locations of most gear, hardware, joinerwork, and equipment—are generally measured from the DWL. Alternatively, though, the designer may specify an extra, imaginary reference line—outside of the hull—and take measurements from it. This line is parallel to the waterlines and either above or below the hull. It's called the *baseline*.

Buttocks

Another set of slices taken through the hull are the *buttock* lines. These lines are the curves that result from slicing the hull from top to bottom and from front to back—like slicing your loaf of bread from end to end along the side (which would no doubt cause the other members of your household some confusion). The majority of lines drawings show three buttock lines, though other variations are common. Almost always, one of the buttocks will fall pretty close to halfway out from the boat's centerline. This is—obviously—one-quarter of the beam out from the centerline, and such buttocks are called—not surprisingly—*quar-*

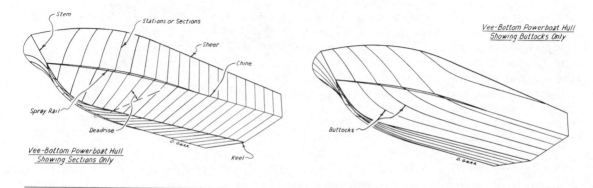

*Vee-Bottom Powerboat Hull
Showing Sections Only*

Stem · Stations or Sections · Sheer · Chine · Spray Rail · Deadrise · Keel

*Vee-Bottom Powerboat Hull
Showing Buttocks Only*

Buttocks

ter-beam buttocks. (See next chapter.) The buttocks help define the hull underbody, and an experienced architect can tell much about a boat's potential performance from their shape. Frequently, the quarter-beam buttock alone will be indicative of speed potential.

Diagonals

There's only one other type of slice taken through the hull. These are the *diagonals.* Unfortunately, although they are very useful, the diagonals cause much confusion. The reason for this is that the diagonals are not slices through the hull at right angles (like sections, waterlines, and but-

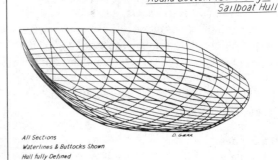

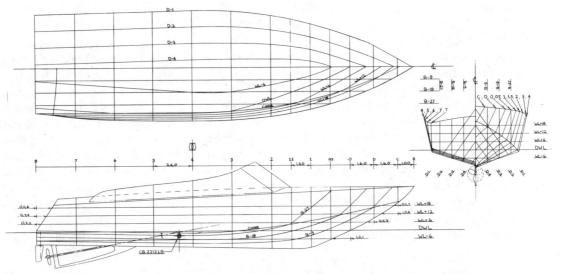

The lines of Sorcerer, *a typical vee-bottom powerboat. Notice that the* sections *in the* body plan *on the right are not symmetrical. The left half of the plan shows the slices through the after portion of the hull; the right half, the front. The diagonals are clearly seen as straight lines sloping down and out in this view. The* buttocks *are the straight vertical lines and the* waterlines *are the straight horizontal lines in the* section *or* body plan.

The lower view of the boat is the profile. *It shows the buttocks, the keel, the sheer, the stem, the chine,*

and the deck at the centerline. The midship section *or* station *is marked by the circle with two intersecting half-circles at station 4.*

Most boats are divided into an even number of stations, *starting with station zero at the waterline where it intersects the stem or bow and working aft. This is an eight-station boat, so midships is at station 4.*

The bottom half of the top view shows the boat in plan *view, or as viewed from above. In the plan view, the curvature of the waterlines, the chine, and the sheer can be seen.*

tocks); instead, they're slices taken—how else (?)—diagonally. This is very much like slicing your poor loaf of bread from corner to corner lengthwise. (By this time your family's probably forbidden you to go near any loaves of bread at all). It's not exactly like this, however, as the diagonal slices on a lines drawing start from the vertical centerline and slope down and out from there.

Some designers consider the diagonals so important that they fair the lines drawing using the diagonals and sections alone, adding the waterlines and buttocks afterward. (Fairing lines is the process of making sure there are no humps or bumps on the hull surface they define.) On sailing yachts in particular, the diagonal approximates the shape that the water "sees" as it flows beneath the hull. In fact, when a boat's heeled over, water must flow under and around the shape defined by these lines. For this reason, a smooth, sweeping set of diagonals, with no humps or hard spots, is something every designer strives for. Frequently, the diagonals of well-proportioned sailing yachts approximate the sections of very large circular arcs for much of their length. Naturally, vee-bottom and flat-bottom craft have bumps in the diagonals where they cross the chine. This is one reason such vessels have somewhat more resistance. Things are seldom this simple though. High-speed powerboats, for instance, actually do much better with the vee-bottom's humps, which—among other things—can help break the water free of the hull, reducing wetted surface resistance.

She's the Same on Both Sides, Isn't She?

It's important to remember that boat hulls are perfectly symmetrical—or at least they're supposed to be. Thus, to simplify the lines drawing only one half of the hull is drawn in (the other side obviously being the same). For this reason, when you look at the section view or body plan, one side of the boat's centerline (usually the right side) shows the section curves or slices of the front half of the hull, and the other side shows the

sections of the after or stern half of the hull. Similarly, when you look at the plan view you'll see waterlines and the sheer line of only one half of the hull. Usually, for convenience, the diagonal lines (curves that result from "slicing" the hull diagonally) are drawn on the opposite side of the centerline from the waterlines in the plan view. This makes the drawing appear somewhat lopsided until you realize that the other half of the plan and section views are not supposed to correspond but instead show different aspects and parts of the vessel.

A Grid for Reference

Since all the slices taken through the hull are perfectly flat planes, they appear as straight lines when viewed edge-on. Thus, the waterlines are regularly spaced straight lines in the sections and the profile view; the sections are straight lines on the plan and profile views; and the buttocks are straight lines on the sections and plan view. All these regularly spaced straight lines form a reference grid for measuring and defining hull shape.

If you look at the lines of *Sorcerer*, you can see the section lines as rows of straight lines in the plan and profile view. Similarly, the waterlines and buttocks appear as straight lines in the section view. By referring to this grid, the builder can locate and identify the shape of your hull at any point. *Sorcerer* is generally representative of a vee-bottom powerboat hull. Her chine is a good example of a line that's curved in three directions. The tip-off is that the chine shows up as a curved line in all three views. In the plan view, it curves in toward the bow. In the profile it curves up toward the bow and in the section view it curves—not surprisingly—up and in.

The drawing of *Madrigal's* lines are that of a typical round-bottom hull. On this drawing, though, the grid lines have been removed. This makes it easier to visualize the sweep or curvature of the hull without the clutter of these grid lines. You can judge a great deal about a hull from such a drawing; however, without the reference grid, building or repairing a boat from such a drawing would be very difficult; accurate measurements are nearly impossible.

You can see the diagonals on both of these drawings. They appear as straight diagonal lines, radiating down and out from the centerline on the section views. On *Sorcerer*'s drawing the curved diagonals have been drawn in above the plan view showing the waterlines. If you look carefully, you can just make out the hump in her outermost diagonal (D-1), at the bow, where it crosses the chine. *Madrigal*'s drawing shows the diagonals below the plan view of the waterlines.

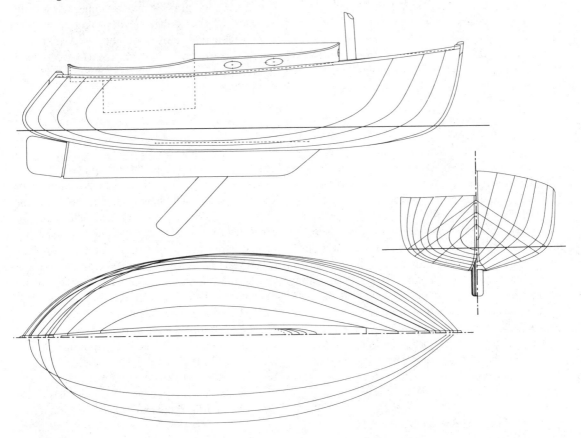

Lines of Madrigal *(see Chapter 9), a round-bottom sailboat. In this drawing, most of the straight reference lines (the station, buttock, and waterlines) have been omitted. This makes it easier to see the sweep of these lines in the views that show them as curves.*

The upper view is the profile, *showing the sheer, keel, and buttock lines. The top half of the lower view shows the hull in* plan *(as viewed from above). The sheer and waterlines are depicted here.*

The lower half of the bottom view shows the curve of the diagonals, which may be seen defined by the three angled, straight lines in the small section *view on the right. The section view shows the cross-sectional shapes of the hull.*

The omission of the straight reference lines makes a drawing like this almost useless for actual building purposes.

CHAPTER 18

Reading Between the Lines

Nothing can be loved or hated unless it is first known.

Leonardo da Vinci

There are so many different sorts of boats, even for the same purpose, that it's often hard to determine which is most suitable. Why is one vee-bottom runabout shaped differently than another of the same size? What's the practical difference between a vee-bottom trawler yacht and a round-bottom one? How does a designer decide on the shape of a particular design, and how can you understand what he or she has done?

There are no simple answers to the above; however, there are many things you can look at that will give you a better handle on a vessel's best use and intended performance. If you know how, armed with a lines drawing, you can read between the lines, seeing many of the things a designer looks for.

Now, many aspects of hull shape depend on aesthetics and accommodations. *Salty Sal,* for instance, could require noticeably different lines (hull shape) if her engine were placed amidships instead of aft to make room for, say, an aft cabin. Similarly the sweep of the sheer and the height of the topsides is frequently controlled by the amount of accommodation volume required, as well as by styling. Still, particularly in the underbody (below the waterline), the lines can reveal volumes about performance and behavior.

Watch the Run

As mentioned in the last chapter, one of the most telling groups of lines in a lines drawing are the buttocks aft. These lines define the shape of the *run*. The *run* is the after half of the underside of a hull. It has a tremendous influence on resistance and speed potential. If you look at the profile view (the view from the side) of a lines drawing, the angle that the buttocks make relative to the horizontal reveals the hull's speed capabilities. For almost all average hulls the quarter-beam buttock (see previous chapter) defines the average angle of all the buttocks. A hull with a quarter-beam buttock that climbs sharply up, say at 15 degrees or so, from the underbody amidships to the stern is

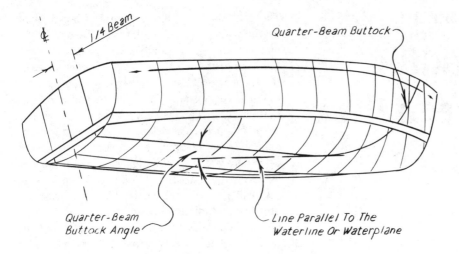

Quarter Beam Buttock Angle

suited for low displacement speeds and load carrying. If, on the other hand, the quarter-beam buttock runs aft flat and horizontal, then you're looking at a design intended for high planing speed. Naturally, buttocks that sweep up at an intermediate angle are meant for intermediate speeds. The faster the boat, the flatter her run (the smaller her buttock angle) should be.

Adjusting for Length

Of course, since longer boats are faster than shorter ones, these speeds and angles are really dependent on length. The way to deal with this is to talk about speed potential in terms of speed-length ratio. This is just actual performance speed in knots divided by the square root of the waterline length, or:

Speed-to-Length (SL) Ratio $= Kts \div \sqrt{WL(ft)}$

Speed-to-Length (SL) Ratio $= Kts \div \sqrt{WL(m)} \times 3.28$

A good general guide for buttock angle is:

	SPEED-TO-LENGTH RATIO	BUTTOCK ANGLE
Planing Boats	2.5 or higher	2° or less
Semi-Planing Boats	1.5 to 2.5	3° to 6°
Displacement Boats	1.5 or less	7° or more

If *Salty Sal* were 40 feet (12.2 m) on the waterline and had a quarter-beam buttock that swept up at 6 degrees, you'd expect her to run at a speed-length ratio of 2 or so. Accordingly, *Salty Sal* could be expected to go about 12 to 13 knots.

Square root of 40 ft. = 6.32
(12.2 m × 3.28 = 40)
6.32 × 2 = 12.6 knots

Now, this doesn't guarantee that she'll actually go this speed; however, her buttock lines indicate that she'd do best in this range. You could install a smaller engine and run her at lower speed, but she'd be more inefficient than a comparable hull with greater sweep to her buttocks—a hull designed to operate at this lower speed. Similarly, you could stuff *Salty Sal* with twin supercharged engines with hundreds more horses than required to move her at 13 knots. *Salty Sal* would go faster—not necessarily much faster—with these monster powerplants, but she'd cause a lot of fuss in the water and waste a great deal of fuel doing it.

Curving the Buttocks

So far, we've assumed that *Salty Sal's* buttocks are straight lines. What if they curve up in profile? Straight-line buttocks are best suited to higher-speed craft, whereas buttocks that curve up (as well as angle up) as they rise toward the stern are intended for low speed. This is why virtually all high-speed powerboats have straight buttocks while nearly all cruising sailboats have buttocks that sweep up in a graceful arc.

Now, though, we have to deal with the trade-off all designers face when shaping the run. Flat, low-angle buttocks are great for going fast, but they're not so good for comfort and seakeeping. Steeply angled and upward-curved buttocks are ideal for comfort and safety at sea, but are only suited to lower-speed craft. Of course, this means that it's particularly difficult to design a really high-speed vessel with the seakeeping abilities of a slower, deeper-hulled boat. You can see that boats with flat, low-angle buttocks will be light skimmers, while steep, angled buttocks lead down to a deep, full, and thus heavy underbody. Making the best compromise for a particular boat and her specific service is the kind of challenge that keeps boat design endlessly interesting.

Line Them Up Neatly

Yet another important aspect of the run is whether the buttocks are parallel to each other or not. If all the buttocks are parallel for most of the length of the run (from midships aft) then the hull underbody has constant deadrise aft. What's that? Well deadrise is the angle the sections of the hull

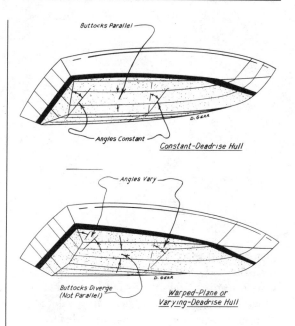

make with the ground (horizontal). A deep-vee craft has lots of deadrise, whereas a flat-bottom skiff has no deadrise at all. (The Off Soundings 34 of Chapter 10 is a modified deep-vee hull, while the Jersey Sea Skiff of Chapter 4 is just that—a flat-bottom skiff.) If you measure the angle of *Salty Sal's* deadrise amidships and find it to be 14 degrees, and then measure it right aft at the stern and get 8 degrees, she has varying deadrise. On the other hand, if the angle was the same all the way from midships to the stern, her deadrise would be constant. The buttocks give you a way to judge this at a glance. If they are all parallel the deadrise is constant; if they run at angles to each other the deadrise is varied.

A Wrong Turn at High Speed

Many years ago designers of planing power craft went off on the wrong tack. They rightly concluded that a flat underbody generates the most planing lift for a given horsepower, so they set out to make their hulls as flat as possible aft—at the

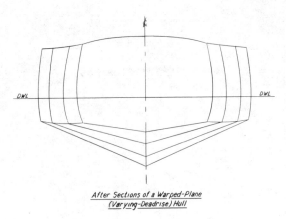

After Sections of a Warped-Plane
(Varying-Deadrise) Hull

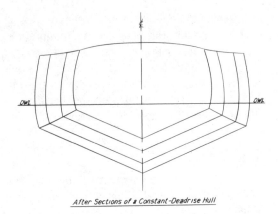

After Sections of a Constant-Deadrise Hull

planing surface. Of course, they quickly discovered that they had to make the deadrise all the way forward—at the bow—very large (sharp) to prevent pounding. Accordingly, these designers started forward with tremendous deadrise (a sharp entry) and decreased the deadrise gradually and steadily as they went aft, until—all the way at the stern—there was no deadrise at all. The bottom of these boat's transoms were dead flat straight across. In other words, they were designing hulls with deadrise that varied over the entire length.

Unfortunately, they didn't realize that this had something of a detrimental effect on water flow under the vessel. As a boat rushes forward over the water, the water flows along under it, pressing upward. When the deadrise varies, the water pushes along the underside of the hull and follows the twist or warp in the underside caused by the changing deadrise angle. As a result, the water not only flows aft, but twists or rotates as well. Forcing all this water to rotate in addition to flowing straight aft takes extra energy; it represents some lost speed and wasted power. These days, most planing hulls have nearly constant deadrise in their run. The deadrise is very pronounced forward and then decreases considerably as you follow it to amidships; however, from there aft deadrise remains pretty constant.

Naval architect Lindsay Lord coined the term *monohedron* for constant-deadrise hulls, and *warped plane* or *warped bottom* for varying deadrise. He was a fervent advocate of constant-deadrise hulls, and claimed that warped underbodies caused a "suction" aft that pulled the stern down and slowed the boat. Although he was essentially correct about the general desirability of constant deadrise, time has shown he was mistaken about the suction. For example, if this mysterious suction existed, you'd be able to drill a hole in the hull bottom and—while speeding along on a plane—have no water come in. This has actually been tried on numerous hulls—warped bottom and constant-deadrise. No matter what type of hull, or where the holes were drilled, the minute they were unplugged a nice jet of water would shoot out of them. You had to stand back to avoid being hit in the eye.

In fact—in spite of its additional drag—moderate warp can, on occasion, be useful. The warp tends to hold a planing hull's nose down—just the opposite of Lord's prediction, by the way. It also gets the hull's center of buoyancy further aft and makes room for heavy engines and gear astern. On craft where obtaining these features is important, moderate warp is desirable. As always, though, it's a compromise—such boats require a bit more power to reach the same speed.

Constant deadrise or parallel buttocks are more important the faster you want to go. Thus, high-speed, race-type planing hulls should, ideally, have buttocks aft so parallel they look as if they were ruled from graph paper. Medium-speed planing sportfishermen and cruisers often have some small degree of warp. Cruising sailboats do not require perfect parallelism, though. Here considerations of appearance and seakindliness can lead a designer to use steep, curved, and unparallel buttocks. Since such craft never go much above hull speed, the drawbacks are slight indeed. Nevertheless, if you had two otherwise identical sailboats, one with constant deadrise and the other with a warped run, the constant-deadrise boat would be slightly faster.

Knifing Through

Buttocks aside, deadrise itself plays an important role in performance and comfort. Because deep-vee hulls have become so successful and popular, many sailors think that this deep-vee (large deadrise) hull shape is *the* most efficient for speed. Surprisingly, just the opposite is the case. The early designers were absolutely right: a flat underbody (with no deadrise at all) is the fastest configuration. The problem here is that a totally flat skiff would literally pound herself and her crew to pieces at top speed in any sort of sea. (Narrow skiffs with sharp entries can be made to go surprisingly fast without excessive pounding.)

Obviously, the more vee (deadrise) the underbody has the softer riding it will be. Such deep-vee hulls essentially knife through the seas. Unfortunately, as the deadrise increases so does the power required to lift the boat out on a plane. Once again, the designer is forced to trade off and compromise between two conflicting requirements: less deadrise, faster but harder riding; more deadrise, slower but softer riding. For planing, generally craft with more than 20 degrees of deadrise in the run are intended for open-water

work, while vessels with deadrises of 8 degrees or less are best as inshore speedsters.

"Bilge!" you say. "Hard or soft?"

Still another aspect of hull shape is hard chine or vee-bottom versus round bottom or round bilge. Actually, there isn't as clear a difference between the two types as you might think. If you take a vee-bottom hull and simply round the corners a bit at the chine, you'll have a round-bilge hull. If the rounding was done to a small, tight radius you'd have a round-bottom hull with a *hard turn of the bilge*. As the radius increases, the bilges get softer and softer (*soft bilges*) until the corner almost disappears altogether. Such vessels have *slack bilges*.

Again, you're faced with conflicting choices. For planing powerboats, a sharp, hard chine is most efficient (it breaks the water clean from the

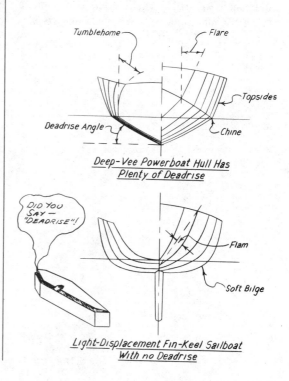

Deep-Vee Powerboat Hull Has Plenty of Deadrise

Light-Displacement Fin-Keel Sailboat With no Deadrise

bottom, reducing wetted surface); however, just as with deadrise and buttock angle, round-bilge hulls are softer riding and more seakindly than hard chines. Properly designed, though, the hard chine can offer an additional advantage; it can act as a spray rail, knocking spray and foam down, keeping water off you and the deck. For sailboats, the hard chine produces additional stability, which adds up to extra sail-carrying power. As usual, there's a drawback—the hard chine increases wetted surface (at displacement speed) and thus generates more resistance than the round bilge. Nevertheless, hard chines are very popular. Not only is the increase in stability for a given beam welcome, but the hard chine (or hard bilge) can make for more usable volume aboard. In some materials, such as metal or plywood, hard-chine vessels are also easier to construct.

In medium-speed boats particularly, the difference between hard-chine and round-bilge hulls can be merely one of aesthetics. Both can be made seaworthy and efficient. The round-bilge version will be a bit easier riding but will have a tendency to roll a bit more deeply, while the hard-chine version will feel steadier but have a slightly snappier roll. Nevertheless, as a general rule, hard chines are for high-speed inshore work and round bilges are for low-speed offshore service.

By now we've defined many of the standard types of boats on the market. It's no accident that high-speed, rough-water boats like, say, Cigarettes, are long with hard chines, constant deadrise, and deep-veed afterbodies. Length, constant deadrise, and hard chines produce speed, while the deep vee aids in soft riding through a chop. Similarly, it's no surprise that heavy trawler yachts are often round bilged, with steeply angled buttocks and deep deadrise. These craft are intended to carry large loads slowly through all sorts of weather. Even high-speed sailing dinghies follow these rules. Such vessels often have have round bilges, but they also have shallow buttocks with constant deadrise and shoal, flat underbodies (low deadrise) for planing.

CHAPTER 19

Speaking Volumes

. . . the aim of exact science is to reduce the problems of nature to the determination of quantities by operations with numbers.

James Clerk Maxwell

Over the past few chapters we've discussed displacement from many angles: how it is the real indicator of boat size, how it affects performance and load-carrying ability, and how it can be distributed. But what exactly *is* displacement? We've seen that it's the weight of a fully equipped vessel, loaded and ready for sea—tanks two-thirds full, two-thirds the usual stores, and full crew.

Thanks to Archimedes

Displacement, though, is more useful and more subtle than simple weight. The tip-off here is the word *displacement,* which comes from its literal (and engineering) meaning—the weight of water your boat (or anything that floats) moves aside as it's lowered into the water. It was crafty old Archimedes who first figured out that, if you catch all the water moved aside (displaced) by a floating object and weigh that water, it'll tip the scales at the object's weight—*exactly!* Accordingly, if you know the true weight of a boat, you also know its exact underwater volume. It's the volume it'd take to hold that weight of water. Similarly, if you know the volume you require for a boat, you know how much she'll weigh. Designers, in fact, use the terms "hull volume," "weight," and "displacement" interchangeably; they really mean the same thing.

Because of the importance of displacement and volume, naval architects spend much of their time calculating and locating volumes (also surfaces). Knowing how much volume is in a hull, how it's distributed, and where its center is located is critical to successful design. Similarly, the architect has to determine the volumes and centers of ballast, fuel and water tanks, and the like. Of course, it's necessary to establish the surface area of the hull that's in contact with the water (wetted surface)—to estimate skin friction—and to determine the areas of planking, bulkheads, and so on—to determine weights. Understanding how this is done can be quite handy for everything from noodling prospective modifications to sketching out your own dream vessel.

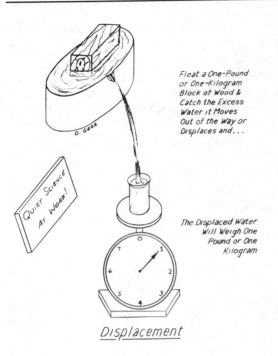

Float a One-Pound
or One-Kilogram
Block of Wood &
Catch the Excess
Water it Moves
Out of the Way or
Displaces and...

D. GERR

QUIET SCIENCE
AT WORK!

The Displaced Water
Will Weigh One
Pound or One
Kilogram

Displacement

The Defining Section

When a designer first lays out the lines of a boat, he or she will frequently start by defining the midship section. This is simply a cross section of the craft as if it had been sliced in half in the middle. An amazing number of things are determined, right off, by this shape—for example, is the boat hard chine or round bilged? Deep or shallow hulled? Flared or straight-sided?

Say Seagoin' Sam—your local boat designer—is working up the lines for your future motorsailer, *Dread Naught.* Sam will, among other things, determine *Dread Naught's* displacement when he draws her midship section. Let's say her midship section has an area below the waterline of 31.4 square feet (2.92 m²). You and Seagoin' have decided on a waterline length of 44 feet (13.4 m). Since a boat's displacement is just the volume of her hull below

the waterline, it's a simple matter to multiply the 31.4 square feet (2.92 m²) of *Dread Naught's* midship section area times her waterline length of 44 feet (13.4 m) to get a volume of 1,380 cubic feet (39.1 m³). This alone does not give the volume of *Dread Naught's* hull; however, it does give the volume of an imaginary object—a prism—the same shape as *Dread Naught's* midship section and exactly 44 feet (13.4 m) long. (In fact, 1,380 cubic feet—at 64 pounds per cubic foot, for salt water—works out to an incredibly high 88,320 pounds of displacement; or 39.1 m³ at 1,025 kg per m³, for salt water, works out to 40,077 kg.)

Of Coefficients and Prisms

Fortunately, there's a very simple relationship between the volume of this imaginary prism and the true displacement of *Dread Naught,* or any other vessel. (Sam will, no doubt, mutter something about the *prismatic coefficient.*) It just so happens that almost every displacement-speed hull requires a prismatic coefficient between 0.51 and 0.56 for best efficiency. (Fifty-four percent is the usual optimum.) *Dread Naught*—in this case—will have 54 percent of the displacement of the imaginary prism. Seagoin' Sam will simply multiply 88,320 pounds times 54 percent to get *Dread Naught's* displacement of 47,770 pounds, or 40,077 kg times 54 percent = 21,640 kg. This is a good figure for a 44-foot-waterline (13.4 m) craft, giving her a displacement-to-length ratio of 250.

Now, the prismatic coefficient is actually indicating how fine, pinched, or tapered the ends—bow and stern—are. A perfectly square scow or barge would have no taper or fineness and so her prismatic coefficient would be 1. Since *Dread Naught*—like most normal boats—comes to a point at the bow, as well as narrowing quite a bit at the stern, her prismatic coefficient is significantly lower.

The Right and Proper Prismatic Coefficient

To find the prismatic coefficient of any boat:

$$\text{Prismatic Coefficient (PC)} = \frac{(Disp\ (lb) \div 64)}{Midship\ Area\ (sq\ ft) \times WL\ (ft)}$$

$$\text{Prismatic Coefficient (PC)} = \frac{(Disp\ (kg) \div 1025)}{Midship\ Area\ (m^2) \times WL\ (m)}$$

Over the last 75 years or so, designers have learned that the faster a boat is intended to go, the higher her prismatic coefficient ought to be, as follows:

	SPEED-LENGTH RATIO	PRISMATIC COEFFICIENT
Displacement-Speed Boats	1.5 or less	0.51 to 0.56
Semi-Displacement Boats	1.5 to 2.5	0.60 to 0.70
Average Planing Boats	2.5 to 4.0	0.70 to 0.72
High-Speed Planing Boats	4.0 and higher	0.72 to 0.78

This makes plenty of sense when you consider the shape of most planing powerboats. Although such craft are quite sharp at the bow, they're usually absolutely square—without taper—at the stern. This additional fullness helps create an efficient planing surface, and shows in impressively larger prismatic coefficients.

Accordingly, if you'd asked Seagoin' Sam to design *Dread Naught* as a 15-knot power cruiser, he'd have picked a prismatic coefficient of 0.62. This would drastically affect the choice of midship section and, naturally, the characteristics of the hull. If, for instance, Seagoin' had used the slower motorsailer's 31.4 square feet (2.92 m²) of midships area he'd have produced a vessel with too much displacement. Thus, Sam would choose a smaller, shallower, and/or narrower midship section of, say, 23 square feet (2.14 m²). In this case, he'd get 40,156 pounds—23 sq. ft. × 44 ft. × 0.62 × 64 lb./cu. ft. = 40,156 lb., or 2.14 m² × 13.4 m × 0.62 × 1,025 kg/m² = 18,210 kg. This works out

well for a higher-speed boat, producing a displacement-to-length ratio of 210.

You Can be a Displacement Detective

Now, all of this can be useful even if you're not designing a boat. If you've ever wondered what the displacement of a particular design is, all you need is her waterline length, waterline beam, and depth of hull. Say you've fallen for a salty hooker—*Varnished Viking*—38 feet (11.58 m) on the waterline, but don't know her displacement. The info sheet says her beam's 12 feet 3 inches (3.73 m) and her draft is 3 feet 11 inches (1.18 m). Of course, no one's told you this design's waterline beam; however, it's usually about 95 to 98 percent of the overall beam. Accordingly, you can estimate *Varnished Viking*'s waterline beam at 12 feet (3.65 m).

Midships Percentages

All that's left is to make a good estimate of *Viking*'s midship area. You guessed it, there's another coefficient to help us out here. It's called the *midship coefficient.* (Seagoin' Sam has probably been making arcane remarks about this as well.) The midship coefficient is just the area of the midship section divided by the area of a rectangle of the same width and depth. An excellent average is 0.65, or 65 percent. Picture the sectional shape of the boat. A perfectly triangular midship section would have a midship coefficient of exactly 0.5 or 50 percent, whereas a perfectly rectangular midship section would have a coefficient of exactly 1.0—the same area as a rectangle—because it *is* a rectangle!

This is just about what you'd find in many barges or scows. The famous racing E-scows have midship coefficients approaching 1.0. Shallow vee-bottom power craft with flattish floors (low deadrise) and flattish-bottom sailboat hulls will usually have midship coefficients of around 0.73, while very sharp deep-vee hulls can have midship coefficients of 0.55 or so. Since *Varnished Viking*

Midship Coefficients

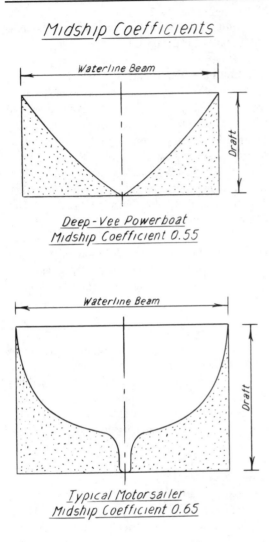

Waterline Beam

Draft

Deep-Vee Powerboat
Midship Coefficient 0.55

Waterline Beam

Draft

Typical Motorsailer
Midship Coefficient 0.65

has an average midship section we'll use a mid-ships coefficient of 0.65 and can figure her midship area to be 30.4 square feet (2.8 m²)—12 ft. WL beam × 3.9 ft. depth of hull × 0.65 = 30.4 sq. ft., or 3.65 m WL beam × 1.18 m depth of hull × 0.65 = 2.8 m².

Varnished Viking is a displacement-speed craft, so we know her prismatic coefficient must be very close to 0.54. A bit of multiplication gives her approximate displacement at 39,920 pounds (18,040

kg)—30.4 sq. ft. midship area × 38 ft. WL × 0.54 = 623.8 cu. ft., and 623.8 cu. ft .x 64 lb./cu. ft. = 39,923 lb.; or 2.82 m² midship area × 11.58 m WL × 0.54 = 17.6 m³, and 17.6 m³ × 1,025 kg/m³ = 18,040 kg.

Volume for Everyone

Soon after Seagoin' Sam has settled on a mid-ship section and waterline length, he'll be ready to start the lines drawing that determines the detail shape of *Dread Naught*'s hull. (Naturally there are many other considerations, like freeboard, flare, and sheer, that Seagoin' will have been working out as well.) From this drawing, Sam will calculate *Dread Naught*'s exact displacement and center of buoyancy.

For some reason, this process gets shrouded in deep mystery. Designers will crank up comput-ers and invoke high-falutin' formulas like Simpson's Rule, the trapezoidal rule, even—brace yourself—Tchebycheff's Rule. Well, you don't need to know any of them. All that's required is simple addition and multiplication. Let's say—for a change—that you'd asked Sam to design a high-speed run-about—*Dynamo Dart*. Sam'll calculate the area of each of *Dynamo Dart*'s sections. If you want to fig-ure her displacement yourself just add up all the section areas and multiply by the distance each station (section) is separated from its neighbor. For *Dynamo Dart* this would work out as follows:

STATION	SQUARE FEET	METERS²
0	0.00	0.00
1	0.40	0.04
2	1.26	0.12
3	2.06	0.19
4	2.70	0.25
5	3.14	0.29
6	3.26	0.30
7	3.26	0.30
8	3.20	0.30
9	3.06	0.28
10	2.96	0.28
total section areas =	25.30 sq. ft.	2.35 m²

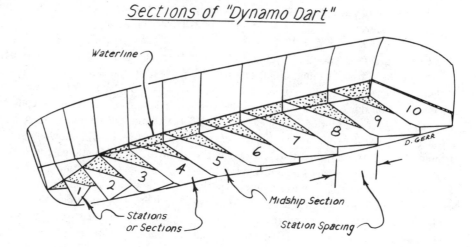

Sections of "Dynamo Dart"

Waterline

Stations
or Sections

Midship Section

Station Spacing

D. GERR

Stations are spaced 20 inches apart, which is 1.67 feet or 50.8 cm. So:

1.67 ft. station spacing × 25.3 sq. ft. section areas = 42.25 cu. ft. displacement and,

42.25 cu. ft. volume × 64 lb./cu. ft. (for salt water) = 2,704 pounds displacement

  or

0.508 m station spacing × 2.35 m² section areas = 1.19 m³ displacement and,

1.19 m³ volume × 1,025 kg/m³ (for salt water) = 1,219 kg displacement.

That's all there is to it—no mystery at all, and you don't need anything more complicated than a simple pocket calculator. What's more, the process is the same for every hull and every type of boat. In fact, you can use the same method to find the volume or weight of ballast, the capacity of oddly shaped tanks, and even the surface area of irregular shapes. All that's required is regularly spaced section areas or, in the case of surfaces, distances.

Finding Station Areas

Of course, you still have to figure the area of each section, which can be a bit trying. Naval architects use a planimeter to ease the chore, but these gizmos cost several hundred dollars and are hardly worth the expense—unless, that is, you plan to open your own design office. You can determine section areas very accurately, however, just by taking transparent graph paper and laying it over the sections. Measure the area of each square—in the scale of the lines drawing—and count the number of squares contained by each of the individual sections. The smaller the squares, the more accurate your measurement, but the more tedious the task. Still, using this method, it won't take you over an hour or two to figure the displacement for any hull you have the lines drawing for.

Where's the Center?

One crucial question remains—where's the center of buoyancy? This is the center of volume of the hull. As we saw in Chapter 16, once a designer knows this he or she can locate the weights of the boat so that her center of gravity falls right over her center of buoyancy—the only way to get a boat to float level.

The Cardboard Buoyancy Calculator

Again, there are all manner of imaginative formulae for locating the center of buoyancy, and, once again, you don't need any of them. Instead, you can locate the center of buoyancy by balancing a piece of stiff paper or cardboard. Draw a straight line on the cardboard to represent the centerline of your boat and then, at regular intervals, draw perpendicular lines to represent the sections. At each section, measure out from the centerline a distance equalling the area of that section—for example 4.8 square feet equals 4.8 inches, or 0.44 m² equals 44 mm. (Make sure you

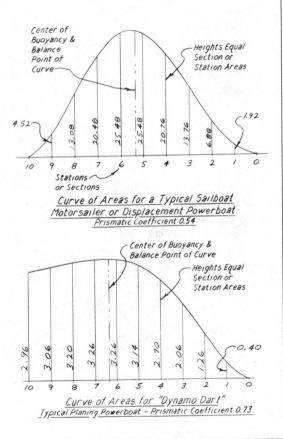

Curve of Areas for a Typical Sailboat
Motorsailer or Displacement Powerboat
Prismatic Coefficient 0.54

Curve of Areas for "Dynamo Dart"
Typical Planing Powerboat – Prismatic Coefficient 0.73

use the same scale and the same method for each section area.)

When you've marked all the section area distances, draw a smooth curve between them—connecting the dots, as it were—and cut the entire shape out. What you've created is a *curve of areas*. This curve shows graphically the distribution of volume in the hull. Not surprisingly, curves of areas with sharp, hollow ends correspond to boats with low prismatic coefficients, and vice versa.

Balance the curve cutout on a ruler edge, and right at the balance point is the center of buoyancy. For *Dynamo Dart* this falls a bit aft of station six. Careful measurement shows that it's 35 percent of the station spacing distance aft of station six, and since you know the stations are 20 inches apart (50.8 cm) on the actual boat, you know that the center of buoyancy is 7 inches (17.8 cm) aft of station six (20 in. × 0.35 = 7 in. or 50.8 cm × 0.35 = 17.8 cm). You now know all you need to calculate the displacement and center of buoyancy of any hull you have the lines for.

So, How Accurate Is All This Estimating?

We can check the accuracy of our earlier method of estimating displacement with the prismatic coefficient. *Dynamo Dart* is a real design on my drawing board. Her overall beam is 4 feet 10 inches and her depth of hull is 11 inches or 0.92 feet (147 cm beam, 28 cm draft). Ninety-eight percent of 4 feet 10 inches is 4.8 feet, which is a good estimate of her waterline beam. (Or, .98 × 147 cm = 144 cm). Since *Dynamo Dart* is a shallow, vee-bottom boat, we can estimate her midships coefficient at 0.73. Accordingly, we'd get a midships area of 3.22 square feet (0.3 m²)—4.8 ft. × .92 ft. × 0.73 = 3.22 sq. ft., or 1.44 m × 0.28 m × 0.73 = 0.3 m².

This is very close to the actual midships area in our earlier displacement calculation. Now, *Dynamo Dart's* waterline is 16 feet 8 inches or 16.67 feet (5.08 m), so the volume of our imaginary prism works out to 53.7 cubic feet or 1.52 m³— 16.67 ft. × 3.22 sq. ft. = 53.7 cu. ft., or 5.08 m ×

$0.3 \text{ m}^2 = 1.52 \text{ m}^3$. As *Dynamo Dart* is a high-speed vessel (speed-length ratio of 4.5), we can figure a prismatic coefficient of around 0.73. Using this, we'd get a displacement of 39.2 cubic feet and 2,508 pounds, or 1.11 m^3 and 1,138 kg.—0.73×53.7 cu. ft. = 39.2 cu. ft., and 39.2 cu. ft. $\times$ 64 lb./cu. ft. = 2,508 lb., or $0.73 \times 1.52 \text{ m}^3 = 1.11 \text{ m}^3$, and 1.11 $\text{m}^3 \times$ 1,025 kg/m^3 = 1,138 kg.

This is less than 150 pounds (80 kg) under our carefully calculated displacement—the weight of one good-sized crewmember—or only 7 percent off. Not bad—you can see how handy this approach can be for extracting hard numbers about the designs you're interested in. For instance, if you knew the displacement of a boat, you could work backwards to find her prismatic coefficient and judge the speeds she was intended for.

Using a bit of common sense, you can learn volumes about the designs you read about in magazines and see on the water. Don't let a few numbers scare you off.

PART 4

How Fast Will She Go?

There was a great difference in boats, of course. For a long time I was on a boat that was so slow we used to forget what year it was we left port in. But of course this was at rare intervals.

Life on the Mississippi, Mark Twain

CHAPTER 20

Power Yardsticks

A 40-knot slipstream seared the cheeks, engines trumpeted, shells whined and some cracked with sonic booms as they whipped close overhead; the boat was clear of the water for a third of her length, and astern the foam rushed away into blackness like a mountain cataract.

Night Action, Captain Peter Dickens

Powerboaters probably spend more time chewing over how fast their boats can go and should be able to go than any other single topic. Getting the most "revs" out of an engine is a high priority. Changing props, "trying a bit of cup," and even fitting new gearboxes are common pastimes.

A question that seldom seems to be asked is, "How fast do you want or need to go, and at what speed does your boat operate best?" These are the critical questions for most powerboats. If your boat's engine doesn't seem quite able to generate its advertised top rpm, this may not be an especially bad thing. It's probably because your vessel is substantially heavier than the relatively stripped-out factory prototype. Thus, your engine can't generate the power needed to push this extra weight at top speed and top rpm.

Of course, if the main reason you own your boat is to blast along at maximum speed, then you'll want to take all the steps required to make your muscle boat operate effectively at full throttle. In this regard, it's particularly important to keep weight down. For most boaters, however, a more leisurely approach yields better results.

To Speed or Not To Speed?

First off, there's the question of how fast you actually want to go. It's not unusual to hear talk about topping 60 knots; however, few yachts really approach this speed. A case in point is a design I worked on several years ago. She was a 32-foot (9.7 m), all-custom, center-console aluminum sportfisherman. Her weight was low; she had no superstructure; and she was long and narrow, with a sharp entry and a beautiful clean, flat run. Even so, with twin 220-hp (164 kw) Yamahas, she seldom exceeds 44 knots at full throttle. Interestingly—with this boat's sophisticated Loran providing accurate speed information—she's had a peculiar habit of passing other boats that were "doing 60."

The fact is that a true 44 knots (50 mph) is *scareeeeaming* along on the water. Even though this sportfisherman was designed with these speeds in mind, it was more comfortable—for the crew and the boat—to slow down to a steady 26 knots or so (30 mph). This is one heck of a respectable clip for cruising. At 44 knots, it was all you could do to keep the chart—folded into a tiny square—from being torn out of your hands by the wind; pounding was not exactly comfortable, and the blast of spray-laden air was, well . . . breathtaking. Exciting, yes; but for how long? Even muscle boats—designed specifically for high speeds—can be pretty rough going at more than 50 knots or so. Spending hours at this speed is like tobogganing down a boulder-strewn mountain for an afternoon's entertainment.

Most of the production powerboats on the market operate best between 18 and 30 knots. Yes, you can push some of them faster, but to what purpose? Except on vessels very specifically designed for high speed, you'd be straining your engine, straining yourself, and burning fuel at a rate that would warm the heart of any OPEC oil minister. Displacement boats, of course, travel quite a bit slower—their speed being largely dependent on their waterline length.

Power versus Weight—The Main Event

For planing boats, the most critical factor determining speed is the power-to-weight ratio. A well-shaped hull and low windage are important, but without enough power even the sweetest hull just won't get up and go. If you look at the Planing Speed chart you can make a good estimate of how fast your boat can be driven with a given engine or engines—either her current machines or the new ones you've been dreaming of installing. Simply divide your boat's displacement (in pounds or kilograms) by her total shaft power (in horsepower or kilowatts) and follow this value up to the suitable line, then run across to get speed in knots. (For inboards, shaft power—the power that actually gets to the prop—is about 95 percent of rated engine power. Current outboard power is rated at the shaft, so no additional deduction is required.)

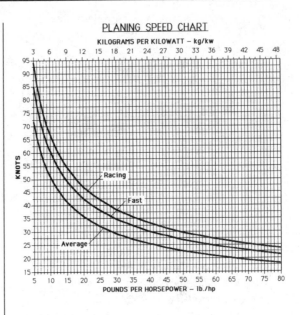

Weigh Your Boat

We've been discussing displacement extensively over the past few chapters, and once again, the trick to getting good answers out of this chart is to use the true weight of your boat when she's loaded and ready for sea. Remember, advertised weights are almost always substantially lower than your vessel's real displacement with you and all your gear aboard. To find real displacement, smaller boats can actually be weighed. Some yards have a scale that can be placed on the hoist during haulout, or—if you can trailer your boat—just drive her over to a truck scale. Remember to fill all tanks about two-thirds full and to keep all your usual gear aboard. Also, don't forget to add crew weight. At 150 pounds (68 kg) or more apiece, a party of six weighs nearly half a ton!

If your boat's too big to be weighed and you can't locate a convenient yard with a scale on their Travelift, you must make the most intelligent estimate possible. One reasonable approach is to take the advertised hull weight, add 10 to 15 percent, plus 150 pounds (68 kg) per crewmember, and:

	POUNDS/ GALLON	KILOGRAMS/ LITER
Diesel Fuel	7.2	0.86
Gasoline	6.1	0.73
Fresh Water	8.4	1.00
(use two-thirds full for all tanks)		

This should give you a pretty fair estimate of your actual ready-for-sea displacement. If you do a lot of cruising or carry a lot of fish or dive gear and so on, you should estimate all these weights as best you can and add them in. Your boat usually weighs more than you think; the longer you've had her, the more gear you've put aboard, so the heavier she is.

Figuring Planing Speed

Still another variable in the Planing Speed chart is the type of hull you have. Most cabin cruisers will fall in the *average* category. Thus, if you know your boat's actual displacement and horsepower, simply divide displacement by horsepower and read across the chart to find your speed with that power plant. Say your *Nelly Belle* weighs 10,000 pounds (4,536 kg) and has an engine delivering a continuous 312 hp (233 kw) at the prop; then *Nelly Belle*'s pounds per horsepower works out to 32, or 19.5 kg/kw (10,000 lb. ÷ 312 hp = 32 lb./hp, or 4,536 kg ÷ 233 kw = 19.5 kg/kw). Reading from the Planing Speed chart, this gives a rather high cruising speed of 28 knots.

If *Nelly Belle* were more of a souped-up cruiser with a lowish superstructure and some racing-boat characteristics (long and narrow, constant deadrise, etc.) you'd read her speed from the *fast* category. If she were a super muscle boat with little or no superstructure and particularly long, lean lines, or an ultralight, stripped-out day runabout, then you'd read her speed from the *racing* category. Be conservative in your estimates though. The faster you want to go, the harder it is to get an engine that will generate enough power.

This is because more powerful engines are bigger and heavier, requiring substantially more fuel. All of this adds weight, detracting from speed.

How Much Power—Really?

Another critical variable is the power that your engine is really capable of delivering to the propeller. Most engine manufacturers rate their engines' hp at top rpm. This is often an impressively large number; but unfortunately, you just can't drive your poor engine this way for long. Most engines are designed to run continuously at around 60 or 70 percent of their top-rated rpm (see Chapter 25). For estimating purposes, you can assume power at 60 to 70 percent rpm is roughly 60 or 70 percent of maximum. Thus, if your engine is rated at 500 hp (373 kw), at 2,800 rpm you'd have to figure on operating at 1,800 rpm on a continuous basis (65 percent of 2,800 revs). At this rpm you'd be generating around 325 hp (242 kw).

As mentioned earlier, even this isn't the actual shaft horsepower your prop "sees." Due to friction in the gearbox, stuffing box, and bearings, you must subtract another 4 to 6 percent for additional lost power. This brings your actual continuously available shaft horsepower down to 312 hp or 323 kw. (Remember *Nelly Belle*: she actually had twin 250 hp (186 kw) engines—500 hp, or 373 kw.) By using a little common sense and following this procedure carefully, you can make a good estimate of how fast you can and should expect your boat (or future boat) to go with her current or future power plant.

A Curvaceous Solution

Now, the professional way to do all this is to go to the engine manufacturer and request performance curves for your engine. These curves show power, fuel consumption, and torque versus rpm. For most purposes you'll want to operate your engine at the position of maximum combined torque and power. Of course, this usually falls somewhere around 65 percent of maximum rpm, but with the performance curves you don't have to guess.

You'll also want to keep an eye on fuel consumption. Light, high-speed gas engines generally deliver the maximum combination of torque and horsepower at a lower percent of top rpm than do heavier, slow-turning engines. Thus, if you're estimating for a light, gas-powered engine, you'd want to assume continuous operation at 60 percent of maximum. A heavy marine or industrial diesel, however, might operate reliably and continuously at as much as 80 percent of maximum rpm. Performance curves take the guesswork out of this.

The Speed of Displacement

Displacement and semi-displacement hulls perform differently than planing hulls. Instead of climbing up over their bow wave and leaving their stern wave behind, these vessels simply push the water aside. Such craft quickly reach a point of diminishing returns when it comes to added horsepower. This is apparent from the Displacement Speed chart.

Let's take a diesel, trawler-type cruiser with a 40-foot (12.2 m) waterline—the *Ocean Queen*. If we assume she displaces 33,000 pounds (14,970 kg)

and has an engine delivering an actual cruising shaft horsepower of 75 (56 kw), then her pounds per horsepower works out to 440, or 267 kg/kw (33,000 lb. ÷ 75 hp = 440 lb./hp, or 14970 kg ÷ 56 kw = 267 kg/kw). Reading off Displacement Speed Chart 1 you'll see that she'll cruise at a speed-length ratio of 1.36 or so. Enter *Ocean Queen's* waterline of 40 feet or 12.2 meters on Displacement Speed Chart 2 and you'll get the square root of her waterline (in feet)—6.3. Multiply 6.3 times the speed-length ratio of 1.36 to find her cruising speed of 8.5 to 8.6 knots. If you run up the 40-foot line (or down the 12.2 m line), you'll find that 8.5 to 8.6 knots falls nicely between the high and low hull-speed lines. Indeed, you can quickly determine standard hull speed for any waterline on Displacement Speed Chart 2.

Costly Power

What would happen if we tripled the power to 225 hp (168 kw)? We'd get 147 pounds per horsepower (89 kg/kw). Sound like a good deal? Well, working through Displacement Speed Charts 1 and 2, you'll find that, at 147 lb./hp (89 kg/kw), the same

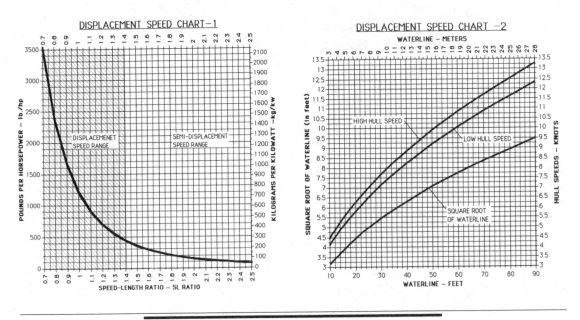

40-foot (12.2 m) waterline boat will go all of 12.8 knots—a gain of a mere 4.3 knots. In other words, you've gained only 50 percent in speed with a 300 percent increase in power and fuel consumption! The faster you try to drive a displacement hull the worse this "strain-gain" relationship gets.

In fact, most displacement hulls just won't go much faster than hull speed (1.3 to 1.4 times the square root of their waterline length in feet. For *Ocean Queen*: $\sqrt{40}$ ft. $\times$ 1.35 = 8.5 knots). Thus, if *Ocean Queen* is a true displacement boat, no amount of additional power will drive her much over 8.5 knots. (Some well-formed displacement hulls can be driven to speed-length ratios as high as 1.45 or 1.5, but it's quite costly in power.) Many power cruisers, however, are of the semi-displacement type. This means their hull shape has been modified slightly to enable them to lift out and plane to some degree. Really heavy, full-bodied craft such as cruising sailboats and workboats, though, will not go faster than hull speed no matter what you do. More power would just be wasted.

Choosing Charts

How do you know when to use the Planing Speed chart or the Displacement Speed charts? Generally, planing begins at speed-length ratios between 2.5 and 3. As a rough guide:

SPEED-LENGTH RATIO TO START PLANING

Light Flat-Bottom Boats Shallow-Vee,	2.5 to 2.7
Modified Deep-Vee Boats Deep-Vee Boats,	2.7 to 3.0
Heavy Vee-Bottom Cruisers	2.9 to 3.1

Find the square root of the waterline from Displacement Speed Chart 2 and multiply that by the speed-length ratio to start planing. If, for example, *Nelly Belle,* had a 28-foot (8.5 m) waterline and was a modified vee-bottom boat, her speed-length ratio to plane would be about 2.8. The

square root of her waterline, from Displacement Speed Chart 2, is 5.3, and 2.8 times 5.3 is 14.8 knots get-up-on-plane speed. As long as the results from the Planing Speed chart predict speed higher than this, it's the chart to use. Otherwise, use the two Displacement Speed charts.

Guzzling Gas, or Getting the Range

Fuel consumption and cruising range are, naturally, greatly affected by engine horsepower. The best way to figure fuel consumption is to look at the performance curves for your engine. You can make reasonably accurate estimates, however, using the following rules of thumb for four-cycle engines:

	GALLONS/ HP/HOUR	LITERS/ KW/HOUR
Diesel Engines	0.055	0.279
Gas Engines	0.100	0.507

Returning to the gas-engine *Nelly Belle,* if she cruises at 2,800 rpm, with her engines delivering 325 hp (242 kw), she's burning 32.5 gallons (123 l) every hour. (325 hp $\times$ 0.10 gal./hp/hr. = 32.5 gal, or 242 kw $\times$ 0.507 l/kw/hr. = 123 l.) Now, it's simple to figure cruising range. We've seen that *Nelly Belle* cruises at 28 knots and that she has a 300-gallon (1,136 l) fuel capacity. At 32.5 gallons per hour, her 300 gallons will last 9 hours and 15 minutes; or at 123 l/hr, her 1,136 liters will last 9 hours and 15 minutes. Twenty-eight knots for 9¼ hours gives a range of 259, say 250 nautical miles.

You'd use the same procedure for diesel engines. Thus, at *Ocean Queen*'s 75 hp or 56 kw (we'll figure around 80 hp or 60 kw at the engine to allow for shaft losses) she'd burn 4.4 gallons (16.6 l) per hour. If *Ocean Queen* also has a 300-gallon (1,136 l) fuel capacity, her running time, at 8.5 knots, would be 68 hours and 15 minutes; and 8.5 knots times 68¼ hours gives a 580-mile range. However, a boat with *Ocean Queen*'s displacement could carry more fuel, say, 600 gallons (2,272 l) giving her a range of 1,160, say, 1,100 nautical miles.

Taking It Easy

An interesting thing happens when you slow *Ocean Queen* down to 7.5 knots—a bit under hull speed. From Displacement Speed Chart-2, we find that the square root of her waterline is 6.32. Divide 7.5 knots by 6.32, for a speed-length ratio of 1.18. Reading from Displacement Speed Chart 1, we find we'd need only 700 pounds per horsepower (425 kg/kw). This works out to a mere 47 shp—50 hp or so at the engine (35 kw—37 kw at the engine). Now, *Ocean Queen* is burning only 2.75 gallons (10.4 l) per hour. With her 600-gallon (2,272 l) tanks she then has a range of 1,630 nautical miles. Not bad—a 40 percent gain in range for a 12 percent drop in speed. You can see that slowing down a bit can pay off in fuel economy and range as well as in comfort. This holds true for high-speed planing boats as well as displacement types—up to the point at which they come off plane. At that point, planing hulls lose efficiency.

Summer Moon—A Cost-Effective Megayacht

Back in Chapter 13, we discussed the benefits of long, lean hulls for high speed. It's possible to combine the benefits of slender hulls with low speed and lower power to get truly breathtaking range and comfort at moderate cost. The drawings show the profile and arrangement of *Summer Moon*. At 81 feet 8 inches (24.9 m) overall and 15 feet 6 inches (1.7 m) beam, her length-to-beam ratio is 5.26 to 1. A displacement of 55 tons gives a displacement-to-length ratio of just 138. Because of *Summer Moon*'s long waterline (72 feet 10 inches—22.2 m) her simple displacement speed is quite high—12 knots. In fact, her slender hull has so little resistance that she can be driven up to a speed-length ratio of 1.7 or 14.5 knots with ease. (This is still hull speed for a very slender hull, not semi-displacement speed. You can find more detailed information on low displacement-to-length–ratio performance in my *Propeller Handbook*.)

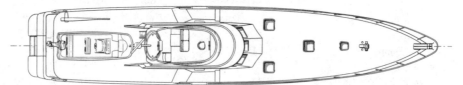

Profile and arrangement of Summer Moon.

LOA	81 ft. 8 in	(24.9 m)
LWL	72 ft. 10 in.	(22.2 m)
Beam	15 ft. 6 in.	(4.7 m)
Draft	7 ft. 0 in.	(2.2 cm)
Disp.	55 tons	

Power	Cat 3408B, 318 hp (237 kw) at 1,200 rpm; 2.0:1 reduction gear
Generators	(2) Northern Lights 20 kw
Fuel	3,200 gal (12110 l) diesel
Water	550 gal. (2080 l)
Speed	14.1 knots max. 9 to 12 knots cruise
Range	2,500 to 5,000 miles

The bottom line here is that *Summer Moon* can be driven at 14 knots with a single 318-hp (237 kw) diesel. This gives her a range of 2,480 nautical miles at 14 knots, 4,000 at 9.2, knots and an incredible 5,100 miles at 8.1 knots! *Summer Moon* can cross any ocean and explore any out-of-the-way region with fuel to spare.

Indeed, *Summer Moon* can be thought of as a cost-effective megayacht. Her hull is welded hard-chine steel (her superstructure's aluminum) for toughness and for inexpensive construction at commercial yards. Additionally, her machinery layout has been kept simple for a craft of this type. Like all long, narrow boats, she has little room for her length, but she has fantastic room for her displacement and cost—she even has a stand-up engine room, workbench, and washer/dryer. Slender hulls offer the most performance for the dollar at high or low speeds, especially when you add in fuel and operating costs. In larger sizes—like *Summer Moon*—they can take you to the ends of the earth in comfort without breaking the bank.

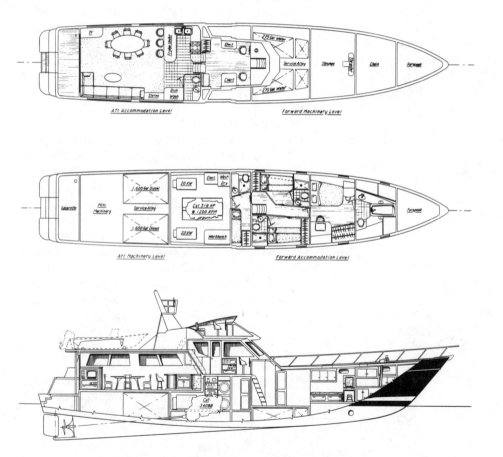

Arrangement and inboard profile of Summer Moon. *Note the privacy for each cabin. The crew's cabin (by the engineroom) is fitted with upper and lower bunks. The engineroom itself has full standing headroom, a workbench, and a separate washer/dryer. The length permits plenty of machinery space, all low down.*

CHAPTER 21

So You Like To Sail Fast?

I wish to have no Connection with any Ship that does not sail fast for I intend to go in harm's way. . . .

John Paul Jones

There's an old saying: "Get any two sailboats together on about the same course and you've got a race." I doubt if any sailor doesn't take pride in how fast his or her vessel can go in the right circumstances. Of course, we know that some craft are just plain faster than others, but why? What makes for speed under sail?

The answer is quite complex. There are myriad factors—sometimes at odds with each other—that yield speed. For instance, a long waterline produces a faster boat. Make this boat narrow as well and you decrease resistance, for a slippery, easily driven hull. Fast, right? Well, not necessarily. If she's too narrow she'll have lost stability and wouldn't stand up to the sail required to drive her. When drawing up a sailboat, a designer is constantly juggling conflicting factors like this to get the best compromise for a given vessel.

Length and Speed

One of the principal factors governing speed for sailboats is length on the waterline. Since the majority of sailboats—especially cruising sailboats—are displacement craft, their top speed is determined as—you guessed it—hull speed ($1.34 \times \sqrt{WL}$ (ft.) = knots, or $1.34 \times \sqrt{WL}$ (m) $\times 3.28$). Unlike powerboats, which have a steady source of power, sailboats operate at their top or hull speed only for that small portion of the time when the wind is blowing fairly hard. Thus, when you speak of a fast sailboat, you have to consider two different sorts of speed potential. The first is the obvious—maximum or top speed. The second is actually more important. This is whether or not a craft can keep sailing well—at a sizable percentage of hull speed—in widely varying conditions. Such a craft will have high average speeds. This is what makes for a *fast passagemaker.*

The Other Factors

Looking into boat speed further, you have to examine the power plant (the sails and rig); resistance (the drag of the hull); and the ability to carry a big enough "engine" (rig)—in other words, stability. This is complicated still further by the fact that vessels of different sizes have radically different proportions of sail area, ballast, and wetted surface; the laws of relativity and similitude are ever busy. To get around this and to be able to compare widely differing boats, designers use *coefficients for comparison*. The most critical of these are the *displacement-to-length ratio, sail area–displacement ratio*, and *sail area-to-wetted surface ratio*.

Displacement-to-Length Ratio

We discussed displacement-to-length ratio in Chapter 14. Briefly, it measures how spread-out the hull volume or displacement is. Longer, narrower hulls have less resistance, and this shows in their lower displacement-to-length ratios. If they have sufficient stability—an important if— low displacement-to-length–ratio hulls are always fastest.

Sail Area–Displacement Ratio

Sail area–displacement ratio (SA/Disp) is simply a measure of power to weight, just as with powerboats. The more sail for a given weight, the more power you have to drive your boat and the higher the SA/Disp ratio. As always, we have to allow for different size boats, so in this case we figure sail area–displacement ratio as sail area (in square feet or meters) divided by displacement (in cubic feet or cubic meters) to the two-thirds power.

Don't worry! This sounds like higher math, but you can find displacement to the two-thirds on any student-grade scientific calculator (simply square a number, then find its cube root), or you can use the accompanying charts. For, say, a 2,800-pound (1,273 kg) sloop, you'd find she was 1.25 tons. Reading from the Displacement to the ⅔ Power charts (or using a calculator) you'd find her displacement to the two-thirds to be 12.6. With this number, you can determine how much

sail you need for good performance. Simply multiply displacement-to-the-two-thirds by the following sail area–displacement ratios:

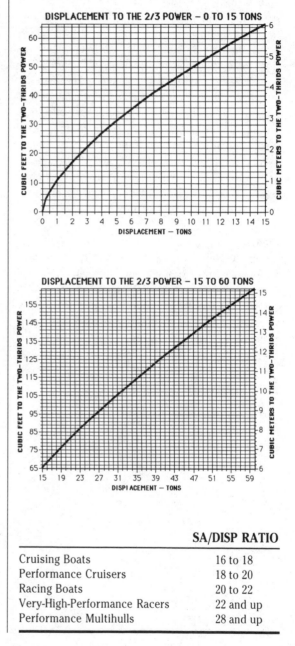

SA/DISP RATIO	
Cruising Boats	16 to 18
Performance Cruisers	18 to 20
Racing Boats	20 to 22
Very-High-Performance Racers	22 and up
Performance Multihulls	28 and up

Generally, boats with SA/Disp ratios below 16 are undercanvased and will be slow. SA/Disp ratios between 16 and 19 are excellent for comfortable cruising. Vessels with these ratios can be relied on to sail fairly well *if* (and this is the big if) they can stand up to their rig. Boats having SA/Disp ratios much over 22 are real flyers. Such ratios are common in multihulls—which are often over 30—as a multihull can generate tremendous stability without lugging along the weight of ballast. If you come upon numbers like this in a monohull, however, you have to assume that you're looking at a boat intended for out-and-out racing. To get a monohull to stand up to this much sail (relative to her weight) you have to make her hull and accommodations very light to cram as much ballast down low as possible.

Figuring Sail Area

In figuring SA/Disp ratio, by the way, you should use the area of your full mainsail (*E* times *P* divided by 2—neglect the roach) plus what's called "100 percent of the foretriangle area." This is simply *I* times *J* divided by 2, or height from deck to jib halyard block times distance from face of mast to headstay chainplate, divided by 2.

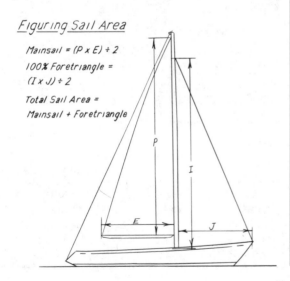

Figuring Sail Area

Mainsail = (P x E) ÷ 2

100% Foretriangle = (I x J) ÷ 2

Total Sail Area = Mainsail + Foretriangle

Don't throw in the area of your spinnakers, bloopers, and gennys. You'd get a pleasingly large number, but since no one else does this, your number wouldn't mean much. (For ketches and yawls add in half the area of the mizzen. For schooners use the full area of foresail, main , and 100 percent foretriangle.)

Sail Area-to-Wetted Surface Ratio

Though you hear a fair amount of talk about the SA/Disp ratio, sail area-to-wetted surface ratio is frequently neglected. This is a shame, as it's important to speed as well. The weight of your boat (her volume) causes resistance due to wavemaking. This is important at high speed—at low speed you only make small waves. The SA/Disp ratio measures your rig's ability to overcome primarily high-speed resistance. For most of us summer sailors, performance in light to moderate air is the ticket. What slows us down in these conditions is resistance due to friction, not wavemaking. Friction is a function of how much hull (wetted surface) is in contact with the water. In fact, this is one of the main reasons that narrow fin-keel boats can be faster than long-keel vessels. Fin keelers have eliminated all the surface area of the keel aft to the rudder and forward to the stem.

Ironically, sail area-to-wetted surface (SA/WS) is the easiest of all the ratios to figure mathematically. Just divide sail area (in square feet or meters) by wetted surface (in square feet or meters)—that's it. If your boat has 540 square feet (50.2 m²) of sail and a wetted surface of 234 square feet (21.7 m²), then her SA/WS is 2.3. Unfortunately, there's no easy way for you to find the wetted surface area of your boat. If you can track down the designer, he or she should be able to give you this information from their files. Most dealers, though, don't have such numbers available, and only a naval architect could measure your hull accurately enough to make it worth the trouble. Nevertheless, SA/WS *is* important. If you're stuck deciding between two designs and can get information on their SA/WS ratios, I'd recommend that you give a lot of thought to the boat with the higher ratio.

As a rule, SA/WS ratios below 2 indicate a boat that will be sluggish in light going. This can be partially remedied by carrying plenty of light sails; however, the same hull with a taller rig would have a better ratio to begin with, and could set even larger light-weather kites. SA/WS ratios between 2.2 and 2.4 are a good average and indicate excellent performance in light weather. Should you locate a boat with a SA/WS ratio above 2.6, you've stumbled on a ghoster *par excellence;* if you're in a light wind area—such as Long Island Sound—pounce.

Does It All Stand Up?

Okay, great, you've found a boat with a low Disp/WL ratio (say, 200) and high SA/Disp and SA/WS ratios (say, 19 and 2.4). She must be fast, right? Well, most likely, but there is still the question of stability. In fact, there is the whole question of speed upwind or VMG (velocity made good) to windward. With insufficient stability, you could spread full sail downwind, but upwind you'd have to reef.

Working Your Way Up

Many cruising sailors say they aren't interested in sparkling upwind performance. I think this is a mistake. No, you needn't go to the lengths that all-out racers do in squeezing out every ounce of upwind speed, but upwind potential determines much of your vessel's overall passagemaking ability. After all, you can make a bathtub sail downwind, but if you want to get from here to there in it you may wait an awfully long time for the wind to shift around and blow from the right direction.

Skimming Dishes

Now, if you have a long, narrow boat with a tall rig, she'll probably do well off the wind. Unless both her hull shape and ballast arrangement are very carefully engineered, however, she won't have stability enough to be at her best upwind. This is where skimming dishes like the Inland Lakes scows come in. Because these boats are so shallow-bodied, they have very low displacement ratios. Because they're so wide, they have the stability to carry plenty of sail—even more so because they carry shifting ballast in the form of crew. On the other hand, skimming-dish craft tend to pound in a chop, and worse still, they can capsize most impressively. These boats are wonderful for day racing, but of course they're not much use for cruising or offshore work.

So, What Makes for Stability?

Figuring the stability of a ballasted monohull is painstaking work. Entire books have been written on this subject. However, the following factors make for increased stability: high ballast ratio (lots of ballast); low ballast placement (deep keel, perhaps with a ballast bulb); low rig weight; hard bilges; and wide beam. The more of these factors a given boat has, the more likely she is to be stiff. If, for instance, you're looking at a long, narrow boat with lots of ballast (say, a 44-percent ballast ratio), a deep keel and hard bilges, all these factors would add up to compensate for her lack of beam; she'd be able to stand up to quite a good press of sail. This—in my opinion—is one of the best formulas for all-around speed under sail in a seaworthy package.

Estimating Stability

In Chapter 15 we saw how to determine stability for an existing boat by using roll timing. If you're noodling a new design and want to determine its righting moment, the best you can do—without having a designer do extensive calculations—is to make an intelligent guesstimate of what that type of vessel's roll time would be. You can then use the stability and wind-pressure-coefficient formulas from Chapter 15 to try out different rigs. The following roll times can be used as a rough guide:

- Heavy motorsailer/cruisers: 25 percent or less ballast ratio, high cabins or wheelhouse—roll time 0.95 overall beam
- Heavy cruisers: ballast ratio between 25 percent and 35 percent, no high cabins—roll time 0.90 overall beam
- Medium cruisers: ballast ratio at least 35 percent, no high cabins—roll time 0.85 beam overall
- Performance cruisers: ballast ratio 35 percent or more, moderately deep keel, no high cabins—roll time 0.80 overall beam
- Average racers: ballast ratio 40 percent or more, deep keels, low cabins or flush decks—roll time 0.75 beam overall
- Special racers (BOC, OSTAR-type): ballast ratio 45 percent or more, extra-deep keels—roll time 0.7 to 0.5 beam overall (without water ballast)

All roll times are related to beam overall in meters.

Note that vessels with an unusual amount of flare—whose beam at the waterline is less than 90 percent of the beam overall—should use 110 percent of the waterline beam, not beam overall.

Ballasted sailboats usually have roll times less than 1 times beam—in meters. They need this stability to carry their rig. Sailboats don't suffer from uncomfortable motion as a result of this rapid roll time, because the force of the wind on their sails and the water on their keel stabilizes them against roll quite nicely.

Influence of the IOR

The current trend in many production boats is to emulate the form of IOR and IMS racers. These vessels can be quite fast, as they have shallow (sometimes almost flat) underbodies combined with plenty of beam and tall, light rigs. Additionally, they have very small, deep, narrow fin keels yielding low wetted surface. All this produces craft that have plenty of power (the ability to stand up to a breeze—especially with the large crew sitting on the weather rail) and low resistance. Unfortunately, wide, shoal-bodied, hard-bilged hulls like this have very lively motion and little stowage space in the bilge.

A cruiser has to examine the trade-offs in this type of craft carefully. Even worse is that the rule penalizes full ends—buoyancy molded into the hull, bow and stern—particularly at the bow. As a result, IOR-influenced designs trim further and further down by the bow as they heel. Eventually, when hard pressed, the stern lifts so far out that it exposes large areas of the rudder. In this condition the rudder ventilates, losing grip on the water and losing steering control.

Getting to the Bottom of Things

After being able to stand up to her rig, reducing leeway (sliding sideways downwind) is the most important factor in increasing a boat's VMG. Presently, there are two approaches to this problem—the brute force approach and the finesse approach. The brute force approach is the old tried-and-true long keel. The idea here is that with so much lateral area, a boat just can't do much in the way of sliding sideways. This works and has worked well for as long as vessels have been going to sea. It has a number of great advantages. It makes for safe grounding, additional low storage space inside, a steady helm and, most important, it works even when you're moving slowly. The long keel's big drawbacks are its substantial wetted surface (compared to the fin keel) and, in racing, its length, which inhibits quick turning.

Fin Keels

The finesse approach is to use a deep, narrow, hydrodynamically shaped fin keel. As we mentioned earlier, such keels reduce wetted surface tremendously. They do have some significant disadvantages though. Grounding out on a boat with such a keel is risky business. Unless the rudder's carefully proportioned to balance out oscillations, the quick helm is tiresome for a cruising sailor. Most significantly, however, such keels rely on hydrodynamic flow to generate lift—just like an airplane wing. This lift force pulls the boat to weather and reduces leeway more effectively than anything else known—at high speed. The problem here is that when vessels with fin keels slow down, especially if slammed to a stop in a strong breeze and chop, they lose the lift generated by flow. With so little lateral area compared to a full keel, there isn't much to keep the boat from sliding downwind. In other words, to be really effective these keels have to be kept moving, and moving well.

Again, this is fine for a racer with plenty of crew, but a cruising sailor will want a compromise—a keel with enough lateral area to resist leeway at low speed but not so long as to create excessive wetted-surface drag. Such keels are also less sensitive to trim and can be kept "in the groove" with less attention. For the sailor interested in fast passagemaking and high average speed with minimum effort, this is the way to go. A bonus is that such a keel is usually long enough to give some real grounding protection.

Once you know a boat's sail area, you can determine if she's got sufficient lateral plane from the following rules of thumb:

LATERAL PLANE AS PERCENT OF SAIL AREA

Total lateral plane, full-keel boats*	12% to 16%
Lateral plane of fin keel only	7% to 10%
Lateral plane of centerboard(s) only	3.5% to 5%
*includes rudder	

Lateral plane areas vary widely; however, if the areas are much less than indicated, you should be suspicious of that boat's ability to hold on without sliding to leeward upwind. If the areas are well above those given, she'll do well in heavy air upwind—assuming adequate stability—but she'll have more wetted surface than ideal for light-air going.

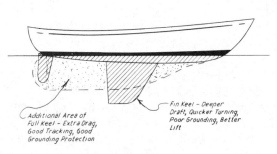

Fin vs Full Keel

Additional Area of Full Keel – Extra Drag, Good Tracking, Good Grounding Protection

Fin Keel – Deeper Draft, Quicker Turning, Poor Grounding, Better Lift

Lift Off

Almost everything we have covered so far applies to displacement monohulls. Happily, there are also planing sailboats—light, shoal-bodied craft with tremendous SA/Disp ratios. True planing vessels have SA/Disp ratios of 37 or higher. With this kind of power and with their flat underbodies, these boats lift out on a plane just as planing power craft do.

Sail Area Equals Horsepower

It's convenient to remember that 5,000 square feet of sail area generates (very roughly) 100 horsepower in a force 4 breeze. Thus, a Laser with 76 square feet of sail is running on a 1.5 hp engine in force 4. This doesn't seem like very much until you realize that, with one crewmember, the whole vessel weighs only 275 pounds. The result is over 180 pounds per horsepower and, using standard powerboat formulas, predicts a speed of 11 knots. For a 12.5-foot-waterline boat, that's smoking along—a speed-length ratio of 3.1. Actually, some planing sailboats are more efficient than this. It's not uncommon for hotter planing dinghies to attain bursts of 14-plus knots. The ultimate is, of course, the windsurfer. These "craft" (?) hold the world speed record under sail at over 35 knots!

For this kind of speed, the formula's always the same: huge amounts of sail and very little weight or wetted surface. To accomplish this, shifting ballast is used. This generates the stability needed for such large sail plans. On a boat like the Laser, crew weight is more than the weight of the entire vessel, and this weight can be shifted to weather by as much as the beam of the boat. The result is tremendous righting moment (great stability) in comparison to the boat's size and weight; the end product—*speed!* Sadly, to accomplish the same thing on a large craft—say, one of 10,000 pounds or 4,500 kg—you'd have to hang a 4½-ton weight 10 feet (3 m) off the weather rail in 20 knots of wind—you couldn't get me aboard!

Extra Hulls

The boats that effectively do this are, of course, multihulls. Their immense beam enables them to stand up to sail plans proportionately as large as those of small planing dinghies, with SA/Disp ratios well over 30. Additionally, long, narrow hulls and low weight give many multis Disp/WL ratios under 70. Add this all up and you get *fast* with a capital F. This doesn't mean that multihulls are "better" than monohulls. It's simply that they excel at this aspect of sailing. If you ever have any doubt, go out on the water some fine summer weekend. Scan the horizon and you'll see the vast majority of sails drifting by at roughly similar speeds. Standing out from all these will be a few that somehow glide by two or three times faster. Even at a distance, you know these are the multihulls.

**Homemade VPP Program—
No Computer Required**

We've now got enough information to make a real stab at predicting speed. This is what VPP (Velocity Prediction Programs) are for. You don't need a computer, though; you can figure the horsepower available from the sail plan and work through the powerboat formulas in the last chapter. For small planing dinghies, take-off or inception-of-planing is at around 2.2 times the square root of the waterline in feet. For a 12.5-foot-waterline Laser, planing will begin at around 7 knots or so. You'd thus use the planing-speed methods for any speed above this. Most small planing dinghies—like the Laser—take off at far higher pounds per horsepower than power craft can. The Planing Speed chart from Chapter 15 doesn't go this low. Instead, you can use the following:

$$Knots = 150 \div \sqrt{Lb./hp}$$
$$Knots = 117 \div \sqrt{Kg/kw}$$

Horsepower for a given sail area, in general, can be derived from the table below.

Swan Song, for example, works out as follows: Her 400 square feet (37.2 m²) of sail would generate about 16 hp or 11.6 kw in force 5. Eight-thousand pounds displacement divided by 16 hp equals 500 pounds per horsepower, or 3,630 kg divided by 11.6 kw equals 313 kg/kw. As Displacement Speed Chart 1 shows, this produces a speed-length ratio of 1.34 (standard hull speed). *Swan Song*'s waterline is 26 feet (7.9 m), so—from Displacement Speed Chart 2—the square root of her waterline is about 5.1; and 5.1 times 1.34 is 6.8 knots. This will, in fact, be very close to *Swan Song*'s speed in a force 5 breeze.

WIND STRENGTH	WIND SPEED IN KNOTS	HP/SQUARE FOOT	KW/SQUARE METER
Force 3	9–10	0.015	0.118
Force 4	13–15	0.020	0.161
Force 5	19–21	0.040	0.312
Force 6	25–27	0.070	0.559

You can use the same method to estimate speeds for any sailboat—displacement or planing. Remember, though, that boats must be large and have great stability to carry all working sail in force 6. You should use force 5 as maximum for average cruising boats. (Boats with wind-pressure coefficients over 1.4 or 6.6 can usually carry full sail into force 6.) We used force 4 for the Laser earlier, because for such small craft, even force 5 is pushing it.

Sizing up Any Boat

The preceding gives you valuable tools for evaluating sailing performance of different vessels. You can estimate speed, check stability and sail-carrying power, and determine if a craft has sufficient lateral plane to make a good course upwind without excessive leeway. You can also—if the spirit moves you—try noodling up your own boat, incorporating the best of all possible features.

PART 5

Fads, Trends, and History

When they went back to Langley's book and examined the table of data on which Langley had based his graph, they discovered that the data did indeed indicate a hump at 30 degrees, but this would have destroyed the smoothness of the curve, so Langley had tagged the datum with an asterisk, keyed to the footnote "Omit."

Wilbur and Orville, A Biography of the Wright Brothers,
Fred Howard

CHAPTER 22

Thanks to the Rule . . .

He had bought a large map representing the sea,
Without the least vestige of land:
And the crew were much pleased when they found it to be
A map they could all understand.

"What's the good of Mercator's North Poles and Equators,
Tropics, Zones, and Meridian Lines?"
So the Bellman would cry: and the crew would reply
"They are merely conventional signs!"

> *The Hunting of the Snark,* "Fit The Second,"
> Lewis Carroll

For over a century we've been inventing rules to rate different boats so that they can race competitively against each other. You'd think with this much time to perfect the idea we'd have gotten it right. But you'd be wrong. At the moment we have the IOR, PHRF, IMS, the meter rule, and even a new Super 12-meter rule. Of course, it's nice that we're so inventive. The IOR is now at Mark IIIa or Mark IIIx-400b, or something. Naturally, the original IOR was written to replace the horrible, outmoded, and downright funky CCA rule, which sort of replaced the Universal Rule, which replaced the Yacht Racing Association's rule, which replaced Thames Tonnage . . .

Now, though these rules were intended for handicapping, they were also intended to enhance and increase boat speed and to make for wholesome, seaworthy boats—vessels that would retain their value and usefulness even after their racing life was over. This is particularly true of most recent rules. (Super 12-meters and C-class cats and such excepted, that is.)

It would be logical to think that if we take some of the most prominent characteristics of modern racers and combined them artfully that we'd end up with *some* vessel—and we would. Let's call her *Flipper Flapper*.

Since we want to spend a fair amount of money on her, *Flipper Flapper* ought to be about 45 feet (13.7 m) long. In the best tradition of most IOR boats, *Flipper Flapper* should have a very short boom. Judging by current trends—no doubt supported by science—*Flapper's* boom should then be about seven feet (2.1 m) long. Like any proper racing boom, *Flipper Flapper's* should droop down at an impressive angle—it looks so, umm . . . depressed that way. In fact, we could add sharp protrusions or spikes to the aft end of the boom to further enhance the dropping boom's great advantage—its unerring ability to locate and make contact with high-flying skulls. Drooping booms offer other seamanlike possibilities. A particularly interesting one is the addition of a large paddle to

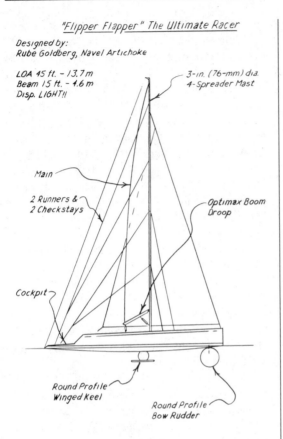

"Flipper Flapper" The Ultimate Racer

Designed by:
Rube Goldberg, Navel Artichoke

LOA 45 ft. – 13.7 m
Beam 15 ft. – 4.6 m
Disp. LIGHT!!

3-in. (76-mm) dia.
4-Spreader Mast

Main

2 Runners &
2 Checkstays

Optimax Boom
Droop

Cockpit

Round Profile
Winged Keel

Round Profile
Bow Rudder

per's mast section to be small—real small. I'd say that with four spreaders we could go with a mast only three inches (76 mm) in diameter and 60 feet (18.3 m) off the deck. Just imagine the hours of entertainment you'll have trying to keep the thing straight. At the end of the season, you'd simply release one of the runners when the wind breezed up at the dock, and down would come the whole rig—no yard bills for unstepping the mast!

Deck layout becomes an interesting question. Some boats have a tee-shaped cockpit, while others seem to favor the open chute at the stern. On *Flipper Flapper* we'll combine the two. This will completely eliminate all the topsides at the stern and transom saving weight and cost. (Saving money is not important, of course, but we can spend the savings on more electronics!) Going overboard to inspect the prop or removing an unwanted crewmember will be easier as well.

the end of the boom. This way *Flipper* will be sure to make maximum use of one of the drooping boom's favorite habits—taking a plunge on downwind courses. Just think of the propulsive benefits.

Flipper Flapper's mast should have at least four spreaders with two separate runners and two separate check stays. By scrambling back and forth to tend all these lines the crew will optimize boat wobble. You may not be familiar with boat wobble; it's the closely held secret of an initiated few. When the boat isn't going fast enough the crew jump up and down and yell a lot. The smartly handled craft responds by bobbing around a great deal and creating an impressive illusion of motion.

The finest thing about having all these spreaders and runners is that they will permit *Flipper Flap-*

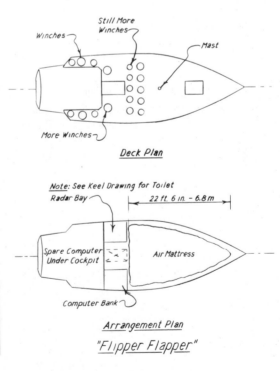

Winches

Still More
Winches

Mast

More Winches

Deck Plan

Note: See Keel Drawing for Toilet

Radar Bay

22 ft. 6 in. – 6.8 m

Spare Computer
Under Cockpit

Air Mattress

Computer Bank

Arrangement Plan
"Flipper Flapper"

Of course, we'll need winches, and lots of them. You may not have heard yet, but a top manufacturer has come out with a five-speed self-coiling winch. Not only does this winch have five gear ratios (1:1, 1:10, 1:50, 1:100, and 1:1,000) but it also coils and uncoils your line for you. The old-fashioned—and downright primitive—simple, self-tailing winch will be found only on character boats and a few scruffy cruisers from now on. I think that four primaries and three secondaries will do nicely for a 45-footer (13.7 m). Naturally, we'll want four or five halyard winches, outhaul winches, barber hauler winches, downhaul winches. . . . Let's face it—you can never have enough winches.

Once upon a time, sailors actually adjusted their rigs by hand. This sort of thing is not for *Flipper Flapper*, though. She'll require a hydraulic backstay adjuster, vang, forestay adjuster, shroud tensioner, and mast step adjuster. Ideally all these hydraulic controls should lead aft to a console of buttons near the helmsman. A practiced hydraulics operator/helmsman will then be able to wiggle the rig around sufficiently to generate his own wind. This should make *Flapper* unbeatable in a calm.

Of course, *Flipper Flapper*'s a sailboat, so she'll need lots of state-of-the-art sails. Mylar-Kevlar headsails should do the trick. Radial,tape-seam, bi-weight, multi-ply construction is a good starting point. Let's see—we don't want to go overboard—but we could use an ultralight number one, then go to a light number one, then a moderately light number one, followed by a light-medium number one, and of course a number-one number one, and then a moderately heavy number-one number one. . . . In these days of intense competition, you see, it's necessary to have a sail for every possible condition. Superb crew work is required to ensure that boat speed is not lost during the numerous sail changes—once every few minutes—called for to keep up with wind shifts and such. A really nice feature of all these sails is that we won't be stuck with them for long. In order to be worth anything at all, they have to be *light*! A

fair life expectancy ought to be three races—maybe two for our really high-tech sails.

Since weight's all-important in a racing boat, we'll not carry anything that isn't necessary. The rule requires a toilet, but it doesn't tell us where to put it. The obvious answer is to make a toilet of lead and put it in the keel. (Why this hasn't occurred to anyone before is beyond me. So far, most racers have limited themselves to installing their heads in the open center of the cabin and taping them shut with duct tape.) Bunks also take up space and weight. The clear solution is a giant inflatable cushion covering the entire interior of the cabin. This should satisfy all sleeping requirements and win the distinction of being the world's only 16-fold berth. Why, the most luxurious yachts in the world don't have bunks that big!

Interior decor's also important, but here we're largely controlled by hull material. Not too long ago *Flipper Flapper* could've been of aluminum—a material with a warm cheery glow. Today, aluminum is passé. What we want is a composite hull—Kevlar and carbon fibers bonded in a matrix of vinylester resin. Again, *Flipper* will have a new innovation—titanium hull reinforcement. Developed by NASA for use on the proposed manned Mars mission, this is really titanium cloth. We can use it to reinforce the hull laminate at high stress areas. Yes it's expensive, but come on—*Flipper Flapper*'s a racing boat; you've gotta' go all out to WIN!

This simplifies the finishing of *Flapper*'s interior. Since we don't want to spend money (remember the electronics) or incur weight for anything as useless as—dare I say it—joinerwork, we'll simply leave the interior totally unfinished. After a hard watch slogging to weather offshore, we'll be able to retire below to the soothing feel of a raw carbon-fiber and Kevlar home. I imagine that the occasional twinkle of a titanium strand poking through here and there will add a pleasing touch. A sign should be posted at all hatches warning crewmembers to wear heavy clothing and gloves to protect themselves from jagged fiber splinters and edges.

Another nice thing about this completely open interior is that it allows all the room you could want for electronics. (Ahh...at last, the electronics!) *Flipper Flapper* should have one of those new systems that combines a radar with a loran, an autopilot, and a computer-stored chart. These gizmos cost only, well...one fair-sized bundle, and they enable you to watch every move your boat makes projected on an electronically generated chart. *Flapper's* secret weapon'll be to tie this device into a Vax microcomputer—mounted on board—that will integrate the information from gyrocompass, hull-speed indicator, and wind indicator to steer *Flipper Flapper* on a better course, in all conditions, than any human could hope to achieve. The next generation of *Flipper* will have an even more sophisticated computer system capable of sheeting, hoisting, and reefing sail. (This system really exists now on the 440-foot (134 m) Windstar sail-assisted cruise ships.) Thus equipped, the next *Flipper Flapper* will be able to out-sail any human in all situations. Naturally, this also leads to the ultimate in crew comfort—you can stay home.

Below the waterline, we'll want to take advantage of all the latest hydrodynamic developments. Both the rudder and the keel should be elliptical in profile. In fact, we ought to go even further and make them perfectly circular. (There, let's see another designer reduce induced drag more than this!)

Thanks to the inventiveness inspired by 12-meter competition, we'll place the rudder forward instead of aft. Actually, we had a number of choices here. Since we know that two rudders are good, logic tells us that three, four, or even 12 rudders would be better. I've always been an admirer of simplicity, though, so—just this once—we won't add anything else. Let's just place the rudder at the bow and eliminate the rudder aft altogether. One really superb advantage of bow rudders is that they act as ideal protection for the hull. Every floating log or lobster pot will meet the trusty bow rudder first. Clearly, this is a small price to pay for total loss of steering control.

Another wonderful lesson from the twelves is wings. By jiminy, we've got to have a pair on *Flipper Flapper*. Of course, we know the great advantage of wings is that they increase lift for a given draft. We wouldn't want to do something as simple as using a centerboard or actually deepening the keel—no indeed. Instead, we'll make *Flapper's* keel only 3 feet (90 cm) deep and her wings a good 16 feet (4.8 m) wide. This offers an interesting challenge to navigation. Not only will *Flipper* draw many feet more when heeled than when upright, but she'll have a tendency to, well...catch on things. Of course, if it works on a 12-meter it must work for us. In fact, the wide-winged keel has a secret advantage—so secret that it has never been acknowledged outside of top design offices before.

What is it? Well, have you ever wondered about the snazzy tactics of the twelves? Why do you think they are doing all that maneuvering? Sure, in the old days, all they were trying to do was to gain an advantage and get ahead. With winged keels, however, the whole game has taken on a new, sinister meaning. Those boats are out there maneuvering to ram each other underwater with their keels. This calls for a skipper and tactician of nice judgement and iron nerve. After all,

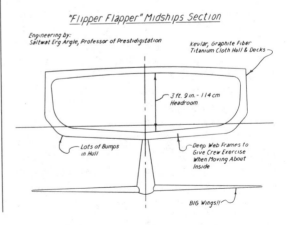

"*Flipper Flapper*" Midships Section

Engineering by:
Saltwat Erg Argle, Professor of Prestidigitation

Kevlar, Graphite Fiber
Titanium Cloth Hull & Decks

3 ft. 9 in. - 114 cm
Headroom

Lots of Bumps
in Hull

Deep Web Frames to
Give Crew Exercise
When Moving About
Inside

BIG Wings!!

this insidious submarine combat is taking place out of sight, under water! One slip and it's down to Davy Jones till next season. Imagine the advantage you'd have with a boat like *Flipper Flapper* under you. You'd need only maneuver within striking distance of a likely foe to neatly shear off his keel or rudder. He'd never know what hit him.

Unfortunately, there isn't room here to go into all of the fine points of designing *Flipper Flapper*. We really can't discuss the reason for the six creases and five bulges in her run. Or why she has absolutely no overhang—none at all. We can't even go into the special seats designed to hold each crewman *firmly* in place on the weather rail—no matter how blustery conditions get. Nope, we don't have time to discuss it all here, but *Flipper Flapper* will be out on the water this summer. If you see her, watch out.

Now, it's not entirely fair to blame boats like *Flipper Flapper* on the racing rules. A large part of the problem is owners and designers who will do anything to win. But the fundamental approach to racing rules has obviously failed to control designs enough to produce wholesome vessels. Neither a contemporary IOR racer nor a current 12-meter has any reasonable value or usefulness after its racing career is over. Often, this career is only a season or two long. (IMS racers are a bit better, but they're already starting down the same beaten path.) These are truly uncomfortable and unseaworthy vessels. And they're anything but cheap. A recent phone conversation with one of Rhode Island's top custom builders gave me a price of 450 grand for a "simple" 45-footer (13.7 m). You couldn't get a quarter-tonner for $300,000, he said. Do we want rules that encourage boats of this cost that are virtually useless in a few short years?

What about speed? IOR boats are faster than most comparable cruising boats. But then they ought to be. They are usually considerably lighter, with newer sails and gear, lots of expensive winches, and a crew of 10 or more tuning, tweaking, and acting as ballast. A fairer indication of how fast these boats are would be to measure them against other racing vessels designed outside the influence of the rule. Just such a comparison of speed occurred in the 1987 BOC race. Singlehander Phillipe Jeantot, skippering *Credit Agricole*, was approaching the finish line at Sydney when *Atlantic Privateer* hove into view and challenged Jeantot to a friendly "drag race" to the line. Now, *Atlantic Privateer* is a 70-foot-plus (22 m) IOR maxi boat, with a crew of 20 or more. *Credit Agricole* is a 60-foot (18.2 m) singlehander. With chutes set on both boats, *Credit Agricole* caught up to and passed *Atlantic Privateer* in short order. What's more, *Credit Agricole*'s lone skipper sat back, unruffled, and watched the whole business as he swept by the IOR maxi under autopilot! Although neither boat is exactly suited to family cruising, I think it's obvious which boat is fastest and easiest to handle.

Still another problem is that the hype associated with racing influences the design of production boats built for you and me. As you can judge from *Flipper Flapper,* winged keels, bow rudders, dozens of winches, and oodles of sails do not make for a comfortable or safe boat. These ideas do *sell* boats, however. Few builders can resist this potential sales appeal. Some bloke from the marketing department will walk into the head office and say: "*Super Hot Rod* just won the Hornblower Cup with a dupple framus on her bow. If we stick a dupple framus on our new model, I can sell hundreds of 'em." Yet there are better, simpler, tried-and-true methods of getting all the benefits these "innovations" are supposed to offer: centerboards and bulbs in place of wings, trim tabs aft of the fin keel (for the diehards) in place of bow rudders. Efficient masts may be made to stand without numerous runners, checkstays, babystays, and related spaghetti. Nothing is wrong with sophisticated design or exotic materials. (I've designed all-Kevlar and all-carbon-fiber vessels and ultralight ocean racers.) What is wrong is when these craft offer less comfort and safety than their predecessors at equal or greater cost.

CHAPTER 23

Speed With Style

. . . you would have thought the boat had two keels—one cleaving the water, the other the air—as the boat churned on through both opposing elements at once. A continued cascade played at the bows; a ceaseless whirling eddy in her wake. . . .

Moby-Dick, "Stubb Kills A Whale," Herman Melville

I've often wondered about roll bars on boats. I can see they'd be useful on race cars and on off-road vehicles, but what are they doing on powerboats? It's not, after all, as if these gizmos will protect you from being crushed by hard water should you capsize. The answer, of course, is that they are some industrial designer's idea of styling—"race cars have them, so put 'em on a boat and she'll look fast." The truth, though, is that these "roll bars" (or radar arches) actually slow the boat down. Their wind resistance at 25 knots or more is phenomenal. In fact, at speeds over 25 knots wind resistance becomes a significant factor. This is why your favorite automaker is spending so much money developing slippery body shapes. A small reduction in surface or appendage area can mean more speed and lower fuel consumption.

Going Forward

Another interesting styling trend is long sloped and rounded cabin sides and fronts. Naturally, one of the reasons for this is to reduce wind resistance, and there's something in this. Such cabins have another interesting feature, however. Try standing on one. Okay, you did it at the dock or in the showroom, now try it at sea while your sloped-cabin *Salubrious Sea Gal* is bucking into a chop. Be sure your man overboard gear is ready to hand.

Nautical Mountaineering

One 100-foot-plus (30-meter-plus) megayacht actually has spiral stairs from the main deck up to the bridge deck. They're beautifully sculptured—neatly smoothed, shiny, and rounded all over. In fact, to further enhance their appearance—or avoid hiding their beauty—the designer completely omitted a handrail. Have you ever tried to climb an ordinary ladder in a seaway? Negotiating this spiral stair would require a full complement of mountaineering gear. I can hear the calls now, "On belay! . . . Ready to rappel!" Styling touches like this are worth your life.

Down Below

Going below on such craft is seldom much help. For some reason, some folks seem to think that crushed velour's the finest way to upholster a power yacht. Settees, chairs, berths, cabin soles, walls, and even ceilings are plastered with this delightful material. Frequently, the exact same color and texture is used everywhere, making it difficult to tell port from starboard or even up from down. A particularly nice feature of crushed velour is its ability to retain salt. Once this stuff gets a good dousing of sea water, it's permapickled.

There's even the occasional all-shag-carpet interior. Getting around in one of these is sort of like being on safari—hacking your way through the tall pile with a machette and referring to a hand-held compass to get your bearings. In fact, simply gluing indoor/outdoor carpeting all over the inside of a boat is one of cheapest and least satisfactory ways to finish off a cabin. If you wander into a vessel fitted out this way, it's a fair indication that quality was a distant second in production considerations throughout. The boat review staff on one magazine I've worked for coined the ideal term for such craft, though they never used it in print for fear of offending advertisers. They called these vessels "rug boats."

The Bloated Boat

Overall proportions aren't immune to this sort of thing, either. I once owned a boat that spent a winter laid up beside *Engulf and Devour* (no kidding). Few names could've been more appropriate. I was always afraid that *Engulf and Devour* would swallow my sloop whole when I wasn't around to look out for her. She was not only enormously wide, but high as well. Large boats are great, but bloated ones? *Engulf and Devour* was almost half as wide as she was long, with a high cabin, a raised wheelhouse, a flying bridge, and a tuna tower. All this is fine for a houseboat, but *Engulf and Devour* was intended for speed. Her engines were . . . well, massive.

Surfing Anyone?

Perhaps, the most instructive thing about *Engulf and Devour* was her wake. Heaven help her if she had to operate in a no-wake zone. For her, there was no such thing. At speed great combers, ideally suited for surfing, curled off her stern—an awe-inspiring sight. If any canoeists or board sailors happened to be in the way, well . . . perhaps we should refer to the local constabulary's list of missing persons. Naturally, all this fuss is not exactly suited to fuel economy or speed. Such a wake is wasted energy and wasted fuel. Further, broad as she was, *Engulf and Devour* would have to slow right down in a seaway. Upwind pounding would get fierce. Downwind, her massive expanse of flat transom would try to broach her at every wave.

Lulworth

Most people don't realize that powerboats of 60 years ago made similar speeds to today's craft, often with less horsepower. The stepped-hydroplane *Bluebird* broke 112 knots with a single 1,250-hp (932 kw) Rolls Royce engine well over a generation ago, and Hickman Sea Sleds—early offshore surface-effect power cats—ran well offshore at speeds over 55 knots more than four decades ago. Modern deep-vee ocean racers can achieve up to 112 knots offshore—which *Bluebird* couldn't—but the versions available to average boaters will seldom make such speeds.

The 40-foot (12.2 m) stepped hydroplane *Lulworth* was used as a torpedo chase boat by the Whitehead Torpedo Company during World War II. She wasn't a stripped-out patrol boat, but a yachty cabin cruiser. Weighing 3.7 tons, she did 36 knots (40 mph) with a single 275-hp (205-kw) engine. This works out to 0.8 pounds per horsepower per knot, or 0.5 kg/kw/knot. By contrast a typical modern high-speed cruiser of 3.5 tons has a top speed of 26 knots with 290 horsepower (216 kw), or nearly 1.0 pounds per horsepower per knot, or 0.63 kg/kw/knot. This is fully 25 percent less efficient.

"*Lulworth*"
Designed by S.E. Saunders
at 34 Knots Some 50 Years Ago

As we've already seen in Chapter 20, the most common way to evaluate boat powering is in pounds per horsepower. *Lulworth,* for example, has 30.1 pounds per horsepower, or 18.2 kg/kw (3.7 tons × 2,240 lb./ton = 8,288 lb. displacement, and 8,288 lb. ÷ 275 hp = 30.1 lb./hp—or, 3,740 kg ÷ 205 kw = 18.2 kg/kw). Now, if *Lulworth* made only 20 knots with this much power per pound she'd be less efficient than she is making her real 36 knots. This shows up in pounds per horsepower per knot, or kg/kw/knot. At 20 knots *Lulworth* would be using 1.5 pounds per horsepower per knot, or 0.94 kg/kw/knot. This is less efficient than the 0.8 pounds per horsepower per knot or 0.5 kg/kw/knot she actually delivers. Pounds per horsepower per knot or kilograms per kilowatt per knot thus gives you a way of comparing the efficiency of powerplants and hulls of different boats.

All of this doesn't take into account that modern engines weigh far less than the machines of *Lulworth*'s day. Additionally, modern materials and construction methods make for proportionately lighter hull structures. A modern version of *Lulworth,* with modern engines and structure, could be faster still.

H.M. Pope III—*Lulworth* Updated

I've had, in fact, the opportunity to design just such a vessel. *H.M Pope III* is a direct descendant of *Lulworth.* With a length-to-beam ratio of 4.2 and a displacement of 19,500 pounds (8,845 kg), *H.M. Pope*'s somewhat wider than, and more than twice as heavy as *Lulworth.* Even so, the *Pope*'s narrow beam—by modern standards—and stepped bottom give her a top speed of 58 knots, with an hon-

Transforms
Compared

"*Lulworth*" Weighs 440 lb.
(200 kg) More Than the
Modern Cruiser!

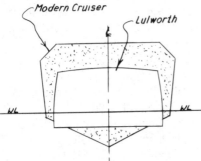

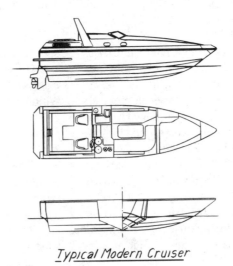

Typical Modern Cruiser

est cruising speed of 35 to 45 knots—higher than *Lulworth*'s top speed! Additionally, with modern engines and construction techniques, the *Pope* exceeds *Lulworth*'s level of efficiency, achieving a fantastic 0.21 lb./hp/knot, or 0.13 kg/kw/knot. (*H.M.*

Pope's 1,600 horsepowers give her 12.2 lb./hp, and 12.2 lb./hp ÷ 58 knots = 0.21 lb./hp/knot—or, 8845 kg ÷ 1,193 kw = 7.41 kg/kw, and 7.41 kg/kw ÷ 58 knots = 0.13 kg/kw/knot).

Part of the reason for *H.M. Pope*'s extra

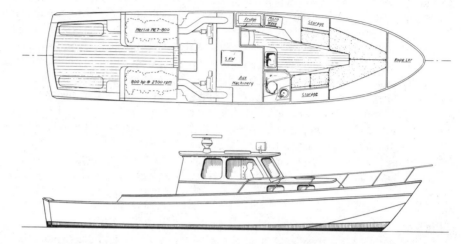

Profile and arrangement of H.M. Pope III.

LOA	42 ft. 9 in.	(13.0 m)
LWL	37 ft. 7 in.	(11.4 m)
Beam	10 ft. 2 in.	(3.1 m)
Draft	3 ft. 3 in.	(1.0 cm)
Disp.	8.7 tons	

Power	Twin Merlin ME7-800s, 800 hp (596 kw) at 2,300 rpm; 1600 hp (1193 kw) total
Generators	Northern Lights 5 kw
Fuel	350 gal (1590 l) diesel
Water	30 gal. (136 l)
Speed	58 kts. max. 30 to 45 kts. cruise

H.M. Pope's inboard profile and wheelhouse arrangement.

weight is that there were no modern gas engines powerful enough to drive her at these high speeds. (The only ones with sufficient power were custom-built racing engines not suited to long-term rugged service.) Accordingly, we had to go with diesels. Just 20 or so years ago, diesels would've been too heavy, but modern turbocharged, intercooled diesels deliver fantastic power for their weight. *H.M. Pope* is fitted with twin Merlin ME7-800s, delivering 800 hp (596 kw) at 2,300 rpm—about the most efficient diesels, pound-for-pound, available in this size. They produce one horsepower for every 2.86 pounds of engine weight, or one kilowatt for every 1.75 kg—far better than even the gas engines of *Lulworth*'s day, and equal to many gas engines today. (A typical 350-cubic-inch/5.7-liter V-8 gas engine delivers 330 hp and weighs 875 pounds—2.65 pounds for every horsepower.)

Slim's the Ticket

One of the most significant differences between *Lulworth* and *H.M. Pope* and most of their modern counterparts is length-to-beam ratio. *Lulworth* has only 8-feet beam on 40 feet length overall (2.4 m beam by 12.2 m LOA) for a length-to-beam ratio of 5 to 1. Our example typical modern cruiser is 29 feet 6 inches overall with 8 feet 2 inches beam (9 m by 2.5 m), for a length-to-beam ratio of 3.6 to 1—a huge difference. (*H.M. Pope* is 4.2 to 1.) In comparing *Lulworth* to the typical modern cruiser, remember that both boats are nearly the same weight, and so nearly the same size. Not only do *Lulworth*'s long, narrow proportions improve speed, but they also improve seakeeping ability. She's able to keep on pounding into a head sea at planing speed long after the wider modern craft would be slowed down. By the same token, *Lulworth*'s exposed transom is only 18.5 square feet (1.7 m²). Our modern cruiser—even though it weighs less—has an incredible 32.2 square feet (3 m²) of exposed transom. (*H.M. Pope* weighs 2.5 times more than our example cruiser and is 13 feet

longer (3.9 m), yet even her transom area is less, at 31 square feet or 2.9 m².) Compared to *Lulworth*, the modern cruiser has 74 percent more transom area, which means that following seas will be able to exert 74 percent more force on the modern craft to slew her around into a broach.

Perhaps the greatest shame is that many folks will look at *Lulworth*'s plumb stem and vertical cabin sides and think she's quaint and slow, when in fact she could blow the doors off many of the boats you've seen. At the same time the rather spacecraft-like architecture of her wider modern counterpart is often mistakenly taken to mean "fast," when just the opposite is frequently the case.

Naturally, the serious race boats are about as narrow as *Lulworth*. Donzis, Cigarettes, and their ilk don't fool around with excess beam and height. It's not necessary to go as low as these craft to get superior cruising speed, however. *H.M. Pope III* shows what a modern version of *Lulworth,* can do. With a bit of rake to her bow and modern cabin, engines, and construction, she's a truly salty and seaworthy cruiser/fisherman capable of maintaining well over 30 knots in rough going.

Needle Boats

This brings us to the question of whether current muscle boats are as efficient as they can be. I think there's room for improvement. What's called for is an extremely long, narrow, light boat—even narrower and lighter than current extra-high-speed craft. I'd call such vessels needle boats.

The numbers for such craft are impressive. If we make the first *Needle* 54 feet (16.4 m) overall and just 6 feet 6 inches (2 m) in beam, she'd displace about 7,500 pounds (3,410 kg), or just 3.3 tons. With a waterline of 49 feet 3 inches (15 m), twin 400-hp (596 kw) gas engines would push her at a sustained 70 knots. (Such engines would operate continuously at just under 320 hp or 238 kw each). This is 80 mph, or fast enough to get you a speeding ticket on any highway in the country. Being low and narrow, *Needle*—like *H.M. Pope*—

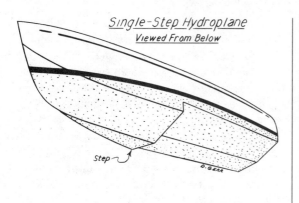

Single-Step Hydroplane
Viewed From Below

step

D. GERR

This view of H.M. Pope's model shows her step clearly.

would be able to maintain her high speed in rougher conditions than comparable wider craft.

If we were to make *Needle* a single-step hydroplane—like *Lulworth* and the *Pope*—her speed potential would increase yet more. This is one approach that'll allow the average yachtsman or yachtswoman to operate a boat that could do better than 80 miles per hour. What's more, at around 800 hp (596 kw), you may be able to afford to blast off in one of these rockets without selling off your family's assets for fuel.

Combining Round Bilge and Hard Chine

In order to achieve the maximum in comfort and seakeeping, *Needle*'s entry or forebody might be round bilged, not hard chined. Five or six feet (1.5 to 1.8 m) forward of the step the round bilge would gradually harden out into the sharp crease

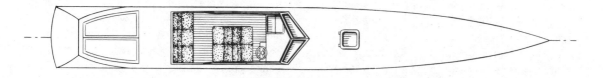

"Needle" a 70-knot Runabout
LOA 54 ft. (16.4 m), DWL 49 ft. 3 in. (15 m), Beam 6 ft. 6 in. (2 m)
Jet-Drive Draft 14 in. (36 cm), Disp. 7,500 lb. (3410 kg)
Power 800 hp (596 kw)

of a true hard chine. In this way, *Needle* would have the best of both worlds—the ease and comfort of a round-bilged entry and the lifting (planing) efficiency of a chine hull's midships and run. (She'd need a substantial spray knocker forward to keep water off the deck.) Additionally, *Needle*'s stern would be well rounded above the waterline. This would reduce the broaching effect of waves striking *Needle*'s already narrow transom to as close to zero as any boat could have.

Yet another potential problem is steering control and appendage resistance. At speeds of 60 knots or so, even a very tiny strut and rudder would cause significant drag. To get around this *Needle* will use twin surface or jet drives. (We didn't install these on *H.M. Pope* because she's a sportfisherman. The surface drives projecting aft would tangle lines and complicate boating fish, while the jets wouldn't fit under a low fishing cockpit.) Not only are these particularly efficient at high speed, but there's no rudder or strut to drag through the water. Extremely long, narrow boats tend to be slow to turn, so *Needle* will be fitted with a small retractable skid fin to increase turning moment. With surface drives that steer like outdrives (or outboards) and her small skid fin, *Needle* will have very quick and positive response to her helm.

At 800 hp (596 kw), *Needle* will be burning around 74 gallons or 280 liters per hour. Four hours of fuel will give *Needle* a cruising range of 200 nautical miles—figuring a conservative cruising speed of 50 knots. This amounts to 300 gallons (1,120 l) of fuel, or a good 1,820 pounds (827 kg). These numbers also give you some idea of what rocket craft like *Needle* are all about. Her engines and drive train will weigh about 2,800 pounds or 1,272 kg (1,400 lb. or 636 kg for each engine). Her composite hull will weigh around 2,100 pounds (924 kg), outfit and gear 700 pounds (318 kg), and if we add in the fuel, we get a total weight of 7,500 pounds (3,410 kg).

The important thing here is that *Needle* is scarcely more than two engines and a fuel tank with a hull hung around them. Actually, as we've been doing in earlier chapters, designers will figure *Needle*'s displacement and performance based on her weight with tanks two-thirds full, or at 1,200 pounds (545 kg). This is just as well, as we have to leave room in her displacement figures for crew. The extra 620 pounds (280 kg) allows for three or four in the cockpit. Of course, with her tanks nearly empty *Needle* will be noticeably faster, and with tanks full she'll be somewhat slower.

An interesting aspect of a boat like *Needle* is that she'll be quite efficient running on one engine, even with that single engine throttled back to two-thirds rpm. Incredibly, under these conditions *Needle* would still be making 39 knots (45 mph)! For *Needle* this would just be loafing along. Running at this mere 39 knots would, however, up *Needle*'s cruising range to 400 nautical miles.

This brings us to still another possibility—a needle cruiser. By settling for 35 knots (faster than most powerboats) and making *Needle*—lets call her *Needle Senior*—just a bit wider and higher, you could have a vessel that would pass nearly every power craft in most sea conditions, while operating on a single 300-hp (224 kw) engine—or perhaps twin 160-hp (120 kw) engines pushing jet drives. *Needle Senior* would have a vee berth, enclosed head, galley, chart table, and small saloon. It would be hard to imagine a better way to get around on the water. You could cover plenty of territory quickly and comfortably, and be able to do so in almost any ordinary weather. In the jet drive configuration, she'd be so shoal (about 14 inches or 36 cm draft) you could take her just about anywhere there's a heavy dew.

The Strong Silent Type

Both *Needle* and *Needle Senior* would have one other important feature—a feature incorporated on *H.M Pope III*—very, very well-muffled engines and soundproofed engine compartments. I don't know why so many owners of high-speed boats seem to like the godawful roar of their mo-

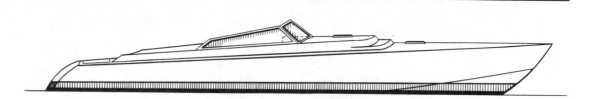

"Needle Senior" a 35-knot Cruiser
LOA 55 ft. (16.7 m), DWL 49 ft. 4 in. (15 m), Beam 8 ft. (2.4 m)
Jet-Drive Draft 14 in. (36-cm), Disp. 9,000 lb (4090 kg)
Power 300 hp (224 kw)

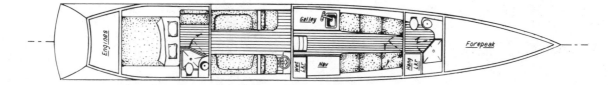

tors. Personally, two or three hours of this kind of racket and I'm ready to jump overboard—not to mention the effect of all this noise on folks out for a quiet daysail or a peaceful fishing junket. A proper power yacht—high or low speed—should make very little fuss or noise at all. Imagine the effect *Needle* would have on onlookers as she glided into a bay at 60-plus knots, making practically no sound. Now, that's style!

Slim is Efficient

It's interesting to compare the efficiency of *Needle* and *Needle Senior* with *Lulworth* and the modern cruiser.

	LB./HP/ KNOT	KG/KW/ KNOT
Typical contemporary cruiser	1.00	0.62
Needle Senior	0.85	0.53
Lulworth	0.80	0.50
H.M. Pope III	0.21	0.13
Needle	0.13	0.08

Needle Senior's just a bit less efficient than *Lulworth*. *Needle* and *H.M. Pope III* are more efficient than either *Lulworth* or the typical modern cruiser, by phenomenal margins.

PART 6

The Iron Breeze

Successful boat design would be a combination of a seaworthy hull and a compact, powerful engine.

U.S. Small Combatants, Norman Friedman

CHAPTER 24

Engine Lore

She was a seven-horsepower, single-cylinder make-and-break, gasoline-fueled monster, built in the 1920s from an original design conceived somewhere near the end of the last century. She was massive beyond belief, and intractable beyond bearing.

The Boat Who Wouldn't Float, Farley Mowat

There was a time—not so very long ago—when if a naval architect needed an engine for a boat, he'd just go ahead and design it. Robert Fulton, John Ericson, and the Wizard of Bristol, Captain Nat Herreshoff, all designed their own engines. This was a certain way to ensure that the engine matched the boat perfectly. Of course, this was back in the days of steam. But even as the new-fangled internal (infernal?) combustion engines made their appearance, many designers continued to draw up power plants specifically for their new creations.

These were heady times. Naphtha, natural gas, and eventually that exotic stuff, gasoline, made it possible to get a whole lot more power from a much smaller machine than had ever been attainable before. Why, the sky was the limit! Imagine being able to power a boat to run at 18 or 20 knots—this was *speed!* These old internal combustion engines were influenced by steam engine design. They had low rpm, large-diameter pistons, and huge flywheels. In fact, an old—now obsolete—rule of thumb for sizing propellers was that prop diameter should equal the flywheel diameter for two-bladed propellers, and for three-bladed props it should equal the diameter just inside the flywheel rim.

These days, no designer would dream of designing an engine from scratch. Instead, we thumb through engine company spec sheets to find the most suitable machine for a given boat. From time to time you'll hear some old codger bemoaning the demise of the "all-marine" thumper. Unlike today's high-speed engines, these big, slow-turning power plants were ideal for driving boats, they'll say. They deliver more low-speed thrust and have less to go wrong with them. This is not really so, however. Such old gas engines were good enough to drive displacement hulls at low speeds, but the power they generated for their weight was very low, at around 50 to 85 pounds of engine weight per horsepower, or 30 to 52 kilograms per kilowatt. Planing boats would hardly have, well, gotten off the ground with these engines and—if you look at the plans of boats from those days—you'll see that a great deal of boat was taken up by power plant.

Current engines are far lighter for the power they produce than similar engines of 60 to 75 years ago. They're also more fuel efficient and generally more reliable—in spite of their many additional moving parts. Still, there's the all-important question, how do you select the best engine for a given job? What's better—gas or diesel, four-stroke or two-stroke, turbocharged or naturally aspirated? To make a stab at answering these questions, we have to look at the different types of engines in more detail.

Gas versus Diesel

One of the most fundamental decisions is choosing between gas and diesel. It's not unusual to hear an almost knee-jerk reaction against gasoline; it can, after all, explode, and it has an electric ignition system that's subject to problems in the wet. Nevertheless, there's much to recommend gas engines on many vessels.

A great advantage of gasoline is that its engines are almost necessarily lighter than diesel engines of the same power. The reason for this is built into the basic working principles of each type of engine—compression versus spark ignition. In other words, gas and diesel engines use totally different methods to get their fuel hot enough to burn.

Putting the Squeeze on a Gas

Temperature is the amount of energy in a given volume of space at a given time, and the energy in a gas is determined by how rapidly its individual molecules are darting around. When gas molecules move more slowly the gas gets colder, until—at some temperature—the gas changes state and becomes a liquid. We can't use the ordinary Fahrenheit or Centigrade temperature scales when investigating this; nature's never heard of

them, and the numbers wouldn't work out properly. Instead, we have to use nature's own scale, relating temperature to absolute zero, in degrees kelvin—K°. (Absolute zero is –459 F° or –273 C°.)

Say, for instance, you have a gas that's about 100 degrees Fahrenheit (38° C), which is 311 K°, at ordinary sea-level air pressure (14.7 pounds per square inch or 1 kg/cm²). Its molecules are zipping around randomly at an average speed of, say, 100 feet per second (30 m/sec.) and are separated from each other by an average distance of, oh, one millionth of an inch (25 nanometers—millionths of a meter). (We're just grabbing numbers out of a hat, but it's the principle that counts.) If we squeezed or compressed this gas into half its original volume, we'd decrease the distance between the individual molecules and at the same time increase the temperature.

Although the numbers vary somewhat for different motors, a good estimate of the temperature increase in internal combustion engines can be made from the following:

Final Temperature (K°) = (Compression Ratio)$^{0.3}$ × Starting Temperature (K°)

In our case, we've compressed the gas into half its original volume, so the compression ratio's 2 to 1 or simply 2, and $2^{0.3}$ = 1.231. For a final temperature, multiply 311 K° by 1.231, which comes to 383 K° (229 F° or 109 C°). The compressed gas molecules are still moving at the same average speed, but they're now much closer together, so there's more energy, quite literally, squeezed into a smaller space. Presto—higher temperature.

Diesel Makes it Work

In the late 1800s a young German inventor named Rudolph Diesel figured that he could use this principle to ignite the fuel in an engine's cylinder, thus eliminating the ignition system. Just squeeze the gas—in this case air—hard enough and it would get so hot that fuel oil sprayed into the cylinder would burst into flame of its own accord. In fact, if the compression ratio from our previous example had been 20 to 1 instead of 2 to 1, the final temperature would have increased to 764 K° (915 F° or 490 C°), more than high enough to set any petroleum fuel ablaze. Obviously, Diesel was onto something. The world of power generation has never been the same since.

A gasoline engine can never approach the high cylinder pressures of a diesel engine, because with this much more volatile fuel such pressures would cause premature and uncontrolled ignition. In fact, such high-pressure ignition can be a problem in some high-compression gasoline engines. It is called pre-ignition or—not surprisingly—dieseling. To avoid dieseling, the maximum compression pressure in a gas engine is kept below 150 pounds per square inch (psi), or 10.5 kg/cm². In a diesel engine, compression pressures must be much higher—between 400 and 700 psi, or 28 to 50 kg/cm².

Another way to look at this is to say that diesels operate at higher compression ratios than gas engines. The compression ratio of an engine is simply the volume in the cylinder with the piston all the way down, at the bottom of its stroke, divided by the volume with the cylinder all the way up, at the top of its stroke. Gas engines operate at compression ratios between 6 and 12 to 1, while diesels operate at compression ratios between 11.5 and 22 to 1.

All this means that forces on the cylinder walls (engine block), piston, connecting rod, crank pin, crank shaft, and so on are substantially higher in a diesel than in a comparable gas engine. To withstand these higher forces, a diesel must be built stronger and thus heavier, which adds up to a more expensive machine.

Pros and Cons

Knowing this, we can get a more realistic picture of the trade-offs between diesel and gas engines. For the same power, gas engines cost less; they are lighter; and they require less force—cranking effort—to get them started. Diesels, on the other hand, don't suffer from pre-ignition; are generally more efficient running at partial load; and being heavier, are usually stronger and more reliable. Add to this the absence of an electric ignition system, and the diesel stacks up as considerably tougher in the marine environment.

Further, diesel fuel—although it *can* burn very destructively—can't explode. This is diesel's biggest and most obvious plus for use in boats. Where gasoline fumes can accumulate in the bilge, just waiting for that errant spark, diesel fumes are no more than good and stinky. In making this comparison between fuels, however, you have to keep in mind that proper venting of the bilge and proper fuel-line, tank, and exhaust installation virtually eliminate the chance of gasoline explosions. Further, gas fumes and exhaust don't smell nearly as bad as diesel, and this is the smell you have to live with all the time, every time you climb aboard.

Indeed, for light, high-speed yachts gas engines are hard to beat. It's not unusual for a gas four-cycle engine to weigh as little as 50 percent of the weight of a diesel of the same horsepower. (Two-cycle gas engines may weigh even less.) This weight savings means more speed with less power, offering lower fuel consumption and a lower-cost engine. It's no accident that most inboard/outboards and virtually all outboards are gasoline engines. The weight and cost of diesels would be far too high for the craft these engines drive. In fact, it would be safe to say that diesel outboards—assuming they were widely available—would cost at least 30 percent more for the same horsepower—not to mention their extra weight. Would you be willing to pay this price? The same is true of inboard boats. When you're ready to write the check for your next *Dream Boat*, you'll find you need less in the bank to cover the cost of a gas-engine craft.

Diesels begin to come into their own on vessels that will see heavy usage over many years and—usually—on boats that don't require extremely high speeds. Few yachts put much more than 1,200 hours of use on their engine per year—many far less. But when usage gets higher than this and/or when boats grow larger—over 35 feet (11 m) or so—diesels start to look much more attractive.

Duty Rating and Engine Selection

Selecting a suitable diesel, however, presents a new set of choices. Four-cycle gas engines are almost always conversions of automobile engines. They are commonly available in just one power rating. Marine diesels are usually marinized truck or industrial engines. They're intended for different grades of duty, and thus the same engine will usually be available in differing power ratings.

If we take, as a typical example, Caterpillar's 3208 engine, we'll find that it is available in 12(!) versions. You could purchase this engine naturally aspirated, turbocharged, or turbocharged and aftercooled. Additionally, you could get each of these three versions rated for either continuous, medium, intermittent, or high-performance duty. The naturally aspirated continuous-duty version of the Cat 3208 delivers 150 brake horsepower (112 kw) at 2,400 rpm, and weighs about 1,740 pounds (790 kg). This comes to 11.6 pounds of engine weight per horsepower, or 7 kg/kw—pretty heavy, but well over 400 percent better than the heavy-weight thumpers some old-timers hark back to so fondly.

At the other end of the spectrum, the high-performance turbocharged and aftercooled Cat 3208 delivers 425 hp (317 kw) at 2,800 rpm, and weighs just 2,080 pounds (943 kg). This is 4.9 pounds of engine weight per horsepower (2.9 kg per kw)—230 percent better than the continuous-duty naturally-aspirated version, and an amazing 1,000 percent better than the marine engines of 60-plus years ago. About the ultimate in diesels is Merlin's 650-7.8 liter engine. Triple-turbocharged, intercooled and aftercooled, it delivers 650 hp

(485 kw)—one horsepower for every 2.38 pounds of engine weight, or one kw for every 1.44 kg!

For most yachts, the high-performance-rating diesel is most suitable. A continuous-duty-rating engine is tuned and set up at the factory to run indefinitely at full horsepower and full rpm. Yep, you could run it with the throttle wide open nearly 24 hours a day, 365 days a year. This kind of operation is intended for industrial generators and compressors. There's not a yacht around that would even begin to need such engine performance. Tugs, lighters, and commercial cargo-carriers sometimes install continuous-rated engines, but even they don't operate at full power *all* the time. Usually, small, heavy-displacement commercial vessels will use medium-duty engines, while patrol craft and lighter work boats will call for intermittent-duty engines. Really fast patrol boats will install the same high-performance engines used on yachts. The weight penalty for using engines rated for more prolonged power output would otherwise make these boats too slow.

The Price of Continuous-Duty Rating

We can see just how much of a weight penalty we'd pay by examining a continuous-duty naturally aspirated engine and a high-performance turbocharged engine of the same horsepower. Say, you've decided that you need twin 200-hp (150 kw) engines to drive your *Delicious Dancer* at speed. We could select two engines from the same manufacturer and see how they stack up. A continuous-duty naturally-aspirated Cummins N-855-M delivers 195 hp (145 kw) at 1,800 rpm, and weighs in at 3,435 pounds (1,568 kg)—over 1½ tons! By contrast, Cummins's turbocharged 6BT5.9-M diesel delivers 210 hp (156 kw) at 2,600 rpm, and weighs just 1,275 pounds (578 kg).

It is sometimes claimed that the extra complexity of turbocharging and intercooling or aftercooling adds too much maintenance, detracts from reliability, and increases cost. In reality, turbocharging and aftercooling allow you to get the same horsepower out of a smaller, lighter, less expensive engine. Even if maintenance costs are higher, you'd have to total up an awful lot of major overhauls to come out ahead with a continuous-duty naturally-aspirated engine for yacht use. Of course, this is exactly why medium-duty and continuous-rated engines become attractive on heavy commercial craft. They do stack up enough engine hours and overhauls to make these heavier engines cost effective. Further, keep in mind that turbochargers have been employed for decades; they are now very well perfected and reliable, and aftercoolers are very simple gizmos indeed, with virtually no moving parts.

Two-Cycle versus Four-

We're still faced with the question of two- or four-cycle engines—which is better? Again, it's not really a question of "better" so much as a question of weight versus horsepower. A four-cycle engine (gas or diesel) delivers a power stroke—not surprisingly—every fourth trip of the piston up or down. By contrast, a two-cycle engine has a power stroke every second stroke of the piston.

A four-cycle engine first draws fuel into the cylinder as the piston descends, then compresses the fuel on the piston's upswing. Next, the fuel is ignited (either by spark or by compression) and the force of the expanding gas delivers the power stroke, pushing the piston back down. Finally, the piston is driven back up again by the inertia of the flywheel and/or the power stroke of other pistons. This drives the burned gases out the exhaust port, at which point the entire cycle begins again.

A two-cycle engine starts with a power stroke.

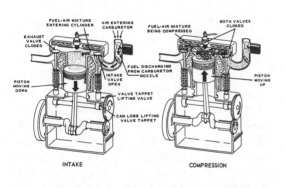

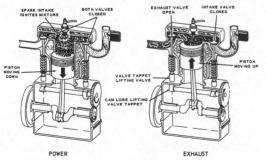

Operation of a four-cycle gas engine.

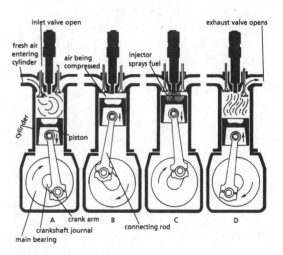

Operation of a four-cycle diesel engine. A is the intake stroke, B compression, C is the fuel injection and ignition, and D is the exhaust stroke. Note that with the air hot enough from compression alone, the fuel ignites as soon as it is sprayed into the cylinder.

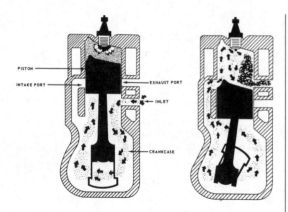

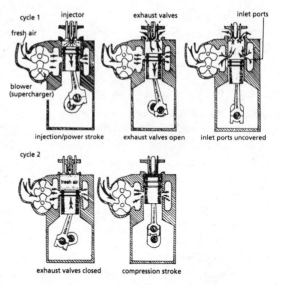

Operation of a two-cycle gas engine. Note how the fuel and air travel through the crankcase to reach the cylinder.

Operation of a two-cycle diesel engine. Unlike two-cycle gas engines, the fuel and air do not pass through the crankcase. (Courtesy Detroit Diesel.)

With the piston nearly at top dead center, new fuel has been sucked into the crankcase beneath the piston, and at the same time the spark or compression ignition takes place in the cylinder above the piston. The expanding gas pushes the piston down, which uncovers the exhaust port, automatically exhausting the burned gases as the piston descends. At nearly the same time, the inlet port is opened allowing the fresh charge of fuel and air—previously admitted to the crankcase below—to be forced into the cylinder above the piston. When the piston rises again, the fresh fuel mixture's compressed, and a new power stroke begins.

The net result is that, in theory, two-cycle engines should deliver twice the power of a four-cycle engine of the same weight. Twice as many power strokes is the same as twice as many pistons. In fact, two-cycle engines do weigh considerably less than four-cycle engines for the same power. This is why most small lightweight engines, such as outboards and lawnmower engines, are two-cycle engines. Four-cycle machines would be too heavy to be conveniently portable.

So why aren't we surrounded with nothing but light two-cycle engines? The answer is that the two-cycle engine isn't nearly as efficient at burning its fuel as the four-cycle machine. This is because in a two-cycle engine the process of getting rid of exhaust gases goes on at nearly the same time as the inflow of fresh fuel and air. Further, because the fuel-air mixture travels through the crankcase, the only way to lubricate a two-cycle machine is to mix its oil with the gas. (Four-cycle engines have a separate sealed lubrication system that's much more efficient.) It's this that gives two-cycle engines their characteristic blue-smoke exhaust.

The result is that combustion's never as clean or as complete as in a four-cycle engine that has a dedicated intake and a dedicated exhaust stroke. Accordingly, although two-cycle engines produce more power per pound or kilogram of engine weight, they use more fuel for each hp or kw pro-

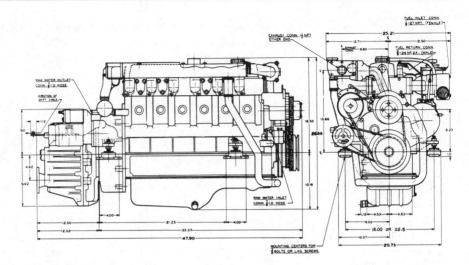

Dimensional drawing of the Westerbeke 100, a four-cycle diesel engine. (Courtesy J.H. Westerbeke Corp.)

duced. In hard usage, you can quickly burn more money in fuel than you'd save by installing a smaller, less expensive two-cycle engine.

Just as with diesel versus gas engines, the trade-off between two- and four-cycle engines is in hours of use and boat speed. Very light high-speed boats can benefit from the low weight of two-cycle engines. Additionally, boats that see limited usage don't require the additional cost of a larger heavier four-cycle engine; however, larger, heavier craft—vessels of roughly 30 feet and over—and boats that are going to see many hours of use for years and years, would be poorly served by saving money on a fuel-guzzling two-cycle engine. Here, four-cycle is the clear winner.

Reliability, RPM, and Piston Speed

Okay, we now have enough information to select the best type of engine for a given boat. Small, light, high-speed craft usually do best with gas engines and/or two-cycle engines, while larger, heavier vessels become candidates for high-per-

formance diesels. Heavy charter yachts, fishing vessels, and patrol vessels might do even better with the still heavier intermittent-duty engines. But how do you choose between two engines of the same type and duty rating, of similar horsepower and weight?

There are many factors to consider. Reliability and ease of repair are certainly two of the most important. There's no easy way to judge this from engine spec sheets. You simply have to keep your ear to the ground and get a feel for the reputations of different manufacturers. What do mechanics think of the engines you're considering? Does the manufacturer have a large dealer network? Are parts and service readily available? Beyond these considerations, however, there are factors you can compare when looking for the most reliable engine. Piston speed and rpm, for instance, give excellent clues to an engine's longevity.

These two factors are directly related. All other things being equal, the faster an engine turns, for a given piston displacement, the more power the engine will deliver. Accordingly, the natural tendency has been for manufacturers to increase their engine speeds to get more horsepower. Unfortunately, the faster turning engine places considerably more wear and tear on its moving parts. If you're comparing two engines of similar weight, horsepower, and cost, the engine with the lowest rpm and piston speed will usually prove to be the longest lasting and the quietest.

Naturally, you can read rpm directly from the manufacturer's literature, but piston speed takes a minute's thought. Each piston goes up and then down again once for each shaft revolution. Thus, if you double the piston stroke and multiply it by the rpm, you'll get piston speed. For example, the Cummins 4BT3.9-M engine has a stroke of 4.72 inches (119.8 mm) and operates at a maximum of 2,800 rpm. Two times 4.72 inches is 9.44 inches or 0.78 feet, and 0.78 feet times 2,800 rpm equal 2,184 feet per minute—or 2 × 119.8 mm = 239.6 mm, and 239.6 mm × 2,800 rpm = 670 meters per minute.

As a general rule, marine engines should not have piston speeds over 2,500 feet per minute (760 m/min.). For really long life, piston speeds of 1,500 feet per minute (470 m/min.) or less are best; however, engines that operate at such low speeds tend to be heavy. When comparing engines, though, make a quick calculation of their piston speed, and keep in mind that the slower piston speed engine will—other things being equal—last the longest. If, for instance, you'd been considering another engine of the same approximate horsepower and weight as the Cummins, but its piston speed worked out to be 2,400 feet per minute (748 m/min.), it would be a good argument in favor of the Cummins.

CHAPTER 25

Let's Talk Torquey: Torque, Fuel Consumption, and How They Affect Your Engine's Performance

. . . this torque reaction may account for the way stars contract into dwarfs and pulsars, or for the way that galaxies pulsate or contract into the incredibly vast and dense, paradoxically named "black holes."

Synergetics, R.Buckminster Fuller

Seven hundred horsepower! The gleaming machine looms before you—it looks like it means business. It draws you in off the main aisle of the boat show. On green-carpeted floor you stalk purposefully around, admiring the flawless paint job, polished hardware, and massive fittings. Why, the exhaust must be 9 inches (23 cm) in diameter. With a tinge of regret, you walk to the other side of the booth to inspect the 150-hp (112 kw) models that fit your vessel. You've been considering repowering, or maybe you're wondering which engine option to have installed in your new boat. Most of these engines have their horsepower posted in conspicuous placards. Should you go for more power? How can you make intelligent decisions about your next engine?

Marine engines are complex gizmos; you can't choose one based on a single number—horsepower—alone. In the previous chapter, we investigated the pros and cons of gas and diesel engines, two-stroke versus four-stroke, power-to-weight ratio, and several other considerations. But we still have to talk torquey . . . excuse me, I mean talk torque.

Power Means Work In Time

Horsepower or kilowatts are—surprise—measures of power, and power is the amount of work done in a specific period of time. Let's say you go and take out three trash cans, lifting them 10 feet (3 m) out of the cellar. The total work you'd have done—as you'd well know—would be 30 foot–trash cans, or 9 meter–trash cans. Since it's obvious that lifting three trash cans 10 feet (3 m) is the same as lifting one trash can 30 feet (9 m), we just multiplied feet or meters times trash cans and presto—work! If you completed this remarkable domestic feat in, say, 2 minutes—no sense lingering over this chore—you'd have been producing 15 foot–trash cans per minute of power, or 4.5 meter–trash cans of power (30 foot–trash cans ÷ 2 min. = 15 foot–trash cans/min—or, 9 meter–trash cans ÷ 2 min. = 4.5 meter–trash cans/min.).

Why do I suddenly feel the urge to collapse in

front of the TV with a cold beer? All we did is divide the total work done by the time it took. This gives power.

Happily for the engineering world, work is not measured in "foot—or meter—trash cans" but in foot-pounds or kilogram-meters. If those cans each weighed 20 pounds (10 kg), then you'd have been delivering 300 foot-pounds per minute, or 45 kgm/min. of power (20 lb. × 3 trash cans = 60 lb., 60 lb. × 10 ft. = 600 ft.-lb., and 600 ft.-lb. ÷ 2 min. = 300 ft.-lb./min; or 10 kg × 3 trash cans = 30 kg, 30 kg × 3 m = 90 kgm, and 90 kgm ÷ 2 min. = 45 kgm/ min.).

Now, a horsepower is defined as 33,000 foot-pounds of work per minute, or 550 foot-pounds of work per second. If we divide your 300 foot-pounds per minute by 33,000 we find that you've been delivering a bit over $\frac{1}{100}$ of a horsepower. Alternately, a kilowatt can be defined as 6,120 kgm/min., or 102 kgm/sec. If we divide your 45 kgm/min. by 6,120, we find that you've been delivering a bit over $\frac{1}{130}$ of a kilowatt. (I don't feel that beer is quite so necessary now.)

Human Power?

It's interesting to note that a first-class male athlete can produce just under 2 hp (1.5 kw) for about 6 seconds, at which time he'll be ready for a nice nap. (Top women athletes produce a bit less, but still plenty more than the average Joe can expect to deliver.) An ordinary fellow, in good condition, can deliver about $\frac{1}{4}$ horsepower (1/5 kw) for 40 minutes or so, and $\frac{1}{6}$ to $\frac{1}{7}$ hp ($\frac{1}{8}$ to $\frac{1}{10}$ kw) for hours at a time. Rowing an average boat at speed takes about $\frac{1}{6}$ hp or $\frac{1}{8}$ kw, which is close to the maximum power output you can deliver continuously. All this might have something to do with the wide popularity of outboard-powered dinks.

The Torque Twist

At any rate, you can see that power—horsepower or kilowatts—is work done in a given time. If you want your *Snazzy Snorkeler* to go faster, you want her engine to do more work in a given time, so you want more power. It would seem that power was *the* thing. But there's a catch. The only way to transfer the power from your engine to the water is through the propeller. You have to convert the power from the engine into a twisting force called "torque." No torque, no propeller rotation, no go. Now, torque's just a force in pounds times a distance. Imagine a 5-foot (2 m) pole projecting horizontally and fastened at one end. Put a 10-pound (5 kg) weight on the free end, and the result is 50 pound-feet or 10 kgm of torque. (In the English system, "foot-pounds" really means the same thing, but "pound-feet" is used for torque to keep from confusing it with the "foot-pounds" of "work.")

The more torque your engine can deliver to the propeller the bigger the propeller it can turn and the more thrust the propeller can generate. Thus you could have two engines with the same horsepower, but one configuration might deliver only 800 pound-feet (110 kgm) of torque to the propeller, while the other delivered 1,600 pound-feet (220 kgm). Even with exactly the same horsepower, the boat with most torque delivered to the prop will be faster or more efficient.

And Now . . . The Tricky Part

So far so good, but here things get tricky. Since power is work done in a given amount of time—as we saw last chapter—one of the simplest ways to get more power out of a particular engine block is to make the engine turn faster. More revolutions per minute mean more work done in that minute. Since it's relatively easy and it works, this is the approach used by most engine manufacturers. Unfortunately, as rpm increases, torque decreases (!)—a classic catch-22. In fact, there's a very simple formula for torque:

Torque (lb.-ft.) = (5,252 × hp) ÷ rpm

Torque (kgm) = (975.17 × kw) ÷ rpm

If you had an engine that delivered 200 hp (149 kw) at 1,800 rpm, its torque would be 583 pound-feet or 81 kgm. Another engine delivering the exact same 200 hp (149 kw), but at 2,800 rpm, would only be generating 375 pound-feet or 52 kgm of torque. This is one heck of a good argument for slow-turning engines (not to mention the fact that such engines run quieter and—broadly speaking—last longer.) There's another big catch here, though. Slow-turning engines are—as we've seen—heavy for the power they produce. On planing boats in particular, you don't want to be lugging around any more weight than you have to. Even on displacement cruisers and sailboats, you want to avoid taking up any more space on board for the engine than is really required, and heavy engines are almost always big engines—expensive too.

This Calls For a Reduction

Luckily there's a way around this dilemma—the reduction gear. Using a reduction gear, you can convert the low-torque, high-rpm power of a fast-turning engine to the slow, high-torque power

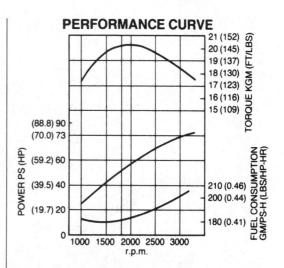

PERFORMANCE CURVE

Engine performance curves for the Westerbeke 70 diesel engine. (Courtesy J.H. Westerbeke Corp.)

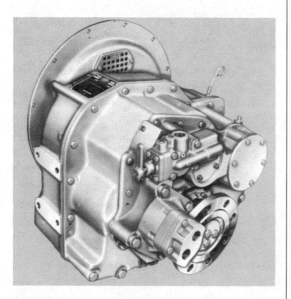

Twin Disc MG-510A reduction gear.

required to swing a large, efficient propeller. You don't get something for nothing, of course; reduction gears do cost money and usually burn up a little extra power—around 3 percent—in friction, but the trade-off is almost always worthwhile.

If we took the same 200-hp (149 kw) 2,800-rpm engine we looked at above and added a 3-to-1 reduction gear, the propeller would see a huge increase in torque. Just subtract 3 percent from power to allow for friction in the gearbox and we're left with 194 hp (144 kw). At the same time, though, we've cut shaft revolutions at the propeller by one-third, to only 933 rpm. The propeller's now receiving 1,109 pound-feet or 150 kgm of torque (5,252 × 194 hp ÷ 933 rpm = 1,109 lb.-ft.—or, 975.17 × 144 kw ÷ 933 rpm = 150 kgm).

And The Torque Falls Off

You can see the importance of torque, which leads to another consideration—how torque falls off at high shaft speeds for a given engine. This has a further effect on engine selection. For almost all internal combustion engines, torque decreases at high rpm. This appears clearly on the performance curves available from most engine manufacturers. Maximum torque usually occurs somewhere between 50 and 70 percent of maximum rpm and maximum power.

If you look at the performance curves of the Westerbeke 70—a typical diesel—you can see that the upper curve shows torque, the middle curve power, and the bottom curve fuel consumption. While the power curve continually increases with faster rpm, the torque curve falls off sharply after about 1,800 rpm. It's somewhere around this rpm—the rpm of maximum torque—that you'll want to run your engine for most efficient service. (The graph gives values for power, torque, and fuel consumption in both English and European units. "PS" is European horsepower, or *Puissance en Chevaux;* KGM is the metric measure of torque, in kilogram-meters; and GM/PS-H is grams per European horsepower per hour.)

Of course, at 1,800 rpm this engine's only delivering about 52 hp (39 kw). You don't need to limit yourself this much. In fact, the curve shows that somewhere between 2,300 rpm and 2,500 rpm would give you between 62 and 68 hp (46 and 51 kw). At the same time, the fuel consumption curve

A Ford V-8 four-cycle gas engine that delivers 285 hp (212 kw) at 4,800 rpm.

This Yamaha V-6 four-cycle gasoline sterndrive puts out 180 hp (134 kw) at 4,600 rpm. Affordable and fuel efficient gas engines like this power more boats than any other type. (Courtesy Yamaha)

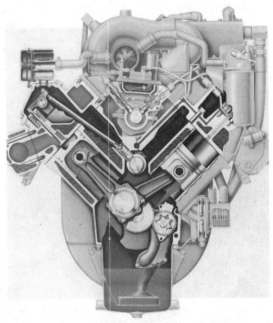

Cutaway view of Caterpillar's 3208-TA turbocharged and aftercooled marine diesel. This pleasure-craft or high-output version produces 425 hp (312 kw) at 2,800 rpm. (Courtesy Caterpillar)

hasn't climbed too steeply. This, then is the ideal cruising speed for this engine—between 2,300 and 2,500 rpm. It's the power delivered at these shaft speeds that controls how your boat will really behave most of the time.

The Turbines That Never Were

The fuel consumption curve brings us to another consideration in selecting an engine: how much fuel your engine burns to deliver each horsepower or kilowatt. This affects both your range and operating costs. (The more you use your boat, the more important this is.) I can remember wandering the 1964 New York World's Fair. It seemed that every automobile and engine maker's exhibit featured visions of a future that would have us all tooling around in cars powered by gas turbine engines: "They're the wave of the future!" Popular car and science magazines were filled with more of the same. Detroit had sunk millions into research and development.

So why, nearly 30 years later, aren't you driving to work in a gas turbine car? Specific fuel consumption, that's why. Gas turbines deliver more power per pound of engine weight than almost any other internal combustion engine. Unfortunately they are, well...fuel hogs, cubed and squared. The bottom line, the make-and-break proposition, for any power plant is how fuel-efficient it is. Even a very light, very inexpensive engine that burns fuel at a tremendous rate will be too costly to operate in the long run—and gas turbines are anything but inexpensive!

Of course, there are applications where engine weight can outweigh fuel efficiency. Airplanes use gas turbines extensively because of their lightness. The M1 tank is driven by turbines—Uncle Sam can afford the fuel bills. A few very high-speed patrol boats and ultra-high-speed megayachts also use gas turbines, but they're almost all fitted with standard diesels as well, for routine operation. Their gas turbines are for sprints only—racing, chases, combat, and related excitement. If they were to run on the turbines regularly, they'd spend almost all their time in port refueling.

Examining The Costs

For you and your *Snazzy Snorkeler,* however, the important thing, when considering two engines of roughly the same weight, cost, power, and torque, is to compare their fuel consumption at operating speed. The Westerbeke 70 curves show that it will consume about 0.419 pounds of diesel per horsepower-hour, or 254 g/kw/hr. You can convert this to gallons or liters per hour by multiplying it by the total power, at the rpm being considered, and dividing by the specific weight of your fuel:

Gal./hr. = *(Specific Fuel Consumption × hp)*
÷ *Fuel Specific Weight*

Liter/hr. = *(Specific Fuel Consumption × kw)*
÷ *Fuel Specific Weight*

The Textron Lycoming TF 40 gas turbine eninge produces 4,600 hp (3,430 kw) at 16, 135 rpm! The 100-foot (30.5 m) Gentry Eagle was fitted with one of these on her attempt to break the transatlantic speed record. How much does one of these machines cost? If you have to ask, forget it.

Two Strokes to the Future?

We've seen that two-stroke or two-cycle engines are lighter for the same power than four-cycle engines. Their problem is that they're fuel hogs and that their exhaust is dirty. Chrysler and Mercury Marine, as well as several other manufacturers, are working on making clean, fuel-efficient two-cycle engines. If they succeed these machines will be the wave of the future.

These engines are known as EBDI (External Breathing Direct Injection). As you can see in the drawing, the Mercury/Chrysler version has gas injected directly into the cylinder after the inlet and outlet ports are closed. This ensures that scavenging (removing) the burned exhaust gases from the last cycle takes place cleanly and completely, before the fresh fuel charge is admitted. It also ends the requirement for mixing oil with the gasoline, which makes for cleaner combustion. EBDI engines should eliminate the inefficiencies that have plagued two-cycle machines.

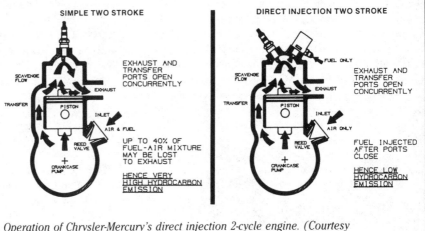

Operation of Chrysler-Mercury's direct injection 2-cycle engine. (Courtesy Mercury Marine and Chrysler Corp.)

SPECIFIC WEIGHTS

	Pounds/Gallon	Kilograms/Liter
Diesel Fuel	7.2	0.86
Gasoline	6.1	0.73

This means that at 2,400 rpm, delivering 68 hp (50.7 kw), the Westerbeke 70 is consuming 3.96, say 4, gallons per hour (15 l/hr.). If *Snazzy Snorkeler* is fitted with a 300-gallon (1,135 l) fuel tank, this translates to 75 hours of continuous operation. With a cruising speed of 12 knots, this would give *Snorkeler* a range of 900 nautical miles. At the same time, if you cruised in *Snazzy* 600 hours per year, she'd be burning about 2,400 gallons (9,080 l). At today's U.S. prices, that's about $2,500 in fuel bills per season.

If another similar engine showed a specific fuel consumption at 68 hp (50.7 kw) of 0.45 pounds per horsepower hour (274 g/kw/hr.), that engine would reduce your range to 838 nautical miles—a loss of 7 percent. This engine would also cost you an additional $175 per year in fuel, or, over the seven or eight years you'll probably own *Snazzy Snorkeler*, an extra $1,300. In fact, the more hours you put on your boat, the more significant specific fuel consumption becomes.

CHAPTER 26

The Care and Feeding of a Power Plant (Of Engine Vents, Fuel Lines, Mufflers and Things)

Cars are normally serviced at regular intervals, but I wonder how many boats' engines receive the same treatment?

Power Boats in Rough Seas, Dag Pike

Almost like a living, breathing creature, your engine needs care and consideration. Throttle it with a clogged fuel line or choke it with insufficient air and performance will falter. Internal combustion engines are much like people doing hard exercise. The perfect conditions for jogging, for instance, are a cool, dry, shady day, at sea level. This is the environment you should try to create in your engine compartment—low humidity, 50° F or 10° C, and oodles of clean fresh air. In reality, such engine room conditions are impossible to achieve, but it's the ideal to strive for.

Give it Air, Give it Air

I'm frequently amazed by the tiny engine vents I see fitted in high-powered craft. On one real 35-foot (10.6 m) twin-diesel sportfisherman—we'll call her *After Burner*—lifting the engine hatch after a hard day's run releases a blast of air almost too hot to bear. In fact, a thermometer placed in *After Burner*'s engine compartment topped out at 135° F (57° C). No wonder this vessel didn't need to turn on its cabin heater until late fall!

The fact is, though, that engine compartment temperatures this high are hot enough to reduce the strength of a wood or fiberglass hull. Further, engines aren't designed to work in this kind of heat—any more than you are. Gaskets and hoses soften or crack in prolonged high temperatures, and your engine can't develop its full power. This is because hot air is less dense than cold air. Quite literally less weight (mass) of air can be forced into the same space when it's hot than when it's cold. Since the amount of power your engine produces depends on the quantity of air crammed into the combustion chamber during each intake stroke, rarefied, lightweight hot air delivers less oomph per gallon or liter of fuel burned than dense, heavy, cool air—no matter how much you turbocharge or intercool.

Most of the information I've come across on the subject of engine-compartment vents was contradictory and unnecessarily complicated. Some systems based vent area on engine compartment volume, others on boat length or beam, while at the same time various engine manufacturers had specific recommendations for their individual engines, which—needless to say—never agreed with the engine-compartment or boat-length methods.

After a fair amount of research, however, I've worked up a pair of simple rules that will allow you to determine if you have sufficient vent area:

Minimum Vent Area (sq.in.) $= hp \div 3.3$

Vent Area (cm²) $= kw \times 2.6$

Minimum Air Flow (cu.ft./min.) $= (2.75 \times hp) - 90$

Minimum Air Flow (m³/min.) $= (3.42 \times kw) - 2.5$

The minimum vent area is the minimum area for natural ventilation without blowers. It makes allowance for standard louvers or grills over the vent openings and for some simple form of baffle box or vent piping. If extensive baffling and/or piping is employed, you'll need to up the minimum area by 20 percent or more.

Vents of this size should provide the air flows indicated by the minimum air flow formulas; however—since you can never have too much air in an engine room—I like to install vents equal to at least 10 percent greater area than recommended, if possible—*plus* forced-air exhaust blowers equal to about one-third the recommended capacity per minute.

After Burner was fitted with twin 325-hp (242 kw) diesels, so she requires a minimum of 197 square inches (1,260 cm²) of vent area (325 hp × 2 = 650 hp, and 650 hp ÷ 3.3 = 197 sq.in.—or, 242 kw × 2 = 484 kw, and 484 kw × 2.6 = 1,260 cm²). The real *After Burner* was fitted with four 4-inch by 5-inch (10 cm by 13 cm) louvered vents, which may seem like plenty, but works out to a bare 80 square inches (520 cm²)—less than half the required minimum. What's more, the air had to travel down long, narrow, twisted ducts to reach her engines. No wonder she ran so hot. In fact, it's a bit of a wonder she kept running at all.

The ideal venting for *After Burner*'s engines would be 10 percent greater than the minimum of 197 square inches (1,260 cm²), or around 220 sq.in. (1,420 cm²), plus a pair of 250 cubic-foot-per-minute (7 m³/min.) exhaust blowers. (The minimum air flow formula recommends 1,697 cubic feet per minute, and 1,697 cu.ft./min ÷ 3 = 565 cu.ft./min., which about equals two 250 cu.ft./min. blowers—or, minimum flow recommendation is 48 m³/min., and 48 m³/min. ÷ 3 = 16 m³/min., which about equals two 7 m³/min. blowers.) These blowers should be wired to run whenever the ignition is turned on, for diesel boats. On gasoline craft they should be turned on *at least* five minutes before engine start, and left on thereafter. This means the blowers must be rated for continuous duty. It also means that you need to check your electric system to ensure it can handle this modest but continuous additional load (a potential problem on some low-powered sailboats, but seldom a difficulty on powerboats.)

Engine-compartment blowers, by the way, should always be set to exhaust—never as intake. If air is forced into the engineroom, it raises the pressure slightly, driving unpleasant engine odors out into the rest of the boat.

Two-hundred-fifty-cubic-feet-per-minute (7 m³/min.) blowers are standard 4-inch-diameter (10 cm) blowers. The exhaust outlets can be led through baffle boxes on the side of the hull, as shown in the drawing. A clamshell vent is installed on the hull exterior over the opening. If the vent runs through the hull side, the clamshell opening should face aft and be angled down about 15 degrees. If the vent is through the transom, the clamshell opening should be angled down and inboard, toward the boat centerline, at about 30 degrees.

Remember that these vent area rules give minimum numbers. You can't have too much engine compartment ventilation. Check the vent area on your existing boat. You'll often find that you have less than the recommended minimum. If at all possible, you should add more vent area or

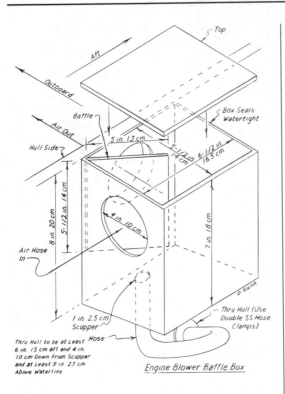

Labels on diagram:
Top
Aft
Outboard
Baffle
Air Out
Hull Side
Box Seals Watertight
5 in. 13 cm
5-1/2 in. 14 cm
6-1/2 in. 16.5 cm
8 in. 20 cm
5-1/2 in. 14 cm
4 in. 10 cm
7 in. 18 cm
Air Hose In
1 in. 2.5 cm Scupper
Hose
Thru Hull (Use Double SS Hose Clamps)
D Gerr

Thru Hull to be at Least 6 in. 15 cm aft and 4 in. 10 cm Down From Scupper and at Least 9 in. 23 cm Above Waterline

Engine Blower Baffle Box

forced ventilation. Your engine will last longer, your fuel consumption will improve, and your engine will smell sweeter too.

Of course, there's one very important proviso here. You can never have too much air in the engine room, but you can easily have too much water! You *must* ensure that water can't find its way below through your new vents—or your old ones either, for that matter. Keeping vent openings fairly high and including water traps and/or baffles is critical. Also, never forget that gasoline engine compartments absolutely *must* be fitted with Coast Guard-approved, explosion-proof exhaust vent blowers. Omitting this little detail is not only downright dangerous, it's also *really* a crime!

A final engine room refinement is to install a solar-powered exhaust vent or two. These vents are independent of the ship's electric system, and run whenever the sun is shining. Thus, even when

you're away from your *Sagacious Sailor,* her engine room is being well ventilated. You'll find a dramatic reduction in mildew, rust, and unpleasant oil and fuel smells.

Vent requirements for sailboats and motor-sailers are exactly the same—an engine is an engine. Remember also to include the total power of all machinery installed in the engine room. If *After Burner* had a 12-kw generator you'd add 18 hp or 13.4 kw for it. (A fair estimate of generator engine power is: hp = 1.5 × rated kw output, or kw = 1.12 × rated hp output.)

Taking the Measure of the Exhaust

Perhaps the least-considered aspect of many engine installations is the exhaust. When you mull over repowering, you investigate whether the engine will fit in the available space, whether the shaft can still be made to line up properly, if the existing engine beds are up to the job, and so on. But the exhaust is frequently an afterthought. This can lead you into difficulties. (I know, it's happened to me several times.) Particularly when converting from gas to diesel, the size of the new exhaust line and its resulting much larger muffler, may make it almost impossible for it to fit—even when everything else does.

Your engine manufacturer will be able to tell

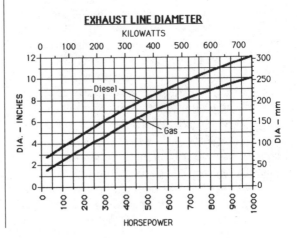

EXHAUST LINE DIAMETER

you the exact diameter for a standard wet exhaust; however, the accompanying chart will give you a very close estimate based on horsepower, and works well for engines from 25 to 1,000 hp, or 18 to 750 kw.

If *After Burner* had been fitted with twin 325-hp (242 kw) gas engines, the chart shows that she'd have required a 5-inch-diameter (13 cm) exhaust tube. Should you decide to repower old *After Burner* with diesels of exactly the same horsepower, however, the chart indicates that she'd need a 6-inch (15 cm) exhaust. That inch (or 2 cm) may not seem like much, but combined with its fatter mufflers and the already cramped space you're fighting in every boat, it can make installing the new, larger exhaust quite tricky. The arrangement drawing of the Off Soundings 34 in Chapter 10 shows her 6-inch (152 mm), twin-diesel exhaust runs. You can see how much space they take up.

Watering the Exhaust

Almost all yachts are fitted with wet exhaust. Engine cooling water is routed into the exhaust line a short distance aft of the manifold. The water not only cools the exhaust piping to safe levels, but quiets the exhaust as well. It is important, however, to have sufficient water flow. Standard marine engines are all set up in this regard at the factory. If you're installing a converted engine, however, the following will give you the minimum safe waterflow:

$$\text{Exhaust-Line Water Flow (gal./min.)} =$$

$$\frac{\text{Engine Displacement (cu. in.)} \times rpm}{66,000}$$

$$\text{Exhaust-Line Water Flow (l/min.)} =$$

$$\frac{\text{Engine Displacement (liters)} \times rpm}{285.7}$$

Smooth Feeding

Also, like any living creature, your engine needs food. Should your fuel line get clogged, you'll hear a few short gasps and then . . . nothing. This can lead to some very interesting situations. Fuel clogs invariably seem to occur when you're in tight quarters and have no time to clear it, or

This fuel piping schematic shows the simplest and most reliable arrangement, suited to almost any craft. If you have no generator, just omit the generator piping. If your vessel is single-engined, simply cross out the second engine and its piping. Small runabouts and day boats can be fitted with a single fuel tank. Larger craft should always be equipped with two or more. It costs a bit more to do this, and some less-expensive large cruisers have only one tank, but this is bad news. Why? If your lone tank springs a leak or becomes clogged or contaminated, you've had it—no more fuel. With twin tanks you can almost always manage to motor home.

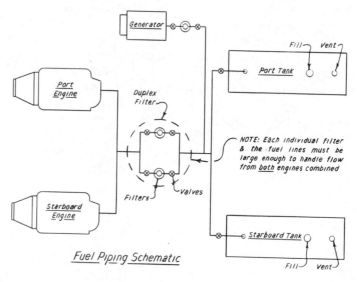

Fuel Piping Schematic

when you're far out with no access to help and a squall is lurking on the horizon. One of the best ways to avoid fuel-line clogs is to rig a double fuel filter. Again, this is not a difficult addition, and it can save you hours of grief.

By plumbing these double filters as shown, you can switch from one filter to the other with the engine running. What's more, you can remove either filter (or both in turn) to clean them without missing a stroke. Sometimes I think this double filter arrangement should be Coast Guard-required equipment. It's also not a bad idea to use a large, deep metal funnel with a screen mesh filter when filling her up. This is especially useful when cruising foreign ports; the fuel standards in some out-of-the way islands are not what they should be.

Tame that Roar

Another consideration is noise. No, it doesn't hurt your engine, but eight or nine hours in company with a whining, trembling power plant can sure make a crew agitated. Your engine will just seem to be working that much smoother if its running quiet. Good engine mounts and a proper exhaust line are essential; however, many sailors don't take the next step, which is to soundproof the engine room.

To accomplish this you have to do two things. First, you should seal the engine compartment as well as possible from the rest of the boat—make sure you don't interfere with ventilation. Gaskets and spring-type lock-down latches or clamps should be fitted on all engine hatches and engine-box covers. Then you should apply proper sound-proofing sheets to the inside faces of the engine compartment bulkheads, overhead, hatches, and so on.

One of the best soundproofing materials is 1 inch (2.5 cm) of open-cell foam (or fiberglass) with 1-pound-per-square-foot (4.8 kg/m^2) lead sheet embedded in it. The foam absorbs much noise energy and the weight or inertia of the lead dampens vibration very effectively. A really first-class job will use 3 inches (8 cm) of foam with lead. A nice feature offered by commercial suppliers of marine soundproofing is a surface coating of aluminized mylar or a similar substance. These tough, smooth surfaces protect the foam and make it far easier to clean.

Sound insulation need not be costly. One- to 3-inch (2.5 to 8 cm) insulation of this type runs about four to six dollars per square foot ($43 to $65 per m^2). A fairly typical mid-sized planing cruiser would require around 40 square feet (3.7 m^2) of sheet foam insulation, or just about $300 to $400 dollars of materials. The difference in peace and quiet can be worth 10 times this. Some luxury yachts go even further. They not only use thicker foam (up to 8 inches or 20 cm at times), but they'll soundproof the hull over the propeller, install sound-deadening mats under the cabin soles, and even place additional soundproofing shrouds around each engine and generator. A few of these vessels—frequently 80- and 90-footers (24 to 27 m)—can thrash their way through a chop at 20 knots plus, yet be so quiet in the saloon that you can enjoy listening to classical music. Now that's the life.

CHAPTER 27

The Case of the Boat That Shook or Engine Nightmare

She thought that she had been similarly frightened once last week, and that the noise was of a mysterious kind—a sound of rustling and of three or four quick beats like a rapid step; while a shock or tremble was communicated to her heart, as if the step had shaken the floor. . . .

Little Dorrit, Charles Dickens

(Although the names and events in the following story may have been changed, oh, just a little, the shaking boat really existed and behaved exactly as described.)

It was a dark, wet morning. Rain spattered on the office windows, and inside the yellow glow from my desk lamp cast angular shadows. I leaned back and contemplated a cold cup of coffee.

The phone rang.

I picked it up.

"Gerr Marine," I answered imaginatively.

"Mr. Archer?" a woman's voice responded. It was soft and throaty but with a definite quaver.

"Nope, Archer . . . aah . . . left the firm a few years ago," I said. "My name's Gerr, Dave Gerr. What can I do for you?"

There was a long pause.

"Umm , Mr. Gerr, I'm in terrible trouble. I . . . I wonder, could I come and see you? I'm just around the corner."

"Sure, come on up," I replied. I heard the phone click and cradled the receiver.

A few moments later the door opened and Effie ushered her in.

She was slender, with auburn hair. The clothes she wore had seen at least three fittings and her makeup had been applied just so, or would have been if her eyes hadn't been red and puffy from crying. She clutched her small handbag tightly as she seated herself.

Effie handed me a card as she turned to go. Her name was Ginger, Ginger Wells, senior claims adjuster for Acme Marine Insurance. I flipped the card onto my desk blotter and tried to look businesslike.

"Tell me about it?" I suggested.

She looked straight at me, and then down at the floor. A vein in her neck pulsed, and she shook herself.

"It's . . . it's one of my claims," she said, "a fellow named Dodge. His boat has terrible problems, just terrible. My . . . my fiancé is the surveyor who approved her for coverage, and if we can't straighten this out, he'll lose his job."

Fiancé, I thought. I wondered if he appreciated the vein in her neck. "Okay," I said, opening my notebook. "Tell me just what's wrong with the boat."

"It shakes," she said.

I stared at her. "You mean it vibrates."

"Well . . . yes, you could call it that, I suppose," she replied. "But really it shakes. When Seymour did the pre-insurance survey he didn't find anything wrong. Everything checked out. All the systems were in order. The hull was sound. We just can't figure it out.

"She's a 40-footer (12 m), the *Lucky Lou*, out of Cascade, New York—on the Hudson." She glanced up briefly. "Mr. Dodge bought her from Drexall Boats on Town Island last year, and he had Seymour check her out. She was delivered a few weeks later, and everything seemed fine until Mr. Dodge called to say that she was shaking. Whenever she was out in any sort of chop with the engine over 1,200 rpm, the boat would shake very badly.

"Seymour went up a couple of times to try and find the problem, but nothing seemed to help."

I'd always liked women who understood boats, and there was no doubt that Ginger knew what she was talking about. The light from my desk lamp flashed across her russet hair, and I briefly considered changing my name to Seymour.

"Look," I offered a bit smugly. "This is the oldest problem around. You've got nothing to worry about. The prop clearance is probably too small. We'll switch the *Lucky Lou* to a prop with more blades and plenty of skew. Check the shaft alignment and maybe try some flexible engine mounts. She'll run as smooth as silk."

To my surprise, she slumped in her chair. Her fingers dug into the leather of her purse.

"Oh, no," she replied. "Seymour tried all that. We tried new propellers, flexible shaft couplings, new engine mounts, realigning the engines. It didn't help . . . It didn't help at all."

That's interesting, I thought. "Can I get up to see the boat?" I asked. "I'd like to take her for a spin, then have her hauled and get a look at her from underneath."

"Oh, would you?" she responded. She sat up, her face brimming with hope. "Do you think you can really figure it out?"

"Sure, doll. Nothing to it," I said, putting on my knowledgeable expression.

It was just two days later that I found myself driving upstate in the blue Chevy. The cold, hard weight of my tape measure felt reassuring clipped to the belt against my hip. Ginger sat beside me admiring the scenery. She had her window open and her hair fluttered elegantly in the breeze. I wondered how a classy dame like this could fall for a scrawny little surveyor named Seymour.

All too soon, we arrived at Ripley Boatyard and were shaking hands with Mr. Dodge—"just call me Bill." We all trooped down the dock to the *Lucky Lou.*

She looked good tied in her slip. Running a critical eye over her, I could appreciate that, whoever her designer was, he could wield a pencil with the best of 'em. The *Lucky Lou* was no gold-plater, but she certainly appeared to be a well-thought-out production motorcruiser. Her deckhouse arrangement was particularly clever. She had more room aboard than most 40-footers (12 meters).

I tended the dock lines as Bill Dodge eased his boat out into the river, and then clambered up to join him on the bridge. The *Lucky Lou* handled smartly and motored steadily. I wondered what the problem was.

"Nice boat," I said. "I like the layout, and she handles well at low speed."

"Yeah," Bill replied. "My wife and I love the arrangement, and she steers very well, but just wait a minute. We're almost out in the chop, and I'll open her up a bit. You'll see."

We'd arranged to take a short hop up the river to Jack's Boat Shop and have the *Lucky Lou* hauled right away. Bill had assured us that the quick trip would be all that we'd need to see the problem in action.

Then it happened. Bill swung the *Lucky Lou* north and pushed the throttle forward. The boat quivered, then started to shake. Ginger tripped and I grabbed her to keep her from falling. I wouldn't have minded helping to steady her a bit longer, but there was too much to do. The *Lucky Lou* was quivering and jumping like she was made of rubber. We could hear things clattering about below.

"Geezuus!" I exclaimed intelligently.

Bill looked at me sharply. He held the throttle up firmly. Clearly, he meant for us to get the full effect.

I decided to take a look below.

The cabin was a shambles. The removable floor panels were jumping out of their places. Pots and pans were crashing about the galley. I knelt on the galley sole to peer into one of the open floor panels. Suddenly something big crashed into my leg. I looked up in disbelief. The refrigerator— nearly a full-size house model—had broken loose from its moorings and walked its way two feet across the floor to threaten me. It teetered back and forth, ready to crush me in an instant.

I jumped up and grabbed it in the nick of time. "Okay!" I shouted up the hatchway. "I'm convinced. Ease her off."

The engine drone slacked and the uncontrollable shaking faded to an uncomfortable throb, with an occasional ragged jerk thrown in for variety. Bill remained at the helm while Ginger and I cleaned up the worst of the mess and muscled the menacing fridge back into its corner.

We clambered back to the bridge and I scanned the river. Sun glinted off the water and a moderate breeze whispered past my ears. It was a fine day, just a bit of chop, and clear sailing. I shuddered to think what could happen if the *Lucky Lou* was caught out in a real blow, when she would need plenty of power just to carry on.

I'd already taken a quick look over her machinery. Her twin Cat-3208s were fine engines and they seemed well installed. Exhaust runs, fuel lines, wiring, and controls all appeared in order. Whatever else Seymour may or may not be, he'd been right about that anyway.

At Jack's Boat Shop, we guided the *Lucky Lou* into the Travelift and I slipped overboard to inspect her props. Bill stood beside me, dodging the water still dripping from her hull.

"These are the second pair of wheels I've had installed," he offered ruefully.

I reached for the solid butt of my tape measure and did a quick check. There was about 20 percent tip clearance between the hull and the prop blades—no problem there. The wheels were four bladed with moderate skew to ease vibration.

"I've had the engine and shaft realigned three times," Bill continued. "Nothing seems to help. I've got an awful lot of money tied up in this old girl." He looked pretty down.

Climbing back on board, I headed below and lifted the engine access panels. As is so often the case, they were ideally sized for a three-year-old. I wondered why the builders of these boats couldn't make their engine access panels larger. *How much could it cost?*

It was tight between the engines too. They were pretty large for the available engine compartment. I had to move carefully to avoid a third-degree burn from the still-hot exhaust manifolds.

Pulling out my flash, I examined the engine mounts. I peered along the hull bottom and started. There were no engine beds! Someone had cut them away. I couldn't believe it. The outboard engine stringers had been cut away so deeply that they were virtually gone! Even the deeper inboard stringers were cut down to just six inches (15 cm) high—the bare minimum. What's more, they'd had notches cut out of them around the engine mounts—a further weakening.

Forward and aft of the engines, the stringers

were plenty deep—eight to 14 inches (20 to 36 cm) high. But at the engines, nothing. Those big powerful Cat diesels were effectively bolted right to the hull bottom!

I twisted my neck to glance overhead, and the reason for this became obvious. The tops of the engines were a scant inch (2.5 cm) or so below the underside of the wheelhouse sole. Somewhere along the line some bright soul in the marketing department at *Lucky Lou*'s builders decided that she'd sell better with bigger engines. The only problem was that there wasn't enough vertical room to fit them. Rather than spend a few bucks and consult with their designer about the change, they climbed inside, measured the required height, and cut the engine stringers away to create all the extra room they needed. It was brilliant. It had cost them next to nothing and produced a boat that was unfit to leave her mooring when it was blowing more than, oh, say two knots.

There was no simple solution to this mess. Engine bearers or stringers have to be long and continuous. The bigger and more powerful the engine the longer and stronger they ought to be. This is particularly true on fiberglass boats. Fiberglass is plenty strong in tension—it has high tensile strength—but it is very low in stiffness—its flexural modulus is low. This is why decks on many fiberglass boats will flex slightly as you walk on them. They're strong enough to support your weight, but they bend as they do it.

Too much flexure, though, is bad news for any structure. Sooner or later, cracks occur. As the flexing continues, the cracks grow and you have a true structural failure. To generate sufficient stiffness, engine beds on FRP boats thus have to be particularly deep, wide, and long. On most glass hulls the engine stringers should run the full length of the bottom. It's also very important that these stringers be shaped in smooth or evenly tapered contours. Sharp corners and hard spots concentrate loads and aggravate vibration, increasing the chance of structural failure. The

Lucky Lou had her engine beds cut off square and sharp just forward and aft of the engines.

To further compound the *Lucky Lou*'s problems, her engine mounts were bolted right into the fiberglass engine stringers. (There were probably steel strips embedded in the glass.) A proper engine mount should use a heavy steel or aluminum angle through-bolted to the FRP engine stringers, and running continuously the full fore-and-aft length of the engines on either side.

A good rule of thumb is to fasten each angle to the stringer with four bolts, whose diameter in inches is equal to:

Bolt Diameter (in.) = Engine Weight (lb.) ÷ 4000

Bolt Diameter (mm) = Engine Weight (kg) ÷ 70

(never less than ⅜ inch or 10 mm)

If the angles are of aluminum they should be about the same thickness as the bolt diameter. If they are of steel, the angles should be about three-quarters of the bolt diameter. The engine mounts should then be bolted to this angle. This system further spreads the loads along the engine beds to reduce flexure and stress concentrations. Even though wood is much stiffer for the same weight than fiberglass, wood boats require much the same reinforcing at the engines. Long, continuous engine beds or stringers are fundamental to sound hull structure and smooth-running boats.

Looking forward and aft of the cuts that had been made in the *Lucky Lou*'s engine beds, I could see that original designer knew what he was about. The basic engine beds had been properly proportioned. They were wide and deep. In fact, a common mistake some builders make is to build their engine beds deep (high) but narrow. This is a durn sight better than no engine beds, as in the *Lucky Lou*, but it concentrates the loads from the engine beds along several narrow strips down the length of the hull. On small, lower-powered fiberglass craft you can get away with this, but as you move up to larger diesels—engines that deliver real torque and plenty of power—you have to be sure to make the engine beds wide to spread the loads even more.

A good rough rule for both fiberglass and wood boats is that each engine bed's or stringer's width should be at least $\frac{1}{40}$ the overall beam of the hull, and at least this same height for most of the length of the vessel. Thus the *Lucky Lou*, with a beam of 14 feet 4 inches or 4.37 m (172 in.—436 cm), ought to have engine stringers at least $4\frac{3}{8}$ inches wide and $4\frac{3}{8}$ inches high (11 cm by 11 cm) for their entire length, except at the engine, where they need to be deeper.

Here, from engine mount to engine mount, the stringer height should be at least $1\frac{1}{2}$ times its width—in the *Lucky Lou*'s case, at least $6\frac{1}{2}$ inches (16 cm) high. In fact, the deeper the better, assuming you have the space. (At the deeper engine stringer section, a fir or ash core should be installed to provide a stronger bearing surface for the mounting bolts.) Naturally, on a vee-bottom hull the outboard stringers are the factor controlling depth. Because the hull is less deep here, the stringers are at their lowest. The inboard stringers are usually quite a bit deeper than the $1\frac{1}{2}$-times rule.

On a wood boat, these stringers are simply made of solid timbers notched over the floors and bolted *securely* in place. (They shouldn't touch the inside of the planking, in most cases.) On a fiberglass boat, the strongest and easiest stringer to fabricate is a foam-core "hat"-section stringer. Foam blocks are easily cut to shape and glued to the bottom inside of the hull. Foam fillets should be glued to the corners of each stringer along both sides where it meets the hull, in order to spread the load even further and to avoid a hard corner in the glass laminate. Then the builder should apply a laminate about equal in thickness to the boat's length overall (in inches or centimeters) divided by 1,600, over the entire foam stringer assembly. At the higher stringer section—around the engine itself—the stringer laminate should be increased in thickness to about equal the LOA (in inches or centimeters) divided by 1,200.

This stringer laminate should run out onto the inside of the hull on either side of the stringer, for about the width of the stringer. What's more, the stringer laminate, where it lies on the hull, should be tapered away in progressively fewer layers of glass, so it ends in a feather edge—again reducing stress concentrations and hard spots. A hull laid up with stringers like this, and following basic rules for fiberglass hull layups, will last a lifetime without giving trouble. (See Chapter 44 for fiberglass-hull rules of thumb.)

Taking out my pad, I made detailed measurements of the inside of the *Lucky Lou*'s engine compartment and then heaved myself back up through her tiny engine access hatch. When I passed along my findings, poor Bill Dodge wasn't much happier than he had been before. It wouldn't be cheap to clear up his problem. Still, at least he finally knew what it was. Grabbing a lift back to our cars, I chauffeured Ginger to her office and headed for a well-earned beer.

Luckily, it turned out that Caterpillar had just come out with their new 3116 engines, which deliver nearly the same power as the original 3208s, but are a good 5 inches (13 cm) lower. The *Lucky Lou*'s old engines were pulled and sold for good value. The engine stringers were built up to proper dimensions, and the new 3116 engines were dropped in. I hear the *Lucky Lou*'s pretty shipshape these days.

I was staring vacantly out my office window several weeks later, when Ginger rang me up. She was in the neighborhood and wanted to say hello. This sounded like a good idea to me. I'd been pondering the best way to break it to her that a guy named Seymour just wasn't for her, anyway.

She swooped in, all smiles, and gave me a kiss on the cheek.

Good start, I thought.

"I don't know how to thank you," she began

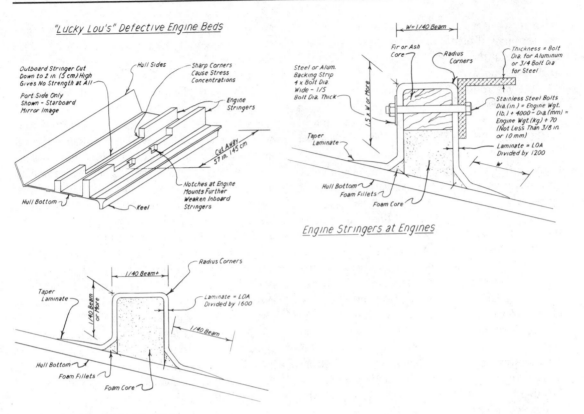

"Lucky Lou's" Defective Engine Beds

Outboard Stringer Cut
Down to 2 in. (5 cm) High
Gives No Strength at All

Port Side Only
Shown - Starboard
Mirror Image

Hull Sides

Sharp Corners
Cause Stress
Concentrations

Engine
Stringers

Cut Away
57 in. 145 cm

Notches at Engine
Mounts Further
Weaken Inboard
Stringers

Hull Bottom

Keel

W = 1/40 Beam

Fir or Ash
Core

Radius
Corners

Thickness = Bolt
Dia. for Aluminum
or 3/4 Bolt Dia
for Steel

Steel or Alum.
Backing Strip
4 x Bolt Dia.
Wide - 1/5
Bolt Dia. Thick

1.5 x W or More

Stainless Steel Bolts
Dia. (in.) = Engine Wgt.
(lb.) ÷ 4000 - Dia. (mm) =
Engine Wgt. (kg) ÷ 70
(Not Less Than 3/8 in.
or 10 mm)

Taper
Laminate

Laminate = LOA
Divided by 1200

Hull Bottom

W

Foam Fillets

Foam Core

Engine Stringers at Engines

Radius Corners

1/40 Beam+

Taper
Laminate

1/40 Beam or More

Laminate = LOA
Divided by 1600

1/40 Beam

Hull Bottom

Foam Fillets

Foam Core

Engine Stringers Not at Engines

breathlessly. "What with the *Lucky Lou* running properly again and with your report, they decided it wasn't Seymour's fault that the construction flaw was undetected in his survey."

I conceded mentally that that kind of structural observation might conceivably be out of the scope of some surveyors' work.

"We're off to my folk's house tomorrow to be married," she continued. "Seymour wanted to stop up to thank you himself. He just had to park the car."

No sooner had she finished than an immense figure loomed in the door. The trim-waisted giant seemed to have to twist sideways to fit his shoulders through the entrance.

"Seymour?" I said.

"Mr. Gerr, am I glad to meet you." His deep baritone rumbled through the office. Damned if his blue eyes didn't twinkle. He reached up to stroke his golden beard a bit shyly, then stuck out an immense paw.

I shook his hand and wished them both well. It turned out that Seymour had bought a charter schooner in the Caribbean and they were both off for the sailing life, for good.

Seeing them out, I returned to my drawing board to contemplate a particularly difficult fuel-tank installation. My right hand would probably take several days to regain its full, natural size.

CHAPTER 28

Outboard Info

Looking ahead to times when Guba II *would land and maneuver on unknown lakes, Archbold had a nine-horsepower outboard motor installed in the rear tunnel hatch. This gave the big plane the ability to slowly approach the shoreline with its Pratt & Whitneys switched off, to turn on a dime, and even to back up. . .*

PBY: The Catalina Flying Boat, Roscoe Creed

We'll probably never know who first thought up the idea of strapping a combined motor/propeller unit to the stern of a boat. The earliest sure evidence is of the Swedish Vulcan company. They manufactured engines for transom mounting in 1891. Unfortunately, these machines drove their propeller through exposed chain drive. Though not especially neat or reliable, it was a start. Others soon got into the outboard act. In England, around 1895, boats were being pushed along by the Watamota (catchy); while in France, folks were installing the Motogodille (motor oar). These later gizmos drove their props through long inclined shafts; they resemble the "homemade" outboards found on the small fishing and utility boats used in the Orient and South America to this day.

A Waterman Pulls it Off

Most likely, it was Cameron B. Waterman—a lawyer from Spruce Harbor, Michigan—who invented the first truly modern outboard engine. He was assisted by George Thrall, who ran a nearby boiler factory. Waterman's idea was to arrange the engine's crank shaft vertically, and then change shaft direction to drive the prop with a bevel gear. The year was 1906. It was simple, reliable, and compact, and it really hasn't been fundamentally improved on to this day. By 1917 some 30,000 units, marketed as the Waterman Porto, had been sold.

Enter Evinrude

Ole Evinrude (I'll bet you've heard that name before), who was running a local machine shop, started building outboards very soon after. Then, at nearly the same time, both Waterman and Evinrude introduced horizontal flywheels (they'd been vertical previously) to ease cranking. The two major U.S. outboard manufacturers of the pre-World War I era were off and running.

Of course, these 2-hp (1.5 kw), single-cylinder 1906 engines were designed to propel small boats at low speed, but outboard size and power grew quickly. In fact, it was Evinrude who—after the war—introduced the revolutionary ELTO (Evinrude Light Twin Outboard). The ELTO was the first two-cylinder production outboard. It offered smoother operation and more power. By the 1930s outboard racing was well established. Small one- and two-man, stepped-hull speedsters were routinely zipping along at 35 to 40 knots. That now-familiar outboard buzz could be heard nearly anywhere water and people mixed.

Outboards are so common these days that it's hard to imagine a world without them. It's not unusual to see an 18-foot, 40-hp (5.5 m, 30 kw) runabout zipping between a 30-footer (9 m) powered by twin 220-hp (164 kw) engines, and a 21-foot (6.4 m) sloop fitted with a 5-hp (3.7 kw) outboard auxiliary. With their great popularity, it's not surprising that I find myself fielding a lot of questions about outboards.

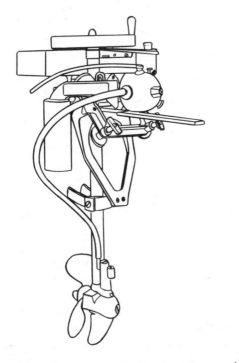

1906 2-hp Evinrude Outboard

How Much Power?

One of the most common of these questions is, "What's the maximum horsepower I can use on my boat?" This can be a complex question leading to plenty of head scratching in the design office. Racing machines—even very small "toy" racing machines—such as midget catamarans and baby three-point hydros can take fantastic amounts of power for their size. Further, very small boats can take more power if they have good planing hulls, rather than displacement hulls, like canoes or modified rowing craft. If we limit ourselves to single-hulled vessels for ordinary use, though, the accompanying charts will be a good general guide. Simply take your boat's length overall (not including pulpits, transom brackets, outriggers, or the like) and multiply it by her beam at the transom. Enter this number on the appropriate chart and read across for maximum recommended horsepower. (Don't use the maximum beam near midships.)

If, for instance, your *Faithful Flipper*'s an 11-foot dinghy with 3-foot 3-inch beam at the transom (3.3 m by 1 m transom beam), her LOA times her transom beam would be 35.75, say 36 square feet (or 3.3 m²). For a displacement boat, this gives a maximum of 5 hp (3.7 kw), which would drive her at a good 4.5 knots or so. If *Faithful Flipper* had a planing underbody, however, you'd read maximum horsepower from the upper dotted line, in which case *Faithful* could handle 15 hp (11 kw). This would move her at about 18 knots. Remember that such a small, open boat can only accept this kind of power in smooth and protected waters.

On the other hand, if your *Fishy Fanny* was 28 feet (8.5 m) overall and 8 feet (2.4 m) transom beam, the chart shows she'd take 370 hp (275 kw). This should push her at something like 30 knots, depending on how much *Fishy Fanny* weighs, of course. Remember that these are maximum powers. Frequently, it's plain inefficient to install so much oomph. The *Offshore Skiff* (see Chapter 2), for instance, is 28 feet overall and 7 feet 2 inches

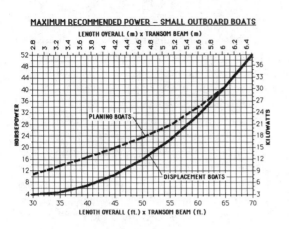

MAXIMUM RECOMMENDED POWER – SMALL OUTBOARD BOATS

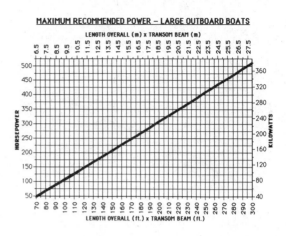

MAXIMUM RECOMMENDED POWER – LARGE OUTBOARD BOATS

in beam at the transom (8.5 m LOA—2.2 m transom beam). The chart indicates she could take something like 315 hp (235 kw), and so she could. The fact of the matter, however, is that a mere 70 hp (52 kw) will drive her at 21 knots, and 150 hp (112 kw) is enough to reach 26 knots. Few folks are really comfortable going much faster in a small, light boat for long periods of time, and those big engines are, well, fuel hogs.

"You had how many people on board?!"

Another question that crops up repeatedly is, "How many people can I safely take on board?" Again there's no simple answer. In fact, the American Boat & Yacht Council and the Coast Guard have some imaginatively complex formulas to try and deal with this problem. For small boats (under 20 feet or 6 meters), however, there's a simple rule of thumb that can serve as a useful guide:

$$Maximum\ Capacity\ (Persons) =$$

$$\frac{Length\ Overall\ (ft) \times Beam\ Overall\ (ft)}{15}$$

$$Maximum\ Capacity\ (Persons) =$$

$$\frac{Length\ Overall\ (m) \times Beam\ Overall\ (m)}{1.4}$$

The result is the maximum number of crew a vessel can carry. (You can also find the answer on the accompanying chart.)

Faithful Flapper, for example, is 4 feet 7 inches (140 cm) in beam overall. Multiply this number by her 11-foot LOA (3.3 m) and you arrive at 50 square feet (4.62 m²); divide by 15 (1.4), and you find your maximum capacity of 3.3—say 4—people. (It's suggested that you round up to the nearest whole number. The Coast Guard—not to mention the local police—frowns on the practice of shipping partial crewmembers.) Similarly, an 18-foot by 7-foot (5.5 m by 2.1 m) Whaler would take 8.5, thus 9 crew. Don't leave your common sense behind when you use this rule. Clearly, a partly enclosed, full-flotation, high-freeboard boat with a broad bottom and hard chines for initial stability can safely carry more folks than an open wooden skiff, without flotation, with soft bilges and low freeboard, even if both boats have exactly the same beam and length overall. Don't overdo it. An overloaded boat is a sure sign that a landlubber's in command.

Keeping the Water Out

Once, while swapping sea stories with my local marine engine salesman, he told me how he'd lost his boat in New York City's East River. Some

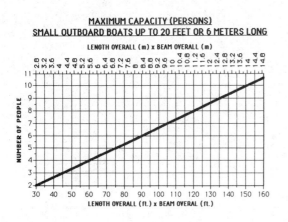

MAXIMUM CAPACITY (PERSONS)
SMALL OUTBOARD BOATS UP TO 20 FEET OR 6 METERS LONG

years ago he'd been cruising along on a fine calm day when his motor quit. Being a motor man, this didn't worry him. He simply tossed his anchor over the stern—not the best anchoring point, but he was young and ignorant at the time—and went aft to have a few words with the recalcitrant machine. The East River is quite deep in places, however, and—with the anchor rode nearly vertical—an anchor fluke snagged something on the bottom.

As my salesman friend sat negotiating with his engine, another vessel motored by. Held down by the anchor rode, my friend's boat couldn't lift to the waves, and even on this dead calm day the wake rolled in, flooding through the outboard cutout. He and his girlfriend bailed like dervishes, but too much river had come aboard. The boat was sitting so low that every ripple washed in, and in a matter of minutes they were left treading water. Happily—if it can be called that—some folks had watched the whole proceeding from the Brooklyn shore. The harbor police had been called; they showed up quickly and rescued both castaways. Though safe and sound, they were plenty steamed, plenty wet, and a bit oily. Meanwhile, somewhere on the bottom of the East River there still lies a fiberglass runabout with a cranky outboard—a menace to submarines entering the harbor.

All outboard boats with transom cutouts can potentially suffer the same fate, especially if they lose power—which is bound to happen someday—in rough conditions. For this reason, any boat that's going to be used in open water must be fitted with a proper transom well. If my friend's boat had been so equipped, he'd never have disturbed the harbor police's coffee break.

Outboard Well Dimensions

The accompanying drawing and the table below give the recommended dimensions for out-

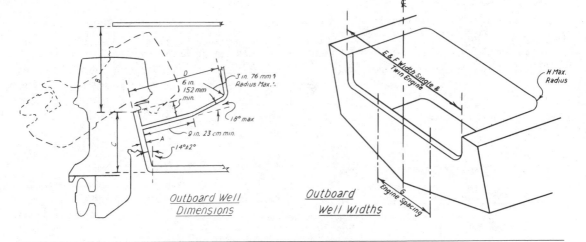

Outboard Well
Dimensions

Outboard
Well Widths

board wells and of the cutout height above the bottom of the keel. You can sometimes get by with a bit less space, particularly on a smaller engine, but this is iffy. Not only does your engine have to be free to swing from hard over to hard over for steering, but it has to be able to pivot up as well, for trailering, for maintenance, and—most important—in case you hit something going full speed.

Of course, the well has to be fitted with scuppers to drain out the stern. Note that the transom height dimension corresponds to the engine's "shaft length." A 15-inch (38 cm) cutout is for a standard-shaft engine; a 20-inch (51 cm) cutout is for a long-shaft, and a 25-inch (63 cm) cutout takes an extra-long-shaft motor.

OUTBOARD WELL DIMENSIONS—ENGLISH

HP	A Transom Thickness	B Cover Height	C Transom Height	D Well Depth
Under 5.5	$1\frac{1}{4}$" to $1\frac{3}{4}$"	$19\frac{1}{2}$"	15"$\pm\frac{1}{2}$"	$13\frac{1}{2}$"
5.5 to 16	$1\frac{3}{8}$" to $1\frac{3}{4}$"	$22\frac{1}{2}$"	15"$\pm\frac{1}{2}$" 20"$\pm\frac{1}{2}$"	$10\frac{1}{4}$"
16 to 61	$1\frac{3}{8}$" to 2"	29"	15"$\pm\frac{1}{2}$" 20"$\pm\frac{1}{2}$"	17"
61 to 85	$1\frac{5}{8}$" to $2\frac{3}{8}$"	$32\frac{1}{2}$"	20"$\pm\frac{1}{2}$" 25"$\pm\frac{1}{2}$"	20"
85 & over	$1\frac{5}{8}$" to $2\frac{3}{4}$"	$32\frac{1}{2}$"	20"$\pm\frac{1}{2}$"	$22\frac{3}{4}$"

OUTBOARD WELL DIMENSIONS—METRIC

KW	A Transom Thickness	B Cover Height	C Transom Height	D Well Depth
Under 4.1	32 mm to 44 mm	50 cm	38 cm ±13 mm	34 cm
4.1 to 12	35 mm to 44 mm	57 cm	38 cm ±13 mm 51 cm ±13 mm	26 cm
12 to 45	35 mm to 51 mm	74 cm	38 cm ±13 mm 51 cm ±13 mm	43 cm
45 to 65	41 mm to 60 mm	82 cm	51 cm ±13 mm 63 cm ±13 mm	51 cm
65 & over	41 mm to 70 mm	82 cm	51 cm ±13 mm 63 cm ±13 mm	58 cm

The final question regarding outboard wells and transom cutouts is their width. Again, you can see the required dimensions on the drawing and the following table.

OUTBOARD WELL WIDTHS—ENGLISH

HP	E Width Single Engine	F Width Twin Engine	G Twin Engine Spacing	H Radius
Under 85	33"	54"	22"	15"
85 plus	33"	60"	26"	20"

OUTBOARD WELL WIDTHS—METRIC

KW	E Width Single Engine	F Width Twin Engine	G Twin Engine Spacing	H Radius
Under 64	84 cm	137 cm	56 cm	38 cm
64 plus	84 cm	153 cm	66 cm	51 cm

With all this outboard info at your fingertips, you should have little trouble selecting and installing the best outboard, or the most suitable boat.

PART 7

Electricity and Water Sometimes Mix

"There is a powerful agent, obedient, rapid, easy, which conforms to every use, and reigns supreme on board my vessel. Everything is done by means of it. It lights it, warms it, and is the soul of my mechanical apparatus. This agent is electricity."
"Electricity?" I cried in surprise.
"Yes, sir."

20,000 Leagues Under the Sea,
Jules Verne

CHAPTER 29

The Case of the Boat That Burned

The grim blackness of the stones told by what the Hall had fallen—by conflagration; but how kindled? What story belonged to this disaster? What loss, besides mortar and marble, and woodwork, had followed upon it?

Jane Eyre, Charlotte Brontë

Aimless and zigzagging bubbles roiled and burbled. Back and forth, back and forth, they wandered the murky surface of Eastchester Bay. Stalwart and forlorn, a pair of antennas projected from the waves. The bubbles were approaching them again. A chill, wet wind cut through my coat. A ragged swell rocked the dock unevenly and I shifted position.

"Gerr?!" the gravelly voice came from somewhere behind me. It didn't sound happy to see me.

"Connor," I replied as I swung around. It'd been a few years, but I'd recognized that voice immediately. I was facing a burly, bull-necked fellow in his mid forties. His nose was red from the wind, and even if you didn't know from direct observation—which I did—you could tell he enjoyed a beer or two at the end of a shift. Sergeant Penn Connor. He was a city cop, one of the detectives who handled marine stuff—vandalism, theft, fraud. He was good, had been at it for years, and—like most city employees—he was overworked.

"You're not on this, are you?" he grumbled hopefully. "I can tell you it's a clear deal. No question about it."

"You sound awfully sure." I tried my best to look cocky.

Connor snorted. "It's a torch job, plain and simple. You're wasting your client's money searching for anything else. Why don't you call it a day and stay out of my hair."

A loud splash showered me with cold water. The diver had popped to the surface and pulled himself out onto the dock in one fluid motion. He spat out his mouthpiece and yanked off his face mask.

Ignoring me, he addressed Connor. "It was the engine room seacock. Last night's storm was too much for it, what with the fire and all. I've got her patched, and we can raise her any time."

"I'm going to be going over her carefully when you get her out." I figured I could ignore the diver, if he could ignore me. I favored the sergeant with a gaze of earnest sincerity.

Connor looked sour. He didn't relish me poking around and slowing up his case load.

"You're not going to make me go through the lawyers, just so I can be a representative of an officer of the court, are you?" I continued before he could reply.

"All right!" He made it sound like an expletive. "She'll be at Miller's Point, Thursday. Call and let us know before you show up, will you. Try being cooperative for once." He nodded to the diver and headed up the ramp to his unmarked car. The flasher—now inactive—was still resting a bit lopsided on the roof.

Gee, all the trappings, I thought.

Since the diver continued to ignore me, I figured I'd show him I could be forgiving and neighborly. "I hear they've been losing police frogmen to giant alligators—the ones that breed in the sewers," I offered. "Want me to stand lookout?" Apparently, he felt up to dealing with alligators on his own. Glancing at me with distaste, he refitted his mask, bit his mouthpiece, and dove back in—a sparkling conversationalist.

Ambling over to the blue Chevy, I aimed for I-95 and Manhattan. I hadn't expected the *Jenny Bell* to be under 14 feet of water when I arrived to inspect her. It didn't look good. I considered if Johnson had scuttled her himself—maybe to hide evidence—but that didn't seem possible; he was in the slammer. Curious. I thought back a day.

Effie had taken the call and interrupted my attempt to decipher a monograph on ship motion that seemed—best as I could make out—to have been written in tensor calculus. "There's a girl on the line, with quite a problem." Effie crooked an eyebrow. "You'll enjoy talking to her."

Suits me, I thought. I hadn't understood anything past the second paragraph anyway. I picked up the receiver. "Gerr," I answered cleverly.

"Mr. Gerr, they've locked my father up," a warm contralto voice replied. "He couldn't have done it. He just couldn't."

Effie had been right, I was going to enjoy talking to her. Even though she was obviously under plenty of strain, she sounded good. I wondered how she'd sound without strain.

"Exactly what did they lock your father up for?" I responded. I thought I did a fair job of making this sort of thing sound routine. "Ms. . . ?"

"Helen. My father's Steve Johnson. I'm Helen Johnson. They locked him up for fraud. They say he set his boat on fire to collect the insurance money. He was having some financial problems and he had been trying to sell the boat, but he'd never do anything like that. I know it. I just know it." She wasn't trying to convince herself. She was convinced.

"Look," I replied, "Tell me the name of the boat, where she is, and how I can get a look at her. Tell me what happened, and give me the name of the boat's insurance company. I'll see what I can find out, and we can meet at my office and go over it."

"Oh, thank you!" she answered. "I know there's got to be some explanation. The insurance people all have their minds made up and I didn't know where else to go. Do you think you can really help me?" She sounded less strained already. I liked the effect.

"Sure, we'll figure it out." I put on my confident voice.

I didn't feel so certain after getting the details. Her father had been trying to sell the *Jenny Bell* for some time. He'd been planning on retirement and needed the money to clear up some old debts. The night of the fire, he'd been seen on board. He'd even been spotted leaving a few minutes before the fire broke out. What was worse, the insurance investigator found that the fire'd been started in the wheelhouse by someone pouring a flammable liquid along the port side by the chart table, and igniting it. Not good. The police had been notified and Steve Johnson had been escorted to the local penitentiary.

After parking the Chevy, I pushed open the office door to be greeted by Effie, who motioned inside. Helen Johnson had arrived a bit early. Hanging up my coat, I walked back to greet her. She stood and met me with a firm handshake.

"Mr. Gerr," she asked, "Did you find anything out?" Her voice was even warmer in person.

I nodded, seated myself, and told her it was nice to meet her, which was so. Generally, I don't have a special thing for blondes, but I decided to make an exception in Helen's case. She had thick, long hair, pale and golden, set off by a surprisingly dark tan. Slightly windburned, her skin crinkled lightly about the corner of her eyes. Her hand, when she shook mine, was a trifle rough. *A sailor,* I thought. She looked like she could handle herself on a boat, and had spent plenty of hours doing just that. I estimated that she'd beat me in a race up a mast without a bosun's chair. A Caribbean vision sprang to mind: her at the helm, me slouched in the cockpit—a book in one hand a cold drink at my elbow. I fought it down.

"I'm afraid the *Jenny Bell*'s sunk," I informed her.

She gasped and slumped into her chair. She didn't carry a bag—it would have been too cumbersome for an athlete like her—so, with nothing else to do, her fingers were getting tangled with each other. "How . . . ?" she started. "It wasn't sunk before. . . ."

"The fire itself didn't sink the *Jenny Bell,*" I explained, "but close to it. She'd been sitting at her slip all right—a parboiled hulk, pumps going full time. The city was getting around to hauling her out, impounding her as evidence, but they didn't move fast enough. Last night's storm was simply too much. A seacock in the charred hull blew, and the pumps couldn't handle the added flow."

"What now?" She looked resigned.

"Well, they're refloating her this evening. I'm going down to look her over Thursday. I'll see what I can dig up."

I continued, "Did you see your father?"

"Oh, yes." She seemed distracted. "A Sergeant Connor took me down to him yesterday evening.

He asked me all sorts of questions, told me it looked bad for Pop, and then wanted to buy me a beer."

Sounds like Connor, I thought to myself. "It was the end of his shift," I informed her. "What did your father say about the fire?"

Helen looked quizzical for an instant, then slumped further. "He doesn't know anything. That evening, he just went aboard to check her and left. Nothing seemed unusual and he didn't know anything was wrong 'til the yard phoned him around one a.m. to tell him about the fire." She looked at me imploringly. "That's not much help, is it?" Desperation was creeping into her tone.

"The police say no one else was seen going aboard, there were plenty of people around to see if someone had, and the fire was noticed just a few minutes after your father left?" I asked.

"Yes." It was a faint wail.

"Look," I asked, "your father's not stupid, is he?"

"Of course not!" she replied, snapping upright. She had a finely honed glare. Hard times or not, she still had plenty of fight.

"Then I don't think he did it," I went on. "It wouldn't make sense. The way the police have it figured, he practically left a neon sign blinking, 'Johnson did it!' It just doesn't add up."

A brief smile flashed at me, and I thought I might try to encourage a longer one sometime.

"You don't look squeamish," I suggested. "Come down with me to see the boat on Thursday morning. Maybe you'll notice something out of the ordinary that I'd miss."

Helen quickly agreed to this, and I saw her out. I decided to be an extra-nice fellow, and called Penn Conner to let him know what time we'd arrive. He didn't seem pleased. Now, is that gratitude?

The *Jenny Bell* sat on her cradle, forlorn and bedraggled. It took quite an imagination to conjure up the fine lines of the proud craft she'd once been. Helen had let out a great sigh when she'd first seen her. The fire had gutted the interior of the hull and completely burned away the wheelhouse roof. The deck and topsides were twisted, buckled, and charred with heat. Only below the waterline was she bright and undamaged.

If the firemen hadn't arrived so quickly, there'd have been nothing left, and no way to tell that the fire had started with a flammable liquid. This point was not in Johnson's favor, but I didn't mention it to Helen, or to Connor either. He was lurking at our elbows, presumably to see that we didn't tamper with the evidence. The smell of burned plastic and evaporating sea water was overpowering.

It was a pleasure to watch Helen scale that rickety ladder—smooth and easy, no hesitation, no uncertainty. She even managed to look graceful picking her way gingerly across the twisted, fragile deck. It was her family's boat, so she was leading us to the wheelhouse where it all started. I followed, swaddled in my coveralls. The cold, hard weight of my flashlight felt reassuringly familiar on my hip. Connor brought up the rear. His heavy footfalls shook the decrepit deck. I wondered that he didn't fall through.

Helen and the sergeant stayed outside—it wasn't very inviting below—while I crept into the wheelhouse. Switching on my flash, I peered about. All was ruin. Still, the bulkheads and cabinetry were roughly in place. I noticed a great deal of electronic equipment forming a sodden, twisted mass over and around what had been the chart table. The fire seemed to have started in a locker to port, in the seat bottom next to the nav station. I knelt to examine it. The outer face had housed the circuit-breaker panel. Not a very big panel for all that electric gear, I mused. I shifted round to get a better view . . .

CRASH!!

The weakened wheelhouse sole gave way under me and I crunched through into the engine compartment below. Still holding my flash, I landed face down in the murky bilge water.

"Gaah!" I spat out a mouthful of the oily brew.

"You all right?" Helen called down anxiously. She'd sprung agilely into the cabin, Conner not far behind.

"Fine, just fine," I replied mournfully. "Felt like a swim, that's all."

I eased myself gingerly to kneeling position and shone about with my flash. Down here, below the waterline, there was little fire damage, only the debris I'd brought down with my fall and the dark bilge water I was crouching in. I'd managed to land neatly between the two engines. Something had made a nice bruise on my left side. I searched for the culprit. It was a bilge pump— brand new by the looks of it. The fire had caused its plastic housing to bulge on one side.

Wait a minute, I thought. *It wasn't hot down here. The fire hadn't even damaged the paint.* I examined the pump more closely. A standard 12-volt DC pump, its float switch had jammed on while the pump itself had clogged. It should have blown a fuse or circuit breaker, but instead it had continued to draw current till it got hot enough to melt the casing. It wasn't likely that this had been a result of the fire. The circuit breakers, being right at the heart of the burning, would have tripped out pretty fast. A bulge like this would have taken some time to develop, and the fire had been extinguished in 20 minutes.

I followed the power line back from the pump. It showed signs of melting even low down in the bilge. The pump had evidently been installed recently and the wiring had been run along the bilge as an afterthought. It progressed straight to port and up into the seat locker where the fire had begun. I could stick my head up through the burned-out bottom of the locker and look at the circuit-breaker panel from inside. There hadn't been enough spare breakers, so whoever had wired the new pump had ganged it up onto another breaker shared with several other items. That wasn't good.

Stamped clearly on the top of the pump was a

requirement for a three-amp fuse. The circuit breaker it had been hooked to was rated far over that to permit all the gear on that line to be run at once. Poor practice, indeed. It's vital that there be enough circuit breakers to handle all the gear installed in a boat—and that the rating of the breakers be low enough so that any single item attached to it will blow it if shorted out. This is especially important if the individual components aren't protected by built-in fuses or circuit breakers of their own.

This had to have been how the fire started, but what about the flammable liquid? I knelt down again and poked around. Something blue and yellow caught my eye. It might have been washed away, but had wedged itself in a corner instead. Picking it up, I found it was the top portion of a melted plastic bottle—a bottle with a yellow body and a blue plastic cap. I placed it back carefully where I'd found it and squirmed my way out of the bilge and onto the deck. Judging by Helen's expression I must have looked like a cross between a coal miner and an accident victim.

"Nice makeup," Connor rasped at me smugly.

Helen frowned at him.

"Hey, Connor," I asked, "The flammable liquid wasn't by any chance naphtha, was it?"

He looked surprised. "Yeah," he replied. "How'd you know? We were sitting on that."

"There's the top third of a melted yellow plastic bottle with a blue cap lying in the bilge. It's exhibit A for the defense," I quipped. "It held lighter fluid or naphtha—same thing. Very flammable, also very handy around the boat. Many folks don't know it, but naphtha's one of the best solvents for dissolving gum, old glue, congealed oils, and such. (A container ought to be aboard most boats—away from electric panels and sources of heat, that is.) Helen's father had a bottle stowed in the seat locker for ready access. There's an improperly wired bilge pump down there. It jammed on, failed to blow its circuit-breaker, and overheated itself and its power cord. The cord ran through the locker next to the plastic lighter-fluid bottle.

Instant fire." I didn't struggle too hard not to seem pleased with myself.

Helen squealed—somehow gracefully—and gave me a hug. Nice. I wondered how she managed to look elegant after being partly smeared with gunk. Connor motioned me back down, and I pointed out the pump, the melted cord, and the melted bottle top, going over the details.

I was sitting at the computer several weeks later battling with a laminate calculation, when Helen breezed in. She looked chipper. Her father had been released just a few hours after I'd finished my investigation.

"You're wonderful," she smiled. She gave me a big kiss on the cheek.

This was a step in the right direction. If I could keep her appreciating my finer points, we'd be set.

"Pop's just collected his insurance check," she beamed. "He's out of the woods. In fact, I think he's looking around for a smaller boat he can afford in his retirement. He just wouldn't enjoy life if he couldn't get out on the water."

"Super," I replied. "Sound's like you're all set." Spring wasn't far off, and I was wondering about asking her out for a sail.

"Penny and I are off for Phoenix," she continued. "I can't wait to get back to the desert."

"The desert?" I responded intelligently.

"Yes, I love the desert and the mountains out West. I spend as much time hiking and rock climbing as I can—especially rock climbing. Penny's put in his 20 years, you know. He's coming out with me to see what it's like."

"That's great," I answered. I can lie with the best of 'em when it's called for. I wondered who the devil Penny was.

"Gerr," the familiar gravelly voice brought me up short.

"Connor?" I said. He had just entered the office.

"Can't thank you enough for straightening out that fire business." He offered me a beefy hand. "It's meant an awful lot to me."

Turning to Helen, he continued, "The car's outside honey. We've got to get going if we're going to make the plane."

You could have knocked me over with a feather.

Helen attached herself to Penn's arm and favored me with a 20-megawatt smile. "Sorry, we've got to run. Thanks again. Be sure to stop by if you get to Arizona." She was already halfway out.

Always quick on my feet, I managed to blurt something about good wishes, and the rest. Connor was trailing after her through the entrance.

"Bye, Penny," I called to him brightly.

He winced and turned to glower at me as he shut the door.

(Although the names and events in the preceding story may be, well . . . invented, the shorted-out bilge pump and fire are from a real insurance claim that occurred exactly as described.)

Circuit-Breakers and Lights

There's one exception to the circuit-breaker-for-every-electric-device rule. Electric components that blow open (leave an open circuit) rather than short when they fail are exempt. In most practical instances this applies to lights (and only to lights). Obviously, it's not necessary to have a breaker for each light fixture. Instead, you need to have a circuit-breaker sized to carry the current draw of all the lights on the same circuit should they all be switched on simultaneously. This can add up to a lot of current. Accordingly, you also must check that the wiring itself can carry this much load without overheating. The circuit-breaker should be sized, in this case, to protect the wiring itself.

CHAPTER 30

Controlling the Flow, Keeping Electrons on the Straight and Narrow

Out of this nettle, danger, we pluck this flower, safety.

Henry IV, William Shakespeare

In almost every respect electricity has lived up to and exceeded the expectations of Jules Verne, who—some 120 years ago—powered the imaginary *Nautilus* with electricity. Many working craft today, in fact, use diesel electric drive and—just as Nemo's *Nautilus* was—are propelled by electricity. Even on ordinary gas and diesel powerboats and sailboats, electricity runs everything from lighting to hair dryers and gizmos that Verne could never have imagined—like onboard computers, GPS, and radar.

Electricity is, indeed, power—the power to do many things quickly, conveniently, and easily. With power, though, comes responsibility, for power out of control is dangerous. It's a sobering fact that more than 25 percent of all boat fires are started by failures in basic DC electric systems. It's tempting to think, "It's only 12-volts; it can't really do much harm." But a short in a 12-volt DC system can produce welding temperatures—temperatures high enough to ignite wood, fiberglass, and fabric almost instantly!

Yet when properly designed and installed, an electric system can be totally safe. You don't have to be an electrical engineer to get a decent feel for whether your boat's electric system is properly laid out. There are many basic things you can look for to ensure that your *High Current*'s safe and secure.

Batteries—the Tanks

Batteries are basically fuel tanks. They store electric power as chemical potential energy, just as your main fuel tanks store heat energy as chemical potential energy. Everyone realizes that a broken fuel line is serious business. A frayed or broken wire is really nothing more than a broken fuel line—dangerous! A rupture at the tank itself is more dangerous still.

Box the Battery

Batteries need to be secured and protected. They must be housed in acid-proof containers of some nonconductive material—usually plastic or fiberglass (in the old days lead). The boxes and batteries must be fastened so they can't shift even if your boat is knocked down in terrific seas. (Imagine your boat lying on her side and heaving up and down rapidly.)

The battery box needs to be enclosed top and bottom. From the bottom it must be liquid tight. (You don't want bilge water getting at the battery and you don't want battery acid getting into the bilge.) The cover protects the battery from drips and sloshes and also keeps metal gear from falling on the terminals and shorting them out.

The battery box mustn't be airtight however. The top's got to provide venting to allow gases to escape. Lead-acid batteries produce hydrogen during charging. Since hydrogen's explosive, improper venting can lead to a real blast!

Protect Your Cables

Batteries are often located near engines; it's important to check that no battery cables are rubbing or chafing on engine parts, engine controls, or hot exhaust lines. It may seem obvious, but insurance companies see this kind of thing all the time. In one case, a fire was started by a starter cable chafing against a wiring harness bracket; in another case a throttle cable—after years of use—wore through a 12-volt cable and shorted to metal fuel tanks!

Should trouble occur, you need a way to shut off the fuel at the source. For diesel or gas fuel tanks, this means a valve near the tank outlet. For batteries, this means a master battery-disconnect switch close to the batteries and *easily* reached. Usually, these are multiple-position rotary switches that allow you to use either one or the other of two batteries (or banks of batteries) or both together, with a built-in OFF position that totally disconnects both batteries from everything else.

The Lonely Cable Rule

Each battery terminal should be lonely—it should have only one cable attached to it. The cable needs to be heavy enough to handle maximum current, and it needs to be fastened with a proper mechanical battery-terminal stud or connector. Using a cheap, cobbled-together connector would be like attaching fuel lines to a gasoline tank with something you dug up out of the scrap bin—foolish!

The one exception is that a single, automatic bilge pump may be powered directly from the battery on it's own separate leads. This independent bilge-pump lead must, however, be protected by it's own fuse or circuit breaker.

Preventing Overflow

As we saw in the story of the burning boat, proper circuit breaker protection of wiring and equipment is essential. The battery cable must run to a distribution panel or circuit board with plenty of circuit breakers or fuses. One of the most common shortcomings of older boats is too small a breaker panel (the problem with last chapter's *Jenny Bell*). Just 15 or 20 years ago, boats weren't fitted with nearly as much in the way of electric gizmos as they are today; their breaker panes were accordingly small. But you *must* have circuit breakers on your panel for each item of equipment. You absolutely cannot gang wires up on a single oversize breaker—it's just asking for a fire. The exception is for light fixtures (see the sidebar in the last chapter). If your boat's breaker or distribution panel's got too few breakers for the job, you simply have to install a larger panel. Believe me, in the long run it's cheap insurance!

Positive Protection

On all boat's DC systems, the hot or active wire is the positive wire. The negative wire is the ground. All your circuit breakers or fuses *must* be on the positive wires. If a breaker's installed on a negative return-to-ground wire, electricity (fuel) will continue to spill into the supposedly protected electric device from the battery through the still connected positive wire. If there's absolutely no other path for the current out from the gizmo all will be fine, but the chances are there *will* be some other path. You'll end up with stray electric current spilling out of some shorted part of the electric device, causing stray current corrosion and possibly a fire.

There should also be a fuse within 7 inches (18 cm) of all terminal or distribution blocks. This protects the wiring bringing power to the terminal block in case of a short there.

Wire Without Fire

Boats—as you've probably guessed—are not houses. Ordinary house wire isn't up to marine service. Sure, it may work for a year or two, maybe three or more, but sooner or later—it's just a question of when, not if—it will deteriorate and fail, leaving you without power or perhaps starting a fire. Since boats move, they work and vibrate. Household wire such as lamp cord or "Romex" has too few strands—sometimes just one solid strand—and improper insulation to stand up to the saltwater environment. Boat wiring must have at least 20 strands in each wire—to take flexing—and the insulation can't contain any paper or fabric. Check to make sure that the wire's approved for marine use.

Sizing Up the Wire

When current flows through a wire it experiences resistance (essentially friction). This resistance builds up heat (as you'd expect from friction). The resistance or friction also robs energy from the electric system. For a given voltage, wire resistance or friction can be reduced by using larger diameter wires or cables, exactly as fatter pipes or wider channels can handle higher water flow with less friction.

Voltage is the equivalent of electric pressure (current is the electric flow rate, like gallons per minute). Power—the power that your gizmo needs to do its job—is just the product of pressure times current flow, or volts (V) times amperes (amps, or A):

$$Power\ (Watts) = Volts \times Amps, \text{ or } Watts = V \times A.$$

Accordingly, higher voltages mean less current is required to transmit the same power, so you can use smaller, lighter, less expensive wire. A winch that drew 50 amps at 12 volts would only draw 18.7 amps at 32 volts. This is a good reason to go with 24- or 32-volt DC systems on boats over 40 or 50 feet (12 or 15 meters). On craft this size, there can be a significant savings in wire cost and weight.

When wire's too small the resistance generates voltage drop (the robbed energy) that can cause gear to operate poorly or not at all. Even worse, wire that's too small will get hotter and hotter under continued load—hot enough in severe cases to start things burning.

The accompanying tables give the wire sizes required to carry 12-volt current with 10 percent and 3 percent voltage drops. Ten percent drop is acceptable for non-critical machinery that's intended for intermittent use of a few minutes at a time. For gear that will be operated for long periods, or for sensitive electronics like radar, 3 percent drop's about the maximum. If your *High Current*'s wire is smaller than recommended, again, you're looking at a potential problem.

Being Well Connected

Marine wiring needs to be well connected. Simple twisted wire splices aren't up to the job. They'll corrode, and the corrosion interferes with the electrical contact between the two pieces. This causes resistance, which—you guessed it—generates heat and voltage drop. Proper mechanical crimp connectors and/or terminal blocks should be used for all connections. You should periodically check all connections to make sure they're clean and tight. If they aren't, you'll run into the same corrosion and resistance problems cause by improper twisted wire splices. Needless to say, wires shouldn't be running in the bilge where they can sit in bilge water. In fact, wherever possible, wiring should be run high up under the deck.

AMERICAN WIRE GAUGE (AWG) SIZES FOR 10 PERCENT VOLTAGE DROP AT 12 VOLTS DC

FEET*	CURRENT (amps)					METERS
	5	10	15	20	25	
20	20	17	15	14	13	6
30	18	15	14	12	11	9
40	17	14	12	11	10	12
50	16	13	11	10	9	15
100	13	10	8	7	6	30
150	11	8	7	5	4	46
200	10	7	5	4	3	61
250	9	6	4	3	2	76
300	8	5	4	2	1	91
350	8	5	3	2	1	107
400	7	4	2	1	0	122
450	7	4	2	1	0	137
500	6	3	1	0	00	152
600	5	2	1	00	000	183
650	5	2	0	00	000	198
700	5	2	0	00	000	213
750	4	1	0	000	0000	229

NOTE: all gauges are of the conductor only, without the insulation.
*distances to and from power source

AMERICAN WIRE GAUGE (AWG) SIZES FOR 3 PERCENT VOLTAGE DROP AT 12 VOLTS DC

FEET*	CURRENT (amps)					METERS
	5	10	15	20	25	
20	15	12	10	9	8	6
30	13	10	8	7	6	9
40	12	9	7	6	5	12
50	11	8	6	5	4	16
60	10	7	5	4	3	19
70	9	6	5	3	3	22
80	9	6	4	3	2	25
90	8	5	4	2	1	28
100	8	5	3	2	1	31
110	8	5	3	2	1	34
120	7	4	2	1	0	37
130	7	4	2	1	0	41
140	6	3	2	0	0	44
150	6	3	1	0	00	47
160	6	3	1	0	00	50
170	6	3	1	0	00	53
180	5	2	1	00	000	56
190	5	2	0	00	000	59
200	5	2	0	00	000	62

NOTE: all gauges are of the conductor only, without the insulation.

Code and Label

Something that's seen on boats all too infrequently is color coding and tagging of wires. Boats have peculiar shapes with many hard to reach corners. If your *High Current*'s fitted with a passel of electric gear, she'll have all manner of wiring running behind and under panels and bulkheads. If there's a problem, how do you know which wire goes to and from where? Not easily, if it hasn't been color coded and tagged. A good winter project is to trace and tag a few items each month. Start with the high-current and critical gear first, and as time permits work your way down to the secondary gear. A couple of seasons will usually see your whole system tagged and marked. What's more, you'll be familiar with the wiring and can check it over for other faults as you go.

Finally, because boats bounce and vibrate so much, all wires must be neatly bundled together and carefully supported not more than 18 inches (45 cm) apart by marine-grade, non-conducting, non-corrosive wire ties and supports. The supports should be lined with a soft non-conductive material to prevent the wire insulation from chafing. Also, wherever wires run through bulkheads or panels, there should be soft ring grommets to protect them from chafing through there.

Final Warnings

A few final items to be aware of: Always use Coast Guard-approved, ignition-protected electric

AMERICAN WIRE GAUGE (AWG) SIZES FOR HIGH CURRENT CABLES 3 PERCENT VOLTAGE DROP AT 12 VOLTS DC

	CURRENT (amps)					
FEET*	100	150	200	250	300	METERS
5	8	6	5	4	3	1.5
10	5	3	2	1	0	3
15	3	1	0	00	000	4.5
20	2	0	00	000	0000	6

NOTE: all gauges are of the conductor only, without the insulation.

devices in gasoline engine spaces. (This is a good idea even in diesel spaces. Diesel can't explode, but a ruptured, pressurized diesel fuel line produces a fine mist that can cause a terrifyingly hot fire if it contacts a flame.)

Never, ever use an automotive battery charger. These chargers don't have ignition protection, and they don't have isolation protection to prevent stray current corrosion.

All the above may sound a bit intimidating; it seems there's an awful lot to go wrong. Indeed, there are plenty of potential pitfalls, but if your DC system observes all the above basic rules, it'll be . . . well, safe as a house!

DIAMETERS OF AWG WIRE

AWG	Inches	Millimeters
0000	0.46	11.684
000	0.41	10.414
00	0.365	9.271
0	0.325	8.255
1	0.289	7.3406
2	0.258	6.5532
3	0.229	5.8166
4	0.204	5.1816
5	0.182	4.6228
6	0.162	4.1148
7	0.144	3.6576
8	0.128	3.2512
9	0.114	2.8956
10	0.102	2.5908
11	0.091	2.3114
12	0.081	2.0574
13	0.072	1.8288
14	0.064	1.6256
15	0.057	1.4478
16	0.051	1.2954
17	0.045	1.143
18	0.04	1.016
19	0.036	0.9144
20	0.032	0.8128

NOTE: all gauges are of the conductor only, without the insulation.

CHAPTER 31

Comprehensible Corrosion: Keeping Your Electrons From Jumping Ship

. . . the advantages offered by a metal structure are somewhat reduced by the threat of corrosion.

Design for Flying, David B. Thurston

Wandering electrons are at the root of the thing. What thing? Everything. You, your next-door neighbor, your boat and her fittings, and just about everything else are essentially held together by electrons. Electrons locked together in chemical bonds produce molecules that make up compounds and complexes of compounds like wood, fiberglass, and metal alloys. When these electrons start moving from place to place, you get chemical reactions. It would be an understatement to say that many of these reactions are beneficial—you wouldn't be breathing without them. In fact, it's just such chemical reactions that drive your battery. However, when electrons start traveling about out of control, you can get corrosion.

Of course, electrons don't simply decide to get up and take a hike. Left on their own—in a neutral environment—the electrons in a given atom or molecule will, very broadly speaking, stay put. (Electrons actually never stay put. They whirl endlessly about their respective atomic nuclei at prodigious speeds in complex probability shells. For our purposes, we can overlook this peculiar hyperactivity, however.) Sea water and air, though, are anything but neutral environments. Sea water, in particular, is filled with charged particles of oxygen, hydrogen, sodium, sodium chloride—you know, table salt—and dozens if not hundreds of trace elements, many of which are also charged particles.

A State of Grace

Now, a charged particle is either an electron all by itself (always negative); or an atom that temporarily has *more* electrons than it can comfortably keep hold of (also negative); or one that has *fewer* electrons than it would normally contain (positive). Chemists call such atoms *ions*. As they're already out of balance—either positive or negative—ions will latch onto or give up electrons at the drop of a hat. (They are always trying to regain a neutral state—sort of a chemical state of grace.) Since sea water's filled with many ions, it forms an ideal medium for carrying electrons around—not free electrons (they can't move effectively in sea water), but electrons that jump ship to hitch a ride on a nearby ion.

This presence of many ions is what makes sea water an electrolyte. There are even better electrolytes, many of which are called acids! Sea water corrodes metals relatively slowly, but concentrated acids are so active that they corrode all sorts of things *fast*—even people. However, it's because acids are so active that they're used as the electrolyte in batteries. You can get more electrical/chemical activity (electrochemical activity) and thus more power out of a smaller, lighter, and more compact unit than you could if you relied on the comparatively inactive sea water.

Unwanted Reactions

Though sea water is less active than acids, it's generally much too active as far as keeping your boat's metal fittings intact. Metals like ordinary mild steel react with the ions dissolved in water. At small local regions on the metal's surface, there are slight excesses of electrons. These electrons react with the dissolved oxygen in sea water to form negative ions, which combine in all sorts of interesting ways with other free ions dissolved in the the ocean until they become neutral.

Every time an electron takes leave of the metal's surface, another electron rushes up from inside to fill the gap. Somewhere, this leaves an electron-starved, or positively charged, area. Here, positive metal ions react with the negative ions in salt water, also dissolving away. All metals behave this way to some degree. Left alone, many metals will wear away completely, losing their electrons and positive ions to electrochemical reactions with ions in sea water.

Oxygen! Oxygen!

Of course, this takes time—on some corrosion-resistant metals, like, say, silicon bronze, a very very long time. Many such metals protect themselves by forming an oxide surface film (using the oxygen dissolved in sea water) that inhibits the electron flow of corrosion. If your boat had nothing but such metals—all nearly similar in chemical composition—and also had no electrical system, you'd have no corrosion problems. Unfortunately, most boats are fitted with several different types of bronzes, in seacocks and propellers; steel shafting;

Corrosion Misnomers or What's in a Name

There's considerable confusion about the proper name for *galvanic corrosion*—the only correct term. Frequently it's called *electrolysis,* or *electrolytic* corrosion. Both are misnomers. Electrolysis is the corrosion or chemical breakdown of the electrolyte—the fluid medium that transfers ions between metals. Obviously, in our case, electrolysis would be breakdown of sea water itself—not of much concern. Electrolytic corrosion is the corrosion produced by externally generated electric currents. It's also known as *stray current corrosion.* Stray current corrosion can be extremely serious. It's a vast subject in itself, however; you may wish to do additional reading about it (see suggested reading).

The Galvanic Series	
ANODIC OR LEAST NOBLE END (Active)	Millivolts (mV)
Magnesium (Mg)	-1730
Magnesium (2% Manganese (Mn))	-1670
Magnesium (9%Aluminum (Al), 1% Mn,1.5% Zinc (An))	-1580
Galvanized Iron (hot dipped)	-1140
Zinc Electroplating	-1130
Cadmium (Cd) Zinc Solder (71%/29%)	-1120
Zinc (Zn)	-1050
Cadmium (Cd)	-860
Cadmium Plated Steel (Cd 0.001 in.)	-860
Aluminum (Marine Alloys 5086, 5083, 6061)	-820
Mild or Structural Steel(A36)	-790
Alloy Steel	-740
Aluminum (forged alloy)	-730
Stainless Steel (316,317,321,347,302,304 – active, oxygen starved)	-550
Tin (Sn)	-500
Manganese Bronze, CA-464 Naval Brass (58%Cu,39%Zn,1%Alum,0.25%Mg)	-450
Naval Brass (60% Copper, 39% Zinc)	-450
Yellow Brass	-450
Admiralty Brass (70% Copper, 29% Zinc)	-360
Copper CA-110 (Cu)	-340
Brass (60% copper, 40% zinc)	-330
Gunmetal (88% Copper, +Tin)	-310
Silicon Bronze (96% Copper, 1.5% Silicon)	-260
Tin Bronze	-260
Lead (Pb)	-240
Copper/Nickel (CA-715 – 70% Cu, 30%Ni)	-200
Aluminum Bronze (90% Copper, 10% aluminum)	-150
Stainless Steel (316,317,321,347,302,304 – passive, oxygenated)	-150
Monel 400 & 500	-110
Titanium (Ti)	-100
Silver (Ag)	-80
Graphite and Carbon Fiber (C)	(+250)
Platinum (Pt)	(+260)
CATHODIC OR MOST NOBLE END (Passive)	Millivolts (mV)

- All measurements taken relative to a silver:silver chloride (Ag/AgCl) elect-rode, at 77 F°.
- The sign of potential applies with the negative (black) probe of the voltmeter connected to the reference electrode, and positive (red) terminal connected to the fitting being tested.
- If uisng a Zinc reference electrode, add 100 mV to the potential. For instance, Silicon Bronze is -260mV, then + 100 mV = -160 mV.
- Average variability of potential is ±40 mV for alloys with iron and/or nickel. ±20 mV for copper based alloys without nickel.
- Readings 200 to 400 mV more negative (more anodic) than given indicate the material is protected.
- Readings at or near those given up to 200 mV above those given indicate the material is unprotected and freely corroding.
- Readings over 400 mV more negative than given indicate overprotection.
- Stray current corrosion is indicated by metals reading more cathodic (more positive) than indicated on the table.

iron and aluminum engine parts; plus a 12-volt DC and/or 110-volt AC electric system.

Electron Losers

If you could keep all these metals and the electric systems isolated from each other, the metal fittings would corrode only at their natural rate, which—if they're proper marine alloys—would be acceptable for a long, long time. We can't do this, however, because some of these items have to be in close contact—bronze props on stainless steel shafts, for instance. Others must

be connected to run the electric system, and to protect from lightning and electric shock.

The problem here is that some metals keep a very loose hold on their electrons compared with others. Aluminum, for instance, will lose its electrons to bronze or copper if there's a good electrical connection—a path for the electrons to travel over. Aluminum, the metal that's losing electrons, is called an *anode,* and bronze, that's gaining electrons, is called a *cathode.* Cathodic metals are also called more "noble" metals. (Presumably this is because they remain serenely unaffected by the chemical activity destroying other metals.)

At any rate, the propensity of one metal to give up its electrons to another when electrically connected while both are immersed in the same electrolyte—in our case sea water—is called their *electrical potential* and it is measured in *volts.* It is this list or table of relative electric potentials that makes up the *galvanic scale* or *galvanic series.* Since most boats have all their different metal fittings electrically connected or bonded together, we have to find some way to keep, for instance, the bronze fittings from eating up all the aluminum and mild steel ones. The solution is the *sacrificial zinc anode.*

An Ode to Anode

Say you had a bronze propeller and a stainless steel prop shaft. When they're firmly fastened together they make good electrical contact. Assuming that the stainless shaft is in its passive state (see sidebar), the bronze is—in this case—less noble (anodic). It will lose electrons to the steel until the stainless shaft acquires sufficient excess electrons to balance out the difference in potential or voltage. If your boat's hauled (out of the water), the process will stop—the difference in potential of voltage will have been neutralized. This is very much like the equalizing of water levels in two buckets filled to different heights. Connect them with a pipe and water will flow from the

Stainless steel appears in two locations on the galvanic scale—one quite noble, and the other fairly anodic. The key to this mystery is oxygen. Most corrosion-resistant marine alloys protect themselves—to varying degrees—by forming a thin surface-layer oxide film. This, as we saw, is generated by interaction with the oxygen dissolved in sea water. Bronze, Monel, copper, and copper-nickel will corrode slightly faster if they lose this film, but will still remain highly corrosion resistant.

Stainless steels, on the other hand, rely chiefly on this oxide film to protect them from corrosion. When stainless is in clean, flowing water containing plenty of oxygen it has no difficulty generating and retaining the oxide film. In this condition it's highly cathodic (noble)—a state that's also called *passive*. Should stainless be deprived of a regular supply of oxygen, however—for instance, pressed for a long time, immobile, against a cutless bearing, smothered by barnacles, or enclosed in a stern tube—it can lose its protective oxide film. In these conditions stainless becomes nearly as anodic as mild steel. Stainless is called *active* in this state, and can suffer severely from pitting corrosion.

higher to the lower bucket until the water levels are equal, at which point flow ceases.

"There's a Hole in the Bucket Dear Liza, Dear Liza . . ."

In sea water, however, the stainless steel (in this case the cathode) continually loses its newly acquired excess electrons to the ions in the ocean. (Returning to our buckets, this would be like having a small hole in the bottom of the lower-water-level bucket.) Thus the electrical pressure (voltage) is never equalized and the bronze prop (the anode) continues to dissolve until there's nothing left but its proverbial grin.

Electron Flooding

If, on the other hand, we were to bond a zinc to the shaft we could protect the propeller. The zinc has so much greater propensity to lose its electrons than either the bronze or the stainless that it floods the entire system with zinc electrons (loosely speaking). This raises the potential of all the bonded metals. As long as all these metals are raised 200 to 250 millivolts (mV) above their natural freely corroding potential, they won't lose many of their own electrons and so won't corrode.

Of course, the zinc will now corrode with a vengeance. It's busy supplying electrons to all the bonded metals. Inside the boat (through the bonding wire, or—in our case—through the metal in the stainless shaft), the zinc's electrons are flowing freely. Outside the boat, the exposed surface of the zinc becomes positively charged. (Remember, it's losing all those electrons to the other metals, which—from there—dissolve into the sea.) This leaves positive zinc ions (zinc atoms stripped of electrons) which are free to react with the negative ions floating around in the water, thus also dissolving away.

Losing From Both Ends

The zinc's losing from both ends—negative electrons through the bonding system to other metals and out into the water, and positive ions directly out into the sea. The greater the quantity and surface area of the other metals our zinc's protecting, the more electrons it puts out and the faster it corrodes. (On some boats—wooden boats in particular—you can have too much zinc and cause harm through overprotection, but this is another story; see sidebar.)

Of course, this process isn't instantaneous, or your zinc would boil away in a flash. It takes time for these chemical reactions to occur, and there's internal resistance in the bonding wire that limits electron flow. Additionally, as this process continues, a thin boundary layer of hydrogen gas (a natural byproduct of stripping oxygen atoms from water, which—of course—is hydrogen and oxygen) forms around the protected metals, insulating them from other ions in the water, further slowing corrosion. Naturally, this protective hydrogen boundary's repeatedly washed away by the motion of the ocean; however, it does help your sacrificial zincs to last longer. In fact, if the amount of zinc anode used is balanced properly against the amount of metal it protects, you will have to replace your zinc just about once a season, when it will be about half eaten away.

Complete Protection?

What we've done then, by bonding all the different metals in our boat together with a sacrificial zinc anode, is to protect them completely from corrosion in the electrolyte (sea water). All we have to do is be sure to replace our zincs once a season, before they wear out, and we have no problems—right? Well, not necessarily. Unfortunately, when plugged into the dock, the bonding system in your boat is nearly impossible to separate reliably from the AC (alternating-current) shoreside power-supply ground. (It would be nice to keep the AC grounding system totally isolated from the protective bonding system and lightning ground but—as a practical matter—there are so many potential paths for current between the two systems that avoiding leakage is very difficult. We have to allow for it instead.)

Wayward Electrons

The problem presented here is that once there's an electrical connection between your boat's bonding system and the shoreside AC green-wire ground, your zincs are no longer protecting just the metal fittings on your own boat. The zinc's protective electrons are now jumping ship, flowing shoreward over the green ground wire. They're trying to protect all the metal fittings on every other boat that's plugged into the

Military Zinc   All zincs are not created equal. Make certain the zincs you buy and install are intended for marine corrosion protection. There are many common zinc alloys which are useless for this, yet occasionally they end up on the market as zinc anodes. It should say in writing somewhere that the zincs you purchase meet military specification, or Mil Spec, Mil-A-18001 J (or higher final letter). This sounds intimidating, but it's standard for everyone. If you don't insist on zincs to this Mil Spec, you're truly buying a pig in a poke. Almost all reputable suppliers will be glad to meet this requirement. In fact, they'll boast of it in their advertising.

same AC ground-wire and—what's more—most of the dock and the rest of the seacoast as well.

Burned Out Zincs

Where your zincs were just large enough to last a season supplying electrons to your boat's fittings, the drain to supply protective electrons to all this additional mass will wear them out in no time flat. In fact, in a really bad situation, you could burn out your zincs in a few weeks. Once your zincs are gone, the next most negative (least noble) metal fittings in your bonding system become the new "sacrificial" anodes. But these are items that you can't afford to sacrifice. A few more weeks after the zincs have gone, and you could easily find your seacocks, propeller, or shaft—depending on their composition—corroded entirely away. All it takes is one corroded, broken seacock to sink you convincingly.

Of course, you could just disconnect the shoreside green ground wire, but whatever happens, DON'T DO IT! That green ground wire's there to provide a path of least resistance to any stray current caused by a fault in the AC power system. As long as it's connected, you're protect-

ed. If you disconnect the ground wire and have a short or fault from the hot AC wire to, say, the metal case of some instrument or appliance, *you* can become the path of least resistance. For example, if you were standing on a wet dock and grabbed the stanchions of a boat with such a fault you could take the place of the ground wire—a shocking experience that would very likely be the last thing you ever did.

The solution on small to medium-sized wood and FRP craft is the *galvanic isolator* (also called—not surprisingly—a "zinc saver"). The galvanic isolator is simply connected in series (in line) with the green ground wire, where it acts as a rectifier. This means that it permits current to travel in only one direction. In fact, galvanic isolators actually allow free current in both directions, but will not allow free current flow from the boat to shore if the potential (voltage) is less than 2 volts. Since your zinc, even when it's working overtime, delivers less than 2 volts, the galvanic isolator keeps your zinc's electrons trapped on board, where they can continue to function as intended. Your zinc can thus protect your metal fittings without corroding away too fast. At the same time,

Overprotection—Too Much of a Good Thing

It's definitely possible to have too much of a good thing. If you have too much zinc, the potentials of your metal fittings can be raised more than –400 millivolts over their "natural" state. Such high potentials mean *overprotection*. Though generally not as serious as uncontrolled galvanic corrosion, overprotection should be eliminated as quickly as possible.

On traditional wood-hull vessels in particular, overprotection can create alkaline byproducts that literally destroy the lignin holding wood fibers together—a condition known as *alkali rot*. Look for whitish or yellowish foamy, soapy gunk around metal fittings on wood hulls. This is a sure sign of alkali rot. Even on FRP, steel, and aluminum hulls, overprotection can cause gas bubbles, destroy paint, generate alkaline solutions that actually eat away aluminum, and lead to hydrogen embrittlement of high-strength steels.

Making Your Zincs Work

It takes some smarts to make zincs work.

1. You must install zincs to protect your boat's metal fittings or hull.
2. The zincs must be in tight, clean electric contact with the metal components they're protecting. (If they're not electrically connected to the bonding system or metal hull, they're useless.)
3. The surface of the zincs must be exposed to the water. You can't paint a zinc anode, ever! You want it exposed, and you want it to corrode. (They're not called "sacrificial zincs" for nothing!)

If your boat's zincs aren't wearing away they're either way, way too large (unlikely indeed), they're not in proper contact with the metals they're protecting, or they're painted over. In any of these cases the boat's zincs would be useless.

Properly sized, zincs should last about a year, at which time they'll be, oh, nearly half gone. You have to remember to check your zincs whenever possible to see that they're firmly attached and corroding properly. You also have to remember to install new zincs at the beginning of every season. Forget, and you'll likely end up replacing your prop or shaft instead—not sound economy!

---

the 110- or 220-volt current carried by your AC system easily travels along the ground wire, giving you full protection from shock in case of a short circuit.

Bridging Empty Space

All-metal boats, and large vessels with complex electric systems, should go one step beyond the simple zinc-saver to protect themselves and their zincs. They should employ *isolation transform-* ers. Isolation transformers eliminate all direct connection between the boat and the external power line. It transfers shoreside electric power to the ship over—unlikely as it may seem—empty space. Instead of using a hard-wire connection, the power is transmitted by magnetic fields over closely spaced (but not touching) coils of wire—a process engineers call inductance. Eliminating all physical connection eliminates the chance for stray or unwanted current flow between ship and shore.

Using the Galvanic Series: Selecting Fittings and Testing for Corrosion

Selecting Fittings Using the Galvanic Series

There are two critically important uses for the galvanic series. First, you should refer to it when installing hardware. *Try to make sure the voltage difference between any two metals, in direct contact in sea water, is less than 0.20 volts or 200 millivolts (mV).* Metals that are less that 200 mV apart corrode each other fairly slowly and need little additional protection. If you must use two metals in contact, farther apart than 200 mV, you need to take steps to protect them, either by insulation (so they're not really in contact) or by using anodes.

Checking Potential (Voltage) to Detect Corrosion

This brings us to the second critical use of the galvanic series. As long as zinc electrons are flooding the other metals, it effectively stuffs them with excess electrons. Rather than lose their own electrons and corrode, the excess zinc electrons are lost first, to be replaced with still more zinc electrons, for as long as there's zinc available. These extra electrons change the charge or potential of the protected metals. And—since electrons have negative charge—the protected metals become more negative. (Metals that are anodic have more excess or easily freed electrons than cathodic metals. Anodic metals thus read more negative than cathodic metals on the galvanic series.)

This process is called *polarization.* It's a change in potential that can be measured quite easily using a portable voltmeter. As long as the measured voltage increase is between −200 and −400 mV (−0.20 to −0.40 volts) above the indicated "normal" voltage shown on the galvanic series, the metal has been polarized enough to be protected from corrosion. Using this information, you can easily spend an afternoon going around your boat testing potentials (polarization or voltages) of various fittings and components to see if they're protected (potential raised −200 to −400 mV) or freely corroding (potential less that −200 mV above the voltage indicated on the galvanic series). It's a good idea to schedule such a test once or twice a year as part of routine maintenance, along with engine overhauls and bottom cleaning.

Using a Voltmeter to Test for Polarization

The test procedure's simple. All you need is a voltmeter with at least one scale that can be set to read with a maximum of 1200 to 1500 millivolts (mV, or 1.2 to 1.5 volts); a silver:silver chloride electrode; and long wire to connect it to the voltmeter. Aboard your boat, chuck the electrode (connected to the voltmeter, of course) overboard and go below with the meter, touching the free probe end to the fittings you want to test. Make a table listing equipment and fittings and their locations, or make a rough schematic drawing, labeling the metal fittings to be tested. Note the measured voltages next to each fitting. If you touch the probe to, say, a manganese-bronze stuffing box and it reads −655 millivolts, it's well protected. On the other hand, if her stainless prop shaft reads −162, it's freely corroding away (it's certainly not connected to any zincs.)

PART 8

Analyzing the Eggbeater

One of the first facts revealed by close observation and the high-speed camera was that wings do not simply flap up and down. Nor do they row the bird ahead like oars. The actual motion is more that of sculling a boat or screwing it ahead by propeller action, a kind of figure-eight movement.

Song of the Sky, Guy Murchie

CHAPTER 32

Power to the Propeller: Propeller Selection You Can Understand

The final answer to all engineering effort in any vessel is in the propeller. . . .

    Seamanlike Sense in Powercraft, Uffa Fox

Somewhere on the stern of your boat is a little metal dingus that doesn't do anything but whirr round and round. On a 40-footer (12 meter) it would weigh little more than 24 pounds (11 kg). But if it weren't there or if it were to be seriously damaged, you'd be well and truly stuck. No dingus, no go. Since the dingus propels your boat, some bright soul christened it "the propeller." They're also affectionately termed "screws," "wheels," and even "eggbeaters."

Many people don't realize that the propeller's barely a hundred years old. None other than John Ericsson—of *Monitor* fame—made one of the first serious attempts at using propellers instead of paddlewheels. His motivation: paddlewheels kept getting shot up and rammed in the Civil War—too vulnerable. Even so, the propeller didn't exactly take the world by storm right off. The best early props could do was about half the efficiency of a paddlewheel. (Some high-tech ideas just fizzle.) A couple of decades after the war, however, we finally figured out how to design a proper prop, one that would work efficiently, and, well . . . the rest is history.

So why is your prop shaped the way it is and how does it work? How big should it be and why? How do a prop's shape and size affect boat and engine performance?

Something Screwy

There are more theories of propeller behavior and performance than you could fit on a shelf full of books—a sure sign that we don't fully understand them. Some of the modern theories dealing with fluid dynamics and the lift generated by flow produce mathematical formulae that would take the breath of the most hardened mathematician. Luckily, the good old "a prop screws its way through the water" approach is just fine for small-craft work. It's direct and straightforward. When your prop rotates, its blades slice through the water at an angle, exactly like the threads of a wood screw working its way into soft pine. (The full name for propellers is *screw propellers*). Just as a wood screw does, your prop will drive forward a certain fixed distance for each complete revolution. This distance is called *pitch*.

If your prop moves forward 10 inches (25 cm) for every complete turn, it has a 10-inch (25 cm) pitch. Since your propeller's firmly attached to its prop shaft, it pushes *that* forward 10 inches (25 cm) as well. The shaft pushes on a thrust bearing (usually in the gearbox) and, you guessed it, the gearbox and engine push against the hull, driving you forward—an excellent reason to have *strong* engine mounts and engine beds.

Twists and Turns

This even explains why propeller blades are twisted as you look at them edge-on. Like any rotating object, the inner part of your propeller (near the hub) travels much less distance each full turn than the tips. If you had a 16-inch-diameter (41 cm) prop, its tips would be traveling along a 50-inch (128 cm) circumference each trip around. By contrast, the root of the blades, right by the hub, would be traveling only an 11-inch (28 cm) circumference each revolution. This is a heck of a difference. Since you don't want the tips of the blades to race ahead of the inner part of the prop, you have to give them a steeper angle so they'll end up at the same place as the blade roots every turn. Carrying this principle all the way down the length of the blades gives them their characteristic twist. It's good to remember that the *pitch* of a propeller is not the same as its *blade angles*. These angles *vary* all along the blade to keep pitch *constant*.

Props Can be Handy

Another critical aspect of propeller shape is *handedness*. A propeller that drives a boat forward when it rotates clockwise—as viewed from astern—is called a *right-handed* propeller. By the same token, a prop that rotates counter-clockwise—as viewed from aft—is *left handed*. You can tell a right-hand prop from a left-hand prop just by

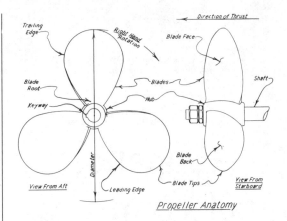

Propeller Anatomy

looking at it. Viewing the propeller from astern, the leading edges of the blades will be farther away from you than the trailing edges. If the leading edges are to your right, the prop rotates clockwise and is right handed. A left-hand wheel will be the opposite.

Right-handed props are almost, but not quite, universal on single-screw vessels. In twin-screw installations, props and engines of opposite hand are used port and starboard. A single right-hand wheel will tend to push the stern of your boat to starboard when going forward (to port going astern). The easiest way to visualize this is to realize that the water at the bottom of the prop's a bit denser and freer to flow (there's no hull above it) than at the top of the screw. This makes the lower blades a trifle more effective, so the prop and the stern walk sideways in the direction of rotation. On a twin-screw craft the screws should be out-turning. The starboard or right prop should be right handed and the port or left prop should be left handed. This has been found to give the best propeller efficiency. If you had a twin-screw vessel with both props the same hand, well . . . I'd rather be somewhere else when you tried to dock. Her stern would be slewing all over the place in low-speed maneuvers.

Shapely Blades

Propeller blades are narrowest at the root and usually broadest about two-thirds of the way out. The amount of blade area that can be driven by a given power is limited, so you have to distribute the area where it will do the most good. Since the tips of the blades are traveling the greatest distance, they can do the most work. Thus, the natural tendency is to try and get all the blade area as far out as possible. Obviously, you can't have tiny little shafts supporting huge plates at the tips. Accordingly, we compromise on the roughly elliptical shape that's most common. The roots of such blades have enough "meat" to support the loads on the middle and tip, while the outer part of the blade's not so big that it gets in the way of the water going to the blade behind it.

The More the Merrier?

This brings us to the question: How many blades? Surprisingly, the ideal is one. A single blade

The standard three-bladed propeller. Blade area is about half the area of a disc with the same diameter, or disc-area ratio is about 50 percent. (Courtesy Michigan Wheel)

does not have other blades disturbing the water flow ahead of it. But trying to get a single-bladed propeller to balance is sort of like trying to clap with one hand. (If you can do this, please let me know). Two blades are the logical answer. Both sailboats that need to reduce drag and very high-speed powerboats sometimes use two-bladed props. The problem with two blades for ordinary craft is that you'd need a whopping big diameter to get all the blade area required to drive you effectively. Enter the standard three-bladed prop. This configuration has proven to be the best compromise between balance, area, and efficiency.

Of course, there are props with four, five, and even more blades. They are useful for two reasons. First, with their extra blades, you can get more area with less diameter. So if you needed a 20-inch (50 cm) screw but only had room for an 18-incher (46 cm), you could use, say, a four-bladed prop. The four-blader (properly sized) would generate almost as much thrust as the ideal three-blader. It would never be quite as efficient, because with the blades closer together, they scramble up each other's water flow—literally getting in each other's way.

Smooth . . . Real Smooth

The best reason to go with more blades is to reduce vibration. Yep, extra blades are real smooth. If your prop's in the habit of kicking up a lot of annoying rhythmic thumping and/or humming, then a wheel with more blades will often go a long way towards curing the problem.

Vibration is just repeated banging. Every time the blades of your prop pass under your hull or by the strut, they cause a change in pressure that generates a push. If the push is strong enough you get a bang. Lots of bangs—vibration. If you have a three-bladed prop that turns at 1,000 rpm, then the blades pass under the stern 3,000 times every minute or 50 times a second—a vibration of 50 cycles per second. Switching to a four-bladed prop, still at 1,000 rpm, would change this to 4,000 times a minute, or 66 cycles per second. The more rapid the cycles the smoother the feel—and the less likely your hull is to resonate (amplify the sound like the body of a guitar) with the vibration.

Which Wheel?

Okay, we know about the propeller's shape, but how do you determine the correct pitch and diameter for your boat? A propeller must meet two completely different requirements. It must match your boat's speed and performance, and it must match your boat's engine.

Because of its shape and weight, your hull requires a certain amount of thrust to push it forward. In order to get her going properly, you need to pick a propeller that will generate as much thrust as possible at the speeds you'll be cruising at most. Take, for example, the single-screw, gas-engine *Svelte Samantha*, which has the following characteristics:

Waterline	28.0 ft.	8.5 m
Beam Waterline	9.34 ft.	2.8 m
Hull Draft	1.5 ft.	46 cm
Displacement	14,200 lb.	6,440 m
Power (max.)	240 hp	179 kw

You can use the Planing Speed chart (Chapter 20) to determine her top and cruising speeds. In *Svelte Samantha*'s case, this works out to 22 knots maximum, and 20 knots cruise. (Obviously, for displacement craft you'd use the Displacement Speed charts.)

Our aim is to have the propeller advance the same distance the boat will at speed. *Svelte Samantha*'s engine is rated at 240 hp (179 kw) at 3,000 rpm, but she has a 2.4-to-1 reduction gear. This means that *Samantha*'s prop is turning at 1,250 rpm (3,000 rpm ÷ 2.4 = 1,250 rpm).

The RPM for Finding Pitch

Now, if we selected pitch at top rpm it would be too great for cruising speed (usually 70 to 80 percent of maximum rpm), while if we used cruising rpm and speed for pitch, the prop wouldn't give us top boat speed. Since we can't change a fixed-pitch prop's pitch, we have to compromise. You should base pitch on boat speed at 95 percent rpm. For most purposes you can guesstimate that power at 95 percent of top rpm will be 90 percent of maximum power. We'll thus assume that *Svelte Samantha*'s running with a shaft rpm of 1,187 at around 216 hp (161 kw). Cruising speed will be bit below this, and you'll still be able to open her up to get top revs when you need to. Again using the Planing Speed chart (Chapter 20), you'd find that—at 95 percent rpm, thus 90 percent maximum power—*Samantha* would be doing 21 knots.

It's important to use an accurate figure for speed. Go over the methods we discussed in Chapter 20. Don't kid yourself that you're going faster than you are. You'll just end up with the wrong prop.

English-Measure Pitching In

Once we know our speed, all we have to do is find the pitch that'll give us the same forward distance traveled per minute as *Samantha* will go at her 21 knots pitch speed (at 95 percent of maximum rpm). Since we know boat speed in nautical miles per hour (knots) and the propeller pitch in inches and rpm, we've got to find some common ground—in this case feet per minute. To convert knots to feet per minute, multiply by 101.3 (to convert miles per hour to feet per minute, multiply by 88). So *Svelte Samantha*'s moving along at 2,127.3 feet per minute (21 knots × 101.3 = 2,127.3 ft./min.). Our prop's turning at 1,187 rpm. If we divide *Samantha*'s speed of 2,127.3 ft./min. by 1,187 rpm we find that our prop should have a pitch of 1.792 feet (2,127.3 ft./min. ÷ 1,187 rpm = 1.792 ft.). Of course, propeller pitches are specified in inches, so we multiply 1.792 feet by 12 and find *Svelte Samantha* requires a screw with a 21.5-inch pitch—without considering slip.

Metric Pitching In

In metric measurement, the common ground mentioned above is meters per minute. To convert knots to meters per minute, multiply by 30.87. So, *Svelte Samantha*'s moving along at 648.3 meters per minute (21 knots × 30.87 = 648.3 m/min.). Our prop's turning at 1,187 rpm. If we divide *Samantha*'s speed of 648.3 m/min. by 1,187 rpm we find that our prop should have a pitch of 0.546 meters (648.3 m/min. ÷ 1,187 rpm = 0.546 m). Of course, propeller pitches are specified in centimeters, so we multiply 0.546 meters by 100 and find that *Svelte Samantha* requires a screw with a 54.6-centimeter pitch—without considering slip.

A Slippery Matter

Of course, water's not really like soft pine. It's a fluid, and so a prop slips or slides a bit as it rotates. This sliding in a liquid is called *slip* or *apparent slip*, and we've got to allow for it to specify the right prop. The only way to find slip exactly is to take your boat out and run her on a measured mile. With her exact speed, you can calculate slip precisely. You can't do this, however, for a propeller that hasn't been installed or even ordered yet. For prop calculations we have to estimate slip. Gerr's Slip Chart is based on a formula I developed. It'll enable you to guesstimate slip fairly accurately.

In *Svelte Samantha*'s case we can enter her speed, at 95-percent rpm, of 21 knots on the chart to find a slip of 0.25 or 25 percent. Subtract this slip from 1 to find the "pitch difference," the percent of pitch *Samantha* really advances through the water each revolution. In our case, 0.75 (1 − 0.25 slip = 0.75). Finally, divide the 21.5-inch (54.6 cm) pitch without slip by the 0.75 pitch difference to find *Samatha*'s pitch with slip of 29 inches or 73 cm (21.5 in. ÷ 0.75 in. = 28.6 in—or 54.6 cm ÷ 0.75 = 72.8 cm).

Bigger is Better

But what about diameter? Except for craft that regularly operate at over 35 to 40 knots, a larger diameter prop's always more efficient than a smaller one. In other words, you'll get more thrust or push with the same engine and a larger-diameter screw. Obviously, you can't have a prop as big as a helicopter rotor. This is because your engine would never have enough power to move it in something as dense as sea water, no matter how slowly. The key here, though, is that the slower the rpms, the bigger the diameter your engine can turn. Shaft speed, not engine speed, is the important thing. Your reduction gear ratio is critical. The greater the reduction, the slower your shaft speed and the bigger your prop can be.

The RPM for Finding Diameter

Diameter's a much larger power-absorbing factor than pitch. Accordingly, where we used power and speed at 95 percent of max rpm to find pitch, we must use maximum rpm and full power to determine diameter. If we used lower rpms, the prop would be so large it would hold the engine back, preventing it from reaching top-rated power. Remember, though, that full-rated power doesn't reach the propeller; there's always some loss in the gearbox and shaft bearings. Once again, 95 percent of full power—not rpm this

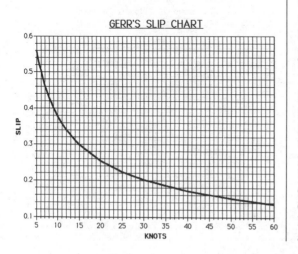

GERR'S SLIP CHART

time—provides a close estimate. For *Samantha,* with maximum rated power of 240 hp or 179 kw, this gives 228 hp at the propeller (shaft horsepower or shp), or 170 kw for finding diameter.

A look at the Propeller–Diameter/Power/RPM chart shows that *Svelte Samantha*'s engine, delivering an honest 228 shaft horsepower (170 kw), can turn a 28-inch (70 cm) prop at 1,125 rpm. We've found that a 28-inch-diameter prop with a 29-inch pitch (or 70 cm by 73 cm) would do the job. Very often a propeller's pitch is specified as a ratio of diameter. In this case, our prop would have a pitch ratio of 1.03 or 1.04 (29 in. pitch ÷ 28 in. diameter = 1.03—or, 68 cm ÷ 73 cm = 1.04). If the pitch and diameter had been the same, the pitch ratio would be 1.00. This is referred to as having a *square wheel.*

Preventing Cavities, or You Must *Never* Forget Blade Area

There's yet another shoal we have to clear. All too often the simple pitch and diameter dimensions are the only factors considered in specing out a prop. This is a *grave* but all too common error. It's vitally important that the propeller have enough blade area to absorb engine power

without causing *cavitation.* (Sounds like something your dentist should fix). Actually, cavitation is bubbles of partial vacuum caused by excessive prop loading. Contrary to common conception, cavitating propellers can generate plenty of thrust. The problem is that these small vacuum bubbles implode with such force against the propeller that they'll cause pitting. These little guys actually suck metal right off the surface of your prop. The pitting leads to uneven wear, bad balance, and vibration—not good stuff.

High-speed powerboats may use special screws designed to cavitate all the time. These are *super cavitating* propellers. Their secret is that they chop off the trailing halves of their blades where the cavitation bubbles often implode—pretty sneaky. You can recognize this sort of prop by its scimitar-like blade shape. Such wheels are useful only on craft going over 35 knots regularly, and they really come into their own only over 45 knots.

How Much Blade Area?

To prevent cavitation you must ensure that your screw's *blade loading* is kept fairly low. What is *blade loading?* Well, if you think about it, your prop's blades essentially push on the water to de-

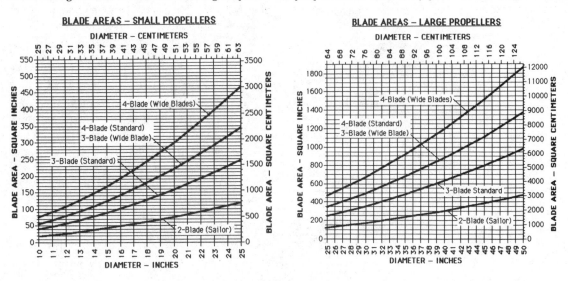

liver a thrust in pounds or kilograms. It's this thrust that drives your *Svelte Samantha* forward. Reading from the Blade Area charts, her 28-inch-diameter (70 cm) standard three-bladed prop would have a blade area of about 310 square inches (2,000 cm²). If her prop were delivering 2,000 pounds (907 kg) of thrust, this thrust—roughly speaking—would be distributed across the surface of the blades.

Svelte Samantha's blade loading would then be 6.4 pounds per square inch (psi), or 0.45 kg/cm² (2,000 lb ÷ 310 sq.in. = 6.4 psi—or, 907 kg ÷ 2,000 cm² = 0.45 kg/cm²). This is generally a good, safe level. Depending on boat speed and propeller depth, safe blade loadings vary from around 5 to 15 psi (0.35 to 1.0 kg/cm²). Happily, you don't have to calculate blade loading; you can determine the minimum blade area required to avoid cavitation from a simple formula I've developed.

Gerr's Blade Area Formula:

$$Required\ Blade\ Area\ (sq.\ in.)\ =\ \frac{100 \times shp}{knots \times \sqrt{knots}}$$

$$Required\ Blade\ Area\ (cm^2)\ =\ \frac{865 \times shaft\ kw}{knots \times \sqrt{knots}}$$

For *Svelte Samantha,* with a shaft horsepower (shp) of 228 (170 kw), and a top speed of 22 knots, this works out to 221 square inches (1,425 cm²).

[100 × 228 shp = 22,800, and the square root of 22 knots is 4.69, 4.69 × 22 knots = 103.2, then 22,800 ÷ 103.2 = 221 sq.in.—or, 865 × 170 kw = 147,050, and the square root of 22 knots is 4.69, 4.69 × 22 knots = 103.2, then 147,050 ÷ 103.2 = 1,425 cm²]

Referring to the Blade Area charts, we can see that this area would be supplied by a standard three-bladed wheel just 23 inches (58 cm) in diameter. The 28-inch (70 cm) prop we selected for *Samantha* has more area, indicating low blade-loading, which, within reason, is fine.

If the blade area at the diameter we'd selected had been too small, we could have called for a wide-bladed three-bladed prop, a four-bladed prop, or even a wide-bladed four-bladed prop to get additional area at the same diameter. If none of these options provide adequate area you've got a real problem. Five or 10 percent less area than recommended will likely generate some small amounts of cavitation—it may be workable, but it's iffy. If blade area's more than 10 percent less than called for, severe cavitation is likely to result—vibration and pitting will probably occur. What you really need is a larger-diameter, slower-turning prop—a different reduction gear and perhaps a modified prop aperture.

Converting to Two or Four Blades

The standard propeller's a three-bladed wheel with elliptical blades, constant pitch, and a *disc area ratio* of 50 percent. (*Disc area ratio* or *DAR* is the total blade area divided by the area of a circle the same diameter as the prop.) The basic system we've been using is for sizing just such a standard three-bladed wheel. To convert to two- or four-bladed, simply multiply by the following factors.

TWO- AND FOUR-BLADE CONVERSION FACTORS

	Diameter	Pitch
Two-Bladed Propeller	1.05	1.01
Four-Bladed Propeller	0.94	0.98

Accordingly, if we were going to fit a four-bladed screw to *Svelte Samantha,* we'd use a 26-inch by 28-inch or 66-cm by 71-cm prop (28-inch dia. × 0.94 = 26.32 in., and 29-inch pitch × 0.98 = 28.42 in.—or, 70-cm dia. × 0.94 = 65.8 cm, and 73-cm pitch × 0.98 = 71.54 cm).

Twice as Screwy

If you have a twin-screw boat, the calculation for pitch is exactly the same as for a single screw.

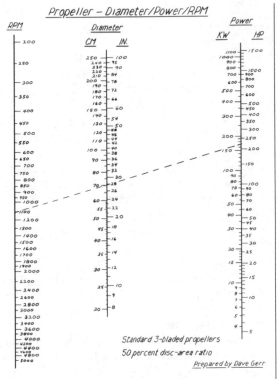

Propeller – Diameter/Power/RPM

RPM	Diameter		Power	
	CM	IN.	KW	HP

Standard 3-bladed propellers
50 percent disc-area ratio

Prepared by Dave Gerr

Note: See full-page chart on page 406.

After all, both props have to advance the same distance as the boat each revolution. In figuring diameter, each engine will swing a prop determined by its individual power and shaft rpm. However, the diameter of each prop can be smaller than in a single-screw installation for the same hull. This is because power and thrust will be divided between two propellers, reducing the blade area required for each.

If *Svelte Samantha* was powered by two engines delivering 108 hp (80 kw) at 1,125 shaft rpm, then, reading from the Propeller–Diameter/Power/RPM chart, each engine could swing a 24-inch-diameter (60 cm) prop. They couldn't handle the 28-inch (70 cm) wheel of the single-screw version, and you wouldn't want them to. In fact, referring to Gerr's Blade Area Formula and the Blade Area

chart, you can see that we'd need only 112 square inches (722 cm²) for each wheel, and this would be provided by a standard three-bladed wheel a bare 17 inches (43 cm) in diameter.

Squeezing a Wheel

There's one more problem we've yet to discuss. What if, as on *Svelte Samantha*, blade loading wasn't a problem but you still needed to swing a smaller prop to fit the available space, keeping the same engine, reduction gear, and shaft rpm. You could proceed as follows: For each 1-inch decrease in diameter, increase pitch 2 inches. Say we had to squeeze *Svelte Samantha*'s prop down to 24 inches (61 cm), at the same power, boat speed, and rpm (with the same engine and reduction gear). We found earlier a 28-inch diameter by 29-inch pitch three-blader (70 cm by 73 cm). Reducing diameter 4 inches (10 cm) means we have to increase pitch 8 inches (20 cm) to 37 inches or 94 cm. This is a pitch ratio of 1.54, which is quite high. Except on high-speed boats (over 35 knots), pitch ratios should be kept under 1.4 for best efficiency. Additionally, props with pitch ratios over 1.5 are often custom orders—expensive!

A better alternative would be to start with the smaller diameter four-bladed screw of 26-inches by 28-inches (66 cm by 71 cm). Reducing this by 2 inches or 5 cm (to 24-inch or 61-cm diameter) would force us to increase pitch by 4 inches (10 cm) to 32 inches (81 cm). The resulting pitch ratio of 1.23 is acceptable. At this shaft speed, you couldn't effectively reduce diameter much further without suffering from a real loss in thrust and efficiency. Smaller diameter really calls for higher rpms.

More on Propellers

All the above will enable you to select a prop for most average boats fairly quickly and accurately. Propeller selection's a complicated business; however, if you really want to do a first-rate job and acquire an in-depth understanding of all the variables, you should get hold of my *Propeller Handbook* (See Suggested Reading section.)

The Strangest Prop

We've only looked at standard fixed-pitch propellers here. There are other sorts of props—surface propellers, contra-rotating propellers, props with Kort Nozzles, and so on. One really bizarre propeller is the Voith-Schneider, or cycloidal, propeller. These doohickies don't look anything like any propeller you've ever seen. They're sort of like vertical paddlewheels. Vertical blades or vanes are arranged in a circle, projecting straight down from the hull bottom. The entire contraption rotates, in unison, while each individual vane or blade oscillates independently. The incredible thing about these engineering marvels is that they'll drive a boat in any direction, even exactly sideways, without rudder or steering thrusters—weird! A few tugs, oceanographic vessels, and some specialized military craft have been fitted with these things. Since they cost about five times more than a normal prop arrangement, I doubt you'll have one on your boat any time soon.

CHAPTER 33

Understanding the Sailboat Propeller— The Art of Compromise

. . . and, as there was no wind, we row'd all the way; . . .

The Autobiography of Benjamin Franklin

Not more than 70 or 80 years ago, it was the exception rather than the rule to find a sailboat fitted with an engine. In those days, crews patiently waited out a calm, routinely managed a huge inventory of light-air canvas, and regularly worked their way into tight slips under sweep and pole, aided only by nice judgment and a keen insight into the vagaries of wind and current. Of course, even back then, engines were being fitted in some larger sailboats. These engines were thought of as auxiliary power, and such craft came to be called auxiliaries—an appelation that has stuck to this day. In fact, the vast majority of production sailboats over 25 or 30 feet (8 to 9 m), are fitted with inboard power and thus, properly speaking, are auxiliaries, or—in higher-powered models—motorsailers.

The Compromise

The advantages of inboard power are legion—no more hours, or even days, of endless slatting about in glassy seas; no more battling headwinds in tight quarters; and easy controlled motoring up to slip, mooring, or dock. But, as always, you don't get something for nothing. All auxiliaries pay a stiff price for this convenience—propeller drag. It's a sad but unavoidable fact that everything that makes a propeller more efficient under power increases its drag when the engine's turned off and you're under sail alone. This is the great compromise confronting anyone wishing to select the best screw for a sailboat, be it auxiliary or motorsailer. If you want a boat to be fast and lively under sail, you have to do everything possible to reduce the drag of the prop. But, if you reduce propeller drag under sail, you simultaneously reduce efficiency under power—a classic catch-22.

Reducing Drag

There are really just two ways to reduce propeller drag under sail. You can make the prop blades themselves as small as possible, or you can hide the prop from as much of the water flow as practical. Ideally, you'd take advantage of both approaches. In fact, this combined approach is one of the reasons for the confusion about whether a prop creates the least drag when it's locked or free to rotate. The simple answer is that a propeller creates less drag when free to rotate. (You must be certain that the gearbox is getting proper lubrication in this condition. If it isn't, you can destroy it quickly. Check with the manufacturer *before* allowing free rotation, if you're not absolutely sure.) However, if the wheel can be locked vertically, hidden behind a skeg or keel, it will produce less drag than when freely rotating. Feathering props also generate less drag when fixed vertically. (Folders, of course, have no tendency to rotate when closed.)

The Conventional Solution

The simplest and oldest method of making a prop smaller to create less drag is to give it fewer blades and to make those blades as narrow as possible. This defines the standard fixed, two-bladed sailor propeller. (As we saw in the last chapter, you can't have a one-bladed screw, because it won't balance. If you think you can solve this one, your fortune may be made.) Standard two-bladed sailboat wheels are inexpensive and reliable. They create far less drag under sail than a standard three-bladed powerboat prop with wide blades. In fact, if the standard fixed two-bladed wheel's hidden behind a keel or in an aperture and is locked aligned vertically behind the deadwood, it creates very little drag indeed.

Small Blade Area Causes Problems

Unfortunately, these narrow blades lead to difficulties under power. Remember, a propeller drives your boat forward by generating a force or push (thrust) on the propeller blades. Let's take the cutter *Windmill,* a typical 45-footer (13.7 m), with a 40-foot (12.2 m) waterline, powered with, say, a 50-hp (37 kw) diesel. Her engine/propeller combination will be delivering around 1,300 pounds (590 kg) of thrust—over half a ton—all delivered through the propeller blades. A standard

two-bladed sailor prop of about 20 inches (51 cm) in diameter (about the right size for this configuration) would have a total blade area of approximately 76 square inches (490 cm²). Since, roughly speaking, the thrust is distributed over this area, it amounts to 17.1 pounds per square inch or 1.2 kg/cm² (1,300 lb. thrust ÷ 76 sq.in. blade area = 17.1 psi—or 590 kg ÷ 490 cm² = 1.2 kg/cm²). This is very high blade loading.

For almost all auxiliary sailboats, top speed is hull speed. For the 40-foot-waterline (12.2 m) *Windmill,* this is 8.5 knots. Using this in Gerr's Blade Loading Formula (from the last chapter) shows that *Windmill* requires a screw with 200 square inches (1,290 cm²) of blade area; and, reading from the Blade Area charts, *Windmill* ought to have a 2-bladed prop about 32 inches (81 cm) in diameter! This is way too large to be fitted on any but specially designed motorsailers.

Low Propeller Efficiency is Sometimes the Best Compromise

Here we face the sailboat propeller compromise squarely. In order to reduce the blade loading and eliminate cavitation, we'd have to increase blade area by making the blades wider and/or using more of them. This, though, would increase drag under sail tremendously. The fact is, though, that most sailing auxiliaries under 50 feet (15 m) or so spend a relatively small portion of their time under power. Few motor more than 100 hours a season; many 50 hours or less. With such a small percentage of time under power, it would not make sense to increase the blade size and thus drag under sail. Relatively low thrust for a given power as well as vibration and some potential pitting from cavitation are acceptable compromises for such vessels.

Feathering Props for Increased Blade Area Without Increased Drag

For larger boats or even for smaller auxiliaries or motorsailers that will power a great por-

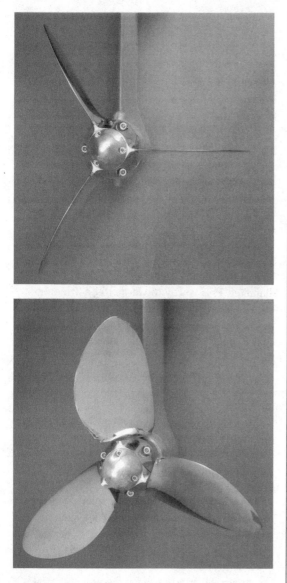

Three-bladed feathering propeller. Note that it has plenty of blade area, but—at the same time—feathers to a low drag shape. (Courtesy ProWell GMBH)

the shape of the blades when they're not in use. This is how we get the feathering and folding propeller. The feathering prop aligns its blades straight fore-n-aft for minimum drag, while the folding wheel's blades fold together almost like the closing of an old-fashioned ladies' hand fan.

In most standard applications, the feathering prop delivers the most thrust. A standard two-bladed feathering screw will have almost 40 percent more blade area for the same diameter when compared to a narrow, fixed, two-bladed sailor type. (On last chapter's Blade Area charts, read about midway between the standard three-blade and the two-blade sailor.) Yet because of it's low drag shape when feathered, the feathering prop will actually have less drag under sail than the fixed two-blader—a 26-incher (66 cm) would provide about 200 square inches (1,290 cm²). A feathering three-bladed prop has, incredibly, about 215 percent more blade area than a fixed two-blader of the same diameter—you can read blade area right off the standard three-blade line on the Blade Area Charts—and will still have slightly less drag than a standard fixed two-blader under sail. Thus, a typical 22-inch-diameter (56 cm) three-bladed feathering propeller would have a blade area of about 195 square inches (1,260 cm²). This is close enough to the recommended 200 square inches (1,290 cm²) to be ideal for an auxiliary or motorsailer.

Every aspect of performance under power will be dramatically improved with this additional blade area, while performance under sail will remain about the same as with a fixed two-blader. This three-bladed featherer is thus an ideal prop for serious voyaging where many hours of motoring or motorsailing are anticipated. A two-bladed feathering wheel—of the same diameter—will have higher blade loadings and thus lower efficiency than the three-blader, but it will still perform better than the conventional fixed two-blader as it still has more blade area. It will also have less drag under sail than either the fixed two-blader or the feathering three-blader. This is a

tion of the time, steps should be taken to increase blade area. In order to do this without increasing drag under sail, we must find some way to change

good compromise screw for the performance-oriented cruiser and the cruiser-racer.

Additional Advantages of Feathering Propellers

Feathering propellers are usually opened or closed either by the torque of the prop shaft or by water pressure. When the prop shaft begins to turn, the blades themselves rotate about their individual axes, almost immediately going from fully feathered to fully open. The best feathering screws have a geared connection between the blades so the blades open evenly and in sync with each other. Additionally, they're fitted with adjustable stops that control the blade angle or pitch at fully open. By adjusting the stop, you can adjust pitch to exactly suit your boat's requirements. (This adjustment can only be made by a diver or with the boat hauled out, of course.) To determine proper pitch, you can use the methods in Chapter 20 to determine how fast you'll go under power, then use the pitch calculations from Chapter 29.

Even more interesting is that feathering propellers are actually *more* efficient than fixed propellers—of any type—in reverse. This is because the individual blades are free to rotate around their axes in either direction. Thus, when the propeller goes into reverse, the blades swing around so their leading edges face the new reversed rotation. For obvious reasons, fixed propeller blades can't perform this trick. They deliver proportionately less thrust in reverse, when they are effectively having their blades driven backwards through the water.

Folding Props for Minimum Drag

At the other end of the spectrum is the racing boat that absolutely must have minimum drag under sail for maximum boat speed. For such craft, even the small drag of a feathering two bladed prop's excessive. Here, the folding propeller comes into its own. Folding propellers have narrow blades and so have small blade areas for a given diameter. Their performance under power—in conventional installations—is thus no better and usually worse than that of the conventional fixed two-bladed wheel. Their great advantage is that, when folded, they create the least drag of any propeller configuration known. As most racers use their engines only a few hours a season—maneuvering into a slip, or powering through a clam on the way to a race—engine/propeller efficiency is relatively unimportant, and the loss of thrust from the narrow folder's small blade area is well worth it in return for the gain of an extra fraction of a knot or so in speed under sail—frequently more than enough for a winning edge.

The Best Sailing Propeller Configuration of All

Interestingly, the folding propeller actually offers the best compromise for true all-around performance auxiliaries, if the boat's specifically designed around this concept. This is due to two things. First, blade area increases very quickly with increased diameter; and second, propeller diameter can be increased if shaft rpm is reduced, even at the same horsepower.

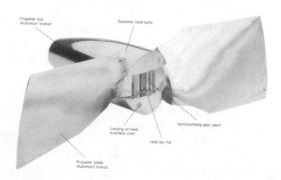

Two-bladed folding propeller shown in open position. Propellers like this offer the lowest drag under sail, but also less thrust under power. The exception is in installations specifically designed for extra-large diameter and low rpm, which allows good thrust under power as well as low drag under sail. (Courtesy Jatstram Ltd.)

We can see how this would work out on our example, *Windmill*. When we first considered her, her 50-hp (37 kw) engine was running at 2,400 rpm, and she was fitted with a 2:1 reduction gear, so her shaft speed was half of this, or 1,200 rpm. Referring to last chapter's Propeller–Diameter/ Power/RPM chart, this would drive a 19.5-inch-diameter (50 cm) three-bladed propeller or—using the two-bladed conversion factors—a 20-inch-diameter (50 cm) two-bladed propeller. We already saw, however, that a 20-inch (50 cm), narrow, two-bladed sailor prop wouldn't have enough blade area for efficient powering.

If, however, we used a larger reduction gear, say 4:1, shaft speed would be reduced to 600 rpm, which would permit using a much larger, 30-inch-diameter (76-cm), 2-bladed folding prop. (Try it yourself on the Propeller - Diameter/Power/RPM chart). Such a screw would have about the same 195 square inches (1,260 cm^2) of blade area as the 22-inch-diameter (56 cm) three-bladed feathering screw we'd arrived at earlier, but less drag under sail than any other configuration. For a sailboat, this is the best of all possible worlds—maximum thrust under power and minimum drag under sail. The catch is that such large-diameter propellers and large reduction gears must be designed in from scratch, as I did on *Quicksilver,* Chapter 5. There's seldom room to retrofit such a system.

Controllable Pitch for Serious Voyagers

True motorsailers over 60 feet (18 m) or so can improve engine/propeller efficiency still further by going to controllable-pitch propellers. These propellers are available in fully feathering models which have as little drag under sail as standard feathering props. The great advantage of controllable-pitch props is just that—their pitch can be adjusted at will from the helm. The plus here is that—when motorsailing—pitch can be tweaked up or down for optimum efficiency at every variation of wind strength, wind direction, and sail combination. On long cruises, the result is

considerable fuel savings, increased range, and higher average speed. Of course, under power alone, pitch can also be adjusted for maximum efficiency—less pitch at the start of a cruise, when heavily loaded with fuel and stores, and more pitch to exactly match the higher speed possible near the end of a trip, when tanks and lockers are nearly empty and the vessel's lighter.

Again, as always, there's a compromise here. In this case it's not in performance, but in price. Well-engineered controllable-pitch propellers are considerably more costly than standard feathering screws, which, in turn, are more expensive than simple fixed, two-bladed sailor props. Further, the pitch control mechanism requires additional regular routine maintenance, which also adds to operating cost. Accordingly, on small motorsailers the additional price of a controllable-pitch propeller is seldom justified. Larger craft, especially over 60 feet (18 m), will usually see a long-term net savings in operating cost as well as gaining increased pleasure from improved overall performance and control.

The Newest Wrinkle

The newest propeller wrinkle I've seen is the patented Autoprop from Brunton's Propellers Ltd, England. This is a totally self-governing controllable-pitch propeller. There's no pitch control mechanism. Instead, the geometry of the blades and their pivoting attachment to the hub is designed to adjust pitch automatically in response to changes in torque, shaft speed, and water pressure—both in forward and reverse.

Data from Brunton's shows considerable improvement in efficiency under power over most other propeller configurations. (There would be no improvement over a conventional controllable-pitch propeller, when pitch was properly adjusted, but the Brunton's prop is simpler. It doesn't require a pitch-control mechanism, and—in theory—automatically adjusts for optimum pitch, freeing you from trying to figure it out.)

The 38-inch-diameter Hundested controllable-pitch propeller and large balance rudder on the 87-foot Frank MacLear-designed cutter Aria. *Note the generous clearance around the prop to optimize water flow to the prop. The rudder and prop are extremely well protected from impact both from grounding and from hitting debris by the keel ahead and the massive skeg below. With a 3:1 reduction gear the prop turns at just 600 rpm at top speed. The large balanced rudder combined with the high-thrust, low-speed prop enable the boat to spin in a tight circle, about 1.3 times her overall length. (Frank MacLear photo)*

At first blush, this seems to be the best of all possible worlds; however, some reports indicate the Autoprop is negatively affected by fouling. The individual blades aren't connected and take their own natural pitch. If one blade has more barnacle growth than another it takes a different pitch, and vibration results. This problem could easily be controlled by diving overboard to clean the prop regularly. (You could use your local bottom-cleaning/diving service.) I've also seen no information on this new gizmo's drag characteristics under sail. It is about certain that folding propellers generate substantially less drag, and it's also reasonable to assume that standard feathering propellers would have slightly less drag under sail as well. The Brunton's Autoprop, then, would seem to be most appropriate for boats that place more of an emphasis on long-distance motorsailing and powering performance, and less emphasis on performance under sail.

CHAPTER 34

Getting the Shaft, Pulling the Prop, and Taking Its Measure

Rose: Could you see anything, dear?
Charlie: Yeah, the shaft's twisted like a
corkscrew, and there's a blade gone off the
prop.

The African Queen, C.S. Forester

For the majority of boats running at average speeds, it'd be hard to come up with a drive system that was simpler, more economical, and more efficient than the propeller. It's far more effective than its predecessors—sternwheels and sidewheels—and, at speeds under 35 knots or thereabouts, props are more efficient than the new-fangled jet drive. (Jets do offer substantial benefits at high speed, or where shallow draft is critical.) To function properly, however, props have to be well treated. They must be installed correctly, have plenty of breathing room, and be mounted on a proper shaft. Fall down in any of these departments and you're in for trouble.

Getting the Shaft

Propeller shafts not only carry the twisting load of the engine to the propeller, but also transmit the full thrust of the prop into the hull. These are hefty loads! A typical 33-footer (10 m) with a 230-hp (170 kw) engine would be delivering a ton of thrust along her shaft. Selecting the correct propeller-shaft diameter is actually a fairly complicated business. Again, you might want to get hold of my *Propeller Handbook* to go into shafting in detail. Happily, for small-craft work, the following rule of thumb will give good results. (For high-powered racing craft and heavy workboats, you'll need to do more detailed checking.) The rule bases shaft diameter on propeller diameter, and works acceptably because the load on the shaft is really controlled by the size of the prop. Simply, shaft size should be equal to prop diameter divided by the following factors:

SHAFT MATERIAL

	Tobin Bronze	Monel 400
Two-Bladed propeller	14.5	18.1
Three-Bladed propeller	14.0	17.5
Four-Bladed propeller	13.1	16.3

We found that *Svelte Samantha*—our example vessel from Chapter 32—took a 28-inch (70 cm) three-bladed prop. Using the above factors, she'd then require a 2-inch (50 mm) tobin bronze shaft or a 1⅝-inch (40 mm) Monel 400 shaft. Note that *Samantha*'s 26-inch (66 cm) four-bladed wheel would take the same shaft diameters using the four-blade factors above; the torque or shaft load's the same for any prop correctly sized for this power/rpm combination. In fact, you can determine shaft diameter simply by entering power and rpm on the Propeller–Diameter/Power/RPM chart (Chapter 32), and then dividing by 14 for bronze or 17.5 for Monel 400.

Holding the Shaft

Just as you need a hefty enough shaft, you also need to support it along its length with shaft bearings—also known as pillow blocks. Too little support creates shaft whip, vibration, and even breakage. You can read maximum bearing spacing for a given shaft diameter from the Propeller Shaft Bearing Spacing chart. *Svelte Samantha*'s 2-inch (50 mm) shaft would require bearings spaced no farther than 6.5 feet or 1.9 meters apart. Again, for high-powered racing craft or heavy workboats, you'll want to use a more exact method. Bearings should not be placed much closer together than necessary. This prevents the shaft from flexing lightly with the hull in a seaway. Bearings shouldn't be closer together than 20 times the shaft diameter.

Giving Your Prop Room To Breathe

All too often you see propellers squeezed into tiny apertures, with blunt square edges blocking the water flow. Without clean water flow, your prop just can't do an honest day's work. When considering the largest diameter wheel you can fit, keep in mind that there should be a clear distance—a *tip clearance*—between the hull and the propeller blade tips of at least 10 percent. *Ten percent is a bare minimum*; 14 to 18 percent is the standard ideal distance, though the bigger the clearance the better—assuming the prop diame-

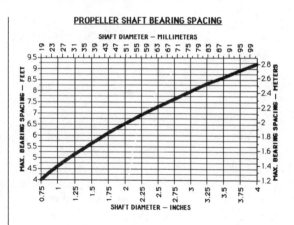

ter's still large enough. For high-speed planing hulls water flow's even more critical. Such craft should have tip clearances of 20 percent. Some of the chief causes of propeller vibration are insufficient tip clearance and poor aperture fairing. They're also nifty fuel wasters. An 18-percent tip clearance for *Svelte Samantha*'s 28-inch (50 cm) prop would be 5 inches or 9 centimeters. Don't forget to fair the edges of the aperture. Your propeller will thank you!

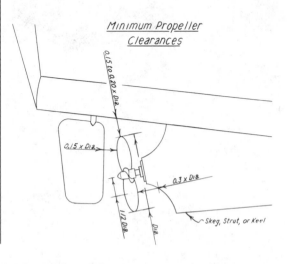

Handling Prop Damage

Like everything else in life, in spite of the propeller's simplicity and efficiency, it's less than perfect. In fact, one of the prop's real drawbacks—one not shared by, say, jet drives—is that the blades can (and do) hit all manner of floating debris and get spectacularly mangled in an instant.

Unless a blade's sheared completely off or a shaft is severely bent, you can usually motor your *Oscill-Eightor* back to port, but vibration will be so horrendous you'll have to slow way down. The only fix is to pull the damaged screws and replace them. (Amazingly, mangled blades can be rebuilt good as new quite economically. But they must be packed off to the prop shop.) All this is an excellent argument for carrying a set of spare wheels onboard. Waiting two to three weeks—or more—for a new set of props to arrive will tend to cut into a vacation cruise.

Removing the Prop

Now, in some small, out-of-the-way yards—like those in the most interesting cruising grounds—the hammer removal technique seems to be favored.

Oops! Who put that beach there, anyway? This is typical prop damage. Incredibly, this prop could almost certainly be rebuilt as good as new. In this case, the rudder's also been mangled. Often, debris will mangle the prop without serious damage to the rudder. Having a spare wheel and a prop puller on board could save your cruise.

The more genteel of these yards will have their mechanic tap with some degree of care on the hub alone, while less retiring yards will have their men whale away on a prop with a heavy metal sledge. Either approach will make anyone who knows about propellers cringe and turn away. Chances are your prop costs as much as—or considerably more than—the VCR sitting in your living room. I doubt you'd let a mechanic try to disconnect it by banging it (even gingerly) with a metal hammer! Propellers are, in fact, finely machined and carefully balanced devices. A metal hammer should never touch *any* part of your prop! Even in removing a damaged prop, banging with a hammer can bend the shaft and further complicate repairs to the blades. (It can also increase the cost of having the wheel rebuilt.)

Prop Pullers are the Answer

For this reason, it makes good sense to carry a well-made propeller puller in your ship's tool chest. Not only will you be able to present it to the yard foreman and insist on its use—if they don't have their own—but it'll enable you to handle wheel changes on your *Oscill-Eightor* yourself. Except on the very largest vessels, this is a job well within the abilities of any boat owner, and is a skill you ought to master for safety and peace of mind.

Prop pullers come in many types and sizes; however, they all serve the same function. They enable you to back off a tight wheel quickly and easily, usually without whacking on it at all. Instead, the prop puller hooks around the back side of the hub (the side facing toward the bow) and then comes forward along the hub between one or more of the blades, to land on the shaft center. Simply tightening down a nut (or nuts, for three-bolt pullers) draws the prop aft and off exactly as a woodworker's C-clamp fastens down. Some prop pullers even look similar to woodworker's clamps.

Getting a Jammed Prop Free

Occasionally a puller won't get a stuck wheel started. In these cases you can tap—on the hub

A clamp-type propeller puller. (Courtesy Dymex, Inc.)

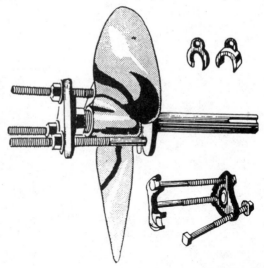

A three-bolt propeller puller. (Courtesy Buck-Algonquin)

only—with a hard rubber or rawhide mallet. Alternately, you can rest a softwood block on the hub and tap on that with a metal hammer. (Never tap on the blades with anything at all.) If your prop still refuses to budge, you can try heat—again, on the hub only. This is a last resort, as heat can change the grain structure of the metal and weaken it. Don't use a welding torch, but a standard shop blow-torch. All you want to do is heat the hub up enough to make it swell and loosen on the shaft. Something around the temperature of boiling water, or slightly more, is all that's called for.

Prop Pulling Step by Step

To remove *Oscill-Eightor*'s prop, you first pull the cotter pin, then loosen and remove the two prop nuts. You'll need to hold the prop immobile while loosening the nuts, and simply putting *Oscill-Eightor*'s engine in gear is definitely not the answer. Instead, place a wood block (or blocks) between her hull and the prop to prevent rotation. Use a standard wrench of the correct size for the prop nuts, and try to apply all turning pressure on the same side as the wood block and towards the block. Applying pressure from the opposite side of the block puts a side load on your shaft that can bend it out of alignment—not generally approved!

Checking the Fit

When reinstalling *Oscill-Eightor*'s prop, you should first check the taper and keyway. Are they clean and straight? Are the key and keyway themselves clean and straight? You can check the match between the internal taper on the hub and the shaft taper by purchasing a small quantity of Prussian Blue (a blue dye) from a local machinist's supply shop. Coat the shaft taper all around with the dye and then fit the prop in place. Rotate

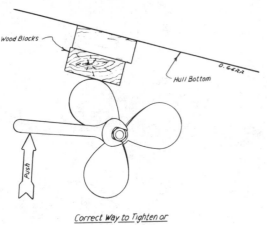

Correct Way to Tighten or
Loosen Propeller Nuts

it a few turns and remove it. Is the dye distributed smoothly and evenly along the inside of the hub? If the dye is concentrated mostly at one end or the other, then the tapers don't match and *Oscill-Eightor*'s prop will wobble on her shaft. The key itself should have an easy, sliding fit. If it's tight you can use fine sand paper or a fine file to grind it down. If it's a sloppy fit, get a new key. They don't cost much, and the key's all that really keeps the prop from spinning freely around on the shaft. (Having a spare key handy is not a bad idea.)

Installing a Prop

If all proves up to snuff, clean off the shaft, the key, and the inside of the hub. Wipe all with a fine film of light oil and fit the hub onto the shaft. Rotate to line up the keyway, and insert the key. Drive prop and key home with some *light* taps with a rubber mallet or softwood block. You're ready to replace the prop nuts.

The Ubiquitous Wrong-Way Prop Nuts

Interestingly, the chances are that your *Oscill-Eightor*'s prop nuts were originally put on backwards. No kidding; they are on most boats. There should always be two propeller nuts: a jam or lock

nut, and the main or load nut. Because it seems natural that the nut directly in contact with *Oscill-Eightor*'s prop is the one that ought to be doing most of the work, many yards install the full-size nut here. This is the wrong way around!

The correct procedure (after you've got the prop and key firmly snugged in place on the shaft) is to install the small, half-height jam nut first—against the hub. Tighten it up as hard as you comfortably can, by hand with a standard wrench. Then, screw on the full-size nut and tighten that down independently—again, as hard as you comfortably can, by hand with a standard-size wrench. Finally, fit the cotter pin, and you're ready to go.

Explaining the Wrong-Way Nuts

Now, I know that many an old sea dog will sit reading this muttering and shaking his (or her) head. (Can experienced woman sailors be "sea dogs"? Perhaps they're "sea cats.") Anyway, the reason the half-height nut goes against the prop—not the other way around—is that, as the second (outer) nut is tightened down, it rotates the nut against the hub very slightly—a fraction of a turn. This unloads the nut against the hub, placing all the load on the top or outer nut. Since the top nut thus does the brunt of the work, it should be the nut with the most threads—the full-size nut. I wouldn't lose much sleep over having the nuts on backwards. It's slightly weaker, but has proven adequate. When you reinstall your own prop, however, you might as well do it right.

Know Thy Dimensions

In addition to knowing how to remove and replace your prop, you ought to know its dimensions—pitch and diameter—and have this recorded on the first page of your ship's log, along with other critical information like engine model, hp, rpm, reduction-gear ratio, shaft diameter, boat displacement, LOA, LWL, beam, draft of hull, draft to bottom of props, etc. Most manufacturers inscribe the diameter and pitch on the prop's hub.

Diameter is always placed first, so a hub marked 20 × 22 belongs to a 20-inch-diameter, 22-inch-pitch wheel. (The metric equivalent would be 50 by 56, for 50-cm diameter and 56-cm pitch.) Unfortunately, hub markings aren't always accurate. On one occasion, I inspected a twin-screw boat. One of her wheels was marked 22 × 23 and the other 22 × 26?! When we pulled the props to check them, it turned out that both were 24-inch diameter and 22-inch pitch!! (The good news was that at least they matched.)

Measuring Diameter

When you remove your prop for routine maintenance or repair, you should check its dimensions. Diameter, of course, is easy. On a two- or four-blader, you can simply measure across the blades. On a three- or five-blader, measure the radius out from the prop center to the tip of one blade; then double the figure. (A reasonably exact way to measure radius easily is to measure out from the side of hub to the blade tip. Next, measure the diameter of the hub and divide that by two. Add this to the hub-to-tip measurement to get radius, and double the answer for diameter.)

Finding Pitch

At first, pitch would seem difficult to measure. Actually, it too is fairly easy. All the measurements can be made with a ruler and a carpenter's square in 15 minutes or so. Take, for instance, *Oscill-Eightor*'s propeller. Place it face up (with the aft faces of the blades up) on a flat table. You'll need a reference line, so take a grease pencil and, with a 12-inch (30- to 50-cm) ruler, draw a reference line along the face of one of *Oscill-Eightor*'s prop blades, along its center from hub to tip. Now measure out from the center any convenient distance and make a tick mark. *Oscill-Eightor*'s props measure 24 inches (61 cm) in diameter, so we'll make the measurement at, say, an 8-inch (20 cm) radius. Draw a transverse line across the blade

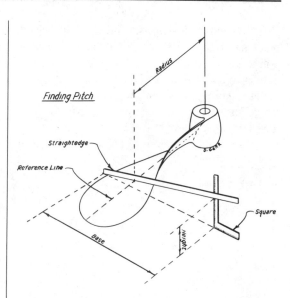

Finding Pitch

face (at right angles to the radius line) through the 8-inch (20 cm) radius mark.

Take any straightedge and lay it on this transverse line so that its bottom edge runs off the prop blade and just touches the tabletop. Place a carpenter's square against the straightedge anywhere along the high side. Note the vertical height from the tabletop at that point, and measure the base—the distance along the tabletop from the point of the straightedge, on the table, to the bottom corner of the square. For *Oscill-Eightor*'s prop we've found a height of 6¾ inches (17.4 cm) and a length along the tabletop (a base) of 13 inches (33 cm). We're ready to find pitch.

Pitch = 6.2832 × Radius × Height/Base

So, (6.2832 × 8 in. radius × 6.75 in. height) ÷ 13 in. base = 26.1 inches pitch, or

(6.2832 × 20 cm radius × 17.4 cm height) ÷ 33 cm base = 66.2 centimeters pitch—nothing to it.

(The metric height's a little different than the English-measure height because the 20-centimeter measurement point—on the reference line—is a bit closer to the hub than the 8-inch measurement point.)

Once you've made the first measurement, you'll find it will take you all of a few minutes to do. Since it's so easy, it's a good idea to take two measurements at two different radii, say, around 30 percent and around 70 or 80 percent of diameter. Also, you can quickly take these two measurements for each blade. Obviously, you ought to get the same pitch for each blade. Sadly, this isn't always the case. Props with unequally pitched blades cause vibration. Happily, this is fairly inexpensive to correct. Most prop shops can adjust pitch and balance blades quickly and economically.

CHAPTER 35

Speed-Demon Drives: Propulsion for High-Speed Craft

"Screws have speeded up!" suddenly reports sound.

All at once it becomes obvious to everyone that the interval between successive pings has decreased. The sound man's report—"Shifting to short scale!" is totally unnecessary.

Submarine!, "Tang,"
Commander Edward L. Beach, U.S.N.

We've been talking a good deal about propellers over the last few chapters, and there's a good reason for this. For most boats, the choice of drive systems is limited. Let's see, there's the propeller, and then there's the propeller. To liven things up just a trifle, you might have the arcane problem of deciding between, oh, inboard props, outboard props, and inboard/outboard props. Of course, there's a good reason for this unanimity of choice. The standard propeller's been so nicely perfected and refined over the past hundred years that it's nearly impossible to beat either in terms of efficiency, cost, or reliability—at least for boats that do less than 35 knots or so.

If, however, your *Dive Bomber* were designed to blast along at 45 knots or more, some interesting things happen that start to make standard props less attractive. Take underwater drag for instance.

Appendages Can Be a Drag

Designers break the force of underwater drag (the resistance that holds your boat back) into two components—hull drag and appendage drag. Hull drag is the resistance of the hull itself and appendage drag is the resistance of all the (what else) appendages—shafts, bearings, struts, rudders, the propeller (or propellers), and anything that happens to be sticking out from the hull into the water flow. (Engineers subdivide hull drag further into wavemaking resistance, wetted-surface resistance, and air resistance. For our purposes here, we can ignore this.)

Obviously, there's not a whole lot you can do about hull drag or resistance. The architect has to design the slipperiest shape he or she can come up with to meet the given speed and service requirements. When it comes to appendage drag though, imagination's the only limit. The smaller the designer can make the appendages, the faster the boat will go with the same power. Ideally, you'd want to eliminate all appendages, which sounds impossible, but we'll see.

Now, on low- and average-speed craft, appendage drag's much less important than on high-speed vessels. This is because the force of resistance increases as the square of the speed. In other words, for the same appendage area, if you double the speed you'd get four times the resistance.

Drag in Hard Numbers

We can see how this works out by comparing the 47-knot *Dive Bomber* with the 15-knot *Stately Stepper*. Say they're both 9,000-pound 35-footers (4,080 kg, 10.7 m) of similar proportions, with standard inboard propeller drives—allowing for the reasonable differences you'd have for such differing speed ranges. The power and resistances involved in driving *Stately Stepper* and *Dive Bomber* are listed below.

A couple of interesting things become apparent right off. First, even though the hulls are about the same size, total resistance is fantastically higher on *Dive Bomber* than on *Stately Stepper*. The difference in appendage resistance is striking; it's increased in real value and as a percentage of total resistance or power used up. On the 47-knot *Dive Bomber* appendage resistance is an impressive 7.6 percent of the total, whereas on the 15-knot *Stately Stepper* appendage drag is only 3.6 percent. Obviously, the faster you go the more im-

portant it is to reduce or eliminate all those things sticking into the water. This is where high-performance drives come in.

Strip Off Those Appendages—Faster, Faster!

How much faster would *Stately Stepper* and *Dive Bomber* go if you could somehow remove their appendages? Well, if we stripped the appendages but kept the same engine and thrust, it'd be the same as if we'd added the horsepower the appendages were using up. In this case *Stepper* effectively would be running on a 67.4-hp (50.2 kw) engine, and *Bomber* would be essentially supercharged with an extra 42 hp to 592 hp—or an extra 31 kw to 441 kw. You can use the speed charts from Chapter 20 to find *Stately Stepper* gains—about a $\frac{1}{10}$ of a knot; hardly noticeable. On the other hand, *Dive Bomber* will go to 49 knots—a gain of 2 knots. And this gain's achieved without burning an ounce more fuel, or installing a larger engine. At higher speeds, the increases are even greater. Ninety- and 100-knot-plus racing machines can see improvements of 4 or 5 knots.

How 'Bout Outboards and Sterndrives?

You might think that outboards or sterndrives would be one approach to reducing appendage resistance, but this isn't the case. It's true that outboards and sterndrives have no rud-

	TOTAL SHAFT HP	TOTAL RESISTANCE LB.	APPENDAGE RESISTANCE LB.	APPENDAGE HP	APPENDAGE %
15-knot *Stately Stepper*	65	800	32	2.4	3.7
47-knot *Dive Bomber*	550	2300	172	42.0	7.6

	TOTAL SHAFT KW	TOTAL RESISTANCE KG.	APPENDAGE RESISTANCE KG.	APPENDAGE KW	APPENDAGE %
15-knot *Stately Stepper*	48	365	14	1.8	3.7
47-knot *Dive Bomber*	410	1040	78	31.0	7.6

ders and no exposed shaft or strut in the water. Unfortunately, the relatively fat lower unit—housing the Z-Drive as it goes down and aft to the prop—not only creates plenty of drag, but also disturbs the water flow to the wheel something terrible.

Get That Prop Out of the Water!

Amazingly, the solution that works is to pull most of the propeller out of the water. Such propellers are called *surface propellers* and are found (not surprisingly) on *surface drives.* Even more interesting is that the first surface drives were used successfully way back in the early 1900s, by Albert Hickman, developer of the Sea Sled. (Sea Sleds were early and very successful surface-effect catamarans. They really haven't been improved on much in 80 some-odd years.) Hickman simply raised the prop shaft and let it run out the base of the transom instead of the bottom of the boat. The result was a propeller that had half of its blades out of the water at any given time—sort of like dipping one blade in each revolution. Hickman's early sur-

Twin Arneson surface drives. The hydraulic-cylinder struts above the drives allow vertical adjustment of drive angle. The hydraulic-cylinder struts, port and starboard, steer the drives like a sterndrive. (Courtesy Arneson Marine, Inc.)

face drives still required rudders, but even so, eliminating the strut and shaft reduced the amount of appendage drag, significantly increasing speed.

After over 60 years of development, surface drives have become even more efficient and reliable. This is particularly so as most modern surface drives are steerable, just like an inboard/ outboard (standard stern drive). As a result, modern surface drives don't even have rudders. In other words, modern surface drives eliminate the drag of the rudder, the strut, the bearing, and the shaft almost completely. (A very short length of shaft just ahead of the prop is in the water flow.) Additionally, propeller drag's reduced by about two-thirds—not bad!

If you're intent on high speed, surface-drive is well worth investigating. Remember, though, that you have to be really serious about going very fast. These systems don't offer significant advantages if you run at less than 35 knots or so, most of the time, and 45 knots or more is the best range. Also, they're quite sophisticated—not cheap!

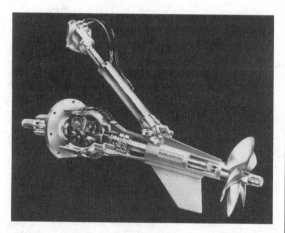

Cutaway view of a single Arneson surface drive. You can see the massive universal joint that permits steering and lifting the drive unit. (Courtesy Arneson Marine, Inc.)

Shallow Drives and No Cavities Too

A nice additional advantage of surface drives is that they require less draft. Accordingly, if you're planning on operating your *Dive Bomber* at supersonic velocities in shoal waters, surface drives have that much more to offer.

Still another advantage is that surface props don't cavitate. Most high-speed craft have very highly loaded props. They have large engines driving small, high-rpm screws. (See Chapter 32.) Low-pressure vacuum bubbles form on the highly loaded blades and implode against them, causing vibration and pitting.

Surface propellers, on the other hand, pop their blades up into the air once every single revolution. As a result the blades are fully aerated. Instead of low pressure vacuum bubbles along the blades, the surface prop actually works with a sheet of air bubbles along the immersed blade—thus no vacuum and no cavitation. If it seems that having air at the prop blades is less than ideal, you're right. However, with high–speed, highly loaded props there's very little propeller designers can do to avoid the gremlins of either cavitation or aeration. Instead they design to work with these nuisances.

The common solution for standard immersed propellers is the super-cavitating propeller—the cleaver or chopper props. These engineering marvels work well cavitating all the time, just as surface propellers work well aerated all the time. The fully immersed cleaver prop, though, doesn't offer the low appendage drag advantages of the surface drives. Ideally , the propeller designer's dream is to invent a high-speed screw that'll work with no cavitation or aeration at all, but don't hold your breath waiting for these babies to hit the market. No one even has an inkling how it could be done.

Jetting Along

Of course, even with surface drives, there are some appendages in the water—part of the propeller and a short bit of prop shaft. There is a drive that eliminates appendages almost completely—the jet drive. Jet drives are basically powerful pumps that suck water through an intake on the bottom of the hull and squirt it out an orifice on the transom. Except for the tiny resistance around the intake scoop, there's not a thing in the water—no appendage drag at all.

A steerable housing at the outlet replaces a rudder, and a reversing gate shuts down over the orifice to deflect the jet ahead instead of astern. This gives the jet drive instant reverse without shifting gears. Even better, jet-drive boats have just about the least possible draft. It's possible to have a jet-drive cruiser of 40 feet (12.2 m) that honestly draws only 18 or so inches (45 cm).

Jet drive proponents sometimes claim that the efficiency of their carefully engineered, impeller-driven pumps is higher than that of any propeller. They're right as far as that goes. What they neglect, however, is the considerable resistance of the water as it flows along the innards of the jet drive's plumbing system.

Jet Pluses

Jets have advantages and drawbacks when compared to surface drives. The jets have even lower appendage resistance, they have shallower draft, and they don't present the menacing nest of flailing blades that surface drives offer at the transom. Jets also can be made to work fairly well at speeds as low as 25 knots (not quite as efficiently as standard props, but close). For shallow-draft, medium-speed, and high-speed craft then, jets are about the best choice. Additionally, jets permit the efficient use of multiple engines, together or one at a time. A standard twin-screw inboard can be run on one engine, but the drag of the idle prop reduces single-screw performance dramatically. With jets you can operate on either engine (or both, of course) without any idle-prop drag at all! The drawings show *Pitan*, a 42-foot (12.8 m) triple-jet-drive patrol/supply boat of my design. By going with three jet drives and three engines, she

A typical modern jet drive unit. This is CastoldiJet's 05 drive mated to Volvo's 167-hp (125 kw) AQ171 gas engine. (Courtesy Castoldi)

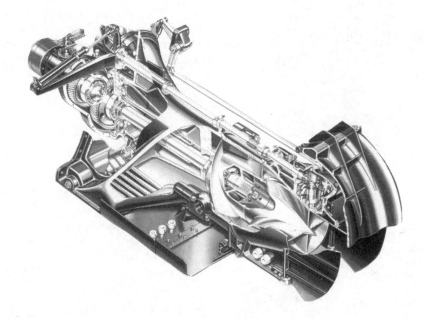

Cutaway view of a jet drive unit. (Courtesy Castoldi)

achieves great flexibility in range and speed. She can operate on one, two, or all three engines, depending on her current mission requirements.

Handy Jets

As if all this weren't enough, modern jets also offer handling advantages. This is because—for low-speed maneuvering—the engine can be left at high rpm with the reverse gate halfway down. Effectively, this puts the boat in neutral with the engine delivering full power. By rotating the steering nozzle left or right while tweaking the reverse gate up or down, the jet can deliver very powerful and precise side bursts on demand. In this mode, jets operate like stern thrusters at low speed—a tremendous maneuvering plus.

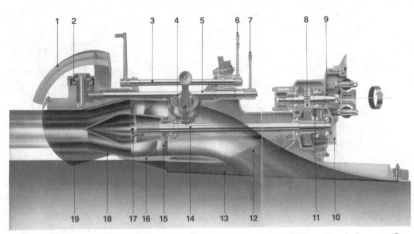

Parts of a typical jet drive: **1.** reverse deflector; **2.** steering deflector control gears; **3.** reverse deflector control shaft; **4.** inspection port; **5.** steering deflector control shaft; **6.** reversing deflector control lever; **7.** steering deflector control lever; **8.** drive gear; **9.** input shaft; **10.** gearbox flange; **11.** clutch; **12.** removable intake debris screen; **13.** jet unit housing; **14.** impeller shaft; **15.** impeller; **16.** impeller housing; **17.** impeller retaining bolt; **18.** nozzle; **19.** steering deflectors. (Courtesy Castoldi)

Profile and wheelhouse arrangement of the jet-drive patrol/supply boat Pitan. *Triple jet drives give her shoal draft and a wide selection of operating speeds and ranges:*

LOA	42 ft. 0 in.	(12.5 m)
LWL	37 ft. 3 in.	(11.3 m)
Beam	10 ft. 9 in.	(3.3 m)
BWL	10 ft. 8 in.	(3.2 m)
Draft	2 ft. 5 in.	(0.7 m)
Disp.	12.6 tons	
Power	(3) Cat 3208-TA, 425 hp	
	(316 kw) at 2,800 rpm	
	Total 1,275 hp (948 kw)	
Drives	(3) Hamilton 291 Jets	
Generator	Northern Lights 8 kw	
Fuel (standard)	625 gal. (2,365 l) diesel	
Water	40 gal. (150 l)	
Speed	40 knots max.	
	26 knots cruise	

Range	
40 knots, 3 engines, standard tanks:	330 miles
26 knots, 2 engines, standard tanks:	620 miles
26 knots, 2 engines, extended tanks:	1,200 miles
18 knots, 2 engines, extended tanks:	1,700 miles

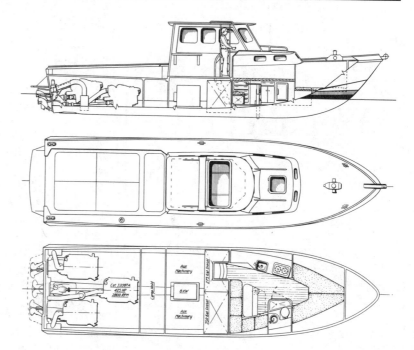

Arrangement, deck plan, and inboard profile of Pitan. *Fuel bladders in her cargo hold give her an additional 820 gallons (3,100 l) of fuel tankage.*

Jammed Up Jets—The Jet-Power Downside

You'd think, with all the above, that jets were *the* answer for high speed; however, they have a significant drawback for operation over 60 knots. Remember, the jet sucks water into a hole—an orifice—in the hull bottom and squirts it out the stern. When a jet boat approaches 60 knots it's moving so fast that water actually gets stuffed or jammed into the orifice faster than it can be used, seriously harming performance. By employing two-stage jets—two impellers, one immediately after the other—and a variable gate on the intake orifice to control inflow—jets have been made to work fairly well up to 90 knots; however, this takes careful engineering. Surface drives don't face the orifice or intake limitation at all; they can be designed to run just as well at 145 knots as they can at 45.

KaMeWa of Sweden manufactures the largest and most sophisticated jet drives currently available. These units are hot numbers on high-speed megayachts. A standard top-of-the-line installation would call for two or three KaMeWa water jets powered by twin or triple MTU diesels (only the best and most expensive engines around). How much does a drive system like this cost? . . . If you have to ask, forget it!

CHAPTER 36

The Boat That Wouldn't Fly

The motor functioned perfectly. Came roars of pop and thunder of motor, with a premier pilot of the air, Gene Shank, at the test try. Just No Dice! She just would not plane.

From *My Old Boat Shop,* Weston Farmer

I was looking at a cold fish. The fact that she was a stunning cold fish—to say the least—didn't help a bit. She and Sam Callard sat directly across from my desk.

"So you see the problem," she went on, all business. Crossing her legs crisply, she arched an eyebrow.

"I think so," I replied. "Mr. Remington's boat won't fly." I tried out my most engaging smile. No luck.

"Precisely," she went on, oblivious. "The boat won't get up on plane, and it ought to. Mr. Remington's got a considerable sum invested in *Valhalla,* and most of that investment will be lost if we can't get her to perform properly." Framed by long black hair, provocative cheekbones and a flawless olive complexion, her dark almond eyes concentrated on mine.

Lizette Lemarque was personal comptroller to Bradley Remington of Remington & Smythe. Apparently, she managed all of Remington's financial affairs, leaving him free for more important concerns. I'd gathered, from my phone conversation with Sam, that both she and he had been responsible for finalizing the sale details on *Valhalla* just under two years ago. Apparently, Remington seemed to feel the problems were somehow their fault.

Her head tilted slightly to one side, she sat prim and erect. I'd been nagged by the feeling that I'd met her before. At that moment I realized why. She looked remarkably like the sculpture of Queen Nefertiti—the one you inevitably find in books about ancient Egypt. Of course, Lizette was a bit younger, but I was in favor of that. It was somewhat inexplicable, as she couldn't be a direct descendant; I'd gathered from a passing comment by Sam that Lizette was French Canadian.

"I handle most of Remington & Smythe's business here in New York." Sam's polished baritone broke the brief silence. "So, since the boat and Ms. Lemarque were both up here, I thought I'd have her speak to you."

Sam was a partner with one of the larger law firms. I'd done some consulting for him before, but he seemed particularly anxious for me to make a good impression. *Remington & Smythe must be a big account,* I thought. After all, he'd recommended me, and if I didn't measure up, it'd reflect on his judgment.

I sat straighter and managed an authoritative expression. "Okay, she's a 56-footer (17 m) built by Green Ocean," I offered. "*Valhalla's* 15-feet (4.5 m) beam and has been heavily customized, with a great deal of extra gear and weight added. She's fitted with twin Caterpillar 3208s delivering a total of 750 horsepower (560 kw). How sure are you about that weight figure? She's probably a lot heavier than originally intended."

"Yes," Lizette answered, "she is heavier than the standard model. They're supposed to weigh 21 tons. *Valhalla's* 27.2. We know for sure because we had her hauled on a Travelift with a scale." Her tone didn't leave any room for doubt.

"Hmm," I mumbled thoughtfully. "Let's see."

I could do the figuring on my pocket calculator, but I didn't want to let Sam down. I swiveled to my computer and brought up the equation processor, making a fine show of tapping keys and manipulating the mouse. Then I turned. "She ought to cruise at about 17 knots," I supplied, "with a top speed of 18 or 18 and a half. That's a difficult speed range for a 46-foot-waterline (14 m) hull—just under full planing speed, or semi-planing." I glanced at Lizette to see if she was bowled over by my computer expertise. It didn't appear so.

"Her top speed's just 11 knots," Lizette stated flatly. "She cruises at 8 to 10. We've had the engine people down to check the diesels. They say that they're working fine and delivering maximum power. We've consulted with propeller manufacturers, and tried several different props. Nothing seemed to help. No one seems to know what's causing the problem."

She turned to Sam briefly for confirmation. He nodded. "Yep, I've been out on her and it feels like she's stuck in a hole—just won't get up and go." He flashed a polished smile at Lizette, and darned if she didn't smile back. I decided she liked Brooks Brothers suits and steely gray hair.

"Can you do anything?" she returned her gaze to me, all business again.

"It'd help a great deal if I had some drawings of the boat, particularly the hull," I said.

"That's one of the problems," Lizette responded. "Green Ocean's out of business. We haven't been able to get any help or information from that direction."

I sighed. Trying to make intelligent decisions about a boat without access to her drawings is like trying to find your way around in a new city without having seen a map, but—in cases like this—it was the rule rather than the exception.

"Okay," I suggested. "Since the boat's here in New York, why don't I go out on her for an afternoon. We can run a measured mile, and get some hard performance numbers. Then, if we can arrange to haul her out, I can take a look at her underbody and see if that gives any clues."

Lizette didn't seem any more impressed by my authoritative manner than she had by my computer expertise or my smile. I was debating trying out hooting like a barn owl to see if that got any reaction, but nixed it. Sam wouldn't have understood.

"That'd be excellent," Lizette said.

Sam looked pleased and a bit relieved.

"We were going to haul *Valhalla* next Wednesday anyway," Lizette continued. "She was scheduled for bottom paint before going south again."

Glancing at my calendar, I admitted I could make it then.

Lizette stood up, lithe and graceful.

It was late afternoon, and Sam took her elbow. "I know a wonderful place for dinner near here," he suggested.

"I'm famished," she answered. "Let's go."

We shook hands—her handshake wasn't cold—and I escorted them both to the door. I could hear her footsteps clicking steadily down the hall. Ruefully, I reflected that I should have tried the barn-owl hoot while I had the chance. Knowing Sam, I wouldn't get another.

Wednesday found us all motoring out on Long Island Sound. It was a chilly, overcast day with an iron-hued sky. But the wind was way down and had been so for a while. There was no hint of swell in the one- to two-foot seas—a good test day. Sam, bustling about like he owned the place, was providing Lizette with a cup of coffee. I was rummaging through my bag, laying out notebook, calculator, and related gear.

"What's that?" Lizette pointed to a round gauge I'd just unpacked.

"It's how I find out if I'm on the level," I replied, trying out a friendly grin.

No reaction.

Sam looked irritated.

I was going to explain that by hooking it up correctly I could determine if I was telling the truth but gave it up. "It's an angle indicator," I replied simply. "I want to see if *Valhalla* is squatting—down by the stern—at maximum speed."

This answer apparently was up to muster.

"We'll be there in a few minutes." It was Captain Herski calling down from the bridge.

I snagged my gear and mounted the ladder.

Glancing at the tachs, I noted they were both right up at 2,800—the maximum. The speedo read exactly as Lizette said—11 knots.

"Okay, Steve," I addressed Captain Herski, "keep the throttles right there for this run." I got hold of my stop watch and squeezed as the mark passed abreast. "Running," I stated.

Four minutes and 58 seconds later we glided by the second mark. I squeezed again and noted the time. Grabbing the angle indicator, I set it against a bulkhead, recording the results. Then we turned and ran back in the opposite direction, at the same rpm. This time it took just 3 minutes and 56 seconds.

Curious, I thought.

We ran the mile three times at 2,800, and then three times each at 2,250 and 2,100. Sure enough, the speedo read 8 knots at 2,100, but something wasn't adding up.

"You've never run a measured mile before?" I asked.

"No," Steve replied. "I've only been on board for a few weeks, so I haven't, but I don't think the last skipper did either."

"What's *Valhalla*'s underbody like?" I inquired hopefully.

"Don't know for sure. I'll see for the first time myself this afternoon. Her draft's on the light side though, if that helps you any—just three and a half feet."

Feeling peevish, I merely grunted acknowledgment. Remington was in Asia on business, and I hadn't been able contact him about his boat's hull shape. I had no drawings, and the current captain was too new to the job to have had a chance to see for himself. *Talk about flying blind,* I thought.

Steve headed *Valhalla* back toward Amalgamated on Town Island, where we were scheduled to be hauled immediately. I asked him to keep the engines up at max for a while and went aft to study the wake.

Certainly Sam had been right. *Valhalla*'s running angle wasn't excessively large, but she sure wasn't planing. Just as he'd said, *Valhalla* seemed to be stuck in a hole. It was as if the hull was being sucked down. Her transom was partially immersed and her wake was an impressive sight. Gray, foam-topped combers curled off *Valhalla*'s quarters. There seemed to be an odd pair of slight rooster tails halfway out from the centerline, each side of the transom.

Sam came back and stood beside me. "Remington wondered if bigger trim tabs might help?" he inquired. "You know, I pressed him to buy this boat because it seemed a better deal than some of the others, from a dollars-and-cents perspective."

"Umm." I made a sympathetic gesture. "I

doubt trim tabs are the solution," I responded aloud, "but I'll know better after I get a look underneath. You don't know if there's anything special about the hull, do you?"

Sam said he didn't, he'd only handled the financial end. He ambled back into the saloon. New blue blazer, sharply creased tan slacks, Timberline boat shoes—*Natty,* I thought.

Not long after, we were guiding *Valhalla* into the Travelift, and I clambered off. I was acutely aware of Lizette, elegant and slender, standing near Sam.

The lift whined and then started its upward climb. I peered along the bottom. The bow came up first. It was unremarkable. Then the stern hove into full view. I whistled.

"She's a tunnel drive!" I exclaimed.

"Meaning?" Lizette asked. She was concerned but cool.

"The propellers are partly recessed up into half-tunnels molded into the bottom of the hull." I pointed.

It was impossible to miss them once you knew what they were. In fact, they were about the largest tunnels I'd ever seen. They cut away a great portion of the underbody aft, blowing the prop wash straight out the transom. That explained the mysterious rooster tails.

I snapped my tape off its clip on my belt and, with Captain Herski's help, measured the bottom and the tunnels. I noticed the speedo impeller didn't seem to be well located.

When I'd finished, Sam escorted Lizette and me to his red Mercedes. Somehow, the car and Lizette seemed to fit. I tried to imagine her in my blue Chevy, but couldn't make it work. Sitting in back, I admired her profile as she turned to speak to me.

"Do you know what the problem is?" she asked.

"I think so," I answered, "but I'd better do some number crunching before I go off on the wrong tack. Can you stop by my office tomorrow afternoon?"

She said she could and Sam said he'd try. He dropped me off about a block from my place. Lizette was apparently going to be treated to another dinner. I wondered how she stayed so trim.

Thursday afternoon, Effie ushered Lizette into my office. She was alone; Sam hadn't been able to cancel a court date, and had said he'd try to stop by later.

Wearing a neat gray suit, she stood eye level to eye level with me in her heels as we shook hands. She seated herself surely and watched me as I got behind my desk.

"I have good news and bad news," I quipped. Grins and smiles hadn't worked so I tried a humorous smirk. Nothing doing.

"Yes." She waited patiently.

"The good news is that *Valhalla's* actually going faster than you think. Whoever installed the speedo impeller put it right behind the depth sounder through-hull. I guess he was trying to run all the instruments to one place, but he should've put them the other way 'round. The impeller's in the wake shadow of the transducer.

"At 2,800 rpm we did one mile in 4 minutes and 58 seconds, which is 12.08 knots, but coming back the other way, we did it in just 3 minutes and 56 seconds. That's 15.25 knots."

Lizette looked confused.

"That's normal," I explained. "There was a 1.58 knot current running, which is why we run both ways—to cancel out the wind and current effect. The average is 13.7 knots. The results were consistent on all runs. In fact, when the speedo's reading just 10 knots at 2,250 rpm, *Valhalla's* actually doing 13.4 knots. At 2,100 rpm she does 12.7 knots. It's not great, but it's not as bad as you thought." I studied her for a reaction.

"But she doesn't go as fast as she should, does she?" she replied. "You said she should cruise at 17 knots, with a top speed around 18."

"That's so," I agreed, "but I didn't know she had tunnel drive. Tunnels are great for reducing draft, but they increase wetted surface drag and reduce planing area. *Valhalla*'s tunnels are unusually large. The configuration might barely have worked on the standard 21-ton boat, but in this case Remington's extras and added weight pushed the hull shape over the edge."

She seemed to want the details so I went on. "It's a common mistake. Some builders forget that you lose planing surface with the tunnels, and then they can't figure out why their boat won't fly. In order to plane, a boat can't be too heavy for her planing surface. After all, it's this underbody area that produces lift, and the more weight the boat has the more lift it needs, so the more planing surface is required.

"At 27.2 tons and 750 horsepower (560 kw), *Valhalla* needs an area of 548 square feet (51 m²) minimum to be able to plane. Actually, 670 square feet (62 m²) would be average, and the drag from her tunnels and the fact that she's operating at semi-planing speed would indicate even more than that might be required. The upper limit would be around 880 square feet (82 m²) of planing surface. That's probably what I'd strive for if I were designing her from scratch.

"*Valhalla*'s real planing surface, after deducting for her huge tunnels, is just 369 square feet (34 m²)—not even close to the minimum. Interestingly, the standard model 21-ton boat would only need 421 square feet (39 m²) of planing surface—still not really up to snuff, but things aren't so bad for the standard model. It can probably get up to 16 or 17 knots."

"Sam and Mr. Remington thought maybe trim tabs would help," Lizette observed.

"Not in this case, I'm afraid," I went on. "Trim tabs keep a boat's nose down. This means that the hull underbody is striking the water at a less blunt angle. It reduces resistance and helps a boat get a few extra knots, while working over the hump and up onto a plane.

"To generate the lift *Valhalla* would need, you'd require giant trim tabs angled way down.

They'd generate lift all right, but they'd also create lots of drag. They'd make nifty brakes." I ventured another smile, but Lizette appeared to be concentrating.

"You could look at it another way," I suggested. "A planing hull's got most of its volume aft for lift. A traditional displacement hull—like a cruising sailboat—has its hull underbody swept up aft, with little or no immersed volume at the transom. This reduces resistance at low speed and moves its center of buoyancy further forward, which is good for seakeeping. But you could never lift a hull like that onto a plane, no matter how big an engine or set of trim tabs you installed. You wouldn't even try.

"In effect, the tunnels in *Valhalla*'s afterbody do the same thing to her hull as the upsweep of a traditional displacement hull's lines aft. She's lost buoyancy and lifting surface aft, and her center of buoyancy's moved toward the bow. *Valhalla* seems to be stuck in a hole because she almost literally is. All she's doing, when you increase power, is building up larger and larger bow and stern waves and settling into them. You noticed that she does 13.4 knots at 2,250 rpm, yet at 2,800 rpm she barely goes 13.7 knots—a three-tenths of a knot increase. In fact, if you gave her a 2,000 horsepower (1500 kw) engine, I doubt if she'd get much above 14 knots." I sat back and waited for everything to sink in.

Lizette's gaze drifted off out the window. "Oh well," she murmured distantly, "at least she's going faster than we thought. I guess we'll have to make the best of it." She remained silent for a moment looking outside. Then she turned and fixed me with a cool look.

"Aren't you going to do any more foolish things on the computer?" she asked. Then she smiled. "I enjoyed the superfluous mouse movement particularly. A lawyer wouldn't have any idea what your were doing, but I have three Macs in my office. I use that equation solver myself every day."

She was grinning, and I learned that dimples and high cheekbones are a remarkably magnetic combination.

"No more quips?" she continued mercilessly.

"Well," I suggested "You've never heard me hoot like a barn owl. It's really something."

"Oh, would you!" she cooed.

The temptation to strangle her was overcome by the realization that if I did, I'd never get to see the dimple/cheekbone combination again. Instead I said, "Alexis Weissenberg's at Carnegie Hall tonight. A friend of mine can't make it. If we dash, I think I can still grab the tickets. I'll do the barn-owl hoot during intermission."

Since she'd nodded an affirmative through her laughter, I got on the phone and arranged to have the tickets left with my friend's doorman.

Lizette had taken the instructions to dash literally. She'd already bounded up to get our jackets, and led the way to the door.

On the way down, we met Sam coming up.

"Where are you off to?" he called as we zipped by.

"Searching for barn owls," Lizette cried back.

Sam looked deeply puzzled.

We settled into the back of a taxi, and I glanced over at Lizette.

"You know my undergraduate degree was in music," she said.

Never having been one to let a well-worn line rest, I replied, "You know Lizzy, this could be the beginning of a beautiful friendship."

She groaned. "Only if you never, ever call me Lizzy," she said.

(Although the names and locations in the preceding story may have been, well . . . manufactured, the boat that wouldn't fly, complete with tunnel drive, rooster tails, and misplaced speed-log impeller, really existed and behaved exactly as described.)

PART 9

Catching the Wind: Sailing Simplified

I suppose I must be one of the few men alive who can remember what life was like in the American Navy of sailing ships. All those fine old ships have sailed away into the Land of Dreams, mounting the swell like great birds. No smoke, no vibration, no noise except the occasional slatting of a reef point against its sail.

The Old Navy, Rear Admiral Daniel P. Mannix III

CHAPTER 37

Getting a Lift

At the bottom, so, and bent them, gently
  curving
So that they looked like the wings of birds,
  most surely.

Metamorphoses, The Story of
Dedaalus and Icarus, Ovid
Translated by Rolfe Humphries

Lift—it must be great stuff; everyone seems to want it. Sailmakers invoke it reverently, naval architects mumble obscure formulas in its name, and even propeller manufacturers will refer to it from time to time.

Of course, if you really wanted to pin the blame for all this lift business on someone, it would have be Wilbur and Orville Wright. They were among the first to actually measure lift, to scientifically attempt to increase it, and to put their results to practical use. They realized that birds fly not because they flap their wings up and down but because their wings have a special shape. Wind flowing over this shape generates lift and . . . eureka, flight! The rest, naturally, is history. Since then we've learned that anything that moves in a gas—air—or a fluid—water, oil, or you name it—follows the same rules. There's no getting away from lift. But why? What exactly does it do? How do you get it?

Yawing About

Take the fin keel of a modern sailboat, *Agile Angel,* for instance. Like all sailboats working to windward, *Agile Angel* doesn't actually move ahead in a straight line. Instead, she crabs forward just a bit sideways, or at a slight angle called *yaw angle.* In other words, her bow's pointing a bit higher (closer to the wind) than *Agile Angel* is actually traveling. This sounds like a waste, but in fact it's beneficial. Because of this yaw angle, the keel's not slicing straight forward but is being driven ahead at a slightly oblique angle to the water. The result is that the symmetrical keel presents an asymmetrical shape to the onrushing water. (Yaw angle is, in fact, the *angle of attack*; without it you couldn't have lift at all.)

**"Round and Round She Goes,
and Where She Stops . . ."**

What the water "sees" as it rushes around the keel is a shape not too dissimilar from an airplane's or a bird's wing, or—for that matter—a sail. The water has a relatively short distance to travel on the leeward (shorter, flatter) side of the keel, but on the windward side the combination of the yaw angle and the shape of the keel makes for a pronounced bulge or curve. This forces all the water on the windward side to travel a greater distance than its counterpart on the leeward side. Initially—remember *initially*—the water traveling across the shorter, straighter side will move faster—there's less surface and curvature to slow it down—than on the highly curved side. Accordingly, when the two flows—from both sides—meet up again at the trailing edge, a vortex or eddy is formed (see Fig. Circ.1). This eddy will break off and trail away in the slipstream; however since, as old Isaac Newton has shown us, every action has an equal and opposite reaction, it causes a counter eddy or current rotation in the opposite direction, around the airfoil itself. You can think of this as the action of two gears (see Fig. Circ. 2). If the trailing-edge eddy rotates counterclockwise, it'll mesh with the water ahead of it (around the keel) by friction, causing it to rotate in the other direction—clockwise. This is the root of the modern circulation theory of lift.

The Circulation that Isn't There

It's this counter-rotation flow of circulation that generates the final, continuous, stable difference in flow speeds that creates lift. This confuses many people, because looked at simply, circulation theory would seem to be saying that the flow of water (or air, for a wing or sail) along the shorter or straighter side of foil (keels, sails, rudders, wings—anything that creates lift in a fluid flow—is a foil) would actually run backwards against the prevailing water flow or wind direction. Obviously, this just never happens.

The mystery's explained easily enough. The counter eddy or circulation isn't actual circulation; instead it's a *potential* circulation or a *circulation field*—similar to, say, magnetic lines of force (see Fig. Circ. 3). If you put a magnet under a sheet

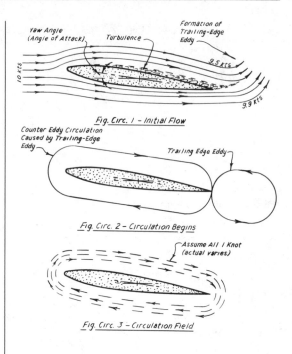

Fig. Circ. 1 – Initial Flow

Fig. Circ. 2 – Circulation Begins

Fig. Circ. 3 – Circulation Field

covered with iron filings, the filings will rearrange themselves to conform to the magnet's lines of force. Similarly, put a foil in a water (or air) flow, and it causes a rearrangement of the lines of flow. Circulation theory simply shows the *potential* effect on flow of a given foil section. Every keel, sail, or foil shape is different; and for various foils and conditions the potential circulation field can be approximately calculated. Then the engineer essentially lays this potential circulation field on top of the undisturbed straight flow, adding the circulation-field speeds to the undisturbed-flow speeds (see Fig. Circ. 4). You can see that the circulation-field flow potential runs in the opposite direction of initial flow on the shorter, straight side—reducing speed; while on the highly curved side the circulation flow potential runs in the same direction as initial flow—increasing speed. The result determines the actual, real-world speed of water (or air) flow around the foil. Just as intuition would lead you to expect, *all* the flow *always* streams aft

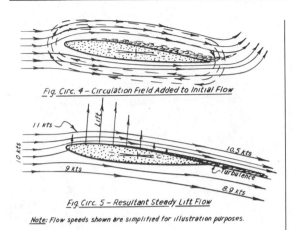

Fig. Circ. 4 – Circulation Field Added to Initial Flow

Fig. Circ. 5 – Resultant Steady Lift Flow

Note: Flow speeds shown are simplified for illustration purposes.

in the direction the water (or wind) was going to begin with; however, the reverse-flow *potential* of the circulation field will reduce the speed of the water (or air) on the smoother, shorter foil side, and will speed up the water on the highly curved longer side (see Fig. Circ. 5). (Confusingly, this steady, continuous circulation pattern is just the opposite of the initial condition that started the eddy, which caused the circulation to begin with.)

When a Vacuum Isn't

What happens next is stranger still. The water (or air, for a wing or sail)—before it encountered the keel or foil—had a specific total amount of energy made up of its combined mass and speed (kinetic energy) and its pressure (static pressure, for the purist). Since the circulation field of the keel/foil has forced the water to speed up to negotiate the longer, highly-curved windward side of the keel, we've increased its speed or kinetic energy.

You can't, however, just get additional energy from nothing. The increase in water speed has to be compensated for by a loss in energy from someplace else. In this case, it's a decrease in pressure. This is weird because—for practical purposes—water and air don't appreciably change density when flowing around a hydrofoil or airfoil at normal speeds. The decrease in pressure is a momentum effect caused by flow. The result, however, is

exactly the same as if there *were* less dense air on the windward side. It's like having a vacuum that isn't there. It's this strange suction effect, caused by foil shape, that generates a circulation field, known as *lift* (see Fig. Circ. 5). Naturally, if there's effectively less pressure on the windward side, there's effectively greater pressure on the lee side. What then happens is that everything in the neighborhood—including the keel itself—tries to rush in "uphill" or upwind and fill up the low-pressure area. As the keel's rather firmly attached to *Agile Angel*'s hull, *Angel*'s drawn upwind as well.

A Real Drag

Having waded through all this, I have to tell you that it's really not quite this simple. We have to face the lift's great adversary—*drag*. Now drag's literally . . . a drag (resistance). Usually, this comes from two sources—friction, and eddies or waves (turbulence).

Friction is—happily—pretty straightforward. As water (or air, for a sail) slides past the keel, or anything else for that matter, it rubs against it, slowing down the flow. Obviously, the less surface in contact with the water, the less friction and the less friction drag or wetted-surface drag. This is one reason that designers are constantly trying to shorten keels. The shorter the keel, the less its surface area and the less the frictional resistance.

Trying to Go Straight

Eddy or wavemaking resistance is somewhat trickier. One of the fundamental causes of eddies is that water—like any self-respecting fluid—tries pretty hard to flow in a straight line. You can force it to bend around a curve for a short time, but sooner or later—usually sooner—it'll break away from the curved surface in an attempt to flow straightaway aft. The minute it does break away, however, it mingles with other water that's also broken away, but at slightly different moments. The result's sort of a mob scene—water milling about every which way in aimless whirlpools called eddies or turbulence. Engineers refer to the smooth flow around the keel as *laminar flow*, and—not surprisingly—they call the broken-away and confused flow *turbulent flow*.

The problem here is that the minute the water's no longer flowing smoothly around the surface of the keel it's no longer generating a difference in pressure, and thus no lift. Even worse, all those eddies whirling around are wasted energy that could have gone into driving *Agile Angel* forward or holding her from sliding off. You guessed it—again, a real drag.

It's this business that gets your local designer muttering arcane equations into his beard. There are literally hundreds of formulas for figuring out the best theoretical foil shape for maximizing lift and minimizing drag. In fact, the favorite way of measuring this is the *lift-to-drag ratio*, which is simply the lifting force (in pounds or kilograms) divided by the drag (resistance) force (in pounds or kilograms). The larger the lift-to-drag ratio, the more efficient the keel—or any airfoil or hydrofoil for that matter.

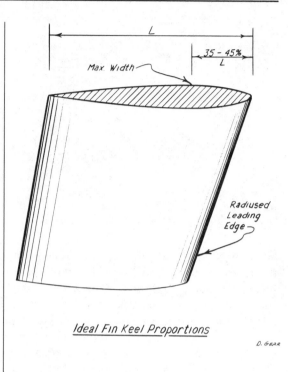

Ideal Fin Keel Proportions

D. GEAR

A Keel Shapes Up

The whole business gets so durn complicated that no two experts seem to agree on the exact best forms for keels; however, most do agree on the best sectional shape for general applications. This is a shape like an elongated teardrop, with the fatter end forward. The leading edge or tip shouldn't be a sharp point, because at the angle the keel operates at, the point would break up the water flow, causing early—and unwanted—turbulence. Instead, the leading edge should be a small radius or ellipse. The widest part of the section should be between 35 and 45 percent of the overall length aft of the leading edge, and the whole shape should taper gradually and smoothly to a point at the stern or trailing edge. For practical reasons, the trailing edge is usually a slight radius as well, since a true point's too fragile and expensive to construct.

Keel Slenderizing

Another thing that most designers agree on is that the thinner the keel the more efficient it will be. This is for two reasons. First, the narrower keel has less frontal area to punch bodily though the water. The second is that the narrower keel has a less pronounced, gentler curve. Accordingly, the water flow finds it easier to follow smoothly along the surface for a greater proportion of the narrow keel's fore-and-aft length. This results in fewer and smaller eddies and so less drag. Interestingly, shorter, wider, more highly curved shapes create more lift; however, they also create proportionately even more drag or turbulence. Thus a longer, narrower keel has a higher lift-to-drag ratio than its wider, fatter counterpart—even though it actually creates less useful side force or lift for a given area.

Leading the Way

Still another way to increase lift and reduce drag is to make keels deep and narrow, like a long, narrow airplane wing. Again, there are two main reasons for this. First, a short section—fore-n-aft—has the water flowing over it for less total distance fore-n-aft. It is thus possible—with a properly designed shape—to keep the water flowing smoothly along this short keel for a somewhat longer portion of its fore-and-aft length. This means that there are fewer eddies or less turbulence and drag. Another way of looking at it is to realize that the smooth (laminar) flow—the only flow useful in creating lift—is at the forward or leading edge of the keel. Accordingly, the deep, narrow keel has more leading edge to generate useful lift than a shallower, longer keel of the same area.

There's no getting around the fact that if you want real upwind efficiency you have to have a good, deep, narrow keel. In fact, if you take two otherwise identical designs and give one a deeper, narrower keel of the same area as its shallow counterpart, the deep-keel vessel will win upwind every single time. Unfortunately, the practical drawbacks are obvious. Few sailors can live comfortably with over 6 or 7 feet (1.8 or 2.1 m) of draft.

Whirlpool Tip-Off

This brings us to the other advantage of a deep, narrow keel and ultimately to the celebrated winged keel. We've seen that the windward side of the keel has effectively less pressure than the lee (downwind) side. This generates lift and causes everything nearby to rush over (upwind) to make up the difference. One of the things that tries to rush over and equalize the pressure is some of the water at the bottom of the lee side of the keel. Since there's nothing below the bottom of the keel to separate the water on the windward and leeward sides, the high-pressure, lee-side water tries to scoot down under the keel and up around to the low-pressure, windward side. In fact, it succeeds in doing so to some extent.

This generates some disgraceful waste. First, it destroys the smooth flow pattern and so eliminates the effective pressure difference along the bottom of the keel. No pressure difference, no lift; thus the entire bottom nine inches to a foot of the keel is generating no lift at all. The other thing this does is to get some really impressive eddies whirling about under and around the bottom tip of the keel. Again, these eddies are all wasted energy, and thus drag. Naturally, someone thought up a high-falutin' name for this phenomenon—*induced drag*. Now that you know what it is, you too can stalk meaningfully about the docks impressing people with obscure references to it. Or you could be sensible and call it "wasteful whirlpools at the tip of a keel, wing, or sail"—same thing.

On a Wing and a Prayer

Anyway, this is what winged keels are all about. The creators of the original 12-Meter Rule realized just how important deep keels are to good windward performance. Their particular solution—to make sure that all boats had an equal chance in this department—was to say no boat can draw more than 9 feet (2.74 m)—period, no exceptions. Well, for years designers tried every trick in the book to increase the *effective* depth of their 12-meter's keel without actually making it deeper than 9 feet (2.74 m) draft. Elliptical shapes, sharp trailing edges, sweep-back angle, and the like are all largely gimmicks to reduce induced drag by infinitesimal amounts—amounts only apparent at the top end of competitive racing.

It was the crafty Aussies, aided by an equally crafty Dutchman, who realized that if you put a fence around the bottom of the keel it would keep the water from flowing around under the keel—an approach familiar to aircraft designers for years. Voilà—markedly less induced drag. Before, without the fence or wings, the bottom foot of the keel was virtually useless except to get the ballast low. Now, the Down-Under designers had gained back most of this useless 12 or so inches (30 cm), and they'd done it in a way so novel that the rule makers had never thought to ban it—as they surely would have, if they'd only known. Indeed, it was just as if the Australians had found a way to get around the rule and use a 10-foot-deep (3 m) keel. What's more, they could fill the fence or wing with lead and thus lower the center of gravity, making their boat stiffer.

Wing Drawbacks

All, however, is not as rosy as it seems. The wings have considerably more than twice the wetted surface or friction drag of a normal keel that is simply made a foot (30 cm) deeper the old-fashioned way. Even worse, wings are a structural nightmare to design and build, they're expensive, and they threaten to hook and catch on things more often than you'd think. In fact, wings are only an advantage when you have an absolute draft restriction. In other words, wings are durn near silly on anything that's not going to race for the America's Cup, and they're not exactly sensible even for that. For the average boat, you can get exactly the same effect by either lowering the keel nine inches to a foot (22 to 30 cm), or by using a centerboard in the keel tip—even a fairly small and simple one.

If you really want to go in the direction of the wing things that seem to have sprouted from so many new production boats, try the Scheel keel. This is naval architect Henry Scheel's patented keel configuration, a configuration that accomplishes exactly the same thing as the wing keels without many of the wing's drawbacks.

Traditional Lift

Now, fin keels aren't the only things that generate lift. Traditional long keels do as well. They simply do it less efficiently—their lift-to-drag ratio's very poor—particularly in light of their much greater area. Rudders also generate lift, and a deep, narrow rudder can be smaller—for less drag—than a wider, shallower rudder, while still producing the same turning force. Don't be fooled, however, into thinking that all the above means that deep-fin-keel sailboats are the only way to go. There are many, many other considerations in choosing a keel configuration, besides lift-to-drag ratio. Remember, in Chapter 21 we considered what happens when a boat and thus her fin keel stops moving. Additionally, there's safety on grounding, shoal draft, steadiness on the helm, and strength and ease of construction—just a few of the many factors that frequently make the traditional long keels attractive. Nevertheless, it doesn't do to forget lift either; it's at work constantly and everywhere. In fact, even propeller blades generate lift.

Propeller Lift

Back in Chapter 32 we investigated propellers in detail and assumed that they screw their way through the water just like a wood screw in soft pine. This approach is more than adequate for figuring small-craft props, but the real experts often look at propeller blades as independent lift-generating wings or foils. Each blade actually functions as an asymmetrical foil shape just like the *Agile Angel*'s keel. Not surprisingly, they pull themselves forward by generating lift. Unfortunately, trying to understand exactly how this functions is a daunting prospect. Not only are the prop blades moving in a circle—instead of a relatively straight line—but they are operating two, three, or more at once—scrambling up the water flow unmercifully. The mathematics required to even begin to make sense out of all this is so horrendous that I get a headache just thinking about thinking about it!

CHAPTER 38

Lift From Cloth: Sails and Their Workings

*Instead of good Russia duck or English
canvas, he had to accept an inferior hemp-
and-jute material called hessians that was
generally used for bagging. . . .*

John Paul Jones, Samuel Eliot Morison

Sailors have been extracting power from the wind for at least 4,000 years—perhaps much longer. At first, the best course anyone could manage was dead downwind. Gradually, however, boats became closer and closer winded. By the time Julius Caesar was crying *"Et tu, Brute?"* mariners were commonly steering as close as 60 or even 55 degrees to the wind—real windward work. The Chinese junk, the Arab dhow, and—somewhat later—the European lugger could, pretty consistently, make good courses as high as these. In all this time and in all the world, however, no one had managed to sail closer than 50 degrees. It just wasn't thought possible.

Today, a sailing yacht that can't point to 45 degrees in average conditions is considered pretty durn pokey. Twelve-meters can be pinched to sail even closer than 35 degrees and high-speed cats can not only point as high as 40 degrees or so, but actually sail faster than the wind. What happened? Why can modern sailors—mariners of the last hundred years or so—do what wasn't even credible for all of time before?

Obviously, there have been a number of technical improvements—better gear, stronger sailcloth, lighter masts, and so on. The most important single improvement, though, the single change that enables modern craft to do the "impossible," is our understanding of aerodynamic lift—exactly as described in the last chapter. The entire rig of a modern sailboat is designed to maximize the lift generated by her sails.

Now, some cruising sailors are prone to say they're not much interested in upwind performance; but this can be a real mistake. The principal reason you find sailing pleasant is that you can sail your trusty *Viqueen* in any direction, regardless of where the ornery wind happens to be blowing. Understanding how your sails generate lift will make it that much easier for you to get *Viqueen* from here to there efficiently and comfortably.

Shape's the Key

The single most critical factor to upwind performance is sail shape. Just as the keels we discussed in the last chapter generate lift as a result of their curvature, sails require the same smooth curvature or camber combined with a suitable angle of attack to perform properly. Cutting a sail to take the best shape is a true art. To do the job right, a sailmaker not only takes into account the characteristics of the sailcloth, but the size and shape of the sail, the type of rig, and the local wind conditions.

What the sailmaker is ultimately after is to make a sail that will fill with the desired smooth, curved shape and hold that shape without distortion in a large range of wind conditions. Additionally, he or she is trying to fine-tune that shape. More depth of camber for greater drive or power, less depth for more tender vessels that can't stand up to the additional heeling force. The location of the point of greatest or deepest curve, called the point of maximum draft, is also critical. The sailmaker wants to keep it from moving too far aft, where it causes excess helm and stalls the airflow.

Cutting for Curvature

The heart of this art is in cutting the individual cloth panels of the sail so they'll naturally take the desired curved shape when sewn together. This is a problem like the one faced by the mapmakers you remember from high-school geography. Just as you can't represent the curved surface of a sphere as a flat surface without adding curvature and distortion, the sailmaker can't assemble a sail to have a curved shape—in three dimensions—without curving the edges of most of the panels. By carefully shaping each panel, your sailmaker can control sail shape very precisely.

Round that Foot

Equally important to sail shape is the luff and foot round. When your sail's laid out flat on the

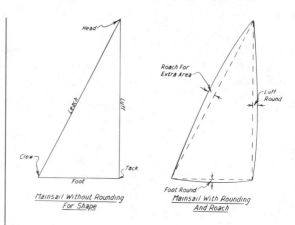

Mainsail Without Rounding For Shape

Mainsail With Rounding And Roach

loft floor the leading edge (luff) and the bottom edge (foot) are cut to a smooth curve—a curve that bellies out from the straight line connecting the corners (head and tack, and tack and clew).

When you hoist your sails on your presumably straight mast and boom, these curves are forced back into the body of the sail, generating a large portion of the desired sail shape. Of course, many masts are not really straight. Mast bend is invoked as the latest in high-tech sail control. Actually, the purpose of controlling mast bend is to control the fullness or depth of camber in your sail. By bending the mast so its middle section bows forward, you'll be pulling the luff round of the sail forward as well. This pulls the excess material of the luff round ahead—out of the body of the sail—and thus makes the sail flatter. That's all there is to mast bend. The sole purpose of all those hundreds of types of backstay adjusters you find advertised is to help you make your sail flatter.

Flattening a Sail

Why make a sail flatter? Well, airfoils—like your sail—generate lift because of their curvature or camber. Thus—within limits—the more camber, the more lift or power. Unfortunately, this greater curvature also creates drag and heeling

Marshall and Stewart Saffer expertly driving their One Design 14 along on a reach in the Mid-Winter Regatta in Miami. Sails for competitive one-design classes require the most expertise from a sailmaker. Since all the boats are the same, every nuance of sail construction, fabric style, and shaping can make a substantial difference. This suit was custom tailored by Sailspar Sailmakers to match the Saffer brothers' lighter than usual weight, enabling them to power to the top of the fleet. (Saffer photo courtesy Sailspar Sailmakers)

force. As the wind grows stronger the heeling force grows too large, forcing you to reef. The problem here is that reefing is a drastic reduction of power. What if you could reduce the heeling force by some intermediate method, without sacrificing so much area? This is just what mast bend is all about. By flattening *Viqueen*'s main you can reduce its heeling force without sacrificing nearly as much drive as you would by pulling in a reef. In fact, most performance sail widgets are aimed at controlling sail shape or fullness.

For instance, cunninghams pull the material of a sail down away from the sail's center, removing fullness or decreasing camber as does tensioning clew outhaul. By tightening the backstay and bending the mast, hauling on the cunningham and the outhaul you can continue to carry full sail, upwind, in considerably greater wind strength than you could with the same sail unflattened, with full draft. Naturally, this means you can work your way upwind faster and, more importantly, safely in stronger breezes—capabilities any cruiser should strive for.

Sag Makes a Bag

Headstay sag, by the same token, increases sail fullness. Since your sail's already been cut to proper depth of camber—allowing for average headstay sag—permitting it to sag more than was calculated on by your sailmaker will add to the effect of the luff round. Where bending the center of your mast forward flattens your sail, the headstay sagging roughly aft (bending back at the center) makes the sail fuller. This makes the sail baggy, creating far more heeling force than is desirable, and moves the draft further back where it's no longer as effective in generating lift. Of course the harder it blows, the more pressure on the headsail and the more the headstay tends to sag. Increasing headstay tension decreases this sag. Unfortunately, you need a whale of a lot of tension, so much so that you can actually bend your boat up at the bow and stern like a banana. On a masthead-rigged vessel, for instance, you'd raise headstay tension by increasing tension on the backstay adjuster. (This, usually, is also increasing mast bend and flattening the main). This tension runs up the backstay over the top of the mast and into the headstay. At the same time, though, you'll be trying to push the mast down through the bottom of the boat. Eventually you reach a point of no return. Any additional tension on the backstay simply bends the boat more (down at the center and up at the ends) without decreasing headstay sag—time to consider setting a smaller headsail.

Now, another critical aspect of lift is that—just as with any airfoil or hydrofoil—the leading edge of a sail is its most effective area. For this reason tall, narrow rigs are most efficient for windward work; they have the most leading edge for a given sail area. As we saw in Chapter 15, this presents your designer with a difficult trade-off. Taller rigs are more efficient, but they also generate more heeling moment. The trick is to strike the right balance between the stability of a given design and the height of her sail plan.

Turbulent Masts

Yet another factor affecting upwind performance is the turbulence created by the mast. Since the mast's usually several hundred times fatter than the sail behind it, it creates a relatively huge wind shadow, destroying much of the lift generating airflow over the sail's leading edge. This has resulted in two trends that have—in racing boats—reached an unhealthy stage. The first trend is to greatly reduce mast diameter. Obviously, if you can make the mast thinner you'll decrease its wind shadow. Reasonably enough, to make a mast thinner you have to add more support, and this support comes in the form of additional shrouds, spreaders, babystays, and running backstays. Unfortunately, all these spreaders and backstays generate additional wind resistance of their own. Even worse, you can easily end up with a rig that's so high-strung that the crew needs to constantly tend it to keep it standing and in the boat—not a safe proposition. Many current IOR racers sport three-, four-, and even five-spreader rigs with two or more runners and/or checkstays. This may improve upwind performance, but it also makes bringing your mast down altogether too, well . . . easy! As a rule, such rigs have no place on proper seagoing craft.

The Case of the Shrinking Mains

The other trend that mast turbulence has created is placing more sail area in the headsail and less in the main. The jib, having only the relatively small headstay ahead of it, experiences significantly less wind shadow or turbulence than the main. In fact, the headstay is merely twenty or so times thicker than the sail—as opposed to the mast's hundreds of times greater width. Accordingly, placing more of your boat's sail area in the headsail will—theoretically—increase the effectiveness of that area's leading edge, and thus lift and windward efficiency.

This works fine to a point; however, large headsails are a bear to handle. Additionally, the

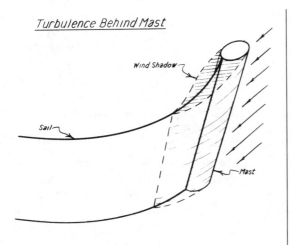

Turbulence Behind Mast

Wind Shadow

Sail

Mast

whole trend to larger headsails has been aggravated by racing rules that don't penalize overlapping sail area sufficiently. Thus, by making the headsails larger, a designer increases not only effective area, but also free (unmeasured) area. The combined effect's been so great that some sizeable vessels have mains that are barely handkerchief-sized.

This is a classic example of how the pressures of racing and racing rules take a basically sound idea and carry it to ridiculous extremes. In actual practice, a large main can be made very powerful. Even allowing for the turbulence of the mast, such mains—if sufficiently large and properly shaped—can be very efficient. What's more, such sails are far easier to handle—on their self-tending booms, well inboard and easy to reef—than the same area in an overlapping genoa that needs a gorilla on a three-speed winch to sheet in.

A Material Difference

Now, in addition to understanding aerodynamic lift, we've also been given a bevy of new and exotic materials for sailmaking. Kevlar and Mylar are the two names that spring immediately to mind, but ordinary Dacron was one of the most important revolutions to sweep the sailing world. Just 40 years ago canvas was—as it had been for centuries—the only real choice for making sails. Now, canvas is good enough stuff, but it's really not all that strong—certainly not in comparison to Dacron. Even worse, canvas stretches considerably under load, and stretch is your sails' worst enemy. You see, all your sailmaker's careful cutting and shaping will be lost forever if your sail stretches beyond intended limits. You'd be left with a relatively formless sack instead of a finely tuned airfoil.

Of course, in the old days part of the sailmaker's craft was to allow for canvas's stretch. They'd cut sails just a bit smaller than their proper finished dimensions, knowing full well they'd stretch to fit. Nevertheless, this was a poor compromise compared to a stronger material with less or—ideally—no stretch. The final bonus—and it is a big one—is that Dacron (unlike canvas) doesn't rot. It used to be that before you could stow your sails and go home, you'd have to hoist them to dry. Overlook this too many times and you'd end up with sails severely discolored by mildew. Ignore this warning sign and your canvas sails would simply rot to pieces. These days, all you do is stuff your sails (wet or not) into a handy bag, loll back on the cockpit seats, and toot for the launch—the easy life.

New Stuff Can Be Good Stuff

Now, many cruising folk are leery of the new materials. There's some reason for this; however, used properly, Mylar and Mylar/Dacron combinations can produce sails that are just as long-lived as Dacron sails, yet at 20 percent less weight and with less stretch. Naturally, this means better performance. Mylar sails have received a bad reputation with regard to longevity because they were, at first, made only for racers. These guys wanted the lightest of the lightest sails that would do the job. As usual, this resulted in flimsy construction and short life expectancy. A Mylar or Mylar/Dacron sail that's been designed specifically for a cruiser or cruiser/racer is constructed much more heavily. These sails don't have to be babied. They can be designed as roller furlers and roller reefers and can be unceremoniously stuffed in a bag—no careful flaking and folding required (though careful flaking and folding's always best, for any sail). They're designed to have the reserve strength to take the abuse cruisers dish out to their hapless sail inventory. With their low stretch, light weight, and superior shape retention, Mylar and Mylar/Dacron sails make for noticeably improved upwind performance, and, being lighter, they're easier to handle.

Of course, not all high-tech ideas work out. Kevlar, as strong as it is, is—in general—not a good material for any sail, particularly a cruising sail. This is because the individual fibers in woven Kevlar cloth cut into each other under load, especially during the rapid, violent bending that occurs when a sail flogs. This weakens the fabric very quickly and adds up to ridiculously short life expectancy. There are a few exceptions—new styles of Kevlar fabric are useful for reinforcing cruiser and cruiser/racer sails. Such sails must be engineered by a sailmaker that really understands Kevlar's drawbacks and uses enough additional strength—over and above racing-sail strength—to make up for Kevlar's rapid degradation in flogging.

On the other hand, Spectra promises to be one of the finest materials ever created for sailmaking. This stuff's so strong and has so little stretch that a sailmaker can almost assume that a Spectra sail will not stretch at all. In other words, it'll keep its best theoretical shape—the precise shape intended by the sailmaker—throughout almost any wind strength. Even better, Spectra is very forgiving of sharp bends, twists, and minor abrasions—Kevlar's pitfalls. What's more, Spectra's easy to work with and not terribly costly, meaning that Spectra sails won't cost an arm and a leg. If you're into performance cruising, club, or IMS racing, this is the fabric of the future; Mylar/Spectra headsails have little more stretch than steel at fantastically less weight.

There is one problem with Spectra; it's so strong that they're having difficulty weaving enough sailcloth from it. You see, ordinary materials, such as Dacron, often have tiny imperfections or blobs on the threads. When these imperfections run through the manufacturer's high-speed looms, the thread simply breaks, and the manufacturer just rethreads and starts up again. Spectra, though, is so strong that when a blob goes through the loom the loom breaks—not the thread. Talk about gumming up the works.

In spite of all this, Spectra is available now. Neil Pride of Hong Kong is making windsurfer sails using this material; while for larger cruising and racing boats, Hood Sailmakers, of—seemingly—all over, and Sailspar of Stamford, Connecticut, have some very interesting, and reliable Mylar/Spectra and Dacron/Spectra reinforced construction approaches—approaches worth investigating if you want to get the most out of your boat. It's interesting to note that windsurfer sails are almost always in the vanguard of sailmaking technology. It's much easier and cheaper to experiment with new construction and new techniques on these small sails than on larger ones. If you want to see what the future may bring, take a good look at windsurfers.

CHAPTER 39

Rigging Rules of Thumb: Demystifying the Rigging Game

No one but an acrobat or a sailor could have got up to that bell-rope from the bracket, and no one but a sailor could have made the knots with which the cord was fastened to the chair.

The Adventure of the Abbey Grange,
Sir Arthur Conan Doyle

Few experiences are more satisfying than standing at the helm, guiding a sailboat upwind in a breeze. The tension from the wheel tugs at your hands as you swoop gracefully from tack to tack. Shading your eyes, leaning over just so, you can gaze up the towering length of the mast, while the windward shrouds hum slightly with the strain and the wind. Something about the symmetry and proportions gives endless pleasure. On a well-designed boat the mast and rigging are just heavy enough to support anything the wind and sea can offer, but no stronger. Excess weight aloft means reduced stability and poor performance, while mast and rigging that are not strong enough guarantee adventures you'd rather not have.

In this age of computers, designers (myself included) frequently fire up the old desktop computer to determine the mast and rigging dimensions. Back in the great age of sail, however, there were no computers, and rule of thumb reigned supreme. For cruisers and family daysailers, there are still many useful rules of thumb that will enable you to estimate mast and rigging size fairly accurately.

Mast Section Width

The most immediate question is how big the mast should be—how wide, how long fore-and-aft, how thick the walls. For standard aluminum masts with a single spreader, a surprisingly accurate rule I developed is to make the transverse mast section width $1/90$ of the mast length from the deck to the headstay. Say our *Prancing Petunia* was a typical 40-footer (12.2 m) with a single spreader rig. The length from the deck (or top of her trunk cabin—if the mast passes through it) to the headstay is 42.5 feet (12.95 m). Then the transverse width of her mast section would simply be 0.47 feet, about $5\frac{3}{4}$ inches or 14.5 cm.

Fore-and-aft Mast Dimension

On a single-spreader rig, the fore-and-aft section of the mast should be about 1.4 times the transverse section. In *Prancing Petunia*'s case this would be 0.66 feet, about 8 inches or 20 cm.

Mast Wall Thickness

Finally, we need to determine the aluminum mast's wall thickness, and this should be about $\frac{1}{35}$ of the mast section width. For our *Prancing Petunia*, with a mast section width of 5.75 inches (14.5 cm), this works out to a wall thickness of 0.16 inches (4 mm). In just a few minutes, we have speced out a 5¾-inch by 8-inch mast section with a 0.16-inch wall, or 14.5-cm by 20-cm mast with a 4-mm wall.

Adjustments for Differing Boats

Of course, a naval architect or top-flight spar-maker will carefully calculate the required mast section from the stability of the boat. He or she will have loads of fun determining moments of inertia and radiuses of gyration, resolving force diagrams, and similar exciting stuff. If you don't have this sort of information and expertise available, however, the above rules of thumb will give generally serviceable results for ordinary cruising boats and daysailers. Remember the word ordinary. If your boat's particularly heavy, it will place greater strains on her rig and thus require a heavier mast. Similarly, if you intend to do serious offshore cruising, you should increase the transverse mast dimension by 5 to 10 percent and then follow the rule of thumb through as before.

How About Two Spreaders?

If *Prancing Petunia* had had a double-spreader rig, she could get by with a narrower mast, but would still require close to the same fore-and-aft mast dimension. Thus we'd use the rule of thumb of a single-masted rig exactly as before, but after finding all the dimensions, we'd reduce the transverse mast section width by 10 to 15 percent. *Prancing Petunia*'s double-spreader mast would then be 5 inches by 8 inches with a 0.16-inch wall, or 12 cm by 20 cm with a 4-mm wall.

Deck-Stepped Masts are Weaker

Another thing to consider in estimating a mast section with these rules of thumb is that masts stepped on deck are not as strong as masts stepped through the deck onto a mast step at the keel. For a deck-stepped mast, you should use the above rules of thumb, but instead of dividing the mast length by 90 to find mast section width, divide by 85. With a single-spreader rig and the mast stepped on deck, *Prancing Petunia* would then take a 6-inch by 8⅜-inch mast with a 0.17 inch wall, or a 15-cm by 21-cm mast with a 4.3-mm wall.

Standard Mast and Rigging Proportions

All the above assume that the overall rigging proportions are essentially standard or average—specifically that the spreaders are located about as follows:

SPREADER LOCATIONS— SINGLE SPREADER RIG

Spreader located between 50 and 52 percent of mast length up from the deck.

SPREADER LOCATIONS— DOUBLE SPREADER RIG

Lower spreader located between 37 and 39 percent of mast length up from the deck.
Upper spreader located between 68 and 70 percent of mast length up from the deck.

Additionally, the shroud angles (the angle each shroud makes with the mast) must be equal to or greater than 10 degrees, and the width or beam between the chainplates (on deck) must be at least equal to $\frac{1}{5}$ of the total mast length from deck to headstay. On *Prancing Petunia* this means the minimum beam between the chainplates (with her 42.5-foot or 12.95-m mast) must be 102 inches or 260 cm.

If all these standard proportions are met—and they will be on most boats—these mast and rigging rules of thumb will give fairly accurate estimates.

Sizing Up the Boom

For simple round aluminum booms, diameter should be about $\frac{1}{45}$ of the overall length, and the aluminum wall thickness works out to $\frac{1}{26}$ of the diameter. On most modern vessels, especially those equipped with vangs, the vertical loads on the boom are greater than the transverse loads. For this reason, elliptical section booms are much preferred. For such booms, the transverse section width is around $\frac{1}{50}$ of the length, the vertical section height is $1\frac{1}{2}$ times the transverse width, and the wall is $\frac{1}{26}$ of the transverse section width.

If *Prancing Petunia*'s boom is 17 feet (5.2 m) long it would then be 4 inches wide, $6\frac{1}{8}$ inches high, with a $\frac{5}{32}$-inch-thick wall, or 10.4 cm wide by 15.5 cm high with a 4-mm wall. A simple round boom would be $4\frac{1}{2}$ inches in diameter, with a 0.17 inch wall, or 11.5 cm in diameter with a 4.4-mm wall.

Estimating the Correct Standing Rigging

After making a reasonable estimate as to mast and boom size, we need to determine the standing rigging sizes. Again, there's a simple rule of thumb: For cruising boats, the total breaking strength of all the shrouds on one side of the boat should equal about 1.1 times the displacement of the boat. Racing vessels and daysailers can get by with the total exactly equalling displacement, while serious offshore cruisers should have a total shroud breaking strength of about 1.2 times the displacement.

One tricky little twist here is that most boats have double lower shrouds. In adding up and figuring the total shroud strength, though, you only use one of the two lowers, not both. The assumption here—and it's proven to be a good assumption, over the years—is that only one of the lowers on each side is really working at any time; however, it may be a different one depending on the angle of sail and trim of the boat.

Let's say that our 40-foot (12.2 m) single-spreader *Prancing Petunia* displaces 20,000 pounds (9,070 kg); then—since she's a standard cruising boat—the total breaking strength of her shrouds should be 22,000 pounds or 9,980 kg.

How Much Load On Each Shroud?

The next question is how to divide the load between the lowers and the uppers. The standard division of load percentages are as follows:

SINGLE-SPREADER RIG

Lower:	60%
Upper:	40%

DOUBLE-SPREADER RIG

Lower:	48%
Intermediate:	26%
Upper:	26%

On a double-spreader rig, the intermediate and the upper shrouds may run separately over the lower spreader to independent turnbuckles and chainplates on deck, or they may combine at the lower spreader into a single shroud ending at a single turnbuckle and chainplate. In this latter case, the combined intermediate and upper shroud would have twice the strength, or 52 percent of the load.

For the single-spreader *Prancing Petunia*, we can see that we'd require an upper with a breaking strength of 8,800 pounds (3,990 kg) and two lowers with a breaking strength of 13,200 pounds (5,990 kg) each. From the wire strength tables, it's now easy to select $\frac{5}{16}$-inch or 8-mm diameter 1×19 stainless steel wire for the two lowers, which have a breaking strength of 12,600 pounds or 5,670 kg; and the upper would be $\frac{1}{4}$-inch or 6-mm diameter 1×19 stainless, with a breaking strength of 8,200 pounds or 3,330 kg.

STRENGTH OF 1×19 STAINLESS STEEL ROPE

Dia.–in.	Pounds	Dia.–mm	kg
1/8	2,100	3	950
5/32	3,300	4	1,500
3/16	4,700	5	2,370
7/32	6,300	5.5	2,860
1/4	8,200	6	3,330
9/32	10,300	7	4,670
5/16	12,500	8	5,670
3/8	17,600	10	8,800
7/16	23,400	11	10,600
1/2	29,700	12	12,570
9/16	37,000	14	16,890
5/8	46,800	16	21,230
3/4	59,700	19	27,090
7/8	76,700	22	34,800

Sizing Up the Headstay

How about the headstay? The rule of thumb is that the headstay should be the size of the heaviest shroud or one size greater. Since we already rounded down slightly on sizing *Prancing Petunia*'s lowers, we should definitely increase headstay size. Accordingly *Prancing Petunia* would take a ³⁄₈-inch or 9-mm 1×19 stainless steel headstay. The backstay—on a masthead rig—is usually one size smaller than the headstay, in *Prancing Petunia*'s case ⁵⁄₁₆ inch or 8 mm 1×19 stainless. On a three-quarter or seven-eighths rig, the backstay doesn't directly oppose the headstay loads. Such headstays largely control mast bend and whip. A rule-of-thumb guide is that they should be the same size as the smallest shroud, in *Prancing Petunia*'s case ¹⁄₄ inch or 6 mm.

We can apply the rigging rule of thumb to double-spreader rigs the same way. In fact, with common sense you can make very good estimates of rigging and spar sizes for nearly any standard single- or twin-spreader boat by adjusting the rigging loads as suggested, and by making proper allowance for such factors as whether the mast is deck-stepped or your vessel's intended for ocean voyaging or inshore gunkholing.

And the Turnbuckles Should Be . . .

As we work our way down to the deck, it becomes necessary to select the appropriate turnbuckles. One way to do this is to pick up one of the manufacturer's catalogs; however, there are even helpful rules of thumb here. For standard open-body type bronze turnbuckles, the screw diameter is usually about twice the wire diameter, the opening between the turnbuckle's jaws is usually about twice the wire diameter, and the clevis pin is usually about twice the wire diameter—can't get a much simpler rule of thumb than this!

Using this rule, we'd choose a turnbuckle with ³⁄₄-inch-diameter (19 mm) screw and a ³⁄₄-inch (19 mm) clevis pin for *Prancing Petunia*'s headstay, ⁵⁄₈-inch (16 mm) screw and clevis turnbuckles for the lowers, and turnbuckles with ¹⁄₂-inch-diameter

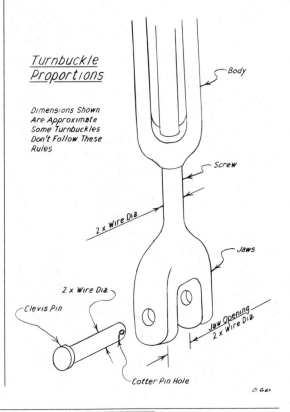

Turnbuckle Proportions

Dimensions Shown Are Approximate Some Turnbuckles Don't Follow These Rules

Body

Screw

2 x Wire Dia.

Jaws

2 x Wire Dia.

Clevis Pin

Jaw Opening 2 x Wire Dia.

Cotter Pin Hole

D. Gei

(6 mm) screw and ½-inch-diameter (6 mm) clevis pins for her uppers. Most turnbuckles will work out very close to these sizes; however, high-strength stainless-steel turnbuckles can be somewhat lighter.

Don't forget the toggles! A toggle should be installed on every turnbuckle between the turnbuckle and the chainplate and at the mast between the tang and the eye on the shroud. Toggles help make up for the misalignments that always occur and always change in every rig as the mast and shrouds bend and sway. Without toggles, even very heavy shrouds will eventually fail from repeated kinking near their attachment points.

Running Rigging

We're still faced with the job of determining the best running rigging sizes. There isn't really a rule of thumb for this; however, the Running Rigging Size chart will give good answers very quickly. For *Prancing Petunia*, at 40-feet (12.2 m) LOA, we find that her main and genoa sheets should be 0.6 inches (15 mm) in diameter (⁹⁄₁₆ inch or ½

inch, or 15 to 16 mm would do nicely); her main and jib halyards and her spinnaker sheets happen to work out to about the same size, about ½ inch (13 mm), while her light spinnaker sheets would be ⁵⁄₁₆ inch or ³⁄₈ inch (8 to 9 mm).

Ordinary three-strand or braided Dacron is fine for all the sheets; however, the rope halyards absolutely must be of the lowest-stretch, highest-quality line available. In fact, the best rope currently available for halyards is Spectra rope—not Dacron at all. This new material has the same stretch characteristics as wire! It is also fabulously strong—so strong in fact that, when specifying Spectra halyards, you should use only 75 percent of the diameter given on the Running Rigging Sizes chart. Thus, we'd call for ⁷⁄₁₆-inch-diameter (11 mm) Spectra halyards instead of the ⁹⁄₁₆ inch (14 mm) braided Dacron. Not only is this slenderer line lighter and freer running than the Dacron, and not only does it have far less stretch, but its reduced diameter means that—even though it's an expensive rope—it really doesn't cost that much more than the fatter Dacron halyard would.

Cleats and Sheaves

As for hardware, remember that all sheaves should be at least 8 times the diameter of their rope—more is better. Cleats should be 12 times as long as the rope diameter, or more. On *Prancing Petunia*, her ½-inch (12 mm) main sheet should run through (at least) 4-inch-diameter (96-mm) sheaves and end at (at least) 6-inch (144-mm) cleats. Again, larger cleats are stronger and easier on the line, and four-hole cleats should be used wherever space permits.

Now, with all this information at your fingertips, you can wade into masting and rigging arguments with plenty of ammunition. Next time your sailing buddy claims that the boat at the next slip is over-rigged, give him a piece of your mind.

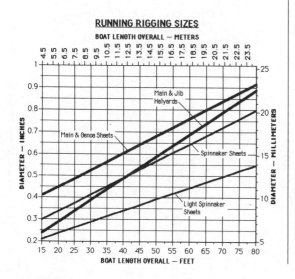

RUNNING RIGGING SIZES

Rigging Your Hull

Rigging loads don't simply stop and vanish at the turnbuckles. It's vitally important that the chainplates be fastened with numerous large bolts and/or tie rods to distribute the load into the boat's structure. Attaching well-made chainplates can be time consuming. It's an easy place for production builders to be tempted to scrimp. When you're considering a new boat ask a lot of detailed questions about how the chainplates are fastened and how the loads from the chainplates are spread out as they go into the hull. Of course, since stability and thus rigging loads increase very rapidly with size (see Chapter 13), this is less of a concern on small daysailers than on larger cruisers.

The author holding two of Holger Danske's massive chainplate weldments. Even though weight is critical on a racer like this, we couldn't make the chainplates any lighter—they would not have been strong enough.

It's also important to keep the hull from distorting at the mast and chainplates. Without proper reinforcement, the mast will push the keel down while the chainplates lift the sides of the hull and squeeze them inwards. These forces combine to lift the deck as well. On one old boat that I owned, the deck actually lifted ¾ inch (19 cm) clear from the bulkheads at the mast. The solution is to install a tie rod between the deck and mast step, and reinforcing knees at the chainplates between the underside of the deck and the inside of the hull.

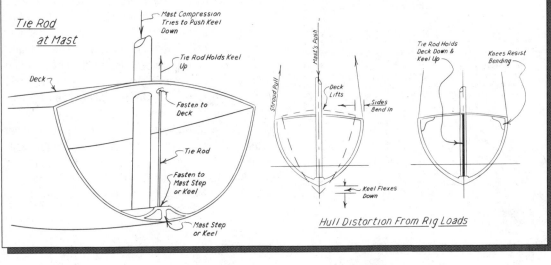

Tie Rod at Mast

Mast Compression Tries to Push Keel Down
Tie Rod Holds Keel Up
Deck
Fasten to Deck
Tie Rod
Fasten to Mast Step or Keel
Mast Step or Keel

Mast's Push
Shroud Pull
Deck Lifts
Sides Bend In
Keel Flexes Down

Tie Rod Holds Deck Down & Keel Up
Knees Resist Bending

Hull Distortion From Rig Loads

CHAPTER 40

The Delicate Balance

It is soon known if the Ship be kept in Equilibrio by the Sails before and abaft the Center of Gravity; for if she be, the Helm may be kept nearly a-midships in smooth Water.

The Young Officer's Sheet Anchor, Darcy Lever

Sailors talk endlessly about helm feel and balance. Often you'll hear a boat described as "hard mouthed," or "light helmed." Of course, these terms refer to the amount of weather or (in some cases) lee helm that a boat carries on various points of sail, and in differing wind strengths—factors that affect steering efficiency and performance. But what exactly is *weather helm* or *lee helm?* How can you adjust for it on your boat, or allow for it in a rig modification?

Facing the Wind

The answers are both simple and complex—simple because the effect is very clear, and complex because many factors interact to create that effect. Weather helm's nothing more than the need to keep your helm to weather—what else?—in order to maintain a desired course. In other words, (on a tiller-steered boat) you have to pull and hold the tiller up to windward to counteract the vessel's tendency to round up into the wind. In moderation, this is highly desirable. In fact, one very important benefit is that this acts as a sort of dead-man's brake. If you suddenly let go of the tiller—in, say, an emergency—it will swing amidships and your craft will head up and (ideally) lie to, in irons.

Another important benefit of moderate weather helm is that it improves upwind performance. The slightly angled rudder deflects the water flow in much the same way that a curved airplane wing deflects airflow. Thus small amounts of weather helm produce additional lift and reduce leeway.

Wrestling With The Tiller

Not surprisingly, you can have too much of a good thing, and too much weather helm is not a good thing at all. This is the condition sailors call "hard mouthed." A vessel with excessive weather helm is slow and tiring to sail. It is tiring because you'll constantly be struggling to hold the tiller up at a large angle—a task that can require considerable strength. Just as unpleasant is that a rudder over at more than 10 or 15 degrees ceases to act as an aid in increasing lift and starts behaving like a brake—an altogether too effective one.

Fingertip Control?

The flip-side of this coin is a boat with helm feel that's so light the merest nudge will swing the tiller wildly. At first this might appear to be the ultimate in fingertip control. Unfortunately, without the slight continuous pressure on the rudder generated by moderate weather helm, you can't really sense your boat's responses. I once owned a boat with helm like this. You could steer her with ease as long as you paid close attention; however, the minute you glanced away she'd wander off course. A helm with feather-light touch like this simply doesn't give you the tactile feedback you need to steer under good control, by the seat of your pants.

Dangerous Helm

Even less desirable is lee helm. Not surprisingly, a craft with lee helm requires her skipper to hold the tiller down (downwind or to leeward) to keep her on course. Not only does this not generate lift to improve upwind performance, but such a boat has no dead-man's brake. If you release the tiller, the vessel will fall off, gathering speed and quite possibly sailing you into serious trouble. Worse still, if you'd been close-hauled with the sheets cleated, you'd end up broadside to the wind with the sails in flat—conditions that make for knockdowns or even capsizes.

Weathercocking

Now, a number of factors affect helm or balance. One of the most significant is the position of the center of effort of the sail plan and its relationship with the underwater area of the boat. A boat that has weather helm essentially weathercocks into the wind like a wind vane. Typically, a windvane's a rod with a small arrowhead on one end and a large feather on the other end. The rod is balanced on its center, and when the wind blows it acts most forcefully on the part of the vane with the largest area—the feather. Accordingly, the feather blows downwind faster than the rod or the arrowhead. Since the rod can't go anywhere it simply pivots around its balance point so that the area of greatest wind resistance is blown downwind and the arrowhead (the bow) points into the wind.

Exactly the same sort of thing happens—or ought to happen—on a yacht. If the center of pressure of the sails (totaled together) falls aft of the center of pressure of the water on your hull's underbody, then your *Natty Nautilus* will—left to her own devices—weathercock into the wind around her balance point—the center of water pressure. This is the general condition that causes weather helm. If the center of pressure on *Natty Nautilus*'s sails is too far aft, she'll have too much weather helm and be hard mouthed. If, on the other hand, the center of pressure of her sails is too far forward, she'll have lee helm. Or, in other words, her stern will tend to point into the wind rather than the bow.

Estimating Lateral Plane

In practice, all this is complicated by the fact that the underbody of a boat is anything but a plain flat shape. It is actually nearly impossible to find where the real center of water pressure lies. There is, however, a very simple method used by most designers for estimating purposes. Trace the profile (side view) of your *Natty Nautilus*'s hull underbody—complete with rudder from the water line down—and cut this shape out on a piece of cardboard (The hull underbody in this case is the silhouette view of every part of the boat below the waterline—the hull itself, the keel, and the rudder.) Balance the cardboard cutout on the edge of a ruler, and use this point as the estimate of the center of pressure on *Natty Nautilus*'s hull. Naval architects call this somewhat imaginary center the *center of lateral plane* or *CLP*.

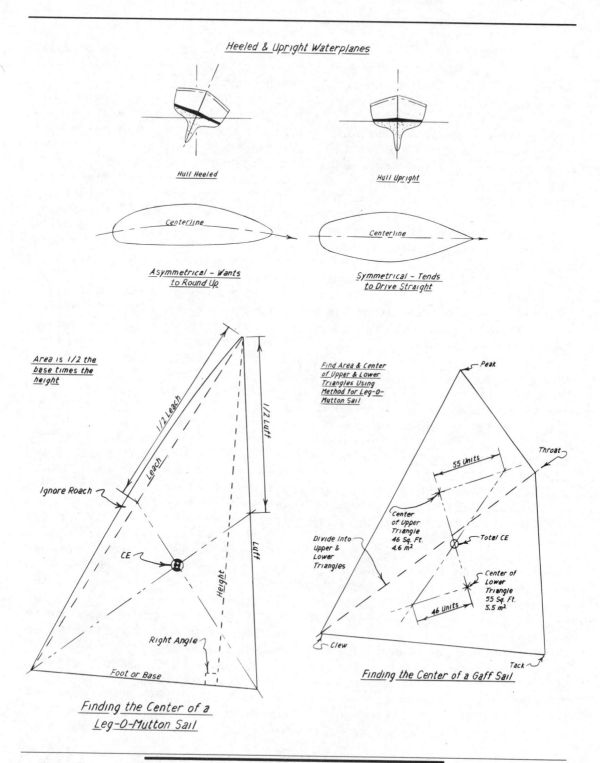

Heeled & Upright Waterplanes

Hull Heeled

Hull Upright

Centerline

Centerline

Asymmetrical – Wants
to Round Up

Symmetrical – Tends
to Drive Straight

Area is 1/2 the
base times the
height

1/2 Leach

1/2 Luff

Leach

Luff

Ignore Roach

CE

Height

Right Angle

Foot or Base

Finding the Center of a
Leg-O-Mutton Sail

Find Area & Center
of Upper & Lower
Triangles Using
Method for Leg-O-
Mutton Sail

Peak

Throat

55 Units

Center
of Upper
Triangle
46 Sq. Ft.
4.6 m²

Total CE

Divide Into
Upper &
Lower
Triangles

Center of
Lower
Triangle
55 Sq. Ft.
5.5 m²

46 Units

Clew

Tack

Finding the Center of a Gaff Sail

Measure That Rig

The next step is to figure the area of the various sails and combine the areas and centers of each individual sail to locate the total center of effort of the entire sail plan. If *Natty Nautilus* were a catboat with a leg-o-mutton sail, this would be straightforward. Ignore the roach, and her sail's a simple triangle. The area's then one-half the base times the height of the triangle. To find the center of effort make a tick mark exactly halfway along two opposite sides and draw lines from these tick mark across to the corner of the triangle that is most directly opposite that mark. The center of effort of this single sail is where these two lines cross. Of course, a sail is no more a flat shape than the hull underbody. Again, designers use this center as a best estimate for the real center of pressure of the wind on the sails—keeping in mind that it is just an approximation.

If *Natty Nautilus* was a gaff-rigged catboat, you'd have to draw a line from the clew to the throat, dividing the sail into two triangles. You could then go ahead and find the area and the center of each triangle just as before. Naturally, adding the areas gives the total area; however, finding the combined center of effort's a bit more complicated.

Draw a line connecting the two center points of each triangle, and then draw two additional lines at right angles (perpendiculars) to this line, projecting out (away) from the center points of each of the two triangles. These lines should project in opposite directions. If the lower triangle was 55 square feet (5.5 m²) and the upper triangle was 46 square feet (4.6 m²), you'd have to represent these areas as distances on the projecting lines. It doesn't make any difference what scale or distance you use as long as you use the same scale on both perpendicular lines, to keep in proportion. You could, say, measure 46 eighths of an inch (5¾ inches) for the 46-square-foot upper triangle and 55 eighths of an inch (6⅞ inches) for the 55-square-foot lower triangle, making a tick mark at

the measured spots. (In the metric system, you could use 5.5 cm for the lower triangle and 4.6 cm for the upper.)

The important thing here is that you measure the distances from the *opposite* triangle on the perpendiculars. In other words, the perpendicular from the center of the 55-square-foot (5.5 m²) lower triangle will show the 55¾-inch (4.6 cm) distance representing the upper triangle and vice versa. Now, all you have to do is draw a line connecting the new tick marks you've made on the two perpendiculars. The point at which this line crosses the original line—the line directly between the two triangle centers—is the center of the full gaff sail.

Of course, this same approach works for combining any areas. (The areas don't have to be touching or even close). If *Natty Nautilus* had been a sloop, the second triangle would be the area of the foretriangle instead of the top half of a gaff sail. (The area of the foretriangle is the area of the triangle made by the headstay, the forward face of the mast—up to the intersection of the headstay—and the distance from the forward face of the mast along the deck to the headstay fitting at the bow.) If you were figuring a ketch or yawl you'd simply find the combined area of the main and jib and then, taking their total area and total center, combine them with the area of the mizzen using the same method. In fact, you could go on with this method to figure the areas and center of effort on any boat, with any number of sails, right up to a full-rigged ship.

Taking the Lead

Once you've completed all this, you have the location of the center of lateral plane and the center of effort. The last step is to see how they relate to each other. To do this, drop a vertical line from the CE down to the waterline and transfer the position of the CLP from the cardboard to the waterline. Measure the distance between them and divide that distance by the full waterline length.

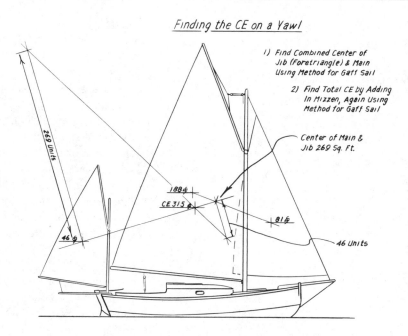

Finding the CE on a Yawl

1) Find Combined Center of
Jib (Foretriangle) & Main
Using Method for Gaff Sail

2) Find Total CE by Adding
In Mizzen, Again Using
Method for Gaff Sail

Center of Main &
Jib 269 Sq. Ft.

269 Units

188 Ş
CE 315 Ş
81 Ş
46 Ş
46 Units

Designers call this the lead (pronounced "leed"). The confusing thing here is that, even though we know that the center of pressure of the sails should be aft of the center of pressure of the hull underbody, almost every boat ever built should have the CE *ahead* of the CLP. In fact, if it weren't ahead you wouldn't have lead at all, but—I suppose—trail. Why is this? Well, remember the CE and CLP are only imaginary approximations of the true centers of pressure on the sails and on the hull underbody. The real centers are much different, and designers have established rules for estimating the amount of lead from these imaginary centers. They are as follows:

PERCENT OF LEAD

Schooner	7%–12%
Ketch	11%–14%
Yawl	12%–15%
Sloop or Cutter	13%–17%

If, for example, *Natty Nautilus* had an 18-foot (5.5 m) waterline and was an average sloop, her lead should be about 15 percent, or her CE should fall 2.7 feet (82 cm) ahead of her CLP. (15% × 18 ft. = 2.7 ft—15% × 5.5 m = 8.2 m). These numbers are average ranges for most vessels, and using them with a little judgement you won't go far wrong; however, there are other considerations that you should take into account in judging the amount of lead.

Factors Affecting Lead

First, the shape of a hull can greatly affect the amount of weather helm a boat has when heeled. This is because as a boat heels her hull presents an asymmetrical shape to the water, tending to make her round up even more than the simple fore-and-aft location of the centers of pressure alone would do. A wide hull with a broad transom and hard bilges will have this effect to a very great degree. (It will be very asymmetrical when

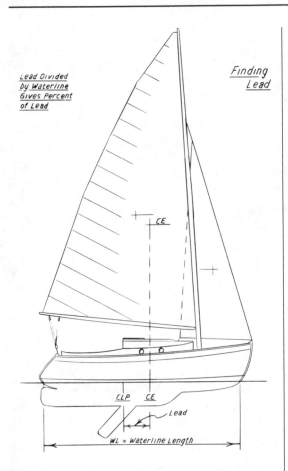

Lead Divided
by Waterline
Gives Percent
of Lead

Finding Lead

CE

CLP   CE

Lead

WL = Waterline Length

ward. Again, for any of the above lead categories, you'd choose from the higher end of the recommended leads for tall-rigged craft and from the lower end for shorter-rigged vessels.

In fact, if all the factors indicated it, you might drop down or go up a bit from the recommended leads. Say your *Galloping Gazelle* was a narrow, slack–bilged, double–ended sloop with a low rig. These factors all indicate that her hull and rig won't generate much additional weather helm due to heel. Thus, for a boat like this you ought to consider using not the 13 percent lead indicated on the low end of the table's recommendations for sloops, but perhaps even 12 percent.

Easy Fixes

If you're not happy with the helm feel on your present boat there are a number of options. One thing that many sailors overlook is that simply changing the way you sheet your sails can alter helm feel. Sheeting the main in too flat, on a sloop, will increase the pressure on that sail and move the wind pressure aft. This is the same as moving the center of effort aft, and it increases weather helm. Accordingly, you could reduce weather helm by sailing with the sheet eased a bit more, and perhaps over-trimming the jib just a mite. The trick is to get the best combination of helm feel and boat speed. Don't worry if your main luffs a trifle at the leach. There's no harm in this if your boat is moving well, and the sails are not actually flogging. Easing the sheets also decreases heel slightly, which decreases hull asymmetry and further contributes to reducing weather helm.

Obviously ketches, yawls, and schooners provide even more opportunities to adjust the effective center of effort by sail trim. For instance, if you wanted to increase weather helm on a ketch you could sheet the mizzen and main as flat as possible, for the wind strength, and ease the headsails some. Similarly—on a sloop or cutter—excessive leach tension cups the after portion of your main, also moving the center of effort aft and increasing helm.

heeled). On the other hand, a narrow double-ender with slack bilges will not be nearly so asymmetrical. Thus, if *Natty Nautilus* were a sloop with a wide hull and hard bilges, you'd be wise to use the larger amount of lead called for in the table to compensate for the additional weather helm generated by the heeled hull shape.

Similarly, a tall rig creates more weather helm than a short one. This is because when the boat is heeled over, the center of the sails is actually way out over the water to leeward. Since the pressure of the wind is—for all intents and purposes—acting at this point, it is as if a giant caught hold of a long lever (the mast) and twisted the boat to wind-

Easing the leach line and sheet can—particularly in combination—make a sizeable difference, reducing weather helm considerably.

The ultimate in helm balance control is found on boats with divided rigs and tandem centerboards, such as the twin-centerboard steel schooner *Papoo* in Chapter 48. On a vessel like this you can adjust helm to exactly suit *any* conditions. For instance, running downwind, *Papoo*'s forward board would be raised and her after board lowered. Her foresail and jib would be flown full-hoist, while her main might be either reefed or furled entirely. Such an arrangement will allow her to run off in confused following seas steadily and surely. Conversely, *Papoo* could heave to with complete certainty dead into the wind by dropping the forward board, raising the after board, dousing the jib and foresail, and sheeting the main in flat (reefed or unreefed.) The intermediate combinations of rig and centerboard arrangements are endless, making such a craft ideal for comfortable voyaging.

Returning to ordinary production craft, if simple adjustments to sheeting and leach tension don't give you the helm feel you're after you can alter mast rake. Raking the mast aft moves the center of effort aft and increases helm, while raking the mast forward will decrease weather helm.

Few production boats will fail to give at least tolerable helm feel using these approaches. If, however, you plan to modify the rig on a boat, taking all the factors above into account will help you strike that delicate balance.

CHAPTER 41

Homemade Self-Steering

I lashed the helm, and my vessel held her course, and while she sailed I slept.

Sailing Alone Around the World, Joshua Slocum

There's nothing quite like a long day's sail—fair winds, clear skies, and lots of time. Pleasant as such a jaunt can be, however, you'll often find yourself wishing for a break. After four or more hours at the helm, well...there are any number of things you might have to take care of. Sometimes you can call for a crewmate to take over; or you could lash the helm and dash through, grabbing that sandwich or what have you. It would be nice, though, if your *Hot Rod* could really steer herself for long periods. You could sit back, a bottle in one hand and a chart in the other, taking in the scenery at your leisure as *Hot Rod* drove herself along.

Notwithstanding Joshua Slocum's *Spray*, just 20 or 30 years ago many sailors still questioned whether or not sailboats could be made to steer themselves effectively. Today, you can buy all sorts of self-steering devices right off the shelf. You have your choice of everything from simple horizontal-axis windvanes to complex servo-pendulum gear to electric autopilots to computers that guide your boat from information received via loran, sat-nav, and GPS. All of these do have one drawback—they cost plenty. You can, however, make your own self-steering system for pennies. In fact, you may very well have everything required on board already. All you need is a snatch block or two (standard blocks will do in a pinch), a few bights of line, and a bit of surgical tubing (bungee chord can be used as a stop-gap).

Most sailors are familiar with wind-vane self-steering gear. Although these rigs are effective, they're complex to install and subject to damage. The homemade self-steering system uses your entire rig as a giant windvane. Not only is your rig, well...always rigged, but you'll be reefing it as necessary anyway. Basically, there are two courses requiring somewhat different setups for our rig—upwind (close reaching to close hauled) and downwind (broad reaching to running).

The Upwind Rig

For upwind courses you have to set your self-steering system so that it pulls your tiller to weather in a puff and lets it fall off in a lull—just as you'd do if you were at the helm. The reason for this is that, in a puff, your boat heels more, which makes her hull more asymmetrical in the water (remember the previous chapter). This requires additional weather helm to keep you on course. The simplest way to do this is to take a line from your main sheet and run it across the boat to a block on the windward side of the cockpit and back down to the tiller. Let's say your *Hearty Hortense* is on the starboard tack (with the wind coming from the starboard side): If the wind freshens, her boom will pay out to port, but as the boom pays out it'll pull on the steering line, which, in turn, will run through the block and haul the tiller to starboard, up—just what we want.

Spring to Leeward

There's one problem here, however. Nothing will prevent *Hearty Hortense*'s tiller from swinging all the way over to starboard (upwind) and staying there. Here's where the surgical tubing comes in. By running the tubing from *Hearty Hortense*'s tiller down to a cleat to port (to lee or downwind) you can create a spring action that resists the pull of the steering line. This also creates the effect you need to control *Hearty Hortense* when the wind decreases. In this situation, the force pulling on the steering line will also decrease, which then allows the elastic tubing to pull the tiller down (to leeward). This naturally corrects for the reduced asymmetry of *Hearty Hortense*'s hull as she comes more upright in the lull. Simply by adjusting the length and tension of the surgical tubing and the length of the steering line, you can adjust your vessel for self-steering in most conditions.

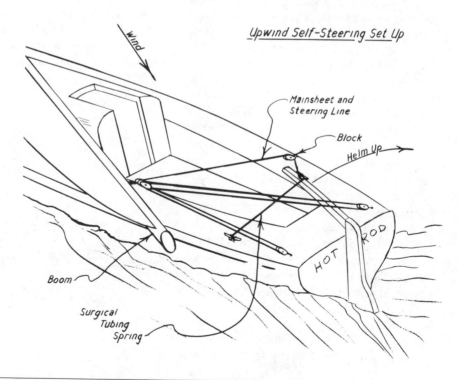

Upwind Self-Steering Set Up

Wind

Mainsheet and Steering Line

Block

Helm Up

HOT ROD

Boom

Surgical Tubing Spring

Fiddling Around

This leads to the one drawback of homemade self-steering—it takes fiddling—sometimes lots of it—to get the adjustment correct. Usually, a couple of afternoons of tinkering will reveal the best set of tensions and lengths for your boat. And once you've got it—you've got it. From then on, you'll be able to set up this gear in a few minutes whenever needed. A good starting place is with the surgical tubing just barely slack when the tiller's amidships. From here, you have two ways to adjust tension. You can shorten the tubing and thus increase tension (while at the same time changing the tiller position at "barely slack"), or you can use heavier tubing or doubled tubing to increase tension without changing the location of "barely slack." Generally, larger boats will do best with heavier or doubled tubing. You may also run into difficulty getting proper adjustment if your mainsheet is used to provide some downward or vanging action. This can cause the tensions on the whole setup to become too large to work well for self-steering. The only way around this is to add a proper and effective vang. If you don't already have a vang installed, though, it's time you got one.

Surgical tubing can be purchased at almost any large pharmacy or surgical supply house. It costs only a few cents a foot (30 cm) and you'll need only four or five feet (1.2 to 1.5 m) at most. Three-eighths-inch-diameter (9 or 10 mm) tubing is a good starting place; however, you may want to get a somewhat larger diameter as well, just in case. Shock or bungee cord doesn't work as well because its springiness is uneven. It will pull very hard at first and then proportionately decrease its pull unevenly. Surgical tubing pulls regularly and is thus much easier to adjust.

Even if you have a store-bought self-steering system, homemade self-steering can be a valuable back-up. Many of the BOC/Globe-Challenge racers, for instance, have been having difficulty with their electric autopilot and (less and less common on these speedsters) their windvane gear—so much

difficulty, in fact, that many boats are carrying as many as six back-up autopilots! This may be fine for a well-financed racer; but you can use homemade gear at less than one-tenth the cost.

The Downwind Rig

So far, we've looked at courses from reaching on up. If, however, you put the helm up and pay your *Hearty Hortense* off, you'll need a new self-steering arrangement. As *Hortense* falls off, the apparent force on her main sheet becomes somewhat less and is thus no longer as effective for steering. Additionally, the main's now less sensitive to wind angle than it was when you were closer winded. The solution's to use the jib sheet as the steering line. In this case, if *Hearty Hortense* has the wind over her starboard quarter, you'd run the jib (or genoa) sheet aft to a snatch block on the port side and back across the cockpit to a block on the starboard side. From here, the jib sheet runs back down to the tiller and becomes the steering line. Just as when sailing upwind, surgical tubing's run from the tiller across to a cleat port.

Now, when *Hearty Hortense* falls off, the jib is blanketed by the main and loses drive. Naturally,

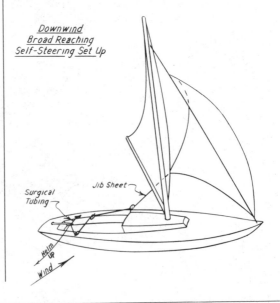

Downwind Broad Reaching Self-Steering Set Up

Surgical Tubing

Jib Sheet

Helm Up

Wind

this eases the jib sheet or steering line and the tubing pulls the helm down, causing *Hearty Hortense* to head up and back on course. If, conversely, *Hearty Hortense* were to head up, the jib would tug harder on its sheet, which in turn pulls on the steering line. This hauls the tiller up and heads *Hearty Hortense* down and back on course.

By using either the upwind main-sheet configuration or the downwind jib-sheet configuration, you'll be able to get your own *Hearty Hortense* to sail herself quite respectably for many hours on just about any course you care to pick. The one course that doesn't work well is dead downwind, especially in light air. The answer's simply to tack downwind. Even if you don't want to stay on a broad reach too long, an hour or two of this will give you plenty of time to relax and take a sandwich break.

Hints and Precautions

It's very important to rig your steering lines and tubing so that you can cast them off pretty durn quick! You never know when you might have to alter course pronto. I've found that a slippery hitch over the cleat does the trick here neatly and, what's more, it makes setting and resetting tension that much easier.

Another useful hint is that you can adjust the amount of pull on the steering line by taking the pull off the mainsheet in various ways. If you've

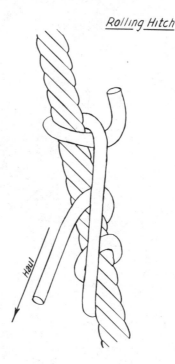

Rolling Hitch

Haul

got a four-part mainsheet and you use the end of the sheet for the steering line, you'll be using only one-fourth of the available force. If, however, you were to clap a rolling hitch around the standing end of the mainsheet (where it attaches directly to the boom) you'd be getting the full force of the wind on the boom to pull directly on the tiller. A rolling hitch on one of the intermediate sheet parts would give you about one-half of the available power. Only experimenting with your boat will tell you what will work best.

Sheet-to-Tiller Steering with a Wheel?

You can even use homemade self-steering on wheel-steering boats. All you need is a spool that you can fasten to the wheel. One half of the spool will accept the line from the steering line and the other half will reel up the surgical tubing spring. The larger the diameter of the spool, the greater the power your system will have; but at the same

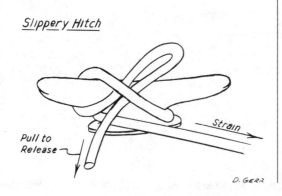

Slippery Hitch

Pull to Release

Strain

D. GERR

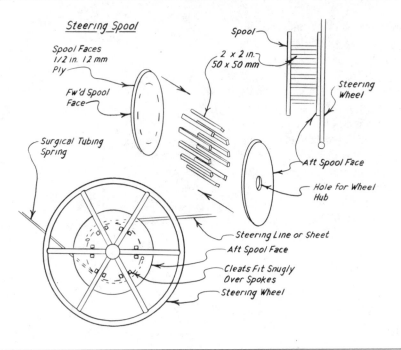

Steering Spool

Spool Faces
1/2 in. 12 mm
Ply

Fw'd Spool
Face

Surgical Tubing
Spring

Spool

2 x 2 in.
50 x 50 mm

Steering
Wheel

Aft Spool Face

Hole for Wheel
Hub

Steering Line or Sheet

Aft Spool Face

Cleats Fit Snugly
Over Spokes

Steering Wheel

The Rice Tensioner

One of the drawbacks to homemade self-steering is the amount of fiddling—tying, untying, retying—while adjusting for proper tubing and sheet tension. Shortly after I'd written about the homemade self-steering system, Charles Rice sent in the neat fix he'd cooked up, pictured here. By replacing the simple surgical tubing strand (or strands) with the rice tensioner, you can immediately and quickly adjust length and tension to suit. You can even add another version of the rice tensioner to the sheet side—without surgical tubing—to adjust that side of the rig. The only drawbacks: a few extra bits of hardware and the need for a bit more cockpit width.

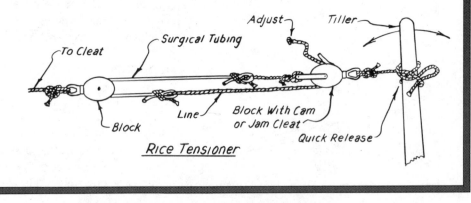

Adjust

Tiller

Surgical Tubing

To Cleat

Block

Line

Block With Cam
or Jam Cleat

Quick Release

Rice Tensioner

time, changes will be in smaller increments. If you're happy with the helm feel of your steering system, try a spool about 40 percent of the outside diameter of your wheel.

If you decide that you want to rig your self-steering system permanently you can make up a nicely finished spool. For most purposes a few feet (a meter or so) of 2 by 2 (50 mm by 50 mm) and a few square feet (half a square meter) of ½-inch (12 mm) marine ply will make a serviceable steering spool.

For a 24-inch (60 cm) wheel, cut two 12-inch (30 cm) circles out of the ply and draw a 10-inch-diameter (25 cm) circle on one side of each one. Then cut a 2 by 2 (50 mm by 50 mm) into ten 9-inch (22 cm) lengths. Screw-fasten the 2 by 2s (50 mm by 50 mm) at equal spaces (every 36 degrees) around the 10-inch (25 cm) circle on one ply face, and then attach the other face to the opposite end of the 2 by 2s. Voilà, you have a spool.

Strengthen the works with three ¼-inch (6 mm) through-bolts, from one ply face to the other, at about 9-inch (22 cm) diameter. Now, cut out a hole in one ply face to fit neatly around the wheel hub and add six or eight small wooden cleats on the aft side of this face to just bracket the spokes. All that remains is to fasten the steering spool to the wheel. You can use some low-stretch line and a couple of cleats. Of course, you'll want to sand and paint the whole contraption.

If you provide a couple of fastening points for both the surgical tubing and the steering line, you can use the homemade self-steering system just as if you had tiller steering. Simply attach the tubing and lines to the spool so that they pull the wheel in the proper direction (the opposite of a tiller) and play with the adjustments until it feels right.

All this will get you well started on homemade self-steering. If you want to dive even deeper into the business, try Dr. John S. Letcher's book *Self-Steering for Sailing Craft,* published by International Marine Publishing Co. Dr. Letcher explains in detail just about every kind of self-steering apparatus you could imagine.

CHAPTER 42

Miracle Rope!

'Ropes indeed!' answered the Elf from the boats. 'Never travel far without a rope! And one that is long and strong and light. Such as these. . . .'

The Fellowship of The Ring, J.R.R. Tolkien

Stretch—the sailor's constant foe. In order to extract power from the wind, you have to hold something up to catch it. But the wind has other ideas; it tries its best to blow it away or knock it down. In response, the ever resourceful sailor lashes his wind-catcher in place at every imaginable spot— the corners, along the top, the bottom, the leading edge, even in the middle. Depending on the rig, nearly everything you could think of has been employed: block and tackle mounted on block in tackle have been lead to capstans where an entire crew could haul a stay tight. Ropes were parceled, served, and tarred. Even chain's been utilized— though I'm glad I haven't been shipmates with one of those arrangements!

Still, in spite of all ingenuity, the durn ropes (not to mention the sails) stretched. In the great age of sail you'd lash everything good and tight, and a few hours of heavy weather later the whole rig would be slacking off again. Even worse, the rigging would slack off when wet and harden up when dry. Of course, if you were content to blow downwind only, this wasn't too bad. (It wasn't too good either.) But if you wanted to work upwind, well, the only way to get anywhere was to keep things well hardened up! Even today the old-time shellback's frustration is remembered; when someone is accused of "slacking off" at work it's a memory of these long gone sailors' travails.

For over 3,000 years seafarers had only a few natural rope fibers available—flax, hemp, jute, cotton. In fact, it was a mere hundred or so years ago that wire rope was introduced and became the material of choice for applications requiring low stretch. For the first time *ever,* the jacktar could tighten up his rigging and keep it that way. Then, suddenly—by the grace of chemical giants like DuPont—nylon, Dacron, and Kevlar were introduced. In only the past few decades, these manmade fibers revolutionized sailing. Dacron's now just about the only material used for sheets and rope halyards. After all, the stuff just doesn't rot. Can you imagine what sailing was like when

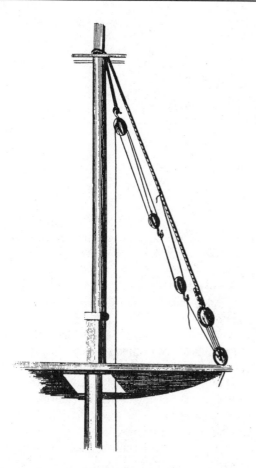

The way it used to be—block and tackle, set on block and tackle, down to the deck and then to the capstan. You could get things pretty tight to start with this way, but—with natural fiber rope—there was no way to keep them taut.

you had to make sure that your rope was dry and well aired before you stowed it or it would literally decay to nothing?

Stretch

Unfortunately Dacron, and particularly nylon, didn't do a great deal for the stretch problem. Both stretch considerably under load. Even the lowest-stretch Dacron stretches a great deal more than does wire rope of the same ultimate strength. Accordingly, standing rigging, halyards, running backstays and such (lines that require low stretch for good sail set and control) have best been made of wire. Of course, wire's a pain in the neck. It's difficult to splice and terribly hard on your hands and gear. Recently, it seemed that Kevlar would come to the rescue. Here at last was a relatively soft rope with truly low stretch.

Kevlar Lets Us Down

Kevlar does have 10 times the strength of steel for the same weight and very low stretch (comparable to steel), but Kevlar's quite expensive, and what's worse, it abrades and cuts itself very easily. In a short time Kevlar can lose a significant portion of its strength to this internal abrasion. Thus Kevlar has a relatively low life-expectancy and must be run over specially grooved sheaves of larger than normal diameter to keep it from failing. Also—though easier on your hands than wire—it's still hard, stiff, and difficult to work.

Spectra to the Rescue

The true miracle material has arrived, however. It's called Spectra, and it's produced by Allied/Signal Corporation. Spectra's not quite as strong as Kevlar. It's merely six times stronger than steel! Steel has a tensile strength of 60,000 pounds per square inch (4,220 kg/cm^2) while Spectra 900 has a tensile strength of 375,000 pounds per square inch (26,360 kg/cm^2). The wonderful thing about Spectra, when used for rope or rope cores, is that it has extremely high abrasion resistance and a long life expectancy under heavy loads and tight bends. It doesn't have to be babied like Kevlar. Even better, Spectra rope has elongation characteristics that equal 7x19 steel wire! And, as if all this weren't enough, Spectra rope has a very pleasant "hand." This means that Spectra line feels nice to the touch. It is fairly soft and supple. It bends and coils easily and is no more difficult to splice than any normal braided line. By contrast, Kevlar line and such low-stretch and prestretched rope as StaySet-X are often particularly uncomfortable to handle.

Currently, Spectra rope's available from Samson Ocean Systems (Samson Rope) as XLS-900 and XLS-800. It is also available from New England Ropes as StaySet-X90 and from Yale Cordage as Maxi Braid Plus, Maxi Braid, and Yale Light. Samson's XLS-900 has a pure Spectra core while XLS-800 has a combined Spectra and aramid core. Both have a Duron polyester braided cover. For most cruisers and cruiser/racers, the XLS-800, which is considerably less expensive than the XLS-900, is more than adequate. You can see the strength and elongation properties of these ropes at various diameters in the chart; however, as a rough guide, Spectra XLS-800 has about the same strength as 7x19 wire rope of one-half the diameter, and the Spectra has about the same stretch! What's more, it weighs considerably less! Actually, Yale Cordage's Maxi Braid isn't just cored with Spectra, it's pure Spectra braid through and through. This rope is so strong that it approaches the strength *and* stretch of wire of the same diameter!

Chuck Your Wire

This means that—for running rigging—you can replace all your wire halyards and runners with XLS-800 or 900, or the equivalent. You won't suffer one ounce of loss in performance. In fact, since the Spectra line will weigh less than the wire, you'll actually improve performance. You'll never again have to worry about wire cuts and meat hooks (those nasty burrs that so often tear your hands and sails).

If you're one of those cruising types who've been using Dacron rope halyards, now's the time to switch to the "high-tech" stuff. Replacing all the halyards on a 30-footer (9 m) with Spectra will usually cost less than a few good dinners on the town, and will give you the same performance and control capabilities as the top racers. Since Spectra's

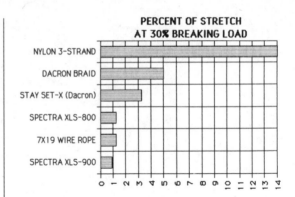

so easy on you and your gear, you don't have an excuse any more. Remember also that since Spectra's so much stronger you can go down a size or more from the rope you were using and still get far less stretch (see Chapter 39). This helps keep the cost down considerably.

Of course, Spectra rope's excellent for almost every application. Outhauls, vangs, cunninghams, sheets, all will yield better control if they are made of Spectra rope. If fact, if you do any racing at all, you'll notice the difference immediately. Actually, some of the new Mylar and Mylar/Dacron sails have so little stretch themselves that, without wire or Spectra control lines and halyards, they will stretch their halyards enough in a puff to harm their set. In one case, a cruiser replaced his old Dacron main with a Mylar/Spectra one. (Spectra's good for sails too.) This fellow had been using prestretched Dacron halyards. They'd been, well, adequate before, but the low-stretch sail put such a strain on the halyard and the Dacron outhaul that you could see them elongate visibly in every puff, and watch wrinkles pucker in and out of the sail. Switching to Spectra halyards cured the problem completely. Even better, it allowed the new sails to develop their full power. Instead of wasting all that energy in stretching Dacron, the full energy of every puff was converted into driving power. You could feel the old girl heel, feather up, and take off!

Comparing Ropes

In comparing rope strengths you should look at two characteristics. One is the strength for a given diameter. This is pretty straightforward and easy to read right off any table. The other aspect to study is elongation or stretch. Most ropes are used at around 30 percent of their breaking strength. Thus, if you have 1/4-inch-diameter (6.3 mm) braided Dacron line with a breaking strength of 1,400 pounds (635 kg) its operating or working load will be around 420 pounds (190 kg)—0.3 × 1,400 lb. = 420 lb., or 635 kg × 0.3 = 190 kg. The key in comparing stretch, then, is to compare how much different ropes stretch at around 30 percent of their breaking strength. Now, stretch is measured in percent of elongation at a given load after so many cycles. Or—in plain english—if you've got a rope that stretches 5 percent at 30 percent load after 50 cycles, you know that this rope will stretch to become 5 percent longer than it was to start with, after it is pulled on with 30 percent of its total rated strength 50 times.

Spectra Looks Good

Using the elongation figures for various ropes you can quickly get a feel for how incredible Spectra is. Seven × 19 flexible wire rope has an elongation of barely 1¼ percent at 30 percent load. Nylon rope elongates a whopping 10 to 15 percent at the same 30 percent of load—almost ten times more! Ordinary braided Dacron line, say, Samson Trophy Braid, stretches 5 percent at 30 percent load. Even the best ultra-low-stretch Dacron elongates a full 3¼ percent at 30 percent load, or nearly 3 times more than wire—not good at all. Samson's Spectra XLS-800, however, elongates only 1¼ percent at 30 percent load—exactly the same as wire! Samson's Spectra XLS-900 actually stretches *less* than some wires. It comes in, astoundingly, at under 1 percent of stretch at 30 per-

WIRE AND ROPE BREAKING STRENGTHS-LB.

	Diameter						
	3/16	1/4	5/16	3/8	7/16	1/2	5/8
Spectra XLS-900	1,900	3,400	5,700	6,900	11,400	12,700	22,900
Spectra XLS-800	1,600	3,000	4,850	6,000	9,700	10,800	19,500
7 × 19 Wire	3,900	6,600	8,200	12,000	16,000		
Dacron Braid	1,150	1,400	2,000	3,000	4,000	6,000	10,000

HALYARD REPLACEMENT CHART

	Boat Size				
	To 22 Ft.		23 to 32 Ft.		32 to 42 Ft.
Wire Diameter	3/32	1/8	5/32	3/16	7/32
Wire Strength	1000	1900	2600	3900	5200
Replace With					
Spectra XLS-900	3/16	3/16	1/4	5/16	5/16
Spectra XLS-800	3/16	3/16	1/4	5/16	3/8

WIRE AND ROPE BREAKING STRENGTHS – KG

	Diameter						
	4.7 mm	6.3 mm	8 mm	9.5 mm	11 mm	13 mm	16 mm
Spectra XLS-900	860	1540	2590	6,900	3130	5770	10400
Spectra XLS-800	720	1360	2200	2720	4400	4900	8860
7 × 19 Wire	1770	3000	3720	5450	7270		
Dacron Braid	520	630	900	1360	1810	2720	4540

HALYARD REPLACEMENT CHART

	Boat Size				
	To 7 m		7 to 10 m		10 to 13 m
Wire Diameter	2.4 mm	3.1 mm	3.9 mm	4.7 mm	5.5 mm
Wire Strength	454 kg	860 kg	1180 kg	1770 kg	2360 kg
Replace With					
Spectra XLS-900	4.7 mm	4.7 mm	6.3 mm	7.9 mm	7.9 mm
Spectra XLS-800	4.7 mm	4.7 mm	6.3 mm	7.9 mm	9.5 mm

cent load. Spectra-cored ropes from other manufacturers have similar properties.

The Future

It's almost frightening to think that materials like Spectra are still nearly 10 times weaker than the theoretical maximum strength obtainable from molecular bonds (remember chemistry—electrons, shells, and all that). I mean, what are the chemists going to come up with next—a fiber that's so strong that you could have halyards no thicker than threads?

PART 10

You Built Her of What!?: Construction for Everyone

Sublime in its enormous bulk,
Loomed aloft the shadowy hulk!
And around it columns of smoke,
upwreathing,
Rose from the boiling, bubbling,
seething
Caldron, that glowed
And overflowed
With the black tar, heated for the
sheathing.
And amid the clamors
Of chattering hammers,
He who listened heard now and then
The song of the master and his men:—

The Building of the Ship,
Henry Wadsworth Longfellow

CHAPTER 43

Even From Cheese Whiz (Almost)

We were an hour on our tour, mostly climbing over obstacles and avoiding paintwork, but examining every discoverable corner and going over the ground from bridge to magazine and fore-peak to tiller flat: We liked the look of her, though she was more like an unfinished factory than a ship.

H.M. Corvette, Nicholas Monsarrat

These days, it's not uncommon to hear of first one material and then another being touted as the best material from which to build a boat. Other materials are heralded as the simplest or the cheapest, or as breakthrough products that have so revolutionized boatbuilding that all boats will be different from now on.

Well, I don't place much stock in all this. Sometimes this kind of talk is generated by someone who genuinely believes that the material he or she is touting really is *the* best. In these instances, I suspect their experience is a bit limited. At other times, this sort of talk is advertising hype from some manufacturer or yard that is—quite naturally—intent on convincing you that its approach and material is the finest available.

Cheese Whiz

Actually, almost all the traditional materials and most of the new materials and approaches can yield a superior vessel if both the designer and the builder understand the structure they're working with. This is the key. Any boat, whether it's of the most advanced construction techniques and materials or of the oldest tried-and-true methods, can be a disaster if the designer and builder don't understand what they're working with. On the other hand, if the designer and builder both understand their chosen construction method, they can produce an excellent vessel out of almost anything— even Cheez-Whiz would nearly do the job.

The Big Three

Basically, there are just three standard materials suitable for boatbuilding: *fiberglass* and the modern *laminates* (including Kevlar and graphite fibers); *wood* (traditional and glued-epoxy); and *metal* (aluminum, steel, and some special metals). You can use many approaches and even combine two or three materials in the same vessel, but this is about it. Now, I'm sure there are a few ferrocement fans reading this; however, ferro's one of the few materials I don't recommend. I'll go into the whys of this in a bit.

Fiberglass

Once upon a time, wood reigned supreme as *the* material for boatbuilding. Today, you'd be about as likely to find a production builder using wood as a factory turning out Model-T Fords. Fiberglass, or one of its many variant laminates, is king. There are numerous reasons for this. First and foremost, fiberglass lends itself very well to mass production with largely unskilled or semi-skilled labor. Second, fiberglass is almost totally inert in the marine environment. FRP just seems to last and last. True, when not maintained, gelcoats may chalk and fittings corrode. Nevertheless, this is essentially superficial damage. The basic glass hull and deck structure—if correctly engineered and constructed to begin with—will remain sound even after years of neglect.

In spite of its absolutely overwhelming popularity, however, fiberglass does have a few major drawbacks. First, aesthetically it lacks the warmth and appeal of wood. It's also unpleasant and nasty stuff to work with. One naval architect likened fiberglass boats to "frozen snot," and another characterized working with glass as "wrestling with eels in tubs of slime." Second, fiberglass has one of the *lowest* stiffness-to-weight ratios of any boatbuilding material. In engineering jargon, its flexural modulus is very low. Since stiffness is one of the most important characteristics of any small boat hull, FRP craft often end up quite heavy (contrary to popular belief). This is because solid glass weighs about 94 pounds per cubic foot (1,504 kg/ m³), as opposed to, say, mahogany's 35 pounds per cubic foot (560 kg/m³)—and the mahogany's considerably stiffer! Accordingly, ordinary glass construction often produces vessels with flexing problems like decks that spring up and down when you walk on them. The builder's trying to save weight (and, not incidentally, cost) by reducing skin thickness.

As we'll see, there are excellent ways to get around fiberglass's structural and aesthetic drawbacks, though. Careful styling and the judicious use of wood trim can eliminate the cold, icebox appearance of fiberglass and produce a very handsome craft. Although they're rarer than they should be, there are a few glass craft that give one the feel of a wood boat. Structurally, the use of various core materials can drastically increase the stiffness of the hull skin. Engineers call this "increasing the section modulus" (catchy). The nice thing about this is that the increase in stiffness comes without much additional weight. Foam, balsa, or even solid wood are all used successfully as core materials. A vessel properly designed and constructed using high-quality cores such as Airex foam can be incredibly strong and light.

Actually, the true "fiberglass" boat may soon be a thing of the past. Technically, "fiberglass" is GRP, or glass-reinforced plastic. Modern designers and builders, however, are now employing such materials as Kevlar (which is not glass) and epoxy rather than the traditional polyester resins. Graphite fibers (not glass either) are even stiffer than Kevlar, and a graphite fiber hull laid up in vinylester or epoxy resin is one of the lightest and strongest structures known to man. In fact, this sort of technology's exactly the same as that used on high-performance fighter plane wings and spacecraft components.

Of course, there's one other great advantage to fiberglass construction—your hull shape's limited only by your imagination. Unlike wood or metal, you can produce highly convoluted and curved parts in glass with relative ease. You can even mass produce such parts economically.

Wood

My personal favorite boatbuilding material is wood. This is for a number of complex reasons. First, aesthetically, wood has a kind of warmth to it, a sort of tactile and visual appeal that no other material possesses. Very few things are as satisfying as the sight of a nicely proportioned sailboat or runabout with varnished topsides and trim. Second, structurally, wood has one of the highest stiffness-to-weight ratios of any material available. It certainly has the highest stiffness-to-weight ratio at moderate cost. All the modern fibers, such as Kevlar and graphite, are quite expensive and unpleasant and difficult to work with when compared to wood.

Wood's great disadvantage is that it decays or rots in the marine environment. Even with this drawback, most boats were made of wood until quite recently, and they still managed to give long and reliable service. In fact, many fisherman still prefer traditional wood-hull craft. They find that—with proper maintenance—these vessels last longer than steel-hulled vessels. The advent of modern marine epoxies, however, has made the wood-epoxy composite boat hard to beat, particularly for custom work. The epoxy-saturated wood's not only stronger than the unsaturated wood, but it's water-vapor impermeable. Basically, wood so treated can't rot. The air and water needed to promote and maintain decay just doesn't get to the wood. At the present level of technology it would be very difficult to build a stronger, lighter, more maintenance-free and attractive vessel than with wood-epoxy composite construction.

There are more ways to go about building a wood-epoxy boat than I could conveniently describe here. Some of the most common are: cold molding (to which there are many different approaches), strip planking, hard-chine plywood, and epoxy-glued lapstrake. Each of these methods has its own advantages and disadvantages. Some are more suited to certain types of boats; others have wider applications. The little-known wood-epoxy lapstrake construction, for instance, is one of the lightest and most beautiful ways to build a boat. Unfortunately, it is also quite expensive, particularly if natural planks and not plywood planks are used.

Even with the advantages of epoxy saturation, though, smaller vessels such as dories, canoes, and guide boats can be built in the old tried-and-true traditional methods without epoxy. Such craft are extremely attractive, long lived, and (if built by a knowledgeable builder) not expensive. To my mind, though, it doesn't make sense to build a large vessel in wood of traditional construction (without epoxy). With their enclosed spaces to trap condensation (fresh water is the worst enemy of traditional wood boats), these craft are guaranteed to begin to rot out in 10 or 15 years. Their value declines and the cost of maintaining them goes up. If the same boat had been constructed with epoxy saturation, its rot resistance and longevity would compare well with fiberglass.

We're not likely to see many wood boats around in the future, however. This isn't because there is anything wrong with wood—far from it. Wood just doesn't lend itself well to mass production (compared to fiberglass, anyway). Since most of us will be buying production boats, they're likely to be of glass.

Steel

If any boatbuilding material doesn't get its just due, it's steel. True, it does have a few disadvantages. One is that it's difficult to build a boat much under 35 feet (10 m) long in steel without making it excessively heavy (although it can and has been done). Another is that steel's expensive to form into compound curvature for a round-bilge hull. Still another is that steel rusts and corrodes.

Nevertheless, steel has some tremendous advantages. One is its almost unbelievable strength and resistance to abrasion and impact. A small boat built of steel is as close to truly indestructible as it's possible to get. Steel vessels have pounded for hours on the rocks in heavy seas and sailed away later under their own "steam." In fact, for a hard-pushed workboat or a vessel expected to take really punishing conditions off soundings, I would recommend steel for reasons of strength alone. Steel's also one of the least expensive materials you can build a boat out of, and it can be worked by welders anywhere in the world. This makes it easy and inexpensive to repair, even in out-of-the-way places. Also, steel can be quite easy to build in, if the design's not round bottom. A vee-bottom or multi-chine vessel can be formed up quite easily by anyone with ordinary welding skills. By using radiused chines and with the aid of a good eye, a designer can make such craft quite beautiful.

In addition, steel's disadvantages can largely be overcome. The proper preparation and treatment of the hull—spraying with hot zinc, for instance—can virtually eliminate and certainly control corrosion and rusting. Careful design can reduce weight, and an experienced builder can produce a very nice, fair, round-bilge steel hull (though the skilled labor required for this somewhat offsets steel's cost advantage).

Aluminum

Most large custom yachts and many first-class workboats are constructed of aluminum these days. This is because aluminum has many of the advantages of steel without some of steel's disadvantages. Aluminum's not as strong as steel; however, because it is lighter, you can build a structure that is just as strong at less weight. In addition, marine aluminum does not "rust" at all, and galvanic corrosion can be fairly well controlled. Further, aluminum's easier to form into a compound-curvature or round-bilge hull. In fact, you can cut marine aluminum with ordinary woodworking sabersaws and bandsaws and form compound curvature with an ordinary hydraulic jack and jig. Though not as hard as steel, aluminum also has tremendous impact and abrasion resistance. This is clearly seen in the way aluminum canoes and runabouts are treated. These boats are routinely run up on rocks and dragged along concrete launching ramps without serious damage. Any dents and dings that do occur can usually be hammered right out.

Even though it doesn't lend itself easily to mass production, aluminum's such a superb material that there are a fair number of production or semi-production aluminum boats available. Additionally, there are also the thousands of stamped-out aluminum canoes and skiffs—the indomitable and indestructible workhorses on nearly every lake and stream in the country.

Unfortunately, aluminum's costly compared to other boatbuilding materials. Also, it can be properly worked only with gas-shielded welding (either MIG or TIG), which requires more complex equipment and skilled welders—neither is cheap. Accordingly, although I've designed a number of vessels in aluminum, I recommend it either for production runs, in which the cost of labor and materials can be spread out and reduced, or for luxury yachts. Of course, this is not a hard and fast rule; some builders have learned MIG welding in a jiffy and have not found the cost of this equipment excessive. Any time light weight combined with toughness and strength are required, aluminum is the material of choice. In fact, if aluminum only had the warmth of wood construction I'd say that it was the perfect boatbuilding material.

The Perfect Marine Metal

Bronze is, and has been for 3,000 years, the finest material in existence for making marine hardware. It is a shame that there's so much aluminum and steel hardware on the market and so little bronze. Bronze is both fantastically strong and resilient and superbly resistant to corrosion in the marine environment. Some high-quality marine bronzes are as strong as steel; others are almost as strong as stainless steel. Aluminum doesn't even come close for this use. What's more, bronze can be worked far more easily than steel or stainless steel and thus formed into lighter, more efficient shapes. Additionally, bronze has a warm golden glow that no other material can approach. If any metal could be said to be warm and appealing, it's bronze.

I was pleased to see that many of the custom fittings on the 90-plus-foot (28 m), cold-molded *Whitefin* were of bronze. I was astonished and dismayed to read a description of this superb vessel in a major sailing magazine that called these bronze fittings "old fashioned and dated in appearance." Not only were these fittings actually quite attractive, but they were almost certainly lighter, stronger, and more efficiently shaped than stainless steel or aluminum counterparts could have been.

The only time to be wary of bronze fittings is on a steel or aluminum boat, where galvanic corrosion's a problem. Otherwise, there is just no better way to go. If you don't like to polish or if you like white-metal fittings, get chrome-plated bronze—now that's Bristol fashion.

Ferrocement

Where steel doesn't seem to get its just due, ferrocement has been touted as the most splendiferous discovery since the Pharohs shipped building blocks down the Nile. Ferro has been particularly attractive to the home builder. It's called cheap, easy to use, and strong. In fact, ferro advocates often claim that ferrocement's as strong as steel, requires no skill and is, at the same time, absolutely the cheapest of building materials.

Unfortunately, although ferro appears cheap in terms of materials, by the time you have added the cost of the skilled labor required to plaster up a fair hull, it is not nearly so cheap at all. Further, constructing the armature, on which the cement is plastered, is an unbelievably time-consuming and laborious task. Imagine yourself facing the wire armature of a 30-footer (9 m). Its broad expanse of surface (over 520 square feet or 48 m²) will stretch out imposingly before you. In order to get the armature tight you have to snug it together

every few inches (10 cm) or less. You'd be facing the individual hand tightening of over 7,000 tiny wires or ties. If you fail to get the armature tightened up *really* well with these ties, the cement shell will end up too thick and the hull will be, quite literally, tons overweight. Actually, little can be done to make a ferrocement hull truly light. These boats are almost invariably much heavier than they should be. What's more, ferrocement has some insidious corrosion problems.

Salt water and oxygen can leach into the cement shell and get to the steel armature. This causes the steel to rust. Since the rust is roughly 16 times the volume of the unoxidized metal, it tends to burst the cement outward and form internal cracks. This problem can develop slowly and not show itself outside for years—until, that is, you really need the strength in severe conditions. Then, when you're counting on it most, the shell can suddenly fail catastrophically.

Of course, there are ways to minimize these problems. As always, if the builder and the designer fully understand the material they are working with, they *definitely can* produce a rugged, long-lasting, high-quality ferrocement boat. Good professional plasterers can produce beautifully fair hulls. Great attention to detail will keep weight down, and the proper additives greatly minimize corrosion. By the time you've done all this, however, you're right back to the cost and labor involved in producing a boat of one of the more common materials, so why bother?

Mixing 'em Up

It's possible to produce very fine vessels using a combination of materials. This is called composite construction. A wood-epoxy boat with bronze floors and knees would be a composite wood and metal vessel. Such a craft could be beautiful, light, and strong indeed. The possibilities are endless. Many lightweight racing sailboats are using extensive aluminum framing to stiffen their light, flexible fiberglass hull shells. Of course you can run into problems. One of the earliest attempts at lightweight metal construction was on *Independence*, a B.B. Crowinshield design. She had a bronze underbody, aluminum topsides, and steel frames. As a result of galvanic corrosion her rivets were so weakened that she would spit them out under sail. Must have been exciting! *Beware!* Don't mix copper alloy and aluminum or ferrous metals, especially below the waterline.

Copper-Nickel

Now, there is one construction material that may truly be the very finest for building boats—at least vessels over 45 feet (14 m) or so. This is copper-nickel. Copper-nickel's very similar in strength and weight to ordinary mild steel. It is thus incredibly tough and rugged. Unlike steel, though, copper-nickel doesn't rust at all. The really incredible thing about copper-nickel is that it requires no bottom paint—ever. It's almost completely and totally nonfouling—forever! In fact, if you didn't want to, you wouldn't have to paint any part of a copper-nickel boat—not ever! Of course, there must be some reason that you aren't completely surrounded by copper-nickel boats, and there is one. They cost dearly. Copper-nickel's expensive, considerably more expensive than even the best aluminum construction. Even so, a few commercial vessels—largely fishing and tug boats—have been built of copper-nickel. The savings in fuel and bottom-cleaning charges (from having a clean bottom *all* the time) can make it worth their while.

CHAPTER 44

Scantling* Rules of Thumb: Estimating Structure and Weight

A safe structure will be one whose weakest link is never overloaded. . . .

To Engineer is Human, Henry Petroski

(Scantlings, in case you're wondering, are the sizes, shapes, and weights of the structural components of a hull.)

Though by now we've seen different, at first glance boats can appear deceptively simple. Floating serenely at their moorings, you might scarcely stop to consider all the factors that interrelate to make them work. Scratch this surface, though, and you're quickly inundated by a morass of calculation—volume, center of gravity, power, and so on. What's worse, all these confounded factors interrelate and affect each other. No sooner have you got a handle on one aspect than you find that the change you were contemplating has affected everything else so much you're back to square one, but facing in a different direction.

Luckily, both you and your naval architect have an easy way to do all sorts of estimating without firing up the old IBM mainframe. Using tried and true rules of thumb and simple formulas, you can answer all manner of questions about your boat, whether you're planning a modification or repair or contemplating a new boat altogether.

Figuring Surfaces

One of the most common problems is estimating your hull's surface area. Not only will this help you figure how much paint you have to buy, but—as we'll see in a bit—you can even use this information to make a fair estimate of hull weight.

DECK AREA = Beam × LOA × 0.75—pretty close. If you have a trunk cabin you can simply add in the area of the cabin sides, plus its front and back, and for a a cockpit well, the area of the well sides.

TOPSIDES AREA = (LOA + LWL) ÷ 2 ×
Freeboard at bow × 0.85 × 2 (for both sides)

HULL UNDERBODY = LWL × WLbeam × 0.82. If you don't know the waterline beam, just take 95 percent of the overall beam. This is usually close to the mark. Sailboats with fin keels and power cruisers with large skegs, keels, or both have to have those areas added, as well as the area of the rudder, when estimating wetted surface—the area you have to paint. (Multiplying their average height by their average length and multiplying by 2—for both sides—will produce a reasonable estimate.)

Construction—How Heavy?

It's handy to be able to estimate how heavily a boat is constructed. Is her planking heavy enough? What thickness of fiberglass laminate is about right for that 30-footer (9 m) you've been admiring. Is she adequately strong or too flimsy?

Wood Planking

A very simple rule for estimating he total thickness of hull planking for a wooden boat (whether she's plank-on-frame or modern cold molded) is as follows:

Plank Thickness in inches =

$$\frac{\sqrt{LOA\ (ft.)} + Beam\ (ft.)}{16}$$

Plank Thickness in mm =
$$[\sqrt{LOA\ (m)} \times 3.28 + (Beam\ (m) \times 3.28) \times 1.58]$$

Deck planking—usually plywood—is about 75 percent of the plank thickness.

Say your *Buoyant Baby*'s 35 feet (10.6 m) LOA, 30 feet (9.1 m)WL, and 11 feet (3.3 m) beam, then her planking should be about 1 inch (26 mm) thick [square root of 35 ft. = 5.92, and (5.92 + 11) ÷ 16 = 1.06 inches—or, 10.6 m × 3.28 = 34.7, square root of 34.7 = 5.89, and 5.89 + (3.3 × 3.28) × 1.58 = 26.4 mm].

If *Buoyant Baby* were planked with a particularly hard, strong wood like teak, she might get by quite well with 7/8-inch (22 mm) plank; in a soft wood like cedar, she'd probably want 1 1/8-inch (29 mm) plank. Further, if *Buoyant Baby* were a heavy boat you'd expect to use planking a bit heavier; conversely, if she were a lightweight, you'd use planking a trifle lighter. *Buoyant Baby*'s deck would be 3/4-inch (18 mm) plywood. Cold-

molded boats can do well with planking 85 to 90 percent as thick as indicated by this method. With a little common sense, this very quick calculation will put you very close to the required plank thickness for almost every ordinary type of vessel.

Wood Framing

The basic structural framing for wood hulls can be estimated as follows:

Transverse frame (standard frames) spacing
= LOA ÷ 34

Frame thickness (athwartships)
= plank thickness × 1.5

Frame siding (fore-and-aft dimension)
= 1.34 × frame thickness

Keel and Stem cross-sectional area
= 12.5 × plank thickness squared, or more

On the 35-foot (10.6 m) *Buoyant Baby*, frames would be spaced 12 to 12½ inches (30 cm) apart, and would be 1½ inches (38 mm) thick by 2 inches (50 mm) fore-and-aft. Her keel should be hewn from timbers or laminated up to have a cross-sectional area not less than 12.5 square inches (80 cm²).

Fiberglass Laminates

For solid FRP hulls there's an even simpler rule of thumb:

$$Skin\ Thickness\ (inches) = 0.07 + \frac{WL\ (feet)}{150}$$

$$Skin\ Thickness\ (millimeters) = 1.8 + \frac{WL\ (meters)}{1.8}$$

with the thickness of the upper topsides about 85 percent of this, and the thickness from the waterline down about 115 percent of this (15 percent greater). In addition, you should increase thickness 1 percent for each knot of boat speed over 10 knots.

If, for instance, we decided to make a fiberglass version of *Buoyant Baby*, we'd get $9/32$-inch (7 mm) laminate from the waterline to about halfway up the topsides, $1/4$-inch (6 mm) laminate for the upper topsides, and $5/16$-inch (8 mm) laminate for the bottom—from the waterline down.

[30 feet WL ÷ 150 = 0.2 inches, and 0.2 inches + 0.07 inches = 0.27 inches; 0.27 inches is about $9/32$ inch thick, and 85 percent of this gives $1/4$ inch for the upper topsides, with 115 percent of 0.27 inches producing $5/16$ inch for the bottom.

Or

9.1 m WL ÷ 1.8 = 5.0 mm, and 5.0 mm + 1.8 mm = 6.8 mm—use 7 mm. Eighty-five percent of this gives 6 mm for the upper topsides, with 115 percent of 6.8 mm producing 8 mm for the bottom.]

This would be for a displacement hull, with a top speed under 10 knots. If *Buoyant Baby* were, say, a 22-knot planing hull, we'd increase the thickness by 12 percent. [22 knots - 10 knots = 12 knots. Add 1 percent per knot over 10 knots or add 12 percent.] The 22-knot *Buoyant Baby* would thus have $9/32$-inch (7 mm) upper topsides, $5/16$-inch (8 mm) middle topsides, and $11/32$-inch (8.7 mm) bottom.

FRP Stiffeners Are Critical

The above rule assumes that the hull has a sufficient number of stringers and bulkheads to produce the necessary stiffness. Usually a series of longitudinal stringers (as described in the next chapter) combined with these skin thicknesses will produce a fairly rugged and reliable hull. There should be five longitudinal stringers about evenly spaced on each side of the inside of the hull, and *at least* five structural bulkheads (more is better) about evenly spaced throughout the length of the hull.

The middle stringer is at the turn of the bilge; two stringers should be run about equally spaced along the inside of the topsides between the bilge and the sheer; and two lower stringers should lie about equally spaced between the centerline or keel and the turn of the bilge. Hard chine craft can omit the middle stringer and simply use a reinforcement at the chine. On powerboats, the necessary engine-bed stringers can take the place of the bottom stringers. (See Chapter 27 for engine-bed stringer proportions.)

Of course, for a proper design job, a naval architect will run detailed structural analysis for the laminate schedule; however—like many rules of thumb—the answers from this simple approach are often quite accurate. You can even take this method one step further and estimate the required thickness for a foam-sandwich or balsa-core hull:

Fiberglass Sandwich Construction

Simply take the thickness for a single-skin fiberglass craft as found above and multiply as follows:

Core = 2.2 times single-skin thickness

Outer Skin = 0.4 times single-skin thickness

Inner Skin = 0.3 times single-skin thickness

In the case of *Buoyant Baby* we'd get:

Core = $9/32$ in. × 2.2 = 0.62 in.; use standard-size $5/8$ in.

Core = 7 mm × 2.2 = 15.4 mm; use standard-size 15 mm

Since it's expensive and difficult to change core thickness and saves very little weight, you'd use this core for the entire hull. However, the inner and outer skins or laminates would be adjusted to match the varying thicknesses calculated for single-skin construction. For *Buoyant Baby* we'd find:

Upper Topsides (single skin = ¹/₄ inch or 6 mm):

Outer Skin = 0.4 × ¹/₄ inch = 0.1 inch, about 5/32 inch

Outer Skin = 0.4 × 6 mm = 2.4 mm

Inner Skin = 0.3 × ¹/₄ inch = 0.07 inches, about ¹/₁₆ to ⁵/₆₄ inch

Inner Skin = 0.3 × 6 mm = 1.8 mm

Middle Topsides (single skin = ⁹/₃₂ inch or 7 mm):

Outer Skin = 0.4 × ⁹/₃₂ inch = 0.11 inches, about 7/64 inch to ¹/₈ inch

Outer Skin = 0.4 × 7 mm = 2.8 mm

Inner Skin = 0.3 × ⁹/₃₂ inch = 0.08 inches, about ⁵/₆₄ to ³/₃₂ inch

Inner Skin = 0.3 × 7 mm = 2.1 mm

Bottom (single skin = ⁵/₁₆ inch or 8 mm):

Outer Skin = 0.4 × ⁵/₁₆ inch = 0.12 inch, about ¹/₈ inch

Outer Skin = 0.4 × 8 mm = 3.2 mm

Inner Skin = 0.3 × ⁵/₁₆ inch = 0.09 inch, about ³/₃₂ inch

Inner Skin = 0.3 × 8 mm = 2.4 mm

Fiberglass Sandwich Framing

FRP sandwich construction requires few internal stiffeners—the core does the stiffener's work. (At least five structural bulkheads, roughly evenly spaced along the length of the hull are required.) The standard engine-bed stringers (as described in Chapter 27) are still essential, however. Because of the lack of stiffeners, sandwich construction saves some labor in fitting out the interior. It also makes the most sensible approach to building FRP deck structures that are stiff enough

to walk on without flexing. Decks are usually the same scantling as the upper topsides for pleasure craft, but the deck core's made 1.2 to 1.5 times thicker than the hull core, to create rigid, non-flexing deck. *Buoyant Baby* would thus take a 3/4-inch to 1-inch (20 to 25 mm) deck core. Workboats will use this core with laminate equal to the middle topsides, sometimes with a few extra layers of mat and roving on the outer skin (the deck proper) for additional abrasion resistance.

You can see that, using this simple approach, you can make a very good estimate of the scantlings required for most ordinary fiberglass vessels. Keep in mind that planing powerboats need 10 to 15 percent additional thickness in their bottoms and plenty of closely spaced stiffeners here to resist their terrific pounding loads. Also, sailboats need lots of heavy transverse stiffeners—similar to wood floors on wooden craft—to reinforce their hulls around the ballast, ballast bolts, and mast step. Usually this rule tends to produce slightly over-strength hulls. For racing craft and light-displacement boats you can reduce laminate thickness by 10 percent or so. If you were dealing with a heavy-service workboat, fishing vessel, tow boat, or such, you'd increase scantlings 10 to 20 percent.

The Standard Laminate

There are almost infinite combinations of possibilities for making up fiberglass laminates—different styles and weights of cloth and different resin can be combined in more ways than you could list in a month of Sundays. In spite of this, the overwhelming majority of boats use the same laminate—alternating layers of 1¹/₂ oz./sq.yd. (48 g/m²) chopped-strand mat and 24 oz./sq.yd (780 g/m²) woven roving laid in standard polyester resin. This combination is proven, reliable, inexpensive, easy to work, and moderately strong for its weight. It's this layup that applies to all the scantling and weight estimates made here.

Estimating Hull Weight

Now that you've got a way to estimate both surface areas and hull scantlings, you can estimate the weight of your hull. All you have to do is multiply the surface areas in square feet by the weight per square foot of the hull material.

Wood Hull Weight Estimate

Mahogany is one of the most common woods for planking. It's strong, easily worked, and relatively inexpensive. Mahogany weighs about 32 pounds per cubic foot (512 kg/m³). Pine, fir, and fir plywood—other common planking woods—also weigh about 32 pounds per cubic foot (512 kg/m³). Teak—if you can afford it—is about 45 pounds per cubic foot (720 kg/m³), and cedar's about 28 pounds per cubic foot (448 kg/m³). Knowing these densities, you can calculate the weight per square foot or per square meter of any hull thickness. This has been done in the accompanying tables. Using them we can estimate the weight of *Buoyant Baby*.

We figured that her hull should have about 1-inch-thick (25 mm) mahogany plank; however she's a lightish boat, so her topsides are only ⁷⁄₈-inch (22 mm) mahogany. Reading from the accompanying tables, we can see that that is 2.34 lb./sq.ft. or 11.4 kg/m².

Say *Buoyant Baby* is an average cabin cruiser: 35 feet (10.6 m) LOA, 30 feet (9.1 m) WL, 11 feet (3.3 m) beam, and 5 feet (1.5 m) freeboard at the bow. Then, using the area estimating method described earlier, her topsides are 276 square feet (25.6 m²). *Buoyant Baby*'s bottom works out to 260 square feet (24.1 m²).

Then:

276 sq.ft. topsides × 2.34 lb./sq.ft. = 646 pounds, and

260 sq.ft. bottom × 2.67 lb./sq.ft. = 695 pounds

Total = 656 lb. + 695 lb. = 1,341 pounds

or

25.6 m² topsides × 11.4 kg/m² = 292 kg, and

24.1 m² bottom × 13.0 kg/m² = 313 kg

Total = 292 kg + 313 kg = 605 kg

Of course, this is just the plank weight for *Buoyant Baby*'s hull planking. A detailed weight analysis would actually calculate the weight of each frame, every stringer, the keel, each floor, the fasteners, etc. For estimating purposes, however, just add 30 percent and you'll be reasonably close. This gives a hull weight of 1,745 pounds (3,840 kg). If you followed the same procedure for *Buoyant Baby*'s deck and cabin you could make a very good approximation of her total structural weight. You'd have to add in the areas and then weights of cabin sides, cockpit wells, and so on, and then add 30 percent for their framing as well. A typical craft of this size would work out around 650 pounds (295 kg), giving a total hull weight of 2,395 pounds (1,089 kg).

From here, you could estimate the proper displacement for *Buoyant Baby*. She's powered with twin 150-hp diesels at, say, 1,200 pounds (545 kg) each. Auxiliary machinery and drive train are about 25 percent more, or 300 pounds (136 kg) for each engine.

Fuel, 360 gallons (1,360 l) = about 2,550 pounds (1,160 kg)

Passengers and crew, 5 people = about 800 pounds (360 kg)

Anchors and deck gear = about 450 pounds (205 kg)

Accommodations = about 900 pounds (410 kg)

Outfit, spares, and gear = about 800 pounds (360 kg)

So, *Buoyant Baby*'s total displacement should come to 10,900 pounds (4,960 kg) in all. Now, one lesson that every designer learns is that boats almost inevitably come out heavier than expected—folks are always adding gear, somehow there are usually more bolts used, more resin, more electronics added, barbecues and hair dryers, and other things left out of the figuring, so another 15 to 20 percent or so should put our *Buoyant Baby* estimate on target—12,900 pounds (5,860 kg).

If *Buoyant Baby* were a keel sailboat you'd have to add the weight of her ballast and of her rig to figure her displacement.

Fiberglass Weight Estimate

As we've seen, the standard fiberglass laminate is composed of alternating layers of 1½-oz/sq.yd. (48 g/m²) chopped-strand mat and 24-oz./sq.yd. (780 g/m²) woven roving. After layup and cure, the finished product's usually around 35 percent glass by weight. Such a laminate weighs in at about 94 pounds per cubic foot (1,505 kg/m³). Thus for a displacement-speed fiberglass *Buoyant Baby*, we can refer to the tables and figure weight just as we did for her wood sister. (A planing-speed *Buoyant Baby* would require somewhat thicker laminates, as we saw earlier.)

For figuring topsides weight we can take the average of the two topside thicknesses—in this case 0.25 inch (6.5 mm), for 1.96 pounds per square foot or 9.78 kg/m². The bottom works out to 2.45 pounds per square foot (12.0 kg/m²). There is much less in the way of additonal interior framing (stiffeners and local reinforcement) in a glass boat, so we only need to add 15 percent to the final result instead of the 30 percent we used for wood construction. Contrary to popular belief, traditional wood construction is nearly as light—it's just 5 to 15 percent heavier—as ordinary single-skin fiberglass. Modern cold-molded wood can be significantly lighter.

If we were to estimate the weight of foam sandwich construction for *Buoyant Baby*, we'd find a real weight saving. The combined thickness of the inner and outer skins is only 70 percent of the single-skin thickness. This means 70 percent of the weight, or 1.37 pounds per square foot (6.7 kg/m²) for the topsides, and 1.7 pounds per square foot (8.4 kg/m²) for the bottom. Actually, we have to add the weight of the foam core. A good average core density is 5 pounds per cubic foot (80.5 kg/m³). Thus *Buoyant Baby*'s ⅝-inch-thick (15 mm) core would weigh about 0.25 pound per square foot (1.2 kg/m²). This brings topsides weight to 1.62 pounds per square foot (7.9 kg/m²) and bottom weight to 1.95 pounds per square foot (9.6 kg/m²).

For framing (stiffeners and local reinforcement) on sandwich boats, add just 5 or 10 percent. When you factor in the small additional framing weight, the fiberglass sandwich boat works out to be lighter than her traditionally built wooden counterpart, with more interior room. Add in total freedom from rot and generally lower maintenance and you can see why so many boats are made of glass. Still, for a one-off boat a modern, well-designed, cold-molded (epoxy saturated and coated) wood boat offers nearly as low maintenance at comparable cost and, yes, even lighter weight for the same strength and stiffness.

Using the above methods—in just a few hours of noodling with a pad and pencil and a pocket calculator—you can now estimate the required structure, weight, and displacement for any design you happen to be considering.

WEIGHTS OF MAHOGANY, FIR, PINE, AND PLYWOOD PLANKING

32 lb./cu.ft. – 512 kg/m³

| Thickness | | Thickness | |
in.	lb./sq.ft.	mm	kg/m²
1/8	0.33	2	1.02
1/4	0.67	4	2.05
3/8	1.00	6	3.07
1/2	1.33	8	4.10
5/8	1.67	10	5.12
3/4	2.00	12	6.15
7/8	2.33	14	7.17
1	2.67	18	9.22
1 1/8	3.00	22	11.27
1 1/4	3.33	26	13.32
1 3/8	3.67	30	15.37
1 1/2	4.00	34	17.42
1 5/8	4.33	38	19.47
1 3/4	4.67	42	21.52
1 7/8	5.00	46	23.57
2	5.33	50	25.62

WEIGHT OF TEAK PLANKING

45 lb./cu.ft. – 720 kg/m³

| Thickness | | Thickness | |
in.	lb./sq.ft.	mm	kg/m²
1/8	0.47	2	1.44
1/4	0.94	4	2.88
3/8	1.41	6	4.32
1/2	1.88	8	5.76
5/8	2.34	10	7.20
3/4	2.81	12	8.65
7/8	3.28	14	10.09
1	3.75	18	12.97
1 1/8	4.22	22	15.85
1 1/4	4.69	26	18.73
1 3/8	5.16	30	21.61
1 1/2	5.63	34	24.50
1 5/8	6.09	38	27.38
1 3/4	6.56	42	30.26
1 7/8	7.03	46	33.14
2	7.50	50	36.02

WEIGHTS OF FOAM OR BALSA CORE

5 lb./cu.ft – 2 kg/m³

| Thickness | | Thickness | |
in.	lb./sq.ft.	mm	kg/m²
1/8	2.08	4	0.01
1/4	0.10	6	0.01
3/8	0.16	8	0.02
1/2	0.21	10	0.02
5/8	0.26	12	0.03
3/4	0.31	15	0.03
7/8	0.36	20	0.04
1	0.42	25	0.05

WEIGHTS AND NUMBER OF PLIES OF FIBERGLASS LAMINATE

Alternating layers of 1 1/2 oz./sq.yd. (48 g/m²) chopped-strand mat, and 24 oz./sq.yd (780 g/m²) woven roving laid in standard polyester resin.

94 lb./cu.ft. – 1,505 kg/m³

Thickness in.	lb./sq.ft.	no. of plies	Thickness mm	kg/m²	no. of plies
1/16	0.49	0.5	1.5	2.26	0.5
3/32	0.73	1.0	2.0	3.01	1.0
1/8	0.98	1.5	2.5	3.76	1.0
5/32	1.22	1.5	3.0	4.51	1.0
3/16	1.47	2.0	3.5	5.27	1.5
7/32	1.71	2.5	4.0	6.02	1.5
1/4	1.96	2.5	4.5	6.77	2.0
9/32	2.20	3.0	5.0	7.52	2.0
5/16	2.45	3.0	5.5	8.28	2.0
11/32	2.69	3.5	6.0	9.03	2.5
3/8	2.94	3.5	6.5	9.78	2.5
13/32	3.18	4.0	7.0	10.53	3.0
7/16	3.43	4.5	7.5	11.29	3.0
15/32	3.67	5.0	8.0	12.04	3.0
1/2	3.92	5.0	9.0	13.54	3.5
17/32	4.16	5.5	10.0	15.05	4.0
9/16	4.41	5.5	11.0	16.55	4.5
19/32	4.65	6.0	12.0	18.06	5.0
5/8	4.90	6.5	13.0	19.56	5.0
21/32	5.14	6.5	14.0	21.07	5.5
11/16	5.39	7.0	15.0	22.57	6.0
23/32	5.63	7.0	16.0	24.08	6.5
3/4	5.88	7.5	17.0	25.58	7.0
25/32	6.12	8.0	18.0	27.09	7.0
13/16	6.36	8.0	19.0	28.59	7.5
27/32	6.61	8.5	20.0	30.10	8.0
7/8	6.85	9.0	21.0	31.60	8.5
29/32	7.10	9.0	22.0	33.11	9.0
15/16	7.34	9.5	23.0	34.61	9.0
31/32	7.59	9.5	24.0	36.12	9.5
1	7.83	10.0	25.0	37.62	10.0

NOTE: The number of plies is the number of pairs of woven roving and mat. Two plies is two pairs of woven roving and mat combined—four layers total; 1.5 plies would be one layer of roving-plus-mat, plus an additional half ply—either one layer of roving only or one layer of mat only.

CHAPTER 45

It's Only Plastic

'What's it made of?' 'Glass sir.'
'GLASS!-GLASS! I won't have you putting glass
on any of my bloody aeroplanes, blast you!'

The New Science of Strong Materials,
J.E. Gordon

Chances are, if you're reading this, you own a fiberglass boat. If not, most of the boats you've sailed (or powered) have almost certainly been glass. In fact, at any boat show, or in any marina, you'll see endless vistas of glass hulls and very little else. It would be hard to believe—if we weren't so used to it—that only 35 years ago a fiberglass boat would have been an oddity. We discussed fiberglass's benefits and its weights and thicknesses in the last two chapters, but what exactly is this glass stuff? What's so good about it? And how does it go together to make your boat?

Combine and Conquer

Fiberglass is a matrix (it would be too simple to say "combination") of glass fibers (fiberglass) and plastic. Actually, the correct technical term for fiberglass is GRP (glass-reinforced plastic) or FRP (fiber-reinforced plastic). The word *reinforced* is the key. Your glass boat's actually mostly plastic. Only around 35 percent of your hull's weight is glass. The rest is polyester or some other more exotic miracle goop.

Imagine that you want to mass produce something as complicated in form as a boat hull. You want it to be strong. You want it to be smooth and fair. And you want it to be cheap to build. Plastic fills the bill pretty neatly, except for the strength angle. You can mold things inexpensively in plastic and you can make them nice and smooth, but if you try bending or flexing most ordinary plastics, well, the stuff breaks. If you could imbed long, thin, high-strength fibers in the plastic your troubles would be over. Presto—fiberglass! Almost all glass production boats are exactly this. A layer of fiberglass is carefully laid out in a mold and saturated (wet out) with polyester resin. The resin's rolled or squeegeed hard into the glass to ensure a tight bond, good resin penetration, and then all excess resin is forced out. Then the next layer is added. This process is repeated again and again until the desired thickness is reached.

Flavors of Glass

Now, fiberglass (the glass itself, that is) comes in a number of different forms. Each form has its particular strengths and weakness. By combining types, a builder can produce the best hull for a particular job.

Mat Matters

Chopped strand mat (CSM)—frequently known simply as "mat"—is literally that. Strands of glass fibers are chopped into short pieces (about $\frac{1}{2}$ to 2 inches or 12 to 50 mm long) and mashed together with a temporary binder called a seizing. The result is—surprise—a matlike material. Because mat's fibers are short and run every which way, it's not particularly strong; however, it's fairly easy to wet out, and—because it's soft, thick, bulky, and a bit spongelike when wet—it's good for bonding to layers of other types of glass. For this reason, the most common way to lay up a hull is with alternating layers of mat and *woven roving*.

Roving About

Woven roving is a heavy, coarse fabric literally woven from bundles of glass fibers. Since the fibers run for long lengths in two specific directions (at right angles to each other) woven roving forms a strong reinforcement. In fact, an all-roving laminate can be nearly twice as strong, for the same weight, as the standard combined roving/mat laminate. It takes great skill and attention to detail, however, to get a high-quality all-roving layup. Without soft spongy mat between the roving layers, it's difficult to make the comparatively hard, flat plies of roving stick to each other reliably. Since the combined roving/mat layup has proved adequate for ordinary boats, very few builders go to this extra expense. (The U.S. Navy frequently specifies all-roving layups, but then the Navy has Uncle Sam paying the bills.)

Whole Cloth

True glass cloth is also quite strong. It is almost exclusively used in small boats and for finish work, though, because it's quite expensive. Unlike woven roving, glass cloth has a very fine weave, not dissimilar to those fiberglass fireproof curtains you can get in department stores. Glass cloth is often used as a surface layer to smooth out the roughness of mat and woven roving. When this roughness shows through on, say, your gelcoat, it's called print-through. The best way to avoid this is to have first a layer of mat and then a layer of light cloth on top of that as the surface for the gelcoat or paint—on a custom boat. Most production builders find they don't need the surface layer of cloth and that a layer of mat alone will usually control print-through. A simple layer of glass cloth on the inside of the hull makes a nice smooth finish, however.

The Goo

The most common plastic for GRP construction is polyester resin. The liquid polyester is mixed with a catalyst and an accelerator to produce a chemical reaction called *polymerization.* (You'd think they could think of something easier to say). Boatbuilders—being more practical—just call it *curing.* What this all means is that the molecules in the plastic interlock with each other to form a very rigid unit. Ideally, the whole hull (or at least its plastic part) is just one long-chain (interlinked) molecule. If you visualize this giant "molecule" warped around all that glass reinforcement, you get an idea why glass boats work so well.

The Glop

Although there are a number of catalysts available, the most frequently used is methyl ethyl ketone reacted with hydrogen peroxide, or MEKP. (This is beginning to sound more like nuclear chemistry than boatbuilding.) MEKP's not fun stuff. It's highly corrosive, and if it touches your skin you'd better wash pretty durn quick. Even more exciting, MEKP's rather volatile. Yep, it can explode. In fact, if the accelerator used to speed up

An Off Soundings 34 being laid up inside the typical female mold. Whenever possible, the molds are set on rollers or in frames that allow them to be rotated so the lay-up is down-handed work. Here, the mold is heeled about 80 degrees to port. You can just make out some of her topsides core material laid on just under and behind the worker's arm. The face mask, air filter, goggles, rubber suit, and gloves are fiberglass's one big drawback. With proper precautions like these, however, it's perfectly safe.

the curing process were to come in direct contact with the MEKP, you'd really have a blast! Accordingly, most polyester resins used in boatbuilding come with an accelerator already mixed in. (Some people just want to spoil all the excitement.)

Fiberglassing For Fun?

The fact is that one of the biggest drawbacks to GRP construction is that it's so unpleasant. Anyone who has ever laid up a glass hull knows that you spend most of every day itching from head to foot because of those blasted fibers, which just get *everywhere*. The chemicals you're using are quite toxic. Even with good ventilation, you are likely to feel lightheaded or dizzy from time to time. Long-term improper exposure to these materials might also do unusual things to any children you may have planned for the future. And, of course, smoking on the job would be more of a risk than most people would care to take—assuming it's a risk you're willing to take anyway.

Glass Plusses

Still, the benefits usually outweigh the drawbacks. A glass hull can be formed up fairly inexpensively. What's more, the designer can draw any weird shape he or she happens to feel like. Compound and complicated sharp curves can be laid up by nearly anyone over a good mold. By contrast, forming the same shape in wood or metal could take the most skilled craftsman days or longer. It might not be possible at all. Also, as we all know, glass boats just don't rot—ever. If you add to that the fact that glass boats are inexpensive because they are so easy to mass produce, well there's no mystery about why your boat and most of your friends' boats are likely to be GRP.

And Now For the Tricky Stuff

Naturally, these are only the basics. Ordinary fiberglass is called *E-glass*. The E-glass and polyester layup or laminate that we've just looked at is not particularly strong for its weight when compared with wood or aluminum; however, it is the standard glass used in boatbuilding. (The weight and scantling rules of thumb from last chapter are based on E-glass.) This is especially true in bending or flexing. Most people take it as a matter of course that a glass boat will have deck or cockpit sections that bend underfoot, or a hull that flexes in a seaway. The same behavior in a wood or metal boat would be cause for alarm. Actually, continued flexing in fiberglass is pretty worrisome too. An area that bends repeatedly will eventually develop hairline cracks that will, sooner or later, become big cracks—also known as failures.

To eliminate this problem, an architect designing a glass boat will constantly try to increase stiffness without increasing weight. There are a number of ways to approach this problem. One is to increase the stiffness and strength of the glass and plastic laminate itself, and the other is to increase the thickness of the hull, deck, or what have you. (You could also do both at the same time).

Stronger than Steel

The first approach takes us into the realm of exotic fibers—Kevlar, graphite or carbon fiber,

and S-glass. It also brings us to the use of epoxy and vinylester resins, which are stronger than polyester. By way of comparison, ordinary glass layups have a tensile strength of around 15,000 pounds per square inch (1,050 kg/cm²). A layup of unidirectional (all the fibers running one way) S-glass laid up in epoxy resin will have a tensile strength of 125,000 pounds per square inch (8,780 kg/cm²)—over eight times stronger! The possibilities here are endless. By combining Kevlar or graphite with S-glass and epoxy resin you can make a boat hull that is nearly 10 times stronger than steel, yet that weighs only a third as much! No wonder they're making bulletproof vests of this stuff. The big, big drawback to these exotic materials is that they *cost*! Graphite is currently selling at around 3 dollars per square foot per layer ($32/m²) as compared with 30 cents per square foot ($3.20/m²) or less for E-glass. Sure enough, graphite is nearly 10 times the strength of glass and more than 10 times the cost.

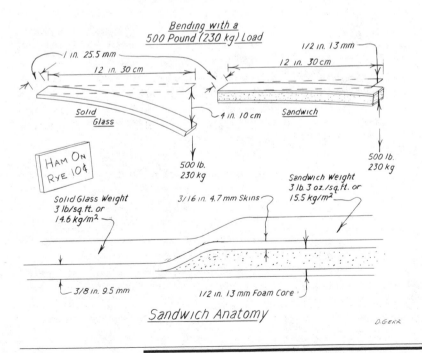

Sandwich Anatomy

D. GERR

Make Me a Sandwich

Luckily, there's another less costly approach to making a fiberglass hull stiffer—make it thicker. Of course, you can't just double the thickness, as you'd double the weight—way too heavy! The solution is to use a core material—*sandwich construction*. This way you have a glass outer shell and a glass inner shell bonded (glued) to a tough but very light sandwich material in between. The increase in stiffness this can produce is astounding. If you had a ⅜-inch-thick (9.5 mm) strip of ordinary solid glass about 1 inch (25.5 mm) wide and a foot (30 cm) long, you'd find that a 500-pound (230 kg) load hung on one end would bend it about 4 inches (10 cm). If you took that same strip and cut it in half to make two layers ³⁄₁₆ inch (4.7 mm) thick you'd have the makings of a sandwich construction hull laminate. Now, if you added a good core, say ½-inch (13 mm) Airex or Klegecell foam, between the two layers and glued it in place firmly, you'd have a much different story. The same 500-pound (230 kg) weight would deflect it barely ½ inch (13 mm)—an eightfold increase in stiffness! I'm not exaggerating when I say that it would seem to be nearly as stiff as a solid iron bar. Yet the foam core's so light that it hardly adds any weight.

Foam sandwiches are not the only kind of sandwich. End-grain balsa's also very effective as a core material. It's light and rigid, just what's called for in your average core. Even better, balsa doesn't soften when hot and has higher compression strength. This makes balsa ideal for coring decks. Foam cores can soften enough in a hot summer sun for you to leave permanent footprints in your deck. Balsa won't play this trick on you.

Wood as a Sandwich

Balsa, plywood, and solid timber are used as sandwich cores and reinforcing cores at mountings for engines and tanks, transoms that support outboards, cabin soles and hatch covers, and so on. Many people are leery of wood cores, fearing they'll rot. I've even seen some terrible cases of this myself. Wood cores, however, are perfectly safe and reliable, if—and only if—they're installed properly. They'll last as long as the rest of a GRP hull, even after damage. The J-Boat line of production sailboats, Black Watch sportfishermen, and Hatteras cruisers and fishermen are just a few of the quality large-production companies that use balsa cores extensively. There are literally thousands of these craft on the water, and I've never seen a wood related core failure on these boats.

The key to success with wood cores of any type is preparation—preparation these quality production builders follow rigorously. The cores absolutely must be pre-saturated with several coats of polyester resin all over *before* installation in the hull. Enough resin has to soak into and coat the wood surface to prevent it from wicking away the resin on the glass layers applied next to the core. If this happens, the glass doesn't bond correctly, and water can find its way in and spread along the surface of the core. Additionally, the glass laminate has to be applied to the core with plenty of pressure, either by hand layup or by vacuum-bagging. Cheap chopper-gun construction and wood cores just don't mix. Steer clear of such craft.

By using sandwich construction and unidirectional S-glass—the least costly of the high-strength fibers—with epoxy resin, a designer can make a GRP hull that's very strong and stiff and also very light, without making it prohibitively expensive. Another nice benefit of sandwich fiberglass hulls is that they're well insulated. You'll never have any trouble with condensation or, for that matter, with keeping her heated in the fall.

You Can String Her Along

The older "conventional" approach to stiffening a solid or single-skin GRP hull is to add—you guessed it—stiffeners—the stiffeners we called for in the last chapter. These are simply longitudinal "frames" running the length of the hull rather than across from side to side. They do, however, work much the same way as the frame of a wooden boat. If your 30-foot (9 mm) *Salty Susan*'s hull was solid glass and only ¼-inch (6.3 mm) thick without any reinforcement, she'd have quite a problem with flexing. There would be nothing to resist bending for the entire width and breadth of her sides. If, however, *Salty Susan* had five roughly equally spaced stringers running along the inside of her hull—located as described in the last chapter—she'd be quite stiff, even with the same 1/4-inch (6.3 mm) hull thickness. Stringers don't provide the insulation of sandwich construction, but they are an effective way to make a reasonably light, stiff glass boat.

Stringer Dimensioning

A reasonable rule of thumb for longitudinal stringers is that they should be ¹⁄₈₀ of beam high (thickness out from the hull), and ¹⁄₃₄ of beam wide. Like the engine-bed stringers from Chapter 27, they should be formed up over foam cores glued in strips along the hull with a the fiberglass laminate laid over them. The layup thickness should equal LOA divided by 2,000, and the laminate should be run out onto the inside of the hull—on either side of the stringers—for a distance of ¹⁄₆₄ beam. To avoid hard corners, the sides of the core are tapered in at a 15- to 20-degree angle.

Networking

Most larger glass boats have a fairly extensive network of stringers reinforcing the hull. Even sandwich hulls will use stringers as well as foam to increase strength around the keel, engines, tank mountings, and other highly stressed areas. Some manufacturers seem to be claiming to have invented the wheel when they declare that their "Ultra Axial Force Grid" is a brand-new way to make a hull strong. Actually, these grids are nothing more than lots of carefully placed stringers—not new at all. On the other hand, any builder who's taking the trouble to make his or her hulls with a well-engineered grid of stringers is probably producing a superior hull.

Lapstrake Fiberglass?

A nifty trick that can be played with single-skin glass hulls is to mold in stringers. All this means is that they build the hull with ridges or joggles to make it more resistant to bending, just like corrugated cardboard. One of the most pleasing ways to do this is to mold a fiberglass hull that looks like lapstrake wood planking. Obviously, there's no reason a glass hull has to be built to look lapstrake, but this approach will make the hull much stronger and stiffer in one shebang—no adding frames or stringers, no sandwich, and no high-tech fibers. It is, however, more difficult for

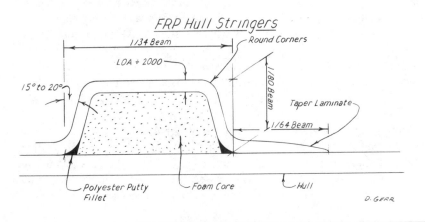

FRP Hull Stringers

1/34 Beam
Round Corners
LOA ÷ 2000
1/80 Beam
15° to 20°
Taper Laminate
1/64 Beam
Polyester Putty Fillet
Foam Core
Hull
D. GERR

the builder to lay up. (It's tough to get a good, tight laminate in all those joggles or corners.)

Another way to get molded-in stringers is to mold in the spray steps on the underbody of a planing power boat. This is a particularly neat solution to the flexing problem, as planing powerboats generate huge loads on their bottoms. Without plenty of stiffening these bottoms would flex and fail pronto. Since spray steps usually improve performance and aid dryness they're an ideal way to add stiffness. Actually, planing boats generate such huge forces when they slam into a wave at speed that they usually combine many of the approaches to increasing stiffness. It wouldn't be uncommon to find a well-built FRP sportfisherman using sandwich construction plus molded-in spray steps and the heavy engine-bed/stringers described in Chapter 27.

Watch Those Sharp Edges

Still another critical aspect of glass hull design is spreading loads. Because glass flexes so easily it's very risky business to have a hard or sharp corner resting directly against a hull or deck. Similarly, engine beds or mast steps and chainplates have to be formed and attached so they don't have any sharp corners or abrupt ends. If the builder doesn't do this, you can have a serious failure indeed. For instance, if your boat's engine beds ended abruptly in the middle of the hull, without being tapered or reinforced at their termination, every time the motor vibrated the corners of the engine bed would effectively drum up and down on the inside of the hull. This is about the same as taking a sharp stick and banging it up and down on a piece of tightly stretched paper. The question wouldn't be whether the hull would fail, but when! A quality builder will spend a great deal of time on fiddley little fastening details to ensure that such loads are well and evenly spread out.

You can see on the illustration of sandwich construction that the change from the single-skin portion to the sandwich region is also smoothly tapered. Because the individual sandwich skins are even thinner than that of single-skin hulls, they're particularly sensitive to hard spots. Look for smooth, tapered transitions of all mountings, bulkheads, and stringers, as well as at the change from single-skin to cored areas; it's a good sign of knowledgeable and careful workmanship.

Temporary Deck Gear

It's not unusual—unfortunately—to find deck hardware, like mooring cleats, simply bolted through the deck. This is downright frightening. Installations like this could best be described as temporary! Many fiberglass decks are barely $3/16$

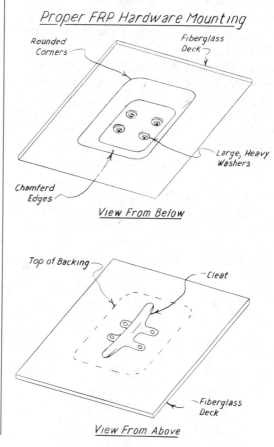

Proper FRP Hardware Mounting

Rounded Corners

Fiberglass Deck

Large, Heavy Washers

Chamferd Edges

View From Below

Top of Backing

Cleat

Fiberglass Deck

View From Above

inch (4.7 mm) thick. Such cleats are just waiting to be torn out. An idea of the kind of forces that a mooring cleat may have to withstand is the debacle at Cabo San Lucas, Mexico, in 1982. Over 60 cruising yachts were anchored, many close to the beach, when an unpredicted storm swept in. The wind veered radically, making what had been a sheltering anchorage a lee shore. Quite suddenly, all these vessels were in danger of blowing up on the beach or onto each other in vicious breaking seas. Although these were no-nonsense cruising boats operated by seasoned sailors—some world famous—many, many boats were lost. Some dragged anchors. Others parted rodes, but quite a few had their chocks, cleats, and even entire windlasses pulled right up out of the deck.

It just isn't possible to install cleats, chocks, and windlasses too strongly! If you're really interested in the quality of construction of a boat you are considering, poke around these deck fittings on the inside, where it's hard to see and to get at them. You ought to find thick, heavy backing blocks with large footprints (areas), and massive washers or backing plates as well. If you don't see this sort of construction, think twice. Ask your broker and builder exactly how these fittings were installed.

Connecting the Halves

A problem that's unique to glass boats is the hull-to-deck joint. Almost all GRP craft have the hull and deck molded separately and joined later in the construction. Obviously, if this joint's not up to snuff . . . well, your boat could split at the seams. Unfortunately, there are more ways to connect a hull to a deck than you can shake a stick at. Even worse, there's practically no way to tell, just by looking, whether a particular hull-to-deck joint is good or bad.

One good strong joint has the top edge of the hull—the sheer—turned inward to form a flange. The deck rests on that, both through-bolted and glued (ideally with epoxy) all along its length. Heavy bolts, say 1/4 inch (6 mm) for 25- to 30-footers (7 to 9 m) and up, closely spaced, 6 or so inches (15 cm) apart, are in order. A substantial rub strip or toe rail covering the joint will help protect it from damage. This too should be well bedded and through-bolted. However, quite a few versions of hull-to-deck joints are used in many different types of craft. Your best bet is to ask around and find out if people have been having trouble with leaks or structural failure in the model you're interested in.

In spite of some of its drawbacks, fiberglass is one of the best compromises you can make in choosing a hull material. In any case, every construction material has its drawbacks. We already have fiberglass car bodies and reinforced plastic airplanes. Who knows, in a few years maybe fiberglass houses will be the norm.

CHAPTER 46

Secrets of Space-Age Hulls: High-Tech Hull Materials That Have Gone Into Orbit

Instead of aluminum the Gossamer Albatross was framed with carbon-fiber tubes fabricated on machines designed and built by MacCready's team. The ribs were made of expanded polystyrene sheet reinforced with carbon fibre.

On Gossamer Wings,
Jim Lepper and Morton Grosser

For millennia we had, oh, about one fiber suitable for the construction of yachts and small commercial craft. That fiber? Why, fiber W, of course: wood. Sure, in the last 80 years or so there were some folks building workboats in steel, and even a few "nuts" building yachts of the stuff, but 95 percent of all small craft were originally trees. Within the last 50 years the boatbuilding world's undergone a revolution. By 1963 fiberglass had begun its clear and unbroken domination of the marine market. After all, as we've seen, glass is tough, easy to shape, and never, ever rots—not bad.

Since the mid seventies, however, there's been a new revolution brewing in the background. Builders started to experiment with new super-high-strength fibers. The chemical wizards at DuPont and Allied Signal began introducing miracle materials—materials with the strength of steel at less than a quarter of the weight. These very same materials are being used regularly to make lightweight aircraft structures—fighter-jet wings, fuselage parts and even space-shuttle components. It's well worth taking a good look at these fibers, as your next boat may be constructed with them.

S-Glass

Actually, the first of these new fibers is simply an improvement on good old fiberglass. The standard glass—the glass we've been basing our figuring and estimating on, and that is used in the vast majority of boats—is known as E-glass. Although you can build a very fine hull of this stuff, it's not really especially strong, particularly in bending or (as engineers like to call it) flexure. In fact, bending strength or flexural strength is different than tensile strength, and you need to look at both.

E-glass's low strength is partly due to the natural limits on the strength of glass itself, and partly to the relatively poor quality of the individual fibers made by the usual manufacturing methods. Not surprisingly, some bright engineer got the idea of improving the quality of E-glass—

making it purer and aligning the fibers more regularly. The result is S-glass, which produces laminates of roughly eight times the tensile strength and four times the stiffness of ordinary glass, when laid up by hand in the usual manner.

Not all this improvement comes directly from increased fiber strength. One of the other drawbacks to ordinary E-glass is that it is either woven (as in woven roving or cloth), or scattered about (as in chopped-strand mat). The result is, relatively speaking, poor tensile strength—even in the significantly stronger roving. Take ordinary woven roving, for example. It's woven in just the same way as the material in your shirt. The fibers run over and under each other crossways. In other words, the fibers have loops or bends in them—over and around each crossing fiber. Now if you take such a material and pull on it, you have to pull the loops straight before the fibers can develop their full strength. To make matters worse, when you do exert enough force to pull the fiber taut, the loops start to cut into each other at all those thousands of crossing intersections. This limits strength severely.

Accordingly, most S-glass is unidirectional. This simply means that instead of coming in woven cloth or mat, the fiber strands are supplied to the builder in neatly aligned and closely packed sheets, with all the fibers running in the same direction. In fact, great care is taken to hold these unidirectional fibers together without any of the crimping caused by a crossing weave. This final product is called unidirectional S-glass (engineers do think of catchy names) and is becoming more and more common in high-performance vessels.

A typical hull laid up with unidirectional S-glass will have one layer applied at 45 degrees to the hull, the next layer applied at 45 degrees but going the other way (like double-diagonal planking), and the layer above that applied running straight fore-and-aft. This makes for strength in all directions by adding up the improved one-direction strength from each unidirectional layer. To make the builder's job easier, unidirectional glass often comes bound together in just this way. Such fabric styles—they're not really cloth or fabric, but what else can you call them?—come precombined at the factory. They're known as bi-axials and tri-axials.

Kevlar

While all this S-glass experimentation was going on, the back-room research teams at DuPont were scheming to produce a fiber so strong that everything else would be made obsolete. (No doubt they're hard at work still—even as you read this.) As usual, they didn't do a bad job. Their miracle fiber: Kevlar—you know, the bullet-proof-vest stuff.

Kevlar laminates have roughly six times the tensile strength of E-glass layups and 2.3 times the stiffness. It's layup tensile strength is actually lower than S-glass pound for pound, but only slightly so. It's great additional advantage is impact and abrasion resistance. Anyone who has ever tried to cut a Kevlar rope knows what a devilishly difficult job this is. Scissors—forget it. Tin snips, wire cutters—only a few times before they become hopelessly dulled. Du Pont even includes a special instruction booklet on proper cutting procedures. Strangely—and disappointingly—Kevlar has no difficulty cutting itself. This weakens it quickly in sails and ropes, but isn't a problem when it's bound in a plastic matrix like epoxy resin.

There's still another advantage to Kevlar. If you take something—anything at all—and bend it back and forth, it'll get weaker and weaker every bend. Finally, it'll snap in two. (For the technically inclined, this is called a structural failure.) As usual, engineers have thought of a snappy name for this—flexural fatigue.

Kevlar laminates have better fatigue characteristics than fiberglass. In plain english, you can bend a Kevlar laminate back and forth more times than a fiberglass one before it fails (and it takes more force to make each bend). This means longer hull life with thinner layups. Even better, Kevlar laminates tend to damp out vibration. Again, in simple English, Kevlar doesn't vibrate as easily as fiberglass, just as foam rubber vibrates less than, say, sheet aluminum. Accordingly, Kevlar makes for less hull vibration—a quieter, smoother-riding boat.

Graphite or Carbon Fiber

I've had more than one client ask me what the difference was between graphite and carbon-fiber hull reinforcing. The answer is none—it's exactly the same stuff. Graphite fibers are just long fibers formed of nearly pure carbon. You'd think, with carbon being so common—you know: soot, charcoal, the building block of life—graphite reinforcing would be inexpensive. Just the opposite is the case, though. Graphite's about the most expensive hull reinforcing material around. The manufacturing process required to generate tight, neatly aligned fibers of nearly pure carbon is costly.

Nevertheless, graphite-fiber layup is fantastically strong. It has over 11 times the tensile strength of ordinary fiberglass layups and, incredibly, over nine times the stiffness. In fact, graphite fibers have about the highest bending strength or stiffness per pound of any material available. It was the availability of graphite fibers that made unstayed masts a reasonable possibility. Because of its high cost, though, only a few obsessed racers are building entire boats of carbon-fiber layups. Instead, graphite's relegated to local reinforcing at high-load areas, and for special components like rudder stocks and masts. Indeed, stayed carbon-fiber masts are roughly half the weight of aluminum for the same job. These stayed carbon masts promise to be *the* biggest single advance in sailing technology since the advent of ordinary fiberglass and Dacron. Reducing weight aloft is so important that no racing boat will be truly competitive without such masts from

now on. Even cruisers will be able to carry more sail and get dramatically improved performance out of the same hull with stayed carbon fiber masts.

Spectra

The newest miracle fiber is Spectra, an invention of the Allied Signal Corporation—one of those mega-giant companies that, for some reason, we don't hear about that often. Spectra's so new—it was only released in the early eighties—that very little work's been done using it for hull layups. Spectra rope, as we've seen, however, is now widely available and is probably superior to every other rope on the market for low-stretch applications.

Although I haven't seen any test results from actual panels of Spectra hull layups, we can estimate the strengths of a Spectra layup from the strength of the raw fiber. A Spectra laminate could be expected to have about 11 times the tensile strength of E-glass and also 6.7 times the stiffness. At first glance, this is not as strong as graphite, but we haven't considered weight. In fact, the real test of a material's strength is how strong it is per pound.

The following table gives tensile strengths, stiffnesses, and weights for our miracle-fiber layups and ordinary structural steel. It assumes that about 40 percent of the laminate is fiber and the rest is resin, which is about normal. The E-glass strengths are for the run-of-the-mill polyester layup, with 35 percent glass, while all the other fibers are laid up in epoxy.

You can see that steel's far stiffer than any of the wonder-material laminates. At the same time, however, steel weighs nearly five times more than even the heaviest of the new-fiber layups. The graph of Comparative Strengths and Weights shows relative values from this table clearly. The graph of Comparative Strengths and Stiffness vs. Weight is even more revealing. This is the simplest way to compare materials. You can see that

TYPICAL LAMINATE STRENGTHS AT APPROXIMATELY
40% FIBER CONTENT

	Tensile Strength		Stiffness or E*		Weight		
	PSI	KG/CM²	PSI	KG/CM²	Lb./Cu.Ft.	KG/M³	
GRAPHITE	170000	11952	12900000	906982	100	1601	
SPECTRA	168000	11812	9400000	660901	82	1313	
S-GLASS	128000	9000	5500000	386698	95	1521	
KEVLAR	90000	6328	3200000	224988	80	1281	
STEEL	60000	4219	30000000	2109260	495	7925	
E-GLASS	15000	1050	1400000	98432	95	1521	

*Engineers know stiffness as the modulus of elasticity, Young's modulus, or E.

steel's tensile strength is so small for its weight that it hardly shows up at all in comparison to our new fibers! This is revolutionary indeed. Even in stiffness versus weight, steel's only about average compared to the new laminates. With its low tensile strength to weight, though, it's not even in the running.(Evaluating stiffness versus weight accurately is more complex than this simple approach. We'll take a more precise look in the next chapter.)

S-glass, Kevlar, and Graphite laminates are all roughly in the same ballpark. S-glass is the least expensive and is a good bet for most lightweight, high-strength hulls. Kevlar's more expensive than S-glass and not quite as strong. With its high abrasion resistance and fatigue resistance, however, it will frequently be superior to S-glass layups, particularly for high-speed powerboat hulls, where vibration and flexing's a continual problem. Graphite's too expensive to consider for an entire hull, but is very useful for local reinforcing. Many of those CSTAR multihulls make liberal use of graphite reinforcing to ensure sufficient stiffness with their very, very thin lightweight hulls.

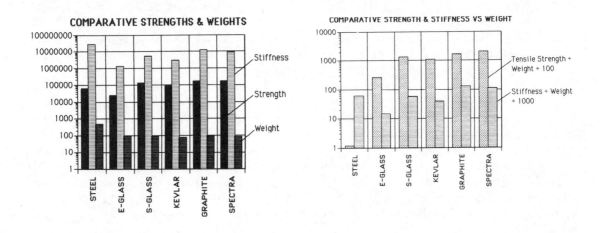

And the Winner Is . . .

Of all the new fibers, the real winner seems to be Spectra laminate. It clearly has the greatest strength-to-weight ratio of all our layups and its stiffness is only slightly lower than the overall stiffness winner—graphite. Why haven't we seen any all-Spectra hulls? Partly, this is simply because Spectra's so new. There just hasn't been time for the experimentation and tooling required. Another problem has been getting good layups with Spectra. Spectra's so light that it tends to float on the resin. This makes for too much resin and thus low strength and high weight. Still, some canoes have recently been built entirely of Spectra laminate. They're almost unbelievably light, weighing just a dozen or so pounds (5 or 6 kg). If the cost of Spectra drops low enough, and if vacuum bagging techniques control the layup problems, I'd expect to see it become the leading edge of the high-speed, high-tech future.

So, What Does All This Do For Me?

The logical question now is, what can these high-tech hull materials do for your next boat? Well, a lighter hull requires less power to drive it. This means your engine or rig can be smaller, cheaper, and easier to handle. If you're a speed-demon, you can keep the same size engine or rig and go faster with the lighter hull. Even if you tend towards the comfy cruiser category, lightweight, high-tech construction has something to offer. The lighter hull structure allows more in the way of accommodations and stores than in a boat of the same displacement but of heavier, traditional construction. Of course, for most ordinary cruising vessels this advantage is slight. The advantage is there—no question—but for craft with displacement-to-length ratios larger than 240 or so, the high-cost of exotic fibers would be hard to justify.

A Warning About Being Thin-Skinned

A final word of warning is in order. When using these high-strength fibers and sandwich construction, the skin thickness required for overall—remember *overall*—structural strength can become almost unbelievably thin, even on quite large vessels. This works out well on paper, but what about hitting a floating log? A well-known designer related a story both amusing and worrisome. A local builder of large (90-foot, 27-meter) high-speed sportfishermen proudly showed him an all-Kevlar, foam-sandwich hull panel that he'd used in a couple of recent craft. The builder explained that his computer confirmed the very, very thin skins (on the inside and outside of the foam) were more than up to the job.

To demonstrate his point, the builder took a hammer and wacked at the sample panel mightily. With the hammer bouncing off harmlessly, he offered it confidently to the skeptical architect. Taking the hammer, the architect turned it claw-side down and—with virtually no force at all—drove it right through Kevlar, the foam, and out the other side. The builder's face turned white. He had a couple of boats out on the water with this layup. The moral—there's always a moral—is that the structural design of high-tech hulls is a complicated business. Before you dash off to build or have built one of these miracle hulls, make sure a good naval architect does a detailed structural analysis.

CHAPTER 47

Believe it or Not, Wood is Best

Next she handed him an adze of polished metal; and then led the way for him to the farthest part of the island, where the trees grew tall, alders and poplars and firs that shot up to the sky . . .

The Odyssey, Homer

Having just spent an entire chapter discussing the wonders of space-age materials, it might seem surprising that—though I frequently design in metal, fiberglass, and high-tech laminates—my favorite boatbuilding material is wood. Part of this is simply due to the aesthetic and tactile pleasure of wood, but mostly it's due to the fact that wood is, in many respects, actually stronger than any material known—even the space-age materials we just examined. What's more, wood's far less expensive and much more pleasant to work with.

Just What is Strength?

How can wood, plain ordinary wood, be stronger than Kevlar and graphite fibers? I know it doesn't seem possible, but it *is* the case. The confusion comes from the meaning of the word "strength." It's important to understand exactly what's being said when someone claims one material's stronger than another. The simple approach we used in the last chapter doesn't give the whole picture. Indeed, I've seen many engineers crunch the numbers for comparing materials incorrectly—going no further than we have so far—and I've seen these results published in tabular form, and accepted without question.

To understand strength and how it's compared we have to understand the different kinds of strength. We've already seen that—for basic structural applications—there are two critical types of strength: tensile strength and stiffness (the modulus of elasticity, or Young's modulus—E). Both are measured in pounds per square inch (psi), or kilograms per square centimeter (kg/cm^2). We can repeat the strength table from last chapter here, but this time—to properly round out the list—include aluminum, the space-age metal titanium, and a good average structural wood, douglas fir. We can also arrange the table in order from the "strongest" to the "weakest" material.

Strength Versus Weight

It appears, at first glance, that wood's anything but "strong"; it's at the very bottom of the

STRENGTHS OF BOATBUILDING MATERIALS

	Tensile Strength		Stiffness or E		Weight	
	PSI	KG/CM²	PSI	KG/CM²	Lb./Cu.Ft.	KG/M³
GRAPHITE	170,000	11,952	12,900,000	906,982	100	1,601
SPECTRA	168,000	11,812	9,400,000	660,901	82	1,313
TITANIUM	150,000	10,546	17,500,000	1,230,401	140	2,241
S-GLASS	128,000	9,000	5,500,000	386,698	95	1,521
KEVLAR	90,000	6,328	3,200,000	224,988	80	1,281
STEEL	60,000	4,219	30,000,000	2,109,260	495	7,925
ALUMINUM	40,000	2,812	10,400,000	731,210	168	2,690
E-GLASS*	15,000	1,050	1,400,000	98,432	95	1,521
DOUGLAS FIR	12,400	872	1,950,000	137,100	32	512

*E-Glass laminate in polyester resin, all other laminates in epoxy.

list. But remember that we have to be careful about what we mean by comparing strength. Since boats—and most structures—require the minimum weight for a given strength, what we really need to compare is how strong each material is for its weight. You'll notice that though wood has the lowest tensile strength, it also has—by far—the lowest weight or density, at just 32 lb./cu.ft. or 512 kg/m³. You can also see that although wood's simple tensile strength is the lowest, its stiffness (modulus) is actually higher than E-glass, which weighs twice as much. How can we compare strength relative to weight? The simplest way—as we did in the last chapter—is to divide the strength or stiffness by density. Doing this will give the following new table:

TENSILE STRENGTH VERSUS WEIGHT

	PSI/Lb./Cu.Ft.	KG/CM²/KG/M³
SPECTRA	2,049	9.00
GRAPHITE	1,700	7.47
S-GLASS	1,347	5.92
KEVLAR	1,125	4.94
TITANIUM	1,071	4.71
DOUGLAS FIR	388	1.70
ALUMINUM	238	1.05
E-GLASS	158	0.69
STEEL	121	0.53

Immediately, we can see that wood moves up in the list. Pound for pound it's stronger in tension than aluminum, ordinary E-glass-FRP layups, and—even though you're used to thinking of steel as being so strong—wood's stronger than steel. Only the high-tech, space-age materials are stronger than wood in tension pound for pound. What if we do the same thing for the modulus or stiffness?

STIFFNESS OR MODULUS VERSUS WEIGHT

	PSI/Lb./Cu.Ft.	KG/CM²/KG/M³
GRAPHITE	129,000	567
TITANIUM	125,000	549
SPECTRA	114,634	503
ALUMINUM	61,905	272
DOUGLAS FIR	60,938	268
STEEL	60,606	266
S-GLASS	57,895	254
KEVLAR	40,000	176
E-GLASS	14,737	65

This time—with regard to stiffness—wood's moved even further up the list. According to this simple analysis, wood's stiffer, pound for pound, than any fiberglass layup, any Kevlar layup, and steel. Aluminum is a hair stiffer pound for pound, but the difference in stiffness is so slight as to be unimportant.

It still appears that wood's less stiff than graphite fiber, Spectra, and titanium. And, sadly, it's this simple analysis that I've seen published by engineers who should know better. There's really more to comparing strength. In fact, in most structures like buildings, airplanes, and boats, stiffness is more critical than pure tensile strength. This is because stiffness determines how much the structure bends under load. In most cases, if the structure's stiff enough not to bend excessively, it's far stronger than necessary in terms of simple tensile loads. Even more important, though, is exactly how stiffness (the modulus "E") is used to determine if a structural member's strong enough to resist bending or flexing in a certain application, when made of a specific material.

Using Stiffness

In almost all cases, to work out the strength of beams or panels in bending, or of columns in buckling, engineers use a variant of one of the following two formulas:

For columns:

Load P = some constants ×

$$\frac{Stiffness \times Moment\ of\ Inertia}{Length^2} = constants \times \frac{EI}{L^2}$$

For beams and panels:

Deflection = some constants ×

$$\frac{Load \times Length^3}{Stiffness \times Moment\ of\ Inertia} = constants \times \frac{PL^3}{EI}$$

Structural Efficiency

The moment of inertia, "I," is a geometric property that describes the distribution of mass in the cross-section of a structural member. We don't have to worry about it here. The important thing is that structural stiffness is related to the material's specific stiffness (its modulus) and the square of the length for columns. For beams and panels it's related to stiffness and the cube of the length. Doing some basic algebraic manipulation will show that for columns structural efficiency's equal to the square root of the stiffness divided by the density of a material, and that for beams and panels the structural efficiency's equal to the cube root of the stiffness divided by the density, or:

$$Column\ Structural\ Efficiency = \frac{\sqrt{Stiffness\ or\ E}}{Density}$$

$$Beam\ and\ Panel\ Structural\ Efficiency = \frac{\sqrt[3]{Stiffness\ or\ E}}{Density}$$

See the sidebar for a more detailed explanation.

Wood Wins

Now that we know how structural efficiency—for stiffness—is determined, it's a simple matter to generate new tables that give structural efficiencies as follows:

STRUCTURAL EFFICIENCY RELATIVE TO WEIGHT: COLUMNS

	$\frac{\sqrt{PSI}}{Lb/Cu.Ft.}$	$\frac{\sqrt{KG/CM^2}}{KG/M^3}$
DOUGLAS FIR	44	0.72
SPECTRA	37	0.62
GRAPHITE	36	0.59
TITANIUM	30	0.49
S-GLASS	25	0.41
KEVLAR	22	0.37
ALUMINUM	19	0.32
E-GLASS	12	0.21
STEEL	11	0.18

STRUCTURAL EFFICIENCY
RELATIVE TO WEIGHT: BEAMS AND PANELS

	$\dfrac{\sqrt[3]{\text{PSI}}}{\text{lb/Cu.Ft.}}$	$\dfrac{\sqrt[3]{\text{KG/CM}^2}}{\text{KG/M}^3}$
DOUGLAS FIR	3.91	0.10
SPECTRA	2.58	0.07
GRAPHITE	2.35	0.06
S-GLASS	1.86	0.05
TITANIUM	1.86	0.05
KEVLAR	1.84	0.05
ALUMINUM	1.30	0.03
E-GLASS	1.18	0.03
STEEL	0.63	0.02

Amazingly—and contrary to everything you've probably read and heard—wood *is* structurally far more efficient than any of the building materials known anywhere! It's even more efficient than titanium and advanced graphite fiber and Spectra composites. In other words—all other things being equal—you can build a lighter structure out of wood than of anything else, for the same stiffness.

Wood Shortcomings

So why aren't airplanes and spacecraft made of wood? Well, airplanes were for many years, through and beyond World War II. Wood, however, isn't the perfect material—there's no such thing. Supersonic aircraft and missiles experience high heat—as do spacecraft—which eliminates wood from consideration. Additionally, there are other factors to consider when evaluating a construction material—abrasion resistance or hardness for one. Wood is very poor here. Aluminum and steel hulls can take a much greater beating against other objects—especially hard, sharp ones, like rocks—than can unprotected wood. Further, they can't burn.

Another consideration is how easy it is to fasten the material together to form your structure, and how easy it is to fasten other materials to it. Wood falls down here too when compared to welded aluminum and steel. Before modern glues, in fact, it was the fastenings that limited wood hull strength, not the wood itself.

Tension Members

Wood's also only moderately efficient in tension. For pure tension members structural efficiency *is* simply the tensile strength divided by the density—as we did at first. Here, high-tensile materials like graphite and titanium are clearly superior. This is part of the reason rigging wire, bolts, and tie-rods are made of metal. Another part is that metal fasteners are harder. Thus they can penetrate the relatively soft wood and remain slender without being easily chipped and broken. Finally, we have to consider volume.

Strength Versus Volume

Because wood is light you can use less of it pound for pound, but the structural piece required will be thick or fat—quite fat—compared to metal or high-tech laminates, which are denser. On the ocean racer *Holger Danske,* for instance, I designed her deep fin keel of a high-tensile steel. In theory, I could've made a lighter keel of wood. (The ballast's in a torpedo/bulb at the keel bottom). In practice, however, a wood keel would have been too fat. I couldn't have formed it into a narrow hydrodynamic shape. It was thus necessary to go with a denser material to get the shape required. Similarly—though again it seems surprising—wood standing rigging would be stronger pound for pound than steel or aluminum. Such rigging would again be too fat, however. It would have too much windage and—interestingly—it would be *too* stiff as well. It's actually necessary for rigging wire to flex and bend with changing load direction. It's this that keeps the rigging in pure tension. Wood standing rigging—assuming such a thing were possible—would be

Wood/epoxy lapstrake construction. Dan Sutherland fitting frames in Madrigal's stern. Her keel and sternpost are clearly visible, as are the laps of each plank.

Epoxy-chine sheet-plywood construction. Michael Powell building his Nester.

Wood/epoxy strip plank construction. The bow of the 60-foot (18.2 m) Holger Danske. Her robust longitudinal stringers and laminated stem are visible. The first eleven strakes (strip planks) are on.

so stiff it would be subject to bending as well as tension, which would quickly lead to failure.

Wood/Epoxy Composite

For modern one-off and semi-production boat hulls, though, I believe that wood/epoxy-composite construction offers the lowest cost, the lightest weight, and the most control over hull shape possible. By gluing up and encapsulating wood in epoxy, the hull becomes essentially one unit, without structural joints or seams and the weakness of local fasteners (a construction known as monocoque). Even better, the wood's totally protected from rot. Yes, even if the epoxy's scratched the wood won't rot except right at the scratch—and even that takes a great deal of time. The water, oxygen, and fungus required to cause rot can't travel into the wood through the damaged part without forcing out some of the material already encapsulated by the epoxy. This material can't be displaced, however, because it has no place to go, still being surrounded and trapped by the epoxy coating.

Labor costs for some types of wood construction are high, however, with cold-molded double-diagonal construction being particularly labor intensive. Wood/epoxy strip plank is the answer. There are many techniques that can be employed to keep labor down on such hulls. Finally, wood's soft, easily-abraded surface can be protected by finishing the hull with a few layers of unidirectional S-glass cloth, which has great abrasion resistance. A hull of this construction is easy to build, light, strong, and long-lived, with low maintenance. As a bonus, wood's a good insulator, so the hull comes with built-in insulation.

Structural Efficiency and Stiffness

To see why structural efficiency is represented by the square root or cube root of the modulus of elasticity divided by density we can start from the basic structural formulas used to determine stiffness. We'll take a look at columns. For a column, Euler's (pronounced "oiler") formula for the load to cause buckling is:

$$P = \frac{\pi^2 IE}{L^2}$$

Where:

P = *the load in pounds or kilograms to cause buckling*
L = *the length of the column*
π ≈ *3.14*
E = *modulus of elasticity*
I = *the moment of inertia (the second moment of area)*

The moment of inertia of a section essentially describes the distribution of mass in a cross-section of a structural member. The moment of inertia I = Ak²
Where:

A = *the area of the cross-section*
k = *the radius of gyration (another description of the distribution of mass in the section)*

Since we're only interested in comparing efficiency, not absolute results, we can drop the constant π^2 (being a constant, it will be the same for every material and shape). Then, we can rewrite Euler's formula to solve for I:

$$I = \frac{PL^2}{E}.$$

continued

Since I = Ak^2 we can substitute this for I; however, as we can chose and compare any section for our column, the radius of gyration can be treated as a constant, and I then = a constant × t^4, where t = the dimension of the section.

Again we can drop the constant, and then we get:

$$t^4 = \frac{PL^2}{E}$$

or, taking the square root of both sides,

$$t^2 = \sqrt{\frac{PL^2}{E}} .$$

Since t^2 represents the section area, the volume of our structure = L × t^2, and weight W = dens × L × t^2, where dens = density (lb./cu.ft., kg/m^3, for instance).

Since

$$t^2 = \sqrt{\frac{PL^2}{E}} .$$

$$W = densL \sqrt{\frac{PL^2}{E}}$$

or

$$W = densL^2 \sqrt{\frac{P}{E}}$$

The efficiency of a structure equals the load carried divided by the weight of the structure, or:

$$Efficiency = \frac{P}{W} .$$

Taking the inverse of our expression for weight (W) and placing the load (P) above it yields:

$$\text{Efficiency} = \frac{P}{W} = \frac{P\sqrt{\dfrac{E}{P}}}{\text{dens } L^2}.$$

This can be rewritten as:

$$\text{Efficiency} = \frac{\sqrt{E}\,\dfrac{P}{\sqrt{P}}}{\text{dens } L^2},$$

Which is the same as:

$$\text{Efficiency} = \left(\frac{\sqrt{E}}{\text{dens}}\right)\left(\frac{\sqrt{P}}{L^2}\right).$$

Now, $\left(\frac{\sqrt{P}}{L^2}\right)$ is the structural loading coefficient. It varies from structure to structure; however, since we're comparing efficiencies of materials for use in the same structure under the same load, this expression is constant and can be dropped. We're then left with.

$$\text{Efficiency} = \frac{\sqrt{E}}{\text{dens}}.$$

You can see that—for columns—the structural efficiency is determined by the square root of the modulus of elasticity divided by the density. A similar analysis will yield :

$$\text{Efficiency} = \frac{\sqrt[3]{E}}{\text{dens}} \quad \text{for panels.}$$

CHAPTER 48

The Ring of Metal— Boats from the Smithy

Gentlemen, I consider it to be your duty to the country to give me an order to build the vessel before I leave this room.

John Ericsson to the Congress of the United States, concerning the ironclad *Monitor,*1861

If you ever wander into a large custom yacht yard—a yard that specializes in vessels over 60 feet (18 m) or so—you'll find that, more than likely, they're building in aluminum. In fact, many of these yards like aluminum so much that—even though they may have started out as wood builders years ago—today they won't bid on a design that isn't metal. By the same token, if you explore some of the commercial building yards dotting our coastline, you'll find they're building in steel. Sure, there are fiberglass and even a few wood commercial builders left, but the overwhelming majority of tugs, barges, fishing trawlers, and the like are built of steel.

Why? What makes metal the material of choice for so many larger craft, and—if metal's so good—why aren't more small yachts made of it?

In the last two chapters we considered tensile strength and stiffness. Both affect the weight of a structure as it's designed to resist its operating loads. For boats, this is the force of the water against its hull, the weights and forces of cargo, the thrust imparted by rig or propeller, and so on. As we saw in the last chapter, though, there are two further considerations. One is impact and abrasion resistance. The other is ductility.

Crash Survival

Steel and aluminum are fantastically tough. You can drag steel and aluminum hulls along rough surfaces, bang them mercilessly against jagged rocks, and chip at them with sharp objects at will. The surface of steel, in particular, is so hard that it's difficult to put more than a scratch on it. In fact, you could take a good-size axe and whale away at a steel-hulled boat without doing much damage at all. Try that on a fiberglass or wood boat and your insurance company will have some interesting things to say to you.

Additionally, steel and aluminum are highly ductile—nope, nothing to do with ducks. A material that is ductile will bend before it breaks—it will stretch or flow like plastic. When you bend a wood beam it will flex evenly, along a relatively smooth curve, for a while and then the wood fibers will reach the point of no return. There, they will snap and the beam will fail, breaking in two. Fiberglass also will crack and fail completely under extreme loads, though it will bend much further—also more easily—than wood. A steel or aluminum beam, however, will seldom fail by snapping in two. Instead, it will just bend more quickly and permanently—the metal fibers will stretch. This adds up to soaking up more energy before failure—a real safety reserve in metal craft. Usually, even very strong impacts will only dent the plating, without causing a puncture or a leak. In fact, anyone who's ever owned an aluminum canoe knows that you can smash these boats against rocks and put huge dents in them without holing the hull. What's more, you can hammer the dents right out again and set off in a relatively smooth boat the next day.

Aluminum boats, when properly designed, will be roughly as strong as wood or FRP vessels at just a bit more weight, and they'll generally take more banging about. Steel craft under 90 feet (27 meters) will be noticeably heavier than wood, aluminum, or fiberglass, but steel's so hard and tough it's about unbeatable for any boat that will take a lot of physical abuse. This alone makes metal construction well worth considering; however, when you add in relative ease of construction, you can begin to see why large custom builders favor metal.

Scrapping the Mold

Fiberglass is a quick and easy material to build in only after very exacting and highly finished molds have been constructed. True production molds are very expensive to produce; complete tooling for a 35-footer (10 m) can run to nearly half a million dollars. This is fine for large-run production craft, where the cost of the mold can be divided among dozens or even hundreds of vessels. For a one-off design, though, it's another

story. (There *are* cost-effective methods for one-off FRP, but all do require some form of mold.)

Working in steel or aluminum, a custom builder can cut the frames from, say, flat bar, right on the loft floor. The keel and stem can be cut out the same way and, when the frames are erected on the keel, viola, the hull shape's fully defined. The builder has no mold to construct, and most of the cutting and shaping's gone into frames that will remain a permanent part of the vessel. All this adds up to substantial labor savings, and labor is the single most expensive component of any construction project.

Forming the Stuff

Aluminum offers the builder still more advantages. It is soft enough to be cut with ordinary woodworking sabersaws and jigsaws (with the proper blade), and it's fairly easy to bend, even into compound curvature. This makes cutting and fitting relatively quick and easy in an aluminum hull. Aluminum's so easy to form that builders won't balk at creating beautiful round-bilge, wineglass-section hulls for sailing yachts or complex, highly-curved superstructures for ultramodern motor yachts.

Because steel's so stiff and so hard, it's considerably more difficult to bend into pleasing compound curvature. Thus in the United States most smaller steel vessels have hard-chine hulls, which greatly reduces the amount of compound curvature required. For most workboats, tugs, and barges this isn't a drawback. A well-equipped builder, however, can produce beautiful round-bilged hulls in steel. Dutch and German builders do this as a matter of course in all manner of craft, ranging from 9-foot (2.7 m) dinghies to 200-foot (60 m) floating palaces.

Compound curvature also adds stiffness to a hull, in just the same way that the curvature of an eggshell makes it stronger. Accordingly, a round-bilge steel vessel with just slightly heavier than normal scantlings is so strong that it is as close to indestructible as it is possible to get.

A Tough Nut

Bernard Moitessier built his famous *Joshua* in round-bilge steel by himself and sailed her all over the world singlehanded. In 1982 the *Joshua* was one of the craft anchored with over 60 other yachts at Cabo San Lucas, off Mexico. When a storm blew up and the wind shifted, dozens of boats—including the *Joshua*—ended up on the beach. Almost every boat that fetched ashore had her hull literally smashed to bits. The *Joshua*—even though she actually had two boats grinding down on top of her—sustained virtually *no* hull damage. Sadly, her wooden hatches and deck structure were destroyed by the yacht on top of her, and this permitted sand and water to sweep through the *Joshua*'s interior. Nevertheless, her steel hull was intact, ready to float off and accept new accommodations.

Round Those Corners

There is an extremely useful intermediate path between true hard-chine and round-bilge construction. The hard corner, where the topsides and the bottom plate meet, can be replaced with a split pipe or even a large radius-rolled plate. (Such plates can be rolled to spec at a mill with rolling equipment, and then trucked to the building site, where the relatively slight final bend and fit can be done on the hull.) Additionally, slight convexity or concavity can be worked into steel along the topsides and bottom without special forming equipment. Properly faired, such a hull's essentially truly round-bilged, specifically designed for easy construction in steel. Not surprisingly, this method is called radius-chine construction.

The drawings show the author's radius-chine design, *Papoo,* a 51-foot (14.4 m) length-on-deck steel pinky schooner displacing 30 tons. A heavy-displacement double-ender like this is nearly indestructible in welded steel construction. Her sections show what a sweet round-bilge hull shape can be achieved with radius-chines combined with small amounts of convexity elsewhere.

You can also see how the hard-chine hull design's converted to a radius-chine hull. The convexity in the topsides and bottom will be easy to form if it's less than 1/40 of the plate width deep at any point.

Metal Joints

Still another advantage of metal boats is that they're all welded. In steel, the weld joint has nearly the same strength as the unbroken metal. This means that—unlike the multiple components of a traditional wooden hull—a welded steel hull's virtually one unbroken piece of metal. For practical purposes, there are no joints to weaken the structure or create leaks. Aluminum welds are not quite as strong; nevertheless, they also create an essentially one-piece construction. Because of the great strength of welds in steel, fittings such as chocks, bitts, cleats, and chainplates can often simply be welded directly into place, with little or no special backing or additional structure built in—yet another labor saver.

Aluminum Costs

The greatest difference between aluminum and steel is cost. When you take stiffness and tensile strength into account, you can say that steel's roughly one-and-one-half times stronger than aluminum, but three times heavier. Accordingly, you can build a lighter structure in aluminum than in steel with the same total strength. Additionally, aluminum's considerably easier to work. It's no accident that you don't see steel jumbo jets trundling down the runway of your local airport. Unfortunately, though, aluminum costs something like 10 times more than mild steel. No wonder it's favored in luxury yachts. There are also fewer suppliers of marine-grade aluminum than of mild steel, which is ordinary building-construction steel used everywhere. This makes aluminum more difficult to order, and it's more difficult to get the exact size and shape of stock required for special pieces.

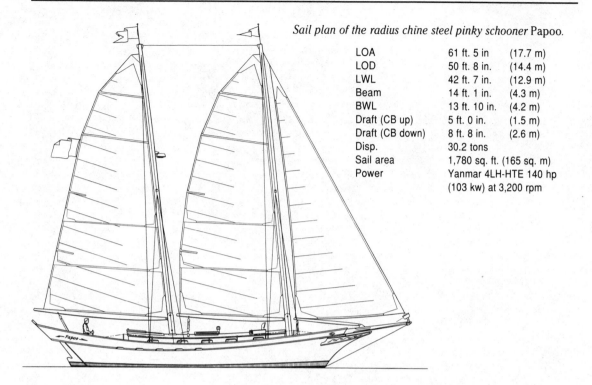

Sail plan of the radius chine steel pinky schooner Papoo.

LOA	61 ft. 5 in	(17.7 m)
LOD	50 ft. 8 in.	(14.4 m)
LWL	42 ft. 7 in.	(12.9 m)
Beam	14 ft. 1 in.	(4.3 m)
BWL	13 ft. 10 in.	(4.2 m)
Draft (CB up)	5 ft. 0 in.	(1.5 m)
Draft (CB down)	8 ft. 8 in.	(2.6 m)
Disp.	30.2 tons	
Sail area	1,780 sq. ft. (165 sq. m)	
Power	Yanmar 4LH-HTE 140 hp	
	(103 kw) at 3,200 rpm	

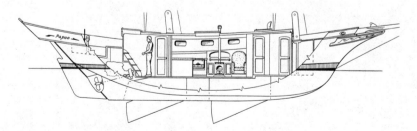

Arrangement and inboard profile of Papoo. Headroom is 6 ft. 7 in. (201 cm) throughout. All berths are 7 ft. (214 cm) long.

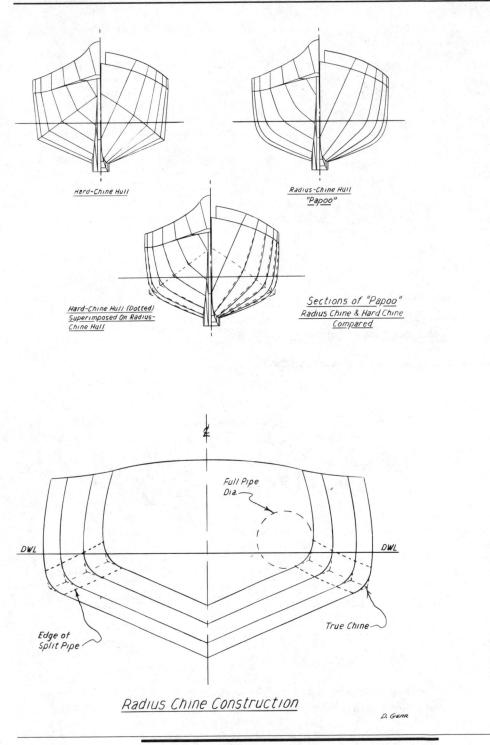

Hard-Chine Hull

Radius-Chine Hull
"Papoo"

Hard-Chine Hull (Dotted)
Superimposed On Radius-
Chine Hull

Sections of "Papoo"
Radius Chine & Hard Chine
Compared

¢

Full Pipe
Dia.

DWL

DWL

Edge of
Split Pipe

True Chine

Radius Chine Construction

D. GERR

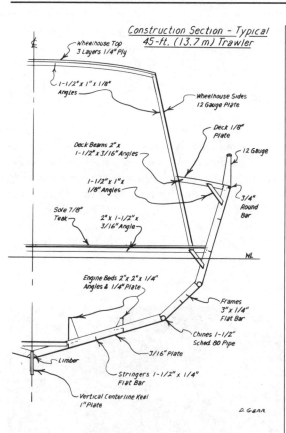

Construction Section - Typical
45-ft. (13.7 m) Trawler

Wheelhouse Top
3 Layers 1/4" Ply

1-1/2" x 1" x 1/8"
Angles

Wheelhouse Sides
12 Gauge Plate

Deck 1/8"
Plate

Deck Beams 2" x
1-1/2" x 3/16" Angles

12 Gauge

1-1/2" x 1" x
1/8" Angles

3/4"
Round
Bar

Sole 7/8"
Teak

2" x 1-1/2" x
3/16" Angle

WL

Engine Beds 2" x 2" x 1/4"
Angles & 1/4" Plate

Frames
3" x 1/4"
Flat Bar

Chines 1-1/2"
Sched 80 Pipe

3/16" Plate

Limber

Stringers 1-1/2" x 1/4"
Flat Bar

Vertical Centerline Keel
1" Plate

D. GEAR

Rusty Buckets?

Of course, some of aluminum's cost disadvantages are offset by the fact that it doesn't rust. Good marine aluminum alloys are so corrosion resistant that they don't even need paint (above the waterline, that is). They can stand years of direct exposure to salt water and air. Steel craft have enough difficulty with rust to force their designers to use heavier plate than is really necessary for strength. This is because the designer will generally assume that about a quarter of the plate thickness will rust away in, say, 15 or 20 years. This is no reason not to own a steel boat. If rust were an intractable problem, all those workboats would be built of something else. Proper surface perpetration, a good paint job, and proper anodes will

give a steel hull years and years of low-maintenance service.

Darn Those Electrons

All metal boats, in fact, face another form of corrosion—galvanic corrosion. The sad fact is that two different metals immersed in sea water form an effective battery. As we saw in Chapter 31, current flows from a metal with plenty of electrons to one with room for more, or from the anode to the cathode. Anyway, if your hull ends up as the anode, it will actually lose metal—electron by electron—and eventually weaken and fail. In fact, poorly designed and poorly protected craft can generate as much current as your car battery, at which rate they will literally eat themselves up in a few weeks or months—shocking, but true. There are excellent proven preventatives for galvanic corrosion, however.

Types of Steel

Say you decide to have your brand-new *Natty Neptune* built at Al's Acme Worldclass Welders. The first thing Al will have to do is order the appropriate materials. If *Natty Neptune*'s to be of steel this doesn't pose much of a problem. Almost all steel boats are fabricated from the most common form of ordinary structural or mild steel, available at any local construction outlet. Sometimes, however, a designer will call for corten steel. Corten's a steel alloy that rusts at a much slower rate than ordinary mild steel. It's a bit more expensive, but, of course it lasts longer. Corten's not stainless steel, which is much more expensive still—far too expensive for hull construction. Corten's thus both rust-resistant enough and inexpensive enough to be worth considering for any steel yacht, particularly one with thin plating. Some builders don't like working with corten steel, however, as it's noticeably harder to bend and form then ordinary mild steel. Occasionally, high-tensile steels such as ASTM-A514 and A440 alloys are specified. They don't offer the additional corrosion protection of corten, however, and are primarily useful for fabricating special high-strength hardware and fittings.

The Right Aluminum

If, on the other hand, *Natty Neptune* were to be of aluminum, the choice of alloy becomes more limited. Only a very small number of the vast array of aluminum alloys available are suitable for marine use. (The alloys used in, say, aircraft or toaster ovens would fail impressively in marine applications). Use the wrong alloy and *Natty Neptune* wouldn't remain natty for long. For hull construction, alloys of the 5000 series are best. Al would probably order most of the plate from the 5086 series of alloys—5086-H32, H111 and H112 is my favorite. This alloy provides some of the best combinations of strength, workability, and extreme resistance to saltwater corrosion, with—for aluminum—moderate cost.

Framing Her Up

Worldclass Welders will loft the hull full size in the usual way. Then they'll mark off the shape of the keel and the transverse frames and bulkheads and simply cut and bend these pieces to the proper shape. It's a fairly simple matter for Al and his crew to erect the frames and bulkheads on the keel/backbone, and presto, he'll have the hull shape fully defined.

The hull of the 87-foot cutter Aria *taking shape at Palmer Johnson. Designed by megayacht specialist Frank MacLear,* Aria *shows what a sweet shape can be fabricated in aluminum. Her transverse frames and longitudinal stringers are clearly visible. Plating has begun at the bottom by the keel. The author spent many challenging years working on vessels like this in the MacLear & Harris design office. (Frank MacLear photo)*

Small shops cut with acetylene torches and special power shears. Aluminum can be cut with an ordinary sabersaw. Large shops often have sophisticated computer-controlled plasma or laser cutters. Some of these machines automatically follow the line of a dark grease pencil, cutting out complex shapes in an jiffy. One builder swears that a fly landed on a marked plate during cutting and was mistaken by the machine for the pencil line. The resulting shape was peculiar, and one can't help considering the fly—it must have been moving right along!

If you wander in to inspect Al's progress at this time, you'll be able to see clearly some of the differences between wood and metal construction. One of the first things you'll notice is that *Natty Neptune* has a large number of longitudinals running from bow to stern. These are called stringers and perform the same function as the stringers or stiffeners on fiberglass craft—providing local stiffness and longitudinal strength. This is required because, even though both aluminum and steel are far, far stiffer than fiberglass, they are so heavy that *Natty Neptune*'s plating must be kept—comparatively speaking—extremely thin. At 45-feet (13.7 m) overall, *Natty Neptune*'s shell plating will be around $^3/_{16}$-inch (4 to 5 mm) thick in steel, and $^7/_{32}$ to $^1/_4$ inch (5.5 to 6.5 mm) in aluminum. This is pretty thin stuff indeed. Without the support of internal stiffeners, a hull this thin would flex, buckle, and oil-can.

Armor Bottoms

A nice feature of some metal hulls is that their bottom plating can be made much thicker than the rest of the hull shell. Weight low down is beneficial to stability and, if the vessel's not a high-speed craft, won't detract from performance. It wouldn't be unusual to find keel bottom plates a full inch (25 mm) thick on many trawler yachts and motorsailers, with bottom plating—sometimes as high as the bilge—as much as $^3/_8$ to $^7/_{16}$ of an inch thick (9 to 11 mm). Such plating's so strong that it requires somewhat less internal stiffening. Additionally, it makes these vessels virtually immune to damage on grounding.

Welding In Spots

Many people think that the framing on a metal vessel is welded continuously along its entire length. Actually, the welds are kept as short as possible, both to save time and labor and—most importantly—to minimize distortion from the heat of welding. Typically, a frame or stringer is welded to the inside of the hull plating for an inch or two (2.5 to 5 cm), then several inches to a foot or more (15 to 30+ cm) is skipped and the next weld's made. Only the watertight joints along the hull, decks, tanks, and such have continuous welds.

This approach is possible because weld joints are so strong. A wood joint made with bolts or screws is safe or reliable up to only 30 or 40 percent of the total strength of the wood. By contrast, most weld joints usually develop at least 85 percent of the total strength of the metal. Many welds in steel are rated at full strength. Such welds are said to be 100 percent efficient or 100-percent welds—not bad. (Wood-epoxy glue joints—properly engineered and assembled—are also 100-percent joints.)

Anatomy of a Weld

You can see in the drawing that a typical V-groove, butt joint weld is filled with solid weld metal between the two plates. When Al's master welder brings his welding rod (on a steel boat) close to the joint, an extremely hot electric arc flows from the metal welding rod to the plate. This melts the metal away, as shown, on either side and also melts the welding rod, which flows into and fills the joint. Later, after the majority of the welding's completed, Worldclass Welders will grind all the exposed surface welds smooth with the same high-speed pneumatic disc sander/grinders used at your local auto-body repair shop.

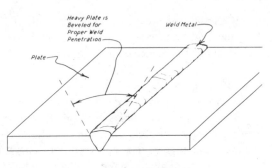

Heavy Plate is Beveled for Proper Weld Penetration

Plate

Weld Metal

Anatomy of a Butt Weld

Aluminum Welds

Now, steel welding rods are covered with a flux coating to help reduce oxidation during welding. In fact, one of the secrets to successful welding's to keep the flux coating from being accidentally scraped or burned off the rod. Aluminum's far more sensitive to oxidation, and simply using flux-coated weld rods isn't enough protection. Accordingly, the same process would be used if *Natty Neptune* were aluminum, except that instead of a weld rod a gas-shielded welder with a welding wire, for the arc, would be used. MIG (metal inert gas) welding is the most common. These welders use a shield of carbon dioxide gas blown out around the weld arc to protect the weld from oxidation. (TIG or tungsten inert gas welding's another, somewhat less common system).

Gas-shielding of welding is both a drawback and an advantage. The drawbacks are that aluminum can only be welded properly indoors, as even small drafts will blow the gas shield away and ruin the weld. By comparison, many commercial steel craft are built out in the open. Further, MIG equipment's expensive when compared to ordinary arc welders. However, as compensation for this, MIG welding in aluminum is nearly three times faster than ordinary rod or stick welding in steel, and what's more the results are usually

cleaner and more even, causing less distortion and requiring less finish grinding.

Spread Those Welds Around

In order to produce a first-class hull with a smooth, fair surface, Al's welding crew will be very careful to weld in small increments scattered widely around the hull. In fact, virtually the entire hull will be tack-welded together first, before any of the final structural and seam welds are made. (A tack weld's a very short, light weld just strong enough to hold things in place during initial assembly).

When the structure's all tacked together, Al's welders will do a few inches or centimeters of final structural or seam weld on, say, a seam amidships to port, then do the same spot on the starboard side. Next, they'll return to the port side and do a bit of another seam at a different location, repeat on the other side, and so on. The reason for this hopping about is that the intense heat of welding causes the hull to expand and shrink as it heats and then cools. If all the welds had been done in continuous unbroken lines, *Natty Neptune* would come out as wrinkled and lopsided as a squashed prune. In fact, the rough washboard appearance of many barges and low-cost commercial vessels are the result of quick welding in long, continuous passes, rather than carefully broken-up step welding.

Muddying the Result

Even with the utmost care, *Natty Neptune*'s hull will almost certainly need additional fairing to come up to yacht standards. After the welds in the hull are ground smooth, the entire hull will be sandblasted and prepared for "mud." This is a mixture of epoxy and microballons (essentially auto body putty). The mud's slathered or screeded onto the hull with long, straight pieces of wood and, when cured hard, ground and sanded to a glass-like finish. The mud fills all the hollows. Of course, if Al's Acme Worldclass Welders has done a good construction job, they won't require much mud. It's not unusual, however, for even experienced builders to use up a few hundred pounds (100 to 200 kg) of the stuff on a 40- to 50-footer (12 to 15m)—a factor that designers have to take into account in their weight calculations.

Built-in Tanks

A nice feature of metal boats is that integral tanks (even fuel tanks) can be fabricated in place as the hull goes together. Since these tanks use the inside of the hull as one of their sides, they take up less interior room and can be located lower down, where they'll help improve stability. Although integral fuel tanks are occasionally found on fiberglass boats, only metal craft have the fire resistance and strength to use them with Coast Guard approval.

The Joys of Insulation

At this point, Worldclass Builders will also be faced with the task of insulating the inside of the hull. Wood and FRP/sandwich–construction boats have their insulation automatically built in. The natural properties of foam and wood create more than enough thermal and sound insulation for anything but Antarctic service. Since metal's such a good conductor of heat and since metal hulls are so thin, metal boats and to a somewhat lesser extent single-skin fiberglass craft must have additional insulation added. It's not unusual to find this omitted from less expensive vessels, but the results are less than pleasant.

One sailor I know was living aboard an uninsulated vessel in the winter. When it got cold outside, the heated air of the cabin generated so much condensation as it struck the cold inside surface of the hull that you could see a constant sweat running to the bilge in rivulets. The interior carpeting was constantly sopping wet—squishing under every step. On one cold night, his wife fell asleep in the forward vee berth. In the morning—though it was warm enough in the center of the berth—she quite literally couldn't get out of bed. The condensation had soaked the edges of the sheets all around and then, in the dead of night, had frozen solid! It may be amusing to recall the effort needed to extricate her after the fact, but it was no fun at the time.

Insulating Wrinkles

Unfortunately, there's no inexpensive and easy way to insulate a metal hull. Specialists can be brought in to spray on a two-part polyurethane foam in only a few hours; however, the builder will have to spend dozens of hours, or even on occasion over a hundred hours, cleaning and trimming the result. Cork about an inch (25 mm) thick can be bonded to the hull in pieces, with wallboard contact cement, but this obviously takes much cutting and fitting. (The cork pieces need to be placed between frames and stringers). Additionally, both the cork and the foam will burn, and so will not meet Coast Guard passenger-carrying requirements, should you decide to operate *Natty Neptune* as a charter vessel. (Cork and foam are acceptable on yachts.) Fiberglass batts about 1½ inches (40 mm) thick can be installed, but his can take even more time than the cork. Acme Worldclass Builders would probably be just as happy if you asked them to forget insulation—it's a costly, finicky job—but if you plan to use *Natty Neptune* anywhere north of the Caribbean, it's a job that has to be done.

CHAPTER 49

Home-Built Boatyard

A Sailor's wonderful handy about the house.

The Nine Tailors, Dorothy L. Sayers

When the wind acquires a chill bite and the days grow shorter, you know that haulout time can't be far off. Those last few autumn sails are golden. Long fall shadows cast the waves in craggy relief and the distant shoreline glows russet with the annual show of color. It would be nice if you didn't have to leave your boat miles away at some yard, if you could keep her near, where you could check on her easily and work on her on a whim. Actually, you can. All you need is a large backyard, and you can store your boat at home. Sure, trailer boats are often brought home, but even 35- and 40-footers (11 to 12 m) can be hauled from your marina to your backyard once a year. Shipping charges are by the mile, so unless you live far from the marina, it seldom costs more—and often less—than the yard storage bill. Of course, once you've got your *Delightful Daisy* home, you'll need proper equipment to keep her safe and to do all the work you might do at the marina's yard. In short, you'll need a home-built boatyard.

Designer Launchings

It's not well known, but launching and handling gear have long been the responsibility of the naval architect. In fact, on large vessels this can be a specialty of its own. Maneuvering craft of this size on land can lead to very interesting problems. A fellow with the inauspicious name of Isambard Kingdom Brunel learned more about this than he cared to well over a hundred years ago. In a day when "large" ships weighed a mere 5,000 tons and were seldom over 350 feet (110 m) long, Brunel's *Great Eastern* loomed massive indeed. She was 680 feet (207 m) long, 82 feet (25 m) beam, and weighed 18,915 tons, nearly four times the bulk of contemporary craft—a sizeable vessel even by modern standards.

Now, Brunel was no novice—he'd already built the two largest vessels in the world, the *Great Western* and the *Great Britain*—but when launching day came for the *Great Eastern,* it was no go. She categorically refused to move off the ways. It took many long weeks for the indomitable Isambard to outsmart and outmaneuver his leviathan and get her wet. The great delay and the tremendous financial drain and uncertainty it created took a terrible toll, however. The owner of the shipyard—a John Scott Russell (one of the founders of the Royal Institution of Naval Architects)—was financially ruined, and Brunel's health failed under the strain. Two days before the *Great Eastern*'s maiden voyage he had a stroke, and he died shortly after.

Cradling

By comparison, handling 30- and 40-footers (9 to 12 m) is a piece of cake. All you need's a little gumption, a bit of elbow grease, and proper equipment, most of which you can make yourself or acquire easily. Naturally, one of the most important requirements is a proper cradle. The cradle supports your boat when she's out of her natural element and keeps her safe. A flimsy or improper cradle is asking for trouble. With a good solid cradle, however, you can slide your boat from

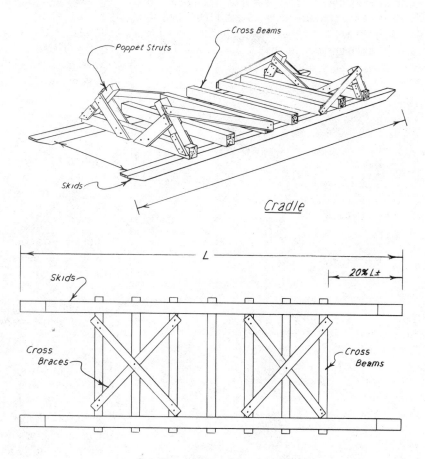

Cradle

Cradle as Viewed from Below

place to place and clamber all over her doing really heavy work without a care.

The drawings show a solid cradle that will live up to these requirements. The entire cradle's built on top of two long fore-and-aft members called skids. Not only do they provide the longitudinal strength required to keep your cradle from getting a broken back, but they act as (surprise) skids. In fact, with your boat sitting in your backyard, in a proper cradle with long skids, you'll be able to drag her around by placing heavy greased planks under the skids and hooking a chain around the forward crossbeam and over the trailer hitch of your station wagon or pickup. (Environmentally aware folks might prefer heavily soaped bards, which work okay, but not quite as well as the greased boards.)

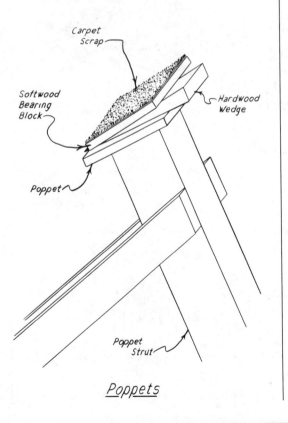

Carpet Scrap

Softwood Bearing Block

Hardwood Wedge

Poppet

Poppet Strut

Poppets

This, by the way, is the reason for the chamfer at both ends of both skids. The cut-away shown is very important in enabling your cradle to slide easily up onto planks or rollers. Rollers, in fact, are another moving option. Two- or three-inch-diameter steel pipes, about 10 percent longer than the width of your skids, will ease shifting the boat and cradle around tremendously. Rollers will work, but only on firm, hard ground, preferably concrete or asphalt. Remember also that, on a sloped surface, a boat and cradle on rollers can take an unwanted trip!

Two Jacks and a Cradle

You'll also usually have to lift the cradle and boat up onto the rollers, which will require a pair of jacks. The procedure is simply to place the jacks on the forward end of each skid and lift them up just enough to slip a couple of blocks under. Ease the jacks down till the skids rest on the blocks, pull the jacks out and repeat the process on the other end. This can go on, back and forth, until you've lifted the entire boat and cradle high enough to do nearly anything you could dream of, but it does require jacks with a lifting capacity about equal to two-thirds your boat's displacement—not cheap, but worth having.

Cradle Construction

The skids themselves define the dimensions of the cradle, and they should be about 80 percent of the length overall of your boat and about 60 percent of her beam between their inside faces. The skids are held together with several crossbeams that are firmly bolted and/or spiked into the skids. The keel rests on the crossbeams, which take most of the weight of your hull. The poppets and poppet struts are only to hold the boat upright *not to support her weight.* In fact, if your *Dauntless Diver* has an unusually shaped keel, you must place blocks on top of the crossbeams, along the centerline, located to fall snugly and evenly under a good long portion of the keel.

The poppet struts are simply cut to the approximate length and angle necessary to match your *Dramatic Dreamer*'s hull shape, with the final adjustment made by hardwood shims and wedges built up and driven home to a snug fit. Remember that the block against the hull should be of a soft wood, like soft pine, and covered with a scrap of carpet. You wouldn't want to scratch *Dreamer*'s flanks. For shipping or during heavy work, the blocking on top of the poppet strut should be tacked in place with a few light nails.

The crossbraces shown on the underside of the cradle are not afterthoughts. They are critical to holding the entire structure rigid. They are spiked and/or through-bolted to the underside of the frame before the poppet struts are installed, and—being relatively thin—can be bent over each other where they cross. Galvanized bolts and spikes are adequate for cradle construction—bronze and stainless would be an extravagant waste of cash—and they should be hefty, say ½ inch (12 mm) in diameter or more. Use heavy ¾-inch-ply (20-mm) gussets and large-diameter washers under bolt and spike heads and your cradle will be a source of strength and security for years. Remember to coat it well with creosote or—for that elegant touch—rugged outdoor-grade oil-based paint.

The timbers in a cradle are sizeable. An excellent source of this type of lumber is building demolition companies. Find them in your business yellow pages and call to ask if they have lumber from demolished buildings for sale. Don't give up if you have no luck with the first call or two. These days, many companies demolish concrete and steel buildings, but sooner or later an old wood-frame loft building comes down to make room for some new mall, or what have you. The demolition companies are then happy to make money by selling off the oodles of massive scrap timbers they'll have on hand. Remember that you don't need yacht-grade stock for a cradle. A light chain saw and a good axe will be helpful in trimming your new-found wood pile into proper lengths. Don't discard the short pieces. Heavy wood blocks and planks are invaluable for blocking and shoring and are worth their weight in, well, wood.

Timber sizes and proportions for cradles can't be set out as an exact science, but the following table will serve as a good rough guide.

BOAT LENGTH	20 FT.	30 FT.	40 FT.
Skids	4" × 6"	4" × 8"	6" × 8"
Crossbeams	4" × 4"	4" × 6"	6" × 6"
Number of Crossbeams	5	7	8
Crossbraces	3/4" × 4"	1" × 5"	1" × 6"
Poppet Struts	4" × 4"	4" × 6"	6" × 6"

BOAT LENGTH	6 M	9 M	12 M
Skids	100 × 150 mm	100 × 200 mm	150 × 200 mm
Crossbeams	100 × 100 mm	100 × 150 mm	150 × 150 mm
Number of Crossbeams	5	7	8
Crossbraces	20 × 100 mm	25 × 50 mm	25 × 150 mm
Poppet Struts	100 × 100 mm	100 × 150 mm	150 × 150 mm

Cover Concerns

Once you've got your *Dramatic Dancer* all set up on her cradle, you have to cover her. Obviously, a simple canvas cover or a blue poly tarp will do, but if you've got serious work planned you ought to erect a better shelter. Short of a permanent shed, an excellent one-season "boat house" can be made from two-by-fours (50 by 100 cm) staked to the ground and covered with 6-mil (0.15-mm) clear polyethylene sheeting. The wood frame should be built up from the ground about 3 to 5 feet (90 to 150 cm) away from the sides of the hull—elbow room! This frame's shaped much like an ordinary house, with vertical sides and a peaked roof. A ridgepole two-by-four at the roof center, and longitudinal two-by-fours at the outer corners and along the ground, add additional rigidity. Vertical two-by-four framing should be placed about every 4 feet (120 cm) with two-by-two frames (50 by 50 cm) in between. Stiffen the whole structure with some diagonal bracing and cover with the polyethylene sheeting. The sheeting should not run all the way to the ground but stop about 4 or 5 feet (120 to 150 cm) up. This permits easy access and good continuous ventilation.

The trick to getting long life out of this thin plastic is to staple it down with long battens on top of the plastic under every staple. This spreads the loads so tears don't start at the staple punctures. At the end of the season, the plastic's ripped off and thrown away, but the frame is disassembled and stored for reuse. It's really a wonderful thing to be able to work continuously on your boat regardless of the weather—no more paint jobs ruined by rain! Even better, the clear plastic sheet acts like a greenhouse. On a sunny day, you'll often find it 10 or 20 degrees warmer under this shelter than outside, with—of course—no wind. When spring rolls around and the temperature rises, you can remove a few bits of the side sheeting to keep temperature from rising too high.

The Simplest Cover

The most common and simplest cover, of course, *is* the blue poly tarp cover. You see them everywhere just haphazardly lashed over unsuspecting

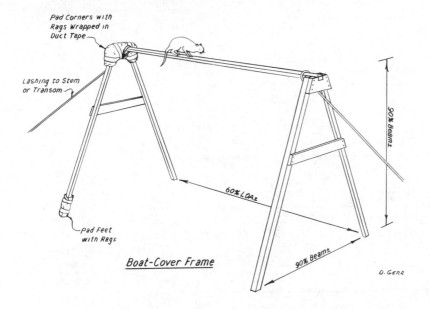

Pad Corners with Rags Wrapped in Duct Tape

Lashing to Stem or Transom

Pad Feet with Rags

60% LOA±

90% Beam±

90% Beam±

Boat-Cover Frame

D. GERR

Finished boat cover, over the frame shown in the drawing, and with the vents installed.

Boat cover ring vent installed in a standard blue poly tarp cover.

craft. For some reason, they're seldom installed on any sort of frame, and they're seldom fitted with any ventilation at all. Without a framework, the cover inevitably sags and forms dents that collect water in pools. Eventually the weight of water either breaks the cover or pulls it partially off. Additionally, ventilation—even for FRP boats—is vital. Without a good supply of fresh air you'll get all sorts of mildew and corrosion. Even worse—should you fail to get your *Dreamer* in the water one summer—she'll be sitting under that unventilated dark blue sheet in the blazing summer sun. The temperature underneath can reach 140 degrees F° (60 C°)! This can play all sorts of havoc with your boat and her gear.

The drawing and photos show a cover and cover frame that's so simple you really have no excuse not to build one. The peak's quite high, so there's no tendency to collect water at all. Usually the width between the feet should just fit inside the toe rail; however, sometimes a high deckhouse interferes. In this case, you can stand the frame—on shortened legs—on the deckhouse top itself. Only the principal fore-and-aft lashing lines are shown on the drawing, but the frame should be securely tied down all over—at the feet, from side to side, and diagonally fore and aft. The pad-

Components of Nicro Fico's boat cover vent.

ding at the fore and aft upper corners is critical; don't stint here.

Finally, you should install a pair of Nicro Fico's boat cover vents high up at the peak. They're easily installed in any cover—plastic or canvas; they don't cost much; and they can be reused over and over for years. A pair of such vents ensures that your *Delightful Dreamer* gets the fresh air she needs during her winter slumber.

A Boathouse for the Building

For those of you who like to dream big dreams, I've shown a drawing of the ideal boat-

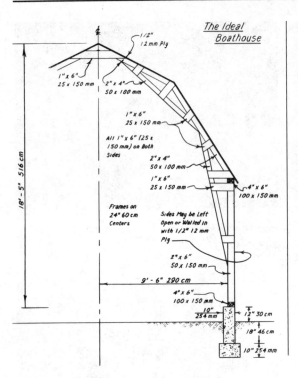

1/2"
12 mm Ply

1" x 6"
25 x 150 mm

2" x 4"
50 x 100 mm

1" x 6"
25 x 150 mm

All 1" x 6" (25 x
150 mm) on Both
Sides

2" x 4"
50 x 100 mm

1" x 6"
25 x 150 mm

4" x 6"
100 x 150 mm

Frames on
24" 60 cm
Centers

Sides May be Left
Open or Walled in
with 1/2" 12 mm
Ply

2" x 6"
50 x 150 mm

9' - 6" 290 cm

4" x 6"
100 x 150 mm

10"
254 mm

12" 30 cm

18" 46 cm

10" 254 mm

18' - 5" 516 cm

house structure. A shelter like this—19 feet (5.8 m) clear width and about 18 feet (5.5 m) clear height—will prove an ideal home for any boat up to 45 feet (14 m), or even, without a flybridge, 50 feet (15.5 m). It should be built at least five feet (150 cm) longer than your boat. As such buildings go, the construction shown is fairly inexpensive and very rugged. Nicely painted, it also looks pretty salty and handsome. The ends of the boathouse should be left open, and only the roof need be finished at first. The side walls may be left off permanently for easy access, or added later, when the urge strikes. Actually, this boathouse would make the perfect destination for your own private launching ramp. You'd just haul your *Dreamy Delia* straight up the bank, along the rails, and right into her house. For those of you lucky enough to live by the shore, this is the ultimate in home boating.

PART 11

People Power or Your Boat Should Fit Like a Glove

I like an aria to fit a singer as perfectly as a well-tailored suit of clothes.

Wolfgang Amadeus Mozart

CHAPTER 50

Room Enough? The Human Dimension

Many other little conveniences may be added, such as a small cooking-stove, book-shelves, gun-racks, etc., but I shall not go into further details. . . .

American Boys Handy Book,
Daniel Carter Beard

The boat biz', like any business, has its share of horror stories. One fellow I know of—a fellow who'd always wanted to get into the marine industry—scrounged together enough dough to go into production building fiberglass 30-footers (9 m). Somehow he'd gotten hooked up with a yard that claimed they'd be able to design the boat as well as construct it. This builder produced some pretty drawings and soon had a fat advance in his pocket. Several weeks later he was gone—yep, skipped with the cash. Of course, the vast, vast majority of builders and designers are a dead honest and hard-working lot, but when—several years after the fact—the victim of this scam showed me the drawings, I didn't know whether to laugh or cry. You see, I could have told him right off that the "designer" didn't have the vaguest idea what he was doing. The accommodations he'd drawn—though they did look pretty—just wouldn't have fit into the hull!

Although this is about as extreme an example as can be imagined, it's not all that unusual to see arrangement plans that are, well . . . really pushing the limit. The designer's faced with two unalterable facts. The first is that the size of people—you and me—remains more or less the same. The second is that the hull encloses only a limited volume and that volume's distributed in a rather peculiar shape—not the easy slab-sided forms that landlubber architects work with.

It is very tempting to look at the arrangement plan of a boat and draw berths, tables, and the like all the way out to the edges of the deck, but it won't do. Since nearly all boats have flare to their topsides, the actual width available for accommodations—low down, where this stuff actually goes—is much less than the total width shown in the plan view or deck plan outline. This is particularly so near the bow, where the hull comes to a point down around the waterline and spreads to a broad vee as you follow it up to the deck. Obviously, the deck plan in this area would show plenty of room and, just as obviously—down in

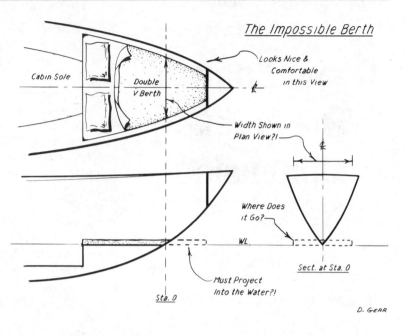

The Impossible Berth

Cabin Sole

Double
V Berth

Looks Nice &
Comfortable
in this View

Width Shown in
Plan View?!

Where Does
it Go?

WL

Sect. at Sta. 0

Must Project
Into the Water?!

Sta. 0

D. GERR

the hull—there'd be virtually no room at all. It was this which popped out at me so quickly when I looked at the nefarious builder's pretty pictures. He'd shown a nice large vee berth all the way up in the bow in the plan view. A quick look at the profile, though, showed that the forward three feet (90 cm) of this berth would have to extend out beyond the bow and right into the water—an interesting trick.

When you're looking through plans in magazines and brochures, you should ask yourself if all the accommodations shown can fit properly into the hull. If there's a huge cabin all the way forward, how did the designer find room for floor space, and how did he or she get sufficient width for the bunk up there in the bow? Even amidships, where the hull's more nearly slab-sided, there can be problems. Does the drawing show the berths drawn all the way out to the deck edge? It's rare to be able to get away with this. Usually there's enough curvature or flare to the hull, even near the center, so that the outboard edge of all berths

has to be at least three or four inches (75 to 100 mm) in from the deck edge—often more.

Designers, even very skilled and responsible designers, are often forced into skirting the edges of the possible by market pressures. They'll get a nice contract to design, say, *The Fireball,* for Speed-Demon Yachts, and then have the marketing manager tell them, "Yes, of course, she has to be fast, but Lightning Builders' *Seasmoke GL* design has seven berths and six heads, so we absolutely have to have eight and seven." The hapless designer will groan inwardly but say, "Heck, if that's what the client wants that's what he'll get." Since the designer knows that no one's ever likely to sleep eight in a 30-footer (9 m), he's not going to worry too much if a couple of the berths are only fit to sleep children.

If you think I'm exaggerating the problem, I'm not. Right now, one of the largest U.S. production builders has a 30-foot (9 m) power-cruiser on the market with six berths. Four measure 5 feet 8 inches (172 cm) long, and the remaining two just 5 feet 4 inches (162 cm)! It seems incredible, but this model is selling. I can only imagine the phone calls to these dealers after new owners come back from their first overnight cruise!

How big does a berth have to be? For that matter, how big does any item of accommodation have to be? Well, obviously, there's some room for variation; however, there are plenty of general rules that will help you evaluate existing designs, or—if you're thinking of modifying your own boat—help you figure out what you can work in.

Single Berths

The absolute minimum width for a berth for an adult is 21 inches (53 cm). Sure, you could sleep in something less than this, but then you could sleep sitting upright too—if you had to. The minimum length is 6 feet 4 inches (193 cm). Now these are minimums. For real comfort, 24 inches (61 cm) wide and 6 foot 6 inches (198 cm) long are the ticket. By way of comparison, a normal single bed—on land—is about 30 inches (76 cm) wide. All berths can be considerably narrower at the foot than the widest part, around the shoulders. The minimum width for the foot of a usable berth is about 13 inches (33 cm). The minimum width at the head—which can be a bit narrower than at the widest part—is about 18 inches (46 cm).

You sometimes hear the claim that a berth can be too wide for heavy-weather comfort. This is only partly true. A berth can never be too wide for comfort in harbor. But you do want to to limit the distance you can roll around during rough weather offshore. The solution is simply to wedge a couple of bolsters or soft duffle bags into a wide comfortable berth. This works like a charm. In this way, a wide berth can easily be made into a narrow one; and of course, it's not so easy to make a narrow one wider.

Double Berths

Many times, I see designs with "double" berths that are hardly wide enough to count as

Escapade *at speed, leaving virtually no wake.*

singles. The minimum width for a comfortable double berth is 44 inches (112 cm). A store-bought double bed is 54 inches (122 cm) wide. Queen-size is a full 5 feet (152 cm) across. The minimum width for the foot of a usable double berth is about 22 inches (56 cm). The minimum width at the head is about 40 inches (102 cm).

Like the single berth, you need a way to divide a double berth into two singles for offshore work. This can be done by making the double berth of two berth cushions, side by side. Install a canvas lee cloth at the center, attached to the top of the berth flat, under the cushions. In good weather, the lee cloth's folded flat under the cushions and you'll never know it's there. When it blows up, you pull the lee cloth up and lash it to the overhead. You now have two snug sea berths. What's more, when the boat heels, say to starboard, one person lays against the side of the hull and the other against the lee cloth, without disturbing the other.

Seat and Berth Headroom

If you have any plans to sit up and read or just look around from a berth or seat you'll have to have a full 36 inches (91 cm) of headroom over the top of the cushion. Sure, a 5-foot 3-inch (160 cm) woman could be happy with only 32 inches (81 cm), but your 6-foot 3-inch (190 cm) friend will swear imaginatively every time he tries to sit up in

Profile, arrangement, and sections of motor launch Escapade, *a vessel that pushes the accommodation limits and gets away with it. Only 25 feet (7.6 m) overall and displacing just 1.7 tons, she has full standing headroom, a private head with shower, and two berths 7 feet (213 cm) long or longer. Note the access to all sides of the engine, and to the tanks.*

LOA	25 ft. 0 in.	(7.6 m)
LWL	24 ft. 4 in.	(7.4 m)
Beam	7 ft. 4 in.	(2.2 m)
Draft	2 ft. 6 in.	(76 cm)
Disp.	1.72 tons	
Power	Volvo 20002 Diesel	
	18 hp (13.4 kw)	
	at 3,200 rpm	
Speed	8 knots max.	
	7 knots cruise	

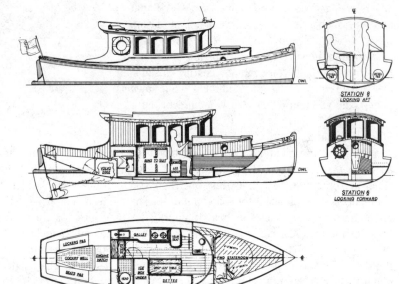

a space this low. Since berth cushions need to be at least 4 inches (100 mm) thick, this means that the top of the berth flat should be 40 inches (101 cm) below the overhead for full sitting headroom. Actually the cushions will compress a bit, so you could perhaps get by with only 38 inches (96 cm); less than this is sort of asking for a headache. Seat cushions can be only 3 inches (75 mm) thick, which assists a trifle in the headroom department. Every inch (centimeter) helps, as—like baseball— working a good arrangement plan into a hull is a game of inches.

Seats

An ideal seat is 18 inches (46 cm) from the top of the cushion to the floor and 18 inches (46 cm)

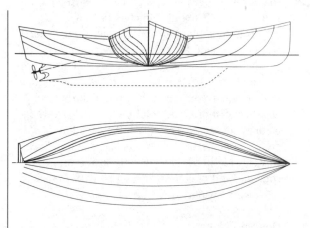

Lines of Escapade. *Her hull is that of a true Whitehall pulling boat—very low resistance at low speeds.*

from the the edge of the seat to the seat back. Most ordinary folk will still be comfortable on seats that are 16 inches and 16 inches (40 and 40 cm)—an excellent and standard marine compromise. On really small boats the seats just have to go lower. The trick here is to increase leg room and rear-end room—the old legs just have to go somewhere. On a normal 18-inch-high (46 cm) seat you need about 18 inches (46 cm) of foot room from the front of the seat forward. If the seat were only 12 inches or 30 cm high (pretty low, but workable for small boats) you'd need at least 24 inches (61 cm) of clearance for the legs and feet to stretch out into, and the seat proper ought to be deeper than usual, say around 20 inches (50 cm) from front to back.

Tables

The smallest table that'll seat and dine four people—two on each side—is 3 feet 2 inches long and 2 feet 4 inches wide (97 by 66 cm). You've probably eaten at slightly smaller tables, with this many people, at a crowded restaurant; however, much less room than this increases the chance of accidentally taking a bite out of your neighbor's elbow. To avoid this—cannibalism ought to be avoided at all costs—each person seated needs about 22 inches (56 cm) of elbow room. Obviously, on a table only 3 feet 2 inches (96 cm) long, elbows will be extending out either end. This is okay unless you plan to seat a fifth or sixth person at either or both ends. In this case, you have to allow a good 27 inches (69 cm) of elbow room for the end folks and the table has to be at least 2 feet 8 inches (82 cm) wide to allow for an extra plate in the center. Finally, there should be 11 inches (28 cm) of knee clearance under the table, from the top of the seat cushions to the underside of the table.

Heads

Why there are so many boats afloat these days with three heads is a mystery to me. Few comfortable homes have three bathrooms. Most families get by quite well with just two. (I've even known folks to get by with only one bathroom in their home! Real pioneer types?) Nevertheless, if the trend continues as it has been, I won't be surprised to see 35- and 40-footers (10 and 12 m) with four heads! I'd prefer one or two, using all that extra volume for regular cabin space—real room. After all, the head is—presumably—the cabin you spend the least time in.

Regardless of the number of heads in your boat, however, the minimum size head compartment's about 24 inches by 34 inches (61 by 86 cm). This makes a room just large enough for a toilet and you. You'll be able to shut the door and sit to contemplate in privacy. A little clever design will enable the addition of a foldaway wash basin and—with real ingenuity—a shower. The latter is accomplished by building a sump in below the head compartment sole and using a telephone-type handheld shower nozzle. Of course, this arrangement will pretty thoroughly wet down everything in the head compartment. To avoid this you'd need a separate shower stall, which would require an additional separate space at least 24 inches (61 cm) square, with full standing headroom.

Passages

Another thing to beware of is doorways and passages that are so narrow you have to sort of ooze through them. The minimum width of a useable passage or door is 19 inches (48 cm) from the waist (30 inches or 76 cm from the floor) and up. Below the waist you can get down to a mere 14 inches (36 cm) wide. A passage this narrow is useable but *tight!* Whenever possible, passages and doorways should be fully 24 inches (61 cm) wide. Twenty-two inches (56 cm) is an acceptable compromise for comfort and space saving.

Galley Counters

Stand-up counters should be 32 to 38 inches high (81 to 96 cm). Standard counter width is 18 inches (46 cm). Less—down to 12 inches or 30 cm—is perfectly usable, but seems skimpy, while more is great (naturally) but hard to get on even the largest of boats. An important aspect of stand-up counters is the kick space. If you look at the bottom of the cabinets supporting the counters in your kitchen, you'll see that there's a cut-out running along the bottom of all of them. Providing this toe room is so important for comfort that virtually every single kitchen cabinet made has them. On a boat, you can get by with a notch 3 inches high by 3 inches deep (7.6 by 7.6 cm) running along the bottom of the cabinet, where it meets the floor (4 inches by 4 inches or 10 cm by 10 cm is the landlubber standard).

Hatches

A proper hatch is 24 inches square or larger. Twenty-two inches square is the bare minimum. Larger hatches not only mean easier access, but more air and light below in fair weather.

Headroom

Full headroom is 6 feet 1 inch (186 cm) under the deck beams or head liner, not an inch or centimeter less. In fact, although I could get by with less, I have enough friends who tower over 6 feet 2 inches (188 cm) to make even 6 feet 1 inch (186 cm) seem low. For small boats, comfortable sitting headroom is about 4 feet 9 inches (145 cm) from the cabin sole to the overhead. Three feet 9 inches (115 cm) is the practical minimum headroom, but this is *cozy!* As a rule, I don't recommend designs with 5 feet 6 inches (166 cm) of headroom or so, though this is sometimes a worthwhile compromise for a portion of the accommodations. This height's just enough to make you think you can stand up, but—of course—you can't. The result is endless knocks on the noggin.

Consumables

Now, there are other dimensions to human design. For instance, you have to allow ample room for storage of gear, food, and water. An average man will consume 6 pounds (2.7 kg) of food per day—including all the unavoidable packaging and disposables. If you're on a week's cruise with two couples this comes to 168 pounds (76 kg) of food. Of course, you need to carry extra food for emergencies, so four people for one week require something over 200 pounds (90 kg) of food. Storage space for all these goods would be at least 6½ cubic feet (0.18 m³)—a couple of fair-sized lockers on most boats.

There's still water. For drinking and hand and face washing only, the average usage is about a gallon (3.8 l) per person per day. For a one-week cruise with four people, this comes to 28 gallons (106 l). Water is so critical to survival and safety, however, that you should always have a huge reserve—at least 50 percent more than the average usage allowance. This brings the requirements of four people for a week to 42-plus gallons (160 l), or just under 6 cubic feet (0.17 m³) of stowage space.

If we add in the space needed to store personal gear—foul-weather gear, clothes, books, bedding, and so on—you can see how quickly storage space requirements build up. This is frequently the greatest failing of apparently roomy accommodations. Such designs often gain an extra berth or a roomier cabin by eliminating locker and stowage space. This looks great on the showroom floor or at the boat show, and it sure sells boats, but—when you go to sea in a craft like this—you'll find there just isn't anyplace to tuck away all the stuff you'd like. The result is that boxes, duffels, and miscellaneous bits of gear end up strewn about out in the open, where they constantly get in the way and cause clutter.

The problem of estimating the quantity of stores required and finding places to put it all is as old as ships themselves. The sailing navies, for instance, had several systems for determining provisions. One allowed each man 3 pounds (1.4 kg) of food per day (they didn't eat as well as we do, nor did they have the complex packaging—cans, for instance—that we do now); 2 pounds (0.9 kg) per day for firewood; 1 gallon (3.8 l) per day of drinking water; plus a fixed allowance of 12 pounds (5.4 kg) for clothes and personal gear, and 28 pounds (12.7 kg) arms and armor. (Hopefully you won't have to allow for arms and armor.) Including storage casks, this worked out to 270 pounds (123 kg) for each crewman for five days. Frequently, the old navies had to transport horses. The rule for them was one horse equals five men—1,350 pounds (614 kg) of stores per horse every five days! Perhaps this explains why so few yachts are equipped to convey horses.

You Never Have Enough Access

Finally, there are "minor" considerations—like access to the engine and steering gear and proper bilge sumps and drainage. Frequently these requirements are given last priority in order to maximize interior room. This is all to the the good until you have gear failure and the only way you can get at the offending machinery is by wedging yourself upside down between the berth and galley table. Such cramped access doesn't exactly encourage routine maintenance either. In fact, you shouldn't even consider purchasing a boat where you can't reach the following for routine repairs:

    engine
    generator
    steering gear
    batteries
    bilge pumps and strainers
    electric panels (front and back)
    fuel tanks and fuel filters

All these items of equipment *must* have *large* access panels installed over and/or in front of them, with quick-release latches, requiring no tools to open. I've surveyed any number of craft where some—often many—of these items couldn't be reached at all! What do you do if the steering gear jams on a boat like this, offshore?

When evaluating boats, keep a sharp eye on the compromises and sacrifices that have been made for additional interior accommodations. All boats and all designs are compromises, but make sure that your boat embodies the kind of trade-offs that match the way you'll use her.

CHAPTER 51

At the Helm: Steering Station Ergonomics

The elevator man—the most experienced crew man was always put on the elevators— stood sideways in the control car so that he could feel the pitch of the ship and correct any rise or fall.

The Great Dirigibles, John Toland

As Yogi Berra once said, "It was *déja vu* all over again." I was standing at the helm of a 27-foot (8.2 m) sportfisherman, speaking to a fellow who was interested in our Off Soundings 34. Practically the first thing he'd done was to clamber over to the helm seat. "This makes me feel short," he remarked, bobbing his head from side to side to explore different viewing angles. "I've got the same situation on my present boat, and also had it on the one before that."

I could see what he was talking about. The helm was such that he had to swing himself up onto a raised bar stool-type seat. Here, his eye was at the right level to see through the windshield, but the minute he stepped down to stand at the wheel his vision was obstructed by the top rail of the windscreen. I tried it myself and it made me feel like a Lilliputian.

What made this *déja vu* all over again was . . . What made this *déja vu* all over again was that I'd just finished a long discussion about this very problem with another client. In fact, it seems I've been hearing this exact complaint—or variation thereof—for years. On far too many boats, if you're tall enough to see over the windshield when standing, then the top rail blocks your vision when you sit, while if you're short enough to see clear through the windshield center seated, then there's that rail again, blocking your view when you stand.

All sorts of dodges are employed to get around this—once the problem has been built in—helm seats that raise and lower like barber chairs; steps installed just under the wheel; slide-out standing platforms; and more. The ideal, though, would be to get the dimensions just so to start with.

Design for Fidgeting

Picture yourself on a normal cruise. You'll walk over to the helm, and—more than likely— motor out of harbor standing up. The extra few inches of eye height help you see around moored boats and such. Further—since you're still on your feet—you can dash over to handle a close-quarter emergency that much faster; you've got a standing start. As you ease out of your anchorage and into the open, you'll bring the old girl up to speed and—it's pretty certain—settle back into your chair. Of course, after a while, you'll get fidgety and stand up again.

More important, when the going gets rough you'll almost certainly stand up again. You can brace yourself better on your feet and, with your knees bent just slightly, absorb the shock of pounding better as well. In these conditions, you want something firm but cushioned to brace your fundement on—a leaning post. In fact, many flat-out ocean racers hardly have true seats at all, but instead very well padded semicircular leaning posts. Strapped into one of these cushioned slots—we can't really call them chairs—your slightly bent knees make excellent spring-type shock absorbers.

An All-Around Solution

When I settled down to work out the detail design for the helm station on the Off Soundings 34 (Chapter 10) I was determined to provide the best of all these variations. I didn't want to use a step to increase standing height, because the step obstructs foot room when seated and makes just one more thing to slip off of or to trip over. I also didn't want to use a high or a variable-height seat. A high seat is a nuisance to get in and out of.

Some years back I'd designed an 18-foot (5.5 m) jet-drive runabout whose seats were low, comfortable, and secure. (She was a 50-knot boat; her seats had better be secure.) With this as a starting point, I worked up the configuration shown in the illustration.

The seat's just 16 inches (41 cm) high—ideal seat height for comfort—and sloped aft for extra back support. In fact, by keeping the seat low, your head is kept well beneath the top of the windshield, providing good protection from wind and

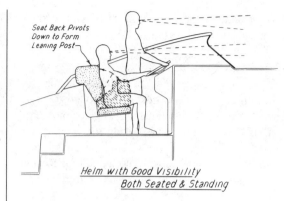

Helm with Good Visibility
Both Seated & Standing

Seat Back Pivots
Down to Form
Leaning Post

spray. At the same time, eye height seated is just about at the middle of the windshield—not barely below the upper windscreen edge, but dead through the clear center of the glass. With this arrangement, you feel like you're in the boat, not perched on top of it, yet you can see easily. Standing up, your entire head's clear above the windshield—100 percent unobstructed visibility (and fresh air) all around.

Standing Around

To create a leaning post for long stints standing at the helm, the seat back flips down. As you can see, the seat back's been made extra thick on top and is heavily padded, front, top, and back. When you're standing and want to lean on something, you just reach behind, grab the seat-back top, give it a tug to release the spring catches, and fold it forward—one easy motion from seat to leaning post. Tired of standing?—reach under the folded-down seat back and shove it up and to the rear. It snaps firmly into its catches—again, one quick motion.

The fellow shown piloting in this drawing's an average Joe, about 5 feet 9 inches (175 cm) tall; however, the configuration works just as well for everyone from a 5-foot 3-inch (160 cm) sylph to a

6-foot 3-inch (190 cm) bruiser. (If you're taller than this, you're on your own.)

Wind Can Be a Blast

Another feature of this helm station is that the top edge of the windshield is rolled down to form an integral wind deflector. On most standard windscreens, the breeze striking the glass is funneled up and aft smoothly. This can make for a perfect continuous blast of spray and air in your face when you stand up high enough to peer over the windshield edge. The wind deflector alleviates this greatly, though not altogether. (There's only so much you can do to reduce the breeze in a 30-knot-plus boat—if you pop your head above the windshield that is.)

Like most sportfishermen, the Off Soundings 34's usually fitted with a tuna or marlin tower with an integral hard top. Canvas and clear acrylic roll-down snap-flaps shelter the whole bridge deck, yet roll up for nearly perfect ventilation when they're not required. Boats with permanently enclosed steering stations, however, require plenty of additional ventilation. In fact, you can get pretty queasy pretty quick in a hot, stuffy wheelhouse while motoring in a beam sea.

Cold-Weather Lobster Machines

Just as I was finishing up the helm station drawings for the Off Soundings 34, a fellow came to me asking for the design of a long, lean lobster boat. He wanted her long and lean for improved speed and comfort in a seaway, and wanted to cruise at 18 to 20 knots. His number-one requirement, however, was super ventilation at the helm. He wanted it to feel wide open in good weather, yet to close down tight when things got nasty.

Now, what we call a lobsterboat, or a Maine lobsterboat, these days, is actually a model that originated in Nova Scotia. In fact, many old-timers still call these boats Novi-boats. The key words here, however, are Nova Scotia and Maine. It's a durn sight cooler up there than it is down on, say, Long Island Sound—never mind points south. Furthermore, the lobsterboats' crews were out in all kinds of bad weather—cold, dank, foggy, blustery, or all of the above. It's no surprise that most lobsterboats are fitted with good solid wheelhouses.

Profile of the lobsterboat Jackpot, *here rigged as a dive boat.*

LOA	36 ft. 0 in.	(10.9 m)
LWL	34 ft. 4 in.	(10.4 m)
Beam	10 ft. 8 in.	(3.2 m)
Draft	3 ft. 8 in.	(111 cm)
Disp.	4.5 tons	
Power	Cummins 6 BT5.9-M Diesel	
	210 hp (156 kw) at 2,600 rpm	
Speed	23 knots max.	
	16 to 20 knots cruise	

Jackpot's *arrangement.*

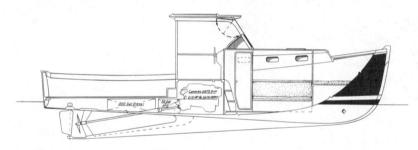

Inboard profile of Jackpot. You can see the upper window panel method of opening and closing.

Opening Her Up

Take one of these fine sea boats out on the Sound some hot, airless summer afternoon and that wheelhouse, so warm and cozy in cold weather, turns into an oven. Even with the usual windows open, it's hard to get it really cool. The solution can be seen on the drawings of *Jackpot*. Although at first glance she appears to have a traditional lobsterboat wheelhouse, you can see that her "wheelhouse" is really just a permanent hardtop. The sides and back are wide open. Forward, the windshield is only half-height. Seated, you look through the clear center of the glass, and your head is below the windshield top for full protection from wind and spray. Standing, you look clear over the windshield. (The seat heights and proportions are almost identical to those of the Off Soundings 34.) Even better, there's a continuous, unobstructed, steady breeze through the bridge deck/helm station, over the top of the half-height windshield.

When it blows up, the upper half of the windshield pivots down from its retaining hook on the underside of the hardtop. This instantly seals off the top of the windshield, converting the half-height windshield into a full-height closed windshield, like those found on any lobsterboat. The sides and back of the bridge deck may be sealed with roll-down canvas and acrylic flaps, making the bridge deck tight and dry enough for the coldest days.

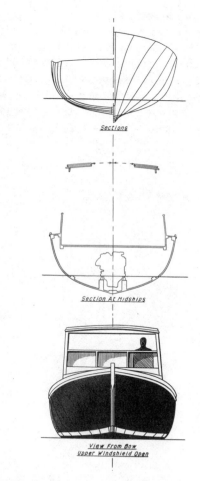

Sections, midships section, and bow-on view of Jackpot. The midships section gives a good idea of how much ventilation space there is at her "wheelhouse."

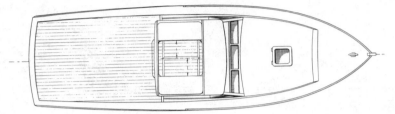

Jackpot's deck plan showing the double-slide opening "sunroof."

Sun Roof Anyone?

To further enhance ventilation, *Jackpot's* "wheelhouse" hardtop's fitted with a huge opening hatch on the centerline. This hatch is like two companion slides that open athwartships, instead of fore-and-aft. (A gasket and drip groove at the centerline keeps things watertight when closed.) With both these slides open, all the warm air in under the hardtop escapes easily. At the same time, enough hardtop's left to provide shelter from the sun. In fact, you can partially open one or both slides, adjusting them for most effective shade, no matter what course you steer or where the sun happens to be. *Jackpot's* thus fitted with the best possible combination of bimini top, hard top, and enclosed wheelhouse.

CHAPTER 52

Staying Afloat

At the end of half an hour a lull allowed
Marlborough *to come round on her course.*
She settled down again slowly, as if she did
not really believe in it, but knew she had no
choice. South-east, it was, and one and a half
knots. It must *bring them home. It had to.*

H.M.S. Marlborough Will Enter Harbor,
Nicholas Monsarrat

In some respect, the first and last job of every boat is to keep you afloat and out of the wet. Most craft do this simply by making sure the water stays out and you stay in. But what if you run into a floating log when you're doing 20 knots plus? Or what if you're knocked down by a terrific gust and swamped? Will your boat remain on the surface then?

The answer, of course, varies from vessel to vessel. Most craft that venture off soundings have strong hulls and decks, watertight cockpits, and robust watertight hatches. They could almost certainly stand a knockdown or being pooped. A major holing, however, would be another story. A eight-inch (20 cm) hole would sink most yachts very quickly. It was just this sort of catastrophic holing that deposited Dougal Robertson and his family in the Pacific. Their vessel, *Lucette,* was struck by killer whales and sank in a matter of minutes. Is there a way to survive such a puncture?

"Prepare to dive! Shut all watertight doors!"

Actually, there are two approaches to keeping your *Salty Dog* on the surface should she be holed. The first is the use of watertight bulkheads. This method is positively ancient. Chinese junks from over a millennium ago were often divided into 12 or more totally separate watertight compartments. It's also tried and true. The *Titanic* notwithstanding, a well-designed vessel with watertight bulkheads is very difficult to sink. This is so much the case that watertight or collision bulkheads are required by Federal regulations in all vessels carrying more than 49 passengers. In smaller craft— under 100 tons—a forward collision bulkhead alone may meet Coast Guard requirements. If you divide a boat into thirds with bulkheads, however, it will usually float with any one compartment flooded. Naturally, the more compartments, the safer you are. The 60-foot (18.2 m) ocean racer *Holger Danske* (see Chapter 21) is fitted with six watertight bulkheads. It would take a truly catastrophic impact to admit enough water to sink her.

The only problem with watertight bulkheads is

that they make it darn near impossible to get from one part of the boat to another from inside. The ancient Chinese junks, for instance, had access to each compartment only from hatches on deck. Sure, ocean liners can have man-size watertight doors, but trying to work one of these contraptions onto your average 50-foot (15 m) cruising yacht will wreak havoc with her nice joinerwork.

Foaming at the Bilges

This brings us to the other approach to staying afloat: Fill your boat with so much foam that she couldn't sink even when chopped to pieces. Actually, most modern powerboats, especially small runabouts, have enough flotation to keep them afloat and level. Some, like the Boston Whaler, really go to town with the foam. Who hasn't seen the ad showing a Whaler cut into three sections with a chain saw, each piece still afloat high and dry? A lot can be said for this. There's no safer place for you to be than on your boat. She has all your supplies and gear on board, she is bigger than your liferaft or you and so easier to spot, and you might even get her patched up and dried out again. Unfortunately, foam flotation, especially full foam flotation, has much the same drawback that watertight bulkheads have. It takes up room—lots of it.

When swamped or holed, your boat can float in a number of ways. She could lie with her decks just awash, she could be somewhat higher out of the water and possibly up by the bow or stern, or she could float so high that it would be difficult to tell that she wasn't in her normal unflooded state.

The Unsinkable Molly Brown

In order for your boat to stay afloat she needs to have a structure that's lighter than water after being swamped or submerged. Here's where we start running into problems. Woods, at least most woods, are lighter than water. A wooden rowing skiff will float no matter what you do to her. Chop her into little pieces and grind them up in your Cuisinart and each piece will still float. If she was of a light wood, like cedar, she'd probably float pretty high as well. But if we made that same hull out of fiberglass, we'd need to add flotation. This is because, as we've seen, glass laminates weigh around 94 pounds per cubic foot (565 kg/m³). Sea water weighs 64 pounds per cubic foot (1,025 kg/m³). Swamp an all-glass boat and she'll sink like a stone.

How Much Foam Do You Need?

Okay then, just add some flotation. In a small unballasted boat without an interior, this is fairly easy. You simply need to float the FRP hull high enough to be about half in and half out of the water—half submerged. We have to end up with sufficient foam to make the combined density of the flotation and the FRP hull equal half the density of water. This works out to 1 cubic foot of 2-pound-density foam for every 45 pounds of fiberglass, or 1 cubic meter of 32-kilogram-density foam for every 721 kilograms of fiberglass.

Now, if your shiny Salty Dog's FRP hull weighs 800 pounds (364 kg) she'll require 17.7 cubic feet of 2-pound-density foam, or 0.5 m³ of 32-kg-density foam. That's a fair amount of space. A box 4 feet by 3 feet by 1½ feet or 100 cm by 100 cm by 50 cm would just fit the bill. A small boat like this doesn't use much interior volume for accommodations and such, so you can use up what room there is for foam—sticking it under thwarts, gunnels, and decks.

You'll Need Plenty

On larger boats the amount of foam required can be quite surprising. This is because you have to make up not only for the weight of the hull, but also for the engine, ballast, and other heavy gear as well. Let's say your 50-foot (15 m) motorsailer Hornblower has a 70-hp (52 kw) diesel. This engine weighs 625 pounds (284 kg). After you add the weights of the tanks, shaft, stuffing box, mounting, controls, and such you can figure around 1,000 pounds (454 kg). *Hornblower* also carries 9,000 pounds (4,090 kg) of lead ballast on 40,000 pounds (18,180 kg) displacement. Additionally, you'd have to add in the weights of her aluminum spars, steel pulpit and life-line stanchions, winches, anchors, chain, and so on. Let's say another 1,200 pounds (545 kg)—it could easily be more.

Now, in addition to floating *Hornblower*'s hull, you need to float all this heavy gear as well. Since they're different densities they require differing amounts of foam:

FOAM FOR HALF-SUBMERGED FLOTATION

Density-2 lb./cu.ft. or 32 kg/m³

Fiberglass:	1 cubic foot for each 45 pounds
Fiberglass:	1 cubic meter for each 721 kilograms
Aluminum:	1 cubic foot for each 37 pounds
Aluminum:	1 cubic meter for each 593 kilograms
Iron and steel:	1 cubic foot for each 32 pounds
Iron and steel:	1 cubic meter for each 513 kilograms
Lead:	1 cubic foot for each 30 pounds
Lead:	1 cubic meter for each 480 kilograms

So, *Hornblower* needs 300 cubic feet (8.5 m³) of foam to float her ballast (9,000 lb. lead ÷ 30 lb./cu.ft. foam = 300 cu.ft.—or, 4,090 kg lead ÷ 480 kg/m³ = 8.5 m³).

For her steel engine and gear (for our purposes and the relatively small amount involved, we'll lump the aluminum gear with the steel) *Hornblower* will need 68 cubic feet (1.9 m³) of 2-pound (32 kg) foam—1,000 lb. engine + 1,200 lb. gear = 2,200 lb., and 2,200 lb. gear ÷ 32 lb./cu.ft. foam = 68 cu.ft.—or, 454 kg engine + 545 kg gear = 999 kg, and 999 kg ÷ 513 kg/m³ = 1.9 m³.

So far, we're up to 368 cubic feet (10.4 m³) of foam and we haven't even added flotation for the hull. How much flotation does the hull require? An architect can calculate the exact hull weight from the plans. A fair estimate, however, can be made by figuring that hull weight is between 30 and 40

percent of displacement for auxiliary sailboats and 45 and 55 percent of displacement for powerboats. In *Hornblower's* case, her fiberglass hull should weigh around 14,000 pounds or 6,363 kg—40,000 lb. × 35% = 14,000 lb.—or, 18,180 kg × 35% = 6,363 kg.

Accordingly, she'd require 311 cubic feet of 2-pound foam, or 8.8 cubic meters of 32-kg foam for her fiberglass hull (14,000 lb. ÷ 45 lb./cu.ft foam = 311 cu.ft.—or, 6,363 kg ÷ 721 kg/m³ = 8.8 m³).

Altogether, *Hornblower* would need 679 cubic feet of 2-pound foam (19.2 m³ of 32-kg foam) flotation to make her float half in and half out of the water when completely swamped.

Locating the Foam

Of course, you'd want *Hornblower* to float level, so you have to locate her flotation evenly along her length. The 311 cubic feet (8.8 m³) of foam to float her hull should be distributed fairly regularly from bow to stern, with a bit more aft to account for the additional hull weight aft, her stern being wider than her bow. The 300 cubic feet (8.5 m³) of foam for her ballast and the 68 cubic feet (1.9 m³) of foam for her engine and gear should be located to float these items. Ideally, you'd want the center of the 300 cubic feet (8.5 m³) of foam (for floating the lead) directly over the center of gravity of the ballast. In practice, however, you can simply be sure to distribute that quantity of foam equally fore-and-aft of the ballast's center.

Another factor in the location of flotation is that it should be as low in the boat as possible. If all of *Hornblower's* flotation was up high, it wouldn't start to take effect until her decks were nearly awash. On the other hand, if we'd placed all her flotation below her waterline, then *Hornblower* wouldn't have to sink much for all of her flotation to take full effect. Small unballasted boats sometimes place their flotation high and asymmetrically distributed (more to one side than the other) to aid in righting after capsize. However, ballasted vessels should have as much flotation low as possible. It's also important to spread the foam out evenly athwartships. This increases stability when swamped and floating on the foam. For a ballasted boat this is not quite as important as getting the foam low. On an unballasted craft going a bit higher with the foam in order to get a good spread athwartships will pay off in stability when flooded.

Heavy Foam

Another drawback to foam flotation is that it's heavy. What?—foam is heavy?! Well, *Hornblower* needs 679 cubic feet (19.2 m³) of 2-pound-density (32 kg) foam, which comes to 1,358 pounds or 616 kg! You see, flotation can not only take up plenty of useful room, but add weight as well. This is yet another reason to get your flotation as low as possible. With its weight low it will not affect stability adversely.

A Full-Flotation Motorsailer

In spite of its drawbacks, full foam flotation's definitely worth consideration. It's a nice feeling of security you get from knowing that no matter what happens, your boat just can't sink. In addition to outboard runabouts, many smaller trailerable sailboats come with varying degrees of flotation. One large production motorsailer with true full flotation is the *Wellington 47*. She's a long-range motorsailer originally of flush-deck design. In order to make room for all the flotation required, Wellington Boats had to alter the *Wellington 47* to a trunk cabin configuration. This allowed for raising the cabin sole and making room for the foam almost entirely below the waterline. A *Wellington 47* with full flotation has so much foam that she'll sink no more than 8 inches (20 cm) when completely swamped. That's it! Not only that, but she is still stable enough to sail when swamped, and all her essential gear and accommodations remain mostly dry. This kind of total flotation can be achieved only in a boat specifically designed for it. Of course, the full flo-

tation does take up room. The foamed *Wellington* has less storage and machinery space than an identical boat would have without flotation; however, with clever design and good layout you can still get by.

In my opinion, the trade-offs for flotation are often worthwhile. A boat like the *Wellington*'s probably as safe as any boat afloat, large or small. She can get where she wants to under sail or power or both. She's ballasted with a good range of stability, and even if her hull were punctured, she'd float—and float quite high.

Can You Foam Your Boat?

If you'd like to figure the amount of foam you'd need to float your boat, you can figure her requirements just as we did *Hornblower*'s. Simply refer to the table for the correct amount of foam for each component of your boat.

Foam comes in many types and densities. You should use the lightest, most rigid foam you can. Avoid leaving voids as much as possible. It's also important to get a foam that doesn't break down or react with gasoline or diesel oil or, of course, salt water.

All the figures above are for 2-pound- or 32-kilogram-density foam; of course, the lighter the foam you use the better. If you use other weights of foam you should multiply the foam amounts given above by the following:

Add 8 percent more foam in cubic feet for 4-lb or 64-kg foam.

Add 10 percent more foam in cubic feet for 6-lb or 96-kg foam.

Add 14 percent more foam in cubic feet for 8-lb 128-kg foam.

Staying High and Dry

Now, the flotation amounts given above will keep you well afloat; however, they won't keep you high and dry. Your boat'll be half in and half out of the water if the foam's installed correctly. In this condition, you'll have a fair amount of water in the bilge, usually well above the floorboards. Dry and intact, most boats float so that two-thirds or more of their structure's above the waterline. To get your boat to float this high when swamped you'd need at least 50 percent more foam than in the tables above. Unless, like the *Wellington,* your vessel was designed around this concept, it's not realistic to be able to work in this much flotation.

The Combined Approach

The most practical way to try to make your current boat unsinkable is to combine a number of flotation techniques. A watertight bulkhead aft of the forepeak and one forward of the lazarette will go a long way to keeping you afloat. If these compartments are fairly large—say, at least 15 percent of the length on deck—they will add considerable reserve buoyancy. Then you can try to find space for foam flotation amidships, low and well spread-out. You may not be able to work in all the foam recommended above, but if you can get in 60 percent of the recommended amount and if your forward and after compartments remain dry, then you'll be pretty certain of staying up.

Another approach is to use air bags as emergency flotation. This is good in that the air bags take up little room until they're needed. They are, though, subject to breakage and failure, which isn't what you want to deal with while your boat's going down. You might consider using a combination of fore-and-aft watertight bulkheads, foam low amidships, and an air-bag system for extra flotation. This way you could use the minimum amount of foam and rely on the air bag to lift your boat higher while you try to patch her up. The total volume of all the flotation systems combined should equal the volume of 2-pound (32-kg) foam you'd need if you were using foam alone.

An interesting wrinkle in flotation is the use of water ballast in sailboats. An all-wood sailboat that relies on water in a low tank for ballast is still absolutely lighter than water. Although ballasted, she'll remain afloat no matter what, just like the all-wood rowing skiff. Only a small bit of additional foam's required to float her high. Unfortunately, water ballast's not very dense, and so its center of gravity's higher than you'd want in most vessels. Still, I owned such a boat for a short time, and it was certainly reassuring to know that she'd always be underfoot, so to speak. In fact, that's the bottom line when thinking about flotation. Next time you're caught out with your family in a nasty blow, or you find yourself having to navigate through floating debris at night, imagine how much more peace of mind you'd have if you absolutely knew that, come what may, your boat just couldn't sink.

PART 12

Getting Where You're Going

I know where I'm goin', and I know who's goin' with me . . .

CHAPTER 53

Rudders: Hitting What You Aim For

It was with a happy heart that the good Odysseus spread his sail to catch the wind and used his seamanship to keep his boat straight with the steering-oar.

The *Odyssey,* Homer
Translated by E.V. Rieu

It's not absolutely necessary to have a true rudder to keep a boat headed in the direction you aim to go. In fact, for millennia, throughout the Mediterranean and all of Europe, boats were steered with oars or paddles hung—almost invariably—off the starboard quarter (the right side of a vessel at the stern). We still do this today on canoes, which—when soloed—are usually propelled with the J-stroke, and are maneuvered by twisting and angling a paddle held off one side of the hull. Since most folks are right handed, it's usually from off of the right side. The old Norse word for this paddle or oar was the "steor-borde"—the steering board, what else. It's from this practice that the term "starboard" has come to mean the right side of a boat.

Also, it's due to this that the starboard side of a boat has traditionally been the captain's side; it was the control side. In the old navies, the officers and important visitors boarded from starboard, while cargo and crew came aboard from port. Even today, a Bristol-fashion yacht will board owner and guests from starboard, and the lowly motor Macks and ship's stores from port.

In the West—from the ancient Phoenician traders, through the Roman Empire, right up to the Norse raiders or Vikings—these steerboards were the only method of guiding a ship. The oldest known evidence of a modern centerline-hung rudder in Europe dates from 1242 A.D. It's a picture on the seal of the North German town of Elbing. I don't know if it compares with the invention of the wheel, but the rudder's certainly right up there on the list of all-time-innovation hit singles. So much more efficient was this newfangled gizmo that within a bare 200 years or so it was nearly universal.

Things progressed a bit more quickly in the Orient. A pottery boat model, from a tomb in Canton, shows an entirely modern centerline rudder. The date—about 200 B.C. The Chinese have been employing rudders for 1,400 or more years before us European barbarians—at least, that's probably how they'd have seen it back when. Curiously, the ancient Chinese word for rudder (a word no longer in use) is roughly transliterated as t'o. It's from an archaic Chinese pictograph meaning branch or tree, or—you guessed it—paddle. Our own word "rudder" comes from the Middle English "rother," meaning . . . paddle. Both civilizations reached the same solution to the same problem, from the same starting point. It just took the West a bit longer, that's all.

On the surface, rudders are simple enough to make you wonder why it took us so long to come up with the idea. We'll take a look at how and why they work and at some little-known aspects of their design, and then give you some insight into checking whether the rudder (or rudders) on your current boat—or on one you're thinking of buying—is up to snuff.

Putting The Rudder To Work

Fundamentally, rudders are no more than a board hung on the centerline of a boat and free to pivot at hinges, called *gudgeons* and *pintles,* along their leading edge; or—alternately—around a vertical shaft, called the *rudder post* or *rudder stock.* (On modern twin-screw craft, the rudders are hung just aft of each propeller.)

If you deflected the rudder blade of your nimble *Sprightly Springer* to one side—say to port—you'd increase the force of the water hitting the port or left side of her rudder, which in turn

would swing *Sprightly Springer*'s entire stern in the opposite direction, to the right or to starboard. Since you've essentially used the force of water flowing past the rudder to kick *Springer*'s stern around to starboard, her bow's now been swung to port, and off *Springer*'ll go to port—presumably what you had in mind when you put her helm over in the first place.

Describing The Rudder

Now, rudders come in many shapes and sizes, so architects have adopted some airplane terminology to help describe them. The depth or vertical height of a rudder's called its *span*. The fore-and-aft length of the rudder's referred to as its *chord*. Designers tend to visualize airplane wings and hydrofoils—like rudders or keels—as growing out from the fuselage or hull; this is, after all, where they're attached. Accordingly, the top of the rudder, near the hull underbody, is known as the *root,* and the fore-and-aft length here is the

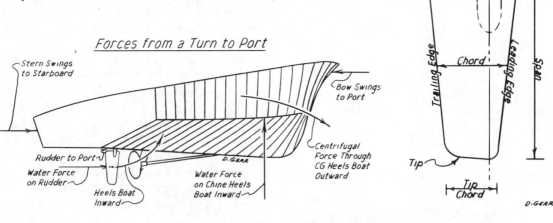

Forces from a Turn to Port

Describing the Rudder

root chord. Similarly, the bottom end of the rudder—farthest from the hull—is termed the *tip,* and the fore-and-aft length at this location's the *tip chord.* (This same terminology is applied to all airfoils and hydrofoils, and could have been used in Chapters 37 and 38, dealing with lift.)

All hydrofoils are more efficient if they're long and narrow than if they're short and squat (as we saw in Chapter 37). It's important to be able to describe this feature clearly as well, and engineers have thought up one of their customarily catchy terms—*aspect ratio.* Aspect ratio is merely the vertical height (the span) of a rudder multiplied by itself (or squared) and divided by the rudder's area. The larger the aspect ratio, the deeper and narrower the rudder. (Finding rudder area doesn't have to be an exact science. To determine the area of the rudder on your boat, just measure its cord (fore-and-aft length) at mid span (mid height) and multiply by the span at mid cord (the average height). The answer won't be precise to the Nth decimal place, but it'll be good enough.)

If your *Sprightly Springer*'s rudder had an area of 1.9 square feet (0.175 m²) and an average height or span of 2.1 feet (64 cm), its aspect ratio would be 2.32 to 1—2.3 [2.1 ft. × 2.1 ft. ÷ 1.9 sq.ft. = 2.32:1—or, 0.64 m × 0.64 m ÷ 0.175 m² = 2.3]. This is a good deep narrow rudder—a high-aspect rudder. An aspect ratio higher than 2.4 gives a still more efficient rudder blade, but adds excessive bending strain on the rudder stock. Such very high aspect ratios should be avoided except on special high-performance craft.

Rudder and Hull Work Together

In turning, a boat pivots roughly around her combined center of gravity and the center of water pressure on her hull forward. The greater the distance the rudder's located aft of this combined center, the greater the lever arm it has to twist the boat around with, and the more effective it can be. Or, for the same steering effect, a smaller rudder can be used, if it's farther aft. Similarly, a boat with a deep forefoot or a steering fin forward will respond more quickly to the helm than one without. This isn't of much importance on average boats, which generally have fairly good proportions for this purpose; however, long, shallow hulls and/or very high-speed planing hulls sometimes benefit greatly from the addition of a small fixed steering or skid fin forward.

Sizing Up The Skid Fin

You have to be careful not to overdo this; too much area forward makes a boat too quick on the helm. In rough seas, such a fin can broach a boat, or cause her to trip and capsize. A good rule of thumb is that the skid fin—when one's required at all—should be about 10 to 15 percent of the length of the boat forward of her center of gravity, and the area of the skid fin should be about 90 percent of the rudder area. (If you have no exact information, you can assume that the center of gravity of a high-speed planing hull is about 60 percent of her waterline length aft of the bow, at the waterline.)

Aspect Ratio and Your Bank

A little-known consideration of rudder design is that rudder aspect ratio affects how your boat banks in a turn. When you put *Sprightly Springer*'s helm over for a hard turn at high speed, centrifugal force acts on her center of gravity, pulling outwards. The center of gravity of almost all planing hulls—in fact of most powerboats of any type—is well above the waterline, which tends to make a boat heel outward. This—when it happens—is an unnerving experience, a sort of drunken, out-of-control sensation. The force of water pressure on the underside of *Springer*'s outboard chine counteracts this outward heel considerably, but the water force acting on her rudder helps as well. The deeper the rudder—the greater its aspect ratio, and the more area it has—the more effective it is in generating the sure-footed inward bank every boat should make as she swings round to a new heading.

Rudder Types

Rudders basically come in two types—*inboard rudders,* or rudders mounted entirely under the hull (see the inboard profile of *Jackpot* in Chapter 51), and *outboard rudders,* or rudders hung on the transom and thus projecting aft of the hull proper (see the *Papoo,* Chapter 48). These two types may each be divided again into *balanced* and *unbalanced rudders.* A balanced rudder has some of its area forward of its pivot or turning point, whereas an unbalanced rudder pivots or hinges entirely at its leading edge, with no area projecting forward at all. (*Papoo*'s rudder is unbalanced, *Jackpot*'s is balanced.)

Inboard and Outboard

For the same rudder shape and area, an inboard rudder's almost always more efficient than an outboard rudder. The hull traps the water rushing over the top portion of the blade, forcing the entire flow here aft and compelling this water to do useful steering work. This is the much-touted endplate effect, and it reduces induced drag, which—as we discussed in Chapter 37—is nothing more than the wasted energy caused by water roiling around the top or bottom edges of a hydrofoil (which, of course, is what a rudder really is). Often, high-speed craft fitted with outboard rudders have endplates (sometimes incorrectly called cavitation plates) fastened to them at the waterline. These reduce induced drag considerably, but such rudders are still less efficient, for the same area, than true inboard rudders.

The great advantage of outboard rudders is their simplicity. It's comparatively inexpensive to attach the gudgeons and pintles outside the hull on the transom, and to run the tiller to steering gear far above the waterline, where watertightness isn't a consideration. By contrast, an inboard rudder usually requires a rudder port and stuffing box through the bottom of the hull, a potential source of leaks which should be inspected several times a season. Further, the outboard rudder allows the propeller to be installed further aft, which permits the shaft angle to be slightly lower (closer to parallel with the waterline) for more efficient thrust.

The Balancing Act

Balanced rudders move the center of water pressure—the force of the water striking the rudder blade itself—forward and closer to the rudder's pivot axis than it would fall on an unbalanced blade. Maximum water pressure occurs at maximum helm or rudder angle, which is about 35 degrees to either side of dead center—70 degrees from hard over to hard over. (At greater angles, ordinary rudders stall, lose effectiveness, and are severely strained by excessive water pressure. Stops should be fitted to keep rudders from turning beyond 35 degrees.) At 35 degrees, when there's the greatest water pressure on a rudder blade, the force is roughly equal to:

1.6 times the rudder area (in square feet) times boat speed squared (in knots). [Pressure (lbs.) = 1.6 × Area (sq.ft.) × Knots²].

or

7.8 times the rudder area (in square meters) times boat speed squared (in knots). [Pressure (kg) = 7.8 × Area (m²) × Knots²].

If our *Sprightly Springer* had a rudder area of 1.9 square feet (0.175 m²) and cruised at 18 knots, she'd generate a rudder force of 985 pounds or 442 kg [1.6 × 1.9 sq.ft. × (18 kts)² = 985 lb—or, 7.8 × 0.175 m² × (18 kts)² = 442 kg]. This is nearly half a ton! You can see why your rudder and steering gear need to be *strong!*

Now, because the water's striking *Sprightly Springer*'s rudder blade from ahead, the leading edge does more work than the trailing edge. (This is so for all hydrofoils and airfoils.) Accordingly, the center of water pressure doesn't fall at the geometric center of the rudder blade as viewed from the side, but at someplace forward of this. In fact, although the position of the center of pressure moves around with changes of rudder angle and boat speed, it usually falls somewhere between 30 and 40 percent of the fore-and-aft length of the rudder (the chord) aft of the leading edge—at the maximum 35 degrees of helm. If *Sprightly's* rudder had a span—vertical height—of 2.1 feet (64 cm) and an average chord of 0.9 feet (27 cm), the center of water pressure would fall about 35 percent of the chord aft of the leading edge, or 0.3 feet (9 cm) aft. *Springer's* unbalanced rudder would thus generate a torque (a force times a lever arm) of 295 pound-feet or 40 kilogram-meters (kgm)—0.3 ft. × 985 lb. = 295 lb.-ft.—or, 9 cm = 0.9 m, and 9 m × 442 kg = 40 kgm.

If *Sprightly Springer* were fitted with a rudder of the same area and proportions, but with a 17 percent balance, the pivot point would be farther aft and closer to the center of pressure—in this case just about ⅞ inch (2.1 cm) away. The balanced rudder would generate a torque of just 69 pound-feet (9.5 kgm)—420 percent less! This results in much easier steering and lighter loads on *Springer's* steering gear, autopilot, and—not incidentally—on her helmsman.

Balance is determined by the percentage of rudder area forward and aft of the rudder post axis. The drawing shows a rudder with 17-percent balance, which years of trial and error have demonstrated to be about ideal. Twenty-percent balance is the maximum. More balance than this moves the center of water pressure ahead of the pivot axis, making the rudder shear wildly and causing uncomfortable, unpredictable steering.

Balanced rudders do have a drawback, especially on slower craft. Since the leading edge projects out from the hull centerline when the rudder's turned, a balanced rudder offers slightly more resistance to the waterflow than an unbalanced one. For powerboats and many racing sail-

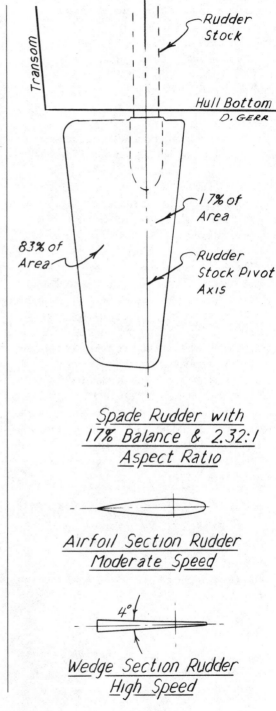

Spade Rudder with
17% Balance & 2.32:1
Aspect Ratio

Airfoil Section Rudder
Moderate Speed

Wedge Section Rudder
High Speed

boats, the advantage of a lighter and more responsive helm makes the balanced rudder hard to beat. For cruising sailboats, however, an unbalanced rudder with a skeg or keel immediately ahead of it offers less resistance and smoother water flow to the rudder.

How Big?

The great question regarding rudders is how big they should be for a given boat. The smaller the rudder, the less drag it creates and the faster you can go. Further, smaller rudders require less steering force and are easier to manage. If the rudder's too small, though, you'll end up with insufficient steering control. Somehow, we've got to nail down the happy medium.

There's no simple solution to this, but the following rules of thumb will put you well in the ballpark. They're for single-screw, single-rudder boats. Twin-screw boats should always have two rudders, each about half the area indicated. Remember that a rudder far aft, on a vessel with a substantial amount of forefoot, skeg, or fin well forward, will be more effective than a rudder located closer to midships. Such a far-aft rudder may be a bit smaller. Conversely, a hull with a long keel that'll resist turning and with its rudder relatively far forward will need somewhat greater rudder area.

Rudder Area Formulas

Average Planing Boat = 0.03 × Waterline Length × Draft (hull only)

Semi-displacement Boat = 0.045 × Waterline Length × Draft (hull only)

Displacement Boat = 0.09 × Waterline Length × Draft (hull and skeg or keel)

Sailboat (deep narrow fin keel) = 0.045 × Waterline Length × Draft (including keel)

Moderate Sailboat (modern long keel) = 0.058 × Waterline Length × Draft (including keel)

Traditional Full Long Keel Sailboat = 0.068 × Waterline Length × Draft (including keel)

Faster boats require smaller rudders than slower ones, as reflected in these rules of thumb, because the force of the water striking the rudder increases very quickly with increased speed. If *Sprightly Springer* were a very fast planing boat, say 45-knots plus, we might well get away with a rudder area only 70 percent as large as that given by the rule of thumb for average planing boats. This would reduce drag due to decreased rudder surface area, increasing *Sprightly*'s top speed slightly.

There's a potential snare here, though. If we fit *Springer* with such a rudder, she'll have enough area to maneuver well at high speed, but not enough to be responsive at low speed or backing down—a classic conflict, and one that's often overlooked. For an all-out race boat this smaller area might be well justified. If, though, *Springer* were, say, a sportfisherman—even though she could make high speeds—she'd spend a great deal of her time trolling at low speed, and doing quick maneuvering, from low speed to high speed, backing down, swinging quick turns, and dashing forward again.

As an average 29-foot (8.8 m) waterline planing boat with a 1 foot 9 inch (53 cm) hull draft, *Sprightly* would require around 1.0 square feet (0.09 m²) of rudder area. For the all-around maneuverability required by a sportfisherman *Sprightly Springer* would need a somewhat larger rudder. She'll lose a bit off her top speed due to the additional appendage drag, but will handle more responsively at reduced speed with the added area. Not only is this important for efficient fishing, but it's critical for safety when caught out in really rough seas that force her to operate at low speed. Planing vessels should have 10 to 20 percent more area than that indicated by the planing boat rule for this service. The other categories of vessels need no additional allowance for low speeds.

The Rudder in Section

Most folks think of the rudder cross-section as being a classic airfoil shape—a rounded entry, maximum width about 30 to 45 percent of chord aft of the leading edge, and a gently convex trailing section terminating at a point. In fact, for sailboats and displacement power cruisers, this is the ideal section shape. As vessels become faster, however, this section becomes less effective. After 30 or 35 knots, the bluntish, rounded leading edge of traditional airfoil sections causes too much turbulence in front of the rudder.

When the rudder's put over, this bluntish leading edge virtually tears the water flow away from the blade, leaving a swirl of eddies along the blade surface. This turbulent flow generates little force or lift and is—in fact—a stall, just like the stalling of an airplane wing in too steep a climb. Accordingly, for high-speed craft, the leading edge of the rudder should be made sharper and sharper and the point of maximum section width moved aft.

Wedge Rudders

Huckins—as in the famous Huckins PT boats—found that a true wedge-section rudder gave the most reliable steering on most planing vessels running at 30 knots and above. Such rudders come nearly to a true point at the leading edge—there's some slight width here for strength—with a perfectly squared-off trailing edge. A wedge angle of about 4 degrees is ideal. Wedge-section rudders do have slightly more drag trailing at dead center than do airfoil-section rudders, but they're much less prone to stalling, and offer more positive steering control at high speed.

Locating the Rudder

On powerboats, the rudder should always be located almost directly behind the propeller. The "almost" is because if you actually place the rudder dead center behind the prop, the mechanic will have to unship the rudder before he or she can pull the prop shaft. (If you ever want to bone up on imaginative cussing, try to be on hand at such an occasion.)

On your single-screw *Sprightly Springer,* with a proper right-hand wheel, the rudder stock should be to port of her prop-shaft centerline, just barely far enough to allow the shaft to slide by the rudder blade. On twin-screw vessels, the two props should be out turning—starboard wheel right-handed and the port wheel left-handed. The rudder stocks should be just inboard of the prop shafts. The rudder stock should also be just far enough astern of the end of the prop shaft to permit pulling the propeller without removing the rudder, but not much further—you want it to be as close to the concentrated propeller wash as possible.

Rudder-Stock Diameter

We've already seen that the loads on *Sprightly Springer's* rudder are about half a ton. Clearly, using a rudder stock that was too small would be asking for trouble. Too fat a rudder stock, though, would create excess drag. The accompanying charts, for solid-bronze rudder stocks, will give you a way to estimate the correct size for a new rudder stock or check on your existing one. If your current stock's substantially smaller than indicated on the chart you might want to have it checked out by a naval architect. (Remember that stainless steel is stronger than bronze, and thus stainless shafts may be roughly 10 percent less in diameter. Also, the charts are *only* for solid bar stocks. Hollow rudder stocks must be fatter, even though they'll be lighter as well.)

Support Your Local Rudder

Rudders are supported in one of two ways: Either they have a shaft projecting from a single bearing in the hull, at the top of the rudder, with no support at the bottom—the *spade rudder;* or the rudder stock continues down into a bearing on the skeg or keel below—bearings top and bot-

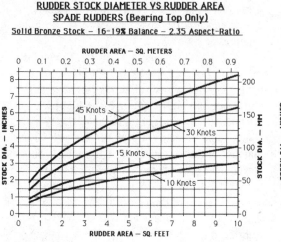

RUDDER STOCK DIAMETER VS RUDDER AREA
SPADE RUDDERS (Bearing Top Only)
Solid Bronze Stock – 16-19% Balance – 2.35 Aspect-Ratio

RUDDER STOCK DIAMETER VS RUDDER AREA
BEARINGS TOP AND BOTTOM
Solid Bronze Stock – No Balance – Aspect-Ratio 1.5 or Greater

tom. Obviously, having two bearings top and bottom is stronger—it eliminates bending loads—and requires a smaller stock. At the same time, though, the drag of the skeg below is undesirable on high-speed craft; the usual trade-off—speed versus strength. Both approaches work well if the stock's strong enough for its configuration and for the boat's speed.

If *Sprightly Springer* were a 28-knot-top-speed craft with a 1.0-square foot (0.09 m²), balanced, spade rudder (supported by only a single bearing at the top), the chart shows she'd require a 1⅞-inch-diameter (48 mm) solid bronze stock (1⅝-inch or 44-mm stainless steel). If, however, she were an 18-knot boat with a rudder supported by bearings top and bottom, and with no balance, she'd need a ⅝-inch-diameter (16 mm) bronze

shaft. (Rudder stocks shouldn't be made less than ⅝-inch (16 mm).) If—on a larger size—this type of rudder were balanced as well as being supported top and bottom, the twisting load would be less and we could decrease diameter a bit further, but the difference would be slight.

We've Only Scratched the Rudder's Surface

All the above, of course, applies to standard rudders. There are new-fangled rudders that behave quite differently—articulated rudders, rudders with trim tabs, and rudders that work at 90-degree helm angles. These latter contraptions double—when needed—as stern thrusters for tight maneuvering. Fitted with these widgets, some tugs can circle in less than their own length!

CHAPTER 54

Tiller Torque— Controlling the Rudder

There's something wrong with the steering. I can hardly turn the wheel.

Sou'west in Wanderer IV, Eric Hiscock

It was—in the age of sail—the test of every deepwater seaman: his ship slogging through a thundering storm; breaking waves crashing across her deck; the watch aloft wrestling with icy, flailing canvas. Cold and exhausting, it was dangerous work. At the helm aft—every sinew taut, their faces contorted with effort and concentration—as many as four or five men might be struggling to master an immense wooden wheel. Should they lose control, their vessel could easily swing broadside to the waves and capsize.

In the previous chapter, we examined the rudder in detail, but you need more than a strong, properly sized and shaped rudder. It's just as important to be able to make it do what you want it to—all the time, every time. What's more, you need to be able to control your rudder without the assistance of four deckhands at the wheel. A modern wheel should have nearly fingertip control. Improperly designed steering systems and steering gear problems can lead to dangerous accidents, even in smooth seas. In rough conditions or at high speeds, such problems can be catastrophic.

Stick it to 'Em

Small and medium-size sailboats have the simplest rudder control system there is—the tiller. This is no more than a simple stick, so there's nothing to go wrong—either the stick's strong enough or it isn't. The accompanying chart gives the minimum height and width of square-section tillers at the widest part—at the rudder— for hand-held wood tillers of various lengths. The tiller should gradually taper and round down from this section to a round end 1¼-inches (32 mm) in diameter—the ideal size for a firm handgrip. A tiller with these proportions will not break even if a 200-pound (90 kg) man falls on it.

Tiller Limits

Tillers, unfortunately, have their limitations. You can only use them from a location directly adjacent to the rudder, and there's also a limit to

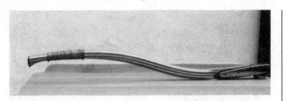

A simple stick? Well, maybe not. Nick Robison fashioned this beautiful S-curve, laminated tiller from mahogany and ash for his Serenade *(see Chapter 9). The French spiral hitching at the hand grip is a nice touch. (Nick Robison photo)*

how large a rudder they can manage without becoming too long. Say your *Right Turn* has a 1.2-square-foot (0.11 m²) unbalanced rudder and cruises at about 20 knots. Using the rudder pressure estimate from last chapter, the maximum pressure on *Right Turn*'s rudder would be about 768 pounds (345 kg). As we saw last chapter, this water pressure effectively acts at an imaginary center of pressure which falls somewhere aft of the rudder post, creating a lever arm. The lever arm for the center of water pressure on a rud-

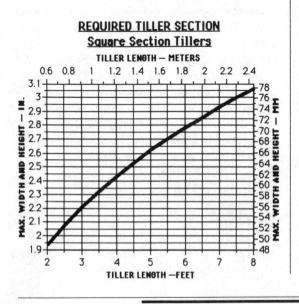

REQUIRED TILLER SECTION
Square Section Tillers

der—relative to the rudder-post axis, at hard-over 35-degree helm—can be estimated as follows:

Balanced Rudder: 0.18 times average fore-and-aft length (chord)

Unbalanced Rudder: 0.35 times average fore-and-aft length (chord)

If *Right Turn*'s rudder is 9 inches (23 cm) fore-n-aft, then the lever arm for the water force (on her unbalanced rudder) is 3.1 inches or 0.26 feet—or, 8 cm. This means the maximum turning force—or *torque*—on *Right Turn*'s rudder is 200 pound-feet or 27.6 kilogram-meters (768 lb. × 0.26 ft. = 199.7, say 200 lb.-ft.—or, 345 kg × 0.08 m = 27.6 kgm).

The Thirty-Pound (13.6 kg) Limit

Now, the greatest force the average Joe (or Jane, for that matter) can exert comfortably on a wheel is about 30 pounds, or 13.6 kilograms. This is really an upper limit, as holding the wheel against a continuous pressure like this will tire you out fast! However, maximum force occurs at hard over, and you'll seldom have the wheel over that far for more than an instant or two. To find how long *Right Turns*'s tiller would have to be to keep the maximum hand force—the force you'll need to steer with—to under 30 pounds (13.6 kg), simply divide the maximum rudder torque by 30 (or 13.6). In *Right Turn*'s case we'd get 6.7 feet or 2 meters. This is too long for many boats. In fact, on most boats over 40 feet (12 m) it gets difficult to arrange a tiller long enough to give sufficient leverage or mechanical advantage—assuming that you didn't want to move the helm station somewhere else anyway.

Wheeling Around

The solution's simple—use a steering wheel. Wheels have built-in mechanical advantage and—even better—they can be located wherever you happen to need them, rather than right aft at the rudder. In the proverbial good old days, there was

Standard sailboat wire rope (cable) steering system, with quadrant. (Courtesy The Edson Corp.)

only one way to get the power from the wheel to the rudder—rope or wire cables. This is still a simple, inexpensive, and reliable system—the standard for sailboats and common, until quite recently, on powerboats. In fact, for rigging your own steering system on any small boat, wire or rope steering's the best bet.

Advantage Mechanical

The wheel size required to keep steering forces under 30 pounds (13.6 kg) can be found by playing with a simple formula:

$$Wheel\ Radius\ (English) = \frac{Rudder\ Torque \times Drum\ or\ Sprocket\ Radius}{30 \times Tiller\ Length\ or\ Quadrant\ Radius}$$

$$Wheel\ Radius\ (Metric) = \frac{Rudder\ Torque \times Drum\ or\ Sprocket\ Radius}{13.6 \times Tiller\ Length\ or\ Quadrant\ Radius}$$

The drum or sprocket radius is the radius of the rope drum or chain sprocket, at the steering wheel, which accepts the steering cable. Drums can be any convenient radius for rope. The smaller the drum or sprocket radius, the greater the mechanical advantage, but the harder it is on the rope or cable. Most modern wheel steerers use bicycle-style, stainless-steel roller chain over chain sprockets instead of a simple drum. For boats up to 35 or 40 feet (10 or 12 m) sprocket radiuses are usually about 1.1 inches (28 mm), and for boats larger than 40 feet about 1.2 inches (30 mm).

Right Turn's Wheel

Trying a 10-inch (254 mm) radius quadrant on *Right Turn,* this works out as follows:

Multiply her rudder torque of 200 lb.-ft. by 12 to get 2,400 pound-inches, and using a 1.1-inch or 28-mm sprocket you'd get:

$$\frac{2400\ lb.in. \times 1.1\ in.\ sprocket\ radius}{30\ lb. \times 10\ in.\ quadrant} = 8.8\ in.\ radius,\ 17.6\ in.\ diameter$$

$$\frac{27.6\ kgm \times 0.028\ m\ sprocket\ radius}{13.6\ kg \times 0.25\ m\ quadrant} = 23\ cm\ radius,\ 46\ cm\ diameter$$

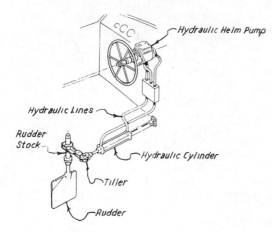

Single helm, single rudder hydraulic steering system. (Courtesy The Edson Corp.)

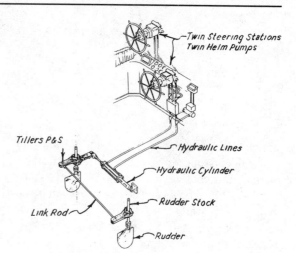

Twin helm, twin rudder hydraulic steering system. (Courtesy The Edson Corp.)

This is quite a small wheel, 18 inches or 45 cm in diameter. You could fit a 20- or 24-incher (50 or 60 cm) if you preferred. On larger boats you're frequently forced to use larger wheels to increase the mechanical advantage. In fact, you can increase mechanical advantage by increasing wheel radius or quadrant (or tiller) radius or both. Increasing quadrant radius also increases the number of turns it takes the wheel to swing the rudder, which brings us to helm quickness.

Quick Turn?

There's yet another important consideration with wheel steering—how quick the helm is. If it took, say, 20 turns of the wheel to swing *Right Turn*'s rudder from hard over to port to hard over to starboard, her steering response would be too slow—way too slow. On the other hand, if her rudder swung from hard over to hard over with just a half turn of the wheel, steering response would be too quick. You'd tend to turn her too far, and every little jerk of your hand would cause a course change.

The ideal number of turns, hard over to hard over, for different types of craft is about as follows:

Runabouts and Small Power Cruisers to 30 ft. (9 m): 1.75 to 2 turns
High-Speed Powerboats (all lengths):1.75 to 2 turns
Power Cruisers 30 to 50 ft. (9 to 15 m): 2.5 to 3.5 turns
Power Cruisers over 50 ft. (15 m): 3.5 to 4 turns
Sailboats 16 to 30 ft. (4.8 to 9 m): 1 to 2 turns
Sailboats 30 to 45 ft. (9 to 14 m): 2 to 3 turns
Sailboats 50 ft. (15 m) and up: 3 to 5 turns

The number of turns from 35 degrees hard over to 35 degrees hard over—also called "lock to lock"—is found from:

$$\textit{Number of Turns Lock to Lock} = \frac{\textit{Quadrant or Tiller Radius}}{5.14 \times \textit{Drum or Sprocket Radius}}$$

Wheel diameter doesn't appear here. It doesn't affect the helm quickness at all. Additional wheel diameter simply increases mechanical advantage, leverage, or power. For *Right Turn,* helm quickness works out as:

$$\frac{10 \text{ in. quadrant}}{5.14 \times 1.1 \text{ in. sprocket}} = 1.77 \text{ turns lock to lock}$$

$$\frac{25 \text{ cm quadrant}}{5.14 \times 2.8 \text{ cm sprocket}} = 1.74 \text{ turns lock to lock}$$

That's quick turning, but good for a boat up to 30 feet (9 m) or so. (The difference between the metric and English results is caused by using a standard 25-cm quadrant rather than a 25.4-cm quadrant that would be exactly equal to 10 inches.) Just playing around with these simple formulas will enable you to pick the right combination of quadrant or tiller size and wheel and drum diameter for any boat you're interested in.

Cable Installation

Cable steering's big drawback is the complexity of its installation. The cables take considerable loads for long periods of time. What's more, those loads oscillate back and forth. Further, the cable itself runs over sheaves at about the same spot constantly, which is the same as bending it back and forth. Flexing anything repeatedly will break it. To control this, the cables must be run over large-diameter sheaves (12 times the wire diameter or greater), and all the sheaves and wire or rope runs must be carefully aligned to ensure smooth operation, with firm cable tension.

If the sheaves get out of line or the cable goes slack, the steering wire or rope can jump out of its grooves and jam—essentially a total steering failure. Clearly, this also means that the steering sheaves must be fastened very securely with heavy through-bolts and substantial backing blocks. If your *Right Turn* is fitted with cable steering, you should check to see that she's equipped with all the above. She should also have quick ac-cess hatches to all the steering gear components—sprocket or drum, cable sheaves and tensioning turnbuckles, and the quadrant or tiller. If she's lacking any of these you've got a steering problem just waiting to happen.

Fluid Power

These days cable steering is found less frequently on power boats. Hydraulics have taken their place. It's not that hydraulics are especially better, but rather that they're much easier to install, particularly with more than one helm station. Most sailboat skippers, in fact, dislike hydraulic steering because—compared to a well-set-up cable system—it gives a mushier helm feel. For power craft this isn't much of a disadvantage. Indeed, it can be a plus; the slight mushiness damps out prop-wash vibrations at the rudder, which cable gear can transmit as a hum or jiggle to the wheel.

Easy Does It

Hydraulics are easy to install because—unlike the finicky alignment and tensioning required by cable systems—the hoses can literally be run any which way. (Kinks and abrasions *must* be avoided; the hoses must be secured with closely spaced supports; and they must be protected from chafe, of course.) Though there are a few hydraulic systems with rotary hydraulic pumps that fit right to the rudder stock, most are simple hydraulic cylinders that attach to a short metal tiller arm that swings the rudder just as you'd turn a traditional wood tiller by hand.

Hydraulic Torque

Since each cylinder model has a fixed throw or stroke, it's designed to work with a standard-length tiller arm. (Using a different length would give you either too much or too little rudder travel—more or less than 35 degrees hard over to hard over.) The cylinder force or power is also fixed by the 30-pound (13.6 kg) limit you can de-

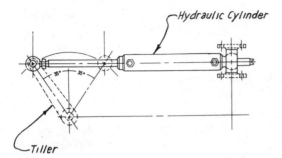

Hydraulic Cylinder

Tiller

Proper alignment of the hydraulic cylinder and tiller.

liver to the wheel and helm-pump unit at the bridge or helm station. (Power assist hydraulic steering is used on large vessels.) Accordingly, once again, you've got a force times a fixed distance—a torque—for each hydraulic cylinder configuration. Obviously, the cylinder/tiller system torque should equal or slightly exceed the maxi-

mum rudder torque. All you have to do is look through the steering-gear manufacturer's catalog and match their torque specifications to your rudder torque to get the correct cylinder.

Locating the Cylinder and Keeping it There

It's important, however, to install the cylinder correctly. Occasionally, it's installed so it's at right angles to the tiller, when the rudder's amidships. This is not good. It puts the cylinder off-angle at either end of its stroke. Instead the cylinder must be installed so that it's at right angles to the amidships tiller location when the rudder's over at 35 degrees either way, as shown in the illustration. (The slight cylinder angle, at dead center, is visible on the arrangement plan of the Off Soundings 34 in Chapter 10.)

Also, the forces on the cylinder mounts can be quite large. For *Right Turn,* a typical hydraulic cylinder would be delivering 250 pounds (114 kg)

Every Boat has a Tiller or A Tiller by Any Other Name . . .

Does your boat have a tiller? You bet. It's easy to think that tillers are found only on small and mid-size sailboats. The only way to effectively twist the rudder stock, however, is by attaching some kind of lever to it . . . *viola*—a tiller! On boats with hydraulic steering the lever that's actuated by the hydraulic cylinder not only *is* a tiller but looks like one. Because the cylinder forces can be quite large, the hydraulic-system tiller can be short and compact, and to take the great strains, it's made of metal (usually steel or bronze) rather than wood. Otherwise, these tillers are no different than wood, hand-held sailboat tillers.

Now, I know that many boats have quadrants, not tillers. It is, in fact, incorrect to call a quadrant a tiller, but that's what a quadrant really is. The only reason it's been, well, rounded off is to keep the steering cable from going slack as it wraps over it. Essentially, the quadrant's a tiller that extends through part of the radius of a circle. The ultimate here is the radial steerer. It—as you can see in the drawing—is a true circle, and the steering cables wrap completely around it. Indeed, technically, a quadrant should be one quarter of a circle (quad for quarter). These days, though, many quadrants are a bit more or less, but then who's checking?

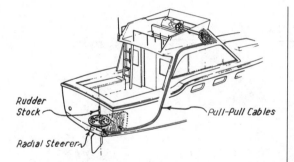

Pull-pull cable steering system, with radial steerer.
(Courtesy The Edson Corp.)

of force—back and forth, back and forth, over and over. This is like having an NFL linebacker stand on something and jump up and down on it over and over for hours and days at a time! Hydraulics are much easier to install than cable systems, but the cylinder had better by mounted double extra strong.

Alternate Steering Gear

There are other steering systems besides simple cable and hydraulic systems. Wheels can be attached to rack-and-pinion steerers or worm-gear steerers. These are both solid machined units that give rugged service and the mechanical advantage needed for large rudder loads. Rack-and-pinion steerers provide positive helm feel or feedback from the rudder like cable steerers. Worm-gear steerers are intended for larger vessels. They were, in fact, first used on large coasting schooners. Their advantage—and their drawback—is that the wheel stays exactly where you leave it when you remove your hands—instant, automatic helm lashing, which can be quite convenient. The drawback, though, is that this eliminates all helm feel or feedback from the rudder. Both rack-and-pinion steerers and worm-gear steerers also have the same disadvantage as the tiller—they must be attached almost directly to the rudder stock aft.

A relatively recent twist on cable steering—it's not much over 20 years old—is *pull-pull cable* steering. It functions the same way as standard cable steering, but consists of cables sliding within cables instead of running over sheaves. This permits you—theoretically—to run the pull-pull cable any which way, like hydraulics. In reality, there are limits. Pull-pull cable steering's an excellent solution for relatively small boats (under 35 feet or 11 meters) in installations where bends can be kept to a minimum. Then, you can run the pull-pull cables in almost as easily as hydraulics. There's generally too much friction and play in these cables for larger boats or more complex runs, however.

Propeller – Diameter/Power/RPM

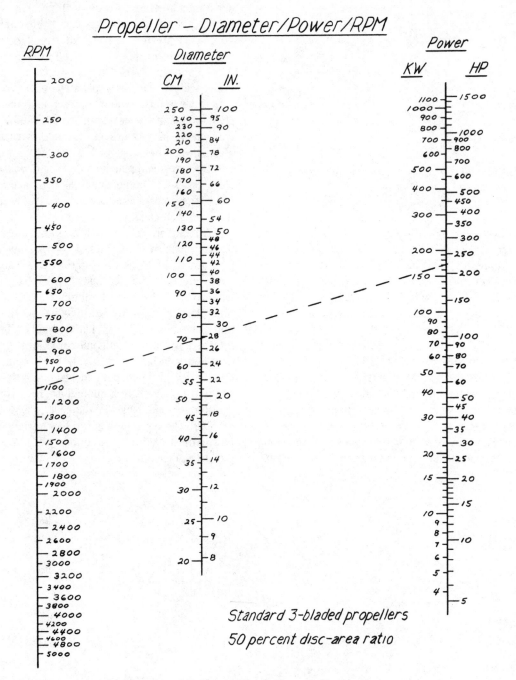

Standard 3-bladed propellers

50 percent disc-area ratio

Note: For a full explanation of chart, see Chapter 32.

Suggested Reading

Boatbuilding, by Howard Chapelle. New York: W.W. Norton & Co.,1941. Along with *Boatbuilding Manual,* the standard reference on wooden boat construction.

Boatbuilding In Your Own Backyard, Second Edition, by Sam Rabl. Centerville, MD: Cornell Maritime Press, 1958. Down-to-earth building and construction information.

Boatbuilding Manual, Third Edition, by Robert M. Steward. Camden, ME: International Marine Publishing, 1987. A clear, concise boatbuilder's reference.

Boatbuilding One-Off In Fiberglass, by Allan H. Vaitses. Camden, ME: International Marine Publishing, 1984. Details most fiberglass construction methods.

The Boatman's Manual, by Carl D. Lane. New York: W.W. Norton & Co., 1979. Navigation, boat handling, maintenance, and more. Read this cover to cover before you set sail.

Boatowner's Mechanical and Electrical Manual, by Nigel Calder. Camden, ME: International Marine Publishing, 1989. The comprehensive reference on all boat's mechanical systems—power and sail. Plainly written filled with detail.

The Boatowner's Sheet Anchor, by Carl D. Lane. New York: Hawthorn Books, 1969. Common sense about every aspect of owning, repairing, building, and operating boats.

Cruising Under Sail, Third Edition, by Eric C. Hiscock. Camden, ME: International Marine Publishing, 1981. Just about the best book on cruising for sailors.

The Fiberglass Boat Repair Manual, by Alan H. Vaitses. Camden, ME: International Marine Publishing, 1988. If you need to fix or plan to modify a fiberglass boat, this book's a good place to start.

Living on 12 Volts with Ample Power, by David Smead and Ruth Ishihara. Seattle, WA: Rides Publishing Co, 1988. Sound advice on safe and economical marine wiring and electric power.

Metal Corrosion in Boats, by Nigel Warren. Camden, ME: International Marine Publishing, 1987. Detailed information on corrosion.

Pocket Cruisers for the Backyard Builder, by Dave Gerr. Camden, ME: International Marine Publishing, 1987. Designs, information, and construction hints for those wishing to build their own sailboat.

Propeller Handbook, by Dave Gerr. Camden, ME: International Marine Publishing, 1989. If you really want to delve into powering and propeller selection, this book will give you detailed information.

Self-Steering for Sailing Craft, by John S. Letcher. Camden, ME: International Marine Publishing, 1974. Detailed explanations of just about every kind of self-steering apparatus you could imagine.

Skene's Elements of Yacht Design, 18th Edition, by Francis S. Kinney. New York:

Dodd, Mead. Even though a bit dated, this has been the standard reference on small-craft design for nearly 50 years.

Skiffs and Schooners, by R.D. Culler. Camden, ME: International Marine Publishing, 1975. Design, construction, and maintenance the old-fashioned way, in plain speaking by a master who really knew how.

Steel Boat Building, Volume I and Volume II, by Thomas E. Colvin. Camden, ME: International Marine Publishing, 1985 and 1986. A truly comprehensive work on steel boat construction.

Traditions and Memories of American Yachting, by William P. Stephens. Brooklyn, ME: WoodenBoat, 1989. A delightful and comprehensive history of sailing and sailing yachts in the United States.

Voyaging Under Power, by Robert P. Beebe. Camden, ME: International Marine Publishing, 1975. If you plan to cruise under power you should get a copy.

Index

Headroom, 23, 40, 373–74, 376
Heads, 375
Headsails, 288–89
Headstay
  sag, 288
  size of, 294
Heave, 121
  rate of, 106–8
Heeling force, 286–87
Heimdall, 53–54
Helm feel and balance, 297–303
Helm station, 378–82
  ventilation in, 380–82
  visibility in, 56, 68, 378–80
Herreshoff, L. Francis, 7, 46, 47, 48, 93, 120
Herreshoff, Nat, 46
Hickman, Albert, 265
Hickman Sea Sleds, 175
H.M. Pope III, 176–78
Holger Danske, 94, 95, 96, 108, 350, 351, 383
Hood Sailmakers, 290
Hoogars (Dutch yacht), 4, 5–9
Horsepower, 153, 155, 192, 193–94
Houseboats, 116
Hull construction
  foam flotation in, 385
  with high-tech materials, 339–43
  metal, 352–61
  structural efficiency and, 346–49
  structure/weight estimates in, 323–30
  titanium, 171, 345, 349
  types of materials in, 317–22.
  See also Fiberglass construction; Wood
    construction
Hull drag, 263
Hull rigging, 296
Hull shapes, 129–34
  basic, 129–30
  constant *vs.* variable deadrise and, 137–38
  deep-vee, 139
  double enders, 58–59
  hard chine *vs.* round bilge, 139–40
  lines drawings of, 130–34
  multi-chined, 130
  run and, 135–37
  volume and, 141–47
  weather helm and, 301–2

Hydraulic steering, 402, 403–5
Hydroplanes, 175–76

Ignition-protected electrical devices, 228–29
Impact resistance, 105
Inboard rudders, 394
Independence, 322
Induced drag, 283
Inflatable dinghy, 77–78
Insulation, 361
Integral tanks, 361
Ions, 230–31
Iron Kyle, 54, 56
Isolation transformers, 236

Jackpot, 381, 382, 394
James, Naomi, 113
Jeantot, Phillipe, 173
Jersey sea skiff, 29–30
Jet drives, 266–69
Jib-headed rig, 64
Joshua, 354
Junks, Chinese, 383, 384

KaMeWa jet drive, 269
Keel
  fin, 162–63, 279
  long, 162, 284
  narrow, 282–83
  swinging, 120
  winged, 283–84
  yaw angle and, 279, 280
Keel boats, 18, 19
Keel line, 130
Ketch, 301, 302
Kevlar laminates, 340–41, 342, 345, 347
Kevlar rope, 310, 311, 312, 340
Kevlar sails, 289, 290
Krivacsy, Steve, 65

Laminar flow, 282
Lateral plane, 163
Launching gear, 362–63
Lead, 301–2
Lead-acid batteries, 226
Leeboards, 4–9, 50–51
Lee helm, 297, 298